P9-CQN-556

USING STANDARDIZED TESTS IN EDUCATION

USING STANDARDIZED TESTS IN EDUCATION

Fourth Edition

William A. Mehrens
Michigan State University

Irvin J. Lehmann
Michigan State University

Theodore Lownik Library
Illinois Benedictine College

Longman
New York & London

LB
3051
.M4653
1987

Executive Editor: Raymond T. O'Connell
Senior Editor: Naomi Silverman
Production Editor: Pamela Nelson
Cover Design: Stephan Zander
Production Supervisor: Judith Stern
Compositor: TC Systems
Printer and Binder: Maple Vail Book Manufacturing

Using Standardized Tests in Education, Fourth Edition

Copyright © 1987 by Longman Inc.

All rights reserved. No part of this publication may be reproduced, stored in a retrieval system, or transmitted in any form or by any means, electronic, mechanical, photocopying, recording, or otherwise, without the prior permission of the publisher.

Longman Inc.
95 Church Street
White Plains, N.Y. 10601

Associated companies:
Longman Group Ltd., London
Longman Cheshire Pty., Melbourne
Longman Paul Pty., Auckland
Copp Clark Pitman, Toronto
Pitman Publishing Inc., New York

Library of Congress Cataloging-in-Publication Data

Mehrens, William A.
  Using standardized tests in education.

  Rev. ed. of: Standardized tests in education. 3rd ed. c1980.
  Bibliography: p.
  Includes index.
  1. Educational tests and measurements.   I. Lehmann,
Irvin J.   II. Mehrens, William A.   Standardized tests
in education.   II. Title.
LB3051.M4653   1986   371.2′62   85-23148
ISBN 0-582-29022-8

    89   90   9   8   7   6   5   4   3   2

Contents

Preface

Decision makers continue to benefit from good tests and testing practices. Further, testing is big business. It has been estimated that 200 million achievement tests are given in the United States each year, and this represents only about 65 percent of all the educational and psychological testing that is conducted.

However, neither all tests nor all testing practices are good. Professionals must be able to make wise judgments about them. Thus, a fourth edition of this text is warranted.

The basic principles involved in the selection, interpretation, and use of tests have not changed much since the first edition of this book was published in 1969. Test users must still be knowledgeable about and able to interpret information in test manuals and other publications regarding reliability, validity, norms, and test use. This edition should not, however, be construed as primarily an updating of earlier forms of various tests discussed in the previous editions. Organizational changes have been made, and there have been, as one would expect, changes in sections that hindsight reveals to be deserving of modification or deletion.

Educators have always been concerned with measuring and evaluating the progress of their students. As the goals of education have become more complex, as the numbers of students have increased, and as the demand by all segments of the citizenry—pupils, parents, taxpayers, and other decision makers—for accountability on the part of educators has grown, these tasks have become more difficult. Recent criticism of the quality of our educational product—students who are unable to read or write effectively, or who lack a knowledge of the fundamental arithmetical processes—as well as the teaching–learning methods employed in our schools and colleges behooves us more than ever before to be concerned about the valid and reliable assessment of our endeavors. The area of educational measurement can be considered as twofold: the construction, evaluation, and use of teacher-made classroom tests and of standardized tests. This text focuses on the latter of these two areas, dealing with both norm- and criterion-referenced standardized tests.

The education of our teachers in measurement is woefully inadequate. Far too many teachers are untrained in the selection, administration, and interpretation of standardized tests, and teacher-training institutions across the nation should provide courses to alleviate this situation.

Although many books are designed for use in basic measurement courses, most attempt to cover the whole domain of topics subsumed under measurement. This book has a more limited goal; it is an outgrowth of the authors' conviction that classroom teachers, counselors, and school administrators must have certain information if they are to select, administer, and use standardized tests correctly. Our basic aim is to provide that information. No formal course work in testing or statistics is necessary to understand the text.

This book can serve as the main text in the first course in standardized testing at either the undergraduate or the graduate level. In either case, the material should be supplemented by detailed examinations of specimen sets of various tests and selected outside readings. This book also is appropriate as a supplemental text in introductory educational psychology courses, methods courses, special education courses, and guidance and counseling courses.

We do not claim to have considered every possible approach to the assessment of cognitive and noncognitive traits. In fact, we have intentionally omitted teacher-made tests and such assessment techniques as observations, ratings, anecdotal records, and sociometry. The selection of topics in this book and the coverage given them have benefited from the advice of many colleagues. At all times, the needs of educators have been foremost in mind.

When we have felt that the topic being considered could not be treated without some theoretical background, we have attempted to present a simple and clear exposition of the theory. When we felt that the topic did not require a full theoretical treatment, we have omitted the explanatory material.

All four editions of the text have benefited from student and instructor reactions. When necessary, we have rewritten material from the third edition so that it will be easier to comprehend. We have tried to obtain simplicity but not at the expense of accuracy.

This fourth edition retains much of the basic organization and coverage of the third edition. Chapter 1 introduces the student to the nature and functions of standardized tests. It includes a section on norm- and criterion-referenced measurement. Chapter 2 examines some basic statistical concepts; Chapters 3 and 4 cover reliability and validity, respectively; norms, scores, and profiles are discussed in Chapter 5. Chapter 6 covers factors such as test anxiety, test-wiseness, and coaching that influence the measurement of individuals.

Because educators make more use of aptitude and achievement tests than they do of interest and personality measures, we have devoted more attention to the cognitive tests. All test information has been updated from the previous edition. Aptitude tests are discussed in Chapter 7, achievement tests in Chapter 8. We have discussed a larger number of achievement tests than aptitude tests because the former are used more frequently in the public schools.

Because school personnel must also know about the noncognitive characteristics of their students, we have examined interest, personality, and attitude measures in Chapter 9. Educators, in general, are more qualified to use interest than personality inventories; because interest-inventory results are of greater educational value, we have stressed them accordingly.

Chapter 10, a new chapter in this edition, covers the assessment of exceptional children. Given the importance and implications of PL 94-142 for measurement, this seems to us a particularly worthy addition.

We have emphasized the key principles to be considered by the user in selecting, administering, and interpreting a particular type of test for his or her specific needs. We have done this by looking briefly at some of the more common standardized tests used in our schools and by evaluating one or more tests in each of Chapters 7, 8, 9, and 10 in a comprehensive fashion. These are not necessarily the best tests available—they are only useful examples. In addition, the reader is not expected to remember the many specifics discussed. Why, then, one might ask, should we cover them? To give the reader some acquaintance with the different kinds of standardized tests available to educators and the way they should be evaluated. We have tried to evaluate the various tests critically, pointing out their strengths and weaknesses, so that users will have some general notion as to what questions they should ask when they select a test; how they should interpret the information presented in the test manual regarding the test's psychometric problems; and what this test has to offer, if anything, over other available tests. To derive maximum value from these brief test descriptions, we strongly urge the reader to have a copy of the test and manual available.

Chapters 11 and 12 (both contained in Chapter 9 in the third edition) include sections on accountability, internal and external evaluation programs, public concerns about evaluation, and a brief look toward the future of testing.

We would like to thank all those who have assisted us in the revision of this book. Comments from students and instructors who used the first three editions as well as comments from several anonymous reviewers of the revised manuscript were of considerable benefit. Naomi Silverman and Jean Anne Cipolla from Longman Inc. assisted in many details, and we thank them for their very competent and cordial professional help. Finally, we would like to thank our typists for their patient and conscientious job.

William A. Mehrens
Irvin J. Lehmann

USING STANDARDIZED TESTS IN EDUCATION

CHAPTER 1

Introduction to Measurement and Evaluation

Decisions, decisions, decisions! They simply must be made. We often must choose among alternative courses of action. And to make wise decisions, one needs information. The role of measurement is to provide accurate and relevant information to assist in wise decision making. Educators and psychologists have been concerned with measurement as a necessary component in both research and practical decision making. The whole field of differential psychology is based on the fact that individuals differ, that these differences are important, and that we need to measure these differences and use this information in decision making. Employers are concerned with hiring, placing, and promoting the best people for the good of the organization and for the welfare of the employees. Educators are concerned with measuring and evaluating the progress of their students, the value and relevance of the curriculum, and the effectiveness of their teaching. As the goals of education have become more complex, this task has become much more difficult.

Education is considered by many to be the most important enterprise in our society. At some time and in some way every citizen is directly involved with education. Because education is such an important enterprise, it is crucial to evaluate its processes and products. Why evaluate? For one reason, taxpayers demand an accounting. If large amounts of their money are spent on a project, they have a right to know the results. Another reason is that students, teachers, administrators, and parents all work hard toward achieving educational goals; it is therefore only natural that they wish to ascertain the degree to which those goals have been realized. The satisfaction of knowing, the removal of ignorance, is an important reason for evaluation. Accurate evaluation is equally important to employers, who must be sure to place the right people in the right jobs. But these reasons are secondary to the basic principle: Measurement and evaluation are essential to sound decision making. Decisions should be based on accurate, relevant information; the responsibility of gathering and imparting that information belongs to professionals, be they educators, psychologists, or personnel directors.[1]

We recognize that some educators and psychologists have somewhat negative feelings toward measurement and evaluation. While God evaluated His work and saw that it was "very good" (Gen. 1:1–31), the critics of evaluation may prefer another Biblical quote: "Do not criticize one another. . . . Who do you think you are, to judge your fellow man?" (James 4:11 and 12). Glass (1975) discusses the paradox that people desire excellence yet oppose the evaluation that makes excellence possible.

Whatever one feels about its value, testing is big business. It has been estimated that 200 million achievement forms are used each year in the United States and that this number represents only 65 percent of all educational and psychological testing that is conducted. On the average, a student will take about six full batteries of standardized achievement tests before graduating from high school (Yeh, Herman, & Rudner, 1980). This is expensive. Rudner (1981) estimates the annual cost to public elementary and secondary schools of achievement testing alone to be at least $24 million. When one adds in aptitude tests and various personality, interest, and attitude inventories, the price tag becomes even higher. These figures do not include any of the costs of testing that occur in industry and governmental agencies other than schools.

Do the benefits outweigh the costs? That surely is debatable. To our knowledge, there have been no cost-effectiveness studies of testing in the public schools. However, Hunter and Schmidt (1982) have done such a cost analysis in business. They suggest that a crucial element of high productivity is the selection of people with high ability for their jobs. They estimate that the difference between the complete use or complete disuse of cognitive

---

[1] We will not always list all job titles of professionals who use tests. At times we will just use *educator*, but it should be thought of as a more inclusive word.

ability tests in making personnel decisions would amount to $80 billion per year in productivity. Others may doubt these figures, and certainly some individuals argue that other factors such as affirmative action, job satisfaction, and so on, must be considered when evaluating the impact of testing.

Whatever you think about the impact of testing as currently practiced, the *purpose* of measurement and evaluation is good, not bad. To repeat, measurement and evaluation are essential to sound decision making.

In this chapter we (1) present a brief overview of some of the more exciting issues to be covered in this book, (2) define important terms, (3) present a classification of standardized tests, (4) discuss briefly the role of information in educational decision making, (5) present some basic functions of standardized testing, (6) discuss some basic considerations of testing and test selection, (7) discuss some practical aspects of testing, and (8) present a guide for reviewing and critiquing a standardized test.

After studying this chapter, you should be able to do the following:

1. Understand and appreciate the variety of interesting issues in measurement and evaluation that will be covered in subsequent chapters.
2. Define and differentiate the terms *test, standardized test, measurement,* and *evaluation.*
3. Classify standardized tests.
4. Recognize that measurement and evaluation are essential to sound educational decision making.
5. Comprehend the functions of standardized tests.
6. Understand what factors need to be considered in selecting tests.
7. Recognize the distinctions between norm- and criterion-referenced measurements.
8. Determine, for a given decision, which types of data are likely to prove most useful.
9. Use some basic information sources when selecting standardized tests.
10. Understand what test and test manual characteristics should be considered in selecting tests.
11. Understand the importance of physical and psychological conditions when administering standardized tests.
12. Know about various methods of scoring tests.
13. Know what questions to ask (and answers to get) when critiquing a test.

ISSUES IN MEASUREMENT AND EVALUATION

We have stressed the point that measurement and evaluation aid in decision making. While we hope this simple statement is unarguable, we do not mean to imply, nor would we want you to infer, that the field of measurement and the materials covered in this text are dull and noncontroversial. There are many exciting and controversial issues of an intellectual, philosophical, political, social, legal, and psychometric nature to be discussed. We believe (as do Stetz & Beck, 1981) that a thoughtful and balanced presentation of the issues is called for. We hope our discussion of these issues can be both objective and interesting. From the quotes below, you should get a flavor of the issues and the intensity of the debate.

1. *Educational and psychological testing represents one of the most important contributions of behavioral science to our society. It has provided fundamental and significant improvements over previous practices in industry, government, and education. It has provided a tool for broader and more equitable access to education and employment. . . . The proper use of well-constructed and validated tests provides a better basis for making some important decisions about individuals and programs than would otherwise be available. (AERA-APA-NCME, 1985, p. 1)*

2. *I feel emotionally toward the testing industry as I would toward any other merchant of death. I feel that way because of what they do to the kids. I'm not saying they murder every child—only 20 percent of them. Testing has distorted their ambitions, distorted their careers. (Zacharias, quoted in Kohn, 1975, p. 14)*

3. *The simple truth is that there has not been, is not now, and will not be any device or scheme which is as efficient as the well-crafted test for capturing relevant samples of human behavior, rendering them in a form that permits analysis, manipulation, and interpretation, and permitting their evaluation as elements in inferential chains leading to diagnosis, understanding, and prediction. And do you know something? Deep down, everyone—even our harshest critics—knows this, for characteristically their diatribes conclude by saying, "but, of course, we have to have tests." (Lennon, 1981, p. 4)*

4. *At least half of the tests currently on the market should never have been published. Exaggerated, false or unsubstantiated claims are the rule rather than the exception. (Buros, 1972, p. xxvii)*

5. *Publishers of standardized achievement tests realize that, from a marketing viewpoint, they dare not spell out exactly what their tests measure. If they did, the test would not be widely purchased, since many educators would find them inconsistent with local instructional programs. Hence, commercial test publishers describe their standardized achievement tests in artfully vague terms, for instance, as a test of "reading comprehension." (Popham, 1976, p. 3)*

6. *Mr. Pulling rambled on about testing being similar to phrenology. He said that this article was occasioned by a desultory contact with some child who took some test in some place and was not rated too bright in mathematics. Nevertheless, this particular individual went to some*

college somewhere *and* somehow *succeeded, all of which prove beyond the shadow of a doubt in Mr. Pulling's logic that* all *testing in* all *places and on* all *levels is similar to the cephalic index of the phrenologists. (Barcley, 1968, p. 4)*

7. *We must listen and attend to healthy criticism of measurement and suggestions for improvement that come from all quarters. However, many of the current attacks on testing do not fall in that category. . . . I would like to focus on them explicitly and label them for what they are:* vicious, destructive, deliberately misleading, *but also* sustained, well-organized, *and* well-financed. *They play on the ignorance of the public, and if allowed to go unchecked, will undermine the whole foundation of our carefully developed and principled field of endeavor. (Anderson, 1980, p. 5)*

8. *IQ and achievement tests are nothing but updated versions of the old signs down South that read "For Whites Only!" (Williams, 1974, p. 32)*

9. *Of the many challenges to a child's peace of mind caused by such things as angry parents, playground bullies, bad dogs, shots from the doctor, and things that go bump in the night, standardized tests must surely be among the least fearsome for most children. (Ebel, 1976, p. 5)*

10. *To a very great extent it is quite reasonable to conclude that the biggest abuse of standardized achievement tests is the level of discourse at which debate on the issue is carried out. (Airasian, 1979, p. 6)*

Throughout this book we will be presenting information and discussions that relate to these ten quotes. We will examine some very general issues, as well as some highly specific ones. For example, we will consider the general value of standardized tests. Probably the most vocal criticism of measurement and evaluation in regard to standardized tests can be found in the January–February 1980 National Education Association's *Reports* article entitled "Teachers and Citizens Protest the Testing Ripoff," which suggests that both teachers and the public at large are opposed to standardized tests. But that is misleading. A survey by Stetz and Beck (1981), for example, indicates that only 16 percent of teachers agreed with the NEA's proposed moratorium on standardized testing. Albert Shanker, president of the American Federation of Teachers, states that the AFT "strongly supports testing":

We do not want to get rid of anything except ignorance. We believe that tests tell us things that are important for students, parents, teachers, colleges, government and the society at large to know. We also believe the public unquestionably has a right to know what we are doing in our schools—how well or how badly. (Shanker, 1980, p. 2)

In general, national polls suggest that parents overwhelmingly feel such tests are useful (Lerner, 1981b).

We are not suggesting that the issue of the value of standardized tests can be settled by popular vote. We are only demonstrating that the issue does exist. Throughout this book we will be discussing the uses and misuses of such tests. We hope you will learn to avoid the misuses of tests. And we hope you will conclude, as we do, that the positive functions of such tests outweigh the negative results that may follow from their misuse.

Another issue in this book concerns minimum competency tests. A large number of states, and local districts within states, are mandating such tests, which students must pass in order to obtain high school diplomas, competency certificates, or grade promotions. In general, the public has backed this expansion of the use of tests. For example, in 1984, Gallup polls of teachers and parents gave the following results:

"In your opinion, should children be promoted from grade to grade only if they can pass examinations?"

	% TEACHERS	% U.S. PUBLIC
Yes	43	71
No	52	25
No Opinion	5	4

"Should all high school students in the United States be required to pass a standard nationwide examination in order to get a high school diploma?"

	% TEACHERS	% U.S. PUBLIC
Should be required	48	65
Should not be required	45	29
No Opinion	7	6

"In addition to meeting college requirements for a teacher's certificate, should those who want to become teachers also be required to pass a state board examination to prove their knowledge in the subjects they will teach, before they are hired?"

	% TEACHERS	% U.S. PUBLIC
Yes	63	89
No	30	7
No Opinion	7	4

Whatever the public's and teachers' opinions, there are a myriad of social, legal, philosophical, educational, and measurement issues related to minimum competency testing.

Other issues discussed in this text include the following:

1. The differences, similarities, and relative value of norm-referenced tests and criterion-referenced tests.
2. The effects of test-wiseness and coaching.
3. The fairness of tests in regard to gender and ethnicity.
4. The definition and sources of "intelligence."
5. The value of diagnosis in teaching.
6. The value of knowledge about pupils' attitudes, values, and interests in providing for optimal learning.
7. The protection of privacy in testing, storing, and disseminating data.
8. The testing of individuals with special needs.
9. The use of tests in selection decisions.

We hope you will enjoy learning more about these issues. You will not get a final, correct answer to each issue. You will receive as objective a discussion as possible from two authors who admit to one bias at the outset: In general, measurement is a good thing and users of tests will make better decisions with appropriate data than without such data.

DEFINITIONS: TEST, STANDARDIZED TEST, MEASUREMENT, EVALUATION, AND ASSESSMENT

The terms *test, measurement, evaluation,* and *assessment* are often used interchangeably, but some users make distinctions among them. *Test,* usually considered the narrowest of the four terms, refers to the presentation of a standard set of questions to be answered. From a person's responses to a series of questions, we obtain a measure (that is, a numerical value) of a characteristic of that person. *Measurement* suggests a broader concept: We can measure characteristics in ways other than by giving tests. Measurement involves using observation, rating scales, or any other nontest device that allows us to obtain information in a quantitative form. The term *measurement* can refer to both the score obtained and the process used.

Standardized tests, the focus of this book, are commercially prepared by experts in measurement and subject matter. They provide methods for obtaining samples of behavior under *uniform procedures*—that is, the same fixed set of questions is administered with the same set of directions and timing constraints, and the scoring procedure is carefully delineated and kept constant. Scoring is usually objective, although a standardized achievement test may include an essay question, and certain unstructured personality inventories are scored in a fashion that is not completely objective. Usually a standardized test has been administered to a norm group (or groups) so that a person's performance can be interpreted by comparing it to the performance of others (that is, the test is norm-referenced). Although some suggest that "norms" be included in the definition of *standardized,* some inventories, such as the Mooney Problem Check List, do not have norms but are ordinarily considered as standardized. And some of the diagnostic achievement tests and "criterion-referenced" achievement tests do not have norms.[2] Some writers seem to think of criterion-referenced tests as not standardized. But if they are commercially prepared, and if administered and scored under uniform conditions, they fit the definition given above, and we consider them in this text.

The term *standardized* does not indicate that the test necessarily measures what should be taught or at what level students should be achieving. However, with the current popularity of criterion-referenced tests, commercial publishers are marketing some achievement tests that perhaps do connote at least minimum standards.

Evaluation has been defined in a variety of ways. Stufflebeam et al. (1971, p. xxv) stated that evaluation is "the process of delineating, obtaining, and providing useful information for judging decision alternatives." Used in this way, it encompasses but goes beyond the meaning of the terms *test* and *measurement.* A second popular concept of evaluation interprets it as the determination of the congruence between performance and objective. Other definitions simply categorize evaluation as professional judgment or as a process that allows one to make a judgment about the desirability or value of something. For example, *Standards for Evaluations of Educational Programs, Projects, and Materials* defines evaluation as "the systematic investigation of the worth or merit of some object" (Joint Committee on Standards, 1981, p. 12).

One can evaluate with either qualitative or quantitative data. Measurement is not the same as evaluation. Two students may obtain the same measure (test score), but we might evaluate those measures differently. Suppose, at the end of fifth grade, two students are both reading at the fifth-grade level. At the beginning of the year, however, one student was reading at the third-grade level and one at the fourth-grade, fifth-month level. Our evaluations of those outcomes are not the same. One student progressed at an above-average rate and the other at a below-average rate.

The term *assessment* is also used in various ways—sometimes it is used synonymously with *evaluation*; at other times it refers more particularly to the diagnosis of an individual's problems.

It is important to keep in mind that we never measure or evaluate people. We measure or evaluate *characteristics* or *properties* of people: their scholastic potential, knowledge of algebra, honesty, perseverance, ability to

---

[2] The differences between norm-referenced and criterion-referenced tests are discussed later in this chapter. Basically, in norm referencing we interpret a score by comparing it to others; in criterion referencing we compare the score to some specified behavioral criterion of proficiency.

teach, and so forth. Evaluating these criteria should not be confused with evaluating the worth of a person. Teachers, parents, and students do not always keep this distinction clearly in mind.

CLASSIFICATION OF STANDARDIZED TESTS

Standardized tests can be classified in many ways. For example, they can be classified according to administrative procedures, such as individual versus group administration, or as oral instructions versus written instructions. However, the most popular broad classification concerns what is measured. We use the following classification of tests:

1. Aptitude tests (general, multiple, and special).
2. Achievement tests (diagnostic, single subject matter, and survey batteries).
3. Interest, personality, and attitude inventories.

The first two categories are considered to contain tests of maximum performance; the third, tests of typical performance. Some people classify aptitude and achievement tests as cognitive measures, and interest, personality, and attitude inventories as noncognitive measures. Because the noncognitive measures have no factually right or wrong answers, they are sometimes called *inventories*. This change in terminology may lessen the anxiety of the test taker. Whether or not these measures are referred to as tests or inventories, they fit the definition of standardized tests presented in the preceding section. The word *test* is used in this chapter to simplify the language. However, it should not be used in the *titles* of noncognitive measures.

INFORMATION GATHERING AND DECISION MAKING

The direct involvement of the citizenry in education means that every person must at some time make educational decisions. Similarly, everyone who works for a living or who hires others makes employment decisions. Some decisions affect many people (for example, federal decisions regarding funding of mammoth projects); others, only a single person (Johnny's decision not to review his spelling list). There are numerous decisions that educators, psychologists, and employers must make, and many other choices that they must assist individual pupils, parents, and the general public in making. Should Susan be placed in an advanced reading group? Should Johnny take algebra or general mathematics next year? Should the school continue using the mathematics textbook adopted this year, revert back to the previous text, or try a new one? Is grammar being stressed at the expense of pronunciation in first-year German? Am I doing as well in chemistry as I should be?

Should I go to college? Should I apply for a job as a salesperson? Should I hire that individual as a salesperson? These are just a few questions and decisions facing educators, employers, employees, parents, and students. Whoever makes a decision, and whether the decision is great or small, it should be based on as much and as accurate information as possible. The more, and more accurate, the information on which a decision is based, the better that decision is likely to be. In fact, many scholars who study decision making define a good decision as one based on all *relevant* information.

Professionals (educators, psychologists, employers) have the important responsibilities of (1) determining what information needs to be obtained, (2) collecting accurate information, and (3) imparting that information in readily understood terms to the persons who must make the decisions—whether students, parents, teachers, college admissions officers, or personnel or counseling psychologists. The philosophy, knowledges, and skills covered in this book should assist the professional in fulfilling such responsibilities. In general, the book deals with the selection, administration, interpretation, and use of standardized tests. The data provided from such tests should help the teacher, counselor, administrator, student, parent, and all those concerned with the teaching–learning process make the soundest educational decisions possible. They should help personnel psychologists make the best selection and placement decisions possible.

The kinds of decisions made are often classified as institutional decisions and individual decisions. *Institutional decisions* are ones in which a large number of comparable decisions are made. *Individual decisions* are ones in which the choice confronting the decision maker will rarely or never recur. In education, institutional decisions are typically the ones the school personnel make concerning the students (for example, homogeneous grouping and college admission). In industry, they are the hiring and promotion decisions. Individual decisions are typically the ones the individual makes about himself or herself (for example, vocational choice). Test information is helpful for both kinds of decision making. Tests per se do not make decisions, but they are one type of information that should be considered in making decisions.

Certainly, no single course in educational and psychological measurement can teach you how to obtain all the information needed to make all the decisions with which you will be confronted, but it can be of considerable help. It can suggest principles and methods of deciding what information would be useful for various decisions and how this information should be gathered. If these principles and methods are applied, it is more likely that the information gathered will be accurate and useful. Numerous existing tests and inventories can be used to gather important data, and there are limitations of measurement data that users should know about.

Occasionally the concepts of measurement and decision making are misunderstood. Some people seem to feel that if a decision leads to a poor outcome, then that shows that the data on which the decision was based should not have been used (that is, do not use selection tests since selection decisions are not perfect). This is not the case. In making decisions we are always taking risks, since we cannot predict outcomes with complete certainty. A good decision is one that is based on all relevant data. This increases the chances of a favorable outcome—it does not guarantee it. The major mistake in decision making is that decisions are too often based on incomplete data. In general there should be a variety of data from diverse sources in order to make the best decision possible. Any moratorium on the use of certain types of data would invariably result in poorer decisions.

FUNCTIONS OF STANDARDIZED TESTS

The functions of standardized tests are many and varied; however, one can in essence sum up their function by saying that they should help in decision making. Throughout their school careers, students make many decisions, and many decisions are made about them. The more (and more accurate) the information on which a decision is based, the better the decision is likely to be.

One way to classify educational and psychological decisions is by the kind of functions they serve (their purposes): *instructional, guidance, administrative,* or *research.* These categories are of course somewhat arbitrary and overlapping. If a decision is made that programmed tests are to be used in all ninth-grade algebra classes, it might be considered either an instructional or an administrative decision. Ordinarily, instructional decisions are thought of as decisions affecting activities that occur in a particular classroom, and administrative decisions as those affecting activities in the total school building or district. If an employer uses a test for a placement decision, that might conceivably be either a guidance or an administrative decision. One shortcoming of this classification system is that different kinds of tests serve different functions within the categories listed above. A two-way classification such as that shown in Table 1.1 is much more meaningful.

The functions, as shown in the table, are explained in more detail within each of the chapters devoted to the different kinds of tests. Note that interest, personality, and attitude tests serve fewer instructional purposes, although these tests can be very useful in the guidance functions of the school.

There have been several studies conducted regarding specific uses of tests by different professionals. For example, Stetz & Beck (1981) asked teachers whether they used standardized achievement tests for eight possible purposes. The purposes, and the percent of teachers who indicated they used the tests for each purpose, was as follows: Individual student evaluation (65 percent), diagnosing strengths and weaknesses (74 percent), class evaluation (45 percent), instructional planning (52 percent), evaluation of teaching

TABLE 1.1

PURPOSES OF STANDARDIZED TESTS*

	Kinds of Tests				
Purposes	Apti-tude	Achieve-ment	Inter-est	Person-ality	Atti-tude
Instructional					
Evaluation of learning outcomes	X	X	?	?	
Evaluation of teaching	X	X			
Evaluation of curriculum	X	X	?		?
Learning diagnosis	X	X			
Differential assignments within class	X	X	?	?	?
Grading	?	?			
Motivation		?			X
Guidance					
Occupational	X	X	X	X	X
Educational	X	X	?	?	X
Personal	?	?	X	X	X
Administrative					
Selection	X	X	?		
Classification	X	X	X		
Placement	X	X	?		
Public relations (information)	X	X	?		
Curriculum planning and evaluation	X	X			
Evaluating teachers	?	?		?	
Providing information for outside agencies	X	X			
Grading	?	?			
Research	X	X	X	X	X

* "X" indicates that a test can and should be used for that purpose. "?" indicates that there is some debate about whether or not a test can serve that purpose.

methods (37 percent), reporting to parents (42 percent), reporting to student (24 percent), and measuring growth (66 percent).

For all the specific functions mentioned, it should be remembered that the *ultimate* purpose of a standardized test is to help in making decisions. Some examples of the kinds of decisions that might be made better by using standardized test results are as follows:

1. Do the pupils in Ms. Perriwinkle's third grade need a different balance of curricular emphasis?
2. What should John, a physically handicapped student, major in in college?
3. Is it advisable for Erskine to take a remedial reading course?
4. Should Billy take a college-preparatory program in high school?
5. Is the phonics method of teaching reading more effective than the sight method?
6. Should Sally be hired as a product engineer?

If knowledge of a test result does not enable a person to make a better decision than the best decision that could be made without the use of the test, then the test serves no useful purpose and might just as well not be given. However, if the test information is used and interpreted correctly, it would be impossible to make poorer decisions using the additional information.

SOME BASIC CONSIDERATIONS IN TESTING AND TEST SELECTION

Because a test, once selected by a school or other agency, is ordinarily used for many years, it certainly behooves the purchaser to consider carefully the problem of test selection. Some of the many questions that always arise are "What kind of information is needed?" "How should this information be obtained?" and if it is agreed that test information would be helpful, "Who should select the tests?" One way to stimulate test use is to have the professional staff who will use the tests help in the test selection process. If teachers are expected to use test information, they should assist in selecting the tests; if guidance personnel will be using test results, they should be involved; and if the principal also plans to use the test results to help in certain decisions, then he or she should assist in the test selection. Test selection should be a cooperative venture by all the professional staff who intend to use the test information.

Many different factors should be considered in selecting a test, such as purpose, administration, scoring, cost, format, interpretation, reliability, and validity. In the rest of this section, we discuss the purposes of testing, norm-referenced versus criterion-referenced measurement, sources of information about tests, and characteristics of tests and manuals.

Purposes of Testing

When deciding which test(s) to select, the first consideration should be a thorough consideration of the purposes for which the testing is to be done. If general uses of the test results are not known in advance, the best decision would be not to test. If, however, specific uses are anticipated, then tests should be selected in a more sensible and systematic fashion. Quite often one can easily decide what general kind of test is most desirable. Aptitude, achievement, interest, and personality tests are not used for exactly the same specific purposes. Although Table 1.1, for example, shows that all kinds of tests can be used for occupational guidance, they obviously do not all serve the same *specific* purpose. Many purposes could fall under the heading of occupational guidance, for instance, and adequate test selection demands more specific planning. Knowing that a test is to be used for the purpose of comparing Jane's interests with the interests of people in various professional occupations would make the selection much easier.

Even knowing precisely the purposes for which testing is done, however, does not necessarily make selection automatic. Suppose you are a seventh-grade mathematics teacher and you wish to measure the achievement of your students in mathematics so you can determine whether they have learned enough material to undertake the eighth-grade math curriculum. Furthermore, suppose you wish to use a standardized test in addition to your own classroom test to help make these evaluations. How do you decide which of the many standardized seventh-grade mathematics tests to administer? To make this decision you must be precise in considering your purposes. One difference in all the tests you might choose from is that they do not all cover the same mathematics content. Some of the tests will cover "modern math." Others will cover the content taught in traditional courses. To make a decision among these tests you have to decide what your specific objectives are and exactly what area of mathematics you wish to test. Although this is a problem of content validity and is mentioned later, it is also a problem of determining just exactly *why* you wish to use the test. It cannot be emphasized too strongly that the first and most important steps in test selection are to determine exactly why you are giving the test, what type of information you expect from it, and how you intend to use that information once you have it.

Norm- and Criterion-Referenced Measurement

One of the major distinctions in standardized achievement tests is whether they (really their scores) are norm-referenced (NRT) or criterion-referenced (CRT). The purpose(s) of testing will help determine which type of referencing is more useful.

There has been much discussion about the distinctions between, and the advantages and disadvantages of, norm-referenced and criterion-referenced measurement. The basic issue concerns *interpretation,* or how we derive meaning from a score, but related to this is a discussion of the different purposes of measurement and techniques of constructing tests.

With respect to *score referencing,* the distinction is one of absolute versus relative meaning. Educators have, at times, been inclined to interpret scores on tests as if they have absolute meaning. Further, they often set a passing score (such as 60 percent) that is the same across different tests. Thus, if Mary scores 62 percent on a spelling test and 58 percent on a mathematics test, one would conclude that Mary did better on the spelling test than on the math test. The trouble with this inference is that it assumes absolute meaning of the scores. If one concludes she "passed" the one and "failed" the other, then two more assumptions are made: that the amount needed to pass can be determined, and that it is equal in both cases. All of these assumptions are open to question.

Since there are so many questionable assumptions involved in the method of interpretation described above, measurement specialists developed the notion of *norm-referenced interpretation*—that of adding meaning to a score by comparing it to the scores of people in a reference (or norm) group. For example, Mary's score of 62 percent in spelling may place her at the 50th percentile in comparison to her classmates (in other words, she scores better than 50 percent of her classmates), whereas her math score of 58 percent may place her at the 80th percentile.

Some people have suggested the norm-referenced approach does not tell us the really important information of what and how much the student has learned. They wish to use the absolute notion of interpretation and have coined a term for it—*criterion-referenced interpretation.*

But if one is to make this type of absolute interpretation, the test must have certain properties. Thus, there seem to be two major types of distinctions made between NRT and CRT. Some professionals talk about the distinction between CRT and NRT in terms of the method of *referencing the score*. Others talk about the difference in the *kinds of tests*. There are many subcategories within each of these types.

It would seem that the distinction between the two types of scores should be clear enough. If we interpret a score of an individual by comparing that score with those of other individuals (called a norm group), this would be norm referencing. If we interpret a person's performance by comparing it with some specified behavioral domain or criterion of proficiency, this would be criterion referencing. To polarize the distinction, we could say that the focus of a normative score is on how many of Johnny's peers perform (score) less well than he does; the focus of a criterion-referenced score is on what it is that Johnny can do. Of course we can, and often do, interpret a single test score both ways. In norm referencing we might make a statement that "Johnny did better than 80 percent of the students in a test on addition of whole numbers." In criterion referencing we might say that "Johnny got 70 percent of the items correct in a test on addition of whole numbers." Usually we would add further "meaning" to this statement by stating whether or not we thought 70 percent was inadequate, minimally adequate, excellent, or whatever.

There is some debate about whether CRT carries with it any implied standard or set of standards. That is, do we reference the performance to a cutoff score (or set of cutoff scores)? It depends on what one means by "criterion" or "standard."

Glaser (1963) was one of the first to use the term *CRT*. At one point he suggests that "criterion-referenced measures indicate the content of the behavioral repertory, and the correspondence between what an individual does and the underlying continuum of achievement" (1963, p. 520). A bit later, though, he states that "we need to behaviorally specify minimum levels of performance" (p. 520). In 1971 Glaser and Nitko defined a criterion-referenced test as "one that is deliberately constructed so as to yield measurements that are directly interpretable *in terms of specified performance standards*" (Glaser & Nitko, 1971, p. 653, emphasis added). However, although often misinterpreted by subsequent CRT advocates, they apparently did not mean the standard was a cutting score. In 1980 Nitko continued to use the 1971 definition but clearly stated that one ought not to "confuse the meaning of criterion-referencing with the idea of having a *passing score* or *cut off score*" (Nitko, 1980, p. 50, emphasis in original). At any rate, everyone agrees that with a criterion-referenced interpretation of the scores the focus is on "what Johnny can do" and the comparison is to a behavioral domain. Whether there should be an implied standard of proficiency or cutoff score(s) is debatable. We suspect most users think of the criterion-referencing of scores in this fashion because of the close association in most people's minds between CRT and mastery testing.

Despite some disagreement about the proficiency aspect, measurement experts generally agree on the basic distinction between norm-referenced and criterion-referenced *score interpretation*. However, there are many disagreements about the distinctions between norm- and criterion-referenced *tests*. The definitions discussed earlier suggest that criterion-referenced tests are constructed to permit inferences from the results of test questions to the entire domain. Other definitions have varied (Ivens, 1970; Harris & Stewart, 1971; Millman, 1974).

Actually, most authors (for example, Popham, 1978, 1981; Hambleton & Eignor, 1979; Nitko, 1980) now admit that *domain-referenced* is the more accurate term. It carries no implication of a cutoff score or standard, which suits those who wish to delete this meaning from *criterion-referenced*. Unfortunately (in our opinion) Popham and others have chosen to continue using the term *criterion*. Their argument for doing so is that "even though in many educators' minds there was more confusion than clarity regarding that measurement notion, it was generally conceded that in criterion-referenced measurement educators had found a new approach to assessment which, for certain purposes, offered advantages over traditional measurement strategies" (Popham, 1981, p. 30). It seems unfortunate to retain a term that educators accept in spite of (or because of) their confusion.

The existing confusion over terms and definitions is partly caused by misunderstanding content validity. (See Chapter 4 for a discussion of content validity. Basically, content validity is related to how adequately the items in a test sample the domain about which inferences are to be made.) Some proponents of CRTs have said or strongly implied that norm-referenced measurement is limited to comparing people and unable to provide any information about what an individual can do—as if the comparison were not based on any content (for example, Samuels & Edwall, 1975; Popham, 1976). (One wonders why they suggest norm referencing CRTs if the process of norming indeed has negative impact on the content!) The debate often is really about the relative merits of "traditional" standardized achievement tests, which "people usually now refer to as norm-referenced tests" (Popham, 1981, p. 24) and tailor-made domain-referenced tests. Some people think that scores from traditional tests cannot be domain-referenced because the domain is not clearly defined and the items are not a random sample from the domain. Although publishers of some standardized tests do describe their content only in very general terms, others provide detailed content outlines. To be meaningful, any type of test score must be related to test content as well as to the scores of other examinees (Ebel, 1962, p. 19). Any test samples the content of some specified domain and has an implicit behavioral element. In norm-referenced measurement, in contrast to criterion-referenced measurement, "the inference is of the form—'more (or less) of trait x than the mean amount in population y'—rather than some specified amount that is meaningful in isolation" (Jackson, 1970, p. 2).

Careful reading of the content validity section of Chapter 4 should convince you that experts in achievement test construction have *always* stressed the importance of defining the specified content domain and sampling from it in some appropriate fashion. For example, in the *Standards for Educational and Psychological Testing* (AERA-APA-NCME, 1985, p. 25), Standard 3.2 for the development of any test states that "the definition of a universe or domain that is used for constructing or selecting items should be described." Thus, all achievement test items, norm- or criterion-referenced, should be keyed to a set of objectives and represent a specified content domain. If they do, the test is likely to have content validity. Although all good achievement tests (those with high content validity) are objective-based, very few can truly be called domain-referenced. In constructing such tests, one defines a content domain (but generally not with *complete* specificity) and writes items measuring this domain. But if any procedure (statistical or judgmental) has been used to select items on the basis of quality, then the test user can no longer infer that a student "knows" 75 percent of the domain because he or she answered 75 percent of the items correctly. The inability to draw this particular inference comes from the use of nonrandom procedures in choosing items. Actually there are few situations where we need to make the pure criterion-referenced interpretation. To know that an individual can type 60 words per minute on an IBM Selectric is a useful datum whether or not the words on the test were randomly chosen from some totally specified domain of words. To know that an individual can correctly add 80 percent of the items on paired three-digit whole numbers asked on a test is useful whether or not those items were randomly pulled from the total set of permutations possible.

Actually, the distinction many authors currently make between "norm-referenced *tests*" and "criterion-referenced *tests*" is based on the degree of precision in specifying the content domain and on the item-generating rules for sampling from that domain. Strong advocates of CRTs argue for very precise specifications of domains and item-generating rules. As they admit, most CRTs are not built with such precision and are not superior to traditional tests in content validity.

The difference between *existing* CRTs and NRTs is most obvious when considering the *breadth of the domain*. The typical norm-referenced achievement test is a survey instrument covering a broad domain, such as knowledge of the basic arithmetic functions of addition, subtraction, multiplication, and division, each with whole numbers, decimal fractions, and common fractions. One could think of 12 subdomains and sample from each when constructing the test. A typical criterion-referenced test would be likely to cover only one of these subdomains, or perhaps an even more specific domain (such as horizontal addition of two-digit numbers to two-digit numbers).

In our opinions, current terminology is quite misleading. We can recognize differences in *degree* as to whether or not a test represents a well-defined domain (is content valid). We can also recognize differences in degree of breadth of the domain. The terms *norm-referenced* and *criterion-referenced* should not be used to categorize tests on either of these bases. We believe the most logical distinction between a NRT and a CRT has to do with whether the comparison of the *score* is made to other individuals' scores (norm referencing) or to some specified standard or set of standards (criterion referencing). In either case we wish to infer from a test score to the domain that the test samples. Only in rare cases can we do this so precisely that we can estimate the percent of items known for the entire domain. That would be the *ideal* goal with respect to content validity. (This should be clearer after you read Chapter 4.) What we *can* do is to make sure the test, whether norm- or criterion-referenced, covers an identifiable set of objectives.

Uses for Norm-Referenced Measurement Most testing and the theory of testing have been based on the norm-referenced approach. Such an approach is useful in aptitude testing where we wish to make differential predictions. It is also often very useful to achievement testing. Many educators would agree with Gronlund's (1971, p. 139) statement: "In measuring the extent to which pupils are achieving our course objectives, we have no absolute standard by which to determine their progress. A pupil's achievement can be regarded as high or low only by comparing it with the achievement of other pupils."

Accepting this view, the purpose of a measuring device is to give us as reliable a rank ordering of the pupils as possible with respect to the achievement we are measuring. Knowing what we do about individual differences, it is obvious that students will learn differing amounts of subject matter even under a mastery learning approach (see, for example, Arlin, 1984). It may happen that all students, or at least a high percentage of them, have learned a significant enough portion of a teacher's objectives to be categorized as having "mastered" the essentials of the course or unit. But some of these students have learned more than others, and it seems worthwhile to employ measurement techniques that identify these pupils. In the first place, students want and deserve recognition for accomplishment that goes beyond the minimum. If we continually gave only minimum-level mastery tests, those students who accomplish at a higher level would lose one of the important extrinsic rewards of learning—that is, recognition for such accomplishments.

Perhaps a more important reason for normative testing than student recognition is in its benefits for decision making. Often, for vocational or educational planning, students wish to know how they compare to others with similar plans. Norm referencing is also necessary in selection decisions. If two physicians have mastered surgery, but one has mastered it better, which one would you want to have operate on you? (For that matter, even if two physicians have equally mastered their training program, you would probably want some norm-referencing information about time to completion. If one physician learns very slowly and takes five time longer than the other one to accomplish a task, you might safely assume that after 10 years of practice, that doctor will not be as up-to-date on current medical techniques as the fast learner.) If two teachers have mastered the basics of teaching, but one is a much better teacher, which one do we hire? If two students have mastered first-semester algebra, but one has learned it much more thoroughly (or faster, time being norm-referenced), which one should receive more encouragement to continue in mathematics? We probably all agree on the answers. If, however, we have not employed evaluation techniques that allow us to differentiate between the individuals, we cannot make these types of decisions. Certainly, norm-referenced measures are the more helpful in fixed-quota selection decisions. For example, if there were a limited number of openings in a pilot-training school, the school would want to select the best of the applicants—even though all may be above some "mastery level" (see Hunter & Schmidt, 1982).

Because standardized NRTs are often broader in focus than CRTs, they are more useful for providing a broad overview of the achievement levels in a given subject matter. They are better for monitoring the general progress of a student, classroom, or school. Although some individuals believe that general norm-referenced tests are insensitive to instruction, they do in fact show gains from grade to grade. Recall, however, that the performance on any test, broad or narrow in focus, can be either norm-referenced or criterion-referenced.

Norm-referenced testing is often considered a necessary component of program evaluation. We have mentioned that CRTs are often narrower in focus than NRTs. Some view this narrow focus as advantageous in program evaluation. We can construct a CRT over the particular program objectives to see if they have been achieved. In evaluating a program, however, we would also wish to know how effective the program is in comparison to other possible programs. Without random assignment of students to programs (which is seldom possible in schools) the comparison needs to be through some norm-referenced procedure that compares the performance of the pupils in the program with a norm group.

Moreover, the more narrow focus of a CRT may not be an unmitigated blessing. At times we desire to evaluate broader outcomes. Consider the following quote by Cronbach:

> In course evaluation, we need not be much concerned about making measuring instruments fit the curriculum. However startling this declaration may seem, and however contrary to the principles of evaluation for other purposes, this must be our position if we want to know what changes a course produces in the pupil. An ideal evaluation would include measures of all the types of proficiency that might reasonably be desired in the area in question, not just the selected outcomes to which this curriculum directs substantial attention. If you wish only to know how well a curriculum is achieving its objectives, you fit the test to the curriculum; but if you wish to know how well the curriculum is serving the national interest, you measure all outcomes that might be worth striving for. (1963, p. 680)

Uses for Criterion-Referenced Measurement   The recent support for criterion-referenced measurement seems to have originated in large part from the emphases on behavioral objectives, the sequencing and individualization of instruction, the development of programmed materials, a learning theory that *suggests* that almost anybody can learn almost anything if given enough time, the increased interest in certification (especially with what are called minimal competency exams), a belief that it is a beneficial procedure to decrease adverse impact, and a belief that norm referencing promotes unhealthy competition and is injurious to the self-concepts of low-scoring students.

If we can specify important objectives in behavioral terms, many would argue, the important consideration is to ascertain whether a student achieved those objectives rather than to determine his or her position relative to other students. Traditionally, the principal use of criterion-referenced measurement has been in mastery tests. A *mastery test* is a particular type of criterion-referenced test. *Mastery,* as the word is typically used, connotes an either/or situation. The person either has achieved (mastered) the objective(s) satisfactorily or has not. Criterion-referenced testing in general could also apply to degrees of performance. Mastery tests are used in programs of individualized instruction, such as the Individually Prescribed Instruction (IPI) program (Lindvall & Bolvin, 1967), or in the mastery learning model devised by Bloom (1968). Such instructional programs are composed of units or modules, usually considered hierarchical, each based on one or more instructional objectives. Individuals are required to work on the unit until they have achieved a specified minimum level of achievement. Then they are considered to have mastered the unit. In such programs the instructional decision of what to do with students is *not* dependent on how their performance compares to that of others. If they have performed adequately on the objectives, the decision is to move on to the next unit of study. If they have not, they are required to restudy the material (although perhaps using a different procedure) covered in the test until they perform adequately—that is, master the material. If instructional procedures are organized so that time is the dimension that varies and degree of mastery is held constant, mastery tests should be used in greater proportion than they are now.

Employing the individually prescribed instruction or mastery model of learning is not the only use for criterion-referenced measures. Such data may also be used to help evaluate (make decisions about) instructional programs. In order to determine whether specific instructional treatments or procedures have been successful, it is necessary to have data about the outcomes on the specific objectives the program was designed to teach. A measure comparing students to each other (norm referencing) may not present data as effectively as a measure comparing each student's performance to the objectives.

Criterion-referenced measures also offer certain benefits for instructional decision making within the classroom. The diagnosis of specific difficulties, accompanied by a prescription of certain instructional treatments, is necessary in instruction whether or not a mastery approach to learning is used.

Criterion-referenced tests can be useful in broad surveys of educational accomplishment such as the National Assessment of Educational Progress or state or local assessment programs.

Cautions in Criterion-Referenced Testing   The 1970s saw criterion-referenced measurement (CRT) revitalized from the 1920 era. Many recent writers (particularly in the more popularized, nontechnical professional journals) have been praising CRT and ignoring some cautions, dangers, and limitations. Although CRT can serve some important functions, it is useful to keep in mind the following points.

1. Criterion-referenced measurement is defined in many ways. The narrow, specific definition is that a CRT allows us to estimate the proportion of questions in a domain that a student would answer correctly. However, very few tests fit this definition, and we should recognize the limitations of making the strong inference from proportion correct in a sample of items to proportion correct in a population of items for most tests that are called criterion-referenced.

2. Many so-called CRTs have no more detailed specification of, or appropriate sampling of, content (content validity) than many NRTs.

3. If we choose items based on sensitivity to instruction (postinstruction minus preinstruction gain scores), then the resultant test is just as content "biased" as if we choose items based on their ability to differentiate between good and poor students.

4. Typically, in mastery testing we would not use items that tap the depth of learning of the few very best individuals. The next step might be to inappropriately exclude from the curriculum the ideas with which only a few students can cope (Gladstone, 1975). All teaching and testing should not be reduced to the minimal mastery level.

5. Many criterion-referenced tests are shorter and therefore less reliable than norm-referenced tests.

6. The questions of how long to make the test and how high to set the cutting score can be answered only by reasonably complicated psychometric procedures that require some fairly specific assumptions about the costs of making errors (Hambleton & Novick, 1973; Millman, 1974; Swaminathan, Hambleton, & Algina, 1975).

7. Criterion-referenced test results do not inform decision makers whether individuals achieve what they should when they should (Grosswald, 1973).

8. Criterion-referenced test prescriptions can be ignored by teachers as readily as they ignore item analyses of norm-referenced tests (Grosswald, 1973).

9. Criterion-referenced tests must be interpreted cautiously. If students fail to master an objective, the fault may be in the instruction, the test items, the standard of mastery, and/or the objective itself (Gronlund, 1973, p. 40).

Comparing the Two Measures   When to use norm-referenced interpretations and when to use criterion-referenced interpretations depends upon the kind of decision one wishes to make. For guidance decisions we should employ both NR and CR interpretations. CRTs are used mostly in achievement testing. Aptitude, interest, and most personality inventories are norm-referenced. This seems appropriate. In general it is probably more useful for people to know how their aptitudes or interests compare with those of others than to obtain some kind of CR score. For selection decisions, NRT is preferred. For classification decisions both CRT and NRT might be used. For placement and certification decisions, CRT might primarily be used. For instructional decisions, it depends mostly upon the instructional procedures employed. For example, if instruction is organized so that time is the variable and students keep at a task until they have mastered it, then we should use mastery testing. This type of instruction is often employed in individualized instruction. If instruction is organized so that time of exposure is constant, students will achieve at different levels, and we should attempt to discern this differential achievement with a test that discriminates, although we might well want to attach both normative and criterion-referenced meaning to the score. Which instructional procedure should be used depends upon the structure and importance of the subject matter being taught.

Surely some subjects are so structured that it is futile to teach higher concepts until basic ones have been mastered. For example, students cannot do long division until they can subtract and multiply at some basic level (although precisely at *what* level is unknown). This is certainly not true of all subjects, however. We do not really need to have mastered (or even have read) *A Tale of Two Cities* before reading *Catcher in the Rye,* or vice versa.

Likewise, as mentioned earlier, some skills or knowledges may be so important that all students should master them, regardless of how long it takes. Knowing how to spell one's name probably fits in this category. But, again, this is not true of all subjects. With regard to this point, Ebel has stated:

> *We might be willing to allow one student a week to learn what another can learn in a day. But sum these differences over the myriads of things to be learned. Does anyone, student, teacher, or society, want to see one person spend 16 or 24 years getting the same elementary education another can get in eight? Should it be those least able to learn quickly who spend the largest portion of their lives in trying to learn? Our present practice is quite the reverse. Those who are facile in learning make a career of it. Those who are not find other avenues of service, fulfillment and success. (Ebel, 1969, p. 12)*

Gronlund (1978, p. 41) made a distinction between objectives that are considered as *minimum essentials* and those which encourage *maximum development*. For the former, one would want to employ mastery testing; for the latter, discrimination testing. Thus for instructional decision making we are suggesting that there is a place for both mastery (criterion-referenced) and discrimination (norm-referenced) testing. The way most schools are currently organized, with time of instruction constant for all individuals and degree of learning the variable, discrimination testing should be prevalent. However, as more individualized instructional processes are used and as more is learned about how various subject matters should be sequenced, mastery testing may become increasingly important. Mastery testing is probably more important in the early elementary grades than later in school.

Finally, we should mention again that many tests are amenable to both norm- and criterion-referenced interpretation. Publishers of some standardized achievement tests, for example, report a norm-referenced score on each subtest and within each subtest report whether a pupil answered each item correctly as well as the percentage of pupils in the classroom, building, district, and national norm group who got the item correct. These item statistics are also frequently collated over items for each objective and the data reported for each objective.

Sources of Information

Once you have determined specifically what sort of information you want to obtain from a test, how can you find out what tests will give this information, and how should you choose among them? There are many sources of information that can assist in this decision. Some of these are Buros' *Mental Measurements Yearbooks* (1938, 1941, 1949, 1953, 1959, 1965, 1972, 1978), *Test in Print III* (Mitchell, 1983), several handbooks from the Center for the Study of Evaluation, a new volume of *Test Critiques* (Keyser & Sweetland, 1984), publishers' catalogs, specimen tests, professional journals, and measurement texts.

A good initial source of information is the *Eighth Mental Measurements Yearbook* (*MMY*) (Buros, 1978). This latest edition lists most of the published standardized tests that were in print at the time the yearbook went to press. Information for each test includes title, author, publisher, publication date, purpose of test, levels, forms, cost, time to administer, and so on. Those tests not reviewed in earlier editions (and those previously reviewed that have been revised) are described and criticized by educational and psychological authorities. The *MMY* also contains reviews of measurement texts, a directory of test publishers, and name, title, and classification indexes of all tests listed. Each school district should own a copy of this book and use it extensively in the test selection process.

Tests in Print III (Mitchell, 1983) is a comprehensive bibliography and index to the first eight books in the *Mental Measurements Yearbook* series. A total of 2672 tests are listed. Each test mentioned in *Tests in Print III* includes the following information:

1. Test title
2. Appropriate grade or age levels
3. Publication date
4. Special short comments about the test
5. Number and type of scores provided
6. Authors

7. Publisher
8. Reference to test reviews in *Mental Measurements Yearbooks*

The Buros Institute (University of Nebraska), publishers of *Tests in Print III* and forthcoming *MMY*s, offers an online computer service through Bibliographic Retrieval Services (BRS). The data base includes the test descriptions and reviews of all the tests mentioned in the *Eighth MMY*, but it is updated monthly with information and reviews on new or revised tests. The data base can be accessed (under the Search Label *MMYD*) through any library that offers the BRS service (see Mitchell, 1984, for a more thorough description). The Educational Testing Service also has information about new and revised tests available through the BRS services.

The Center for the Study of Evaluation (CSE) sources include the handbooks *Preschool/Kindergarten Test Evaluations, Elementary School Test Evaluations,* and *Secondary School Test Evaluations.* The secondary level comprises three separate volumes: one for grades 7 and 8, one for grades 9 and 10, and one for grades 11 and 12. There is also a handbook for higher-order skills, so there exist six handbooks in all. The approach used in these handbooks is to rate potential tests for various instructional objectives in terms of the tests' validity; appropriateness; ease of administration, scoring, and interpretation; reliability; range of coverage; and fineness of score gradations.

As mentioned, another source is *Test Critiques* (Keyser & Sweetland, 1984). While so far only Volume 1 has been published, Volumes 2 and 3 are in press. These works all give critical reviews of tests in much the same fashion as the *Mental Measurements Yearbooks.*

Sources of information about unpublished or little-known instruments can be found in such references as *A Sourcebook for Mental Health Measures* (Comrey, Backer, & Glaser, 1973), *Measures for Psychological Assessment* (Chun, Cobb, & French, 1976), and a two-volume *Directory of Unpublished Experimental Mental Measures* (Goldman & Busch, 1978; Goldman & Saunders, 1974). Sources about instruments for children include two handbooks in *Tests and Measurements in Child Development: Handbooks I and II* (Johnson & Bommarito, 1971; Johnson, 1976).

Test publishers' catalogs are a particularly good source for locating new and recently revised tests. These catalogs provide basic information about the purpose and content of the test, appropriate level, working time, cost, and scoring services available. An important piece of information not provided in all publishers' catalogs is the copyright date (or norm date).[3]

After some promising tests have been located by searching the *Mental Measurements Yearbooks,* the CSE handbooks, and the publishers' catalogs, the tests must be examined before a final selection is made and large

---

[3] Addresses of test publishers are listed in Appendix A.

quantities are ordered. For a very nominal price most publishers will send specimen sets of tests. These sets usually include the test booklet, answer sheet, administrator's manual, and technical manual, as well as complete information on cost and scoring services. Careful study of the set is essential in determining whether a given test meets the specific purposes a teacher has in mind. For example, a seventh-grade modern-math teacher may receive a brochure describing a modern-math achievement test. From published reviews as well as from the descriptive literature provided, this test seems to be appropriate. But is it? Even though the professional reviewers approve the test from a technical standpoint and praise its modern content, the test may still be inappropriate. The seventh-grade teacher may stress fundamental operations in set theory, but the test may have only two items devoted to testing this concept. The teacher may skim over binary operations, but more than 25 percent of the test may be devoted to this topic. The teacher may stress commutative, associative, and distributive properties without resorting to technical jargon. Although measuring these same properties, the test may assume the pupils' understanding of this mathematical language. This disparity between what the test is designed to measure and what the teacher actually teaches will not be evident except by detailed examination of the test and the test manual.

In addition to providing the information that can be obtained from a specimen set, several publishers have regional representatives who will visit the school and answer any questions the testing committee may have about their tests. It would be wise to consider inviting such representatives to a testing committee meeting before making a final selection. These representatives typically are quite well qualified, often having an M.A. or a Ph.D. degree in the field of educational measurement.

Other sources of information are the test reviews found in the professional periodicals. Journals such as the *Journal of Educational Measurement*, the *Journal of Counseling Psychology,* and *Measurement and Evaluation in Counseling and Development* typically carry reviews of some of the more recently published or revised tests. *Educational and Psychological Measurement* publishes a validity studies section twice a year. The bulk of the articles in this section are reports of studies using various standardized instruments for predictive purposes. Textbooks on measurement also usually include information on various tests.

It should be obvious that an abundance of sources of information about tests is available. These sources should be used to a considerable extent. It makes test selection both easier and better.

Characteristics of Tests and Manuals

Several characteristics of tests and test manuals must be considered when selecting tests. Some of the data regarding these characteristics may be found in published reviews, such as in Buros' yearbooks; some may be found in publishers' catalogs; some must be obtained from the technical manuals. Unfortunately, all relevant information is just not available for some tests. The *Standards for Educational and Psychological Testing* (AERA-APA-NCME, 1985) is a guide that recommends certain uniform standards for tests as well as standards for the *use* of tests. These standards are intended to apply to most published devices for diagnosis, prognosis, and evaluation. They do not apply to devices used only for research, but rather to those that will be used as an aid in practical decision making. The standards make recommendations on six specific topics for developers and for users.

The importance of the individual recommendations made in the *Standards* is indicated by two levels: primary and secondary. At different places in this text we discuss many of the points made in the *Standards*. Nevertheless, serious developers, selectors, and users of tests should review these standards with care. Most reputable publishers pay close attention to the standards in developing their tests and in preparing their manuals. If the publishers have good data on the norms, reliability, validity, and other characteristics of their tests, they typically provide the information in the manual. If the manual does *not* have such information, it seems reasonable to infer that the test developer did not do an adequate job in investigating these important qualities of the test or that the data are such that the publisher prefers not to report them.

PRACTICAL ASPECTS OF TESTING

The range of practical tasks begins with test selection but also includes administration, scoring, and interpretation. These are aspects that, although separate tasks, should be taken into consideration along with such factors as reliability and validity at the time of test selection. These factors will therefore be considered in terms both of their importance in test selection and of their unique aspects in the whole process of test use.

Test selection should be guided in part by such factors as ease of administration and scoring, availability of norms, availability of equivalent or parallel forms, and the test's ultimate utility (utility depends upon the test's reliability and validity). Other things being equal, one will wish to select the test that is easiest to administer and score and the one that is accompanied by the most detailed manual outlining the procedure to be followed. Factors considered in this section are administration, scoring, cost, and format. Interpretation is covered in various chapters. Reliability and validity are covered in Chapters 3 and 4.

Administration

A characteristic of the standardized test that distinguishes it from the teacher-made test is that the standardized test has a uniform procedure with respect to administration. This procedure refers to the physical arrangements made for the actual testing as well as to the directions to be employed in administering the test. Conditions prior to the actual testing also are relevant.

Administrative Decisions and Details   It may seem condescending to spell out the specifics in administering a testing program. We do want to emphasize, however, that even small details are important. Many a testing session has been less than ideal because someone overlooked a detail. An adequate number of tests, answer sheets, and pencils should be available. (*Education Week* [1984] reported that in one county over 10,000 answer sheets were misread because pencils with an insufficient graphite core had been used.) The administrator must be familiar with the test being given; an administrator's test manual is necessary. Enough time must be allowed for the test. A suitable room (well lighted, quiet) must be made available. Adequate seating space must be provided. A watch or clock with a second hand is frequently needed. The presence of a trained proctor is often necessary. And staff must be given directions about what to do with those little gummed labels containing numbers which are returned from the scoring services. Two topics that deserve some additional discussion are scheduling the tests and preparing the faculty and students for the testing.

Scheduling Tests.   There are many views on the question of the time at which tests should be administered. Some practitioners feel that all tests should be administered in the morning, when most people are physically and mentally at their peak. Others believe that tests should never be given on Mondays or Fridays. Some people think that tests should be administered at the same time of the year that the tests were given to the standardization sample; others feel that interpolations or extrapolations of the norm data can be made valid to correct for differing time conditions.

In general, time of the day and day of the week are not too important. It would probably be best not to give the test right after lunch or right before a pep rally for the homecoming game, but no valid evidence suggests that some days or times of day are particularly bad. *However, it is important in achievement testing to try to administer the test at the same time of year as when the norming was done.* Assume that the normative data for a test were gathered in October. The norm group's seventh-graders might have a mean raw score of 85; the eighth-graders, a mean raw score of 125. Can one predict from these data what a mean raw score for the norm group's seventh-graders would have been if they had been tested in June (nine months after the norm group was actually tested)? Some test companies would answer affirmatively and provide interpolated norms depicting this mean to be 115 (three-fourths the distance between 85 and 125). However, in some subjects it might well be that at the end of the year, seventh-graders perform better than beginning eighth-graders because the latter forget during the summer months. This illustrates one of the dangers of attempting to use the interpolated norms of test companies—norms arrived at mathematically rather than empirically. For this reason it is best to administer achievement tests at the same time of year as the actual norm data were gathered. Another possibility is to choose a test having norms gathered during the time of year the teacher wishes to test. (Most tests have normative data for fall and spring.)

Suppose a choice must be made between two equally valid achievement tests. They differ only insofar as the time normative data were gathered— fall and spring. Which test should be used? This is indeed an important point to consider. If the data are to be used to assist the teacher during the regular school year, it might be advisable to test in the fall. Adams has suggested five basic advantages of testing in the fall.

> (1) It permits the teacher to obtain a complete test record for each student. When students have been tested the preceding spring, pickup testing is necessary for new entrants. (2) The data are up-to-date. During a long vacation, many students lose in varying degrees their proficiency in certain skills; on the other hand some students have gained in reading achievement through their summer reading. Others may have gained in skill subjects through attendance at summer school or through special tutoring. (3) Fall testing places the emphasis on the analysis of student needs, rather than the evaluation of teaching. (4) More time is available for the administration and scoring of tests and the analysis of results. End-of-year pressures can result in tests being filed away without being used. (5) Up-to-date test results can be used as a basis for grouping students for differentiated work or special corrective instruction. Moreover, scores on survey tests serve as a starting point for the use of supplementary diagnostic methods to determine specific retraining needs. (1964, p. 499)

Thus, in fall testing, we use the results as input data. Spring testing is more useful as accountability outcome data. We can use it for such purposes as determining the school's standing in comparison with other schools in the district, state, or nation; in making future curriculum and instructional decisions; as research data in evaluating teaching effectiveness; and in helping to determine which students are in need of summer instruction. All in all, the time of testing will depend, in large part, upon the uses to which the data will be put. Recall that this decision may relate to which test to use, since interpolated norms can be misleading.

In addition to scheduling the time of testing, someone has to decide on the place of testing. Test administrators often neglect to ensure that pupils take the test under similar physical testing conditions. In other words, they sometimes fail to consider the seating arrangements, the ventilation, the heat, the lighting, and so on. There is no doubt that an individual's test score can be somewhat influenced by the physical conditions under which the test is taken. All pupils should take the test under conditions that duplicate as closely as possible those that existed when the test was standardized. (It is usually assumed that these conditions have been optimal.)

After decisions have been made as to when and where the tests are to be given, exact schedules should be given to all educators in the school so that they will not plan other activities (such as field trips) for the same time. Of course this requires two-way cooperation. The test director should not schedule tests to conflict with other scheduled activities (such as the pep rally for homecoming).

Preparing Faculty and Students.   Each year teachers and other school personnel should have a brief in-service workshop describing various aspects of the testing program. Suggested topics for this program include the following:

1. Why the school gives standardized tests.
2. A brief description of each test—what it measures and its intended purpose.
3. How test results can assist the classroom teacher.
4. How to administer standardized tests.

The first and third topics often are inadequately covered in these workshops, yet they are important. Teachers sometimes resent the amount of instructional time lost to standardized test administration. If the teachers could see how the data were to be used, they might be less resentful of tests and of the time necessary to administer them properly.

The last topic (how to administer standardized tests) is significant, because in all likelihood teachers will serve as test administrators. We feel that for most group tests, the ordinary classroom teacher is capable of administering the test without any formal or specialized training beyond an in-service workshop. What must be stressed is that the directions in the test manual must be followed exactly (Yamamoto and Dizney, 1965). For example, if test A has three subparts and the manual states that part 1 is to be given first, test givers must administer part 1 first even though they think that it would be better to administer the test in a different order. Deviating from the directions given may make the norms provided misleading. Some specific dos and don'ts follow:

DO

- Read the test manual and study the test at least two or three days before the test is administered.
- Adhere explicitly to the directions for administration printed in the test manual.
- Be sure that you are using the correct form or level of the test.
- Call the test publisher *before* the test is administered if you have any questions or note any inconsistencies in the test manual.

- Make sure that you are using the correct answer sheet if you are having the test scored by the publisher or some external agency.

DON'T
- Deviate from the printed directions—that is, do not ad lib the directions even though you have given the test many times.
- Deviate from the specified time(s), give hints, clarify the meaning of words, and so on.
- Minimize the importance of the test even though you may personally feel it is useless. Never make a statement such as "I'm sorry we have to waste time on this test, but the school board has ordered me to give it."

An example of a simplified method of administering tests is called CAST (Controlled Administration of Standardized Tests, sold by MSRD, a subsidiary of the Psychological Corporation). CAST uses cartridge playback equipment to ensure fair presentation to all examinees. Starting and stopping signals as well as the test directions are presented by the tape so that timing and directions are both controlled with complete accuracy.

Occasionally instructions to the students concerning guessing are vague. Because it is not always made clear, test administrators are frequently asked if a penalty is imposed for guessing. If the test giver knows how the test is to be scored (that is, whether or not a guessing formula will be applied) but the directions read to the students are vague, any questions that students raise about the use of guessing formulas must be answered without giving additional information. This could be done, for example, by the administrator's saying something like, "The directions suggest that . . ." and then rereading the directions. Any direct answer providing more information than the original instructions would destroy the test makers' attempt to establish a certain mental set.

Students also need to be prepared for taking standardized tests. People usually perform better at any endeavor, including test taking, if they approach that experience with a positive attitude. Yet test administrators frequently do not establish a positive mental attitude in those being tested.

We know that test anxiety influences optimum performance. It is the task of the administrator to prepare the student emotionally for the test. Students should be motivated to do their best, but should not be made unduly anxious. If students are made aware of the benefits they will derive from accurate test results, the information should do much toward setting the proper emotional climate (see Karmos & Karmos, 1984; Taylor & White, 1982).

Besides the motivating factor, other characteristics of students may affect their test performance but are not related to what the test is attempting to measure. For instance, all individuals have certain personality traits that govern their test-taking behavior. Students also vary in their degree of test-wiseness or in their ability to pick up cues from the format of a test item or of the test itself. To equate for this variable, it would be best to attempt to have all students at approximately the same level of test-taking sophistication. Books such as those written by Millman & Pauk (1969) and Juola (1968) are useful in teaching students some test-taking skills. Those interested in reviewing more literature on the topic of test-taking skills are referred to Moore (1971) and Slakter, Koehler, & Hampton (1970a & b). Many school districts and state departments of education have prepared guides to test taking. Two of the better examples are pamphlets from Michigan (Caswell, 1981) and Florida (Hills, 1981). In Chapter 6, more will be said about the various factors that can affect an examinee's score.

Ease of Administration   In the selection of tests, ease of administration as well as the adequacy of the directions presented must be considered. The nature of the test with respect to time limits will also influence the selection of one test over another. If one test takes 75 minutes to administer but consists of three parts, the longest of which takes 30 minutes, and another test takes 55 minutes but must be given at one time, class schedules may dictate which test should be used, because most schools operate with periods from 30 to 50 minutes. Any test that necessitates a change in the school's operating procedure should be considered carefully before being selected. Naturally, if the so-called inconvenient test is a much better test, it should be selected regardless of the slight inconvenience that might result.

Test users must critically examine the test manual and assess the adequacy of the directions for administration. The test publisher has an obligation to furnish a manual describing standard testing conditions, as well as norms and directions that are clear and concise. On the other hand, administrators must provide for standard testing conditions and qualified test givers. Only when these conditions are met will students be able to perform maximally according to clear and concise instructions that both they and the examiner fully comprehend.

Scoring

A variety of scoring devices are currently available. Briefly, there are two widely used methods: (1) hand scoring, either in the booklets themselves or on separate answer sheets, and (2) machine-scored answer sheets. The manner in which the tests are to be scored depends, at least in part, on the availability of special scoring equipment or on the monetary resources to have the answer sheets scored by the test publisher or by an independent scoring service.

Hand Scoring   Hand scoring is primarily used in the preschool or primary grades, because this method is relatively easy for the children to understand. Here the subject is asked to perform a task such as "Cross out the thing that doesn't belong in this group" or "Draw a line from the wagon to the horse," and the pupil proceeds to record the answer directly in the test booklet. The test booklets are then hand-scored. Pupils can also record their answers to multiple-choice test items on a separate answer sheet, and a punched key can then be placed over the answer sheet to obtain the score. This key is nothing more than the regular answer sheet with the correct responses punched out. The teacher places the key over the pupil's answer sheet and counts the number of blackened spaces to determine the number of items answered correctly. One advantage of separate answer sheets is that the test booklet can be used repeatedly, which reduces the cost of test administration.

Machine Scoring   The simplest way to score select-type objective test items is to have pupils record their responses on a separate answer sheet and then have the answer sheet machine-scored. Although separate answer sheets make scoring easier and more reliable, they are *not* recommended for young and slow-learning children because of the inconclusive evidence regarding their appropriateness with such children (Cashen & Ramseyer, 1969; Clark, 1968; Gaffney & Maguire, 1971; McKee, 1967; Moore, 1960; and Ramseyer & Cashen, 1971). Machine scoring of test booklets is available for use with young children. When a separate answer sheet is used, pupils must remember the question that they are answering (especially if they skip one) and the answer selected, and then transfer the answer accurately to the answer sheet. Such a task may be too demanding for very young children (kindergarten and first-graders definitely). If separate answer sheets are used, the pupils must be taught how to use an answer sheet, should be given practice with it, and should be given examples on the test. It would be helpful for the teacher also to give examples on the use of the answer sheet before the test begins.

When feasible, we recommend the use of a separate machine-scorable answer sheet for efficiency and accuracy. A disadvantage of machine scoring is that, unless directions are given explicitly and followed by the student, scoring errors will occur. The errors can be minimized by a preliminary screening; however, the time required for correcting sloppy and/or smudgy papers may prove costly. This need for re-marking or correcting can be almost entirely eliminated by careful administrative directions and practice before the test is taken.

Although schools with either small testing programs or a small enrollment would not be in a position to justify the expenditure of funds to purchase or lease sophisticated test-scoring equipment, simpler versions are available to them. In the past few years, small, relatively inexpensive scoring machines have appeared, with prices varying from about $1000 to $3000.

For volume users, commercial firms will provide test-scoring services for a very nominal charge. In addition to scoring the tests, publishers make available a variety of reporting services, including information on classroom, building, and district averages. For a small charge, state universities or large school districts will also score answer sheets. Those considering the processing of separate answer sheets by machine should compare the costs and services offered so that they will be able to process their answer sheets most economically.

Although such factors as validity, reliability, availability of norms, equivalent forms, and ease of administration and scoring are all to be considered seriously in test selection, two other minor points should also be evaluated in selecting a test: cost and format.

Cost

Cost should be only an ancillary factor in deciding which test is to be employed. Other things being equal, of course, the teacher or counselor should select the test that will have the lowest per pupil cost in terms of administration and scoring. However, validity, reliability, norms, an adequate manual, and the like are all more important than cost. Just as in any purchase, one test at ten cents may be a good buy, whereas another at six cents may be too expensive. We should consider *what* we are getting for our money rather than *how much* it will cost us to provide an adequate and meaningful testing program in our school.

Format

Just as we should not judge a book by its cover, so should we not judge a test by its initial appearance. Nevertheless, whenever possible we should select the test that is most attractive in appearance and that is printed in clear type of a size appropriate for the grade level. If illustrations are used in the test, they should be of high quality. Too often tests used at the preschool or primary level contain illustrations that are fuzzy, hazy, and ambiguous. When the quality of reproduction is such that pupils might answer incorrectly because of the illustrations used rather than because they do not know the correct answer, we should look for a better test.

REVIEWING AND CRITIQUING A STANDARDIZED TEST

We have discussed some basic considerations and practical aspects of test selection. Before selecting a test, it may be helpful to use the same format for reviewing several competing tests. The following factors should be considered:

1. Purpose(s) of testing in the local school district.
2. Purpose(s) and recommended use of test as stated in the manual.

3. Grade level(s) of test.
4. Availability of alternate forms.
5. Copyright date of test.
6. Format.
7. Cost.
8. Content appropriateness.
9. Administration ease.
10. Scoring ease and expense.
11. Types of scores provided.
12. Adequacy of the norms (including recency).
13. Test reliability.
14. Test validity.
15. Instructional and interpretative aids provided.

Many of these factors have already been discussed. Others (reliability and validity) are discussed in Chapters 3 and 4 respectively. In each of Chapters 7, 8, and 9, we have thoroughly critiqued at least one test according to most of the factors listed above. After finishing the study of this text, it is hoped that you will be able to critique a test comprehensively enough so that you are able to select the best test for your purpose from among the competing tests. (For a proposed set of guidelines for evaluating criterion-referenced tests see Hambleton & Eignor, 1978.)

SUMMARY

The following statements summarize the major points of this chapter:

1. A variety of controversial, intellectual, philosophical, political, social, legal, educational, and psychometric issues exist in measurement.
2. The term *test* refers to the presentation of a standard set of questions to be answered.
3. The concept of *measurement* is broader than that of testing. We can measure characteristics in ways other than by giving tests.
4. Evaluation is the process of delineating, obtaining, and providing useful information for judging decision alternatives.
5. Standardized tests are commercially prepared instruments for which administrative and scoring procedures are carefully delineated by the authors. Typically, norms are provided as interpretive aids.
6. Standardized tests are classified as (a) aptitude tests, (b) achievement tests, and (c) interest, personality, and attitude inventories.
7. Measurement and evaluation are essential to sound educational decision making.
8. Every person must at some time make educational decisions.
9. A good decision is based on relevant and accurate information. The

responsibility of gathering and imparting that information belongs to the professional (educator, psychologist, employer).

10. Standardized tests serve as aids in instructional, guidance, administrative, and research decisions.
11. In test selection, the first step is to determine the purposes for which testing is to be done.
12. Norm referencing is used to interpret a score of a person by comparing it with those of others.
13. Criterion referencing is used to interpret a person's performance by comparing it to some specified behavioral criterion.
14. To be most meaningful, a test score should be related to both norms and criteria.
15. The principal use of criterion-referenced measurement is in mastery testing.
16. An achievement test should be based on specified content (must be content-valid) whether one employs norm or criterion referencing.
17. A *pure* criterion-referenced test (also called a *domain-referenced* test) is a test consisting of a sample of questions drawn from a domain in such a fashion that one may estimate the proportion of questions from the total domain a pupil knows based on the proportion of test questions answered correctly. Few tests fit this narrow definition.
18. Typically, the objectives sampled in a criterion-referenced test are more narrow in focus than the objectives sampled in a norm-referenced test.
19. Norm-referenced measurement is necessary for making differential predictions.
20. If pupils differ in achievement levels, normative information can often assist in decision making.
21. Norm-referenced testing is often considered a necessary component of program evaluation.
22. Whether norm-referenced or criterion-referenced measurement is used depends upon the kind of decision one wishes to make.
23. The *Mental Measurements Yearbooks, Tests in Print III,* various CSE handbooks, publishers' catalogs, specimen sets, professional periodicals, and measurement textbooks are all fruitful sources of information about tests.
24. In administering a standardized test, the uniform procedure specified in the administrator's manual must be followed.
25. Whether standardized tests should be given in the fall or the spring depends upon the uses to which the data will be put. Fall testing is more useful if input data are desired. Spring testing is more useful in providing outcome data. Testers should choose a test normed at the same time of year that they plan to administer it.
26. Both faculty and students need preparation before standardized tests are administered.

27. Responses may be made either directly on the test or on a separate answer sheet. Separate answer sheets should not be used for children below grade 3 unless special instructions and practice have been given.
28. In comparing tests for test selection, some sort of systematic procedure should be followed. Several factors to consider are suggested in the text.

POINTS TO PONDER

1. What educational or psychological decisions should be made without a consideration of standardized test data? Should any decisions be made in the absence of data?
2. Is the decision about whether a person attends college an individual or an institutional decision? Can it be both?
3. Should public school educators be concerned with the *research* functions of standardized tests? Has too much class time been devoted to this function?
4. In determining who should be admitted to Honors Algebra, should norm-referenced or criterion-referenced measurement be considered?
5. Test administration involves many aspects. What factors must the examiner be alert to during the test administration? (*Hint:* Cheating is one such factor.)
6. You are responsible for selecting a standardized achievement survey battery for your elementary school. You have finally narrowed your selection to Test A. At the staff meeting, you announce your choice. One of your colleagues challenges your selection and states that Test B is equally good. What kinds of evidence or support should you present in defense of your choice of Test A?

CHAPTER 2

Some Basic Statistical Concepts Related to Testing and Test Selection

KINDS OF SCORES
SHAPES OF DATA DISTRIBUTIONS
MEASURES OF CENTRAL TENDENCY
MEASURES OF VARIABILITY
MEASURES OF RELATIONSHIP

When given a set of scores, one may have difficulty in determining their meaning. If people are going to use data successfully in decision making, they must have some knowledge of how to describe and synthesize data. In this chapter we discuss various kinds of data distributions and some of the concepts of basic descriptive statistics, such as measures of central tendency, variability, and relationship.

After completing this chapter the student should be able to do the following:

1. Comprehend the differences between nominal, ordinal, interval, and ratio data.
2. Recognize the relationship between the shape of the data distribution and the relative positions of measures of central tendency.
3. Determine the mean and median of a set of test scores.
4. Understand how the measures of central tendency differ and the significance of those differences.
5. Determine the variance and standard deviation of a set of test scores.
6. Know the relationship between standard deviation units and the area under a normal curve.

7. Interpret the Pearson r as a measure of relationship.
8. Appreciate the value of the information presented in this chapter to educators, psychologists, and others who wish to describe or interpret data.

KINDS OF SCORES

Data differ in terms of what properties of the real number series (order, distance, or origin) we can attribute to the scores. The most common—though not the most refined—classification of scores is one suggested by Stevens (1946), who classified scales as *nominal, ordinal, interval,* and *ratio* scales.

Nominal Scales

A nominal scale is the simplest scale of measurement. It involves the assignment of different numerals to categories that are qualitatively different. For example, for purposes of storing data on computer cards, we might use the symbol "0" to represent a female and the symbol "1" to represent a male. These symbols (or numerals) do not have any of the three characteristics (order, distance, or origin) we attribute to the real number series. The 1 does not indicate more of something than the 0. Some psychologists do not wish to consider the nominal scale as a scale of measurement, but others do. It depends on how one defines measurement. If measurement is defined as "the assignment of numerals to objects or events according to rules" (Stevens, 1946), then nominal data indicate measurement. If, on the other hand, measurement implies a *quantitative* difference, then nominal data do not indicate measurement.

Regardless of how we define measurement, nominal data have some uses. Whether or not categories (such as sex) are ordered, it is often helpful to know to which category an individual belongs.

Ordinal Scales

An ordinal scale has the order property of a real number series and gives an indication of rank order. Thus, magnitude is indicated, if only in a very gross fashion. Rankings in a music contest or in an athletic event would be examples of ordinal data. We know who is best, second best, third best, and so on, but the ranks provide no information with regard to the differences between the scores. Ranking is obviously sufficient if our decision involves selecting the top pupils for some task. It is insufficient if we wish to obtain any idea of the magnitude of differences or to use the process to perform certain kinds of statistical manipulations.

Interval Scales

With interval data we can interpret the distances between scores. If, on a test with interval data, Shelly has a score of 60, Susan a score of 50, and Sally a score of 30, we could say that the distance between Susan's and Sally's scores (50–30) is twice the distance between Shelly's and Susan's scores (60–50). This additional information is obviously of potentially greater use than just knowing the rank order of the three students. It has been hotly debated whether or not most psychological data really have the properties of an interval scale. (See, for example, Coombs, 1964.) In general, however, educators and psychologists have treated (interpreted) most test data as being interval measurement.

Ratio Scales

If one has measured with a ratio scale, the ratio of the scores has meaning. Thus, a person who is 7'2" is twice as tall as a person who is 3'7". We can make this statement because a measurement of "0" actually indicates no height. That is, there is a meaningful zero point. Very few (if any) psychological measures provide ratio data. (Occasionally a psychologist will suggest that something like attitude can be measured on a ratio scale, since a neutral attitude could be considered a meaningful zero.) Note that in the interval-data example of Shelly's, Susan's, and Sally's scores, we could not say that Shelly had twice as much of the characteristic being measured as Sally. To make such a statement would require that one assume a score of "0" to actually represent *no amount* of the characteristic. In general, if a person received a score of zero on a spelling test, we would not interpret the score to mean that the person had *no* spelling ability. The same is true of any other test.

Educators, then, usually interpret (treat) test data as representing interval but not ratio scales, although when using percentiles only ordinality need be assumed. Assuming we obtain a set of scores having properties of interval data, what can we do to aid us in interpreting these scores?

SHAPES OF DATA DISTRIBUTIONS

Distributions of scores can assume many different shapes. When only a small number of scores are plotted, the shape of the curve will be very uneven or irregular. With a large number of scores, the curve is ordinarily expected to take on a more smooth or regular appearance. The shape of this smooth curve will depend both upon the properties of the measuring instrument and the distribution of the underlying characteristic we are attempting to measure. Four types of distributions most frequently discussed in educational and psychological measurement are *normal distributions, positively skewed distributions, negatively skewed distributions,* and *rectangular distributions.*

A normal distribution is a bell-shaped curve, as shown in Figure 2.1. There has been considerable discussion in the past about whether human characteristics are normally distributed. Evidence of physical traits like height and weight lend some support to those who take the position that such characteristics are normally distributed. It is debatable, though, whether any reference can be drawn from this observation about the distribution of psychological characteristics. The distributions obtained from tests cannot be used as evidence of the distribution of the trait itself, because the test-score distributions may be influenced greatly by the characteristics of a test. For example, very difficult or very easy tests will not produce normal distributions of scores. Whatever the truth about the underlying distribution of a characteristic for humans in general, classes of 20 to 50 students are *not* likely to be distributed normally with respect to any attribute. The test results from the large norm groups used for standardized tests are likely to appear more normal. (We arc not concerned about whether this is due to the normal distribution of the characteristic we are measuring or is an artifact of the properties of the measuring instrument.) We will discuss further some properties of the normal curve when we consider measures of central tendency and variability and types of scores.

In a positively skewed distribution (see Figure 2.2) most of the scores pile up at the low end of the distribution. This might occur, for example, if we gave a test that was extremely difficult. Or if we were plotting teachers' salaries and most of the teachers had very little experience (thus having relatively low salaries), we might obtain a positively skewed distribution.

A negatively skewed distribution is shown in Figure 2.3. In this case the majority of scores are toward the high end of the distribution. This could

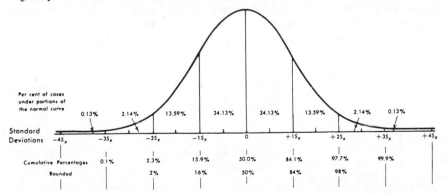

Figure 2.1   Chart showing the normal curve and the percent of cases under various portions of the normal curve. (Reproduced from *Test Service Notebook* No. 148 of the Psychological Corporation.)

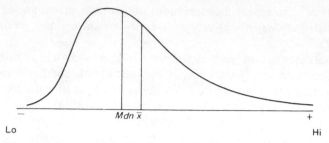

Lo   Hi

Figure 2.2   A positively skewed distribution. (Mdn = median; $\bar{X}$ = mean)

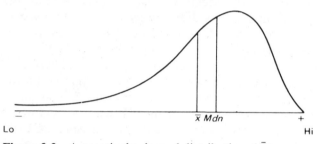

Lo   Hi

Figure 2.3   A negatively skewed distribution. ($\bar{X}$ = mean; Mdn = median)

occur if we gave a test that was easy for most of the students, such as a mastery test. Or if we were plotting teachers' salaries in a school district where most of the teachers were experienced and were close to the maximum on the salary schedule, we would expect such a distribution.

A rectangular distribution will result if the same number of people obtain each of the possible scores (see Figure 2.4). This would occur, for example, if percentiles (a type of test score) were plotted (see Chapter 5).

In the next section we relate measures of central tendency to score distributions.

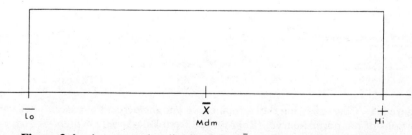
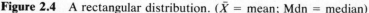

Figure 2.4   A rectangular distribution. ($\bar{X}$ = mean; Mdn = median)

MEASURES OF CENTRAL TENDENCY

It is often valuable to summarize characteristics of a distribution of test scores. One characteristic of particular interest is a *measure of central tendency,* which gives some idea of the average or typical score in the distribution. For example, you might wish to know the typical temperature in Miami, Florida, during the month of January. Or if you took an examination in measurement, surely you, as a student, would wish to know not only how you performed on the examination, but also how well, in general, the other students performed. You would want some measure of central tendency to help interpret your own score. When you teach, of course, your students may desire the same information. We discuss two measures of central tendency—the *mean* and the *median*—that present this type of information.[1]

Mean

The mean ($\bar{X}$) is the arithmetic average of a set of scores. It is found by adding all the scores in the distribution and dividing by the total number of scores (N). The formula is

$$\bar{X} = \frac{\Sigma X}{N} \qquad\qquad (2.1)$$

where $\bar{X}$ = mean
X = raw score for a person
N = number of scores
Σ = summation sign, indicating that all Xs
in the distribution are added

An example of computing the mean is given in Table 2.1.

Median

The median (mdn) is the point below which 50 percent of the scores lie. An approximation to that point is obtained from *ordered* data (scores listed from high to low) by simply finding the score in the middle of the distribution. For an odd number of scores, such as 25, the approximation to the median would be the middlemost score, or the score below which and above which 12 scores lie (actually $12\frac{1}{2}$ if the middle score is split and half of it is considered to be above the midpoint and half below). That is, the median is considered to be the 13th score. For an even number of scores the median would be the

---

[1] The *mode* is occasionally used as a measure of central tendency. It is the most frequently occurring score in the distribution. Because it can be greatly influenced by chance fluctuations, it is not recommended.

TABLE 2.1

HYPOTHETICAL DISTRIBUTION OF IQ SCORES FOR A CLASS OF 20 STUDENTS*

IQ Scores (X)	
185	
185	
83	
83	
82	
81	$N = 20$
81	
80	$\Sigma X = 1780$
80	
80	$\bar{X} = \dfrac{\Sigma X}{N} = \dfrac{1780}{20} = 89$
78	
78	Mdn = 79
78	
77	
77	
76	
74	
74	
74	
74	
$\Sigma X = 1780$	

* This distribution is, of course, very atypical. It is used to illustrate the principle of how extreme scores can influence the mean but not the median.

point that lies halfway between the two middlemost scores. The median for the data in Table 2.1 is 79, halfway between the 10th and 11th scores.

Comparisons of Mean and Median

Statisticians generally prefer the mean as the measure of central tendency. The mean takes into account the actual numerical value of every score in the distribution. The median is preferred if one desires a measure of central tendency that is not affected by a few very high or very low scores. Table 2.1 presents a *hypothetical* distribution of IQ scores where the median rather than the mean would be considered a better indicator of central tendency. The mean of 89 is a misleading figure, greatly influenced by two students with very high scores. Note that in this case the mean (89) is actually six points above the third highest score (83)! The median of 79 is a much more representative figure.

If you will reexamine the distributions presented in Figures 2.1 through 2.4, you will note that there is a relationship between the shape of the distribution and the relative placement of the mean and the median. For normal and rectangular distributions (or for any distribution that is symmetrically shaped), the mean and the median coincide. In a positively skewed distribution the mean will give the highest measure of central tendency. In a negatively skewed distribution, just the opposite occurs. Thus, for classroom tests or teacher salary distributions, one could create a different impression by presenting a median instead of a mean. But for standardized test results with fairly normal distributions, it would matter little which measure of central tendency was used. The mean is most often employed, however, since it can be used in the calculation of other statistics, such as the standard deviation and correlation coefficients, discussed below.

MEASURES OF VARIABILITY

To know only a person's raw score is of little value. To know that a person's score is so much above or below the mean is of some value. If one has an indication of the variability of a distribution of scores as well, much more information is obtained. (To go back to the example of the temperature in Miami, knowing only the average temperature is not nearly so useful as also knowing something about the variability of the temperature.)

The measures of variability most often used in testing are the *standard deviation* (S) and the *variance* (S^2).[2] These two have a very precise mathematical relation to each other: The standard deviation is the square root of the variance. This relation is indicated in the symbols by use of the exponent 2 when indicating variance. The variance can be computed by[3]

$$S_x^2 = \frac{\Sigma(X - \bar{X})^2}{N} \qquad (2.2)$$

where the subscript x identifies the score distribution (here the X scores) whose variance is being computed and all symbols on the right-hand side have been previously defined.

Equation 2.2 is sometimes called a *definitional formula*. Expressed in words, it states that the variance is the arithmetic average (notice that we are summing several values and dividing by the number we sum, just as when computing the mean) of the squares of the deviation scores from their mean. The $(X - \bar{X})$, then, is known as a *deviation* value showing the distance

---

[2] Occasionally the range (high score − low score + 1) is used, but this measure, like the mode, is very unstable.

[3] When *estimating* the variance of a population from a sample, one uses $N - 1$ instead of N in the denominator to get an unbiased estimator. Typically in using test data for *descriptive* purposes, we do not estimate the population variance but rather present the variance for the given scores. Thus, N is the appropriate denominator.

between a person's score (X) and the mean $(\bar{X})$. Equation 2.2 is easy to use if the computing is done by hand. (Rounding $\bar{X}$ to the nearest whole number, while destroying accuracy somewhat, makes hand computation quite easy. Computational formulas are available in most statistics texts. Many inexpensive calculators have built-in variance and standard deviation programs and a user need only push the appropriate buttons.)

The standard deviation (S_x) is obtained by taking the square root of the variance. The standard deviation, then, is

$$S_x = \sqrt{\frac{\Sigma(X - \bar{X})^2}{N}} \tag{2.3}$$

Two examples of computing the variance and the standard deviation are illustrated in Table 2.2.

To carry out the computation using the equations given, the following steps are completed using Example A as an illustration.

1. Compute the mean by adding all the X scores and dividing by the total number of scores. $\Sigma X = 2000$, $N = 20$, so $\bar{X} = 100$.
2. Subtract $\bar{X}$ from each individual's X score $(X - \bar{X})$ (e.g., for the first individual in Example A, $X = 109$, so $X - \bar{X} = 109 - 100 = 9$).
3. Square these $(X - \bar{X})$ numbers to get an $(X - \bar{X})^2$ for each individual (e.g., $9^2 = 81$).
4. Add the column of $(X - \bar{X})^2$ scores. This value, $\Sigma(X - \bar{X})^2 = 480$, is the numerator of Equation 2.2.
5. Divide $\Sigma(X - \bar{X})^2$ by $N(480/20)$ to get the variance $(S_x^2 = 24)$.
6. Take the square root of the variance to obtain the standard deviation $(S_x = \sqrt{24} = 4.9)$.

A new student with an IQ score of 120 (assume all IQ scores were obtained from the same test) who joins a class of pupils with IQ scores as shown in Example A in Table 2.2 will be 20 points above the mean and 11 points above the second pupil in the class in measured aptitude. A student who joins a class with scores as shown in Example B will still be 20 points above the mean, but three pupils in the class will have higher measured academic aptitude. The class depicted in Example B will be much harder to teach than the class depicted in Example A, because of the extreme variability in academic aptitude of the students.

The standard deviation is used to describe the amount of variability in a distribution of scores. No number by itself has any absolute meaning with respect to large or small. The numbers can be used to compare the variability of two or more groups. Although the standard deviation can be computed for any size distribution, it is particularly useful for reporting the variability of large sets of scores, such as the norms on standardized tests, because of the relationship between the standard deviation and a normal distribution. In a

TABLE 2.2

TWO DISTRIBUTIONS OF IQ SCORES WITH EQUAL MEANS BUT UNEQUAL VARIANCES

Example A				Example B		
X	$(X - \bar{X})$	$(X - \bar{X})^2$		X	$(X - \bar{X})$	$(X - \bar{X})^2$
109	9	81		185	85	7225
108	8	64		147	47	2209
107	7	49		121	21	441
105	5	25		108	8	64
105	5	25		106	6	36
103	3	9		104	4	16
102	2	4		103	3	9
101	1	1		103	3	9
101	1	1		102	2	4
101	1	1		101	1	1
99	−1	1		99	−1	1
99	−1	1		96	−4	16
97	−3	9		91	−9	81
97	−3	9		83	−17	289
96	−4	16		82	−18	324
95	−5	25		80	−20	400
95	−5	25		74	−26	676
94	−6	36		74	−26	676
93	−7	49		71	−29	841
93	−7	49		70	−30	900

$\Sigma X = 2000 \quad \Sigma(X - \bar{X})^2 = 480$

$N = 20 \quad \bar{X} = \dfrac{\Sigma X}{N} = \dfrac{2000}{20} = 100$

$S_x^2 = \dfrac{480}{20} = 24$

$S_x = \sqrt{24} = 4.9$

$\Sigma X = 2000 \quad \Sigma(X - \bar{X})^2 = 14{,}218$

$N = 20 \quad \bar{X} = \dfrac{\Sigma X}{N} = \dfrac{2000}{20} = 100$

$S_x^2 = \dfrac{14{,}218}{20} = 710.9$

$S_x = \sqrt{719.9} = 26.66$

normal distribution a specified percentage of scores fall within each standard deviation from the mean. As can be seen from Figure 2.1, about 68 percent of the area under a normal curve (or 68 percent of the scores if the normal curve depicts a distribution of scores) falls between $\pm 1 S_x$ (that is, plus or minus one standard deviation from the mean); 95 percent between $\pm 2 S_x$ (the 95 percent interval is actually $\pm 1.96 S_x$, but for practical work it is often computed as $\pm 2 S_x$); and 99.7 percent between $\pm 3 S_x$. More is said about this relationship between a normal curve and the standard deviation in the discussions of reliability and validity in Chapters 3 and 4. Also, one uses the standard deviation in obtaining various types of scores. More will be said about this in Chapter 5.

MEASURES OF RELATIONSHIP

If we have two sets of scores from the same group of people, it is often desirable to know the degree to which the scores are related. For example, we may be interested in the relationship between mathematics test scores and GPA. (Do people who do well in mathematics also, in general, do well in other areas in school?) Or we may be interested in other relationships such as that between test scores and IQ scores or GPA and IQ scores. We will also be interested in relationships between two sets of scores when we study the reliability or validity of a test. (See Chapters 3 and 4.) The Pearson product moment correlation coefficient (r) is the statistic most often used to indicate this relationship. It can be calculated from the formula

$$r = \frac{\Sigma[(X - \bar{X})(Y - \bar{Y})]}{NS_x S_y} \qquad (2.4)$$

where X = score of a person on one variable
Y = score of same person on the other variable
$\bar{X}$ = mean of the X distribution
$\bar{Y}$ = mean of the Y distribution
S_x = standard deviation of the X scores
S_y = standard deviation of the Y scores
N = number of pairs of scores

The value of r may range from $+1.00$ to -1.00. When an increase in one variable tends to be accompanied by an increase in the other variable (such as aptitude and achievement), the correlation is positive. When an increase in either one tends to be accompanied by a decrease in the other (such as age and value of a car), the correlation is negative. A perfect positive correlation (1.00) or a perfect negative correlation (-1.00) occurs when a change in the one variable is *always* accompanied by a commensurate change in the other variable. A zero (.00) correlation occurs when there is no relationship between the two variables. Table 2.3 illustrates the computation of r using Equation 2.4. Again, many calculators have built-in correlation programs.

How close to 1 (positively or negatively) an r must be in order to indicate that a significant relationship exists is difficult to specify. It depends upon how one defines significance. Significance may be considered in either a statistical or a practical sense. For example, a correlation coefficient of .08 (say, between teaching method and grades) is statistically significant (not due to random error) if the number of cases used to compute the correlation is sufficiently large. But this correlation is so low that it has no practical significance in educational decision making.[4] The scattergrams in Figure 2.5

---

[4] However, low but statistically significant correlations could be of practical significance if a decision vital to life, such as in medical research, is pending.

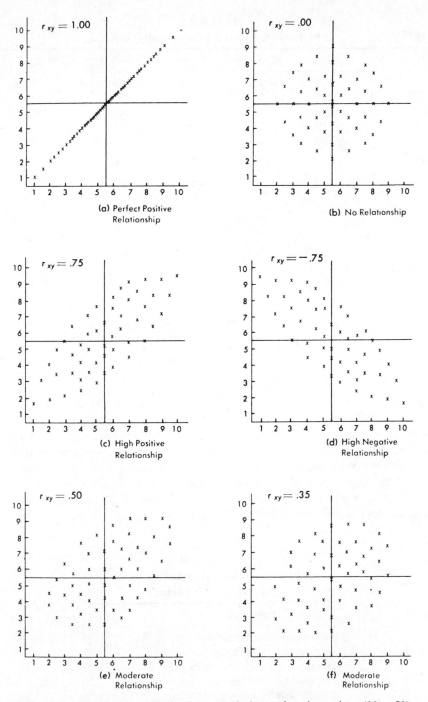

Figure 2.5 Scattergrams indicating correlations of various sizes ($N = 50$).

TABLE 2.3

THE CALCULATION OF *r* USING EQUATION (2.4)

X	Y	$X - \bar{X}$	$(X - \bar{X})^2$	$Y - \bar{Y}$	$(Y - \bar{Y})^2$	$(X - \bar{X})(Y - \bar{Y})$
50	45	20	400	16	256	320
49	50	19	361	21	441	399
30	25	0	0	−4	16	0
11	10	−19	361	−19	361	361
10	15	−20	400	−14	196	280
150	145		1522		1270	1360

$$\Sigma X = 150 \qquad \Sigma Y = 145$$

$$\bar{X} = 30 \qquad \bar{Y} = 29$$

$$\Sigma(X - \bar{X})^2 = 1522 \qquad \Sigma(Y - \bar{Y})^2 = 1270$$

$$S_x = \sqrt{\frac{\Sigma(X - \bar{X})^2}{N}} = \sqrt{\frac{1522}{5}} = \sqrt{304.4}$$

$$S_y = \sqrt{\frac{1270}{5}} = \sqrt{254}$$

$$R = \frac{\Sigma(X - \bar{X})(Y - \bar{Y})}{NS_xS_y} = \frac{1360}{5\sqrt{304.4}\,\sqrt{254}} = .98$$

depict the amount of relationship for various correlation coefficients. (A *scattergram* is a plot showing each individual's scores on both X and Y.)

Obviously, we do not expect all different sets of variables to have equal degrees of relationship. Correlations vary considerably in size, and the value of a given correlation must be interpreted in part by comparing it to other correlations obtained for similar variables. For example, a correlation of .85 would be considered somewhat low if one were correlating two equivalent forms of an aptitude test. However, a correlation of .70 between scholastic aptitude test scores and college grade point averages would be interpreted as

TABLE 2.4

TYPICAL CORRELATION COEFFICIENTS

FOR SELECTED VARIABLES

Variables	*r*
Two equivalent forms of a test	.95
Intelligence of identical twins	.90
Height and weight of adults	.60
High school and college GPA	.50
Intelligence of pairs of siblings	.50
Height and intelligence	.05

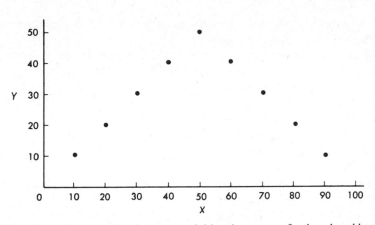

Figure 2.6   A scattergram showing two variables that are perfectly related but with a zero Pearson product moment r.

quite high. Table 2.4 gives some typical correlation coefficients for selected variables. The more experience you obtain, the more you will know what degree of relationship is expected between different variables.

Two cautions should be mentioned concerning the interpretation of correlation coefficients:

1. Correlation coefficients are *not* an indication of cause and effect. One can find all sorts of variables that are related but have no causal relationship. For example, for children the size of the big toe is slightly correlated with mental age—yet one does not cause the other. They are correlated simply because they are both related to a third variable: chronological age.

2. The Pearson product moment correlation is a measure of linear relationship. In Figure 2.6 there is a perfect relationship between variables X and Y. The Pearson r, however, is zero. If it is suspected that two variables have a relationship other than linear, a different index of correlation should be computed.[5] A relationship somewhat such as that in Figure 2.6 might be found if X were stress and Y were performance on some task (although it would not be perfect).

SUMMARY

The following statements summarize the major points of this chapter:

1. Data can be classified as nominal, ordinal, interval, and ratio data.
2. The shape of a distribution of scores depends both upon the properties of

---

[5] An explanation of curvilinear relationships is found in W. A. Hays (1973), *Statistics for Psychologists* (2d ed.). New York: Holt, Rinehart and Winston.

the measuring instrument and the distribution of the underlying characteristic we are attempting to measure.

3. The mean and the median are measures of central tendency. They give an idea of the average or typical score in the distribution.
4. The mean is generally preferred by statisticians as the measure of central tendency, but the median is easier to compute and is therefore sometimes preferred by classroom teachers.
5. For distributions that are fairly normal (such as those obtained from most standardized tests results), it matters little which measure of central tendency is used.
6. The variance and the standard deviation are measures of variability. They give an indication of the spread of scores in a distribution.
7. The standard deviation is the square root of the variance.
8. The Pearson product moment correlation coefficient is the statistic most often used to provide a measure of relationship. The values of the coefficient may range between -1.00 and $+1.00$, indicating perfect negative and perfect positive relationships, respectively. A value of 0 (zero) indicates no relationship.
9. There are two major cautions in interpreting correlation coefficients:
   a. They are not an indication of cause and effect.
   b. The ones studied in this chapter are only measures of linear relationship.

POINTS TO PONDER

1. Assume that you are the teachers' representative at a salary-negotiating session with your school board. If you wish to show the low salary of teachers in the system, would you use the mean or the median salary? Why?
2. If a negatively skewed distribution of test scores is obtained, what, if anything, can be inferred about the "true" distribution of the characteristic being measured?
3. Which of the scattergrams shown in Figure 2.5 would you expect to obtain if you were studying the relationship between
   a. chronological age and intelligence?
   b. car age and car value?
   c. height and weight?
   d. aptitude test scores and college grade point average?
4. What does a correlation of .11 mean to you? Would it (or could it) be significant to a cancer researcher? How?

CHAPTER 3

Reliability

DEFINITION OF RELIABILITY
CLASSICAL THEORY OF RELIABILITY
STANDARD ERROR OF MEASUREMENT
ESTIMATES OF RELIABILITY
FACTORS INFLUENCING RELIABILITY
RELIABILITY OF DIFFERENCE SCORES
RELIABILITY OF CRITERION-REFERENCED TESTS
RELIABILITY AND TEST USE

Every measurement device should possess certain qualities. Perhaps the two most important technical concepts in measurement are reliability and validity. These concepts are presented in this chapter and the next one. Although validity is the more important concept, reliability is discussed first, because validity includes reliability to some extent and therefore the structure of the subject matter makes that order of presentation a little more straightforward.

The only statistics needed as a background for understanding this chapter have been presented in Chapter 2. For those readers who have the necessary statistical background and prefer a more sophisticated treatment of the topics, we highly recommend Cronbach (1971), Cronbach, Gleser, Nanda, & Rajaratnam (1972), and Stanley (1971b).

After studying this chapter the reader should be able to do the following:

1. Recognize some sources of error variance in educational and psychological measurement.
2. Understand the theoretical concept of reliability as the ratio of true-to-observed score variance.
3. Recognize that the standard error of measurement can be derived from the theoretical reliability formula.
4. Understand the meaning of the standard error of measurement and interpret score bands.
5. Obtain various estimates of reliability and understand how these estimates differ.

6. Recognize several factors that influence reliability estimates, and understand the nature of the influence.
7. Understand and interpret the reliability of difference scores.
8. Appreciate the importance of reliable data for decision making.

DEFINITION OF RELIABILITY

Reliability can be defined as the degree of consistency between two measures of the same thing. This is more of a conceptual (or layperson's) definition than it is a theoretical or operational definition. Any measurement device provides only very limited data. What we hope is that a person's score would be similar under slightly different conditions. For example, if we measure a person's weight, we would hope that we would receive almost the same measure if we use a different scale or weigh the individual one day later. If we measure a person's level of achievement, we would hope that the score would be similar under different administrators, using different scorers, with similar but not identical items, or during different times in a day. In other words, we wish to generalize from the particular score obtained to the score we might have received if conditions had been slightly different.

In physical measurement we can ordinarily obtain very reliable measures. This is true primarily for three basic reasons:

1. Physical characteristics can usually be measured directly rather than indirectly.
2. The instruments used to obtain the measures are quite precise.
3. The traits or characteristics being measured are relatively stable.

Even in physical measurement, however, there is some unreliability or inconsistency. If we are interested in determining the reliability with which we can measure a person's weight, we may proceed in a variety of ways. We may, for example, have a person get on and off a scale several times, and we may record the weight each time. These recorded weights may differ. The person may stand somewhat differently on the scale from one time to the next, a factor that would influence the reading, or the person doing the measuring may not read or record the numbers correctly.

Another method of checking the consistency with which we can measure weight is to record the weight of a person as obtained on ten different scales and to compare these values. The values may vary for the reasons just given. They may also vary because of whatever differences exist in the scales. Thus, one would expect to obtain a somewhat more variable (less consistent) set of values.

Still other methods of checking the consistency of weight measures would be to weigh a person on ten successive Saturday mornings (1) on the same scale each time or (2) on ten different scales. With these two procedures one would have an additional source of variance from those already mentioned: the stability of the person's weight from one week to the next.

In all methods mentioned so far we would be obtaining information about consistency by determining how much variation exists in a specific individual's score (intraindividual variability). This variability is commonly expressed as a *standard error of measurement* and is explained in a later section.

Another approach to studying consistency would be to have a whole group of people weigh themselves twice (changing scales and/or times and/or the reader and recorder of the measure) and determine whether the relative standing of the persons remains about the same. This would give us an estimate of the *reliability* (or interindividual variability) of the measure. In educational or psychological measurement it is often unrealistic, or indeed impossible, to measure a single person repeatedly, so no direct measure of intraindividual variability can be obtained. Reliability theory, however, gives us ways to estimate this intraindividual variability through interindividual variability data, as we see in the subsequent two sections. Thus there are many different procedures for estimating the consistency or reliability of measurement. Each procedure allows a slightly different source of variation to affect the values obtained.

A pupil's test score may vary for many reasons. The amount of the characteristic we are measuring may change across time (trait instability); the particular questions we ask in order to infer a person's knowledge could affect the score (sampling error); any change in directions, timing, or amount of rapport with the test administrator could cause score variability (administrator error); inaccuracies in scoring a test paper will affect the scores (scoring error); and finally such things as health, motivation, degree of fatigue of the person, and good or bad luck in guessing could cause score variability.

The variation in a person's scores is typically called *error variance,* and the sources of the variation (for instance, trait instability, sampling error) are known as *sources of error.* The fewer and smaller the errors, the more consistent (reliable) the measurement. With this general background, let us turn to a brief discussion of the theory of reliability.

CLASSICAL THEORY OF RELIABILITY

The classical theory of reliability can best be explained by starting with observed scores (X). These are the scores individuals obtain on the measuring instrument. These observed scores may be conceptualized as containing various component parts. In the simplest case we think of each observed score as being made up of a "true score" (T) and an "error score" (E) such that

$$X = T + E \tag{3.1}$$

where X = observed score
T = true score
E = error score

The true score is similar to what some psychologists refer to as the "universe score" (see Cronbach, Gleser, Nanda, & Rajaratnam, 1972). The true score is unobservable, and the term can be a bit misleading. The true score is that portion of the observed score not affected by *random* error. Any systematic error (such as a scale always weighing everyone two pounds too heavy) does not affect reliability or consistency, and so in reliability theory, it is considered part of the "true," stable, or unchanging part of a person's observed score.

People, of course, differ from one another with regard to both their true scores and their observed scores. Since the errors are assumed to be random, theoretically the positive and the negative errors will cancel each other, and the mean error will be zero. If the errors are random, they will not correlate with the true scores or with each other. By making these assumptions, we can write the variance of a test as

$$S_x^2 = S_t^2 + S_e^2 \tag{3.2}$$

where S_x^2 = variance of a group of individuals' observed scores
S_t^2 = variance of a group of individuals' true scores
S_e^2 = error variance in a group of individuals' scores

Theoretically, reliability (r_{xx}) is defined as the ratio of the true score and observed score variances

$$r_{xx} = \frac{S_t^2}{S_x^2} \tag{3.3}$$

Reliability, then, tells us to what extent the observed variance is due to true score variance. The symbol r_{xx} is used for reliability, because so many of the reliability estimates are computed by the Pearson product moment correlation coefficient (r) procedure. The double x subscript is used to indicate measurement of the same trait. Equations 3.2 and 3.3 are basic formulas from which most of the commonly written expressions concerning reliability and the standard error of measurement (see the following section) are derived. Rewriting (3.2) as $S_t^2 = S_x^2 - S_e^2$ and substituting into 3.3, we get

$$r_{xx} = 1 - \frac{S_e^2}{S_x^2} \tag{3.4}$$

Reliability is often expressed in this fashion.

STANDARD ERROR OF MEASUREMENT

Solving Equation 3.4 for S_e, which is called a *standard error of measurement*, we get

$$S_e = S_x\sqrt{1 - r_{xx}} \qquad (3.5)$$

This is an estimate of the measure of intraindividual variability mentioned earlier. Since we often cannot test a person repeatedly, this statistic is typically estimated from group data, using Equation 3.5. It is frequently conceptualized, however, as the standard deviation of a single person's observed scores (from many administrations of the same test) about that person's true score on that test. Theoretically, the true score (T) of an individual does not vary. If we retested the same person many times, there would be some inconsistency (error), and therefore the observed scores (X) of this single person would vary, sometimes being greater than T and sometimes less. Making the assumption that the errors within a person's score, across testing sessions, are random, the positive and negative errors will cancel each other, and the mean error will be zero. Thus, the mean of the observed scores over repeated testings is the individual's true score $(\bar{X}_i = T_i)$, where the subscript i refers to the individual.

It is assumed that, over repeated testings, the observed scores for an individual will fall in a normal distribution about the person's true score. The standard deviation of the observed scores across repeated testings should become clear if we examine Equation 3.2.

$$S_x^2 = S_t^2 + S_e^2$$

If we think of these values as being obtained from the data for a single individual over many testings, then the true score does not change, and hence $S_t^2 = 0$. Changing the notation of S_x^2 to S_{xi}^2 to indicate the variance of a single person's observed scores over repeated testings, we get

$$S_{xi}^2 = 0 + S_e^2$$

$$S_{xi} = S_e$$

Note that this holds only for the case where S_{xi} represents the standard deviation of a person's observed scores over repeated testing. If a test has any reliability at all, S_e will be smaller than the S_x for a *group* of individuals, each tested once, because as a group their true scores will vary, even though for each *individual* $S_t^2 = 0$.

To reiterate: The standard error of measurement is conceptualized as providing information about the variability of a person's scores on repeated testings. Ordinarily, we do not give a person the same test many times, because it is uneconomical and because these repeated testings could result in changes in the individual (fatigue, learning effects). Thus, the standard error of measurement is usually estimated from group data. Using group data and Equation 3.5, we obtain only one standard error and interpret every individual's score using this same standard error. This interpretation could lead to slight misinterpretations, particularly if the group is fairly heterogeneous. The better commercially published tests report different standard errors of measurement for different homogeneous subgroups along the continuum of the trait being measured.

Some publishers report standard errors of measurement which have been derived in a way differently from Equation 3.5. One such approach is a procedure developed by Lord (1957). The equation using his procedure is

$$SE_{Xi} \doteq \sqrt{\frac{1}{n-1} X_i(n - X_i)} \tag{3.6}$$

where SE_{Xi} = standard error for individual i
n = number of items in the test
X_i = observed score for individual i
$\doteq$ = an approximation

We can see from Equation 3.6 that a person's standard error is dependent upon only two things: that person's score, and the number of items in the test. Using this formula, people will have different standard errors. Equation 3.6 offers some theoretical advantages over Equation 3.5 and is used by some commercial test builders.

Another estimate of the standard error of measurement is based on the information function from an approach called *item response theory* (*IRT*). This method also differs somewhat from the classical theory previously discussed. As with Lord's formula, using this approach produces slightly different estimates of the standard error of measurement for students with different abilities. Some researchers also believe that this technique has some theoretical advantages over the classical approach. All three approaches mentioned above are used by publishers. Although the formulas (and the assumptions made in their derivations) differ, all the estimates can be interpreted in essentially the same way.

The standard error of measurement has an interpretive advantage over the reliability coefficient in that it allows us to state how much we think an individual's score might vary. The standard error of measurement is often used for what is called *band interpretation*. Band interpretation helps convey the idea of imprecision of measurement. Because it is assumed that the errors are random, an individual's observed scores will be distributed normally about that person's true score. Thus one can say that a person's observed score will lie between $\pm 1S_e$ of his or her true score approximately 68 percent of the time, or $\pm 2S_e$ of his or her true score about 95 percent of the time (see Figure 2.1). Of course we do not know the true score, but one can infer with about 68 percent (or 95 percent) *certainty* a person's true score to be within $\pm 1 S_e$ (or $\pm 2 S_e$) of the observed score. (Note that this is *not* the same as saying a person's true score is within those limits 68 [or 95] percent of the time. The true score is fixed and either is or is not within the given interval. But we can talk about how certain we are that the true score is within a given interval.) The interval $X \pm 1 S_e$ is ordinarily the band used when interpreting scores to others.

Suppose, for example, that a scholastic aptitude test has an r_{xx} of .91 and an S_x of 15. Thus, using Equation 3.5,

$$S_e = S_x \sqrt{1 - r_{xx}}$$

$$= 15\sqrt{1 - .91} = 15\sqrt{.09} = 15(.3) = 4.5$$

The band interpretation of the above computed standard error of measurement of the observed score would be as follows: If Susan obtains a score of 112, we could be about 68 percent confident that her true score lies between 112 ± 4.5, or 107.5 to 116.5. We would be about 95 percent confident that her true score lies between $112 \pm 2(4.5)$, or between 103 and 121. Similar interpretations would be made if the other approaches to computing the standard error of measurement were used.

ESTIMATES OF RELIABILITY

Now that we have defined and discussed reliability conceptually and theoretically, let us consider the operational definitions of reliability. How do we obtain estimates of the theoretically defined reliability? Given one set of observed scores for a group of people, we can obtain S_x^2. From Equation 3.4 we can see that one must get an estimate of either r_{xx} or S_e^2 in order to solve the equation. Ordinarily, one estimates r_{xx} first and then uses Equation 3.5 to estimate S_e.

The methods used to estimate reliability differ in that they consider different sources of error. Many different approaches can be used to estimate reliability, but the more common ones reported in test manuals are listed below.[1] (Note: Not all types are reported in any *one* manual.)

1. Measures of stability.
2. Measures of equivalence.

---

[1] Methods 1, 2, 3 and 4(a) all use the Pearson product moment correlation coefficient r. It is not obvious why this should be a reasonable estimate of reliability as defined in Equation 3.3. Space does not allow us to present all algebraic derivations. However, given the assumption that the error is random error and that the two distributions have equal means and variances, it can be shown that Equation 3.3 is equal to Equation 2.4 for the Pearson product moment coefficient. Thus, a correlation coefficient is a good estimate of reliability to the extent that the assumptions are met.

3. Measures of equivalence and stability.
4. Measures of internal consistency.
   a. Split-half
   b. Kuder-Richardson estimates
   c. Coefficient alpha
   d. Hoyt's analysis of variance procedure

Measures of Stability

A measure of stability, often called a *test–retest* estimate of reliability, is obtained by administering a test to a group of persons, readministering the same test to the same group at a later date, and correlating the two sets of scores.

With this type of reliability estimate, we can determine how confidently we can generalize from the score a person receives at one time to what he or she would receive if the test had been given at a different time. There are various possible time intervals. The estimate of reliability will vary with the length of the interval, and thus this interval length must be considered when interpreting reliability coefficients. Therefore, when stability reliability is reported in a test manual, the time interval between testings should always be specified, as well as some indication of the relevant intervening experiences. Any change in score from one setting to the other is treated as error (it is assumed that the trait measured is stable). This is analogous to weighing a person at two different times and ascribing to error the difference in the two recorded measures. The difference may be due to the person's standing on the scale somewhat differently; it may be due to the scale's breaking (becoming inaccurate) between measures; it may be due to a mistake in reading or recording the numbers; or it may be due to an actual weight change (trait instability) over time. In this type of estimate we cannot isolate which of the sources of error contribute to the difference in performance (weight). What is really being measured is the consistency over time of the examinees' performances on the test.

The stability estimate is often difficult to obtain and interpret in psychological measurement. Many psychological tests are reactive measures (Webb et al., 1981). That is, the very act of measurement causes the person to change on the variable being measured. The practice effects from the first testing, for example, will likely be different across students, thus lowering the reliability estimate. On the other hand, if the interval is short, there may be a strong recall or memory effect. That is, students may mark a question the same as before, not because they decide again that that is the correct answer but just because they remember marking it that way previously. This memory effect would tend to make the retest reliability estimate spuriously high. Problems such as memory are usually of less concern for tests in the psychomotor domain, but could be troublesome in tests in the cognitive and affective domains.

Measures of Equivalence

In contrast to the test–retest procedure, the *equivalent forms* estimate of reliability is obtained by giving two forms (with equal content, means, and variances) of a test to the same group on the same day and correlating these results. With this procedure we are determining how confidently we can generalize a person's score to what the individual would receive if he or she took a test composed of similar but different questions. Here, also, any change in performance is considered error, but instead of measuring changes from one time to another, we measure changes due to the specificity of knowledge. That is, a person may know the answer to a question on form A and not know the answer to the equivalent question on form B. The difference in the scores would be treated as error. This procedure is somewhat analogous to weighing a person on two *different* scales on the same day. Here, we are unlikely to have much of a difference score (if any) due to weight change, but a difference could exist because two different scales are being used.

In constructing equivalent tests, care must be taken that the two measures are equivalent in a statistical sense with equal means, variances, and item intercorrelations. But the equality of content is also important. (Sometimes the term *parallel* is used instead of *equivalent* to connote the similarity of content.) The same table of specifications in building the test (see Chapter 4) should be followed for both forms. The items should be of similar difficulty and of the same format (for example, multiple choice), and administrative instructions should be the same for both tests.

Equivalent forms of a test are, of course, useful for reasons other than estimating reliability. For curriculum and/or student evaluation the teacher might want to administer a posttest covering the same type of material presented in a pretest. Using an equivalent form instead of repeating the same test helps reduce teaching for the test (in a specific pejorative sense), as well as reduce the memory effects noted earlier. Or one might wish to use equivalent forms of a personality inventory in evaluating the effects of therapy.

The stability and equivalent forms methods of estimating reliability are quite different and may give different results. Which, then, should be used? The method chosen depends on the purposes for which the test is administered. If we wish to use the test results for long-range predictions, then we wish to know the coefficient of stability. For example, in order for a scholastic aptitude test in grade 9 to predict college GPA (grade-point average), the scores must be fairly stable. And in order for a personality test given to

Peace Corps candidates to predict how well they will be able to adapt to the rigors of life in a highly unfamiliar setting, the scores must be quite stable. If they are not, we would fail in long-term predictions. Thus, we desire a reliability estimate to reflect any trait change as error so that our confidence in any prediction would be appropriately tempered by a lower reliability coefficient.

If the purpose of giving a test is not for making long-range prediction but rather, say, for making inferences about the knowledge one has in a subject-matter area, then the tester would be primarily interested in a coefficient of equivalence. In this case we are less interested in how stable the knowledge is over time and more interested in whether we can infer or generalize to a larger domain of knowledge from a sample. If there was a marked change in score from one equivalent form to another, then the score on either or both forms is due, in large part, to specificity of knowledge. Inferences to the domain of knowledge from a score so influenced by the properties of a specific sample are hazardous. This fact would be reflected by a low equivalent-forms reliability estimate.

Measures of Equivalence and Stability

People are sometimes concerned with *both* long-range prediction and inferences to a domain of knowledge. Actually they are more likely to be concerned about these than about only stability. For example, the measurement of constructs[2] such as intelligence, creativity, aggressiveness, or musical talent is probably not dependent upon a specific set of questions. If it is, the construct is not of very much interest. We would like to know whether a different, but similar, set of questions asked at a different point in time would give similar results. In that case a coefficient of *equivalence and stability* could be obtained by giving one form of the test, and after some time administering the other form and correlating the results. This procedure allows for changes both in scores due to trait instability and in scores due to item specificity. This estimate of reliability is thus usually lower than either of the other two procedures.

Measures of Internal Consistency

The three estimates of reliability previously discussed require data from two testing sessions. Sometimes it is not feasible to obtain these kinds of data. However, it is possible to obtain reliability estimates from only one set of test data. With the exception of the split-half method, these estimates are really indices of the homogeneity of the items in the test, or the degree to

[2] *Constructs* are unobservable phenomena, both inferred from and used to help explain an individual's behavior.

which the item responses correlate with the total test score. If there is a high degree of internal consistency, then it is reasonable to assume that had another set of similar questions been asked, the results would have been comparable.

Split-Half Estimates   The split-half method of estimating reliability is theoretically the same as the equivalent-forms method. Nevertheless, the split-half method is ordinarily considered as a measure of internal consistency, because the two equivalent forms are contained within a single test. That is, instead of administering an alternate form of the test, only one test is administered. In estimating reliability, a subscore for each of two halves is obtained, and these two subscores are correlated. In most cases the Pearson product moment correlation coefficient (described in Chapter 2) is used. This correlation coefficient ($r_{1/2\,1/2}$) is an estimate of the reliability of a test only half as long as the original. To estimate what the reliability of the whole test would be, a correction factor needs to be applied. The appropriate formula is a special case of the Spearman-Brown prophecy formula.

$$r_{xx} = \frac{2r_{1/2\,1/2}}{1 + r_{1/2\,1/2}} \qquad (3.7)$$

where r_{xx} = estimated reliability of the whole test
$r_{1/2\,1/2}$ = reliability of the half-test

Thus, if two halves of a test correlated .60 ($r_{1/2\,1/2}$ = .60), the estimated reliability of the whole test would be

$$r_{xx} = \frac{2(.60)}{1 + .60} = \frac{1.20}{1.60} = .75$$

The advantage of the split-half method is that, to estimate reliability, only one form of the test need be administered only once.

The Spearman-Brown prophecy formula assumes that the variances of the two halves are equal. If they are not, the estimated reliability of the whole test will be greater than that obtained by other methods of internal consistency. Thus, one of the problems that exists in the split-half method is how to make the split. This problem can be approached in a variety of ways. But if one really attempts to make the two halves equivalent (and parallel), it requires all the same efforts necessary to construct two equivalent forms (except that only half as many items are needed). Ordinarily, the test is split into two parts by a preconceived plan (for example, odd items versus even items) without statistically attempting to make the two parts equivalent.[3]

[3] In consulting other materials, such as test manuals for standardized tests, the reader may see references made to Rulon's, Guttman's, or Flanagan's split-half procedures. If the two halves of the test have equal variances, the results will be the same by using their methods as by using the procedure discussed here. If not, they will give slightly lower reliability estimates.

Kuder-Richardson Estimates   If items are scored dichotomously (right or wrong), one way to avoid the problems of how to split the test is to use one of the Kuder-Richardson formulas. The formulas may be considered as representative of the average correlation obtained from all possible split-half reliability estimates. K-R 20 is the formula used most extensively. The K-R 20 formula is as follows:

$$r_{xx} = \frac{n}{n-1}\left[1 - \frac{\Sigma pq}{S_x^2}\right] \tag{3.8}$$

where n = number of items in test
$\quad\quad p$ = proportion of people who answered item correctly (if, for example, on Item 1, 6 of 30 people answered the item correctly, p for this item would be $\frac{6}{30}$ = .20)
$\quad\quad q$ = proportion of people who answered item incorrectly ($q = 1 - p$; if p = .20, q = .80)
$\quad pq$ = variance of a single item scored dichotomously (right or wrong)
$\quad\quad \Sigma$ = summation sign indicating that pq is summed over all items
$\quad S_x^2$ = variance of the total test

Coefficient Alpha (α) and Hoyt's Analysis of Variance Procedure   Coefficient alpha and Hoyt's methods yield results equal to K-R 20. They have been mentioned here only because you will probably see references made to them in the literature. Stanley (1971b) discusses both procedures in more detail.

Comparison of Methods

Table 3.1 presents a comparison of the different methods of estimating reliability. As can be seen, more sources of error can occur with a coefficient of

TABLE 3.1
**SOURCES OF ERROR REPRESENTED IN DIFFERENT
METHODS OF ESTIMATING RELIABILITY**

	Method of Estimating Reliability			
Source of Error	*Stability*	*Equivalence*	*Equivalence and Stability*	*Internal Consistency*
Trait instability	X		X	
Sampling error		X	X	X
Administrator error	X	X	X	
Random error within the test	X	X	X	X

equivalence and stability procedure than with any other method. Thus, reliability estimated by this procedure is likely to be lower. In choosing a standardized test or in interpreting its results, it is not sufficient to merely look at the numerical value of a reliability estimate. One must also take into account which estimate is being reported.

FACTORS INFLUENCING RELIABILITY

As has been pointed out, the specific procedure (equivalent forms, test–retest, and so on) used will affect the reliability estimate obtained. Other factors will also affect the reliability estimates. Four of these are now discussed: test length, speed, group homogeneity, and difficulty of items.

Test Length

In the discussion of the split-half method of estimating reliability, a specific case of the Spearman-Brown prophecy (Equation 3.7) was illustrated. The more general expression of this equation is

$$r_{xx} = \frac{Kr}{1 + (K - 1)r} \qquad (3.9)$$

where r_{xx} = predicted reliability of a test K times as long as original test
r = reliability of original test
K = ratio of number of items in new test to number of items in original one

Thus, if a test has an original reliability of .60 and if the test was made three times as long ($K = 3$) (for instance, going from a 20-item test to a 60-item test), we would predict the reliability of the lengthened test to be

$$r_{xx} = \frac{3(.60)}{1 + 2(+ .60)} = .818$$

As previously stated, when $K = 2$ (as in the case of split-half reliability), the Spearman-Brown prophecy formula makes the assumption that the two subtests are equivalent. A more general way of stating this assumption is that the items added to a test must be equivalent to the items already in the test.

Just as adding equivalent items makes a test more reliable, so deleting equivalent items makes a test less reliable. A test may have very high reliability but may be too long to be usable. Equation 3.9 can also be used to estimate the reliability of a test shorter than the original. For example, if one wishes to know what the estimated reliability of a test half as long as the original would be, $K = \frac{1}{2}$ could be used in the equation.

Speed

A test is considered a pure *speed* test if everyone who reaches an item gets it right but no one has time to finish all the items. Thus, score differences depend upon the number of items attempted. The opposite of a speed test is a power test. A pure *power* test is one in which everyone has time to try all items but, because of the difficulty level, ordinarily no one obtains a perfect score. (Items in a power test are usually arranged in order of difficulty.) Few tests are either pure speed or pure power tests. However, to the extent that a test is speeded, it is inappropriate to estimate reliability through the methods of internal consistency, and the measures of stability or equivalence should be used.

It is easy to see that, in a pure speed test, if the items were split into odd and even, then a person who got *n* odd items right would get either *n* or *n* − 1 even items right. (For example, a person who answered the first 30 items correctly would get 15 odd and 15 even items right. A person who answered the first 31 items correctly would get 16 odd and 15 even items right.) If all examinees marked an even number of items, the correlation between the two split-halves would be 1. It would be slightly less than 1 if some examinees marked an odd number of items. Thus, odd-even reliabilities of speeded tests are spuriously high. Typically, other internal consistency estimates also are too high, since some items are reached by some pupils but not by others, a factor that tends to increase the mean interitem correlation. If a test is speeded, reliability should be computed by one of the methods that requires two administrations of the test (or tests).

Group Homogeneity

A third factor influencing the estimated reliability of a set of scores is group homogeneity. Other things being equal, the more heterogeneous the group, the higher the reliability. The reason for this can be best explained by referring to a definitional formula for reliability, such as Equation 3.4.

$$r_{xx} = 1 - \frac{S_e^2}{S_x^2}$$

There is no reason to expect the degree of consistency of a person's observed score to vary as a result of group characteristics. Because S_e^2 is conceptually thought of as the variance of a person's observed scores about his or her true score, S_e^2 should remain constant with changes in group heterogeneity. But S_x^2 increases with group heterogeneity. If S_e^2 remains constant and S_x^2 increases, r_{xx} increases. Thus, in considering tests for selection purposes, it is important to note the heterogeneity of the group from which the reliability was estimated. If the reported reliability was estimated on a group of sixth- through ninth-graders and if the test was then administered to only seventh-graders, it would be safe to conclude that because the students in the seventh grade are more homogeneous, the reliability of the test for those seventh-graders would be considerably lower than the reported reliability.

Difficulty of Items

The difficulty of the test, and of the individual items, also affects the reliability of the set of scores. Since traditional reliability estimates are dependent upon score variability, tests in which there is little variability among the scores give lower reliability estimates than tests in which the variability is large. Tests which are so easy that almost everyone gets all the items correct or, conversely, so hard that almost everyone gets all the items wrong (or a chance score if guessing is involved) will have little variability among the scores and will tend to have lower reliability.

RELIABILITY OF DIFFERENCE SCORES

Is John really better in numerical ability or in verbal ability? Did Susan gain significantly in reading ability this year? Whose arithmetic skill is better, Jane's or Bill's? To answer each of these questions, we need to consider whether there are reliable differences between two observed scores. We wish to know how appropriate it is to generalize from an observed difference to a "true" difference.

Unfortunately, difference scores are much less reliable than single scores. The errors of measurement on each test contribute to error variance in the difference scores, and the true variance that the two tests measure in common reduces the variability of the difference scores (see Thorndike & Hagen, 1977, pp. 98–100). Theoretically the reliability of difference scores (like reliability of single sets of observed scores) is the ratio of two variances. In this case, reliability is equal to the true variance of the difference scores divided by the observed variance of the difference scores. If two tests have equal variances,[4] the reliability of a difference score can be computed as follows:

$$r_{\text{diff}} = \frac{\dfrac{r_{xx} + r_{yy}}{2} - r_{xy}}{1 - r_{xy}} \qquad (3.10)$$

where r_{diff} = reliability of the difference scores
r_{xx} = reliability of one measure
r_{yy} = reliability of other measure
r_{xy} = correlation between the two measures

[4] The assumption of equal variances is somewhat restrictive. A formula which does not make that assumption can be used, but the points made in this section can be understood better using the simple formula given here.

From this equation it can be seen that three variables affect the reliability of the difference scores: the reliability of each of the two measures and their intercorrelation. To obtain reliable difference scores, we need tests that have high initial reliabilities and a low intercorrelation. For example, if the two tests had reliabilities of .90 and .86 ($r_{xx} = .90$, $r_{yy} = .86$) and if they had an intercorrelation of .20 ($r_{xy} = .20$), the reliability of the difference score would be

$$r_{\text{diff}} = \frac{\dfrac{.90 + .86}{2} - .20}{1 - .20} = \frac{.68}{.80} = .85$$

However, if the reliabilities of the tests were the same but the intercorrelation was .80, the reliability of the difference score would be

$$r_{\text{diff}} = \frac{\dfrac{.90 + .86}{2} - .80}{1 - .80} = \frac{.08}{.20} = .40$$

As can be seen, the intercorrelation of the two tests can have quite an impact on the reliability of the difference scores. A drop in the reliability of the difference scores also would occur if the reliabilities of the tests were lower.

Significance of Difference Scores

A commonly suggested caution in standardized test manuals is that a difference between two scores should not be interpreted as significant unless the lower score plus one standard error of measurement of that score is less than the higher score minus one standard error of measurement of that score. In other words, if one uses the band interpretation of scores discussed in the section "Standard Error of Measurement," it is only when the two bands do not overlap that one assumes a significant difference exists between the scores (See Figure 5.3).[5]

In interpreting difference scores, two types of errors can be made: (1) interpreting an observed difference as a true one when in fact it was due to random error (type I error) or (2) interpreting an observed difference as due to chance when in fact a true difference exists (type II error).

A type I error may be considered one of overinterpretation; a type II error, one of underinterpretation (Feldt, 1967). If one follows the commonly suggested procedure of interpreting the scores as not different if the $X \pm 1S_e$ bands of the two scores overlap, then the chance of a type I error is quite small (around .16 if the S_es of the two tests are equal). This kind of interpretive guideline, if followed, increases the chances of making a type II error.

[5] Formulas for computing the standard error of difference scores can be found in the second edition (1975) of this text.

Publishers and educators evidently feel that a type I error is more costly, and so risks of making it should be minimized. (See Feldt, 1967, for a further discussion of this point.)

Gain Scores

A special type of difference score that has received considerable attention from many of the advocates of accountability and program evaluation is a gain (or change) score. In education we often wish to know how much our students have learned (gained) from a particular instructional process. In psychology, we often wish to know how much our clients have changed as a consequence of therapy.

Statistically, we can estimate the reliability of a gain score by using Equation 3.10. In measuring gain, the r_{xx} would be the pretest, r_{yy} the posttest (which may be the same test or an equivalent form), and r_{xy} the correlation between the pretest and the posttest. One particular problem with gain scores, however, is that r_{xy} is usually reasonably high, thus reducing the reliability of the gain scores. We could, of course, attempt to construct intentionally a posttest so that r_{xy} would be low and r_{diff} high, but then we are faced with the logical dilemma of whether the difference score is really a change in whatever characteristic was being measured on the pretest. If r_{xy} is low, maybe the pretest and posttest are not really measuring the same thing and therefore the difference is not a gain. Bereiter (1963) refers to this as the unreliability-invalidity dilemma. There are many other troublesome aspects of measuring gain. Refer to Cronbach & Furby (1970), Cronbach, Gleser, Nanda, & Rajaratnam (1972), Harris (1963), Overall & Woodward (1975), Rogosa, Brandt, & Zimowski (1982), Stanley (1971b), and Zimmerman & Williams (1982) for more technical treatments of this topic.

The major points to be kept in mind are that (1) difference scores are less reliable than single scores; (2) gain scores are in general the least reliable of all difference scores; (3) although difference or gain scores may be too unreliable for use with individuals, they may be reliable enough for making decisions about groups (group means are always more reliable than individual scores because the random errors of the individual scores tend to cancel themselves out, thus making the mean reasonably accurate); and (4) anyone who intends to use difference (or gain) scores for important educational decisions is well advised to study the references given in the preceding paragraph.

RELIABILITY OF CRITERION-REFERENCED TESTS

As mentioned in Chapter 1, the purpose of a norm-referenced test is to discriminate among individuals or compare them to one another. The purpose of a criterion-referenced test is to compare each individual to some standard. For criterion-referenced interpretation of test scores, student variability is not essential. In fact, if all students receive a perfect score on a mastery test, we would be happy. Yet, since classical reliability depends upon the existence of differences among students' observed scores, the classical reliability of such a mastery test would be undefined.

Let us rewrite slightly the basic definitional formula (Equation 3.3) for reliability.

$$r_{xx} = \frac{S_t^2}{S_x^2} = \frac{S_t^2}{S_t^2 + S_e^2}$$

If the variability in true scores is reduced, the ratio is reduced and classical reliability goes down. At the point where S_t^2 (true-score variance) is reduced to zero, reliability is zero except for the situation where S_e^2 (error-score variance) is also zero, so that everyone receives the same observed score. Then the denominator would be zero, and the ratio would be undefined.

It has therefore been argued that classical estimates of reliability are not completely appropriate for criterion-referenced measures, particularly for that subset of criterion-referenced measures called mastery tests. Yet the concept of a precise measure—one which has a small standard error of measurement—is still important. We do wish to measure with as much precision as possible, and we should have estimates to tell us what precision we have obtained.

Whereas in classical test theory we are interested in the precision of the score, in criterion-referenced interpretation we are sometimes interested in the precision of the score but at other times only in the precision of the decision. For example, in mastery testing, our decision is to categorize individuals as masters or nonmasters. We are really more interested in the precision of the decision than in how precise a score is. Different mathematical formulations are needed to estimate the reliability of a decision than to estimate the reliability of a score.

More work still needs to be done in the conceptual and operational definitions of reliability where criterion referencing is used. For both criterion-referenced and gain-score measurements, where we may not be interested in maximizing the differences between individuals, classical reliability estimates may yield values that present a very pessimistic picture of the precision of the measuring instrument. Excessive emphasis should not be placed on them in judging the technical adequacy of such scores.[6]

---

[6] Various formulas have been developed for estimating the reliability of criterion-referenced tests. Discussion of these is beyond the scope of this book. We refer interested readers to Berk (1980a), Hambleton, Swaminathan, Algina, & Coulson (1978), Huynh (1976), Livingston (1972), Subkoviak (1976), and Traub & Rowley (1980).

RELIABILITY AND TEST USE

A question often asked in measurement courses is: How reliable should a test be in order to be useful? This question cannot be answered simply. The answer depends upon the purposes for which the test is to be used. No major decision should be made on the basis of a single test. If the decisions the scores will help make are extremely important and/or irreversible, then the reliability goes down. At the point where S_t^2 (true-score variance) is reduced so important and/or is tentative and reversible. If a measure is to be used to help make decisions about individuals, then it should be more reliable than if it is to be used to make decisions about groups. Although there is no universal agreement, it is generally accepted that standardized tests used to assist in making decisions about *individuals* should have reliability coefficients of at least .85. (Classroom- or teacher-constructed measurement devices may often have lower reliability than this. Thus, important decisions should not be made on the basis of only one test.) For *group decisions,* a reliability coefficient of about .65 may suffice. *These are only guidelines.* There are no absolutes; the best test available should be used. A more relevant factor is the consideration of how good a decision can be made without the help of the test data. If there is very little other information on which to base a decision, and a decision must be made, it may be helpful to use a test with low reliability instead of no test. (A test with low reliability may still have some *validity* and can therefore be useful.) On the other hand, if a good decision (or accurate prediction) can be made without any test data, it may not be worthwhile to give a test, even though it is reliable.

In standardized test selection, a crucial matter for the reader of a test manual is to be able to understand the reliability information reported. (This, of course, implies that reliability data are reported in the test manual.) A knowledge of the concept of reliability, different estimates of reliability, and effects on these estimates should help lead to such an understanding.

The kinds of reliability data to be expected in a test manual depend on the type of test and on how it is to be used. For general aptitude tests, the most important kind of reliability estimate would be a stability estimate. Because aptitude test results frequently are used to help make long-range predictions, it is important to know how stable the aptitude results are. (If the test scores are not stable, they cannot predict themselves, much less a criterion.) For multiple aptitude tests it is also essential to have data on the reliabilities of the subtests and the difference scores. Equivalence and internal consistency estimates are also of value for interpreting any aptitude test, since one should have some information regarding the homogeneity of the content and the degree to which the scores are dependent upon particular questions.

For achievement tests, equivalence reliability estimates seem almost essential. One wants to infer from the responses to a specific set of items the degree to which a person has mastered the essential skills and/or knowledge in a much larger universe. Moreover, it would be valuable to have some indication about the homogeneity of the content. Thus, internal consistency estimates should also be provided. If no equivalent form of a test exists, one can, given certain assumptions, make inferences about how well one can generalize to the domain from an internal-consistency estimate. Recall that this is not appropriate for speed tests. As with multiple aptitude tests, achievement test batteries should provide data on subtest reliabilities and on the reliabilities of difference scores. Inasmuch as most achievement tests are intentionally designed to fit the curriculum, and students learn those materials in differing amounts and rates, it is not expected that these scores will remain constant. Hence, long-range stability coefficients would be rather meaningless.

For noncognitive measures (such as measures of interests, attitudes, and personality), the types of reliability information needed varies. For example, if one wishes to use an interest test to predict long-term job satisfaction, then one must assume that interests are stable, and information relevant to this assumption is needed. On the other hand, a test giver who wishes to obtain a measure of a transient personality characteristic (such as temporary psychological depression) should not expect high-stability coefficients. Instead, the administrator might look for internal consistency reliability.

In addition to indicating the type(s) of reliability estimates obtained, the manual must also provide other information. It is essential to know the characteristics of the sample on which the reliability estimates were computed. The sample size, its representativeness, and the mean and standard deviation of sample scores should be known.

Standard errors of measurement (and how they were obtained) should be provided. Separate age and/or grade estimates should be reported. Even within an age or grade level, different S_es should be reported (for example, an aptitude or achievement test should report separate S_es for students performing at the high, middle, and low levels).

SUMMARY

The principal ideas, conclusions, and implications presented in this chapter are summarized in the following statements:

1. *Reliability* is the degree of consistency between two measures of the same thing.
2. Some examples of sources of inconsistency, or error variance, are trait instability, sampling error, administrator error, scoring error, and errors within the person.
3. The standard error of measurement (S_e) is the estimated standard deviation of a person's observed scores about his or her true score. When we

know a person's observed score, we can place a confidence band of $\pm 1S_e$ about this score and say that we are about 68 percent confident that the true score will be in that range.

4. There are many estimates of reliability. Those discussed in this chapter are categorized as measures of (a) stability, (b) equivalence, (c) stability and equivalence, or (d) internal consistency.

5. Measures of stability are obtained by administering a test to a group of individuals, readministering the same test to the same individuals at a later date, and correlating the two sets of scores. Any change in score from one time to another is treated as error.

6. Measures of equivalence are obtained by giving two forms of the test to the same group on the same day and correlating these results.

7. Measures of equivalence and stability combine the previous two procedures.

8. All measures of internal consistency require only one administering of the test.

9. The different methods of estimating reliability consider different sources of error. Which should be used depends upon how one wishes to use the results of the test.

10. In general, longer tests are more reliable.

11. Internal consistency estimates should not be used for speeded tests.

12. Reliability will be higher when a test is given to a heterogeneous group.

13. Difference scores are less reliable than single scores. A gain score, a special type of difference score, is particularly unreliable.

14. Traditional estimates of reliability depend upon true-score variance. For criterion-referenced measures, where we are less interested in true-score variability than we are in norm-referenced measures, the traditional estimates of reliability are not completely appropriate.

POINTS TO PONDER

1. All measurement is subject to error. List at least eight types of errors of measurement.

2. Why should the split-half method of reliability not be used with speeded tests?

3. Which set of values shown below gives the higher reliability for *difference scores*?
   a) $r_{xx} = .80$, $r_{yy} = .90$, and $r_{xy} = .75$
   b) $r_{xx} = .80$, $r_{yy} = .90$, and $r_{xy} = 0$

4. A test manual reports a corrected split-half reliability of .75. What does this mean? What is the correlation between the two halves of the test?

CHAPTER 4

Validity

KINDS OF VALIDITY EVIDENCE
METHODS OF EXPRESSING VALIDITY
FACTORS AFFECTING VALIDITY
VALIDITY AND DECISION MAKING
VALIDITY GENERALIZATION
VALIDITY AND TEST USE
VALIDITY OF CRITERION-REFERENCED TESTS

The *degree of validity* is the single most important aspect of a test. A useful oversimplification is to think of validity as truthfulness: Does the test measure what it purports to measure? For a test to be valid, or truthful, it must first be reliable. If we cannot even get a bathroom scale to give us a consistent weight measure, we certainly cannot expect it to be accurate. Note, however, that a measure might be consistent (reliable) but not accurate (valid). A scale may record weights as two pounds too heavy each time. In other words, reliability is a necessary but not a sufficient condition for validity. (Neither validity nor reliability is an either/or dichotomy; there are degrees of each.)

Validity can be best defined as the extent to which certain inferences can be made from test scores or other measurement. The *Standards for Educational and Psychological Testing* (AERA-APA-NCME, 1985) states that validity "refers to the appropriateness, meaningfulness, and usefulness of the specific inferences made from test scores. Test validation is the process of accumulating evidence to support such inferences" (p. 9).

In discussing validity, it is useful to think of two general types of inferences: (1) making inferences about performance other than that measured and (2) making inferences about a property (behavioral domain) of the person measured. The first is a *statistical* inference, the second a *measurement* inference (Guion, 1983). When a score is used to infer other performance, we are, in a sense, *predicting* performance and knowing the degree to which the prediction or inference is accurate depends on *criterion-related validity* evidence.

When a test score is used to make an inference about a property or behavioral domain (for instance, level of knowledge of physics, or amount of motivation) of the person measured, we can think of the test score as *representing* the property of the person. This is a reasonable inference to the extent that the test items actually do represent the behavioral domain. Tests that represent can further be differentiated as *samples* or *signs*. The distinction is based on the degree to which we can *define* the behavioral domain being sampled. If the items are drawn from a clearly defined universe, we speak of this as a sample. If the universe is not clearly defined, we speak of the test as a sign. Samples *describe* the domain, signs help *explain* the domain. An example of a test that *samples* a domain would be one in arithmetic computation. Not all possible arithmetic combinations and permutations would be on the test—only a sample of them. However, the inference we wish to make is typically to the total domain. An example of a test that serves as a sign would be the Rorschach inkblot test. The administrator is not interested in inferring to how a person will respond to a domain of inkblots but rather to inferring to personality characteristics that were not sampled. For tests to serve as samples we need high *content validity evidence*; to serve as signs we need high *construct validity evidence* (see the following section).

Since a single test may be used for many different purposes, there is no single validity index for a test. A test that has some validity for one purpose (a particular inference) may be invalid for another.

After studying this chapter the reader should be able to do the following:

1. Understand the relationship between reliability and validity.
2. Understand the basic kinds of validity evidence.
3. Interpret various expressions of validity.
4. Recognize what factors affect validity and how they affect it.
5. Recognize the relationships between test validity and decision making.

KINDS OF VALIDITY EVIDENCE

The latest *Standards for Educational and Psychological Testing* (AERA-APA-NCME, 1985) discusses three categories of validity evidence:

1. Content validity.
2. Criterion-related validity.
3. Construct validity.

Although the *Standards* uses the above three labels, it goes on to say that "the use of the category labels should not be taken to imply that there are distinct types of validity . . ." (p. 9). As suggested in the introduction, different types of inferences can be made, and the justification for them frequently requires different types of validity evidence. Current authors stress that it is important to keep in mind that it is the *evidence* that can be labeled as valid or invalid. We should not really think in terms of different kinds of validity, although we, as other authors, do on occasion use the labels without adding the word *evidence* each time. We discuss each of the three kinds of validity evidence as well as two other terms you may encounter: face validity and curricular/instructional validity.

Content Validity Evidence

As mentioned earlier, one purpose of a test (or other measurement) is to make an inference about a property or behavioral domain of a person. A test serves as a *sample* of the domain if the items are drawn from a clearly defined universe. Content validity is related to how adequately the content of, and responses to, the test samples the domain about which inferences are to be made. This has been stressed for many years. For example, three decades ago Lennon (1956, p. 294) defined validity as "the extent to which a subject's responses to the items of a test may be considered to be a representative sample of his responses to a real or hypothetical universe of situations which together constitute the area of concern to the person interpreting the test."

Content validity is particularly important for achievement tests. Typically we wish to make an inference about a student's degree of attainment of the universe of situations and/or subject matter domain. The test behavior serves as a sample, and the important question is whether the test items do, in fact, constitute a representative sample of behavioral stimuli.

In judging content validity, we must first define the content domain and universe of situations. In doing so, we should consider *both* the subject matter and the type of behavior or task desired from the pupils. Notice that in Lennon's definition content validity is ascribed to the subject's responses rather than to the test questions themselves. Both content and process are important. The test user makes inferences to a *behavioral* universe. (For simplicity in writing from now on, we call the universe to which we wish to infer the *content domain*. Remember, however, the inferences are to *behavior*.)

There has been some debate about how explicitly the content domain needs to be defined. In most cases it is probably desirable to define the domain as specifically as possible in terms of a complete, finite, set of behavioral objectives. This is easier for some subject matter areas than others. For example, elementary school mathematics may be more easily defined totally than British literature. The more thoroughly defined the domain, the closer we come to being able to build a domain-referenced test (see Chapter 1). But for many subject matters we cannot define the total domain with complete specificity. This, of course, means we would not have perfect content validity, but it does not necessarily mean that the content validity is inadequate. A reasonable expectation is that the test constructor specify with considerable detail the subject matter topics and pupil behaviors the test is designed to sample. We talk more in Chapter 8 about test blueprints or tables of specifications for achievement tests. These are two-way grids designed to aid in constructing tests so that all appropriate topics and behaviors will be sampled in the proper proportions. If those grids are carefully constructed and carefully followed in building the test, this will do much to ensure adequate content validity.

Table 4.1 is an example of a two-way grid of the content of a natural science exam and relates the content to the level of objectives as defined by Bloom (1956).

TABLE 4.1

TWO-WAY TABLE OF SPECIFICATIONS FOR AN EXAMINATION IN NATURAL SCIENCE

	*Level of Objectives**				
Examination Content	*Knowledge*	*Comprehension (Translation, Interpretation, Extrapolation)*	*Application*	*Analysis*	*Total*
1. Methods of science; hypotheses concerning the origin of the solar system	5	2		3	10
2. Minerals and rocks	5	5			10
3. Changes in land features	4	4	2		10
4. Interpretation of land features	2	2	6		10
5. Animal classifications	2	4	4		10
6. Plants of the earth	4	4	2		10
7. Populations and the mechanisms of evolution	3	3		4	10
8. Variation and selection		1	5	4	10
9. Facts of evolution and the theory that explains them		2	2	6	10
10. Evolution, genetics, and the races of mankind		3	4	3	10
Total	25	30	25	20	100

* Objectives are based on Bloom's taxonomy.

SOURCE: C. H. Nelson. 1958. *Let's Build Quality into Our Science Tests*. Washington, D.C.: National Science Teachers Association.

The content could, of course, be delineated into finer subdivisions. Whether this needs to be done depends upon the nature of the content. A good rule of thumb to follow in determining how detailed the content area should be is to *have a sufficient number of subdivisions to ensure adequate and detailed coverage.*

Notice that in the table there are numbers in certain cells and blanks in other cells. Note also that the totals of the last column and of the bottom row amount to 100. These numbers give the percent of the test questions in each cell of the table of specifications.

There is no commonly used numerical expression for content validity. Content validity is typically determined by a thorough inspection of the items. Each item is judged on whether or not it represents the specified domain. Although a detailed, systematic, critical inspection of the test items and table of specifications is probably the single best way to determine content validity, such inspection does have some drawbacks. It is subjective and does not yield any quantitative expression. Two persons—whether or not they have the same understanding of the content domain—may well make different judgments about the match of the items to the domain. Of course, interjudge agreements of ratings could be calculated (Tinsley & Weiss, 1975).

The task of subjectively judging content validity is made easier if the test author defines the universe and the sampling process. Displaying the table of specifications and the number of items from each category would greatly facilitate this judgment. The procedures followed in developing the table of specifications as well as the methods used for classifying the items should also be described. These procedures might include using curriculum specialists as expert judges and reviewing current texts, curricular guides, and the like.

In addition to expert judgment, there are other procedures for estimating content validity. One method, similar to one discussed in the chapter on reliability, indicates the close relationship between one type of reliability and content validity. Recall that with reliability we wished to know how confidently we could generalize from the particular score obtained to the score we might have received under different conditions. Likewise, in content validity we are interested in how adequately we can infer from a particular score to a larger domain. In either case we wish to *generalize*. Thus, building two tests over the same content, giving both to the same set of pupils, and correlating the results tells us something about both equivalent form reliability and content validity. In fact, Ebel (1975) has suggested that instead of content validity we might better use terms such as *content reliability* or *job sample reliability*.

As Brown (1983) points out, in one sense content validity is a general property of a test. A test *author* who defines the content domain and writes items to represent the domain succeeds to some degree in attaining his or her goal. From the point of view of a test *user,* however, content validity is situation-specific. Does the test sample the domain to which the user wishes to infer? Is there a proper balance among the subcategories (if any) of the domain? It should be emphasized that an achievement test may have high content validity for one user and low content validity for another.

For example, not all teachers (even those teaching the same course titles in the same grade) are necessarily teaching the same domain of subject matter. For that reason they should construct their own evaluation instruments to ensure that their tests have adequate content validity for their particular courses, if that is the domain to which they wish to infer. However, if they wish to make inferences to a broader domain of knowledge than that covered in a specific course, then the test should sample from that broader domain. A standardized achievement test may have good content validity for that broader inference.

Criterion-Related Validity Evidence

Criterion-related validity pertains to the empirical technique of studying the relationship between the test scores or other measures (*predictors*) and some independent external measures (*criteria*), such as scholastic aptitude test scores and college grade point average. Some writers make a distinction between two kinds of criterion-related validity: concurrent validity and predictive validity. The only procedural distinction between these pertains to the time period when the criterion data are gathered. When they are collected at approximately the same time as the test data, we speak of concurrent validity. When they are gathered at a later date, we have a measure of predictive validity.

A second distinction is a logical rather than a procedural one and is based not on time but on the purpose of testing or the inference we wish to make. In predictive validity we are actually concerned with the usefulness of the test score in *predicting* some future performance. In concurrent validity we are asking whether the test score can be *substituted* for some less efficient way of gathering criterion data (such as using a score from a group scholastic aptitude test instead of a more expensive-to-gather individual aptitude test score).

Although concurrent and predictive validity differ in the time period when the criterion data are gathered, they are both concerned with prediction in a *generalizability* sense of the term. In criterion-related validity, as in content validity and reliability, we wish to determine how well we can *generalize* from one score to other scores. In reliability we were asking how confidently we could generalize to another measure of the same characteristic. In content validity we wish to generalize from a sample to a total domain. In criterion-related validity we are asking how confidently we can generalize (or predict) how well a person will do a *different task*. For example, a college admissions test may include verbal analogy items. Admissions officers are not directly interested in how well a student can perform on these items; rather they wish to measure this characteristic because it predicts a relevant criterion: college success.

The distinction between a test as *representing* versus *predicting* is not completely clear. The same test could be used for both types of inferences. A test sampling the mathematics concepts taught in grade 7 could be used as a description of level of achievement in seventh-grade mathematics; it could also be used to predict success in eighth-grade mathematics.

Measuring the Criterion   In studying criterion-related validity, the conceptual and operational (measurement) aspects of the criterion must be examined closely. For example, suppose we wish to determine the degree to which scores on a certain aptitude test predict "success in school." Success in school is, then, the criterion. How do we measure success in school? Traditionally, educators have used grade point average (GPA) as the operational definition of school success, but most realize that this is not a completely adequate definition. Other criterion measures, such as graduation versus withdrawal from school, are possible. Similar situations exist if we are trying to predict success on a job. In this case, supervisor ratings are often used as a criterion measure, even though they have many inadequacies. If a test score did not correlate well with the ratings, we would not know for sure whether the test did not predict on-the-job success or whether the supervisor could not rate it accurately, or both.

One of the most difficult tasks in a study of criterion-related validity is to obtain adequate criterion data. Gathering such data is often a more troublesome measurement problem than constructing the test or predictive instrument. *Criterion measures, like all other measures, must have certain characteristics if they are to be considered adequate* (see Brown, 1983, pp. 101–102). First of all, they should be *relevant*. That is, the criterion measure should actually reflect the important aspects of the conceptual criterion. There is no point in obtaining a criterion measure that really does not reflect the criterion. The degree of relevance of the criterion measure is a value judgment, and not everyone will agree on any specific case. Some educators, for instance, argue that success in college should mean the amount of knowledge acquired after four years in college and that grades are a good (or at least the best available) measure of such knowledge. Others believe that amount of knowledge is a good definition of success, but feel that the grading system employed does not allow one to infer amount of knowledge from GPA. Still others may feel that success in college means marrying well, making good contacts, or something else. To these people, grades would be an irrelevant criterion measure of school success.

A second desired characteristic of a criterion is that it be *reliable*. Just as test reliability affects the degree of correlation between it and the criterion, so does the reliability of the criterion affect the correlation. A general theoretical relationship is that the maximum relationship obtained between two variables is equal to the square root of the product of their respective reliabilities. Or

$$r_{xy} \leq \sqrt{(r_{xx})(r_{yy})}$$

where r_{xy} = correlation between predictor (x) and criterion (y)
$\qquad$ (a common method of expressing criterion-related validity)
$\qquad r_{xx}$ = reliability of the test
$\qquad r_{yy}$ = reliability of the criterion

Thus, the reliability of the criterion affects criterion-related validity every bit as much as the reliability of the predictor.

A third characteristic of the criterion measure is that it be unbiased, or free from contamination. Criterion contamination occurs when the criterion score is influenced by the knowledge of the predictor score. Suppose that in September a ninth-grade math teacher gives and scores a test designed to predict success of her pupils in ninth-grade math. If her knowledge of these predictor scores consciously or unconsciously affects the grades (criterion scores) she assigns at the end of the year, then we have criterion contamination. The best way to avoid this problem is to make sure the rater supplying the criterion scores has no knowledge of the predictor values.

Construct Validity Evidence

Construct validity is the degree to which one can infer certain constructs in a psychological theory from the test scores. If an instrument has construct validity, people's scores will vary as the theory underlying the construct would predict. Construct validity is important for tests purportedly measuring such characteristics (constructs) as intelligence, motivation, assertiveness, compulsiveness, paranoia, and others. A simplified example may help.

People who are interested in studying a construct such as creativity have probably hypothesized that creative people will *perform* differently from those who are not creative. It is possible to build a theory (or theories) specifying how creative people (people who possess the construct creativity) behave differently from others. Once this is done, creative people can be identified by observing the behavior of individuals and classifying them according to the theory. (They could be rated rather than classified.)

Now, suppose one wishes to build a paper-and-pencil test to *measure* creativity. Once developed, the creativity test would be considered to have construct validity to the degree that the test scores are related to the judgments made from observing behavior identified by the psychological theory as creative. If the anticipated relationships are not found, then the construct validity of the inference that the test is measuring creativity is not supported.

A lack of a relationship could occur for several reasons. For example, the test may not really measure the construct of creativity, or the psychological theory specifying how creative people behave may be faulty. Theoretical psychologists are probably more apt to believe that the test rather than the theory is faulty. Even though this is the more probable reason, psychologists should be a little more willing to reexamine their theories if empirical evidence does not support them.

Construct validity is an important concept for the educators and psychologists who are doing theoretical research on various constructs. Those with such interests surely need to delve further into the topic than we have in these few paragraphs. We suggest Cronbach & Meehl (1955), Brown (1983), and Anastasi (1982) as good references for further study.

Some authors contend that all validity evidence is construct validity evidence (for instance, Cronbach, 1980; Tenopyr, 1977). They believe that almost always the inference one wishes to make goes beyond the simple descriptive statement strictly allowed in content validity. A very strict interpretation of content validity is that one can infer from the number of items in the test answered correctly to the number of items in the total domain that one *would answer* correctly. Recall that the items should sample both content and responses. Strictly speaking, one can infer from a sample of responses to multiple-choice questions to a domain of responses to multiple-choice questions. If one wishes to infer that the student *knows,* has the *ability,* or is *able* to answer a certain percent of items correctly then, so the argument goes, one is inferring something about an underlying construct (see Linn, 1980). This is a subtle distinction that may at times be useful and at times counterproductive. The difference between performing in a certain way and having the ability (a construct) to perform in a certain way is not one we typically make in everyday language. To infer that a level of performance represents some hypothetical construct may only encourage mysticism (Ebel, 1974). But the reminder of the *narrowness* of a content validity inference is appropriate. A person who performs well on a test of addition of two-digit numbers horizontally arranged is likely to do well on a test with different combinations arranged in the same way. It is probably reasonable to infer that the individual has the "ability" to add such combinations. If a person has a low score on the test, the content validity inference to the domain of questions *asked the same way* is appropriate. It would *not* be appropriate, however, to infer that the individual could not (or lacked the ability to) perform vertical two-digit addition problems.

The important thing to remember is that there should be some evidence— or at least good logic—for the inference we wish to make. Whether we term that evidence content or construct validity evidence is only semantic.

Face Validity

People sometimes use the term *face validity,* but it should not be confused with content validity. Face validity is not really validity at all in the technical sense of the word. It simply refers to whether the test looks valid "on the face of it." That is, would untrained people who look at or take the test be likely to think the test is measuring what its author claims? Face validity often is a desirable feature of a test in the sense that it is useful from a public acceptance standpoint. It a test appears irrelevant, examinees may not take the test seriously, or potential users may not consider the results useful. (Occasionally, in assessment in the affective domain, one wishes to conceal the purpose of assessment in order to diminish faking. In these cases, reduced face validity could lead to increased criterion-related or construct validity.)

Curricular/Instructional Validity

The terms *curricular validity* and *instructional validity* are being used increasingly in the literature. Curricular validity relates to the question of the degree to which the test content is covered in the curriculum materials. Instructional validity is a more restrictive term and relates to the degree to which the test content is actually taught. (At times the terms are used interchangeably.) Instructional validity is certainly important if one wishes to make inferences about instructional effectiveness. We would surely not wish to infer from a low test score that instruction was ineffective if the content of the test did not match the instruction. We could, however, make an inference about the appropriateness of the instruction or curriculum (or the test) based on the match or lack of match of the content.

Curricular validity is considered by many to be important for any type of minimal competency test required for, say, high school graduation. It seems unfair to withhold a diploma from someone who did not learn something that was not covered in the curriculum. This seems true to many even if no inference is made regarding instructional effectiveness.

The problems of obtaining evidence of curricular/instructional validity are myriad. For example, if one wishes to teach for transfer or understanding, then the students should be able to perform on tasks that depart somewhat from the specific tasks practiced in the classroom. How much the questions can differ from the instruction and still "match" is a matter of judgment, but most would agree we should not have to limit the test to questions measuring recall in order to have curricular validity.

It is much more difficult to obtain evidence on instructional validity than curricular validity. The reason is that evidence about a match between curricular materials (such as textbooks) and test questions does not necessarily mean the materials were covered in class or even assigned out of class. Some would suggest that to gather good evidence of instructional validity would require full-time unbiased observers in the classroom. To "prove" that the material in a state-mandated minimal competency test was covered would require full-time observers in every classroom in the state! Such a requirement is clearly unreasonable.

Some individuals even argue that the observers must go beyond observing *what* is presented since presentation is not the same as effective teaching (Hills, 1981, p. 161). We think that such a requirement is far too stringent. Notice that we carefully used the word *covered* rather than *taught* in the previous paragraphs. One of course could argue that if the student has not learned, the teacher has not taught. But then, no test would have instructional validity for a person who did poorly on the test! That would be an illogical conclusion.

Fisher (1983) and Hardy (1984) describe the procedures that their two states (Florida and Alabama) used to establish that their high school graduation examinations were instructionally valid. (Other states have done similar studies.) The Florida study included an analysis of content in the curriculum by every district in the state, an audit of the district reports, a survey of all the teachers in the state, and a survey of students asking them whether they had been taught the material. These procedures were upheld in court as providing sufficient evidence that the test had adequate curricular/instructional validity (*Debra P.,* 1983).

The Alabama study (Hardy, 1984) asked teachers of grades 7 through 10 to report the proportion of students in their classes who had received instruction on each competency. (Limiting the survey to teachers of those grades was appropriate because the required competencies were considered to be skills typically taught by the ninth grade.) As of this writing, there has not been a legal challenge to the Alabama examination. As Hardy points out, "There is inadequate case law to establish precedent on what might be considered appropriate and sufficient evidence of instructional validity for a test to be used as a requirement for high school graduation" (p. 292).

Content Validity vs. Curricular Validity

Some individuals have suggested that curricular validity should be considered a subcategory of content validity. In fact, an appellate court ruling on the *Debra P.* case stated that "an important component of content validity is curricular validity" (1981, p. 6770). We think this is a misuse of terms and only adds to some confusion that already exists between the two. We agree with Yalow and Popham (1983), who argue that instructional/curricular validity issues are really issues regarding the adequacy-of-preparation for a test. As they state, "*adequacy-of-preparation is not a component of content validity.* Not only is it not a component of content validity, it is not a form of validity at all'' (p. 12). In the *Debra P.* court case, for example, the concern about instructional validity had to do with the action to be taken based on a high school senior failing a basic skills test. Yalow and Popham argue that the *inference* that such a student does not possess the basic skills was not at issue: ''Adequacy-of-preparation is not necessary for one to make sensible inferences about what scores signify'' (p. 13).

Recall that content validity relates to the adequacy of the sampling from the domain to which one wishes to infer. Frequently that domain does and should go far beyond the domain of materials actually taught. For example, critics of standardized achievement tests have sometimes based their criticism on the lack of a perfect match between the test and the curriculum/instruction of a particular school. They occasionally argue that because the match is not perfect, there is inappropriate content validity and the test should not be used. This is not necessarily so. It depends on the inference one wishes to make.

To suggest that a test must have curricular validity in order to have content validity would restrict us to making inferences about whether students know the specific materials on the curriculum. As Mehrens (1984) notes: ''At times we wish to infer to the specific objectives taught by a specific teacher in a specific school. More commonly we wish to infer to a general domain'' (p. 9). For example, ''If parents wish to infer how well their children will do in another school next year they need to infer to a general domain, not to the perhaps narrow and idiosyncratic domain of a single teacher's objectives'' (p. 11). Certainly, as Cronbach (1963) observes: ''In course evaluation, we need not be much concerned about making measuring instruments fit the curriculum. . . . An ideal evaluation might include measures of all the types of proficiency that might reasonably be desired in the area in question, not just the selected outcomes to which this curriculum directs substantial attention'' (p. 680). As Green (1983) points out: ''If the students have learned fundamental skills and knowledge and understand it, they will be able to answer many questions dealing with material not directly taught . . . generalized skills and understandings do develop. . . . Since all the specifics can never be taught . . . this development is highly desirable and tests . . . should try to assess it. This can only be done by having items that ask about content *not* directly taught'' (p. 6).

In conclusion, at times we want evidence of curricular/instructional validity; at other times we do not. It all depends on the domain to which we wish to infer.

METHODS OF EXPRESSING VALIDITY

The methods discussed below are used in expressing both criterion-related and construct evidences of validity. As mentioned before, there is no common numerical expression for content validity evidence, and curricular validity evidence usually involves a survey of teachers, students, and/or curricular materials. However, it should be kept in mind that one must obtain many indices before feeling justified in suggesting that any degree of construct validity has been demonstrated.

Correlation Coefficients and Related Expressions

The Pearson product moment correlation coefficient (r) is probably the most common procedure used in reporting validity. A fairly standard notation is to use the symbol r_{xy} for correlations representing validity coefficients. (Recall that r_{xx} is used for the reliability of measure X.) The x subscript stands for the test score (predictor); the y subscript, for the criterion measure. For example, a correlation coefficient of .60 (r_{xy} = .60) between Scholastic Aptitude Test scores (X) obtained in eleventh grade and college freshman GPAs (Y) may be reported. This correlation indicates a substantial relationship for this type of prediction and therefore we could say that the Scholastic Aptitude Test has considerable predictive validity with regard to college freshmen grades.

The relationship between the test and the criterion is often expressed by using algebraic modifications of the correlation coefficient. One such expression is $(r_{xy})^2$—that is, the squared correlation between the test and the criterion. A squared correlation is called a *coefficient of determination*. An often-heard expression is that $(r_{xy})^2$ indicates the proportion of criterion variance accounted for by the test. Thus, in the above example, where r_{xy} = .60, $(r_{xy})^2$ = .36. Therefore 36 percent of the variation in college freshman GPA can be accounted for (predicted) from knowledge of the aptitude test scores.

Another statistic often reported is the *standard error of estimate* ($S_{y.x}$). The symbol is read "the standard deviation of Y for a given value of X." It can be computed by

$$S_{y.x} = S_y \sqrt{1 - (r_{xy})^2} \qquad (4.1)$$

where S_y = criterion standard deviation. The value $S_{y.x}$ can be used to set confidence limits about an estimated criterion score, just as the standard error of measurement (S_e) is used to set confidence limits about a true score. The equation (commonly called a regression equation) used to estimate the criterion score (Y) is

$$\hat{Y} = r_{xy} \left(\frac{S_y}{S_x} \right) (X - \bar{X}) + \bar{Y} \qquad (4.2)$$

Of course, in order to use this equation (or compute any correlational data), we must have data for a single group of people on both the X and Y variables. If we have such data, why would we be interested in predicting Y

from X? Why not just look at the Y score to see what it is? The answer is that we build the equation from one group's scores to use in predicting Y scores for other similar groups. The group we use for test-validation purposes should not be the same as the group for which we use the test in decision making. For example, suppose we wish to validate a Scholastic Aptitude Test (X) for the purpose of predicting college success (Y) (operationally defined as a college GPA) at Michigan State University (MSU). We would gather data on the Scholastic Aptitude Test for high school (say grade 12) students. We would follow these students through MSU and determine their college GPA. We would then have the X and Y data. We would use this information for assistance in predicting college GPA for *future* groups of high school students. If we gathered Scholastic Aptitude Test data in 1980 and college GPA data in 1984 (or more likely, GPA data in 1982 at the end of the sophomore year), then we would use these data to predict college GPAs for the 1985 high school graduating class.

Suppose we wish to predict Melinda's GPA at MSU from knowledge of her score on a Scholastic Aptitude Test. Assume her aptitude test score (X) is 52, $\bar{X} = 50$, $r_{xy} = .60$, $S_y = 0.8$, $S_x = 10$, and $\bar{Y} = 2.4$. Melinda's predicted GPA score would be

$$\hat{Y} = .60 \left(\frac{.8}{10} \right) (52 - 50) + 2.4 = 2.496 \cong 2.5$$

It is desirable to know how much confidence can be placed in this predicted GPA. Since the standard deviation of the GPA distribution (S_y) is .8, by using Equation (4.1) we see that $S_{y.x} = .8\sqrt{1 - (.60)^2} = .64$. Recall that $S_{y.x}$ is the estimated standard deviation of the Y (criterion) scores for all people with a given X score. In this case, we are saying that the Y-score distribution for all people with an X score of 52 will have a mean of 2.5 ($\hat{Y} = 2.5$) and a standard deviation of .64 ($S_{y.x} = .64$). By assuming that this distribution of Y scores is normal, we say that about 68 percent of the people with an X score of 52 will obtain a GPA (Y score) of 2.5 $\pm$ .64. Ninety-five percent of them will obtain a GPA between 2.5 $\pm$ 2 (.64). In setting confidence limits on Melinda's GPA, we can say that the chances are about 68 in 100 (odds of about 2 to 1) that Melinda's actual GPA will be between 2.5 $\pm$ .64. We can be about 95 percent confident (odds of 20 to 1) that her actual GPA will be between 2.5 $\pm$ 2 (.64). We assume that $S_{y.x}$ will be the same for every value of X (this is called the assumption of homoscedasticity), so we would use the value of $S_{y.x}$ found in the above example (.64) in setting confidence bands about any predicted Y score. The 68 percent confidence band is always the predicted Y score ($\hat{Y}$) $\pm$ $1S_{y.x}$; the 95 percent confidence band is always $\hat{Y} \pm 2S_{y.x}$; and the 99 percent confidence band is $\hat{Y} \pm 2.58S_{y.x}$.

Before leaving this section on expressing validity using correlational procedures, recall two points made in Chapter 2: (1) correlation does not signify cause and effect; (2) the Pearson product moment correlation coefficient is a measure of linear relationship. If we believe that the relationship between X and Y is not linear, we should use some other measure of association.

Finally, this section and the example in it were written as if one were predicting a person's Y score (and therefore making a decision about that person) on the basis of a single piece of data (X score). Such a situation should seldom, if ever, occur. We used the single-X example because it is easier to conceptualize. Typically, a decision maker would use a variety of predictor data. Equations similar to 4.2 exist to assist us in such predictions. They are called *multiple regression equations,* indicating the use of more than one X score per person. For example, we might wish to predict college grades from *both* knowledge of high school rank (HSR) and a Scholastic Aptitude Test score. Both of these variables would then be used as data in the equation. If we thought that other variables would assist in the prediction, we would use them also. Perhaps data on a scale measuring academic motivation would increase our ability to predict. Perhaps data on race or sex would assist. Any (or all) of this additional data could be used in an equation predicting college success. (Sometimes, if variables such as race or sex are used, they are termed moderator variables.) Further discussion of multiple regression is beyond the scope of this book. Interested readers should refer to a book such as Kerlinger and Pedhazur (1973).

At times it is appropriate to use a technique called *multiple cutoff scores* rather than multiple regression. In such a case, a decision may be made "against" an individual who falls below the cutoff score on any one of the measures. Whether to use multiple regression or multiple cutoff score techniques relates to the question of compensatory qualifications. If a deficiency on one characteristic (skill) can be compensated for by an excess on another characteristic, then it is more appropriate to use multiple regression techniques. However, for some jobs, an excess in one skill cannot compensate for a deficiency in another. In such cases, multiple cutoff scores should be used. For example, although a high school math teacher should know basic mathematics and be able to relate to high school students, an excess of relating skills cannot compensate for a deficiency in math knowledge, or vice versa. In such cases, one needs to use multiple cutoff approaches.

Sometimes people get confused about the multiple cutoff approach. The data may be gathered sequentially, and the individual being tested may make the cutoff score on all but the last test. Critics will look at this final decision point and argue that the decision was inappropriately made on the basis of a single piece of data. Not so. Several pieces of data were used. But, because of the noncompensatory skills needed, a negative decision can be made if the cutoff score on one measure was not achieved. Of course, it would be permissible and perhaps even wise to give individuals several chances to pass. How many chances depends upon the relative cost of false rejections and false acceptances (see pp. 94–97).

Expectancy Tables

Ordinarily students, teachers, and other test users find expectancy tables easier than correlation coefficients to understand and interpret. A hypothetical expectancy table is given in Table 4.2. Column 1 gives the Scholastic Aptitude Test score in percentile rank form (a percentile rank is the proportion of individuals who score below a given score). The numbers in columns 2, 3, and 4 of the table represent the percent of people within each of the five categories of the test who achieved college freshman GPAs of D or higher, C or higher, and B or higher, respectively. Although such a table is usually understood by high school students, two limitations (or possible misinterpretations) should be noted. First, the column giving the size of the group is important. From column 5 we can see that the percentages for the last row were based on only ten people. Percentages based on such a small number of people are subject to extreme fluctuation. Second, the table should not be interpreted as if a person in the bottom fifth (0–19) on the Scholastic Aptitude Test has no chance of receiving a GPA of C or greater, or that a person in the middle fifth (40–59) has no chance of receiving a GPA of B. The table shows only that of the group sampled, no students fell in these cells of the table. Using a different sample, we would expect to find slight deviations in our predictions.

Counselors would be well advised to build expectancy tables such as Table 4.2 for their own school system. The tables can be very useful in helping students make decisions about college attendance. However, one must remember that just as there can be errors in prediction with regression equations, so there can be with expectancy tables. Like correlation data, expectancy tables do not prove cause and effect and can be built using more than one predictor variable.

TABLE 4.2

SAMPLE EXPECTANCY TABLE*

(1) Percentile Rank on the Scholastic Aptitude Test (National Norms)	Chances in 100 of Freshman Obtaining an Average Grade of			(5) Size of Group (n)
	(2) D, or higher	(3) C, or higher	(4) B, or higher	
80–99	99	81	32	100
60–79	95	52	12	100
40–59	80	15	—	60
20–39	50	—	—	30
0–19	30	—	—	10

* Expectancy table for first-year GPA, based on Scholastic Aptitude Test scores of freshmen entering Central College in the fall of 1982.

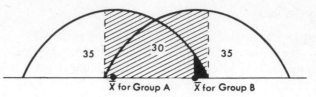

Figure 4.1   Diagram showing percent overlap between groups using two different definitions.

Discriminant Statistics

Other methods of expressing validity employ various statistics describing the degree of difference between groups (t tests, F tests, the discriminant function, and the percent of overlap are examples of this type of statistic). To learn to compute these statistical values requires more statistics than are presented in this text. However, the test user need only understand that these procedures allow for a numerical expression of the degree to which various groups perform differently on the test. If we wish to use a test to differentiate (classify) people with various psychiatric disorders (as in the Minnesota Multiphasic Personality Inventory) or to differentiate between various occupational interest groups (as in the Strong Campbell Interest Inventory), it is important to know how successful the test is in that endeavor.

The percent of overlap is one of the more common methods used by test publishers to express the difference between groups. If two groups have a 30 percent overlap on a test, 30 percent of the total number of people in the two groups have scores higher than the lowest score in the better group and lower than the highest score in the poorer group. Assume that in Figure 4.1 there are 50 people in group A and 50 in group B. Of these 100 people, 30 (30 percent) have scores in the lined area, so there is a 30 percent overlap.

Another way of expressing overlap is to determine the percent in the lower-scoring group who exceed the mean of the upper-scoring group. This is illustrated in the solid portion of Figure 4.1. As can be seen, a much smaller percent of overlap is obtained when it is defined in that fashion. In reading studies that report an overlap statistic, one has to note carefully which definition the author is using.

FACTORS AFFECTING VALIDITY

Many factors can affect any of the validity measures previously discussed. Of course, a major factor affecting validity measures is the actual relationship between the two variables being measured. If height is actually unrelated to intelligence, then the *measures* of height and intelligence should be unrelated. However, it is possible for two variables *actually* to be highly related but *measures* of them in a particular *sample* of people to indicate the contrary. This could occur for several reasons. For example, there may be an actual relationship between knowledge of eighth-grade mathematics and success in ninth-grade algebra. Yet a *test* of eighth-grade mathematics may not correlate with ninth-grade success. This might be because the test is too hard or too easy, because the students did not try while taking the test, and/ or because the test may simply be a poor test of knowledge of eighth-grade mathematics. These same things could all be true of the criterion measure also.

As already stated, the reliabilities of both the predictor (often a test) and criterion measures are important. The less reliably we can measure either the predictor or the criterion, the lower the validity coefficient. Recall that $r_{xy} \leq \sqrt{(r_{xx})(r_{yy})}$. Since r_{yy} is often fairly low, r_{xy} must be fairly low. Another factor is the heterogeneity of the group(s) with respect to both test data and criterion measures. As with reliability coefficients, other things being equal, the more heterogeneous the group, the higher the validity coefficient. Thus, it may not be reasonable, for example, to expect the Miller Analogies Test scores and grades in a doctoral program to be highly related, since the doctoral candidates are fairly homogeneous with respect to both variables. A low correlation due to homogeneity is especially likely to occur when the group on which the correlation has been obtained has already been screened (selected) on the basis of the test (or some other measure that correlates with the test score). For example, if all those who took an algebra aptitude test took algebra regardless of their test score, we would anticipate obtaining a higher correlation between test score and grade than if only those who scored in the upper half of the test could take algebra. For group-difference statistics such as percent overlap, significant differences are more likely to be found if each group is homogeneous but different from the other group(s).

The problem of *interpreting* validity coefficients on groups already screened or selected is particularly troublesome. Ideally, in investigating the validity of an instrument for predicting job performance or educational success, scores from an *unselected* group of applicants should be used. For example, one should study the relationship between the scores on a scholastic aptitude test of all applicants for college and their later success in college. But many colleges will not allow all applicants to be admitted. (Probably no employer would hire all applicants unless there was a real shortage of workers.) Thus, the validity study must be conducted with a more homogeneous group than the group of future applicants on which decisions will be made.

A paradox exists with respect to validity. In evaluating a test to determine whether it will assist in decision making, we want the test to have high validity coefficients on *unselected* groups. However, if we then *use* the test data to help make wise selection decisions, the validity coefficient among the selected individuals may be quite small. The more successful the test is as a selection device, the smaller will be the validity coefficient within the selected group, provided that the proportion being selected is small.

If we originally evaluate the usefulness of a test using a *selected* group, or if for legal or other reasons (see the section "Fairness of Tests to Minority Groups" in Chapter 12) we are forced after the fact (that is, we have used it for selection purposes) to prove the test is valid, the good *use* of a test decreases the validity coefficient. That is, if we accurately select *out* those who will not succeed and select *in* only those who will succeed, we are successfully decreasing the validity coefficient among the selected *in*-group. As Fricke (1975) points out, good personnel practices will produce low correlation coefficients among the selected individuals. Unfortunately many users of tests do not understand this and at times incorrectly assume that low correlations among selected individuals indicate that the test was invalid for making the original selection decisions.

In addition to the decreased correlation due to the restriction of range that occurs following selection, the shape or form of the relationship between the predictor and criterion variables also plays an important role. The scattergrams in Figure 4.2 illustrate these points. Let X be the predictor and Y the criterion. Assume that the horizonal line a represents the minimum criterion score necessary to consider an individual successful. Let the vertical line b represent the predictor score necessary to be selected. The elongation (very little scatter around a line) and general slope of the oval shapes indicate the degree of relationship between X and Y. If the pattern of scores is quite elongated and sloping, the correlation is high. If there is considerable scat-

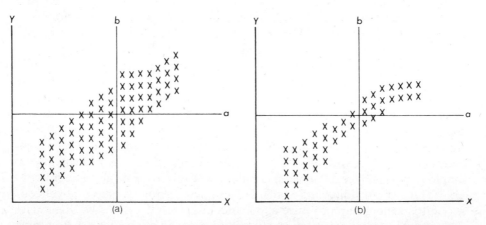

Figure 4.2   (a) Scattergram showing a high degree of relationship between X and Y for total range of X scores and a smaller degree of relationship for scores to the right of line b. (b) Scattergram showing a high degree of relationship for the total range of X scores and zero relationship for scores to the right of line b.

ter, the relationship is low. If the slope is zero, there is no relationship. In Figure 4.2a and b the overall correlation between X and Y is quite high (although for Figure 4.2b we would not use the Pearson product moment correlation coefficient). After restricting the range through selection, we have a much lower degree of relationship in Figure 4.2a, but it is still positive. There is essentially no relationship between X and Y in Figure 4.2b after selection (for scores to the right of line b). This would be the case in situations where one needed a certain amount of characteristic X in order to be successful in endeavor Y, but "more of X" would not help a person to be more successful in Y. This might be true, for example, if X was a measure of reading comprehension and Y a job requiring that one can read well enough to comprehend instruction manuals but in which further skills in reading are irrelevant. One could *validly* use the reading test to select out those who could not read at a high enough level to perform their tasks. But, after the test was *wisely* used for that purpose, there would be no correlation between X and Y for those accepted applicants.

Thus, we see that just as the size of the reliability coefficient can be affected by so many variables, so too can the validity measures. To interpret validity data correctly, it is necessary to be aware of these various factors.

Let us take one more example to illustrate these interpretation problems. Suppose a correlation of 0.20 is found between college GPA and some measure of success as a teacher. (In this example GPA is the predictor variable X, and success as a teacher is the criterion variable Y.) How should this fairly low correlation be interpreted? Those not aware of the factors discussed in this subsection might assume that the data indicate that knowledge of subject matter is irrelevant to teaching success. This assumption, of course, is a possibility, but there are many other possible (and more likely) reasons for the low correlation. Perhaps grades do not actually measure knowledge of subject matter. Perhaps the criterion measure of teaching success does not actually measure what we really mean when we think of a successful teacher. Perhaps our measure of neither X nor Y is reliable. Perhaps our sample is too restricted in range on either the X or the Y variable. Or perhaps a relationship exists such as that depicted in Figure 4.2b, and we have only graduated (or hired) teachers to the right of line b. (Perhaps once teachers know enough mathematics they can teach it, but to know a lot more advanced mathematics is irrelevant for teaching success.)

Before we could reasonably infer which of these "perhaps" statements is most likely, we would need information on the grading practices of the college, the reliability of the GPAs, the reliability and at least the *content* validity of the measure of teaching success, and the variability of the sample studied on each measure. To really know *empirically* the degree to which knowledge of subject matter influences teaching success, we would have to be willing to let people teach with all degrees of knowledge from none on up. Rather than do that, we probably would rather assume that we can *logically* infer that knowledge of subject matter is related to teaching success, and that the low correlation cited above is due to one or more of the many factors discussed.

VALIDITY AND DECISION MAKING

Let us assume that a test manual reports a correlation coefficient of 0.50 between scores obtained on a mathematical aptitude test administered in the eighth grade and scores in a ninth-grade algebra course. Will this information have any effect on the kind(s) of decisions made? What if the school's policy is to have all students take ninth-grade alegbra in heterogeneous classes? In this case the benefits derived from the test score information could be used only for instructional purposes. If the school's policy is to have all students take ninth-grade algebra and if students are also grouped homogeneously, then the test score information can be used for both instructional and administrative purposes. If the school's policy is to permit students to select either ninth-grade algebra or general math, then the test score information could be used for instructional, administrative, and counseling purposes. For any of these decisions—instructional, guidance, or administrative—the important question is whether or not better decisions could be made by using test score results in addition to other data already available (for example, teacher recommendations and previous school grades). This is an empirical question, one we would not necessarily expect the ordinary classroom teacher or counselor to answer. However, all educators should be cognizant of the following factors that are likely to make test score information useful and efficient.

1. *Availability of other data.* Tests should be used only if better decisions can be made with the data than the best decision one would make without them. This improvement in decision making is often referred to as incremental validity. How much better the decisions would be if they are based on the data than if they are based on chance alone is not the relevant consideration. One never, or almost never, is forced to make a decision on the basis of no information. If fairly valid decisions can be made without test data, then the probability that the test data will improve the accuracy of the decision decreases. If the probability of making a correct decision without the test data is very low, then it may well be beneficial to give the test, even though it has only a modest correlation with the criterion.

2. *Cost of testing and faulty decisions.* Decisions are subject to two kinds of errors: (1) *false rejections*—that is, predicting failure when success would have occurred, and (2) *false acceptances*—that is, predicting success when failure is the result.[1] The value of a test is dependent upon the difference

---

[1] Some authors use the terms *false positives* and *false negatives* for these two errors. The terms used here seem less confusing.

between the cost of testing (including such factors as the cost of purchasing the test, student and examiner time, and scoring) and the saving in the cost of errors that result from using the test. In the algebra example, a student could take algebra and fail, or not take algebra even though he or she could have passed it. The decision whether the test information is worth gathering depends upon the cost of these errors and whether the reduction in these costs by using the test is greater than the cost of gathering the data. The concepts of available data, incremental validity, and cost effectiveness often lead to *sequential* testing and decision making. In the algebra example, one may well be willing to use already available data, such as previous grades, to make decisions for a fair number of individuals. For example, in a particular school one may decide that *all* students with less than a B average in seventh- and eighth-grade math should *not* take algebra. There may be another set of students for whom the school personnel are willing to recommend ninth-grade algebra without the knowledge obtained from a mathematical aptitude test. Only those students for whom a decision could not be made would take the aptitude test. In general, in sequential testing and decision making one uses already available data first, gathers relevant data that are fairly moderate in cost for more decisions, and uses expensive data-gathering techniques to make decisions about only a few individuals. Figure 4.3 illustrates a basic sequential decision-making strategy. As mentioned earlier, one of the misunderstandings about sequential decision making is that some people only look at the last data point in the sequence and think the decision was made on only a single piece of data. Actually sequential decision making usually results in *more* data being collected; one can often afford to gather *more* types of data for the same cost because not all data are gathered for all individuals. (Although we have used an educational example, all of these same principles apply to employment testing also.)

Once data are gathered, the decision regarding where to set the cutoff score depends upon the relative cost of the two errors. If a false rejection is more expensive than a false acceptance, then the cutoff score should be lower (that is, the selection ratio should be higher) than if the reverse is true. Suppose, for example, we have the relationship between Y (success in col-

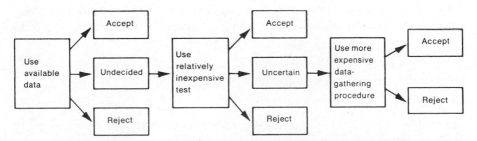

Figure 4.3   A basic sequential decision-making strategy.

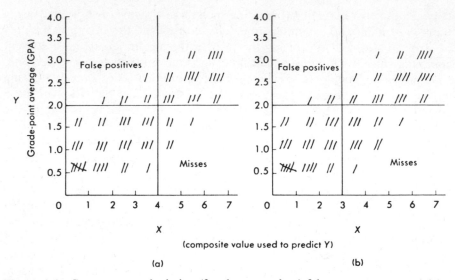

Figure 4.4   Scattergrams depicting (for the same data) false acceptances and false rejections for cutting scores of 4 and 3, respectively, when a GPA of 2.0 is required for success.

lege defined as GPA equal to or greater than 2.0) and X (some numerical value derived from a combination of variables such as test score information or past grades) represented by the scattergram shown in Figure 4.4a. Here each tally above the horizontal line (defining success in college) and to the left of $X = 4$ (the minimum admission score) would represent a false rejection. Every score below the horizontal line and to the right of the X cutoff score would be a false acceptance. The other tallies would represent correct decisions.

If the decision maker considered the costs of the two kinds of errors to be equal, then the proper approach would be to minimize the total errors and therefore to set the cutting score at 4, as is shown in Figure 4.4a. This would give six false rejections and five false acceptances (or 11 total errors). If, however, it was decided that false rejections are three times as costly as false acceptances (in terms of loss to society, for example), then the proper cutoff score should be changed. If the cutoff score were kept at 4, we would have

6 false rejections at a cost of 3 units each = 18 cost units
5 false acceptances at a cost of 1 unit each =   5 cost units
                                              23 cost units

A cutoff score of 3, as in Figure 4.4b, would produce 15 total errors but only 21 cost units, as follows:

3 false rejections at a cost of 3 units each = 9 cost units
12 false acceptances at a cost of 1 unit each = <u>12 cost units</u>
                                                21 cost units

This simple example illustrates again that test information does not make decisions but is used (often in conjunction with other information) to help set probability values. Many decision strategies other than the simple one illustrated here might be adopted. In some cases, for example, a person might decide that false rejections are not costing anything and might simply wish to obtain the highest possible ratio of successes to failures *among those selected*. Or, more likely (especially in industry), the person may wish to maximize some *mean level of output*, and thus would *not* simply count a success as a success but would weight the *degrees* of success differentially (likewise for failures). In the latter case, the evaluator would decide whether the cost of testing is worthwhile by comparing the mean utility value for all those hired using the test to help make decisions versus the mean utility value of those who would be hired without the test data. If this *difference* is greater than the cost of the test, then it is cost-effective to give the test. The general point to keep in mind is that once we have set some utility values on the various outcomes of the alternatives, we can combine probabilities and utilities to arrive at better decisions. Of course, we need to keep in mind that although from a theoretical measurement point of view we ideally obtain data such as the data presented in Figure 4.4, we often do not in practice. Typically colleges simply do not admit, and industries do not hire, people below the cutting score. Thus, we do not know what the data to the left of the cutting-score line are really like. However, it is possible to make mathematical estimates of these data. One report (USES, 1983), for example, estimates that by using the General Aptitude Test Battery for maximal decision making, the U.S. Employment Service could "help improve the productivity of American industry on the order of 50 to 100 billion dollars" per year (p. v).

3. *Selection ratio*. In the example dealing with ninth-grade algebra, it was pointed out that if all students were required to take ninth-grade algebra, the test data would be of no value for selection purposes. If conditions are such that almost everyone is to be selected, then the data will not be so valuable in selection decisions as in cases where the selection ratio is lower.

4. *Success ratio*. Another factor affecting whether test data are likely to improve decision making is the success ratio (the proportion of people selected who succeed). The success ratio depends in part upon the selection ratio. Other things being equal, the smaller the selection ratio, the larger the success ratio. The success ratio, however, is also highly dependent upon base rates (Meehl & Rosen, 1955). *Base rates* refers to the proportion of people in the general population who fall in a certain category. If 99 percent of the general ninth-grade population can succeed in ninth-grade algebra,

one can predict success with 99 percent accuracy simply by predicting success for everyone. It would take a very valid test to enable one to predict more accurately than that. If only 1 percent can succeed, an analogous situation exists. Base rates in clinical psychology are often so high or low (for example, the proportion of people who commit suicide) that tests cannot improve prediction. In educational and industrial decisions the base rates are often somewhat closer to 50 percent, the value that best enables a test score to improve the predictive accuracy.

VALIDITY GENERALIZATION

An important issue in educational and employment settings is the degree to which criterion-related evidence of validity that is obtained in one situation can be generalized (that is, transported and used) to another situation without further study of validity in the new situation. If generalization is limited, then local criterion-related evidence of validity may be necessary in most situations in which a test is used. If generalization is extensive, then situation-specific evidence of validity may not be required. (AERA-APA-NCME, 1985, p. 12)

Historically, there has been a belief that the validity of an inference from a test (at least in an industrial setting) should be situation-specific. Thus, people making criterion-related validity inferences from test scores were encouraged to conduct their own local validation studies. The evidence for the belief in situational validity was that validity coefficients varied considerably across situations. More recently, that belief has been challenged. Many analysts have concluded that the reason for the varying and usually quite modest correlations were the result of statistical artifacts, due to (1) sampling error inherent in small sample sizes, (2) criterion and test unreliability, and (3) restriction in the range of test scores.

In a 1979 conference on validity, Hunter, a leading advocate of and researcher on validity generalization, began his presentation as follows: "I have come not to present theories but to verify them" (1980, p. 119). In that paper, he made a strong argument, backed by evidence, for the belief in validity generalization. In general, the audience was receptive but felt that perhaps Hunter was overly enthusiastic. As Novick pointed out: "I think you have taken us down the right road—perhaps a bit too far" (1980, p. 126).

Subsequent to that 1979 meeting, a fair amount of additional research has been done on validity generalization, and many industrial psychologists currently believe that local validation is no longer *necessarily* required. At the 1984 annual convention of the American Psychological Association, psychologists could be seen wearing a button that said, "VG is contagious." Recent research results suggest that test validity is in fact stable across jobs and settings. A recent U.S. Employment Service report has provided evidence to suggest that "cognitive ability is a valid predictor of job performance for all jobs" (USES, 1983, p. 14).

While we basically support the notions of validity generalization, we do think it possible for local users to put too much faith in such a notion. The *Standards* seems to put the issue into a nice perspective:

> *The extent to which predictive or concurrent evidence of validity generalization can be used as criterion-related evidence in new situations is in large measure* a function of accumulated research. *Consequently, although evidence of generalization can often be used to support a claim of validity in a new situation, the extent to which this claim is justified is constrained by the available data. (AERA-APA-NCME, 1985, p. 12)*

Standard 1.16 states that

> *When adequate local validation evidence is not available, criterion-related evidence of validity for a specified test use may be based on validity generalization from a set of prior studies, provided that the specified test use situation can be considered to have been drawn from the same population of situations on which validity generalization was conducted. (AERA-APA-NCME, 1985, p. 16)*

For a local user of test data, the sensible way to go is to gather local validation data if feasible. If not feasible, assume you can generalize to your specific inference only if prior studies suggest that such generalization is appropriate. We believe that a great deal of relevant evidence exists. However, at this time, the evidence is probably greater for educational uses than it is for industrial/employment uses of tests. (Actually, the evidence is almost overwhelming with respect to tests predicting success in future educational endeavors. A test that predicts success in one school almost invariably predicts success in another school.)

VALIDITY AND TEST USE

Just as people wish to know how reliable a test should be, they also wish to know how valid a test should be. The same answer must be given: It depends upon the purposes for which the test is to be used. Naturally, one should select the best test possible. Suppose, however, that no test allows us to make very valid inferences for our purposes. Does that mean we should not test? To decide, we must answer the incremental validity question raised in the preceding section: How much better a decision can we make by using the test information in addition to all other information than we could make just from the other data alone? Once we answer this question, we must inquire whether this increase in accuracy of prediction is sufficiently greater to justify the use of the test. Theoretically, this can be answered by cost-analysis procedures if we could specify the cost of faulty decisions. It is stressed here that in education a test is seldom used to assist in only one decision. As Cronbach (1971, p. 496) has stated: ". . . in educational testing the information is usually placed in the student's file and used for many later decisions: admission, choice of major, selection of courses, career planning, etc. A test with multiple uses can repay a cost that would be unreasonable if a test were to be used once and forgotten."

Validity is a matter of degree, and a test has many validities, each dependent upon the specific purposes for which the test is used. Eventually the validity of any test is dependent upon how it is used in the local situation; therefore educators and personnel directors should, where feasible, conduct their own validity studies (although, as mentioned, the evidence for validity generalization is impressive).

Publishers of standardized tests also have a responsibility to conduct and report research on the validity of a test. Just as for reliability, the kinds and extent of validity data that one should expect to find in a test manual depend upon the type of test and the use(s) the publishers advocate for it. As discussed previously, for achievement tests content validity evidence is by far the most important type of validity evidence. Depending upon their use, aptitude, interest, and personality measures should probably have evidence of criterion-related validity. If one wishes to use test data as evidence to support or refute a psychological theory, then construct validity evidence is necessary.

In addition to reporting the type(s) of validity evidence, the manual must provide other relevant information. The characteristics of the group(s) from which the evidence was obtained must be reported in detail. Tables of specifications and their rationale should be given in support of content validity claims; standard errors of estimates should be reported for validity coefficients, and a large number of studies should be reported if a claim is to be made for construct validity.

Three points should be reemphasized in reference to validity and test use. First, it is extremely unlikely that any test will ever have perfect validity for any decision. Some errors are bound to occur. Our goal is to minimize errors in decision making, but one should *not* conclude that a test is invalid because it is possible to point to incorrect inferences made with the use of test data (for example, "I scored 88 on an intelligence test and a counselor told me I couldn't succeed in college, but I now have a Ph.D.; therefore all intelligence tests are invalid."). The crucial question in validity is *not* whether errors will be made in individual cases—the answer is invariably "Yes." The crucial question is whether fewer errors will be made by using a test in addition to other data than would be made using just the other data.

Second, although the examples used here have tended to be for selection decisions, remember that many decisions are for placement or classification rather than selection. It is necessary for all these kinds of decisions to have some data supporting the criterion-related validity of a test. But sometimes discriminant statistics are more relevant than correlational data.

Finally, when we gather information that will be useful in decision making, we are, in one sense of the word, using the data to make predictions. We predict what will occur if we decide on various alternative strategies. In education we would be well advised to concentrate on how to upset negative predictions. We typically use the predictive information not primarily for making a passive prediction but rather for directing action toward desirable outcomes. This goes along with what we said earlier about the difference in predictive validity before using the test and the predictive validity after using the test data for wise decision making. We should be striving to use adaptive strategies that will result in upsetting negative predictions that would have resulted under traditional treatments. But to do this we need to have the test data in order to identify which students need special attention. If we can use the data to make decisions that result in positive outcomes for those for whom we *originally* predicted negative outcomes, we should feel gratified. But we should not conclude from this that the test either was not valid or did not serve a useful function. The test did just what it was designed to do—identify individuals who needed special attention.

VALIDITY OF CRITERION-REFERENCED TESTS

The issue of the validity, like the reliability, of criterion-referenced tests has been a source of considerable disagreement among psychometricians. Since criterion-referenced tests are used primarily in the area of achievement testing, a major concern is the content validity of the test. In this respect criterion-referenced tests should always match or excel norm-referenced tests. Why? Because the *universe of behaviors or achievement is usually more narrowly defined in criterion-referenced tests, and the rules for sampling from this universe (item-generating rules) are often more precisely defined.* The content validity of criterion-related tests thus constructed ought to be almost assured. Such a test would have what Mosier (1947) termed *validity by definition* or what Ebel (1961) referred to as *meaningfulness*.

However, if results of criterion-referenced tests are to be used in instructional decision making, some empirical (criterion-related) validity evidence must be provided.[2] We practically always wish to "generalize beyond the universe of content defined by the item generating rules" (Jackson, 1970, p. 13). For example, if one is using the results of a mastery test to decide

----

[2] The terms *criterion-referenced testing* and *criterion-related validity* can be confused. *Criterion* has a different meaning in each term. In the former it refers to some measure of proficiency on the test itself; in the latter it refers to a different characteristic, which is estimated from the test score.

whether to allow a student to proceed with the next unit of study, some evidence ought to be provided to show that people just below the cutoff score do not do so well in the subsequent material as do people above the cutoff score.

If one uses correlational approaches to establish the criterion-related (predictive or concurrent) validity of criterion-referenced tests, the potentially small variability of criterion-referenced test scores (discussed earlier) will attenuate the validity coefficient just as it would the reliability coefficient. For this reason the discriminant statistic approaches are likely to be more useful. (See Hambelton & Novick (1973), Harris et al. (1974), Millman (1974), Swaminathan, Hambleton, & Algina (1975), and Linn (1980), for more complete discussions of the validity of criterion-referenced tests.)

SUMMARY

The principal ideas, conclusions, and implications presented in this chapter are summarized in the following statements:

1. Reliability is a necessary but not sufficient condition for validity.
2. Validity can be defined as the degree to which certain inferences can be made from test scores (or other measurements). Since a single test may have many different purposes, there is no single validity index for a test.
3. Validity evidence is typically categorized into three kinds: content, criterion-related, and construct validity.
4. Content validity is related to how adequately the content of the test samples the domain about which inferences are to be made.
5. Criterion-related validity pertains to the technique of studying the relationship between the test scores and independent external criterion measures.
6. In order to study criterion-related validity, it is important to have a good measure of the criterion. This measure should be relevant, reliable, and free from bias.
7. Construct validity is the degree to which the test scores can be accounted for by certain explanatory constructs.
8. *Curricular validity* and *instructional validity* are terms used to express the degree to which test material has been covered in the curriculum or has actually been taught. They are not validity at all in the conventional sense of the term.
9. Various methods of expressing validity include the correlation coefficient, the coefficient of determination, the standard error of estimate, and expectancy tables.
10. Various factors affect validity—for example, reliabilities of the predictor and criterion measures, group heterogeneity, and shape of the relationship.

11. Various factors affect whether a test is valid enough to be useful in decision making—for example, availability of other data, cost of testing and faulty decisions, selection ratio, and success ratio.
12. A fair amount of evidence exists suggesting that in many cases one can generalize from a criterion-related validity study done in a particular setting to other settings.
13. The content validity of criterion-referenced tests should match or excel that of norm-referenced tests.
14. The correlational approaches to determining validity are not appropriate for criterion-referenced tests to the extent that the variability of the score distribution is constricted. Therefore, discriminant statistic approaches are more likely to be useful.

POINTS TO PONDER

1. Is a reliable test valid? Why?
2. If you were permitted evidence on only one type of validity, which would you select for each of the following tests: an intelligence test, an art test, an achievement test, an interest inventory, an attitude inventory? Why do you think that knowledge of this type of validity is most germane?
3. You wish to use an algebra aptitude test to help decide who should take ninth-grade algebra. Two tests (A and B) are equal in every respect (cost, format, ease of scoring) except for their reliabilities and predictive validities:

	Test A	Test B
Reliability	.84	.95
Validity	.85	.80

Which test should you choose?
4. Do you agree with the statement "Criterion-referenced achievement tests *must* demonstrate criterion-related validity?" Explain.

CHAPTER 5

Interpreting Test Scores

NORMS
TYPES OF NORM-REFERENCED SCORES
TYPES OF CRITERION-REFERENCED SCORES
PROFILES

In Chapters 3 and 4, we discussed the reliability and validity of sets of scores. In this chapter we will discuss the interpretations of various types of scores. Most readers will realize that a raw score (number correct) on a test provides very little information. For that reason, the interpretation of the score is almost always facilitated by some type of transformation of the raw score that provides a frame of reference. Two such frames of reference are *norm*- and *criterion*-referenced. We discussed this issue briefly in Chapter 1. Recall that in the former, our frame of reference is the scores of an identifiable "norm" group. In the latter, the frame of reference is some performance standard. It is not necessary to review here the debates about nonstandard terminology, and the relative values of the two types of referencing. The two types of referencing are used by most publishers of tests, and professionals need to be familiar with both. Thus, we will present some specific types of norm- and criterion-referenced scores that you may come across as a professional and that you should understand and be able to explain to others.

After studying this chapter, the student should be able to do the following:

1. Know the basic definitions of the terms presented.
2. Appreciate the value of a norm group as an aid in interpreting test scores.
3. Evaluate the adequacy of a set of norms in terms of recency and representativeness.
4. Judge what would constitute a relevant norm group for a specified purpose of testing.
5. Recognize when different norm groups should be used.
6. Judge the adequacy of the norms description in a test manual.
7. Distinguish between norm-referenced and criterion-referenced scores.

8. Interpret various types of derived scores.
9. Recognize the limitations of various types of derived scores.
10. Interpret various profiles.

NORMS

In norm-referenced interpretation, a person's score is compared to the scores of some clearly specified group, called the *norm group,* or reference group. There may be more than one such specified norm group for any test. A table showing the performance of the norm group(s) is called a *norms table,* a set of *norms,* or (more commonly) *norms.* Norms tables typically show the relationship or correspondence between *raw scores* (the number correct on the test) and some type of *derived scores.* (Table 5.1 is an example of the types of norms tables found in manuals.) Before discussing several types of derived scores, let us first consider the need for norms, how to obtain an appropriate norm group, some various types of norm groups, what test manuals should report about norms, and how to use norms.

Need for Norms

In Chapter 1 we discussed briefly the differences between norm- and criterion-referenced measurement. Criterion-referenced measures have a place in specific types of instructional training programs, but, in general, normative referencing is of more value. There are very few educational situations in which criterion referencing *alone* is sufficient. Even if the test itself is composed of all behaviors to which we wish to infer, we usually desire normative data.

Suppose we have a 100-item test composed of all possible permutations of multiplying two one-digit numbers. If Johnny took this test and got 75 answers correct, we could clearly make a criterion-referenced statement: Johnny knows 75 percent of the material. But to know how others performed on the test would certainly help us to interpret his score. If others of his age and education can typically receive 100 percent and have been able to do so for two years, his score would take on quite a different meaning than if he is the only one in his age group who can score higher than 50 percent on the test. Norms, then, are important in that they tell us how others have performed on the test.

An Appropriate Norm Group

To be appropriate, a norm group must be *recent, representative,* and *relevant.*

TABLE 5.1

PERCENTILE NORMS FOR FORMS V AND W: DAT

Raw Scores

MALES (N = 5800+)

Percentile	Verbal Reasoning	Numerical Ability	VR + NA	Abstract Reasoning	Clerical S and A	Mechanical Reasoning	Space Relations	Spelling	Language Usage	Percentile
99	49–50	40	87–90	44–45	87–100	67–70	58–60	88–90	46–50	99
97	47–48	39	83–86	43	75–86	65–66	56–57	86–87	44–45	97
95	44–46	37–38	80–82	42	67–74	63–64	54–55	83–85	41–43	95
90	42–43	35–36	76–79	41	60–66	62	51–53	80–82	38–40	90
85	40–41	34	72–75	40	57–59	61	48–50	77–79	36–37	85
80	38–39	32–33	69–71	39	54–56	59–60	46–47	74–76	34–35	80
75	36–37	31	65–68	38	52–53	58	44–45	72–73	32–33	75
70	34–35	29–30	62–64	37	50–51	57	41–43	69–71	31	70
65	32–33	28	59–61	36	49	56	39–40	67–68	29–30	65
60	30–31	26–27	56–58	35	47–48	55	37–38	65–66	28	60
55	28–29	25	53–55	34	45–46	54	35–36	62–64	27	55
50	26–27	23–24	49–52	33	44	52–53	32–34	60–61	25–26	50
45	24–25	22	46–48	32	43	51	30–31	57–59	24	45
40	22–23	20–21	43–45	31	41–42	49–50	27–29	54–56	23	40
35	20–21	18–19	40–42	30	40	48	25–26	52–53	21–22	35
30	18–19	17	36–39	28–29	38–39	46–47	23–24	49–51	20	30
25	16–17	15–16	33–35	27	37	44–45	21–22	46–48	18–19	25
20	15	13–14	30–32	24–26	35–36	41–43	19–20	44–45	16–17	20
15	13–14	11–12	26–29	20–23	33–34	38–40	17–18	41–43	14–15	15
10	11–12	9–10	22–25	15–19	30–32	34–37	15–16	37–40	12–13	10
5	9–10	8	19–21	10–14	26–29	29–33	13–14	34–36	10–11	5
3	7–8	6–7	16–18	7–9	19–25	25–28	11–12	31–33	8–9	3
1	0–6	0–5	0–15	0–6	0–18	0–24	0–10	0–30	0–7	1
Mean	27.1	23.5	50.6	31.6	45.8	50.8	33.4	60.0	25.8	Mean
SD	11.5	9.4	19.5	9.2	13.9	10.5	13.3	15.7	9.6	SD

SOURCE: Reproduced by permission from the *Differential Aptitude Tests Administrator's Handbook Forms V & W*. Copyright © 1982, 1972 by the Psychological Corporation. All rights reserved.

Recency Other things being equal, tests with recent norms are preferred. This is particularly true in the area of achievement tests. If we do a better job of instructing, or if we change our curricular emphasis, the achievement of ninth-grade students in a social studies test three years from now might be quite different from the achievement of present ninth-graders. Of course, as the content of a curriculum changes, not only the norms but the test itself becomes outdated. This is usually obvious to a test user who is competent in the subject matter.

A less likely detected obsolescence of norms occurs when the content of the test is still relevant but the characteristics of the reference group have changed. This may be true, for example, in a college that changes from a restricted to an open admissions policy. A prospective first-year student may have quite a low test score in comparison with that of first-year students admitted under a restrictive policy; on the other hand this student's score may be quite high relative to that of first-year students admitted under an open policy. Many other less obvious changes in society could also make an older reference group no longer appropriate.

One caution to be mentioned here is that the recency of the norms group on a published test cannot be judged by the copyright date of the test manual. Any change in the test manual allows the publisher to revise the copyright date of the manual, although the later date may not be an indication of the recency of the norms.

Representativeness There are two sources of error in any normative statement about a person's score. One, the error of measurement, was discussed in Chapter 3. It is due to the imprecision or unreliability of the test or testing process. The second, the sampling error, is due to the inadequacies of the sample. A *population* refers to a specified *group* of individuals (for example, all fifth-graders in the United States). A *sample* is a smaller number of people selected from the population and actually tested. In this section we are concerned with the adequacy of the sample. In the following section we consider the relevance of the population sampled.

One consideration of some importance in sampling is the size of the sample. Any sample should be large enough to provide stable values. By "stable" we mean that if another sample had been drawn in a similar fashion, we would obtain similar results. Most of the more popular published tests have samples of adequate size.[1]

Another important factor is the kind of sampling. A large sample alone is not sufficient. If a sample is biased, making it larger does not solve the

[1] The stability of the sample does not depend only on the number of students. It also depends upon clustering procedures. Thus, for example, the number of *schools* sampled, as well as the number of *students,* is relevant to the stability estimates. More technical details with regard to sampling can be found in Angoff (1971).

problem. The sampling procedure must be correct. Space does not permit us to delve into sampling techniques extensively. In general, however, stratified random sampling is the best procedure where the stratification is done on the most relevant independent variables. The relevant independent variables (such as age, sex, socioeconomic status, race, size of community, and geographic location of the subject) would vary from one kind of test to another. Perhaps the most troublesome problem in sampling is that one is dependent on the cooperation of the sample chosen. If cooperation is poor, so that the proportion of the original sample for which scores are obtained is too low, then the obtained scores may be from a biased sample. Fortunately, most schools cooperate with agencies desiring to obtain a norm group. Unfortunately, the agencies do not always tell us what proportion of the originally chosen sample did cooperate and how they differed from the noncooperators.

A study by Baglin (1981) suggests that a considerable proportion of schools decline to participate. Those who participate are more apt to be using the publisher's tests or instructional materials than those that decline. Thus, the "national norm" may be biased in favor of schools having a curriculum related to the test content. This would be likely to produce a more difficult set of norms than a truly national norm. That is, those who participate in the testing should, as a group, do better than nonparticipants would have done. Thus, pupils would receive a lower norm-referenced score than they would have in a truly national sample.

A technique too often employed is to sample by convenience rather than by a particular technical sampling procedure. For example, schools in which one has professional contacts or those which have previously cooperated are often chosen because these procedures are convenient. Such a chosen sample *may* not be biased, particularly if the data in the sample are appropriately weighted. Nevertheless, the likelihood that such a sampling procedure will produce biased results is great enough that we should be leery of norms built in such a fashion.

Relevance   The relevance of the norm group depends upon the degree to which the population sampled provides an appropriate comparison. Is it comparable to the group with which users of the test wish to make a comparison? If, for example, a tester wishes to compare a student's ability with that of students who intend to go to college, then the norm group should be a sample of students who wish to go to college and not a sample from a general population. Since a test may be used for several different purposes, it is usually necessary to have more than one norm group. For example, it may be useful for a female high school student to have her interests compared with those of *all* people in a given occupation, *and* to have her interests compared with those of all *women* in an occupational group.

Types of Norms

Some of the more common types of norms are discussed briefly here.

National Norms   The type of norms most commonly reported by test publishers and used by educators are *national norms*. These norms are almost always reported separately by the different age or educational levels for which the test is constructed. Occasionally they are reported separately by sex. National norms can be used with all types of tests but are probably most useful for general scholastic aptitude and achievement tests. They assist in keeping one from forming too parochial a view. Suppose Mary attends a school district where the students all come from professional homes. The school, Mary's parents, and Mary herself may get quite an unrealistic picture of Mary if she is compared only with others in that district. She may be in the bottom fourth of that district but in the top 10 percent nationally.

Most major test publishers who report national norms have employed reasonably satisfactory sampling procedures. Nevertheless, there is still the obvious limitation of school cooperation, some tendency to choose samples for convenience, and the always-present sampling error. Thus "national norms" are not completely comparable to each other, and it is not really possible to compare a pupil's scores on two different tests unless the data were *gathered on the same sample*. Many testing companies do use the same sample for norming both an aptitude and achievement battery, thus allowing intertest comparisons.

One other point should be mentioned. National norms for educational tests are most often gathered in school settings. Since 100 percent of the population is not in school, we do not have a truly national sample. The higher the grade level, the lower the proportion of children that are in school and the more biased the sample. This is not really a handicap in making educational decisions, but it is a point we need to remember if we wish to interpret the data as literally representative of the nation.[2]

Thus, as useful as national norms may be, they certainly do have some limitations. The most serious one is that often they simply do not provide the comparison data or permit us to make the interpretation we need. We would be much better able to counsel students who planned to take auto mechanics at Dunwoody Technical Institute if we knew how their aptitude in auto mechanics compares with that of students presently in Dunwoody.

Special Group Norms   For many decision-making purposes, highly specific norms are the most desirable. Norms such as "first-year education students

[2] Related to this point, we must remember that in any international comparisons of achievement, the samples are drawn from schools, and the United States has a greater proportion of youth attending school than do other countries. In such studies, we are often comparing the top 75–85 percent of our youth to the top 20–30 percent of the youth in some other country.

at state colleges," "high school juniors," or "students who have taken two years of French" may be the comparison we are most interested in. We are likely to want such special norm groups for specific aptitude tests such as mechanical, clerical, and musical, and for specific subject-matter tests such as first-year Spanish, music appreciation, and chemistry. Such special norm groups are also useful for tests designed for the physically or mentally handicapped. Intelligence tests designed for the blind or the deaf obviously need to have special group norms.

One test frequently used by educators involves a special type of norm group that needs some explaining. The College Board Scholastic Aptitude Test (SAT) uses what is called a *fixed reference* group. This fixed reference group comprises the approximately 11,000 people who took the test in 1941. A common set of items (an anchor test) used in a previous test is included in each new SAT test. Then, through a series of equating procedures, the new form can be equated back to the 1941 test.[3] By using this fixed reference group, changes in the candidate population over time can be detected. There is, of course, a danger of misinterpreting the scores. A person who scores 500 on the SAT is scoring at the mean. But it is a very special mean, one calibrated to be equal to that of the 11,000 students who took the test in 1941. It is *not* the mean for all students who took the test more recently.

Local Norms   If some intraschool comparisons or intracity comparisons are desired, many people prefer local norms. Although such comparisons could be made by using national norms, the users might find it more difficult to make the comparison with the data in that form. If test scoring is done by machine—whether by a test company or locally—local norms can be constructed easily. In general, it is worth the slight extra charge to have these local norms prepared. This facilitates test score interpretation to the teacher, the parent, the student, and the community.

School Mean Norms   If we are interested in comparing the mean performance of a school (or total school district) to that of other schools, we must use school or total district mean norms. *It is not appropriate to compute a mean for a school district and interpret it by using the norm tables based on individual pupil performance.* The variability of school means is far less than the variability of individual scores, and the individual norm tables would therefore give an underestimate of relative school performance for above-average schools and an overestimate of relative school performance for below-average schools. Not all test publishers provide school mean norms for those who wish to make such comparisons. If not provided, such comparisons cannot be made (of course, the local district can compute the school

---

[3] The various techniques of equating and calibrating test scores are not dealt with in this book. The interested reader is referred to Angoff (1971).

means for the schools in that district and build local school mean norms for those specific schools).

What Test Manuals Should Report

The users of test information must be very cautious in their interpretation of the norms provided by the test publisher. Questions such as the following must be considered: How representative are the norms? What were the characteristics of the standardization and norming sample? How old are the norms? Are the norms useful for the kinds of comparisons to be made? These questions must be satisfactorily answered before one can correctly and meaningfully use the norm data, but test manuals do not always provide the data necessary to answer them. If the information is not available in a manual, it may be found in a technical supplement. At any rate, the norms should not be accepted on faith.

A manual may state that it has a "national" sample without providing the data necessary for users to judge for themselves the adequacy of the sample (norms). The norm group must necessarily consist of those who are willing to be tested, and the test manual should state the refusal rate. The users must then decide how this information will affect their interpretations. Many older tests were often normed so that the norm data really represented, say, only the Midwest, or only the East Coast, or only the Far West. Generally, the newer tests, particularly those published by the larger reputable companies, have adequate norm data. Highly sophisticated sampling procedures have been worked out so that a representative sample can be obtained if the publishers are willing to go to the effort to achieve such an end.

Using Norms

Normative data aid greatly in the interpretation of test scores, but there are also dangers of misinterpretation or misuse of norms. It would be a misuse, for example, to interpret national norms as special group norms, or vice versa. Perhaps the greatest mistake is to interpret norms as standards. *Norms are not standards.* Norm information tells us how people actually perform, *not how they should perform.* Comparing a person's score with a norm group does not automatically tell us whether the score was above or below the level at which it *should* be. It tells us only how the person performed in comparison with others. A description in relative terms is not an evaluation.

One of the most ridiculous but frustrating criticisms of the schools is the complaint that there are so many students "below norms." For example, half the sixth-graders read "below grade level"! Terrible? Of course not. If *norm* is used as a synonym for *average,* half the students *must* be below the norm. There is no way the schools can do such a good job that less than half the students will be below average.

Also, when evaluating output—such as scores on an achievement test—input must be considered. Input includes such things as previous instruction on the variable being measured, as well as family, community, and school characteristics. We talk more about the relationship between input and output in the section on accountability in Chapter 11. But output should always be interpreted in relation to input. As mentioned in Chapter 1, we would evaluate two fifth-graders' scores quite differently if in the preceding year one had scored at the third-grade level and the other at the fourth-grade, fifth-month level.

One final point: The output on standardized achievement tests should be interpreted in view of the local curricular and instructional objectives. If the local objectives differ from the ones followed by the test maker, any interpretation of the result must be made in light of this fact. More is said about this in Chapter 8.

TYPES OF NORM-REFERENCED SCORES

To know a person's observed score (raw score) on a measuring instrument gives us very little information about his or her performance. As stated in Chapter 2, to know how that person's score compares with the mean score of an identifiable group norm (group) is of more value. If one has an indication of the variability of the distribution of scores in the norm group as well, much more information is obtained. If a person's raw score is changed into a score that *by itself* gives normative or relative information, we can present the information more efficiently, since the mean and standard deviation need not also be reported. Such expressions as *kinds of scales, kinds of norms, types of scores,* and *derived scores* have been used to refer to those various transformations of raw scores into scores that have normative or relative meanings.

Derived scores are useful, then, in comparing a person's score with those of others—that is, in making *interindividual* comparisons. A second use is in making *intraindividual* (within-individual) comparisons. It is not possible, for example, to compare directly the test score, GPA, and IQ measures. It is first necessary to transform all data into comparable units. (Of course, comparability of the norm groups is also necessary.)

The following example illustrates the importance of derived scores in interpreting data. Assume Irwin, an eleventh-grade boy, has received the following *raw scores* on the Differential Aptitude Tests (DAT).

These data, in and of themselves, tell us nothing about how Irwin compares with others of his age, since we have no idea how other children score. But do they even tell us anything about whether Irwin is better in one subtest

	VERBAL REASONING	NUMERICAL ABILITY	ABSTRACT REASONING	CLERICAL S AND A
Raw Score	32	29	32	42

	MECHANICAL REASONING	SPACE RELATIONS	SPELLING	LANGUAGE USAGE
Raw Score	42	36	64	30

area than in another? Do we know if Irwin is better in spelling than in language usage? No, because we do not know the total number of questions on each subtest, nor whether some subtests have easier questions than the others. Some type of derived score is necessary for both inter- and intraindividual interpretations.

Another use of derived scores is to assist in a meaningful combination of data. Sometimes the teacher wishes to combine various pieces of information to make a single decision about an individual. An example would be to combine results of term papers, quizzes, and examinations to arrive at a final grade. The question is: How does the teacher weight the various pieces of data? By converting all scores to derived scores, a weighting scheme can be carried out.

The types of norm-referenced derived scores that are most likely to be used by psychologists and educators can be divided into two basic types: relative position status scores and developmental level scores. The relative position status scores discussed below include percentile ranks, linear z and T scores, normalized z and T scores, normal curve equivalent scores, deviation IQ scores, and stanines.[4] The developmental level scores we will discuss are grade equivalents, mental age scores (and the related ratio ''IQ'' scores), and scaled scores. We will also discuss expectancy scores, which, depending on the metric used, could be either status or developmental level scores.

Relative Position Status Scores

Percentiles and Percentile Ranks   A *percentile* is defined as a point on the distribution below which a certain percentage of the scores fall. A *percentile rank* gives a person's relative position or the percentage of students' scores

---

[4] The literature on transformed scores is not consistent with regard to terminology. In general, normalized z scores are not used as such but are found only as an intermediate step to normalized Ts. Some refer to a normalized T score with just the symbol T and use z to refer to what we have called a ''linear'' T.

falling below that individual's obtained score.[5] For example, let us assume that John has a raw score of 76 on an English test composed of 100 items. If 98 percent of the scores fall below a score of 76, the percentile rank of the score of 76 is 98 and the 98th percentile is a score of 76. Thus 76 is the point below which 98 percent of the scores in the distribution fall. This does not mean that the student who has a percentile rank of 98 answered 98 percent of the items correctly. If this score is equivalent to the 98th percentile rank, it means that 98 percent of the students who took the test received a score below 76.

Percentile ranks have the advantage of being relatively easy to compute and fairly easy to interpret. (Occasionally, people will confuse percentile ranks with percentage correct, but the distinction can be easily explained.) In explaining a national norm percentile rank to a child, the teacher will say, for example, "Your percentile rank of 85 means that you obtained a score higher than 85 out of every 100 students in a representative sample of eighth-graders in the nation who took this test."

As with other derived scores, both intra- and interindividual comparisons can be made from percentiles. For example, referring to a percentile norm table (see Table 5.1) for the DAT values given earlier for Irwin, we find the following percentiles.[6]

	VERBAL REASONING	NUMERICAL ABILITY	ABSTRACT REASONING	CLERICAL S AND A
Raw Score	32	29	32	42
Percentile	65	70	45	40

	MECHANICAL REASONING	SPACE RELATIONS	SPELLING	LANGUAGE USAGE
Raw Score	42	36	64	30
Percentile	20	55	55	65

We can now see how Irwin's scores in each subtest compare with those of other eleventh-graders (interindividual comparison) as well as how his scores in the different subtests compare with each other (intraindividual comparison). As can be noted, the *order* of Irwin's raw scores was meaningless information.

Percentile ranks have a limitation in that the size of the percentile units is

---

[5] Statisticians differ somewhat in the precise definitions of these terms, but these differences are minor and need not concern us. Some use the terms *percentile* and *percentile rank* interchangeably.

[6] Some would call these *percentile ranks*. The DAT manual refers to them as *percentiles*.

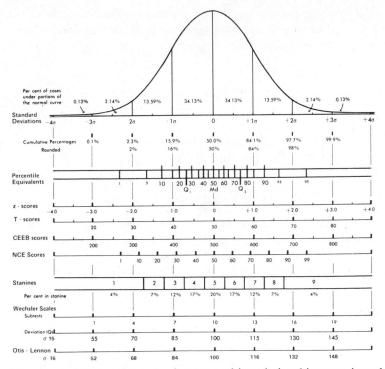

Figure 5.1 Chart showing the normal curve and its relationship to various derived scores. (Reproduced from *Test Service Notebook* No. 148 of the Psychological Corporation.)

not constant in terms of raw-score units.[7] For example, if the distribution is normal, the raw-score difference between the 90th and 99th percentiles is much greater than the raw-score difference between the 50th and 59th percentiles (see Figure 5.1). Thus a percentile difference does not really represent the same amount of raw-score difference in the middle of the distribution as it does at the extremes. Any interpretation of percentile ranks must take this fact into account. We can be more confident that differences in percentile ranks represent true differences at the extremes than at the middle of a normal distribution. This problem can be alleviated somewhat by presenting the information on a graph, called a *normal percentile chart,* that "accounts for" the unequal units. Some publishers do use this type of visual reporting scheme (see Figure 5.3, p. 000). Of course, the ordinal nature of the percentile rank units means that one cannot treat them further statistically. But this is not a relevant limitation with respect to interpreting the scores to others. In general, the percentile rank is one of the best types of

---

[7] Except in the unusual case where the raw-score distribution is rectangular.

relative position status scores to use in interpreting test scores to others. A type of derived score that does not have the limitation of unequal units is the linear *standard score,* discussed below.

Linear *z* and *T* Scores   *Linear scores* (frequently called *standard scores*) are transformed scores for which the resulting set of values has a distribution shape identical to the original raw-score distribution. In other words, if the original raw scores are plotted on one axis and the transformed scores on another, a straight line will connect the plotted points. The linear *z* score is the basic standard score. The formula for a linear *z* score is

$$z = \frac{\text{raw score} - \text{mean}}{\text{standard deviation}} = \frac{X - \bar{X}}{S_x} \tag{5.1}$$

As can be seen from the formula, a person whose raw score is equal to the mean will have a *z* score of zero. If a person has a raw score that is one standard deviation above the mean, the *z* score will be $+1.0$. Thus, *z* scores are standard scores with a mean of zero and a standard deviation of 1.

Linear *T* scores are derived scores with a mean of 50 (the *T* score if $z = 0$) and a standard deviation of 10. The formula for a linear *T* score is

$$T = 10z + 50 = 10 \left(\frac{X - \bar{X}}{S_x} \right) + 50 \tag{5.2}$$

Theoretically the *T* score has no advantage over the *z* score, or vice versa. One is simply a linear transformation of the other. Practitioners often prefer *T* scores, because then negative numbers and decimals can generally be avoided.

Table 5.2 shows the computation of the linear *z* and *T* scores for an individual with a raw score of 85 on a test that has a mean of 100 and a standard deviation of 15.

When scores are *normally* distributed, there is a precise mathematical relationship between *z* and *T* scores and other derived scores. Recall that in a normal distribution, approximately 68 percent of the scores fall between $\pm 1 S_x$, 95 percent between $\pm 2 S_x$, and 99.7 percent between $\pm 3 S_x$. Since a *z* score has a standard deviation of 1, approximately 68 percent of the *z* scores

TABLE 5.2
COMPUTATION OF LINEAR *z* AND *T* SCORES

$$X = 85 \qquad \bar{X} = 100 \qquad S_x = 15$$

$$z = \frac{X - \bar{X}}{S_x} = \frac{85 - 100}{15} = \frac{-15}{15} = -1$$

$$T = 10z + 50 = 10(-1) + 50 = -10 + 50 = 40$$

will be between ±1, 95 percent between ±2, and 99.7 percent between ±3 in a normal distribution. As Figure 5.1 illustrates, a person who scores one standard deviation above the mean has a z score of 1 ($T = 60$) and is at about the 84th percentile.

Most norm groups for standardized tests are quite large, and the distribution of their scores often approaches normality. Thus, linear z and T scores for most standardized tests can be interpreted as if they relate to percentiles, as shown in Figure 5.1. Classrooms of 50 pupils, however, *do not* typically present normal distributions, and the relationship depicted in Figure 5.1 would not be accurate.

Normalized z and T Scores   When raw scores are *normalized*, the shape of the distribution of the transformed (normalized) scores is normal, regardless of the shape of the original distribution.[8] Test publishers often provide normalized scores, and the wise test user should be able to discern the difference between these and linear-transformed scores. If normalized z and T values are given, the relationship between these values and percentiles as shown in Figure 5.1 is accurate, regardless of the shape of the raw-score distribution. Thus, knowing that a person had a normalized z of 1, we would know that he or she was at about the 84th percentile. This interpretation could not be made with a linear z of 1 unless the original raw-score distribution was normal. (It should be emphasized that the relationships shown in Figure 5.1 hold for a normal distribution of raw scores, not for all raw-score distributions.)

Normal Curve Equivalents (NCEs)   *Normal curve equivalents (NCEs)* are normalized standard scores with a mean of 50 and a standard deviation of 21.06. Only integers from 1 to 99 are assigned. Normal curve equivalents are like normalized T scores in that they have a mean of 50. However, NCEs are constructed to have a standard deviation of 21.06 instead of 10. This value was selected so that percentiles of 1 and 99 are equivalent to NCEs of 1 and 99. NCEs are related to stanines in that there are approximately 11 NCEs to each stanine. The formula for NCEs is

$$NCE = 21.06 \text{ (normalized } z) + 50 \qquad (5.3)$$

NCEs have been used in ESEA Title I Evaluation reports. It is too soon to know how popular they will be in other settings. They may be confused with percentiles if they are communicated to nonmeasurement-trained persons.

---

[8] It is not an objective of ours that readers of this text be able to normalize raw scores. However, for those who wish to do so, proceed as follows: Rank the raw scores, convert them to percentiles (percentile ranks), and look up the corresponding z score in a conversion table (found in almost any basic statistics or test theory text). A normalized z can be converted to a normalized T by using Equation 5.2.

Deviation IQs   The intelligence quotient (IQ) is one of the most misunderstood concepts in measurement. Much of this confusion exists because of a misunderstanding of intelligence tests. (In Chapter 7 we consider what an aptitude or intelligence test supposedly measures, and how the scores can be interpreted usefully.) Part of the confusion, however, exists because people do not understand the type of score typically used to report the results of intelligence tests—that is, the IQ. Originally, the IQ was actually a quotient (a ratio). It was found by dividing a person's mental age by his or her chronological age and then multiplying by 100 ($IQ = MA/CA \times 100$). (See the section "Mental Age Scores" below.)

The ratio IQ has many inadequacies. Because of these, most test constructors now report *deviation IQs*. Deviation IQs are computed separately for each age group within the norm sample. These are not literal intelligence quotients. They are transformations much like the z or T values (usually normalized) discussed earlier. Typically, these deviation IQs have a mean of 100 and a standard deviation of 15 or 16, although some tests have standard deviations as low as 12; others, as high as 20. The fact that standard deviations vary from test to test is just one of the reasons why we cannot compare two individuals' IQ scores unless they have taken the same test. A score of 128 on a test with a mean of 100 and a standard deviation of 12 has a higher z score than a score of 130 on a test with a mean of 100 and a standard deviation of 16.

Stanines   *Stanines* are derived scores with a mean of 5 and a standard deviation of 2. Only the integers 1 to 9 occur. In a normal distribution, stanines are related to other scores, as shown in Figure 5.1. As can be seen, the percentages of scores at each stanine are 4, 7, 12, 17, 20, 17, 12, 7, and 4, respectively. Whether or not the original distribution is normal, stanine scores are typically assigned so that the resultant stanine distribution is the 4, 7, 12, 17, 20 . . . 4. Thus, a plot (histogram) of the stanines would approach a normal distribution, and we can think of stanines as normalized scores. (Some authors round the percentages slightly differently and present the percentages as 4, 8, 12, 16, 20 . . . . 4. This is slightly less accurate but easier to remember, since one can use the "rule of four." That is, one starts with 4 percent for stanine 1 and adds 4 percent for each subsequent stanine up to stanine 5 [20 percent] and then subtracts 4 percent for each subsequent stanine.)

Stanines have no particular technical advantage over other types of derived scores. They are less precise than others because so many different raw-score values may be grouped into the same stanine score. For example, individuals at the 41st and 59th percentile rank would receive the same stanine. A supposed advantage of stanines is that if two scores are *not* interpreted as being reliably different unless there is at least one stanine score between them, there is less of a tendency to incorrectly infer a difference between two scores when no true difference exists. We believe it preferable to use confidence bands rather than stanines in this fashion. Stanines do represent the finest discrimination that can be made on one column of an IBM card, but this is a minor point. The major reason we present them is that they are frequently used in reporting the results on standardized tests, and a competent professional should be able to interpret such scores.

Summary of Relative Position Status Scores   While all the scores we discussed in this section have properties that make them the preferred score in certain situations, experts generally agree that, in interpreting the meaning of a score to a layperson, the *percentile rank* is the best score to use. If data from a test that reports one of the other types of scores are being presented, the professional should convert the score to a percentile rank and relay it to the individual. Most publishers will report percentile ranks, so the professional can obtain them easily from the test manual.

Developmental Level Scores

For *developmental level scores* a normative comparison of an individual's score is made against the average scores obtained by individuals at different points (for instance, age or grade) in their developmental progress. Such scores, which are sometimes used for those characteristics that develop systematically across age or years of schooling, are quite different from the relative position status scores discussed earlier. Developmental scores should *not* be used if one is interested in comparing a pupil's performance with that of others in a particular reference group such as a specific grade. Developmental scores *must* be used if the purpose is to compare a pupil's performance with a series of reference groups that differ developmentally in the characteristic being measured.

As indicated earlier, the major types of developmental scores are (1) grade equivalents, (2) mental age scores, and (3) scaled scores.

Grade Equivalents   *Grade equivalents (GEs)* can be explained best by an example. If a student obtains a score on a test that is equal to the median score for all the beginning sixth-graders (September testing) in the norm group, then that student is given a grade equivalent of 6.0. A student who obtains a score equal to the median score of all beginning fifth-graders is given a grade equivalent of 5.0. If a student should score between these two points, linear interpolation would be used to determine the grade equivalent. Because most school years run for ten months, successive months are expressed as decimals. Thus, 5.1 would refer to the average performance of fifth-graders in October, 5.2 in November, and so on to 5.9 in June.

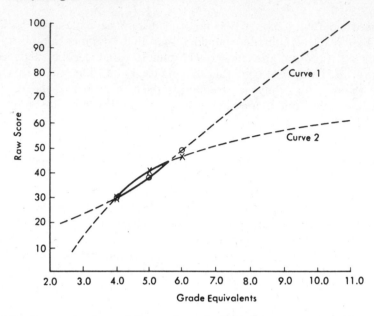

Figure 5.2   Curves for determining grade equivalents from raw scores. (O = population median raw scores for grades 4–6; X = sample raw scores for grades 4–6)

Grade equivalents suffer from at least four major limitations. One of these limitations is the problem of extrapolation. When a test is standardized, normally one does not use students of all grade levels in the normative sample. Suppose a particular test is designed to be used in grades 4, 5, and 6. Ordinarily the norming would be done on only these three grades.[9] Now, if the median sixth-grader receives a grade equivalent of 6.0, half the sixth-graders must have a grade equivalent higher than this. How much higher: 7.0, 7.8, 9.0, 12.0? We do not know. Since the test was not given to students beyond the sixth grade, there is no way of knowing how well they would have done. However, we can estimate—and that is just what is done. A curve can be constructed to show the relationship between raw scores and grade equivalents, as in Figure 5.2. The actual data (that is, the median raw scores for each grade) are available only for grades 4, 5, and 6. However, the curve can be extrapolated so that one can guess at what the median raw scores would be for other grade levels. The extrapolation procedure is based on the assumption that there would be no points of inflection (that is, no change in the direction) in the curve if real data were available. This is a very unrealistic assumption.

[9] Some publishers would norm on a wider range—perhaps grades 3 through 8. The problem of extrapolation would still exist, but to a lesser degree.

Another problem in extrapolation relates to sampling error. Study the two curves in Figure 5.2. Let us assume that curve 1 is accurate for grades 4 through 6. That is, given the whole population of students in these grades, the median raw scores would fall as indicated by the circles on curve 1. However, because of sampling error (that is, not having a group with the same median as the population) within grades 5 and 6, we may obtain the medians shown by the Xs on curve 2. The differences between the medians of the two curves are well within the range of sampling error we might expect. Now, when these two curves are extrapolated, we get completely different estimated grade equivalents. For example, a raw score of 60 is given a grade equivalent of 7.0, using curve 1 (the one we assumed accurate), whereas it would get a grade equivalent of about 10.3 if curve 2 is used. Thus small sampling errors can make extrapolated grade equivalents very misleading.

A second limitation of grade equivalents is that they give us little information about the percentile standing of a person within a class. A fifth-grade student may, for example, because of the differences in the grade equivalent distributions for various subject matter, have a grade equivalent of 6.2 in English and 5.8 in mathematics and yet have a higher fifth-grade percentile rank in mathematics.

The third limitation of grade equivalents is that (contrary to what the numbers indicate) a fourth-grader with a grade equivalent of 7.0 does *not* necessarily know the same amount *or* the same kinds of things as a ninth-grader with a grade equivalent of 7.0. For example, a bright fourth-grader who can do very well on an arithmetic test requiring speed and accuracy may perform as well as the average seventh-grader. A weak ninth-grader may be poor in speed and accuracy and may perform at the seventh-grade level on a test demanding those skills. Yet those two students, receiving equal scores on an arithmetic test, do not know the same things about mathematics in a more general sense.

A fourth limitation of grade equivalents is that they are a type of norm-referenced measure particularly prone to misinterpretation by the critics of education. As we have mentioned, norms are not standards, and even the most vocal critics of education do not suggest that everyone *should be* above the 50th percentile. Yet people talk continually as if all sixth-graders should be reading at or above the sixth-grade equivalent!

Finally, grade equivalents have no interpretive value beyond the eighth or ninth grade. They are appropriate only for those subjects that are common to a particular grade level.

Of the characteristics of GEs discussed above that make them subject to misinterpretation, the one that has received the most attention is the fact that a GE of, say, 9.0 obtained by a sixth-grader does not tell us that the student can perform at a level equal to the average ninth-grader on ninth-grade content. But because the scale so "obviously" seems to say that, GEs are frequently misconstrued. A scale somewhat similar to the GE—a Grade Development Scale (GDS)—has been developed by Cole (1982) for *The 3R's Test*. It has been developed using a different empirical procedure from what publishers typically use. Cole suggests that the interpretation that a fourth-grader with a GDS of 9.0 has the same kinds of mathematical skills as the average ninth-grader is more apt to be a correct one for the GDS than for the typical GE. It should be noted, however, that the GDS has all the other limitations of GE scores. It will likely have shrinking units, it is not very appropriate beyond ninth grade, it will not be comparable across school subjects, and it may well be misinterpreted as a standard.

Grade equivalents remain popular in spite of their inadequacies. They do provide the frequently desired developmental data, and educators are under the impression that such scores are easily and correctly understood by both children and parents—an unfortunate assumption. It is probably not too dogmatic to suggest that grade equivalents, although useful if used in conjunction with other kinds of scores such as percentile ranks, should never be used alone in reporting scores to students or parents. And, as noted, they are not at all useful at the high school level where different students study different subjects.

Mental Age Scores   To obtain mental age scores, publishers give the test to representative samples of individuals at different ages and plot the results. The mean (or median) raw score for individuals in a given age group is then assigned that mental age. For example, if on a test, the average score for 4 1/2-year-olds is 26, then the score of 26 is assigned a mental age of 4 years, 6 months. The same process is used for other specific age groups. Interpolation and extrapolation are used to determine the mental age equivalents for all the other raw scores.

Mathematical and conceptual problems with using mental age scores are the same as for grade equivalent scores. First of all, difficulties may occur in the interpolation and extrapolation of the data points. Second, the size of the mental age unit does not remain constant with age. Rather, it tends to shrink with advancing years. Thus, the distance between the mental ages of 3 and 4 represents a larger developmental difference than between the ages of 12 and 13. Also, there is some disagreement as to when one's mental age quits growing. Some psychologists may use 16 as a maximum mental age, whereas others may prefer 18. Because of the drawbacks in mental age scores and their interpretations, they should be used with great caution.

Nevertheless, there are circumstances when a careful explanation of a person's mental age may be useful. For example, to enable a parent to understand the degree of retardation of a 10-year-old child, it may be helpful to use a developmental level scale. That is, it may be better to tell a parent that the child functions mentally like an average 7-year-old than to say that the child performs better than 3 percent of a sample of 10-year-olds. Or it may be preferable to communicate to a parent of a gifted 4-year-old that the child functions mentally like an average 8-year-old than to say that the child functions mentally better than 99.9 percent of a representative sample of 4-year-olds. Both of these examples assume, of course, that the psychometric methods of obtaining the mental ages were good enough to make the scaled mental ages of 7 and 8 reasonably accurate. In deciding whether to use mental age scores, one must consider both the drawbacks and the alternatives.

A type of score that has been derived from the mental age is the IQ, or intelligence quotient. As mentioned in a previous section, the IQ was originally a quotient that was found by dividing mental age by chronological age and then multiplying by 100. One of the weaknesses of the quotient approach was that the standard deviations of the IQs were not constant for different ages, so that an IQ score of, say, 112 would be equal to different percentiles at different ages. A second problem was that opinions varied about what the maximum value of the denominator should be. As mentioned, *when* a person's mental age quits growing is controversial. Thus, ratio IQ scores are seldom reported at the current time. The deviation IQ scores discussed earlier are much more popular.

Scaled Scores   Scaled scores could be considered either developmental scores or criterion-referenced scores, depending both upon how they are constructed and how they are used. The scaled scores that most publishers report are most commonly used for developmental comparison purposes. Constructors of these scores frequently claim that they have ''equal units'' and are free of many of the problems associated with GE scores. While there is considerable debate about the psychometric properties of these scales (see Hoover, 1984), it is probably true that because the scales are based on some arbitrary numbering system, the scores are less likely than GE scores to be misunderstood as *standards*. However, the arbitrary numbering system makes it likely that they will not be understood at all.

The scaled scores, like GE scores, are particularly useful when one wishes to equate the raw scores from various *levels* of the same subtest. They would be useful, for example, if we wished to equate the score of Sarah, who took an out-of-level test, to the score we think she would have achieved had she taken the appropriate level test. This equating across levels and the resultant common scale are potentially useful for researchers who wish the scores to have certain mathematical properties.

As mentioned, the supposed advantage of the scaled scores over GE scores is that they have equal units. This claim is made because of the mathematical techniques used for constructing the scales. These techniques require certain assumptions to be made, however, and there is considerable debate about the reasonableness of these assumptions (see Hoover, 1984, and Burket, 1984). The techniques most frequently used are one of the scaling models developed by Thurstone or Thorndike, or, more recently, an item-response theory model (see the next section). For example, the Stanford Achievement Test uses the one-parameter (Rasch) item-response theory model. The Comprehensive Test of Basic Skills uses the three-parameter item-response theory model. You would need to study the technical manual of the test you are using to understand just how the publisher calculated the scaled scores and what they mean. Unless you are doing research, you probably will not be using these scores. Grade equivalents are preferable for most *developmental level* test interpretations.

Item-Response Theory.   While the basics of item-response theory (sometimes called Latent Trait Theory or item characteristic curve theory) have been around for a long time, there has recently been a sharp increase in the advancement and use of the theory. One basic advantage of the theory is that if the mathematical model being used holds, the difficulty value of the scaled items does not depend on the particular sample of pupils in the standardization group and the ability estimates of the pupils are independent of the sample of items they were administered. The scaled scores of both items and people are considered to be "sample-free." Thus, once the items are scaled, one can compare the scores of people on some characteristic even though all the people did not take the same items.

There are different mathematical models used to do the estimation. The two most common ones are the one-parameter (Rasch) model and the three-parameter model mentioned before. The mathematics will not be dealt with here. However, you should note that when items are scaled with the one-parameter model, the pupils' scaled scores will be in exactly the same rank order as the raw scores. However, in the three-parameter model the particular questions answered will influence the scaled score, and two individuals could get the same number of questions correct yet obtain different scaled scores. While this may seem disconcerting, you might note that more traditional scoring has, on occasion, been criticized just because two individuals who each got 15 items correct—but *different* items—received the same score!

Arguments about using the one-parameter (Rasch) model versus the three-parameter model can get quite heated. They need not concern you. The three-parameter model is more mathematically sophisticated but requires more computer time and a larger sample size than the one-parameter model. As mentioned, the Comprehensive Test of Basic Skills uses the three-parameter model, and so pupils can get the same number of items right yet obtain different scores.

Summary of Developmental Level Scores   Mental ages, grade equivalents, and scaled scores all suffer from some major weaknesses in their psychometric properties and ease of misinterpretation. Nevertheless, there are times when it is necessary to communicate a developmental level to others. If a developmental level score is chosen, one must explain the score very carefully, including a discussion of common misinterpretations. In general, you will probably choose a developmental level score over a relative position status score fairly infrequently.

TYPES OF CRITERION-REFERENCED SCORES

The preceding discussion has focused on norm-referenced score interpretation—that is, how an examinee's score compares with the scores of other people in an identified norm group. There are instances, though, in which a criterion-referenced interpretation may be preferred. It should be emphasized that the method of referencing is *not* an either/or dichotomy. Often it may be desirable to make *both* a norm- and a criterion-referenced interpretation of the score. As mentioned earlier, in criterion-referenced interpretation the score focuses on what the individual can (does) do rather than on the relative position of the person with respect to others. For this reason many measurement specialists, including us, would prefer to use the term *domain-referenced* or *content-referenced,* but unfortunately *criterion-referenced* appears to be the most popular term.

In what situations or with which tests one should use norm-referenced interpretation and/or criterion-referenced interpretation is a subject of considerable debate. We discussed it briefly in Chapter 1, but cannot delve into that dispute in any detail. However, most educators and psychologists would agree that norm referencing is used primarily to communicate levels of performance on aptitude tests and most personality and interest inventories. It is the relative degree of these constructs that is of interest. Furthermore, the behavioral domains of such constructs as intelligence, compulsivity, and hypochondriasis, are simply not defined with enough precision to use criterion-referenced interpretations. For achievement tests one might wish to use either a norm- or a criterion-referenced interpretation of the scores, depending on the particular decision one is trying to make.

In criterion referencing, the definition of the domain is very important. Without a clearly defined domain of material to be tested, criterion (or domain) referencing of the score is not possible. As pointed out in Chapter 1, the domain (or content) is likely to be most clearly defined on achievement tests of basic skills at the elementary grade levels. Once the domain is defined, it is necessary to establish some procedure that will meaningfully report the level at which the individual has achieved on the domain. The most commonly used methods are (1) percent correct and (2) "mastery" or "nonmastery" scores.

Percent Correct Scores

The easiest scale to compute and understand is the percent of items that an individual got correct. If items are not all worth the same number of points, the scale can be modified to allow for a calculation of the ratio of total points earned to maximum points possible. If one has devised a test that is truly domain-referenced, it would be theoretically possible to infer from the percent that an individual got correct on a test to the percent of the total domain that the individual knows. Of course, most domains cannot be defined with such precision that the test literally represents a random sample of items from that domain. But the more thoroughly the domain is defined and the better the sampling is from that domain, the closer we can come to making that type of inference. (That is, if the test has good content validity, a domain-referenced interpretation makes some sense.)

However, even with a good domain definition and sampling of items from that domain, it is possible that the items in the test are more or less difficult than the average of the items in the domain. Ordinarily we cannot check this out because the total domain of items does not actually exist; it exists only as a hypothetical construct. Further, most constructors of criterion-referenced tests use some sort of item analysis procedure in selecting items for their tests, thus guaranteeing that the selected items indeed do not represent the domain of possible items.

Although percent correct scores are still used with some frequency, they have all the problems that caused measurement experts to advocate abandoning them years ago.

Mastery/Nonmastery Scores

One of the most common uses of criterion-referenced test scores in education is to measure mastery learning. In mastery learning, the basic notion is that students do not advance to new material until they have mastered the prerequisite material. The problem of defining what is meant by mastery on a test can be handled by setting a cut score in some fashion. Nitko (1983) correctly points out that any test can have a cut score. That does not necessarily mean one can make a criterion-, domain-, or content-referenced inference from the score. but if a test adequately represents a domain, and if a cut score can be set on some defensible basis, then one can say that those above the cut score have "mastered" the material, and those below the cut score have not "mastered" the material.

This whole approach dismays many measurement experts, for two important reasons. First, mastery is not really an either/or dichotomy. In most situations there are clearly degrees of mastery. Second, the methods used to set cut scores are arbitrary. There are two counterarguments to these concerns. (1) Although mastery is a continuous, not dichotomous, construct, we are often forced to make dichotomous decisions. For example, we do need to decide what a passing score is on a driver's license examination. We do need to decide whether an individual has enough knowledge of a current unit of material to begin studying the next higher unit. We do need to decide who knows enough to graduate from high school. Even if everyone graduates, there has still been a categorical decision as long as the philosophical or practical possibility of failure exists. If one can conceptualize performance so poor that the performer should not graduate, then theoretically a cutoff score exists. (2) Although setting a cutting score may be arbitrary, it need not be capricious. Setting cut scores on tests is usually less capricious a choice than many other categorical decisions that are made in life.

In a basic text on standardized tests, we cannot explicate in any great detail all the methods that have been proposed to set cut scores. Summaries of these procedures can be found in Livingston & Zieky (1982), Mehrens (1981), or Shepard (1980). These techniques can be categorized in a variety of ways. One fairly common approach to categorization is as follows:

1. *Standards based on absolute judgments of test content.* Qualified judges inspect the test content and decide what percentage of correct answers indicates mastery. Several specific methods use this general approach. However, the techniques used can lead to quite different results.
2. *Standards based on judgments about groups.* The standard is set by looking at the performance of individuals in an identified group or groups. If one can identify two contrasting groups—one composed of masters and one composed of nonmasters—they can be given the test, and the cut score can be set based on the intersection point of the two distributions. If one can identify a group of "borderline" masters, they can be given the test and the standard set at the median, thus passing 50 percent of the borderline group. (Of course, one could choose to pass some other percentage of minimally competent individuals.)
3. *Standards based on norms.* The cut score is based on the percentage of students who would be considered nonmasters. To some, setting a cutoff score by a normative approach seems to be contradictory to the purpose of criterion-referenced testing. However, as Shepard (1980) points out, "qualitative judgments about the excellence or adequacy of performance depend implicitly on how others did on the test" (p. 456).

Currently, most standard-setting approaches use some combination of procedures from categories 1 and 3. If you are using tests for which a cut score has been established by the publisher, you will want to look closely at the methods the publisher used in arriving at the cut score. It may not be the most appropriate cut score for your specific situation. If you become involved in setting a cut score on a test, we urge you to check the references above prior to attempting such a process.

Summary of Criterion-Referenced Scores

Recall from your study of validity (Chapter 4) that to make inferences from a score to a domain (content validity inferences), the domain should be well defined and the test should be an adequate sample from that domain. If that is true, one can employ both normative and criterion referencing. They are not mutually exclusive or contradictory to each other. Recently there has been an increase in the use of criterion referencing. This is due primarily to the increased use of mastery or minimum competency tests. The interpretation of either percent correct or mastery/nonmastery scores seems straightforward. However, remember that both types of scores have limitations. Percent correct scores obviously depend on the difficulty of the items in the test. Mastery scores obviously depend on the method employed to determine what the cutoff score should be.

Expectancy Scores

In Chapter 1 we discussed the difference between measurement and evaluation. A test score (for instance, Lucile's percentile rank is 75) represents measurement. When an interpretation or a judgment is made about the score (for example, that is good), that is evaluation.

The tester could, and often should, make different evaluations of the same test score made by different students. To interpret a test score, the tester should have information about other relevant variables. For an achievement test, one such relevant variability is scholastic aptitude. Many test publishers norm their scholastic aptitude and achievement tests on the same sample. They can then provide a derived set of scores that indicate the *expected* score on an achievement test based on a scholastic aptitude score. (Some publishers base the expectancy score on other variables as well, such as race and sex. The mathematical techniques of the equating also differ with publishers. We do not discuss these differences here.)

These expectancy scores help answer the question of whether a child's achievement is as high as could be reasonably expected. Discrepancy scores may be provided showing the difference between an individual's actual achievement and expected achievement.

Discrepancy scores can be useful in dealing with an individual child. Such scores for groups of children can help in making curricular or instructional decisions about a class, building, or school district. However, such scores need to be interpreted with caution. In the first place, there is considerable debate about whether aptitude tests are really much different from achievement tests. (We discuss this further in Chapters 7 and 8.) They most assuredly are *not* pure measures of *innate* ability. They are, in part, measures of developed ability, and some of the same environmental factors that influence the scores on achievement tests also influence scores on aptitude tests. Thus we should *not* form *fatalistic* expectations and conclude that children with low scholastic aptitude scores are innately stupid, and should not therefore give up trying to teach them. (Actually, expectancy scores may keep us from doing this, because many students indeed *do* achieve higher scores than expected, thus showing it is possible.) Nevertheless, since schools do *not* have control over many of the factors that affect both scholastic aptitude and achievement scores, educators should not unduly chastise themselves for low achievement test scores if the expectancy scores are low; nor should they feel particularly virtuous about high achievement scores if the expectancy scores are high. The discrepancy between expected achievement and actual achievement is a better measure of school impact (or absence of impact) than achievement data alone.

A second caution regarding discrepancy scores is that, since achievement scores and expectancy scores are highly correlated, the difference scores are extremely unreliable. This is particularly important to remember when interpreting an individual pupil's discrepancy score. The difference has to be quite large before we should interpret it as being due to more than chance variation. Publishers usually only encourage you to interpret these scores as significantly different from achievement scores if the differences are larger than one standard error of measurement.

PROFILES

When we wish to present two or more scores for the same person (or groups of people), we do so by means of a *profile*. Of course any such comparison is meaningless unless the raw scores have all been converted to the same type of derived score based on the same norm group. When a test is composed of several subtests (such as multifactor aptitude tests, achievement batteries, or many personality and interest inventories), these subtests will have been normed on the same sample, and meaningful profiles can be constructed. Some test companies norm different tests on the same sample, and derived scores from these tests can also be meaningfully compared.

In addition to a common norm group and type of derived score, some index of error should be portrayed on the profile. This has been done in different ways (and sometimes not done at all), as we shall see in the following examples.

Profile sheets should also contain complete information about the test, such as the title, form, and level; the name of the person tested; the date of the test; and the raw scores from which the scaled scores were derived.

Figure 5.3 shows a profile on the Differential Aptitude Tests. The scale used is a percentile scale, but it is plotted on a *normal percentile chart*. These are profiles for which the scores reported are in percentiles, but the dimensions are such that equal linear distances on this chart represent equal

DIFFERENTIAL APTITUDE TESTS

G. K. Bennett, H. G. Seashore, and A. G. Wesman

School NORTH PORT HS

System NORTH PORT PUBLIC   Counselor HERMAN DAVIS

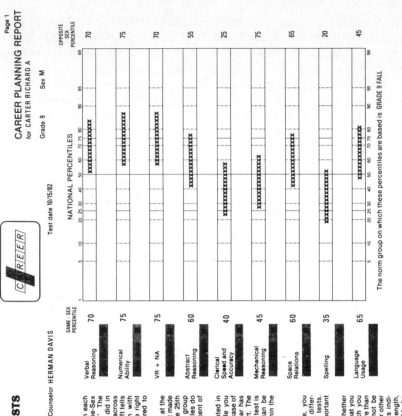

Test	SAME-SEX PERCENTILE	OPPOSITE SEX PERCENTILE
Verbal Reasoning	70	70
Numerical Ability	75	75
VR + NA	75	70
Abstract Reasoning	60	55
Clerical Speed and Accuracy	40	25
Mechanical Reasoning	45	75
Space Relations	60	65
Spelling	35	20
Language Usage	65	45

NATIONAL PERCENTILES

The norm group on which these percentiles are based is GRADE 9 FALL

Form V

Process Number 001-0012-001

YOUR PROFILE OF DAT SCORES

The numbers that tell you how you did on each test are in the columns marked "Same-Sex Percentile" and "Opposite-Sex Percentile." The higher the number for any test, the better you did in that area as compared to students in your grade across the country. The column of percentiles on the left tells where you rank on each test in comparison with students of your own sex. The column on the right shows how you rank on each test as compared to students of the opposite sex.

If your percentile on one test is 80, you are at the top of 80 percent of the group—only 20 percent made higher scores than yours. If you scored in the 25th percentile, this means about 75 percent of the group did better than you on the test. These percentiles do NOT tell you how many questions (or what percent of them) you answered correctly.

On your profile, a bar of X's has been printed in the row for each test you took. The percentile you earned is at the middle of the bar, except in the case of extremely high or low percentiles, where the bar has been shortened so as not to run off the chart. The reason for the bar instead of a single X is that a test is not a perfect measure of your ability. You can be reasonably sure that you stand somewhere within the area covered by the bar.

HOW BIG A DIFFERENCE IS IMPORTANT?

Since tests cannot be perfectly accurate, you should not place too much importance on small differences between the percentiles for any pair of tests. The bars of X's help show the more important differences.

Look at the bars for any two tests to see whether their ends overlap. If they do not, chances are that you really are better in the kind of ability in which you scored higher. If the bars overlap, but not by more than half their length, the difference may or may not be important. To help you decide, consider with other things you know about yourself agree with this indication. If they overlap by more than half their length, the difference between the scores can probably be ignored; your ability is really about the same in both areas. You can use this method of looking at the overlap of the bars to compare any two abilities, whether they are listed next to each other or not.

Continued on back.

130

The report printed below is based on your answers to the *Career Planning Questionnaire* and on your aptitudes as measured by the *Differential Aptitude Tests*. Remember that this report tells you how things look at the present time, and that your interests and goals may change. To help you in understanding the report, descriptions of the tests are printed on the reverse side of this form, followed by the groups of school subjects and activities, and the groups of jobs and occupations.

In your Career Planning Questionnaire you indicated that you are 14 years old, a male in the 9th grade, and that you expect to graduate from a four-year college. Furthermore, you said that your grades put you in the second quarter of your class. Among the groups of school subjects and activities, you said you liked the following: Technical Subjects, Mathematics, and Biology.

You indicated that your first choice of career goals was in the group called: Business—Administration. Most people who do this kind of work have had the amount of education you plan to get. Also, they have aptitudes like yours. However, the school interests you reported are different from those of most workers in this area. While this occupational choice seems reasonable in terms of your educational plans and tested abilities, you may want to consider some field of work closer to your stated interests.

You indicated that your second choice of career goals was in the group called: Engineering and Applied Science. People who do well in this field work usually like the school subjects and activities you like. Also, the kind of education they have matches your plans for school. However, their scores on the aptitude tests are related to this field are often higher than yours. In view of this, you may wish to reconsider this occupational choice and look into other fields of work that would be more suited to your particular abilities.

You indicated that your third choice of career goals was in the group called: Business—Analytic. This field of work is related to the school subjects and activities that you like. It also matches your educational plans and your pattern of aptitude test scores. It appears that this field is a good career choice in terms of your interests, abilities, and educational plans.

Other occupational areas that match your pattern of abilities and school subject preferences:

Business—Sales and Promotion
Visual and Performing Arts
Medically Related

Copyright 1982, 1973, 1972 by The Psychological Corporation.   All rights reserved.

Any lack of agreement of your present occupational goals with the kinds of school subjects and activities you like, or with your tested aptitudes, suggests that you might reconsider your career plans. The *Occupational Outlook Handbook* (published by the U.S. Department of Labor, and available in most public and school libraries), your school counselor, your parents, and other interested and informed adults may be useful sources of information and helpful to you in making decisions about what to try out and what to aim for.

DATA SERVICES DIVISION
THE PSYCHOLOGICAL CORPORATION
HARCOURT BRACE JOVANOVICH, PUBLISHERS

Figure 5.3 Individual Career Planning Report from the Differential Aptitude Tests. (Copyright © 1982, 1972 by The Psychological Corporation. All rights reserved.)

differences between scores. (Note: Both same-sex and opposite-sex percentiles are reported.) The distances between the percentiles correspond to those portrayed in Figure 5.1. The significance of differences is discussed in the text accompanying the profile in Figure 5.3. Although this discussion is for the student and is in nontechnical language, it is related to the discussion of the reliability and standard error of difference scores discussed in Chapter 3.

Figure 5.4 shows a profile for the Iowa Test of Basic Skills (ITBS). This profile permits the charting of growth on the ITBS for an individual across 10 different administrations of the test. The scaled scores are really grade equivalents, so a value of 65, for example, means the fifth month of the sixth grade—usually expressed as 6.5. Although this type of profile has the obvious advantage of showing growth, it also has several disadvantages:

1. The scaled scores are spaced close together so that the profile is flattened in appearance.
2. Grade equivalents are used; although these are useful for considering growth across time within a subtest, they can be misleading if one wishes to compare a student's subtest scores at one point in time. (See the discussion under "Grade Equivalents.")
3. No provision has been made on the profile for displaying error of measurement.
4. There is no place to record the raw scores.

Increasingly, publishers of standardized tests will provide computer printed narrative test result reports to accompany the derived scores and profiles. For example, publishers of the Iowa Test of Basic Skills have prepared such reports for pupils, parents, and teachers. The reports offer information in a form easily understood by pupils and parents and are a useful supplement.

Profile Analysis

In addition to using profiles for making intraindividual comparisons, the tester may wish to compare the total profiles of two or more persons or to compare a single individual's profile against various criterion groups. The topic of such profile analyses is beyond the scope of this book. In general, multiple regression procedures could be used to weight and combine the separate scores so that a best prediction can be made of a single criterion. This approach is simply a mathematical extension of the regression procedure discussed in Chapter 4. Discriminant analysis procedures and similarity scores can be used if the tester wishes to determine in which criterion group the individual's profile best fits. Interested readers should consult such references as Cooley (1971), Prediger (1971), and Rulon, Tiedeman, Tatsuoka, & Langmuir (1967). Discriminant analysis procedures are most likely to be

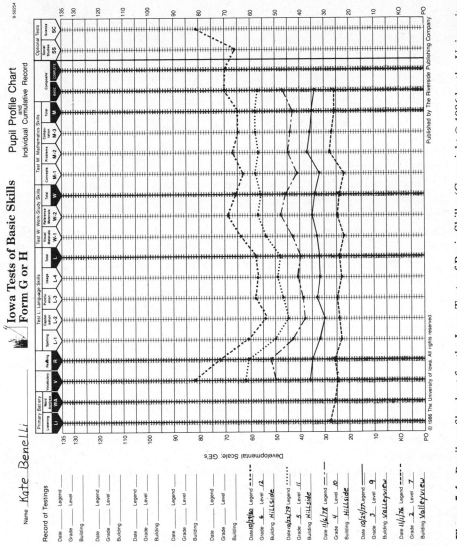

Figure 5.4 Pupil profile chart for the Iowa Tests of Basic Skills. (Copyright © 1986 by the University of Iowa. Reprinted by permission of the publisher, The Riverside Publishing Company, 8420 Bryn Mawr Avenue, Chicago, IL 60631.

133

used with interest and personality inventories and are especially helpful in counseling based on the test data.

SUMMARY

The following statements summarize the major points of this chapter:

1. Normative data are an important aid in interpreting scores.
2. Norms should be recent.
3. Norms should be sampled from a larger population in such a manner that the sample is representative.
4. The population sampled should be relevant.
5. The type of norm most commonly used by test publishers is the national norm.
6. Special group norms or local norms are often more meaningful than national norms.
7. School mean norms should be used if one is interested in comparing one school district's performance with those of other school districts.
8. Norms are not standards.
9. Norm-referenced scores can be divided into relative position status scores and developmental level scores. Both types are potentially useful and serve somewhat different purposes. Relative status scores are more frequently used and less subject to misunderstanding.
10. A percentile rank for a person indicates the percentage of students' scores falling below the individual's obtained score.
11. Percentile ranks are easy to interpret but have the disadvantage of unequal units.
12. z and T scores are derived scores with means of 0 and 50, and standard deviations of 1 and 10, respectively.
13. NCEs are derived scores with a mean of 50 and a standard deviation of 21.06.
14. Deviation IQs are standard scores with means of 100 and, depending on the test, with standard deviations usually (but not always) of 15 or 16.
15. Stanines are derived scores with a mean of 5 and a standard deviation of 2.
16. When scores are normally distributed percentiles, z, T, stanine scores, and NCEs have the relationship depicted in Figure 5.1.
17. Grade equivalents have several major limitations. The technical limitations are due to extrapolation and absence of any information regarding the shape or variance of the grade-equivalent distribution. Practically, grade equivalents are likely to be misinterpreted as indicating the actual grade level at which a person is performing and/or as standards of performance.

18. Mental age scores are subject to most of the same limitations as grade equivalents.
19. Scaled scores are supposed to have equal units, but this claim is disputed by some. Scaled scores are useful for research but not for reporting scores to others.
20. The criterion-referenced scores used most frequently are percent correct or a mastery/nonmastery classification.
21. Expectancy scores are derived scores usually based on the regression of aptitude on achievement. Such scores are useful in helping answer the question of whether a child's (or school mean) score is about at the level that could be reasonably expected. Such scores need to be interpreted with caution.
22. Profiles are useful aids in interpretation when we have several scores for the same individual.
23. In order to use profiles, scores must all be converted to the same type of derived score and must be based on the same norm group. In addition, some index of error should be portrayed on the profile.

POINTS TO PONDER

1. Can norms be recent and representative without being relevant? Explain your answer.
2. Do the following numbers look reasonable? Explain.

Lori's national percentile	95
Lori's local percentile	85
The school mean percentile of Lori's school	35

3. What additional information might you need to compare your score on the midterm (43) and your score on the final (62)?
4. Given a normal distribution of raw scores, which of the following standard scores is furthest from the mean?

$$T = 65$$
$$z = -2.0$$
$$\text{percentile rank} = 90$$
$$\text{stanine} = 7$$

5. Figure 5.3 shows that a clerical speed and accuracy raw score of 36 is equivalent to a percentile of 40. However, a space relations raw score of 26 is equivalent to a percentile of 60. How do you account for this wide discrepancy in percentiles? How would you explain this to Jane and her parents?
6. Would you use a profile chart such as Figure 5.4 to discuss Ben's progress with his parents? Explain.

CHAPTER 6

Factors Influencing Measurements of Individuals

TEST ANXIETY
TEST-WISENESS
GUESSING
COACHING AND PRACTICE
RESPONSE STYLES
OTHER FACTORS AFFECTING AN EXAMINEE'S TEST
  PERFORMANCE

Most teachers will have encountered at one time or another, examples of students whose test performances defy nearly all of their expectations.[1] One student, for example, may appear somnolent and uncomprehending in class, may be unable to give coherent answers to the teacher's questions, and yet perform brilliantly on tests. Another, who is keen, alert, and interested in class, and who gives every appearance of understanding the material taught, encounters disaster when confronted by a test. Are the teacher's judgments wrong, and should they be discarded in favor of the more "objective" information provided by the tests? Our answer is "No," and we would counsel teachers not to jump too quickly to conclusions in such a situation but to exercise caution in their efforts to reconcile conflicting information.

It is often difficult for teachers to accept the fact that a student can have a good understanding of what is taught and yet consistently perform poorly on tests. Our aim in this chapter is to consider some of the extraneous factors that can influence the performance of students on tests and in measurement situations generally. And what makes a factor extraneous? For a test to

---

[1] Although we use teachers and pupils in many of our examples, one could easily substitute examiner and examinee, respectively, or psychologist and client.

provide a valid measure, a person's score should be determined by his or her achievement in that particular content area, and by nothing else. Some characteristics of the person (motivation to learn, general ability, study habits) and some characteristics of the environment (competence and dedication of the teacher, parental support and encouragement) will surely have their influence on achievement and therefore, one would hope, on test scores. But there are other factors that may affect test scores, about which we might be less happy. If a person does poorly on a test because of an inability to comprehend the test instructions, because of an inappropriate guessing strategy, because of poor apportionment of testing time, emotional disturbance, anxiety, or environmental distraction, we can only conclude that the test does not measure that student's achievement as accurately as it should, and therefore that the validity of the test as a measure of achievement is lessened.

In interpreting test scores, a person should have some awareness of the various factors that can have detrimental effects on measurement, and be willing to take these into account if there is an indication that any of them might be seriously influencing an individual's test performance. For example, when a child's test score is at variance with the teacher's knowledge of the child, we urge the teacher not to dismiss that knowledge as "subjective, unreliable, and disproven by the test score," but instead to look more closely and to see if the disparity can be accounted for. It is in keeping with the emphasis of this book that we urge teachers to use test information to *add* to their previous knowledge of a child, but not to replace it.

After studying this chapter, you should be able to do the following:

1. Identify the major extraneous factors that can detrimentally affect the measurement of individuals' achievement and ability.
2. Recognize situations where these factors could be important.
3. Take these factors into account when interpreting the performance of an individual on a test.
4. Understand the positive and negative roles played by anxiety in the test situation and know how to limit and control its negative effects.
5. Understand the nature of test-wiseness, and know the major skills involved.
6. Be familiar with major research results concerning test-wiseness, and find ways to minimize the contribution of test-wiseness to test-score variance.
7. Evaluate the seriousness of the problems that result from guessing on objective tests.
8. Understand and avoid all the common major misconceptions about guessing on objective tests.
9. Distinguish among the major types of programs commonly referred to as "coaching."

10. Evaluate research results on the effectiveness of coaching for standardized aptitude and achievement tests.
11. Adopt a rational and informed view with respect to public controversy over the propriety and the effectiveness of coaching on the various college and professional school entrance exams.
12. Understand the different types of response styles and their effect on a person's test score.
13. Understand the role that the sex, age, personality, race, and other characteristics of the examiner can play in affecting a person's test scores.

TEST ANXIETY

The challenge presented by a test is reacted to by people in a variety of ways. There are those whose competitive spirits are "fired up" by such a situation, and whose enthusiasm for meeting any challenge is translated into maximal performance. Others may suffer a mild degree of anxiety, and yet find that the resulting tension enhances their powers of concentration (in just the same way that some athletes give their best performances when they are nervous and "keyed up" for a big occasion). Yet other students may become so anxious that they are unable to perform at all well, and may suffer physical distress (such as nausea) as well as emotional disturbance. We are all familiar with the stereotype of the student who "goes to pieces" in the examination situation. It may not be common, and it may be that some students simply find it a more palatable excuse for poor performance than lack of preparation, but it can happen.

Alpert and Haber (1960) distinguished between these two kinds of response to stress, calling them "facilitating" and "debilitating" anxiety. They found moderate negative correlations between the two measures. The anxiety of most concern to teachers and to measurement experts is debilitating anxiety, since it may result in students performing on tests at levels that are lower than warranted by their knowledge or ability.

What causes students to become so anxious in the test-taking situation and what can be done to minimize its detrimental effect on performance? Research on test anxiety has not been particularly helpful in providing answers to these questions. Correlation studies, for example, which have consistently shown moderate negative correlations between measures of test anxiety and scores on achievement and aptitude tests (see, for example, Spielberger, Anton, & Bedell, 1976; Tryon, 1980) do not, as is sometimes supposed, establish that anxiety *causes* poor performance. Indeed, as has often been pointed out (for example, Hopkins and Stanley, 1981, p. 145; Anastasi, 1982, p. 36), the opposite implication (that poor performance causes test anxiety) is equally consistent with the data, and, depending upon one's presuppositions, perhaps equally plausible. Attempts to resolve the question of causality by designing experimental studies in which anxiety is induced in some students but not in others (Chambers, Hopkins, & Hopkins, 1972) cannot resolve the issue either, since the tendency toward anxiety that has built up in a student over a school career is clearly a quite different phenomenon from anxiety that is artificially induced and short-term. (We have seen no examples, and we trust that there are no examples, of experimental studies in which the induced anxiety is long-term.)

But we would argue, further, that the question is unresolvable not only because of the constraints of research methodology, but that it is unresolvable logically and conceptually. As we have mentioned previously, not everybody reacts in the same way to anxiety, and it seems likely that causal mechanisms operate quite differently for different people. Certainly John's anxiety may have contributed to his doing badly on a test, and certainly Glenn's history of low achievement may make him anxious whenever he has to take a test. But it is also likely that both effects occur within the one person—that a history of poor achievement can lead to test anxiety, which in turn contributes to poorer subsequent achievement. We do not need to wait for research to answer the "chicken-and-egg" question before we confront the practical problem of what to do about the problem of poor performance accompanied by excessive anxiety.

And the anxiety can be excessive indeed. According to a report in *The Age* (1977), 341 students committed suicide in Japan in 1973, the majority attributed to fear of failure on the University Entrance examinations. Where a student's whole future depends on a single examination, anxiety is not just a problem, it is probably the only rational response. Administrative arrangements would minimize the possibly unfortunate effects of anxiety if

1. important decisions were made on the basis of performances on many occasions, not just one, and
2. the more important the decision, the greater the opportunities that are provided for students to redeem themselves if they appear or believe themselves to have performed below their capabilities.

These recommendations are consistent with a recognition of the likelihood and nature of measurement error, to which we have given attention in Chapter 3.

Within the classroom, there are many things that the teacher can do, not the least of which is the adoption of a warm and encouraging attitude toward students, and particularly toward any students who show indications that they are traumatized by fear of failure on the test. For those students who appear to evidence test anxiety, teachers can give one of the many test-anxiety scales on the market (for instance, Sarason's Test Anxiety Scale and Alpert's Achievement Anxiety Test); if it is determined that a pupil is truly test-anxious, appropriate remedial action can be initiated or, at the very least, the subject's anxiety can be taken into account when the test score is being interpreted. It is essential to recognize that whether or not the fears are justified, they are real and their effects can be real. Testing will be less anxiety-provoking if it is a familiar experience, so that to base decisions as much as possible upon a larger number of tests is advisable both psychometrically and psychologically.

We have no magic prescription by which teachers can "cure" excessive anxiety. A great deal depends on the attitude of the teacher. If tests are perceived by the students as being the "club" that the teacher uses to keep them in line, then of course their confidence in the teacher and the tests will be diminished. If tests are seen as a way to "trap" students, anxiety and fear of failure are natural responses. Teachers who, by their attitudes and their actions, convey the message "I want you to do well; I have confidence that you can do well; my purpose in testing you is to provide you with the opportunity to do well" will not provoke anxiety and fear of failure.

Finally, it is our experience that students are made anxious by uncertainty. Teachers who "spring" tests on students without warning, teachers whose tests are so unpredictable that the students do not know what to expect, teachers who leave students "in the dark" as to what is expected of them, and teachers whose marking is based on whimsy, all create anxiety by their measurement incompetence. While it is true that these slips relate primarily to teacher-made classroom tests, nevertheless the atmosphere fostered in the classroom by teacher-made tests may permeate into the standardized test arena. Teachers who prepare students adequately for tests should not find that their students are overly anxious about tests. The student who has not learned well and knows it should expect failure but not fear it. The student who has worked well will have a justifiable fear of failure if the teacher lacks the skill to do an adequate job of test construction and test score interpretation. Increased measurement competence on the part of the teacher has many benefits; lessening students' unwarranted anxieties is just one of them. (See Sarason, 1980, and Tryon, 1980 for an excellent discussion of test anxiety and its treatment.)

TEST-WISENESS

A growing body of research evidence suggests that the ability to handle testing situations is a source of test-score variance over and above that which can be attributed to subject-matter competence (for a comprehensive review of research literature on test-wiseness, see Sarnacki, 1979).

The most widely accepted definition of test-wiseness is that proposed by Millman, Bishop, & Ebel (1965) in the first comprehensive and widely circulated analysis of the concept: Test-wiseness is "a subject's capacity to utilize the characteristics and formats of the test and/or the test-taking situation to receive a high score (p. 707)." The wide acceptance of this definition implies that test-wiseness is regarded as a set of cognitive skills, although few would deny that the willingness to draw upon those skills is determined largely by attitudes. While some students will call upon every resource at their command in order to "beat the examiner," there are surely others to whom the possibility would never occur.

The analysis by Millman, Bishop, & Ebel (1965) focused on two aspects of test-wise behavior: (1) those independent of test constructor or test purpose, including use of time, strategies for avoiding errors, sensible guessing tactics, and the use of deductive reasoning to eliminate incorrect alternatives in multiple-choice tests; and (2) those specific to particular tests or particular examiners. The latter involve recognizing test-construction errors and examiner idiosyncracies that can help to "give away" the answer, and "reading the examiner's mind" when the intent of the question is not clear. As noted earlier, standardized tests are generally less prone to "item-error" (such as ambiguity, clues to the correct answer) than teacher-made tests. Hence, only the aspects of test-wiseness independent of the test constructor should be operative in standardized tests.

Following the work of Millman, Bishop, & Ebel, there has been something of an explosion of research in the area. Measures of test-wiseness, developed by Gibb (1964), Millman (1966), Slakter, Koehler, & Hampton (1970a) and Diamond & Evans (1972), have focused on those strategies that are directed toward improving one's score on multiple-choice tests. Research has established the following:

1. Test-wiseness can be effectively taught (Gibb, 1964; Slakter, Koehler, & Hampton, 1970b). But Keysor, Williams, & Van Mondfrans (1979) found that for a select group of college students, training appeared to have little effect.
2. The teaching of test-wiseness results in small score increases on many achievement tests (Wahlstrom & Boersma, 1968; Moore, 1971; Callenbach, 1973; Kalechstein, Kalechstein, & Docter, 1981).
3. Test-wiseness conveys a greater advantage when the test is multiple-choice (Rowley, 1974; Smith, 1982) and when it is poorly constructed (Bajtelsmit, 1977).
4. Test-wiseness increases with age (Slakter, Koehler, & Hampton, 1970a) and with experience in taking tests (Kreit, 1968).
5. Although logically independent of achievement, test-wiseness has moderate positive correlations with measures of achievement (Rowley, 1974) and intelligence (Diamond & Evans, 1972). Since test-wiseness is a set of cognitive skills, this ought to be expected.

What to do about test-wiseness? The answer seems obvious enough. It is neither possible nor desirable to take test-wiseness skills from those who already have them. It is both possible and, we believe, desirable to teach test-wiseness to those who lack it. The evidence indicates that a little instruction and experience in answering the types of questions being used can be quite effective, especially for elementary and intermediate school students. The writing of essays has long been regarded as a valuable skill that is worth teaching; the anwering of other types of test questions should be seen in the same light. We concur with Ebel (1965b), who declared that "more error in measurement is likely to originate from students who have too little, rather than too much, skill in taking tests (p. 206)."

GUESSING

Many individuals believe that guessing is a major factor in determining scores on objective tests, and most of us have heard such tests (especially multiple-choice) referred to in jest as "multiple-guess." But how serious a problem is guessing, and how concerned should test developers be? Is it true that some students can increase their scores substantially by being "lucky," while other, less fortunate beings are condemned to suffer "the slings and arrows of outrageous fortune"? In this section, we will give some attention to the research findings that relate to the effects of guessing, the gains made by guessing, and the means advanced as ways of counteracting guessing.

Why Do Examinees Guess?

Although the answer is obvious enough, we think the question needs to be asked in order to provide some perspective to the discussion that follows. Examinees "guess" because they do not have enough knowledge or ability to provide an answer about whose correctness they are certain. It follows, therefore, that there is more than one kind of guess—in particular, we would like to distinguish the "blind guess" (where examinees choose an answer *at random* from among the alternatives offered) from the informed guess (in which examinees draw upon all their knowledge and abilities to choose the answer *most likely* to be correct). Those who express concern about the effects of guessing often seem to assume that what takes place in the examination setting is blind guessing. There may be situations in which this is true (as where the test is totally unsuited to the ability levels of the examinees), but such evidence as is available (particularly Ebel, 1965b) indicates that the amount of blind guessing that occurs in normal circumstances is very small indeed. Students who are motivated to do their best will use every scrap of information at their disposal to seek out the right answer, will eliminate implausible alternatives to the extent that they are able to, but will rarely find themselves in situations where blind guessing is all they can do. To the extent that guessing occurs on multiple-choice tests (as of course it must), logic and evidence combine to suggest that it is informed guessing that predominates.

Those who dislike blind guessing (for whatever reason, be it ethical, aesthetic, or psychometric) should not allow this dislike to transfer itself to informed guessing, which is a different phenomenon altogether. Informed guessing is not morally reprehensible—if so, we, the authors, and almost everybody we know, are moral reprobates, since virtually all the decisions we make are based on informed guesses about the consequences. Nor does informed guessing detract from test validity, and there are good reasons to think that validity can be enhanced by informed guessing. Multiple-choice tests are sometimes thought to be insensitive to "partial knowledge" because items are scored zero or one, and the student who has some knowledge, but not enough to pick the correct answer, scores zero—as does the person who has no knowledge at all. But this analysis considers only one item, not the test as a whole. If students are encouraged through test directions and scoring to use their partial knowledge in making informed guesses, where necessary, those with higher levels of partial knowledge will be correct more often than those with lower levels. Thus, although a single item appears not to reward partial knowledge, the test as a whole will reward it, provided of course that attempts are not made to prevent examinees from using their partial knowledge in making informed guesses. It is for this reason, we suppose, that research has found no way of substantially improving the measurement of partial knowledge beyond that afforded by the multiple-choice test (see, for example, Traub & Fisher, n. d.). Those who think that examinees should answer only multiple-choice items when they *know* the correct answer might give some thought to the parallels that exist between multiple-choice and essay tests. On a multiple-choice item, examinees lacking complete knowledge will give either an informed guess (if they have some partial knowledge), or a blind guess, or an omit (if they have no knowledge at all). On an essay question, students lacking complete knowledge (that is, every student?) will give an incomplete or at least an imperfect answer. Students lacking any knowledge (if that is possible) will either omit the question or try to use whatever verbal skills they possess to give the best possible answer. "Bluffing," "waffling," "padding," and various less polite terms are used to describe this strategy, and it is not confined to those with little or no knowledge. All students who want to do well on a test can be expected to do whatever they can to make their answers convincing. We commend to the reader a wonderful letter written by Stephen Leacock, the Canadian humorist, to *The Daily Princetonian* (Leacock, 1938), in which the author describes his approach to written (essay) examinations. Attesting to the success of the strategy, he recalled:

There, one can see how easy it is. I know it from my own experience. I remember in my fourth year in Toronto (1891) going into the exam room and picking up a paper which I carelessly took for English Philology. I wrote on it, passed on it, and was pleasantly surprised two weeks later when they gave me a degree in Ethnology. I had answered the wrong paper. This story, oddly enough, is true.

We do not suggest that our classrooms are full of young Stephen Leacocks. But we do suggest that bluffing and guessing should be seen as parallel problems, and that bluffing is probably a matter that warrants greater concern. Why? There are two reasons. The first is that we suspect, without firm evidence, that there is more to be gained by bluffing on an essay test than there is by guessing on an objective test. Second, and more important, we can feel well assured that whatever advantage a student may gain from lucky guessing is only transitory—next time it will be somebody else's turn to be lucky, and, in the long run, luck of this kind evens itself out. (If it does not, then it is not luck, but something else. For example, if Lois consistently "guesses" more successfully than Jim, we will soon have to accept the conclusion that Lois is not guessing—at least not blindly—and that Lois really does know something that Jim does not.) But with bluffing we have no such assurance. Those who bluff most successfully today will do so tomorrow, and the next day, and the next day, since bluffing and associated verbal skills are clearly more highly developed in some people than in others. We therefore argue that guessing, to the extent that it advantages or disadvantages anyone, has effects that are relatively minor and, in the long run, fair. Bluffing on an essay test is a greater measurement problem than guessing on an objective test.

How Much Is Gained by Guessing?

On a single multiple-choice item, there is no question that luck can play an important part—it can of course make the least knowlegeable examinee score as well as the most knowledgeable. From this, does it follow that the same is true of a test, which is merely a collection of such items? Of course not. The merest knowledge concerning the operation of chance is all that is needed to see why. Consider the following example. Brian is taking a 40-item, four-alternatives multiple-choice test (most standardized aptitude and achievement tests use the multiple-choice format), about the content of which he knows absolutely nothing. If Brian guesses blindly on every item, we would expect him to score 10 out of 40. What is the chance that Brian will guess well enough to gain a perfect score? Almost none—his chance of getting a perfect score by guessing is 1 in 1,200,000,000,000,000,000,000,000. If a score of 30 is passing, his chance of passing is 1 in 2,000,000. Lengthening the test would reduce the odds even further. These figures take on more meaning if we realize that if all citizens of the United States were to take such a test every day of their lives and guess on all items, we could expect one perfect score to be produced, on the average, every 15 years. If Brian is serious about wanting a perfect score, we suggest that study would be a more advantageous strategy.

In the light of this knowledge, it is clear that "guessing lucky" is just not an adequate explanation of any student's high score, nor is bad luck a believable excuse for a low score. Luck in guessing may raise or lower a particular student's score by a mark or two, but it will not make any notable difference unless the test is unreasonably short.

The Prevention of Guessing

Those who see guessing as a problem to be dealt with have frequently thought it desirable to discourage students from guessing, both by means of the instructions given when the test is administered and by scoring the test in such a way as to penalize those who guess incorrectly (commonly known as *formula scoring* or, less aptly, *correcting for guessing*). We recognize that many standardized tests do not employ formula scoring and that the issue of formula scoring is more relevant to teacher-made tests. However, we believe that in order for teachers and others to be able to take a position on the matter, they should understand why we do not favor any correction for guessing.

Why Prevent Guessing?   There appear to be at least two reasons for wanting to discourage guessing. The first involves the ethical/moral belief that guessing is wrong and/or sinful because it is a form of gambling, or because it reflects the intention to deceive. We do not share this view. The second major reason is that guessing can affect the psychometric properties of the test. On theoretical grounds, one could argue that guessing should, by adding a source of random variance to test scores, decrease both reliability and validity (Lord, 1963). But empirical studies into these questions have been unable to produce consistent evidence either way (Blommers & Lindquist, cited in Ebel, 1965b; Sabers & Feldt, 1968; Traub, Hambleton, & Singh, 1969; Hakstian & Kansup, 1975).

There is, however, a long line of research which indicates that instructions *not* to guess have different effects on different students, and that these differences are then reflected in their test scores. Students who have been shown to be disadvantaged by such instructions include those whose personalities have been described as "submissive" (Votaw, 1936), "characterized by introversion, rumination, anxiety, low self-esteem, and undue concern with the impression they make on others" (Sheriffs & Boomer, 1954), and unwilling to take risks (Slakter, 1968). The reason is simple; even with the application of a correction (see the next section), those who obey the "do-not-guess" instructions are disadvantaged, and those who disregard the instructions profit from so doing.

Formula Scoring   Associated with "do-not-guess" instructions, standardized test publishers *could* but seldom do use a scoring formula that is in-

tended to nullify the effects of blind guessing. In its most common form, the
formula is

$$S = R - \frac{W}{A - 1} \tag{6.1}$$

where S = corrected score
R = number of right answers
W = number of wrong answers
A = number of alternatives per item

With four-choice items, then, the effect of the formula is to penalize the
examinee one-third of a point for every wrong answer. Justice is said to be
done because an examinee who guesses blindly on four items could expect,
on average, to choose one correct answer and three incorrect answers. The
point gained from the one correct answer is exactly cancelled out by the
point lost from the three incorrect answers, and so the examinee who
guesses is no better off and no worse off than the examinee who omits. From
the point of view of the examinee, the expected reward from (blind) guessing
is identical to the expected reward from omitting. If this were all there was to
it, the examinee could be indifferent to the choice.

But other factors come into play. First, as pointed out previously, the
guessing that takes place on multiple-choice tests is overwhelmingly informed guessing, in which the probability of success is substantially greater
than chance. Even when examinees believe they can do no better than
chance, the evidence is that they can do substantially better (Wood, 1976;
Cross & Frary, 1977; Rowley & Traub, 1977; Bliss, 1980). In these circumstances, the expected reward from answering is greater than that from omitting, and the most honest advice to examinees would be that they should
answer every question on the test, even if the test instructions tell them
otherwise!

Problems arise because some examinees are more easily intimidated (by
instructions, penalties, and so on) than others, and we should be aware that,
particularly in the case of a true-false test, where the "correction" for a
wrong answer is enough to cancel out a previous correct answer, the penalty
can appear particularly severe. Those examinees who are most intimidated
by this situation will omit questions that they could and should have answered, and their scores will suffer as a result. Slakter (1968a) was correct in
referring to the scoring formula as a "penalty for not guessing."

It seems (Traub, Hambleton, & Singh, 1969) that a correction formula of
the form

$$S = R + O/A \tag{6.2}$$

where O = number of omits

has somewhat different psychological effects. Examinees are, in effect,
promised a chance score on any item they omit, rather than a penalty for any

wrong answer. Apparently this is less inhibiting to the timid examinee. On a highly speeded test, where unrestrained guessing could be a problem, it makes it clear to the examinee that no advantage can be gained by randomly answering the uncompleted portion of the paper.

In general, we would counsel against the use of formula scoring. The benefits in terms of psychometric qualities are small and frequently undetectable, and the price—that the test scores will be confounded with unwanted personality factors—too high.

Misconceptions About Formula Scoring   Before leaving the subject of guessing, it seems worthwhile to give attention to some of the misconceptions that abound. We will discuss them only briefly.

1. *Formula scores rank examinees quite differently from number-right scores.* Wrong. Correlations between formula scores and number-right scores are usually above .95 (see, for example, Ebel, 1972, p. 252) and will reach 1.00 if all examinees can be persuaded to answer all questions.

2. *Formula scores compensate the unlucky guesser.* Wrong. The penalty is determined only by the number of wrong answers, not by the examinee's belief while giving those answers. A person who is unlucky in guessing will have more wrong answers and be more heavily penalized than an equally knowledgeable examinee who guesses with greater luck.

3. *If a guessing penalty is applied, examinees should omit questions if they judge that their probability of success is at chance level.* As pointed out before, examinees' probabilities of success are usually greater than they believe, and it is in their interest to attempt all items, regardless of their perceived likelihood of success.

4. *The penalty penalizes only guesses.* Wrong again. If examinees answer a question wrongly in the genuine belief that it is correct, not only do they fail to score on that question but they lose a fraction of a mark from somewhere else—a penalty for a "guess" they did not make!

Conclusions on Guessing

Although we must, in fairness, acknowledge that not all writers agree with us (see, for example, Hopkins & Stanley, 1981, p. 152), we believe that the evidence is strong enough to justify the recommendation that the correction for guessing *not* be used, and that test instructions include the recommendation that all examinees should attempt all questions, even if they do not think they know the answers. The only exceptions we see are (1) a highly speeded test, where examinees are not expected to complete all items, and (2) a diagnostic test, where the examinees' interests are best served by revealing their strengths and weaknesses rather than by striving to maximize their scores. Finally, we assert that guessing on multiple-choice tests is not the serious problem it has often been thought to be, and that compared to "bluff-ing" on essay tests, it pales into insignificance.

COACHING AND PRACTICE

Questions concerning the effects of coaching and practice on test perfor-mance cannot be neatly separated from those related to test-wiseness. Par-ticularly for test-inexperienced examinees, a major benefit of both coaching and practice is familiarity with the nature of the task. Taking tests is like any other activity in that one is likely to perform better when the nature of the task is familiar and well understood.

It should be obvious to our readers by now that lack of test-taking skills can only result in test invalidity, since it will lead the test user to a false inference—that an examinee lacks certain skills, when in fact the examinee had the skills but did not demonstrate them in the test situation. No test results can be valid (lead to accurate inferences) unless all examinees are sufficiently experienced and familiar with the testing situation to be able to demonstrate the skills that they possess.

Research on the effects of coaching and practice has been scattered and difficult to interpret. There are many reasons for this, but the major difficulty comes from the wide range of meanings ascribed to both terms. *Practice* may refer to a single test-taking experience or to extensive drill on similar test items. *Coaching* can mean any of the following (Anastasi, 1982):

1. *Test-taking orientation.* Materials designed to help the student become familiar with the type of test being used and comfortable in the test-taking situation. Good examples are *Taking the SAT* (College Entrance Examina-tion Board, 1978) and *A Guide to Test Taking as Easy as . . . 1 2 3* (Michi-gan State Board of Education, undated, but released in 1981). Each is de-signed with the expressed aim of enabling students to perform as well as they are able to on a specific test or testing program. Materials such as these are typically made as widely available as possible, and to the extent that they are effective they would have the effect of improving the quality of measure-ment by reducing the unwanted variance due to differences in familiarity with the test-taking task. Nearly all standardized cognitive tests, especially those designed for testing young children, have numerous practice tests and examples. Also, some test publishers are now offering films, filmstrips, and other materials to acquaint examinees with the test and the testing environment.

2. *Coaching.* Used in this context, the term generally refers to relatively short-term "cramming" sessions, sometimes commercially motivated, sometimes intended to advantage students at one or more schools compared to the bulk of examinees. "Coaching" courses for college admissions tests

have concerned the College Board and other groups for many years. Often they consist of extensive practice ("drill") on sample items or on items similar to those in the test for which the coaching is designed.

3. *Instruction.* This generally refers to longer-term programs of instruction in broad cognitive skills similar to those tested. It differs from coaching in that it is intended to improve a person's performance on the whole range of abilities that the test samples. While we recognize that programs will occasionally be found that have elements of both instruction and coaching, most are fairly clear in their intentions.

Questions about coaching, practice, drill, and so on must concern us from the ethical as well as from the practical point of view. In order to clarify some of the ethical issues, we find it useful to distinguish between the *domain* of behavior represented by a test and the *sample* of behavior chosen— the items on the test. The domain may be defined very explicitly in terms of behavioral objectives, as in some criterion-referenced tests; in terms of broad content areas, as in many standardized achievement tests; or in terms of very broad classes of behavior (such as inferential reasoning or analogies), as on many tests designated as aptitude tests. However explicitly defined the domain may be, the distinction is clear: The domain refers to the class of behaviors about which inferences are being made; the items on the test merely sample that domain.

Test-taking orientation, as we have defined it above, will, to the extent that it is successful, remove some of the obstacles that might cause the test taker's performance on the test to inaccurately represent his or her performance on the domain. It is in the interest of the test takers, because it will prevent their scores from being inappropriately low. It is in the interests of the test user, because its effect is to lessen the likelihood of false inferences about examinees, and so improve the validity of the measurement process. *Instruction,* to the extent that it is effective, will improve the examinee's performance on the domain of behaviors, with one result being improved test performance. If the test is used to predict a criterion, improved performance over the domain should result in increased performance on the criterion. *Coaching,* which attempts to increase the test score without improving domain performance, does raise ethical questions, because it is the only one of the three that aims explicitly at deception. And it may not be in the interests of the examinees, if its intention is to have them admitted to a program or occupation for which the best conceivable prediction (from performance over the domain) would be that they are unsuited. We think the ethical implications should be clear to the reader.

But what of effectiveness? First, we must point out that research evidence, particularly concerning the effects of instruction and coaching, is tenuous at best. The reason for this lies in research methodology. Many studies have been conducted that compared coached to uncoached groups,

but since those in the group receiving the coaching are normally there because they want to be there, and those not being coached are there because
they do not want to be coached, it is difficult to make any inferences from
such studies. For those interested, Messick (1980b, Chapter 2) has summarized research of this type. No firm conclusion can be reached. (See also
Messick & Jungeblut, 1981.)

True experimental studies, in which examinees are randomly assigned to
experimental and control groups, are rare, because of the ethical and practical difficulties involved. The most recent (Alderman & Powers, 1980) found
that special programs already in place in the eight secondary schools studied
brought about an increase of around 8 points, on average, on the SAT scale
of 200–800. This is very small (about one-twelfth of a standard deviation)
and less than the improvement normally made on a second testing. There
was a problem with this study in that the special administration of the test
that was arranged for the study did not "count" in any real sense, so that
students may not have been as motivated as they normally would be when
taking the SAT. But the findings are consistent with the general thrust of
other, less carefully designed research, which are that the best that can be
hoped for from any programs of coaching, test-taking orientation, or practice is an improvement of about one-fifth of a standard deviation, and most
yield less than this (Hopkins & Stanley, 1981).

In recent years there has been something of a furor over the question of
the effectiveness of coaching for the SAT. Most of the attention has focused
on an article by Slack & Porter (1980a), in which the authors examined
literature on coaching and the SAT and concluded with a triumphant flourish
that the SAT scores are "unrelated to the quality of [students'] minds" (p.
172); that the SAT is coachable; and that it should therefore be replaced by
standardized achievement tests (which presumably would be more coachable than the SAT).

The controversy surrounding this sweeping conclusion (see, for example,
Jackson, 1980; Messick, 1980b, 1981; Slack & Porter, 1980b) has clarified
several important points, and there is much of value to be learned from it.

First, we note that Slack & Porter (1980a) assume that an aptitude test
measures some innate, unchanging quality of the individual that is not affected (or, at least, not appreciably affected) by that individual's experiences. This is, of course, a naive view of the nature of aptitude, which
contrasts most strongly with modern thinking. Anastasi (1982) points out
what should be obvious: "All tests reflect what a person has learned. An
individual's test performance is a sample of what he or she is able to do at the
time" (p. 1086). The notion, then, that achievement tests are coachable and
that aptitude tests are not, is false. There are good reasons to hope that the
former would be more responsive to instruction than the latter, but the
difference is a matter of degree. For reviews of the conceptual distinction
between achievement and aptitude, consult Chapter 7 or Anastasi (1982).

The best available recent summaries of research on coaching, with particular reference to the SAT, are those by Messick (1980b, 1981). Messick, in focusing on the regularities that do exist among the seemingly disparate results, has made many telling points. In particular, he has emphasized that questions about the effectiveness of coaching are questions of degree (How much coaching? What kinds of coaching? How much improvement?) rather than simple yes–no questions (Does coaching work?). To this end, he has sought what he calls relational rather than categorical answers. In particular he has shown that the score gains that can be expected increase with the time spent, that there are diminishing returns for increased coaching time, and that the verbal section (SAT-V) is less responsive to coaching than the mathematical (SAT-M). This is to be expected, since the SAT-M is more strongly curriculum-related than the SAT-V. But Messick has also made a very cogent point about the research that has been done. Short-term coaching programs have typically been of the "cramming" kind referred to earlier, while long-term programs have concentrated more on instruction in broad cognitive skills. Summaries such as that by Slack & Porter (1980a) have confounded the two factors *nature* and *duration* of the coaching or instruction given. Even given the diminishing returns earlier, it is not possible to conclude that a program can be made more effective by making it longer—it may be that increased effectiveness comes only with an increase in time allocation *and* a shift in emphasis to instruction in broad cognitive skills. And if it proves to be the case that the most effective way to improve one's SAT score is to improve one's ability across the broad repertoire of skills tapped by the SAT, who would be unhappy about that? Certainly not the Educational Testing Service, nor, we would hope, its critics.

Often mistaken for coaching—that is, a purposive treatment—is the effect of repeating a test or taking a parallel form of the test. As might be expected, those examinees who repeat the test receive higher scores on the second administration (Hutton, 1969; Nevo, 1976; Wing, 1980). Wing found that on repeating the test, examinees did slightly better on the numerical-type items than they did on the verbal-type items, although they improved slightly on both. We believe that test users need not concern themselves too much with the effect of repeating a test, since only infrequently are examinees given the same or a parallel form of an aptitude or achievement test. When they are, users should interpret the second test score accordingly.

RESPONSE STYLES

We will use the term *response style* to refer to a characteristic of individuals, apart from achievement or ability, that consistently affects their manner of responding to a test. On noncognitive measures the problem can be quite serious, and the term *response set* is usually preferred. For cognitive tests, we have already met several important response styles. Test-wiseness is a response style; test-wise students have their own repertoire of ways of dealing with test items, and if these strategies are well learned and consistently applied, they can constitute a style of response that distinguishes those examinees from others. The tendency or propensity to guess is another response style; some students will always guess when the opportunity arises, while others consistently pass up the opportunity, preferring to omit a question if they are unsure. Both test-wiseness and guessing can have consistent effects on examinees' test scores.

Of those we have not yet considered, perhaps the most important response style is speed of work, sometimes referred to as the *speed versus accuracy* response set. Examinees have distinct preferences regarding the speededness of tests. Some work best, and prefer to work, under highly speeded conditions, while others are favored by conditions that allow them to work slowly and deliberately through a test, without having to worry about the passage of time. Tests can, in fact, be arranged on a continuum, with "speed tests" at one end and "power tests" at the other. An example of a pure speed test would be one where no pupil finishes in the allotted time. On a pure speed test, it is assumed that the items are so easy that errors contribute at most insignificantly to score variance, and speed of response is the sole determining factor. On a power test, in comparison, sufficient time is allowed for all students to finish the test—in practice this might be accomplished by allowing extremely generous time limits or by having no time limits at all.

On standardized tests, the teacher does not have control over the amount of time allowed. It is advisable, however, for teachers to inspect the answer sheets to see whether the students had sufficient time to attempt all questions. If not, test givers should bear in mind that the test measures, in part, speed of work, and that low scores can result from slow work as well as from poor work.

There are a set of response styles that are particularly unique to noncognitive tests—that is, attitude, interest, and personality measures. Some of these are the examinees' predisposition to select the neutral category when an agree–disagree continuum is used, social desirability, acquiescence, and the like. These will be discussed more fully in Chapter 9.

Some other examples of response set, especially operative in aptitude and achievement tests employing a multiple-choice format, are the tendency for the examinee to choose the answer in the middle or at the top or at the bottom, to select the longest (or shortest) alternative as the correct answer, and so on. It should be obvious that many of the response-set problems can be controlled by adhering to the principles of good test construction.

OTHER FACTORS AFFECTING
AN EXAMINEE'S TEST PERFORMANCE

In Chapter 1, we discussed the effect of such administrative factors as environmental conditions, training of test administrators, test scoring, and the establishment of rapport between the examiner and the examinee on an examinee's test performance.

So far in the present chapter we have discussed the impact of such factors as guessing, coaching, and test anxiety on examinees' test scores. In essence, the factors we have considered are related either to something inherent in the test, the testing conditions, or the personality of the examinee. There are, however, another set of factors—such as the *examiner's* race, sex, expectancy level, personality, and socioeconomic status—that may have an effect upon an examinee's test performance.

Examiner Effects

What do we know about examiner effects? Generally, they are more operative—that is, they have a greater effect—on individually administered tests than on group-administered tests; on younger children than on adults; on intelligence or semistructured and projective tests than on achievement and interest tests; on emotionally disturbed and handicapped children than on normal children; when the test results are being used to make significant rather than trivial decisions (for instance, in determining whether a felon is sane enough to stand trial for murder, rather than in deciding whether to award students a $50 college scholarship); and on tests where the stimuli are ill-defined and the responses scored subjectively.

We will now consider race, sex, expectancy, and other examiner effects in more detail.

Race   The numerous studies on the effect of the examiner's race on the examinee's test performance have, for the most part, shown that it is negligible. Graziano, Varca, & Levy (1982) reviewed 29 studies to learn whether the examiner's race affected the examinees' intelligence test performance and concluded that "these studies provide no consistent or strong evidence that examiners of different races systematically elicit different performance in black and white examinees" (p. 491). Jensen (1980), after reviewing 37 studies done between 1936 and 1977, as well as studies and reviews by Sattler (1970, 1974, 1982) and Sattler & Gwynne (1982), also concluded that the race of the examiner is not an important factor influencing an examinee's performance on mental ability tests. Although one might expect to find a significant examiner–examinee interaction for individually administered in contrast to group-administered tests (establishment and maintenance of rapport is more crucial in the former), Sattler & Gwynne (1982) found that this was not so.

In summary—contrary to popular misconception, especially among minority group members—the race of the examiner has very little impact on the examinee's test performance. One should not jump to the conclusion that the examiner's race could not influence a person's test performance because it could. However, in standardized tests, at least, the test directions are so specific that we should not expect to find a difference between a well-trained black examiner testing white children and vice versa.

Sex   Once again, one might expect that males would obtain higher test scores when examined by a male examiner and that females would do better with a female administrator. Research, however, does not corroborate this theory. Although Rumenik, Capasso, & Hendrick (1977) found that when an examiner was dealing with sensitive, sexually related items, the sex of the examiner could affect the examinee's responses, they generally observed, for most personality and intelligence tests, that no sex effect existed. Whereas Black and Dana (1977) noted that female examiners obtained higher WISC scores from children, Cieutat and Flick (1967) found no sex effect when the Stanford-Binet was used. Thus the results are somewhat contradictory.

Expectancy   Another area of conflicting or uncertain evidence is the examiner's *expectancy,* or the expectancy effect.

Although Rosenthal and Jacobson (1968) claimed that teacher expectancy affected the mental ability scores that pupils received, their conclusions were disputed because of faulty methodology (Barber & Silver, 1968; Snow, 1969; Elasoff & Snow, 1971). Cronbach (1975) and Jensen (1980) among others contend that teacher expectancy has no effect on pupils' mental ability test scores.

Somewhat contradictory conclusions are voiced by Sattler (1974), Sattler, Hillix, & Neher (1970), and Sattler & Winget (1970), who found that examiners scoring WISC tests gave more favorable treatment (credit for the answer) to the responses that supposedly came from brighter pupils and gave lower scores to those they thought came from the duller pupils (the examiners did not administer the tests; they only scored them).

Thus the expectancy effect studies yield, at best, inconsistent results. Since we really have no evidence to conclude that there is such a thing as examiner/scorer bias, we should be aware that it *may* exist and govern our interpretations of test scores accordingly.

Other Variables   An examinee's test performance may also be affected by the examiner's personality; by certain examiner characteristics such as age, training, and experience (Cohen, 1965; Dyer, 1973); and by the examiner's behavior before and during the test administration. Exner (1966) found, for example, that test takers performed significantly better on an intelligence test when the examiners were "warm and kind" than when they were "cold and impersonal." The significant interaction between the examiner's and examinee's personalities may sometimes be quite specific—so that, for example, a particular examiner might affect Billy but not Peter primarily because the personalities "mesh" in one case but not in the other. It has also been shown that motivated students who are examined by trained examiners (and taught how to mark the answer sheet) do better than their counterparts who are not motivated, are not trained to take tests, and are tested by untrained examiners.

Summary of Examiner Effects

In conclusion, the results are clear about the effect of certain examiner variables on examinees' test performance. The examiner's race has a negligible influence on the examinees' test performance, whereas the data with regard to the role of the examiner's sex and expectancy are inconclusive. It is apparent, however, that examiner and other situational variables are a greater confounding factor on personality tests, especially projective tests, than on cognitive tests. In fact, it has been found that only subtle variations in the phrasing of instructions and in examiner–examinee relationships can markedly alter examinees' performance on projective tests (Masling, 1960; Klopfer and Taulbee, 1976).

SUMMARY

The principal ideas, conclusions, and implications of this chapter are summarized in the following statements:

1. Some students' test performance may defy a teacher's expectations. This is sometimes due to extraneous factors that can influence the test performance.
2. In interpreting test scores, one should be aware of and take into account the various factors that may have detrimental effects on measurement.
3. There are two kinds of response to stress, facilitating and debilitating. Debilitating anxiety may result in examinees scoring lower on tests than knowledge or ability warrant.
4. Teachers can do a variety of things to minimize debilitating test anxiety. Relying on a variety of data-gathering devices (observation, teacher-made and standardized tests, rating scales) rather than on the results of just one or two tests should help decrease test anxiety.

5. Test-wiseness is the ability to utilize the characteristics and formats of the test and/or test-taking situation to receive a higher score than the level of ability or knowledge warrants.
6. Test-wiseness can be effectively taught—especially to younger children; it results in small score increases on many achievement tests; it produces a bigger increase for poorly constructed tests than for well-constructed tests; and it increases with age and test-taking experience.
7. Teachers should attempt to teach all of their students to be test-wise.
8. Informed guessing is the practice of examinees using partial knowledge to arrive at an answer. Informed guessing should be encouraged.
9. Blind guessing is not likely to have much impact on the score of a test unless the test is very short.
10. In general, we recommend against using formulas to "correct for guessing." In fact, we recommend that the instructions of all standardized aptitude and achievement tests should encourage all examinees to attempt all the questions.
11. The terms *coaching* and *practice* have both been used in a variety of ways. Generally one thinks of coaching as a short-term cramming session.
12. Most measurement experts attempt to differentiate between test-taking orientation, coaching, and instruction. Test-taking orientation and instruction are good things to do. Coaching is a questionable ethical practice and may well not be in the best interests of the examinee.
13. Coaching is of some, but quite limited, usefulness in raising test scores.
14. Response styles such as *speed versus accuracy,* the tendency to answer true, and positional response styles can be controlled through good test construction and administrative procedures.
15. Repeating a test or taking a parallel form will usually result in examinees receiving a higher score on the second administration.
16. The race of the examiner has a neglible effect on the examinees' mental test performance.
17. The data concerning the influence of the examiner's sex on the examinees' mental test performance is inconclusive.
18. Studies on teacher/examiner expectancy effects yield inconclusive data.
19. A variety of factors associated with the examiner—personality, interaction with the examinee, age, training—can affect examinees' test performance.

POINTS TO PONDER

1. Suppose you were given a class to teach and you found that nearly all of your students were from other countries. Although their English was perfect, they were totally inexperienced in taking tests. Sketch an outline

of what you would want to teach them about tests so that they could cope adequately in the United States school environment. (Choose a grade level with which you are familiar.)

2. Respond to the following students' explanations of their performance on tests:

   a. "I just guessed. If I passed, I suppose I must have guessed lucky."

   b. "I knew nothing about the third question. I passed it by bluffing."

   c. "I never do well on examinations—I get so nervous that I just go to pieces."

   d. "I think I must be born unlucky. My friends seem to be able to do well on objective tests by just guessing, but it never works for me."

   e. "I always do badly if it's multiple-choice. As soon as you put two or three alternatives in front of me, I become confused."

   f. "I was just unlucky. I knew most of the course, but on the examination we were asked only a few of the things I knew."

CHAPTER 7

Standardized Aptitude Measures

INTRODUCTION
INDIVIDUALLY ADMINISTERED TESTS OF GENERAL INTELLIGENCE
  (APTITUDE)
GROUP TESTS OF GENERAL APTITUDE
MULTIFACTOR APTITUDE TESTS
SPECIAL-APTITUDE TESTS
USING APTITUDE TEST RESULTS

This chapter is divided into six major sections. An introductory section covers (1) definitions of intelligence, (2) the structure of intelligence, (3) the etiology of intelligence, (4) the stability of intelligence, (5) the distinctions and similarities between intelligence, aptitude, and achievement tests, and (6) the classification of aptitude tests. The second section discusses some individually administered intelligence tests; the third section covers group tests of general aptitude; the fourth, multifactor aptitude tests; the fifth, special-aptitude tests. The final section is devoted to a discussion of some of the uses of aptitude tests results.

After studying this chapter, the student should be able to do the following:

1. Know some of the basic definitions of intelligence.
2. Understand some of the theories of the structure of intelligence.
3. Understand that both genetics and environment affect aptitude test scores.
4. Interpret the data on the stability of intelligence.
5. Compare the terms *intelligence, aptitude,* and *achievement.*
6. Know about some of the more popular individual intelligence tests and their advantages and limitations.
7. Know about some of the more popular group tests of intelligence.
8. Evaluate a general aptitude test.
9. Discuss the concept of culture-fair testing.
10. Understand the desired characteristics of a multiple aptitude test.

11. Know about some of the more popular multiple aptitude tests.
12. Evaluate a multiple aptitude test.
13. Recognize the existence of special-aptitude tests and the purposes they are designed to serve.
14. Recognize some instructional, guidance, administrative, and employment uses of aptitude test results.

INTRODUCTION

That society should assist each individual "to achieve the maximum of which he or she is capable" is a motto often heard in educational circles. But behind that simplistic, well-meaning phrase lurk perplexing problems. How do we know what a person's capabilities are? Can we define *capacity*? Can we measure capacity? Does a person have a general capacity to acquire knowledge, or are there many different capacities, each specific to a given type of knowledge? Is capacity constant over time? If not, what conditions affect capacity? These are all relevant questions. Unfortunately, all psychologists do not agree on all the answers. Nevertheless, for the past eight decades psychologists have been using various labels such as *capacity, intelligence, potential, aptitude,* and *ability* to identify a construct (or set of constructs) that seems to be able to predict various kinds of behaviors. The tests designed to measure this construct (or set of constructs) vary to some extent because test authors may not define a construct in the same way or indeed may be talking about different constructs.

Definitions of Intelligence

In discussing definitions of *intelligence,* it is useful to consider the common-sense, psychological, and operational or measurement definitions of the term. Most of us use the term *intelligence* in everyday language. We think we can differentiate between highly intelligent individuals and those at the opposite extreme. We make these differentiations on the basis of the individuals' behaviors. If a person can time after time select an effective course of action under difficult situations, we are apt to conclude that person is intelligent. Sternberg, Conway, Ketron, & Bernstein (1980) found that the views of laypersons concerning intelligence are quite well formed; that they are frequently used both in self-evaluation and in the evaluation of others; that they are closely related to existing psychological theories of intelligence; and that they are quite strongly related to intelligence as measured by an "IQ" test. The common core of peoples' beliefs about what constitutes intelligence includes problem-solving ability, verbal ability, and social competence.

A fairly recent psychological definition of intelligence is given by Cleary,

Humphreys, Kendrick, & Wesman (1975, p. 19), who define intelligence as "the entire repertoire of acquired skills, knowledge, learning sets, and generalization tendencies considered intellectual in nature that are available at any one period in time." Most research evidence would suggest that a hallmark of intelligence is the ability to generalize information from one situation to another (Campione & Brown, 1979). Sternberg, a leading theorist on intelligence, suggests that "intelligence can best be understood through the study of nonentrenched (novel) kinds of tasks. Such tasks require subjects to use concepts or form strategies that differ in kind from those to which they are accustomed" (1981, p. 1). He and other theorists have been using a cognitive psychologist's information-processing approach to the study of intelligence. (See also Chi, Glaser, & Rees, 1982; Sternberg, 1984; Wagner & Sternberg, 1984.) This approach to the theoretical study of intelligence, if successful, should ultimately lead to tests which would provide useful information for understanding and therefore improving individuals' learning processes.

Under current psychological definitions, intelligence is *not* a capacity but rather a behavioral trait that is, at least in part, dependent upon past learning. This approach is good in that it helps us avoid a "reification" of the concept. Intelligence is not something people have, like brains and nervous systems. Rather it is a description of how people behave. Operationally, intelligence is what an intelligence test measures. Though often scoffed at by people who do not understand the concept of operational definitions, this statement is neither meaningless nor bad. If a test measures acquired behaviors that psychologists agree can be labeled intellectual, then the test would be considered a *good* operational definition of intelligence; if it does not, it would be considered a *poor* operational definition. Although the various intelligence tests differ somewhat from each other with respect to what behaviors they measure, the correlations among the scores from such tests are typically quite high, and all such tests "measure a cluster of intellectual traits demanded in modern, technologically advanced, societies" (Anastasi, 1982, p. 182).

Cleary and colleagues (1975) claim that an intelligence test contains items that sample the components of their definition and that the definition is not circular because "there is a consensus among psychologists as to which kinds of behaviors are labeled intellectual" (p. 19). Although there is room for some debate about that last point, most psychologists would probably concur. The reason for potential debate is that intelligence is an "open" concept. That is, "the number of activities legitimately characterized as indicators has never been listed—would indeed hardly be capable of being listed" (Butcher, 1968, p. 27). Even if we could agree completely on a list of behaviors, we might well disagree on how these are structured. In the following subsection we discuss various theories on the *structure* of intelligence.

Recall from Chapter 4 that tests can be either *samples* or *signs*—the former if the items are drawn from a clearly defined universe, the latter if they are not. Since intelligence is an open concept and the universe of "intellectual behaviors" is not clearly or totally defined, intelligence (aptitude) tests are signs, not samples. For tests to serve as signs, we need high construct validity, and the data gathered in the process of construct validation help us to understand the concept. The reading of this chapter plus the validity information in the technical manual of any intelligence (aptitude) test being used will aid in the understanding of what is being measured by that particular test and how that information is likely to be useful.

To understand more fully the uses and misuses of the various instruments typically identified as intelligence (aptitude) tests, it is first necessary to study briefly the various theories of the structure and development of intelligence. We will curtail this discussion drastically. Whole books have been written on the subject; many of the best known are cited in the text.

Theories of Intelligence Structure

The formal movement in testing intelligence began in the latter part of the nineteenth century with Sir Francis Galton. Galton believed that tests of sensory discrimination and reaction time were estimates of intellectual functioning, and his tests were largely of this type. James McKeen Cattell, an American psychologist, also theorized that differences in sensory keenness, reaction speed, and the like would reflect differences in intellectual functioning. Cattell (1890) introduced the term *mental test* in 1890.

Binet and Henri (1896) began their research on intelligence by measuring such traits as memory, attention, and comprehension. In other words, they measured complex functions rather than the unitary characteristics (such as reaction time) previously employed. Although their research involved many different kinds of tasks, they conceptualized intelligence as a very general trait, defining it as the ability to adjust effectively to one's environment. Binet & Simon (1905) developed the first individual intelligence test (the Binet Scale), designed to be a global measure of intellectual level.

Although many other psychologists have conceptualized intelligence as a general characteristic, several opposing theories have developed. The controversy of whether mental ability can be measured meaningfully by a single score still continues. A variety of positions have been taken in the past 60 years (see McNemar, 1964; Humphreys, 1967; Resnick, 1976). Spearman (1927) developed a two-factor theory, suggesting that intelligence is composed of a general factor (g) and many specific factors (s_1, s_2, . . . s_n). Thurstone (1933) developed a theory of multiple factors (f_1, f_2, . . . f_n), which led to his test of Primary Mental Abilities. Vernon (1961) suggested a hierarchical structure of abilities, starting with a general factor that is divided into two major group factors: verbal-educational and kinesthetic-mechanical. These major group factors are a little less general than Spearman's *g*, but more general than Thurstone's group factors. Under each major group factor there are minor group factors; and under each of these are specific factors.

R. B. Cattell (1963, 1971) has proposed a theory that suggests that intelligence is composed of both a fluid component and a crystallized component. The fluid component is the more general, and a person with a large amount of fluid intelligence would do many different tasks well. It is conceptualized as an abstract, essentially nonverbal, and relatively culture-free mental efficiency. Crystallized intelligence is more closely linked to the culture or environment and represents a person's ability to achieve in more specific tasks related to the culture. It is more similar to achievement (Cattell & Horn, 1978).

Guilford (1959, 1967, 1969), in a structure-of-intellect (SOI) model, postulated many factors of intelligence. He categorized these factors under three broad dimensions according to (1) the process or operation performed, (2) the kind of product involved, and (3) the kind of material or content involved. He then subclassified under each of these dimensions five operations, six types of products, and four types of content. Seeing the three main headings as faces of a cube, he ended up with 120 (4 × 6 × 5) cells within the cube, each representing a different aspect of intelligence. Guilford claimed to have demonstrated empirically that 82 of the 120 different structure-of-intellect factors exist (Guilford, 1967). He argued that each factor should be tested separately and that tests giving a single score are somewhat misleading.

Although Guilford's SOI model received much attention, most psychologists consider it to be more of theoretical interest than of practical value. Just because the model is *logical,* it does not follow that tests could be constructed to correspond to every cell of the cube. And even if such tests could be constructed, they would not necessarily be of any value. Vernon (1964) and Hunt (1961) are both very pessimistic about the predictive value of any such tests. Hunt states flatly (p. 301) that tests of these highly specific factors have no predictive value in any situation. Some educators (for instance, Meeker, 1981) have advocated using the SOI model for *diagnostic* purposes. Theoretically, examining the profile of scores for an individual would allow strengths and weaknesses in cognitive functioning to be identified in a highly specific manner. In practice, however, the tests developed from (or scored according to) the SOI model have such severe psychometric limitations that they are better reserved for research purposes than educational or clinical purposes (Clarizio & Mehrens, 1985).

Piaget (see O'Bryan & MacArthur, 1969; Pinard & Sharp, 1972; Uzgiris & Hunt, 1975) believed that a child's intelligence develops in sequential stages, each stage identifiable by ways of thinking. He divided the evolution of thought into four major periods: sensorimotor (birth to age $1\frac{1}{2}$ or 2 years), preoperational (from $1\frac{1}{2}$ to 7), concrete operational (from 7 to 11 or 12), and formal operational (from 11 or 12 to 14 or 15).

Jensen (1968a, 1970a, 1973a, 1980) advocates a two-level theory of mental ability. Level I ability consists of rote learning and memory. It is the ability to register and retrieve information. Level II is characterized by mental manipulations, conceptualizations, reasoning, and problem solving. Level II is similar to the general factor (g) or Cattell's concept of fluid intelligence. Jensen (1980, 1982) and Jensen and Munro (1978) have revived the earlier notion of Galton's that reaction time (RT) and movement time (MT) are related to intelligence. They report a series of research findings showing that both RT (particularly choice RT) and MT correlate with scores on intelligence tests. (MT is not correlated with intelligence in normal adults but it is with children and retarded adults.) As Jensen suggests, this study of RT and its correlates "brings us closer to the interface of brain and behavior—the point at which individual differences in intelligence must ultimately be understood" (1982, p. 308).

From the preceding discussion it should be evident that there are many different theories concerning the structure of intelligence. Some theorists believe that intelligence is a general attribute; others think that there are many different aspects to intelligence. However disconcerting it may be, we must accept the fact that psychologists cannot agree on the real nature of intelligence. Although theoretical psychologists generally adopt the view that there are specific factors of intellect, most believe that is also a general factor. There are two primary reasons why many psychologists feel that the concept of general intelligence cannot be abandoned. First, whenever a whole battery of current cognitive tests is given to a sample of people, a set of positively correlated scores results. This phenomenon of correlation among separate tasks is one of the most pervasive and stable findings of psychology and "virtually forces attention to the questions of general intelligence" (Resnick, 1976, p. 7). Some individuals have suggested that we need specific ability measures that are not correlated with intelligence. Snow suggests that this is an absurd position, stating that "we simply cannot make believe that there is no such construct as intelligence reflecting variations in an organization of fairly generalized learning abilities. The concept has as much scientific status as does the concept of gravity" (1984, p. 12). Second, a general factor of intelligence is the best predictor of future general academic performance. It is primarily for the latter reason that most practical psychologists are still inclined to use tests of general intelligence.

As a result of the disagreement about the structure of intelligence, there are a wide variety of tests that are often subsumed under the phrase *intelligence tests* (as we see later, *scholastic aptitude tests* and *ability tests* are often preferred terms). They do not all measure exactly the same thing. An important implication is that when selecting and interpreting an intelligence test, the user must be completely aware of the author's definition of *intelligence*.

Etiology of Intelligence: Heredity or Environment?

Because psychologists cannot agree on what intelligence is or how many intellectual factors there are, obviously they cannot agree on the etiology of intellectual differences. The score on any test of ability is a result of how well a person performs on that instrument at a particular time. An intelligence test measures acquired behavior. An acceptance of this statement does *not* rule out genetic influence. Being able to run the 100-yard dash in 9.2 seconds is also acquired behavior, but speed may partly be genetically based. Being able to throw a 16-pound shot put 50 feet is acquired behavior, but strength may partly be genetically based. Likewise, scoring well on an intelligence test is due to acquired behavior, but intelligence may partly be genetically based.

Ignoring the possibility of chance errors for purposes of this discussion, we must ask: Why was that person able to perform as he (or she) did? Is the behavior on an aptitude test due to an individual's heredity or environment? Or does it really matter? For some purposes of testing, the preconditions affecting the test performance may not be relevant. If the purpose of a test is to use the results simply to predict some future behavior, then the question of the usefulness of the test is an empirical one. However, educators seldom wish solely to predict. In fact, as stated before, educators are, or should be, in the business of attempting to upset negative or unfavorable predictions by changing the school environment. (This is not always easy, if at all possible.) If we are effectively to change our educational process as a result of the predictive evidence, then it may well be helpful to understand why individuals perform as they do. For this reason, some understanding of the heredity-environment controversy is necessary.

A great amount of research has been done in an attempt to resolve the heredity-environment controversy. Many of these studies compared correlations of intelligence tests scores between identical or fraternal twins reared together or apart, and between other subjects hereditarily linked but in different environments. Erlenmeyer-Kimling & Jarvik (1963) reviewed 52 such studies, yielding over 30,000 correlational pairings. The average correlations of their studies are shown in Table 7.1.

Most psychologists would interpret such data as being supportive of a strong genetic base for performance on intelligence tests. Without going into detail, it may be said that by far the most popular current opinion is that there is an interaction between heredity and environment. The original question, "Which one of these factors affects an intelligence test score?" was replaced by "Which one contributes the most?" This question, in turn, has

TABLE 7.1
SUMMARY OF COMPARATIVE DATA
ON IQ CORRELATIONAL STUDIES

Category	Median Coefficient
Foster parent–child	.20
Parent–child	.50
Siblings reared together	.49
Fraternal twins	.53
Identical twins reared apart	.75
Identical twins reared together	.87

been replaced by "How do heredity and environment interact to affect test scores?" Psychologists do not yet have the complete answer to this question, and, since the publication of a paper by Jensen (1968b), some have returned to the question of *how much.* Whether heredity contributes about 80 percent to the variance of scores on an intelligence test in the population, and environment 20 percent, as some suggest, is hotly debated. (These estimates are called heritability ratios.) Schoenfeldt (1968) obtained estimates of heritability as low as 0.26 and concluded that "genetic components are not as large a proportion of the total variance as previously believed" (p. 17). Vernon (1979, p. 200) believed that research converges on the estimate that roughly 60 percent of the variance is genetic, 30 percent environmental, and 10 percent an interaction between the two. Herrnstein (1982) stated that "virtually all specialists on the heritability of IQ estimate a value somewhere in the range of 50 percent to 80 percent" (p. 72). Jensen (1984) reported that recent research in the Soviet Union, Poland, East Germany, and other communist countries obtained heritability estimates falling between 0.60 and 0.80. Jensen finds these data "virtually indistinguishable from those of behavioral-genetic researchers in capitalist countries" (p. 462).

The debates about heritability ratios arise partly because psychologists look at different mathematical formulas in computing the ratios. Although we cannot delve into those problems in this text, we can discuss briefly some pitfalls in interpreting these ratios. First, it must be emphasized that these are *estimates* of the proportion of the total *variance* (see Chapter 2) of a trait (say, intelligence) that is attributable to heredity in a *population* of people. Such a ratio tells us nothing about what proportion of a *single* individual's intelligence is due to heredity, nor can that be determined. Jensen (1969a), for example, states this clearly. Since the heritability ratios apply to populations, each applies only to a particular population at a particular point in time. As social conditions vary, so should heritability estimates. For example, if all U.S. citizens lived in environments that were *equal* (not necessarily identical) in their impact on intellectual development, then none of the variance in the intellectual differences could be due to environment; all would be due to genetic differences, and the heritability ratio would be 1.0. If our environments are becoming more equal, then the heritability ratio should be getting higher. Some environmentalists have trouble accepting this mathematical fact. They would like to have environments (with respect to impact on intellectual development) become more equal but hate to think of the proportion of variability as being increasingly genetic in origin.

Some individuals like to ignore the heritability-estimates debate entirely. Since both genetics and environment contribute to our intelligence, and since they interact in this contribution, these individuals argue that it is pointless to talk about which factor contributes most. No one would suggest that the nervous system in immune from genetic influence. Likewise, no reputable writer would suggest that a person's environment does not at least partially influence his or her score on an intelligence test. Such things as malnutrition or prolonged intellectual deprivation in the home environment, especially early in life, can inflict severe damage on intellectual growth.

One final point needs to be made. Many people seem to feel that it is better to accept the environmental side of the debate because it is more optimistic. If individuals have a poor environment, we can change that and thereby increase their intelligence. If intelligence is genetically based, it is unchangeable. *Neither of these statements is necessarily true.* Severe environmental deprivation can inflict permanent damage (see Ausubel, 1968, p. 246). And even if the damage is not necessarily permanent, it does not follow that we know enough about how to manipulate the environment to succeed in reversing the damage. Likewise, *genetic* does not mean *unchangeable*. A classic example is the low intelligence resulting from phenylketonuria (PKU), a gene-based disease. Special diets low in amino acid phenylalanine prevent the accumulation of toxic metabolic products in the brain, and intelligence can develop to a fairly normal level. Remember, high heritability of a trait should not be automatically equated with a low level of modifiability.

Social Class, Race, and Intelligence   It has long been known that relationships exist between social class and intelligence and race and intelligence. The reasons for these relationships have been much debated. The linkages conceivably could be due to genetic factors, environmental factors, test bias, or any combination of the three.

Jensen (1968b) published an article "Social Class, Race, and Genetics: Implications for Education" in the *American Educational Research Journal*. A year later he published an invited paper on the same general topic in the *Harvard Educational Review* (Jensen, 1969a). These papers have caused more public controversy among educators and psychologists than any other two articles in recent history. The subsequent issue of the *Harvard Educational Review* carried rebuttals by other psychologists and a rejoinder by Jensen. The whole series of papers has been reprinted in paperback book form (*Harvard Educational Review*, 1969). Other references on this same topic are Jensen (1970b, 1973a,b, 1980), Eysenck (1971, 1979), Herrnstein (1971), Shockley (1971, 1972), Gage (1972), Block & Dworkin (1974a,b), Kamin (1974), and Cronin et al. (1975). As Loehlin et al. (1975, p. 3) point out, when questions on social class, race, and intelligence are examined in a society riddled with unresolved tensions in these areas, "it is not surprising that the result should be a massive polemic in which personal conviction and emotional commitment often have been more prominent than evidence or careful reasoning." It is difficult to discuss the controversy raised by the Jensen papers, especially in a brief space, without being misunderstood— and we certainly do not wish to be misunderstood on such an important and emotional issue. Jensen's original papers were scholarly reviews of the available evidence on causes of intellectual differences. Jensen came to the conclusion that within the white race, the heritability index (the proportion of variance on intelligence test scores due to genetic reasons) is about .80. This conclusion parallels that of many other investigators, but of course is not accepted by all.

Correlations between socioeconomic status (SES) and scores on intelligence tests within a race are typically around .3 (see Coleman et al., 1966; Jensen, 1980). This is not as high as many people seem to believe. Most psychologists believe that at least part of this correlation is due to genetics. That is, groups differing in SES would, on the average, differ in their genetic endowment of intelligence.

The major types of *evidence* supporting the position that differences in SES are related to genetic differences in intelligence are of course indirect but include such findings as (1) children who score lower on intelligence tests than their fathers go down in social class, whereas those who score higher go up in social class (Waller, 1971) and (2) childhood intelligence determines about three times more of the variance of adult educational level than the father's educational and occupational levels combined (Li, 1975).

Briefly, the rationale for the belief that SES is related to genetic differences in intelligence is as follows: If social mobility is in part a function of individual differences in ability, which in turn are in part genetically based, then status differences will tend to be associated with genetic differences. As Loehlin et al. (1975, p. 167) point out, this is not (contrary to what some people think) an assertion of heredity castes, as in an aristocracy. It is quite the opposite, since social mobility is the *key* to the genetic sorting out process in each generation.

In general, the position on the relationship between SES and intelligence has not been attacked (Eckland, 1967; Gottesman, 1968; Herrnstein, 1973) by psychologists, although some social critics seem to feel that intelligence tests serve the (perhaps intentional) purpose of preserving social class privileges (see Bowles & Gintles, 1974). This criticism, of course, ignores evidence such as that presented by Waller and Li. Further, it ignores one of the original purposes of such tests. Originally, testing was cherished by those who hoped test use would result in one's birth, family, wealth, and connections counting for less and merit counting for more. Indeed, the evidence shows that is what has occurred.

The issue of the causes of the relationship between race and intelligence is much more controversial. Jensen, for example, has argued as follows:

> *There is an increasing realization among students of the psychology of the disadvantaged that the discrepancies in their average performance cannot be completely or directly attributed to discrimination or inequalities in education. It seems not unreasonable, in view of the fact that intelligence variation has a large genetic component, to hypothesize that genetic factors may play a part in this picture. But such an hypothesis is anathema to many social scientists. The idea that the lower average intelligence and scholastic performance of Negroes could involve, not only environmental, but also genetic, factors has indeed been strongly denounced (e.g., Pettigrew, 1964). But it has been neither contradicted nor discredited by evidence.*
>
> *The fact that a reasonable hypothesis has not been rigorously proved does not mean that it should be summarily dismissed . . . the preponderance of the evidence is, in my opinion, less consistent with a strictly environmental hypothesis than with a genetic hypothesis, which, of course,* does not exclude the influence of environment or its interaction with genetic factors *[italics added]. (1969a, p. 82)*

Some people have agreed with Jensen, and some have attacked his position with vigor. Many did not see how evidence on heritability could provide a basis for social or educational policy. Cronbach stated that Jensen "does not see that, in writings for educators, it is pointless to stress heredity. The educator's job is to work on the environment; teaching him about heredity can do no more than warn him not to expect easy victories. Heritability of individual differences is not his concern" (1969, p. 197).

Jensen countered this point as follows.

> *I submit that the research on the inheritance of mental abilities is relevant to understanding educational problems and formulating educational policies. For one thing, it means that we take individual differences more seriously than regarding them as superficial, easily changed manifestations of environmental differences. (1969a, p. 239)*

Anastasi (1973), who leans toward the environmental position, agrees with Jensen on the *importance* of the topic. "It is only through a clear understanding of the operations of hereditary and environmental factors in behavior development that we can contribute toward effective decisions for the individual and for society" (p. 9).

Those interested in further exploring opinions on this topic should refer to Mackenzie (1984) and Loehlin et al. (1975). Several reviewers have considered the work of Loehlin and colleagues to be one of the most comprehensive and balanced reviews of the race and intelligence issue so far published. Their "final" conclusions are as follows:

1. *Observed average differences in the scores of members of different U.S. racial-ethnic groups on intellectual-ability tests probably reflect in part inadequacies and biases in the tests themselves, in part differences in environmental conditions among the groups, and in part genetic differences among the groups. It should be emphasized that these three factors are not necessarily independent, and may interact.*
2. *A rather wide range of positions concerning the relative weight to be given these three factors can reasonably be taken on the basis of current evidence, and a sensible person's position might well differ for different abilities, for different groups, and for different tests.*
3. *Regardless of the position taken on the relative importance of these three factors, it seems clear that the differences among individuals within racial-ethnic (and socioeconomic) groups greatly exceed in magnitude the average differences between such groups. (Loehlin et al., 1975, p. 239)*

These authors follow these conclusions with what they believe to be several social and public policy implications. Two of these are as follows:

1. Given the large overlap in ability distributions, it would be both unjust and incorrect to label individual members of one group as inferior to members of another.
2. Although measured intelligence is an important variable, we must always remember that it is very far from being all-important in determining what life will be like for most persons in the United States at the present time. It is easy to make too much of these differences—whatever their origin.

Much *incontestable* evidence demonstrates that there is considerable overlap between groups. Jensen himself argues strongly that his paper is concerned only with *group* differences. Every psychologist knows that we *cannot* draw *any* definite conclusions about an individual's intelligence on the basis of race or socioeconomic class. Unfortunately, some individuals, including teachers and counselors, do this, but it is hoped that readers of this book will not be among those. A wider discussion of how this problem affects testing and what steps have been taken to adjust for cultural differences is found in a later section ("Culture-Fair Tests of Intelligence") and in Chapter 12.

Stability of Intelligence

Because intelligence is now generally considered to be influenced by both heredity and environment, it logically follows that as a person's environment changes, so might intelligence—or so at least might his or her score on an intelligence test, which is an operational definition of intelligence.

The extent to which intelligence is a stable or variable construct is very important. If there were no stability to intelligence test scores, then the test would be a useless instrument. On the other hand, if intelligence test scores were completely stable, then we might adopt fatalistic attitudes concerning a student's educational prognosis.

Research findings suggest that intelligence test scores are very unstable during the early years of a person's life. (See Bloom [1964, pp. 52–94] and McCall, Appelbaum, & Hogarty [1973] for excellent reviews of the longitudinal research.) Bayley (1949) found no relationship between intelligence measured at age 1 and age 17. Generally, preschool tests administered after the age of 2 have moderate validity in predicting subsequent intelligence test performance, but infant tests have almost none (see, for example, McCall, Hogarty, & Hurlburt, 1972).

Certainly the tested intelligence of children under 4 years old is quite unstable.[1] It is hard to know whether this instability is caused primarily by imprecise measuring instruments, trait instability, or both. With increased age, the stability of intelligence test performance increases rapidly. Bayley (1949) found a correlation of .71 between mental age at age of 4 and at age 17. "This justifies our taking preschool IQ's seriously" (Cronbach, 1970, p. 231). In general, longitudinal studies have suggested that intelligence is a fairly stable characteristic after age 5. Bayley (1949) found the correlations between intelligence tests' scores at ages 11 and 17 to be .92.

Most of the research on the stability of intelligence has used individual intelligence tests. Longitudinal research using group verbal and nonverbal tests shows that (1) below age 10 stability in group test scores is less than for individual tests, (2) verbal group test scores are more stable than nonverbal scores, and (3) after grade 7 there is hardly any difference between the stability of individual and group verbal tests (Hopkins & Bracht, 1975).

In spite of the reasonably high stability coefficients for groups of children, individuals may show considerable growth or decline in intelligence test scores. Honzik, Macfarlane, & Allen (1948) reported that between ages 6 and 18, the scores of 59 percent of the children changed by 15 or more IQ points. Studies such as this should impress upon us the fact that, although scores on intelligence tests are reasonably stable and therefore useful as *guides* in both short- and long-term decision making, scores can and do fluctuate, and permanent decisions (or labeling) should not be made solely on the basis of intelligence test performance.

Several books (see, for example, Engelmann & Engelmann, 1968) and a

---

[1] Data such as these have led one colleague to suggest that the best estimate we can obtain of a young child's intelligence is to take the average of the parents' intelligence. One would not have to lean heavily toward the hereditarian position to make this statement. Familial characteristics may be just as much due to environment as to heredity.

few research studies (see Pines, 1969) have suggested that through proper intensive early stimulation, one can succeed in raising the intelligence of children. One study conducted by Hunt reported that having mothers of disadvantaged children watch the administration of intelligence tests and afterward coach their children on the test items resulted in an average gain of 30 IQ points (Pines, 1969). One must be very careful about drawing any conclusions from such data, which may be misleading to both theoreticians and practitioners. Biehler offered the following analogy to help clarify the point.

> *Assume . . . that a particular child has extremely poor vision. If you helped this child memorize the materials used in testing his vision, would you be improving his sight? With training he could pass the test with a perfect score, but would he see any better? What might happen if on the basis of the test the child was placed in a situation in which he had to have perfect vision? Would he be able to perform satisfactorily? Or would it make more sense to get an* accurate *estimate of his sight and assist him to make the most of the actual vision he possessed? (1971, p. 447)*

Besides the problem of teaching to the test, there has been some professional concern about the adequacy of the research and the inability to replicate the studies showing that early intervention produces any major changes in intelligence test scores. Also, there have been reservations expressed regarding "the ease with which tentative information may become virtual fact" (Sommer & Sommer, 1983, p. 983). For example, the Milwaukee Project, begun in the late 1960s, reported an average difference of 24 IQ points between an experimental group and a matched comparison sample of children who had not been given an enrichment program. An investigation by Sommer & Sommer showed that this research was widely discussed in textbooks even though the original findings were never subjected to journal review and have not been replicated. Moreover, according to a review by Herrnstein (1982), the "media seem unwilling to publish anything that might challenge the certitude with which editors, politicians, judges, and others insist that we know how to increase measurable intelligence" (p. 71).

Ignoring the poor research, and the research based on direct teaching for the test, there is some evidence suggesting that a *marked* change in environmental conditions is needed to affect a test score greatly after the first five formative years. This is one reason why there has been so much emphasis on programs such as Project Head Start, Sesame Street, and Electric Company.

There also has been some controversy concerning the stability of adult intelligence. Wechsler (1955), testing a cross-sectional sample of adults, found that the verbal aspects of intelligence increase until age 30 and then begin gradually to diminish. However, his method of sampling was somewhat faulty because the educational levels of the various age groups were not comparable. The younger groups had a higher educational level than the older groups, and this could have accounted for the differences he found. Bayley (1955), using longitudinal evidence, concluded that there is continued intellectual growth until 50. A safe conclusion would be that general intellectual functioning does not automatically decrease with age. The environment of adults may serve to increase or decrease their intellectual performance, but barring health problems, 50-year-old men and women may well have as much intellectual ability as they had at age 25 (Jarvik, Eisdorfer, & Blum, 1973). Of course we do not mean to deny the evidence suggesting that if one lives long enough, a decrease in at least some intellectual characteristics is likely to occur. But decrement is not a necessary concomitant of aging and is not caused by aging per se (see Baltes & Schaie, 1976; Horn & Donaldson, 1976).

Intelligence, Aptitude, Ability, or Achievement

The terms *aptitude, ability, intelligence,* and *achievement* are used interchangeably by some, while others suggest that subtle shades of meaning distinguish them. The first three terms are usually considered to have the most meaning in common.

The difference between the terms *aptitude* and *intelligence* is not at all clear, but some distinctions have been made on two separate bases. One distinction is whether the measure we obtain is considered a *general* measure. If so, the test is frequently called an intelligence test. If the test measures *multiple* or *specific* factors, it is more apt to be termed an aptitude test. Thus, we might conceptualize different measures of intelligence (aptitude) as lying on a continuum, with global measures falling at one end and specific measures at the other. At some point along the continuum we could arbitrarily change the label of the construct we are measuring, from intelligence to aptitude. Although this schema has been suggested by some, it certainly is not universally followed. It does present some difficulties, because some tests are considered measures of a general factor, yet report subscores.

Another distinction between the meaning of the two terms has a historical basis. During the time intelligence tests were first being developed, many psychologists thought of intelligence as being an innate characteristic not subject to change. This assumption is invalid. However, the term *intelligence* unfortunately still connotes complete innateness to some people. To avoid the implications of innateness, many test makers prefer to use the term *aptitude*. Because such aptitude tests are most useful in predicting future school success, some have suggested that the phrase *scholastic aptitude tests* is the most honest and descriptive. Others prefer to refer to all such tests as measures of learning ability.

Test publishers seem generally to agree with those using the terms with a more narrow meaning. Thus they have modified the titles of their tests, moving in general away from the terms *intelligence* and *aptitude* and toward the use of the term *ability*. For example, the *Otis-Lennon School Ability Test* was previously referred to as the *Otis-Lennon Mental Ability Test*. The *Cognitive Abilities Test* was previously called an intelligence test, and the *Short Form Test of Academic Aptitude* was previously called a mental maturity test (Lennon, 1980). Yet, as Lennon (1980) points out, "there is a certain equivocation or ambivalence on the part of their [the tests'] authors as to whether the tests continue to be intelligence or mental ability tests, or should be regarded only as measures of school learning ability" (p. 3).

As mentioned, aptitude, ability, and intelligence are probably considered more similar to each other than they are to achievement. Whether aptitude and achievement should be thought of as separate concepts has been the subject of much debate. Kelley defined the *jangle fallacy* as "the use of two separate words or expressions covering in fact the same basic situation, but sounding different, as though they were in truth different" (1927, p. 64). He believed that intelligence and achievement tests were examples of the jangle fallacy. Many psychologists from his time to the present have also believed that the two types of tests are quite similar. Carroll (1974, p. 287), however, notes that we must distinguish between aptitude as a *construct* and *indicants* of aptitude. He states:

> *[I]t is difficult to see why there should be any great difficulty in distinguishing between aptitude and achievement as concepts . . . if aptitude for a learning task is measured prior to an individual's engaging in a task, and if achievement on the task is measured after a given amount of exposure to the learning task, the concepts of aptitude and achievement are operationally distinguishable. (Carroll, 1974, p. 287)*

Whether or not, or to what extent, the *measures* of aptitude and achievement differ is more debatable. Kaiser (1974, pp. 345–346), for example, believes that the measures might well be different based on what he admits are two very nonscientific sources:

> 1. *I have been writing test items . . . for more than 20 years, and I know damn good and well when I am writing an achievement item. . . .*
> 2. *Over the years I have consulted with approximately 40 million teachers . . . and all of them, without exception, firmly believe that achievement relative to aptitude can be measured; indeed, they claim to measure it all the time. . . . Can 40 million teachers be wrong? Not completely, is my guess.*

There is certainly no hard-and-fast rule that allows us to distinguish an achievement test from an aptitude test by cursory examination of the test format. Further, both tests do measure behavior, and the behavior measured is acquired rather than innate. However, aptitude and achievement tests do frequently differ along several dimensions:

1. General aptitude tests typically have broader coverage than achievement tests.
2. Achievement tests are more closely tied to particular school subjects.
3. Aptitude test items are more likely to be ones that are dependent upon maturational level (such as copying a diamond) than achievement test items.
4. Achievement tests typically measure recent learning, whereas aptitude tests sample learning from all times in the individual's past.
5. Studies generally show that aptitude tests have higher heritability indices than achievement tests.
6. The purpose of aptitude tests is to predict future performance; the purpose of achievement tests is to measure the present level of knowledge or skills.

It has often been said that the best way to predict future performance is to examine past performance. If this is true and if aptitude tests are best able to predict future scholastic success, how do they differ from achievement tests? The common distinction that achievement tests measure what a pupil has learned (or past learning activities) and that aptitude tests measure ability to learn new tasks (or future performance) breaks down if past learning is the best predictor of future learning.

Thus, some people suggest that the difference is not in what the tests do but in the author's purpose and method of constructing the test. A certain achievement test may be a better predictor than a particular aptitude test for some specified purpose. If, however, the author originally constructed the test for the purpose of predicting future performance, then the test is called an aptitude test. If the purpose of the author is to measure recent learning, then the test is considered an achievement test, even though it may well be a very successful predictive instrument.

Aptitude and achievement tests are sometimes classified according to the degree to which the tasks within a test are dependent upon formal school learning. For example, a test of knowledge in English, mathematics, or science would be considered an achievement test. A test of abstract reasoning abilities based on figure analogies would be considered an aptitude test. Since most vocabulary is learned in everyday contexts rather than through direct instruction, vocabulary tests are likely to be considered aptitude tests (Sternberg, 1984). Obviously, the distinction is a matter of degree. Some aptitude tests are more like achievement tests than others. As the test tasks become more and more dependent upon specific educational instruction, the test becomes more and more an achievement test. Thus, we have a continuation of the distinction between the terms *achievement* and *aptitude* on the innate–environmental continuum. Being more dependent on specific school instruction, achievement tests are more environmentally influenced than aptitude tests.

In Chapter 5 we mentioned that publishers of some tests provide expectancy scores. These are derived scores that indicate the expected score on an achievement test based on a scholastic aptitude test score. *Discrepancy scores* are sometimes computed showing the difference between actual achievement and expected achievement. This information may be useful for evaluation purposes. Publishers providing such scores should be using aptitude measures that are as independent of specific instruction as possible. Further, they need to explain carefully in their manuals the differences they perceive in the two constructs and the (typically low) reliability of the discrepancy scores.

In summary, several possible distinctions have been suggested between aptitude tests and achievement tests. An author whose purpose is to develop a predictive instrument will no doubt call it an aptitude test. If the purpose is to develop an instrument to measure past performance, it will be called an achievement test. For the latter goal the test items will be based on past school instruction; for the former goal, that may or may not be the case. However, regardless of what an author calls a test, its uses may vary. Many achievement tests, like aptitude tests, are used to predict. This is ordinarily quite appropriate. However, aptitude tests are certainly better at predicting general academic performance, and because they typically take much less time to administer, they do it more efficiently.

Classification of Aptitude Tests

Aptitude tests can be classified in a variety of ways. One classification is verbal versus performance (language versus nonlanguage) tests. Although the verbal tests and language tests have similar connotations, performance tests and nonlanguage tests can be quite different. A performance test usually requires the subject to manipulate objects to complete a specified task. (An example might be to fit a puzzle together.) Nonlanguage tests are those in which the subject is not required to use or understand the language. However, the subject need not be required to manipulate objects in a nonlanguage test. In spite of their differences, performance tests and nonlanguage tests are alike in that both are relatively independent of specific educational instruction. Test authors, however, do not always use these terms as appropriately as they should. In order to determine what a test demands, one should look at both the items themselves and the test manual, not only at the name of the tests or subtests.

For purposes of discussion, aptitude tests are subdivided into four categories: (1) individually administered tests that give a general measure of intelligence[2] (or aptitude), (2) group-administered tests that give a general measure

---

[2] The use of the term *intelligence* in no way implies that the authors of this book believe that intelligence test scores are solely measures of an innate characteristic. We know that is not true.

of aptitude, (3) tests that give measures of multiple aptitudes, and (4) tests that are measures of some specific kind of aptitude.

Individuals are often looking for a single measure of ability that will enable them to make a general prediction about future vocational or educational success. Tests of general intelligence best suit this purpose. For those wishing to make differential predictions, then a multiple aptitude test might be better. If they wish to predict success in a specific vocation or course, a specific aptitude test may be most appropriate. The following four sections are devoted to a consideration of the four categories just mentioned.

INDIVIDUALLY ADMINISTERED TESTS
OF GENERAL INTELLIGENCE (APTITUDE)

For the most part, educational institutions, business, and industry make use of group tests of scholastic aptitude. However, it is occasionally more appropriate to administer an individual intelligence test. All individual tests are valuable as clinical instruments. An examiner can observe the examinees' approach to problem solving, their reaction to stress, and their general test-taking behavior patterns, thereby having the opportunity to gain valuable information. Individual administration allows the psychologist not only to observe more closely but also to control the behavior of the individual. This generally leads to more reliable measurement and a better understanding of the factors underlying the subject's behavior.

Control, as used here, has a positive connotation. Process variables, such as the motivational level of the examinee, should be controlled. The outcome variables (responses) may also be controlled somewhat. However, this can be overdone. The amount of freedom a test administrator has in clarifying the questions so as to elicit the proper response is, appropriately, somewhat limited. When we suggest that individual administration leads to more reliable behavior, we are, of course, assuming that the test is correctly administered. Test scores could vary as a result of variability among administrators. However, reliability of administrators is high if they are correctly trained.

The most popular individual intelligence tests are the Stanford-Binet and the various Wechsler tests. A fairly new test, the Kaufman-ABC, is being heavily promoted and shows promise of becoming quite popular. These instruments, as well as examples of some infant and preschool scales and some performance scales, are discussed in this section. However, because this book is designed to serve only as an introduction to standardized tests, these individual tests are not covered in great detail. For fuller coverage of individual intelligence tests, see Anastasi, 1982. Proper administration of individual tests requires a great deal of training. To be adequately trained, a person needs a basic knowledge of psychology, in addition to at least one course in individual testing with much practice under supervision.

Stanford-Binet

The present Stanford-Binet test is an outgrowth of the original Binet-Simon Scales. As previously mentioned, Binet was convinced that measures of simple sensory and motor processes were of little value as measures of intelligence. When Binet was charged with the task of identifying the mentally deficient children in the Paris schools, he collaborated with Simon to publish the 1905 scale, which consisted of 30 tasks of higher mental processes arranged in order of difficulty. This scale was revised in 1908 and the tasks were grouped into age levels. For this reason, the Binet is referred to as an age scale. Thus, the score of a child could be expressed as a mental age. The test was again revised in 1911.

Although several American revisions of these scales were published in the United States, the one that gained the most popularity was the Stanford revision, published in 1916 (Terman, 1916). A second Stanford revision appeared in 1937, and a third revision in 1960 (Terman & Merrill, 1937, 1960). A new set of norms was published for the third edition in 1972. All three revisions followed essentially the same format. A series of tasks was designed at each of several age levels. For average individuals, administrators start at a level just below the chronological age of the subject. They then work downward, if necessary, to lower age levels until the subjects pass all the tasks within that age level, called the *basal* age. Examiners then proceed upward from their original starting place to a level at which the subjects miss all the tasks, called the *ceiling* age. An individual's total score (mental age) is computed by adding to the basal age appropriate weights for the items answered correctly up to the ceiling age.

The 1960 edition of the Stanford-Binet Form L-M (with its 1972 norms) is not really a revision but a combination of the best items of the two forms of the 1937 edition. It groups the tasks into age levels ranging from age 2 to superior adult. In the Stanford-Binet the emphasis is placed on the knowledge of words and the comprehension of written material throughout the test—especially at the higher age levels. The few instances of performance-type items are to be found at the lower age levels. In addition, scattered at the various age levels are tests designed to measure memory and ability to follow directions.

Intelligence scores using the 1972 norms are computed as deviation IQ scores with a mean of 100 and a standard deviation of 16. In other words, they are derived scores (Dev IQ = $16z + 100$). One can also obtain mental ages (MAs) for the Stanford-Binet. These are obtained using the same procedures as in the 1960 and 1937 editions.

By most technical standards, the Stanford-Binet is a soundly constructed instrument. Most of the reported reliability coefficients are over .90. They do, however, tend to be somewhat lower for the younger subjects. This test, like other intelligence tests, is most useful in predicting future scholastic success. The predictive and concurrent validity coefficients using such criteria as school grades and achievement test scores tend to fall between .40 and .75.

Perhaps the most limiting aspect of the test is that it is primarily a measure of verbal ability. Another drawback is that some of the tasks are somewhat outdated. Recall that the 1960 revision used items from the 1937 scale. The popularity of the test is indisputable. Thorndike (1975) reports that from 1960 to 1972 the test was administered to about 800,000 persons a year. The amount of research done on the Stanford-Binet can be attested to by the fact that Mitchell (1983) lists 1793 references to professional journals and books regarding the test.

The fourth edition of the Stanford-Binet Intelligence Scale is scheduled to be published in 1986 by the Riverside Publishing Company. The authors of the new revision are Robert L. Thorndike, Elizabeth P. Hagen, and Jerome M. Sattler, all well-known leaders in the measurement of intelligence. In a draft manual (Thorndike et al., n.d.) the authors suggested that the 1960 edition had two major strengths. One was its adaptive-testing format and the other was that it provided a continuous scale for measuring cognitive development from ages 2 through 18. Both of these features have been retained. The major weakness of the third edition was that no theoretical model of intelligence was used in constructing the scale.

The fourth edition is built on a model of intelligence that allows for an analysis of the pattern as well as the overall level of an individual's cognitive development. The theory is similar to both Vernon's (1961) and Cattell's (1963) theories discussed earlier. The test is based on a three-level hierarchical model with a general reasoning factor (g); three broad factors (crystallized abilities, fluid-analytic abilities, and short-term memory); and three more specific factors (verbal reasoning, quantitative reasoning, and visualization). There are a total of 15 tests for the fourth edition—nine have evolved from previously used item types and six tests are based on new item types. Figure 7.1 depicts the theoretical model and the 15 different tests. Separate scores will be available for each of the 15 tests plus a verbal reasoning score, an abstract/visual reasoning score, a quantitative reasoning score, a short-term memory score, and a complete composite score.

Because the test has not been actually published at the time of this writing, it is obviously too soon to speculate on its acceptance or its psychometric features. The authors suggest that because of the adaptive testing format and wide range of item difficulties, the test will be particularly effective for appraising people at both the lowest and highest extremes of cognitive development.

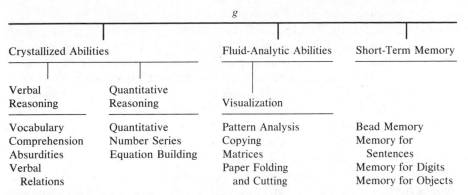

Figure 7.1 Cognitive ability factors appraised in the fourth edition of the Stanford-Binet

Wechsler Scales

The major competitors of the Stanford-Binet are the Wechsler Scales. The first form of the Wechsler Scales, published in 1939, was known as the Wechsler-Bellevue Intelligence Scale. This scale was specifically designed as a measure of adult intelligence. The Wechsler Intelligence Scale for Children (WISC) was first published in 1949 and was revised (WISC-R) in 1974. The original WISC was designed for ages 5 through 15; WISC-R spans the ages 6 through 16. In 1955 the Wechsler-Bellevue was revised and renamed the Wechsler Adult Intelligence Scale (WAIS). It was revised in 1981 and is currently referred to as the WAIS-R. The Wechsler Preschool and Primary Scale of Intelligence (WPPSI) was published in 1967 and is designed for children of ages 4 to 6½.

WAIS-R   The WAIS-R (for ages 16 to 74) is composed of 11 subtests grouped into two scales: Verbal and Performance. The verbal scale consists of six subtests: Information, Digit Span, Vocabulary, Arithmetic, Comprehension, and Similarities. The five performance scale subtests are Picture Completion, Picture Arrangement, Block Design, Object Assembly, and Digit Symbol.

An individual's score is based on the number of items answered correctly. For this reason, the WAIS-R is referred to as a *point scale*. (The items are not classified by age level, as in the Binet.) Each subtest score is expressed in comparable units, permitting intra- and interindividual comparisons. Deviation IQ scores with means of 100 and standard deviations of 15 can also be obtained for the Verbal and Performance Scales as well as for the total. An interesting aspect of these deviation IQ scores is that they are obtained separately for different age groups. IQs were computed separately for different age groups intentionally so that, even if intelligence does decline with age, the average intelligence scores for each age group are equated. The norms sample for the WAIS-R was controlled for sex, race, geographical region, occupation, and education.

The WAIS-R is considered to give a very reliable total score measure of adult intelligence. The separate subtests, being quite short, have lower reliabilities. Because the intent of Wechsler was to get a total or global measure of intelligence, he suggested that a profile interpretation of the scales for normal subjects would not be meaningful. There is some debate about the use of the subtest scores as clinical data. A limitation of the WAIS-R is that it has a rather high floor and low ceiling, making it a poor measure of extremely high or low levels of intelligence. Many studies support the usefulness of the test in predicting various criteria. Unfortunately, validity data are not included in the manual.

WISC-R   The WISC-R (for ages 6 through 16) follows the same format as the WAIS-R, giving subtest scores and verbal, performance, and total IQs. The WISC-R contains 12 subtests. Two of these (Mazes and Digit Span) are used only as alternates. The 10 commonly used subtests are Information, Similarities, Arithmetic, Vocabulary, Comprehension (these comprise the verbal scale), and Picture Completion, Picture Arrangement, Block Design, Object Assembly, and Coding (these make up the performance scale). The first five listed are scored on the verbal scale, and the last five listed under the performance scale. Actual administration alternates verbal and performance subscales. The norms sample for the WISC-R was stratified on age, sex, race, geographic region, and occupation of head of household. Like the WAIS-R, no validity data are in the manual.

WPPSI   The WPPSI (for ages 4 to $6\frac{1}{2}$) contains 11 subtests, one of which is an alternate. Eight of these are downward extensions of WISC subtests. Sentences replace Digit Span in the Verbal section, and Animal House and Geometric Design replace Picture Arrangement and Object Assembly in the Performance section.

WPPSI has been standardized on a sample that includes 14 percent nonwhites. Its biggest faults are that (1) it is too difficult for the lowest performing 4-year-olds and (2) the test is somewhat long for young children.

Kaufman ABC (K-ABC)

The Kaufman Assessment Battery for Children (K-ABC), published by American Guidance Service in 1983, is an individually administered test for children from ages $2\frac{1}{2}$ to $12\frac{1}{2}$ years. It is somewhat different in scope, format, and process from the Stanford-Binet and Wechsler Scales. The K-ABC provides standard scores with a mean of 100 and standard deviation of 15 for four global areas: sequential processing, simultaneous processing, mental processing composite (sum of previous two), and achievement. The distinction the authors make between the mental processing and achievement scales is much like Cattell's (1971) distinction between fluid and crystallized abilities (see p. 162).

There are a total of 16 subtests across the various ages, but a maximum of 13 is administered to any one child. At age $2\frac{1}{2}$ only 7 subtests are administered. The total set of subtests are as follows:

Sequential Processing Scale
  Hand Movements, Number Recall, Word Order
Simultaneous Processing Scale
  Magic Window, Face Recognition, Gestalt Closure, Triangles, Matrix Analogies, Spatial Memory, Photo Series
Achievement Scale
  Expressive Vocabulary, Faces & Places, Arithmetic, Riddles, Reading/ Decoding, Reading/Understanding

All of the achievement subtests also use standard scores ($\bar{X} = 100$, $S_x = 15$), but the mental processing subtests report what the authors term *derived scores*, with a mean of 10 and a standard deviation of 3.

The K-ABC also provides national percentile ranks and stanines, subtest age equivalent scores, arithmetic and reading grade equivalents, and sociocultural percentile ranks.

The K-ABC has met with mixed reviews. Mehrens (1984) felt it was a good test. His review noted some particularly noteworthy features including (1) the theoretical bases for the test, (2) the completeness of the manuals, and (3) discussions on the statistical significance and psychological significance of difference scores. Some limitations Mehrens listed had to do with (1) incomplete normative data, (2) the lack of any long-term stability reliability data, (3) lack of clarity in how to use the sociocultural norms, and (4) a lack of definition of *bias*. (The authors imply that bias is a lack of differences in means across ethnic groups.)

Hopkins & Hodge (1984) give the K-ABC a somewhat more negative review and conclude that the "K-ABC fails in its attempt to improve on current measures, and may not have done as well" (p. 107).

The fall 1984 issue of *The Journal of Special Education* is devoted to a close look at the K-ABC. This issue should be consulted by those who have a special interest in this new test.

Individual Performance Scales

A test is called a *performance* test if the tasks require a manipulation of objects (for example, making geometrical configurations with blocks) rather than an oral or written response. This type of test is most helpful in assessing the level of intellectual functioning for people who have language or communication difficulties. Those who speak only a foreign language, who are deaf or illiterate, or who have any type of speech or reading disability are unable to perform adequately on the instruments discussed in the preceding section. In some instances, then, performance scales must be used as replacements for other tests. It should be pointed out, however, that performance scales were originally conceived as supplements to, rather than substitutes for, the more verbally weighted tests. Some examples of performance scales are the Pintner-Patterson Scale, the Cornell-Coxe Scale, the Arthur Point Scale, the Cattell Infant Intelligence Scale, the Merrill-Palmer Scales (for preschoolers aged 2 and up), and the Leiter Adult Intelligence Scale. Although a variety of tasks can be, and are, used, some of the more commonly used subtests require (1) manipulating small objects to form designs, (2) tracing and copying, (3) solving mazes or puzzles, (4) following simple directions, and (5) completing formboards.

Performance scales are most useful with young children and/or the mentally retarded, because verbal tests are not very accurate for these groups. Although scales of this kind can be very helpful in assessing the level of intellectual functioning, they are not very predictive of immediate scholastic success and are therefore seldom used in the schools.[3] If they are used, they should be given only by qualified personnel.

Infant and Preschool Mental Tests

As mentioned earlier, the measures of intelligence prior to age 5 do not correlate very well with the measures obtained at a later point in a person's life. McCall's (1980) summary suggests that scores from tests given during the first 6 months of life essentially are uncorrelated with later scores. At ages 7 to 12 months, the scores correlate about .26; at 13 to 18 months, about .40; and at 19 to 30 months, about .50. These somewhat low correlations are not entirely due to imprecision of the measuring instruments. (Split-half and alternate form reliabilities of the tests used at early ages are reasonably high.) The low correlations between earlier and later testings of intelligence are also caused by the instability of the construct of intelligence from early childhood to adult and/or the nonidentity of the constructs being measured.[4] That is, the change in intelligence test scores may occur because the construct of intelligence is affected radically by environmental conditions; or the change may occur because the tasks on intelligence tests, being different at different age levels, actually measure different aspects of intelligence; or the

---

[3] Performance tests measure abilities that are different from those measured by verbal tests such as the Stanford-Binet. Correlations between verbal and performance tests range from .50 to .80.

[4] Because the constructs measured at two different ages may, indeed, be different, many people would speak of the low correlation over time as a lack of validity rather than a lack of stability reliability.

change may occur because of a combination of these and other factors that are continually interacting. For example, preschool tests are performance tests rather than paper-and-pencil tests. Is, then, a change in score the result of a qualitative or a quantitative change in mental functioning? The question is a difficult one to answer, and the answer one gives depends in part upon which theory of the structure of intellect one accepts (Stott & Ball, 1965).

Doing experimental research and armchair philosophizing on the reasons for the low correlations may be enjoyable and beneficial to the experimental and theoretical psychologists. Yet practitioners have a legitimate point if they question the value of early testing. Because early intelligence testing does not allow us to do an accurate job of predicting future development, the use must be justified on the basis of measuring present developmental status. That is, these tests are really similar to achievement tests, and their use must be justified, if possible, on that basis.

Because the nonspecialist will not be involved with infant testing, these kinds of tests will not be reviewed here. However, there are many such tests. A fairly recent survey lists 61 tests for infants (Katoff & Reuter, 1979). The Stanford-Binet and WISC-R are two of the most popular tests for children under 6. The WPPSI has gained in popularity. The McCarthy Scales of Children's Abilities is appropriate for children from ages $2\frac{1}{2}$ to $8\frac{1}{2}$ years. It is a popular device, providing a measure of general intellectual functioning (general cognitive scale) as well as a profile of six other scales (verbal, perceptual-performance, quantitative, numerical memory, memory, and motor). The McCarthy Screening Test, adapted from the McCarthy Scales of Children's Abilities, is specifically designed to help schools identify children between 4 and $6\frac{1}{2}$ years old who are likely to need special educational assistance. Other preschool and infant tests are the Columbia Mental Maturity scale, the Bayley Scales of Infant Intelligence, the Goodenough-Harris Drawing Test, the Gesell Schedules, the Cattell Infant Intelligence Scale, the Ammons Picture-Vocabulary, the Peabody Picture Vocabulary Test, the Pictorial Test of Intelligence, and the Merrill-Palmer Scales.

A test based on the conservation aspect of Piaget's developmental theory of cognitive structure is the Concept Assessment Kit—Conservation. Most reviewers consider the kit useful for demonstrating Piaget's theory but not established enough to be viewed as more than an experimental test (see Buros, 1972, pp. 810–813). Students interested in more details on these preschool scales should check various editions of Buros.

Summary of Individual Tests

The field of individual intelligence testing is dominated by four tests: the Stanford-Binet, the WAIS-R, the WISC-R, and the WPPSI. The K-ABC may eventually take its place in this group. These tests are technically sound and are useful both as predictors of future academic success and as clinical assessment devices. In comparing individual tests with the group tests to be discussed, the major disadvantages are that individual tests are expensive to give and require a highly trained administrator. The major advantages are: (1) individual tests are generally more reliable; (2) they are potentially more useful in clinical settings—a qualified administrator can learn more about a person from an individual test than a score indicates; (3) they can be used with individuals who may be unable for reasons of shyness, reticence, or anxiety to perform validly on a group test; and (4) although many individual tests are highly verbal, they do require considerably less reading ability than most of the group tests to be discussed in the following section.

GROUP TESTS OF GENERAL APTITUDE

As mentioned earlier, educational institutions, businesses, and industry use group aptitude tests far more extensively than individually administered intelligence tests. Although in many schools the actual tests may be administered by a counselor or someone else with advanced training and in industry by an industrial/organizational psychologist, most group tests are designed so that any teacher with a minimum of training (such as in-service training or a basic course in standardized testing) should be capable of the administrative task.

Many group tests, designed to give a measure of general aptitude, actually yield scores on two subtests. These may be given such titles as verbal and nonverbal scales or language and performance scales. In considering the use of subscores, one must keep in mind the continuum from global to specific measures mentioned earlier. It is always hard to know just when to consider a test a measure of general aptitude and when to consider it a measure of multiple aptitudes. The classification is not solely dependent upon the number of subscores. The author's definition of aptitude or intelligence and the method of constructing the test are primarily what determines the classification.

Most authors of tests that have two subscores, such as verbal and nonverbal, are really attempting to measure the *same* construct (general scholastic aptitude) with two separate procedures rather than to obtain measures of two separate aptitudes. Tests giving a whole series of subscores are typically attempting to measure *different* aspects of intelligence and are referred to as multifactor aptitude tests. These are considered in the following section. In this section we discuss the tests that are group-administered and are considered as measures of general aptitude even though they may report more than one score.

Group tests are usually classified according to grade or age level. Some tests have different levels, each level being appropriate for certain grades. For school purposes there are advantages to using such tests. The same construct is being measured at all levels of the tests, and norm groups are chosen to be comparable from one level to another. This permits comparison of measures obtained over a period of time.

It is impossible to list all appropriate group tests for each grade level. Because most group aptitude tests measure essentially similar skills (verbal and nonverbal), we discuss only a few of the more commonly used tests. Finally, a short subsection on culture-fair tests is included.

Primary and Elementary Level (Grades K–8) Group Aptitude (Intelligence) Tests

Although some individually administered tests attempt to measure the intelligence of very young children, group tests should ordinarily not be used for children under 5 (preschool children). Because children of this age have difficulty following the detailed directions necessary for group-testing procedures, they need individual supervision. For 5- and 6-year-olds, group testing is feasible, but it is necessary to keep the number within a group as small as possible. It is suggested that no attempt be made to administer tests at the primary level to groups of more than 10 to 12 children.

Actually there is some difference of opinion on whether or not it is worthwhile to give aptitude tests to children in the very early grades. If only a few children are to be tested for specific reasons, individual intelligence tests are often used. As discussed earlier, the long-range reliability (stability) of these tests for young children leaves much to be desired. For this reason it is debatable just how useful the scores can be. Some persons argue that such measures can be helpful to the teachers in grouping their students. Others feel that any grouping should be very flexible and that scores on an aptitude test serve only the ill-advised purpose of making educators' decisions too rigid at this early school level. Decisions about grouping should be flexible. Using test information need not contradict this principle.

At any rate, several group tests are appropriate for these early grade levels. These tests require little or no reading or writing on the part of the student. Responses are marked directly on the test booklets, because it is difficult for young children to use separate answer sheets. Most of the items are of the type that require the student to mark the correct picture (see Figure 7.2).

Tests at the elementary level (grades 4–8) give more stable results and are therefore more useful than primary level group tests. The tasks in these higher levels are generally more verbal. All the tests mentioned below, except the Boehm, contain levels suitable for the high school grades.

We have chosen to review one of the tests in this section a bit more thoroughly to illustrate some of the important aspects to consider in test selection and use. Our choice of the Cognitive Abilities Test is not meant to imply that we consider it the best test available. We have tried to point out

Part I. Classification   (The child must decide which picture does not belong with the others by abstracting the principle involved.)

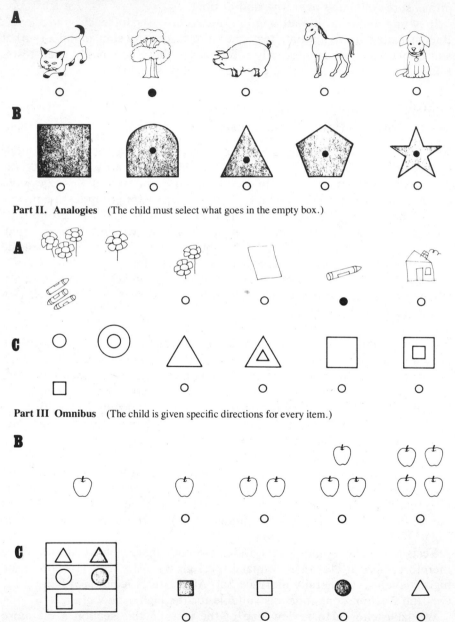

Part II. Analogies   (The child must select what goes in the empty box.)

Part III Omnibus   (The child is given specific directions for every item.)

Figure 7.2   Specimen items from the Otis-Lennon School Ability Test. (Copyright © 1979 by Harcourt Brace Jovanovich, Inc. All rights reserved. Reproduced by permission.)

previously in this book that a test must be evaluated in accordance with its intended use. No test is best for all possible uses. The Cognitive Abilities Test is considered to be technically well constructed, but so are many others. The CAT has been chosen as a representative example of those well-made tests that cover a wide age range.

Cognitive Abilities Test (CAT)   These tests are authored by Thorndike and Hagen and published by the Riverside Publishing Company, 1982.

Grade Level and Content.   There are two separate batteries: the Primary Battery (K–3) and the Multi-Level Edition (grades 3–13). The Primary Battery has two levels. Because the primary tests consist of pictorial materials and oral instructions, ability to read is *not* a prerequisite for accurate assessment. There are four subtests: oral vocabulary, relational concepts, multimental (one that doesn't belong) concepts, and quantitative concepts. The authors have attempted to include tasks that are based on content that children of this age group are likely to have experienced but to use this content in a new way. The test measures the following eight skills and competencies (Thorndike & Hagen, 1982, pp. 5–6):

1. Ability to comprehend oral English.
2. Ability to follow directions.
3. Ability to hold material in short-term memory.
4. Possession of effective strategies for scanning pictorial and figural stimuli to obtain either specific or general information.
5. Possession of a store of general information and verbal concepts.
6. Ability to compare stimuli and detect similarities and differences.
7. Ability to clarify, categorize, or order familiar objects.
8. Ability to use quantitative and spatial relationships and concepts.

The Multi-Level Edition is bound into a single booklet and grouped into eight overlapping levels. The Multi-Level Edition has three batteries separately administered. The Verbal Battery has four subtests: Vocabulary, Sentence Completion, Verbal Classification, and Verbal Analogies. The Quantitative Battery has three subtests: Quantitative Relations, Number Series, and Equation Building. The Nonverbal Battery is entirely pictorial or diagrammatic and has three subtests: Figure Analogies, Figure Classification, and Figure Synthesis. For most students, the Nonverbal Battery is not quite as good a predictor of school performance as the other two batteries, but it does "permit an appraisal of abstract intelligence which is not influenced by disability in reading" (Technical Manual, 1982, p. 8). Sample items for all subtests are shown in Figure 7.3.

Types of Scores.   The Primary Battery provides deviation IQ scores, percentile ranks by age and grade, and stanines by age and grade. The Multi-Level Edition provides standard age scores (SAS) and percentile ranks and

---

Sample Items from Verbal Battery Subtests

Vocabulary: Which word means most nearly the same thing as wish?

  wish   A agree   B bone   C over   D want   E waste

Sentence Completion:

  The fire is _____.

  A wet   B green   C hot   D running   E round

Verbal Classification:

  Think in what way the words in dark type go together. Then find the word on the line below that belongs with them.

                    mouse   wolf   bear

  A rose   B lion   C run   D hungry   E brown

Verbal Analogies:

                    big→large : little→

  A girl   B small   C late   D lively   E more

Sample Items from Quantitative Battery Subtests

Quantitative Relations:

  Mark A if the amount in Column A is *greater* than that in Column B.

  Mark B if the amount in Column B is *greater* than that in Column A.

  Mark C if the amount in Column A is exactly *equal* to that in Column B.

              Column A   Column B
              $3 + 2$ $2 + 3$

Number Series:

  1   2   3   4   5   →   A 4   B 5   C 6   D 7   E 8

  Equation Building: In this test, you will try to discover how to put numbers together to make true equations or number sentences. You are to discover how to put together *all* of the numbers and signs given in a problem in a way that gives you *one of the answer choices supplied in that problem.*

  2   3   1   +   +   A 4   B 5   C 6   D 7   E 8

Figure 7.3 Sample items from Cognitive Abilities Test, Form 3. The examples of Cognitive Abilities Test items are sample items reproduced from Form 3 of the Cognitive Abilities Test Copyright © 1982. Reprinted with permission of the Publisher, THE RIVERSIDE PUBLISHING COMPANY, 8420 Bryn Mawr Ave., Chicago, IL 60631. All rights reserved.

Sample Items from Nonverbal Battery Subtests

Figure Classification: Each question starts with a set of figures or drawings that are alike in some way. You are to figure out how they are alike, and then find among the answer choices on the right the figure that belongs with them.

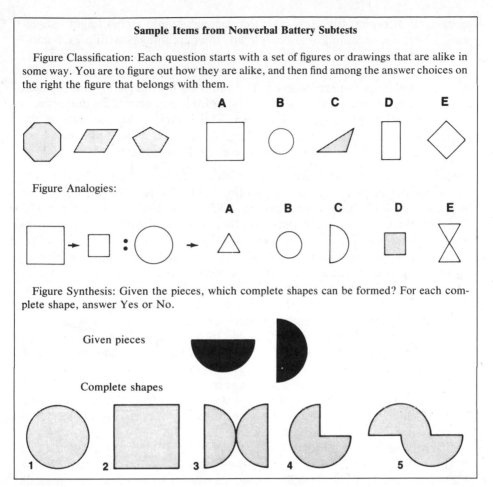

Figure Analogies:

Figure Synthesis: Given the pieces, which complete shapes can be formed? For each complete shape, answer Yes or No.

Given pieces

Complete shapes

Figure 7.3 (continued)

stanines both by age and grade for each of the three batteries. The SAS is a normalized standard score with a mean of 100 and a standard deviation of 16. (Historically this type of score frequently has been referred to as a deviation IQ score.)

Norming.   The CAT Multi-Level Edition was normed during the fall of 1977 and the spring and fall of 1978. The Primary Battery was normed in 1978. The CAT was normed concurrently with the Iowa Tests of Basic Skills and the Tests of Achievement and Proficiency in both public and Catholic schools. The sample was quite large, with approximately 18,000 students per grade for the Multi-Level Edition and 2800 to 7800 students per grade for the Primary Battery. The sample was stratified by school size (seven levels), geographical region (five regions), the socioeconomic status (eight categories). After the sampling was completed, the percentages within each category were adjusted by weighting to make them closer to the actual national percentages. In addition to the above stratification variables, the public/nonpublic balance was considered. The sampling procedure for this test was meticulously planned and executed. The norm group should be quite representative of the nation's schoolchildren. The Technical Manual lists all the schools that participated in the sampling. (Most other major publishers take similar care with their sampling plans for widely used tests.)

Reliability.   Internal consistency reliability data computed separately per grade for the Primary Battery are around 0.90. The K-R 20 reliabilities for the Multi-Level Edition cluster around 0.95 for the Verbal Battery and 0.93 for both the Quantitative Battery and the Nonverbal Battery. Standard errors were estimated using item response theory. Information functions (the reciprocal of the error variance, so that the standard error is the square root of the reciprocal of the information function) were calculated for each item and added to give the information functions of the test at each of a series of raw score levels. Although this procedure was discussed only briefly in Chapter 3 because of its relatively complicated mathematics, it is generally considered to be theoretically preferable to the standard error of measurement formula given in this text. It provides a separate standard error for each raw-score level.

The standard errors in SAS units range from 2.9 to 10.8 in grades 4, 7, and 10, depending upon raw score. The largest standard errors are at the extreme high and low raw-score levels. For the middle range scores, the standard errors range from 2.9 to around 5.3.

Stability reliability estimates over a six-month interval average around 0.91 for the Verbal Battery, 0.86 for the Quantitative Battery, and 0.85 for the Nonverbal Battery. Stability estimates over two- and four-year periods were in the middle .80s for the Verbal Battery, low .80s for the Quantitative Battery, and middle .70s for the Nonverbal Battery.

Reliabilities of the difference scores among the batteries averaged about 0.74 for Verbal versus Quantitative, 0.79 for Verbal versus Nonverbal, and 0.71 for Nonverbal versus Quantitative.

Validity.   Under content validity the authors write that the

> *test can be characterized by the following statements and that these characteristics describe behavior that it is important to measure for understanding an individual's educational and work potential:*
>
> *1. The tasks deal with abstract and general concepts.*
> *2. In most cases, the tasks require the interpretation and use of symbols.*
> *3. In large part, it is the relationships among concepts and symbols with which the examinee must deal.*

4. *The tasks require the examinee to be flexible in his or her basis for organizing concepts and symbols.*
5. *Experience must be used in new patterns.*
6. *Power in working with abstract materials is emphasized, rather than speed." (Technical Manual, 1982, p. 35)*

Criterion-related validity evidence includes correlations with achievement tests and with school grades. The CAT Verbal Battery generally correlates (concurrently) with the various subtests of the Iowa Tests of Basic Skills (ITBS) in the high .70s and low .80s. It correlates with the ITBS composite score in the high .80s. The Quantitative Battery has slightly lower correlations (except with the math subtest of the ITBS). The Nonverbal Battery has slightly lower correlations, with the subtest correlations ranging from the low .60s to the low .70s, and the correlations with the composite in the low .70s. Correlations between the CAT and the Tests of Achievement and Proficiency range from the high .60s to the low .80s. Predictive data from grade 5 CAT scores to grade 9 ITBS scores are 0.82 for CAT Verbal with ITBS composite, 0.77 for Quantitative with composite, and 0.67 for Nonverbal with composite.

Concurrent validity correlations between CAT and grade-point average range in the low .40s to .60 across grades 7, 9, and 11. The Quantitative Battery tended to correlate the highest. There were only minor differences in the correlations across ethnic groups (white, black, Hispanic, and Asian) and sexes. Predictive validity coefficients between grade 5 CAT scores and grade 9 GPA ranged from 0.52 for the Nonverbal Battery to 0.63 for the Quantitative Battery. The Asian students generally achieved marks in the ninth grade above what would have been predicted (on the basis of a regression equation for whites), while black males had lower grades than those predicted. Thus, under one definition of *bias,* the CAT is biased against Asians and in favor of black males.

Construct validity evidence includes correlations with the Stanford-Binet (low .60s to high .80s, depending on subtest and age level). The correlations were somewhat higher for older children than younger ones, and the Verbal Battery correlated the highest of the three with the Stanford-Binet.

Correlations with four subtests of the Differential Aptitude Test (DAT)— Verbal Reasoning, Numerical Ability, Abstract Reasoning, and Space— were also reported. These ranged from 0.74 for the correlation between CAT Verbal and DAT Verbal to 0.40 for CAT Verbal and DAT Space.

A factor-analytic study shows a substantial general factor running through all the subtests. The authors summarize the results of the study as follows:

> *In summary, it seems to say that each one of the three batteries gives a substantial measure of some common factor of abstract reasoning; that the Verbal Battery represents in addition a word knowledge factor and the Nonverbal Battery a factor of a figural or visualizing nature; and that the*

three quantitative tests measure largely the general factor and a set of specific quantitative skills. (Technical Manual, 1982, p. 41)

Interpretation and Use.   The final section of this chapter, "Using Aptitude Test Results," will deal with the interpretation and use of all the types of aptitude tests described in this chapter: general, multifactor, and specific. In discussing here the uses of the Cognitive Abilities Test, we will mention only three unique characteristics and explain their function, rather than outline all possible uses of the CAT. These are unique in the sense that they are not common to all group-administered general aptitude tests. We do not mean that no other group aptitude tests would have them.

First, the continuous multilevel approach (with norms showing the comparability of levels) has two advantages: (1) it allows one to use tests of appropriate difficulty and (2) it allows one to observe an individual's relative intellectual growth over time.

Second, the Nonverbal Battery, "a test whose items involve neither words nor numbers and which, through its use of geometric or figural elements, measures a 'fluid' type of ability that is not bound by formal school instruction" (Technical Manual, 1982, p. 5), allows one to make an estimate of ability that is unaffected by reading skill and less susceptible to the influences of formal schooling than are the other two batteries.

Third, because both the Iowa Tests of Basic Skills and the Tests of Achievement and Proficiency are standardized on the same norm group as the CAT, a comparison between level of achievement and aptitude is possible.

This fairly thorough review of the CAT was presented as an example of what you should look for in choosing a group general aptitude test. The CAT compares well with other tests of the same type. We would classify it as one of the better measures of its kind.

Finally, some readers may wonder why this test has been classified as a general aptitude test instead of a multifactor aptitude test. After all, it does report three separate scores from three separate batteries. As we mentioned earlier, the classification of some tests is rather arbitrary. We have followed the classification procedure used in Buros (1978). In a sense, this test is a cross between a general and a multifactor aptitude test.

On the next pages we will discuss very briefly four additional general aptitude tests.

Boehm Test of Basic Concepts (BTBC)   Published by the Psychological Corporation (1969), the BTBC contains two forms and one level: K–2. The test is composed of 50 items divided into two 25-item booklets. Testing time is from 30 to 40 minutes. The norms are the percent passing each item, by grade and socioeconomic level.

This test differs from the traditional group test of mental ability, although Buros (1978) classifies it as such. The publisher's catalog classifies it as a readiness test (Psychological Corporation, 1984). The test can be considered a cross between an aptitude test, a readiness test, a diagnostic test, and a criterion-referenced achievement test. This instrument is a picture test "deisigned to appraise the young child's mastery of concepts that are commonly found in preschool and primary grade instructional materials and that are essential to understanding oral communications" (Psychological Corporation, 1984, p. 118). The fact that this test supposedly can serve as a useful guide in instruction of specific content makes it unique among the more traditional aptitude tests, which are not helpful in *specific* instructional guidance. For thorough reviews of this test, refer to Buros (1972, pp. 625–629) and Dahl (1973).

Otis-Lennon School Ability Test (OLSAT)   Also published by the Psychological Corporation (1979), the OLSAT is a revision of the Otis-Lennon Mental Ability Test. The name change from "Mental" to "School Ability" was made because " 'School Ability' is considered a more accurate description of what is measured and of the purposes for which the test is intended" (Psychological Corporation, 1979, p. 68). There are two forms (R, S) and five levels (Primary I—Grade 1; Primary II—Grades 2–3; Elementary—Grades 4–5; Intermediate—Grades 6–8; and Advanced—Grades 9–12). No pupil reading is required in Grades 1–3. All items were reviewed by a minority group panel for ethnic bias as well as for possible sex bias. Norms were developed concurrently with the Metropolitan Achievement Tests. A school Ability Index and a Predicted Achievement Range in terms of the Metropolitan grade equivalents are provided.

School and College Ability Tests, Series III (SCAT III)   This test was developed by Educational Testing Service, published by Addison-Wesley, and marketed by California Test Bureau (1980). It contains three levels (grades 3 through 12), with two forms available at each level. The SCAT III is composed of two separate parts: Verbal and Quantitative. A total score is available also. The Verbal portion is composed of verbal analogy items. The Quantitative portion is composed of items that involve comparing the magnitude of two mathematical entities. The publisher's catalog and the SCAT Manual both suggest that, among other uses, the test can estimate growth in abilities over time. (This is an explicit recognition that abilities are developed. It was probably stated to counter some critics' charges that the publishers imply, or at least users infer, that tests measure inborn abilities that are fully developed at birth. It is, of course, somewhat of a bizarre charge. Surely no one either implies or infers that, any more than one would imply or infer that we are born at our full height.) Evidently, however, the publishers do not believe that there is much individual variation in mental development across the high school years, because they also suggest that grade 9 SCAT III scores may be used to estimate twelfth-grade Scholastic Aptitude Test

(SAT) scores. (As you should realize after studying Chapter 3, individual differences in growth of abilities across four years would decrease the accuracy of the prediction.)

The SCAT III is co-normed with the Sequential Tests of Educational Progress (STEP III), and SCAT/STEP Discrepancy Tables are available.

Test of Cognitive Skills (TCS)   Published by the California Test Bureau/ McGraw Hill (1981), the TCS is composed of five levels (grades 2 through 12). The TCS has four subtests: Sequences, Analogies, Memory, and Verbal Reasoning. Scores are provided for each subtest and for the total test. The total score is called the Cognitive Skills Index. The TCS is a major revision of the previously used Short Form Test of Academic Aptitude (SFTAA). Note that the word *aptitude* is not in the title of the TCS. The publisher's catalog describes the TCS as a "measure of skills important to success in the school setting" (Publishers Test Service, 1984, p. 36). Further, the publishers state that the Cognitive Skills Index (the total score) "indicates a student's overall ability or academic aptitude" (p. 36).

High School-, College-, and Adult-Level Group Tests

Many tests (such as several reviewed above) have levels appropriate for students from primary through grade 12. Some are designed for even higher levels. When choosing a test for a certain age level, one should be careful to assure that the ceiling on the test is adequate. If, for example, a test is to be administered to a group of above-average high school seniors, it would be best to use a test designed for college students as well as high school seniors so that the test has an adequate ceiling.

Two programs that are particularly useful in predicting college success at the undergraduate level are the following.

ACT Assessment Program   The American College Testing Program (ACT) is an independent, nonprofit educational service organization. The Assessment Program is the major service of ACT; approximately 1 million college-bound students participate in the program each year. The main purposes of the Assessment Program (1983, p. 1) are to do the following:

1. Help students present themselves as persons with special patterns of educational abilities and needs.
2. Provide information to help students select college majors and make educational and career plans.
3. Provide students with information about their college choices.
4. Provide dependable and comparable information for precollege counseling in high schools and for on-campus educational guidance.
5. Provide colleges with student admissions/enrollment data.

6. Provide colleges with information about students' high school records.
7. Provide estimates of a student's academic and out-of-class abilities.
8. Help colleges place freshmen in appropriate class sections in introductory courses in English, mathematics, social studies, and natural sciences.
9. Help colleges identify students who would profit from special programs such as honors, remedial, and independent study.
10. Help colleges estimate whether a student should be considered for advanced placement and further examination.
11. Help colleges examine and improve their educational programs.
12. Provide information useful in granting scholarships, loans, and other kinds of financial assistance.

The ACT Assessment Program has four tests, a Student Profile Section, and an Interest Inventory. The tests—in English, mathematics, social studies, and natural sciences—"emphasize problem-solving and reasoning abilities rather than the rote recall of facts" (American College Testing Program, 1984, p. 1). Scores range from 1 to 36, with 20 being the median score of college-bound, first-semester high school seniors. (Standard deviations range from 5 to 7.) The Student Profile Section asks for the information that a college typically requests on its application form, such as high school grades, vocational choice, and educational major. The ACT Interest Inventory provides six scores: Social Service, Business Contact, Business Detail, Technical, Science, and Creative Arts.

In the fall of 1976 ACT launched a national program called the Proficiency Examination Program (PEP). The ACT-PEP includes 49 college-level proficiency examinations in a variety of subjects. The tests are designed to certify a student's level of knowledge in specific courses and, like the CLEP exams, discussed in the following section, may be used by colleges as a basis for awarding college credit.

In addition to the Assessment Program and the Proficiency Examination Program, ACT provides a Student Needs Analysis Service, an Educational Opportunity Service, a Career Planning Program, and the Assessment of Career Development.

College Entrance Examination Board   The College Entrance Examination Board (CEEB) is "an association of schools and colleges that concerns itself primarily with the movement of students into college. The chief purpose of the College Board is to increase access to that movement and to make it more equitable and efficient" (*Report of the Commission on Tests,* 1970, p. 11). The operational phases of the CEEB are conducted by Educational Testing Service (ETS). Although the CEEB's services are not restricted to college entrance examinations, it is best known for three such exams: Preliminary Scholastic Aptitude Test (PSAT), Scholastic Aptitude Test (SAT), and a series of Achievement Tests.

The PSAT is basically a shortened (1 hour and 40 minutes) version of the SAT. It has replaced the National Merit Scholarship Qualifying Test (NMSQT) and is referred to as the PSAT/NMSQT. The PSAT/NMSQT reports two scores, verbal and mathematical. The scores range from 20 to 80. About 1.4 million students take the PSAT/NMSQT each year.

The SAT is a three-hour objective test. It is considered a test of ability, not of factual knowledge. Verbal, mathematics, and English scores are provided. In addition, separate scores on the reading comprehension and vocabulary subtests of the verbal tests are reported. Scores range from 200 to 800. About 1 million seniors took the SAT in 1983–1984.

The CEEB Achievement Tests are a series of one-hour tests. These tests are in a variety of subject-matter areas such as American history, social studies, biology, chemistry, physics, English composition, two levels of mathematics, and several foreign languages. As in the SAT, scores range from 200 to 800.

Many colleges require that applicants take the SAT and three of the Achievement Tests. Some colleges request specific Achievement Tests: others allow prospective students to choose among them.

Besides the admission tests already mentioned, the CEEB offers many other services. One such service is the Advanced Placement Program (APP). The APP is based on the belief that many students can complete college-level courses while still in high school. The program provides outlines of college-level courses and administers and grades three-hour exams based on these courses. As of 1983, the APP offered exams in 24 introductory college courses in 13 fields. In early 1984 the program offered an exam in computer science. About two-thirds of all college and universities accept the exam grades for college credit advanced placement.

Another service is the College Level Examination Program (CLEP). CLEP allows colleges to grant credit by examination, and nearly 1800 colleges use this service. The CLEP exams are of three types: General Examinations, which measure achievement in English composition, mathematics, natural sciences, humanities, and social sciences–history; Subject Examinations in 47 (at present) undergraduate subjects; and Brief Tests, which are shorter versions of the subject exams and are used not to give individuals credit but to evaluate groups of students.

Other services that CEEB provides are the Career Skills Assessment Program (see Chapter 9), the Comparative Guidance and Placement Program, the College Scholarship Service, the Student Descriptive Questionnaire, and the College Locater Service. Some of these services have been added as a response to recommendations from the *Report of the Commission Tests* (1970). This commission, after reviewing criticism of current tests and their use, concluded that the CEEB should broaden its scope. The commission felt that the three functions the CEEB should serve were distributive, educative, and credentialing functions.

Culture-Fair Tests of Intelligence

Intelligence tests have often been severely criticized for their "cultural biases." This term has been defined in so many ways, however, that one can never be completely sure what the criticism means. There are three common interpretations of cultural bias. To some, a test is considered culturally biased if different subgroups obtain different mean scores on the test. To others, a test is culturally biased if it measures different constructs (or achievements) for different subcultures. Still others consider the issue of cultural bias in terms of differential prediction equations and/or different selection ratios or success ratios. (The entire spring 1976 issue of the *Journal of Educational Measurement* focused on the issue of bias in selection procedures. See Flaugher, 1978, for a nontechnical summary discussion.)

Many measurement experts prefer the third definition, since it focuses on the fair *use* of tests rather than on the tests themselves. (See Chapter 12 for more information on the fair use of tests.) Nonmeasurement specialists who are critics of testing are more likely to use the first definition (for example, tests are unfair to blacks if the mean score for blacks is lower than the mean score for whites). Measurement specialists are more likely to prefer the second definition to the first. A test is biased if it measures something different in different subcultures. Now, a test biased in the second sense will probably (but not necessarily) be biased in the first sense. The logic is much less compelling in the opposite direction. To clarify these points, let us use two examples—one of physical measurement and one of educational measurement.

If we wish to determine how fast people can run the 100-yard dash, we may measure this by timing people on this very task. Now, if blacks obtain a faster mean time than whites (or vice versa), the measure is biased under the first definition. However, if the task is measuring the same thing for both races, it is not biased in the second sense.

If we wish to determine whether first-grade children know the rank order of a set of numerals, we might ask a question such as "Which of the following numbers represents the least amount: 13, 17, 19, 21?" If a lower percentage of Hispanic students answer the question correctly than whites, the test is biased in the first sense. Is it biased in the second? It depends. If both the Hispanic and the white students who miss the question do so because they do not know the concept of ranking numerals, the question is *not* biased in the *second* sense. If, however, some of the Hispanic students and none of the whites miss the question because they do not know the meaning of the word *least,* the question *is* biased in the sense that it is measuring knowledge of vocabulary for (some) Hispanics and knowledge of the rank order of the numerals for whites.

Clearly the second kind of bias is undesirable. It leads to incorrect and harmful inferences to assume that individual children (or groups of children) are inadequate in one area when in fact they have been measured (unknowingly) on something else. Test constructors try to avoid building tests that will have such biases. Research evidence (Jensen, 1976, 1980; Reynolds, 1980, 1982) tends to indicate that publishers are generally quite successful in minimizing this kind of bias. Sattler (1982, p. 360) states: "The evidence, gathered from many studies and with a variety of intelligence tests and ethnic minority groups, points to one conclusion: *Intelligence tests are not culturally biased. They have the same properties for ethnic minority children as they do for white children*" (italics in original).

Some writers would not concur with this interpretation (see Williams, 1974; Zoref & Williams, 1980). Publishers cannot build tests that are fair in the second sense for all possible uses and misuses. If an intelligence test in the English language is given to a child who speaks only Spanish, surely the test is measuring something different from intelligence for that child. We cannot blame publishers for such a ridiculous misuse or accuse them of building a culturally biased test.

What about the unfairness of tests in the first sense—that is, of different means for different subcultures? We have already alluded to some difficulties with that definition, but it is nevertheless frequently used. Indeed, people have attempted to build tests that are "culturally fair" in that sense of the phrase. As already discussed, a person's environment (subculture) can affect his or her test score. People of different nations as well as people in different subcultures within the United States place different values on verbal fluency, speed, and other characteristics that influence the scores on intelligence tests. Suppose people in one subculture are less verbal than those in another subculture and that the test used requires verbal skills. Is the test fair to those of the first subculture?

In the past, psychologists have attempted to develop tests that are free from cultural influences. Failing in this—no test can be free from cultural influences—an attempt has been made to construct tests that are equally fair to members of all cultures. In the attempt to achieve this cultural fairness, these tests have included tasks that involve nonsense material, or tasks that should be equally familiar or unfamiliar to all cultures. Frequently such tests have liberal time limits to deemphasize speed. Nonverbal items are used more than verbal ones. Examples of tests of this type are the Cattell Culture-Fair Intelligence Test and the Davis-Eells Test of General Intelligence of Problem-Solving Ability. Figure 7.4 presents sample items taken from Scale 2 of the Cattell Culture-Fair Intelligence Test. Complete verbal directions are read to the subjects so that they understand the task. The items do not appear to be unfair to any culture. However, the research evidence suggests that these tests are not culturally fair if by this phrase we mean that groups from one culture score as well on the tests as groups from another culture.[5]

[5] For substantiation of this statement, see the reviews in the *Fifth* and *Sixth Mental Measurements Yearbook* (Buros, 1959, 1965) of the two tests mentioned.

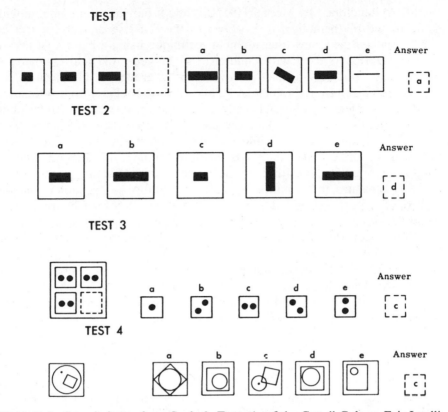

Figure 7.4 Sample items from Scale 2, Form A, of the Cattell Culture-Fair Intelligence Test. (Reprinted with permission. Copyright © 1949, 1960, by the Institute for Personality and Ability Testing, P.O. Box 188, Champaign, Illinois 61820, U.S.A. All rights reserved.)

It is very hard, if not impossible, to devise a test that will show no difference between such groups. Contrary to what many critics believed, stress on verbal skills in our current tests is not the primary cause of group differences. Flaugher (1970) has cited a number of studies showing that the greatest difference in the performances of blacks and whites is on nonverbal items. Even if we could devise a completely culture-fair test, would it be a worthwhile attainment? Some argue yes, claiming that such a measure would be relatively independent of cultural influences and therefore as nearly correlated to innate ability as possible. Others argue that to mask existing group differences by eliminating all items measuring these differences is to delimit the usefulness of the test (Tannebaum, 1965, pp. 722–723).

A somewhat different approach to developing a culturally fair instrument is a technique known as the System of Multicultural Pluralistic Assessment

(SOMPA) developed by Mercer (1977). While it has much in common with some of the mathematical approaches to the fair use of tests, it can be conceptualized as a new measurement technique using a battery of instruments. SOMPA is used with children 5 to 11 years old and compares a child's score not only against a national norm group but also against the scores of children from a similar social and cultural background. Information for the assessment is gathered from two sources: a test session with the child and an interview with the child's principal caretaker, usually the mother. The test sessions with the child include administering the WISC-R, the Physical Dexterity Tasks, and the Bender-Gestalt test. Information obtained from the mother includes data on the Sociocultural Modalities, which purportedly measure the distance between the culture of the home and the culture of the school; an Adaptive Behavior Inventory for Children; and a Health History Inventory. Using multiple regression equations based on the additional data, the WISC-R is "corrected." Mercer compares this correction to a golf handicap (Fiske, 1976). She feels that *uncorrected* scores should be used to determine immediate educational needs, whereas the *corrected* scores should be used to determine a child's "latent scholastic potential." Mercer wants to use the *corrected* scores to avoid labeling children as retarded and to use the *uncorrected* scores to make educational decisions. This may or may not work. One danger, of course, is that users will come to regard the "corrected" scores as reflecting reality in a way that they clearly do not. Children who have not learned certain skills or capabilities, for whatever reason, remain without those skills or capabilities even after the statistical correction is made. To treat the children as if they have them, or to ignore their absence on the grounds that "They're no worse than other children of similar background" does no service to the children at all.

Another danger is that many states currently distribute special education funds on the basis of the number of children classified as retarded. Whether the label can be removed without the loss of the additional funding available for special educational needs is as yet undetermined.

The debate as to the usefulness of a culture-fair test or one mathematically "corrected" to equate for varying cultural backgrounds depends on how we want to use the instrument. Some people wish to get a measure of innate ability (whatever that is) and argue as follows:

1. There are no genetic differences in intelligence among subcultures. (As mentioned earlier, this point has been debated by psychologists. However, there is certainly no compelling scientific reason to reject this assumption, and there are some good humanitarian reasons for accepting it.)
2. Tests that are measures of innate ability will show no differences between subcultures.
3. Therefore, tests that show no differences between subcultures (or can be equated on the subculture) are tests that measure innate ability.

The logic breaks down in going from point 2 to point 3. If A implies B, it does *not* follow that B implies A. We simply cannot (at the present time) obtain measures of innate ability.

Other people, who believe that innate ability can never be measured with a paper-and-pencil test, wish to use intelligence tests primarily as predictive instruments. If the environmental effects of one's culture are related to the criterion we are attempting to predict, then to eliminate these cultural differences would reduce substantially the validity of the test.

Most specialists take the position that if culture-fair tests could be developed, in general they would be less useful measures than the presently existing assessments that are influenced by environmental factors. We further discuss the testing of minority groups in Chapter 12.

MULTIFACTOR APTITUDE TESTS

As already mentioned, some psychologists contend that intellect is a general characteristic and that a single score can adequately represent the degree to which a person possesses intelligence. Others subscribe to a multifactor theory of intelligence, but argue that the measurement of these multifactors adds little, if any, to the predictive validity of single-factor tests. The advocates of multifactor testing generally support it on both theoretical and practical bases.

Many schools, employment agencies, and businesses administer multifactor aptitude tests. What are the reasons for this popularity of multifactor tests? Is the popularity justified? What are the characteristics of these tests? What are their advantages and limitations?

The development of factor-analytic techniques has certainly been the major technical development affecting the popularity of the multifactor theory.[6] Rather than simply argue whether intelligence is general, multifactor, or composed of many specific abilities, a factor analysis can be made on many different kinds of ability tests. If only one factor is obtained, then we have some support for the theory of general intelligence. If many factors are obtained, the multifactor theory is supported. If we obtain as many factors as kinds of tests, the specific aptitude theory is supported.

Some of the multifactor tests have been constructed by choosing items that have high correlations with other items in the *same* subtest but low correlations with the items (and subtest scores) in the *other* subtests. This results in a set of subtests that are internally consistent but which have low intercorrelations with each other. This should be a major characteristic of

[6] Factor analysis is not covered in this book, other than noting that the intercorrelations between the tests determine the number of factors. If the tests are all highly correlated with each other, for example, we have only a single factor. If, at the other extreme, the tests do not correlate at all with each other, then we have as many factors as tests.

any multifactor test. Of course, the use of test construction techniques to develop a multifactor test does not enable us to argue that obtaining a set of factors proves the actual existence of the factors within a person.

Another aspect that has led to the increased popularity of multifactor aptitude tests is the vocational and educational counseling movement. The discovery of differential abilities within a person should certainly facilitate vocational and educational counseling. But does it? Some argue that identification of differential abilities is helpful in counseling only to the extent that this knowledge allows us to predict differentially how well an individual will be able to perform in various educational curricula or vocational tasks. The degree to which multifactor tests enable us to predict differentially is an important aspect in determining their usefulness.

In general, the data indicate that multifactor aptitude tests are not very good for *differential* prediction. This is not solely because of test inadequacies in subdividing intellect into its component subparts. Another problem is that the criteria (for example, job success) are not solely dependent on specific aspects of intelligence. Thus, although we may be able to obtain measures of numerical ability and verbal ability that are distinct, there simply is not any criterion that differentially demands one aptitude and not the other. Therefore, there is little evidence of differential predictive validity. Whether this makes multifactor tests no more useful than the less expensive and less time-consuming tests of general intelligence depends on the degree to which one believes that a more precise *description* is useful in counseling, regardless of whether it increases predictability. As with any belief, there are differences of opinion on this. It is not a belief easily subjected to scientific verification.

Examples of Multifactor Aptitude Tests

In a survey of secondary schools, Engen, Lamb, & Prediger (1982) reported that 66 percent of the schools administer the Armed Services Vocational Aptitude Battery (ASVAB), 34 percent used the Differential Aptitude Tests (DAT), and 24 percent used the General Aptitude Test Battery (GATB). These three widely used multifactor aptitude batteries are discussed briefly here. The Differential Aptitude Tests, published by the Psychological Corporation, is reviewed in more detail than the other two because of the wealth of material available about the test.

Differential Aptitude Tests (DAT)

Grade Level and Content. The DAT has been designed for use in grades 8–12. There are two forms of the test, and each form has eight subtests: Verbal Reasoning (VR), Numerical Ability (NA), Abstract Reasoning (AR), Clerical Speed and Accuracy (CSA), Mechanical Reasoning (MR), Space Relations

(SR), Spelling (Sp), and Language Usage (LU). (The last two subtests are more appropriately considered achievement tests, because they are more closely tied to the curriculum.) The authors of the test also report a ninth score, VR + NA, which is interpreted as a measure of general scholastic aptitude. Examples of some of the practice items are shown in Figure 7.5. Of course, these examples are easier than the actual items in the subtests, although they are identical in form.

Types of Scores.   Percentile ranks and stanines can be obtained for the eight subtests and for the combined raw scores on the verbal reasoning and numerical ability tests.

Norming.   Separate sex and grade-level (8–12) norms are provided. The testing of the normative sample was done in the fall. However, the authors also provide spring (second-semester) norms for grades 8–11. These spring norms were obtained by interpolating between the fall norms of successive grades. Because the accuracy of these interpolated norms is debatable, it is better to administer the test in the fall and to thus avoid having to use the spring norms.

Reliability.   Split-half reliability coefficients computed separately for each sex and each grade are reported for both forms for all subtests except the clerical speed and accuracy subtests. Because this subtest is speeded (remember that others are timed but supposedly unspeeded), an alternate form reliability is reported. The reliability coefficients for the separate subtests range from .87 to .97 for boys and from .83 to .96 for girls.

Validity.   The research on the prediction of course grades is summarized according to subject areas. English grades are best predicted by VR + NA and by the LU and VR scores. Mathematics grades are best predicted by the VR + NA combination or by NA alone. Science grades can be best predicted by VR + NA, VR, NA, or LU subtests. Social studies grades can be predicted about equally well, using VR + NA, VR, NA, or LU subtests. The four major subject-matter areas can all be predicted with a fair amount of success. However, all four major subject-matter areas can be predicted successfully using the same score: VR + NA. Thus, the *differential* validity of the DAT in predicting course grades is not substantiated.

The prediction of achievement test results follows essentially the same pattern as the prediction of course grades. Again, the subscores on the DAT are fairly good predictors, but they are not very adequate in differential predictions. The data showing the relationship between DAT scores and educational and occupational groups indicate the same thing.

The concurrent validity showing the correlation between the VR + NA score and tests of general intelligence reveal consistently high correlations. The correlations, ranging mostly in the .70s and .80s, are as high as the

ABSTRACT REASONING

Each row consists of four figures called Problem Figures and five called Answer Figures. The four Problem Figures make a series. You are to find out which one of the Answer Figures would be the next (or the fifth one) in the series of Problem Figures. Here are two examples:

In Example X, note that the lines in the Problem Figures are falling down. In the first square the line stands straight up, and as you go from square to square the line falls more and more to the right. In the fifth square the line would be lying flat, so the correct answer—chosen from among the Answer Figures—is D. Therefore, the circle for D has been filled in on line X of your Answer Sheet.

CLERICAL
SPEED AND ACCURACY

This is a test to see how quickly and accurately you can compare letter and number combinations. On the following pages are groups of these combinations; each test item contains five. These same combinations appear after the number for each test item on the Answer Sheet, but they are in a different order. You will notice that in each test item one of the five is **underlined**. You are to look at the **one** combination that is underlined, find the **same** one after that item number on the Answer Sheet, and fill in the circle under it.

The following examples have been marked correctly on your Answer Sheet. Note that the combination marked on the Answer Sheet must be exactly the same as the one that is underlined in the test item.

Examples

V. <u>AB</u> AC AD AE AF   Y. Aa Ba <u>bA</u> BA bB

W. aA aB BA Ba <u>Bb</u>   Z. 3A 3B <u>33</u> B3 BB

X. A7 7A B7 <u>7B</u> AB

MECHANICAL REASONING

Find the space for Mechanical Reasoning on the Answer Sheet.

This test consists of a number of pictures and questions about those pictures. Look at the two examples below, to see just what to do.

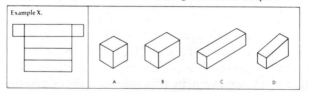

Example X.

Which person has the heavier load? (If equal, mark C.)

SPACE RELATIONS

This test consists of 60 patterns which can be folded into figures. To the right of each pattern there are four figures. You are to decide which **one** of these figures can be made from the pattern shown. The pattern always shows the **outside** of the figure. Here is an example:

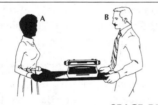

In Example X, which one of the four figures—A, B, C, D—can be made from the pattern at the left? A and B certainly cannot be made; they are not the right shape. C is correct both in shape and size. You cannot make D from this pattern. Therefore, the circle for C has been filled in on line X of your Answer Sheet.

Figure 7.5 Examples of practice items from some of the subtests of the Differential Aptitude Tests, Forms V and W. (Copyright © 1982, 1972 by the Psychological Corporation. All rights reserved. Reproduced by permission.)

correlations between most tests of general intelligence. Thus it certainly appears that the VR + NA score serves the same purpose as general intelligence test scores, and little would be gained by administering the DAT and a test of general intelligence in the same grade.

An interesting (and perhaps surprising) finding is the low correlations between the subscores on the DAT and the Kuder Preference Record scores. In general, interests and aptitudes are not highly correlated and, as the DAT Manual points out, it is risky to base counseling on interest scores without having some information on a person's aptitude scores.

As mentioned in the introduction to this section on multifactor tests, one of the characteristics such tests should have if they are to be successful in differential prediction is low intercorrelations of the subtests. Although the average (across grades) intercorrelations of the DAT are reasonably low (average about .50), most users would probably wish lower intercorrelations.

Interpretation and Use.   The administration of the DAT in grade 8 or 9 can provide information that is relevant to the decisions a student must make concerning future educational plans. The general lack of differential predictive validity does not mean the test is useless. The subtests do predict a variety of criteria, and the descriptive value of the subtest scores is not to be underemphasized.

Many counselors appreciate the fact that students who would perform at a low level on a test of general intelligence may do well on some of the subtests of the DAT. Thus, the counselor can say something positive about the student's abilities, and the student leaves the counseling interview with a better self-concept than if one could only interpret the low score on a general intelligence test. The combined score (VR + NA) serves very well as a measure of general intelligence. A casebook prepared by the Psychological Corporation is valuable to counselors in interpreting the profile differences to students, although it is badly in need of revision (Bennett, Seashore, & Wesman, 1951).

An optional service of potential value to counselors and students is the DAT/Career Planning Program. This program consists of a Career Planning Questionnaire and the DAT Career Planning Report, in addition to the DAT itself. The questionnaire collects data on student status, interest, and goals. A computer compares these data with the results of the DAT and prints out an interpretive report, which may confirm the appropriateness of the student's occupational choices in terms of abilities, interests, and plans, or which may suggest alternative occupational areas. The publisher suggests that the report can be used by counselors in interviews with students and parents, and/or can be given to students for further discussion and study at home.

General Aptitude Test Battery (GATB)   This test, which is available from the United States Government Printing Office (1946–1977), is designed for grades 9–12 and for adults. GATB has 12 tests and yields the following nine scores: intelligence, verbal aptitude, numerical aptitude, spatial aptitude, form perception, clerical perception, motor coordination, finger dexterity, and manual dexterity. These aptitudes are not completely independent, because some of the subtests are used in determining more than one aptitude score.

Correlational studies (see Hunter, 1983) suggest that the GATB has three general factors: a *cognitive* factor (intelligence, verbal, and numerical), a *perceptual* factor (spatial, form perception, and clerical perception), and a *psychomotor* factor (motor coordination, finger dexterity, and manual dexterity). Because the perceptual factor can be predicted very accurately by the other two factors, it adds little to the predictive power of the battery. A nonreading adaptation of the GATB, called the Nonreading Aptitude Test Battery, was published in 1969. It produces the same nine scores from 14 tests.

The GATB has been widely used by the United States Employment Service (USES), and the tests are available to nonprofit institutions (such as public schools) for counseling purposes. Specific occupations have been grouped into job families, and multiple cutoff scores (a series of minimum scores) have been established for the three most relevant aptitudes for each family. These scores are used in predicting job success. The multiple cutoff approach has been criticized for its noncompensatory attributes and the fact that no relative probabilities of success are available to assist in guiding those who exceed the cutoff scores in more than one job family. Further, some evidence suggests that the relationships between the tests and job performance is linear (Schmidt, Hunter, McKenzie, & Muldrow, 1979). Thus, multiple regression would produce more optimal predictions.

The USES has already completed 515 validation studies on the GATB and is continuing to do research on the GATB. It is considered by many to be a very well constructed instrument. The total time required for testing is about $2\frac{1}{2}$ hours.

Armed Services Vocational Aptitude Battery (ASVAB)   Published by the United States Military Enlistment Processing Command (USMEPCOM) in 1984, this test is designed for use both in high schools and junior colleges, and for selecting and classifying all enlistees at the Armed Forces Examining and Entrance Stations. Form 14 of the test is intended for use in high schools. It has 10 subtests as follows: General Science (GS), Arithmetic Reasoning (AR), Word Knowledge (WK), Paragraph Comprehension (PC), Numerical Operations (NO), Coding Speed (CS), Auto & Shop Information (AS), Mathematics Knowledge (MK), Mechanical Comprehension (MC), and Electronics Information (EI). The total testing time, including administrative time, is about 180 minutes. There is a total of 334 items.

The ASVAB-14 yields three academic composite scores and four occupational composite scores. The academic composites are Academic Ability, Verbal, and Math, and indicate potential for further formal education. The Academic Ability composite was derived logically and the other two academic composites through factor analyses. The occupational composites—Mechanical & Crafts, Business & Clerical, Electronics & Electrical, and Health, Social, & Technology—indicate level of aptitude for career areas. All occupational composites were based on regression analyses of criteria from military training programs on the ASVAB subtest scores. The composites, however, are based on weighting the relevant subtests equally.

The ASVAB norms are based on subsamples of a 1980 reference population from the Profile of American Youth study. There are norms for eleventh graders, twelfth graders, two-year college students, and a random sample of youth between the ages of 18 and 23. If the test is given to tenth graders, there is no relevant norm group, and they would be compared to the eleventh-grade norm group. The test is not currently being recommended for ninth graders.

The alternate-form reliabilities of the composite scores range from 0.84 to 0.95. These are acceptably high. However, it should be pointed out that there is overlap in the subtests that constitute the various composites. For example, three of the four occupational composites have the Arithmetic Reasoning subtest as a component of the composite, and two of the composites have Electronics Information as a component of the composite. Given the overlap, the intercorrelations between the occupational composites are quite high, ranging from 0.68 to 0.93 for students in grades 11 and 12. The reliability of the difference scores between composites is therefore not necessarily very high.

The validity data for the ASVAB are based primarily on studies done in the military, where the criteria were performance in training programs for a variety of military occupations. Some evidence from validity generalization studies suggests the ASVAB may also be reasonably valid for civilian occupations that are counterparts to those in the military. Because of the relatively low reliability of difference scores and the pervasive problem of multifaceted criteria mentioned earlier, we should not expect much *differential* validity.

The results given to the students present total youth population percentile scores, and grade/sex percentile scores. The counselors also receive opposite-sex and total grade normative information on the counselor section of the results sheet. Counselors will need to determine whether this information should be shared with the students. Probably at times it should be and at other times not, depending on the purpose of the counseling session and the ability of both the counselor and the student to understand the different norming groups and the implications of the data.

As mentioned earlier, the ASVAB is used by about twice as many schools as use the DAT. This is probably true, in part, because the test is available at no cost or obligation to the schools or to the students. The widespread use of the ASVAB by schools has been somewhat controversial, however. Many points have been made to support using the ASVAB: it is free, the test provides some useful data for vocational counseling, and it is particularly helpful for those students who are considering entering the military (the largest single employer of high school graduates). Of the students that take the ASVAB in high school, approximately 15 percent enter military service. The results of the ASVAB are used by the military to assist in recruiting and to stimulate interest in the services. (This could be seen as either a positive or a negative aspect, depending upon one's point of view.)

On the negative side, some measurement experts have considered the previous edition of the ASVAB (the ASVAB-5) to be less psychometrically sound than some of the other multifactor aptitude batteries. While the ASVAB-14 is too new to have been reviewed by many psychometric experts, probably the weakest aspect of this test is the relatively sparse amount of validity evidence for predicting success in civilian jobs or training programs. However, the ASVAB-14 is an improvement over its predecessor, which was quite popular. Local school districts evidently feel that, as a free item, it was "worth the price." Certainly for those schools with a sufficiently large number of juniors and seniors considering military service this test may be a potentially useful tool.

Other Multiaptitude Batteries   Other multiaptitude batteries include the Comprehensive Ability Battery, the Guilford-Zimmerman Aptitude Battery, and the International Primary Factors Test Battery. Reviews of all these can be found in Buros (1978).

SPECIAL-APTITUDE TESTS

A special aptitude is usually defined as a person's potential ability (or capacity to acquire proficiency) in a specified type of activity. Special aptitude tests were developed primarily for help in making vocational and educational selection decisions as well as for counseling. Compared to multifactor aptitude tests, they are probably more useful in selection (or placement) decisions and generally less useful in personal counseling for individual decision making.

Although many kinds of special-aptitude tests could be mentioned in this section, we do not discuss any particular test because readers will not all be interested in the same areas. There are tests of Vision and Hearing, Mechanical Aptitude Tests, Clerical and Stenographic Aptitude Tests, and Musical and Artistic Aptitude Tests. Those interested in a more thorough coverage of any test or area of testing should turn to the sources of information about tests discussed in Chapter 1. We will now briefly discuss aptitude tests for specific courses and professions and tests of creativity.

Aptitude Tests for Specific Courses and Professions

Aptitude tests developed for particular school subjects such as algebra and foreign languages have been used extensively in the past to help individual pupils with their curricular choices. In recent years, however, this popular practice has diminished. Research has shown that such tests generally do not significantly increase the predictive validity over what can be obtained by a general mental ability test, the relevant subscores on multifactor aptitude tests, or achievement test batteries. Because these latter tests are usually given in the schools, it may well be a waste of time and money to administer special-aptitude tests.

Many special-aptitude tests, such as the Law School Admissions Test and the Medical College Admission Test, have also been developed in recent years for use in various graduate and professional schools. These tests are designed to be of appropriate difficulty (harder than general aptitude tests for adults) and emphasize the abilities of importance to the particular profession. Although these tests are usually slightly better predictors than general aptitude tests, their major advantage lies in their security. Many general aptitude tests could be obtained in advance by an enterprising person wishing to obtain a high score, thereby gaining admission into a professional school. The security of the professional test rules out this sort of endeavor as a factor in admission decisions.

Tests of Creativity

Some who subscribe to the general theory of intelligence suggest that creativity is an aspect of general intelligence and need not be measured separately. Others realize that, although tests of general ability are best able to predict future school success (that is, grades), it is likely that creativity is a distinct ability. Research seems to indicate that whereas a person has to be reasonably intelligent to be creative, the converse does not hold.

We feel that more research on attempts to measure creativity and to investigate its correlates is warranted. There is now available enough evidence to suggest that creativity is something unique and not necessarily correlated with ability to perform well in an academic setting. (However, it is a misconception that creative children do poorly in schoolwork. Research shows that, as a group, creative children do quite well in school.) There are many potential benefits available if the construct of creativity can be effectively isolated and measured. Creative people are important for an advancing society. If creativity can be further understood, if the identification of creative people becomes possible, and if creativity can be taught in the schools, society is sure to benefit.

At the present time there are few creativity tests on the market. The tests that do exist should be considered only as research instruments, and much more work is needed in the area before we can really feel comfortable with the results these tests give us. For further reading on this interesting topic, refer to Getzels & Jackson (1962), Torrance (1962, 1965), Wallach & Kogan (1965), Guilford (1967), Crockenberg (1972, pp. 27–46), and Magnusson & Backteman (1978).

USING APTITUDE TEST RESULTS

Considering all the types of aptitude tests discussed in this chapter, it can confidently be said that the average child will take at least three aptitude tests before graduating from high school. A college-bound student may easily take five or more. How are these tests being used? Are they helpful or harmful?

The public has been much concerned with the uses and possible *misuses* of aptitude tests. This final section, devoted to the uses of aptitude tests, also contains warnings against potential misuses.

Table 1.1 lists some various purposes of standardized tests under four headings: instructional, guidance, administrative, and research. The use of aptitude tests under each of these categories is discussed in more detail here. We will also discuss the use of such tests in employment.

Instructional Uses

The ability level of students in a particular class should enable a teacher to evaluate the appropriateness of the class materials. A teacher should not teach the same kind of material in the same fashion to two classes, one in which the students have a mean scholastic aptitude score of 85 and the other in which the students have a mean scholastic aptitude score of 120. Neither should two students within the same class who differ widely in ability have similar assignments. Thus, knowledge of general aptitude test scores enables a teacher to make better decisions about the kind of class material presented to each student.

If educators gain more knowledge in the area of aptitude-treatment interaction (see Cronbach & Snow, 1969), scores on aptitude tests may become even more helpful in designing appropriate instructional strategies. However, it is likely that if aptitude tests are to be maximally effective in such a task, they will need to be somewhat different from those currently most popular (see Chi, Glaser, & Rees, 1982; Glaser, 1973). We should remember that current aptitude tests are much more useful for prognosis than for diagnosis.

An argument that has occasionally been voiced against the use of aptitude tests for instructional purposes is that teachers will use low aptitude scores as an excuse for not attempting to teach the students—"The students can't learn anyway" attitude. Unfortunately, it is probably true that some teachers have this attitude. Aptitude test scores should be used in helping teachers form realistic expectations of students; they should not be used to help teachers develop fatalistic expectations.

However, in agreeing that this potential danger of testing exists, we do not think it should be overemphasized. The teachers in slum schools who do not try their hardest because of preconceived ideas that their students cannot learn have not obtained their ideas of student deficiency primarily from aptitude test scores. Such factors as the parents' educational level, socio-economic status, race, and occupation all contribute to teachers' opinions concerning a child's aptitude. Goslin (1967), a noted sociologist, in a comprehensive survey of teachers' opinions about tests, found that less than one-fourth of the teachers felt that abilities measured by intelligence tests are more important than other qualities for predicting school success. He also found that teachers tend to view intelligence tests results as being more influenced by environmental factors than by innate capacities. Whether or not this is true, Goslin's findings suggest that teachers are not likely to become fatalistic about a person's innate ability from intelligence test score information. Goslin summarized the problems of teachers' opinions concerning the nature of intelligence as follows:

Leaving for a moment the question of whether or not intelligence or aptitude tests actually measure innate capabilities to any substantial degree, we may conclude that there are likely to be certain advantages for the school system and for pupils in it if teachers are unwilling to accept the presupposition that a pupil's score reflects his inherent (and therefore, presumably, unchangeable) abilities. How one reconciles this proposition with the facts in the situation, namely, that intelligence tests do measure innate abilities to some degree, however, is less clear. It is probably unrealistic to consider seriously attempting systematically to dupe teachers into thinking that tests do not measure innate abilities or that there are no such things as genetically influenced individual differences in capacity for learning. . . . In attempting to hide the fact that individual differences in learning capacity do exist, such a policy may result in teachers and others using less appropriate measures . . . to make inferences about the intellectual capacities of children (pp. 131–132).

Knowing that Denny has a scholastic aptitude DIQ of 80 and that his father is an unemployed alcoholic, the teacher may conclude (correctly or incorrectly) that Denny will have trouble learning in school. If the teacher accepts these factors in the spirit of a challenge and makes every effort to help Denny—fine. If the teacher adopts a fatalistic attitude toward Denny—bad. However, there is no more compelling reason to blame the test for the improper attitude than to blame the teacher's knowledge of all the other facts.

Let us make this point clear. *Aptitude tests can help teachers develop realistic expectations for their students.* While we do not condone—in fact we condemn—teachers who develop fatalistic attitudes toward the learning abilities of their students, we do not think aptitude tests should be made the scapegoat. We admit this potential misuse of tests. There is little evidence, however, to suggest that teachers' attitudes toward the learning potential of their students are unduly influenced by test results. A 1973 Teachers Opinion Poll of NEA members shows, for example, that six teachers in 10 thought that group IQ (their term—we prefer *scholastic aptitude*) test scores predicted poorly or not at all the ability of physically handicapped pupils. Three teachers in four thought the test predicted poorly or not at all the ability of socially or culturally different pupils. However, seven in 10 thought the tests predicted very well or fairly well the ability of pupils other than the handicapped (Teachers Opinion Poll, 1974). Obviously, the teachers sampled in this poll are not (as a group) overinfluenced by test results. Airasian, Kellaghan, Madaus, & Pedulla (1977) found that in less than 10 percent of the cases standardized achievement tests results alter Irish teachers' perceptions of their students.

Research shows that a child's classroom behavior counts more than standardized tests in teacher judgments about students (Kellaghan, Madaus, & Airasian, 1980; Salmon-Cox, 1981). Moreover, the teachers tend to raise, but not lower, their ratings of students' performance as a result of receiving standardized test results. It must be remembered, however, that if we use any kind of data (including aptitude tests) to label children, we must be sure not to misuse the labels. *Labels must be treated as descriptions rather than as explanations.* Too often a label is treated as an explanation.

Improvement in aptitude test scores should not be used in evaluating learning outcomes or teaching, because these scores should be relatively unaffected for formal school learning. However, knowing something about the ability level of the students in a class or a school *can* help teachers determine whether the students are learning as much as is predicted from their ability level. Although some people object to the term *underachiever* (for, really, it is just an overprediction), it is nonetheless helpful to know that a person is not performing as well as could be predicted on the basis of ability scores. If a whole class or school is performing less well (say, for example, on a standardized achievement battery) than would be predicted from aptitude test scores, then this *may* be due to inadequate teaching. (See the section in Chapter 5 entitled "Expectancy Scores.")

Guidance Uses

Aptitude test scores can be useful in vocational, educational, and personal counseling. These test scores are useful in vocational counseling because the educational requirements of some jobs require considerable general ability. The correlations between general aptitude scores and success in training programs tend to run between 0.40 and 0.50 (Ghiselli, 1966). These correlations would be even higher if there were no restriction of range because the scores were used for selection into the training programs. (See Chapter 4.) McCall (1977) found that aptitude scores obtained on a sample of children between 3 and 18 years old predicted educational and occupational status when the sample was age 26 or older.

General aptitude tests often provide useful data for dealing with problem children. An overactive first-grader, if very bright, may be bored and need to be challenged more. Or the child may be totally incapable of doing first-grade work and therefore causing trouble because of frustration. If the child is of average intelligence, perhaps emotional problems are the reason for the overactivity. An individually administered intelligence test can often provide the best data available for judging which of these competing hypotheses is most tenable.

Multifactor aptitude tests are often used in counseling to give students a better idea of their differential abilities. As discussed, the measurement of these differential abilities does not necessarily improve differential prediction, but it does lead to a fuller understanding of one's self.

For guidance, as for instructional purposes, there are some possible misuses of aptitude test scores. The problem of treating test scores as fatalistic predictors still exists. Counselors, teachers, and in fact all school personnel should remember that their job, in part, is to attempt to upset negative predictions.

A problem related to educators' becoming fatalistic is the development of a fatalistic attitude in children. A popular topic of conversation is the importance of developing a good self-concept in the students. There is no doubt that students should be self-accepting and feel that others accept them also. If a counselor interprets a low test score so that the student feels unworthy, that is indeed unfortunate. One of the advantages of a multifactor aptitude test is that a student usually performs at an acceptable level on some of the subtests, and these scores can and should serve as morale builders for the student.

As with other possible misuses of test results, we feel this problem of low aptitude scores resulting in poor self-concepts can be overemphasized. Just as test scores are not the major factors in forming teachers' opinions about the learning abilities of children, so also low aptitude test scores are probably much less influential than other factors in contributing to an undesirable (inaccurately low) self-concept. In fact, a review of relevant research by Rosenholtz & Simpson (1984) shows quite clearly that young children typically overestimate their own abilities, but their estimates begin to relate to actual classroom performance by about second grade. This shift to realism may be considered good or bad, depending on one's views. The shift is certainly not due to aptitude test results, because aptitude tests are not routinely given prior to grade 3 or 4. Children of all grade levels are found to spend considerable time determining their academic status in comparison with their classmates'. Tests often seem to be blamed for educational problems that were not caused by the tests to begin with. To be sure, there is some relationship between what individuals think they can achieve and what they will achieve. Nevertheless, it is a generally held position that counselors should help students obtain and accept an accurate self-concept, not an inaccurately high one. Proper interpretation of aptitude tests can be useful in this endeavor (Hodgson & Cramer, 1977). We agree totally with Carroll & Horn (1981), who state that "far from being abused by overuse, the science of human abilities is underexploited in diagnosis, counseling, and evaluation" (p. 1019).

Administrative Uses

Aptitude tests can be used in many ways by the administration. Some selection, classification, and placement decisions, such as who should be admitted to kindergarten early, who should be placed in the enriched classes, who should be placed in the remedial classes, and who should be admitted to colleges, are decisions that may be made by counselors or school psychologists who rightly may not consider themselves as administrators. Nevertheless, these are administrative decisions.

As with almost any use of aptitude tests, there are accompanying potential misuses. Some persons charge that the major misuse of tests in administrative functions is that decisions made on the basis of test scores are often treated as if they were permanent and irreversible. If a child is put into a remedial class in, say, grade 3, there is too often a tendency on the part of the administration, having once made a decision, to forget about it. The child then gets lock-stepped into a curriculum.

Now, although we do not support administrative inflexibility in the reconsideration of decisions, we should consider whether the use of test scores is really the causative factor of this inflexibility. We must admit that in some cases it is. Some people simply place far too much faith in test scores, and this results in too much faith in the correctness of decisions—so they are made and then forgotten. However, not all, or not even most, inflexibility can be charged to test score misuse. Many of the decisions made would be incorrectly treated as permanent, even if there were no test score data on the students. It is worth noting that if a decision must be made, it should be based on as much evidence as possible. Not to use test information in making decisions because of possible misuse is cowardly, foolish, and even unprofessional.

There are also some who argue against the use of aptitude tests for various decisions, because they do not think the decision must, or should, be made at all. However, if a test is used to help implement a policy that is considered incorrect by some, there is no reason to blame the test. For example, a sizable group of educators is against ability grouping. If the policy, right or wrong, is to group on the basis of ability, it is appropriate to use an aptitude test to help decide who should be placed in what group. Some have argued that tests are unfair to different subgroups, and therefore the test results should be ignored when doing ability grouping. However, although we do *not* advocate using *only* test data, Findley (1974) reported that Kariger has shown that such a process would result in *less* separation of upper and lower SES students than if other factors in addition to test scores are used—for example, teacher grades, study habits, citizenship and industry, and social and emotional maturity. As Findley explains, "stereotypes of upper and lower SES children held by school personnel result in further separation between groups than the tests alone would warrant" (p. 25). We emphasize that this example is not meant to advocate ability grouping or decisions made only on test data. It does suggest that blaming *tests* for what may be considered harmful social separation is inappropriate. However, with respect to aptitude testing and grouping, we should make one important point. It is becoming increasingly clear that some educationally deprived children are being inappropriately labeled as retarded and are therefore placed in special classes. Any time an aptitude test score is used, the administrator must keep in mind the environmental conditions under which the child was reared. Whether or not special classes are desirable for mentally retarded children, it certainly is not desirable to *misplace* a child into such a special class.

Let us take another example. Some people are opposed to the use of scholastic aptitude tests in college selection decisions. It is sometimes unclear whether they oppose the notion of selecting students on the basis of predicted success in college or the use of scholastic aptitude tests in assisting in that prediction. If the former, that is a philosophical point and should be argued separately from whether tests help in predicting success. If the latter, the critics should read the research literature. As Samuda (1975) states, "the evidence about college entrance tests as predictors is no longer a subject of legitimate dispute. The studies have been widespread, they number in the thousands, and the results are consistent. By and large, the higher the test scores, the more successful the students are in college" (p. viii). In fact, there is also evidence that academic aptitude at time of college admission is significantly related to occupational level later in life (Lewis, 1975).

But don't aptitude tests serve to keep the lower SES students out of college? Were they not, in fact, designed to do that? The answer to both questions is *no*. As to the latter question, as Cronbach indicates in an excellent historical analysis, "Proponents of testing, from Thomas Jefferson onward, have wanted to open doors for the talented poor, in a system in which doors often are opened by parental wealth and status" (1975, p. 1). With respect to the former, evidence suggests that the testing movement has accelerated the breakdown of classes by identifying able individuals from the lower strata who might otherwise have gone unnoticed (Tyler, 1976). The reason some people may doubt this is that they read potentially misleading statements on this topic such as "Men with high test scores *tend to come from* economically and socially advantaged families" (Jenks, 1972, p. 221, italics added). What Jenks should have said is that people from upper SES groups *tend to score higher* than do individuals from lower SES groups. It has been estimated that of youths in the top quarter with respect to scores on intelligence tests, 33 percent come from the working class, 42 percent come from the lower-middle class, and 25 percent come from the upper and upper-middle classes combined (see Havighurst & Neugarten, 1975). Thus, lower SES students are not kept out of college because of their aptitude test scores. Fricke (1975) demonstrated that if admission to the freshman class at the University of Michigan had been determined *entirely* by academic aptitude test scores of high school seniors, a *majority* of freshmen would have come from low SES backgrounds rather than the 10 or 15 percent that is typically the case. Using only the presumed "biased" test scores would not decrease but *increase* by a factor of four or five the number of low SES students. Again, we are not advocating the use of only test scores to make decisions. We are pointing out that it is not low test scores that are keeping low SES students (in general) out of college. At any rate, because of the proven validity of scholastic aptitude tests for predicting college success, if there is a policy, right or wrong, to limit college enrollment to those with some minimal level of scholastic aptitude, it is not incorrect to use aptitude test scores to *help* determine who should be admitted to college. Far too often the cry of test misuse is raised because the lamenter is against the policy that the correct use of test scores helps implement rather than because the test is not being correctly used under the existing policy.

The uses of aptitude test results for public relations and for providing information for outside agencies do have some very real potential pitfalls. Occasionally, news releases are made concerning how schools compare with each other in the average ability of their students. Although this sort of public relations may momentarily "feather the cap" of some school official, the chances that the public understands the release are dim indeed, and one is hard put to verbalize any real advantages of this sort of public release of information.

The issue of whether schools should provide an individual's aptitude test score to outside agencies is a cloudy one. The question is whether such information is to be treated as confidential. If so, then it should not be released without a student's permission. But does the consent have to be explicit, or can it be implied? For example, if a student applies for a job that requires security clearance, is the application to be interpreted as implied consent for the release of school records? This question cannot be discussed in great detail in this book. The safest procedure (both morally and legally), however, is not to release test information to any outside agency without the explicit consent of the student and/or the parents.

Another possible use of aptitude tests is for relevant supplementary information in curriculum planning and evaluation. An idea of the general ability level of the school should help educators decide, for example, how much relative emphasis to place on college preparatory curricula.

Finally, some administrators feel that aptitude tests can be useful in deciding which teachers to hire or promote. Whereas there is obviously a relationship between aptitude test scores and the obtaining of a teacher's certificate, there is little known evidence suggesting a relationship between aptitude test scores and on-the-job performance for certified teachers. Thus, hiring or promoting on this basis has little merit.

Research Uses

Aptitude test scores can be used in research in many ways. Ordinarily the scores are used as independent variables (variables that influence the variable being studied) in a research design. For example, in evaluating instructional procedures many researchers would wish to use some aptitude measure as an independent variable. Some research—such as that investigating the environmental effects on intelligence—treats the scores as dependent variables (the variables one wishes to influence). Because this book is not designed for the researcher, we preclude further discussion of this topic.

Employment Uses

As we mentioned briefly in Chapter 4, on validity, there was an earlier belief that aptitude tests seemed to predict success in some jobs and in some settings but that the validity coefficients seemed to be situation-specific. It has also been suggested by psychologists and educators that scores on aptitude tests given to children were predictive of school success but not much else. Recent research and reviews of the literature have refuted both of those positions.

With regard to the second point, Willerman writes as follows: "The results . . . clearly confirm the view that outstanding accomplishments can be predicted from IQ tests obtained in childhood, . . . if one were looking for a single childhood augury of outstanding later accomplishment, one could not do better than to obtain an intelligence test measure on the subject'' (1979, p. 332). We should not infer from this that we should select job applicants based on childhood IQ scores. However, it does support both the stability and cogency of early aptitude for life success.

The validity of aptitude tests in employment situations has been studied extensively throughout the years. Current opinion is that psychologists made incorrect inferences from the early studies showing positive but not necessarily high or statistically significant validity coefficients. It is now generally concluded that most findings of low validity were due to statistical artifacts such as small sample size, unreliable criterion data, and restriction of range. Using such techniques as meta-analysis, we currently can conclude that ability tests do, quite consistently, predict subsequent job and job training performance. Schmidt & Hunter, who have done much of the theoretical and statistical work in this area, flatly state that ''professionally developed cognitive ability tests are valid predictors of performance on the job and in training for all jobs in all settings'' (1981, p. 1128). While this strong statement has not been proven to everyone's satisfaction, they do back it up with an impressive amount of evidence.

Not only do aptitude tests predict job performance, but they do so better than any other single predictor. Hunter & Hunter (1983) summarize a set of validity studies where all the studies used supervisor ratings as the criterion. Table 7.2 shows the mean validity coefficients of various predictors for entry-level jobs where training would follow hiring; supervisor ratings were

TABLE 7.2
**MEAN VALIDITIES OF VARIOUS PREDICTORS
FOR ENTRY-LEVEL JOBS***

Predictor	Mean Validity	Number of Correlations	Number of Subjects
Ability Composite	.53	425	32,124
Job Tryout	.44	20	—
Biographical Inventory	.37	12	4,429
Reference Check	.26	10	5,389
Academic Achievement	.21	17	6,014
Experience	.18	425	32,124
Interview	.14	10	2,694
Training and Experience Ratings	.13	65	—
Education	.10	425	32,124
Interest	.10	3	1,789
Age	−.01	425	32,124

* Adapted from Hunter & Hunter (1983).

the criterion data. As can be seen, ability is, on the average, the best predictor. The findings in this table must be taken quite seriously. They are based on a large number of correlations. Further, the criterion is one which might reasonably be influenced by interpersonal skills of the same type that might influence interview results. In spite of that, the mean validity for interviews was far down the list.

Whether or not one uses ability tests in employment decisions can have a tremendous impact on productivity. Hunter & Schmidt (1982) applied a utility model to the entire national workforce and estimated that the gain in productivity from using cognitive tests as opposed to selecting at random would amount to a minimum of $80 billion per year! They equate this gain as being roughly equal to total corporate profits, or 20 percent of the total federal budget. While these estimates are based on a few assumptions that are open to some debate, there can be no doubt but that the use of ability tests can result in more effective hiring and that effective hiring procedures can have a substantial impact on national productivity.

SUMMARY

The major points of this chapter are summarized in the following statements:

1. The definitions, structure, etiology, and stability of intelligence are all unsettled issues in psychology.
2. Current definitions of intelligence stress that it is a behavioral trait that is, at least in part, dependent upon past learning.
3. Theories regarding the structure of intelligence have ranged from the idea of a general factor of intelligence to the conceptualization of many specific factors. These various theories have resulted in many different kinds of tests, classified as tests of general intelligence, multifactor aptitude tests, and special-aptitude tests.
4. Both heredity and environment affect intelligence test scores.
5. In general, intelligence measures are not very stable in early childhood, but by the age of 5 or so they begin to stabilize.
6. The most popular individual intelligence tests are the Stanford-Binet and the Wechsler instruments. The Kaufman-ABC is a recently published test which may well become popular. Specialized training is required to administer and interpret these tests correctly.
7. Individual tests can be better used with those who, for motivational or other reasons, do not perform accurately on group tests. Furthermore, more clinical information can be obtained from individual tests.
8. Teachers are generally qualified to administer group tests of intelligence.
9. Some attempts have been made in the past to build culture-fair intelligence tests. These results have largely failed if we define *culture fairness*

as the equality of mean scores for various subcultures. Even if culture-fair tests could be devised, the usefulness of such measures is open to question.

10. Multifactor aptitude tests are used by the majority of school systems. Although designed to be differentially predictive, they have not been very successful in that respect. Nevertheless, they have remained a popular tool of the counselors to assist students in understanding themselves better and as a catalyst for career exploration.

11. Many kinds of special-aptitude tests exist. They include mechanical, clerical, musical, and art aptitude tests; tests for specific courses and professions; and creativity tests.

12. Aptitude test results can be used by teachers, counselors, administrators, and employers. They can also be misused. Unfortunately, the negative attitude the public correctly displays toward test misuse has been overgeneralized and extended to the tests themselves. There can be no doubt but that the wise use of aptitude tests benefits society.

POINTS TO PONDER

1. Which theory of intelligence do you subscribe to? What are the advantages and limitations of accepting this theory?

2. Project Head Start implicitly makes an assumption that environment plays a significant role in intellectual development. If research shows that programs like Head Start are ineffective, must we conclude the assumption is incorrect?

3. Can you write an item that you would defend as being a measure of aptitude and not a measure of achievement?

4. A married couple wishes to adopt an infant. They request assurance that the infant possesses a normal intelligence. What should the social worker tell this couple?

5. List five specific situations where group intelligence tests would be more appropriate than individual intelligence tests. Do the same for the converse situation.

6. Assume that two randomly chosen groups were given the Stanford-Binet at age 4. One group (group A) of students received nursery school instruction that included tasks similar to those asked on the Stanford-Binet. The other group (group B) received no such instruction. On retesting at age 5, group A performs significantly better. Does this tell us anything about the stability of intelligence, the effects of environment on intelligence, or the validity of the test?

7. Why do you think there are no multifactor aptitude tests published for the early elementary grades?

8. What are the advantages and limitations of using a multifactor aptitude test rather than a set of special-aptitude tests covering the same constructs?
9. What are the instructional advantages (if any) of being able to correctly identify highly creative children?
10. Given the question "What can books be used for?" a student responds, "To build fires." Is this a creative answer? Support your contention.

CHAPTER 8

Standardized Achievement Tests

DIFFERENCES BETWEEN STANDARDIZED AND TEACHER-MADE
  ACHIEVEMENT TESTS
CLASSIFICATION OF STANDARDIZED ACHIEVEMENT TESTS
EXAMPLES OF STANDARDIZED ACHIEVEMENT TESTS
CRITERION-REFERENCED STANDARDIZED ACHIEVEMENT TESTS
STANDARDIZED ACHIEVEMENT TESTS IN SPECIFIC SUBJECTS
STANDARDIZED ACHIEVEMENT TEST SURVEY BATTERIES
USING ACHIEVEMENT TEST RESULTS

What is an achievement test? How do standardized achievement tests differ
from teacher-made achievement tests? Are there achievement tests for all
subject matter areas? Will the Stanford Achievement Test be valid for my
purpose? What use can be made of achievement test results? What are some
of the factors that must be considered in the selection of a standardized
achievement test? These are some of the questions that the classroom
teacher, counselor, and school administrator can be expected to ask and
should be able to answer. This chapter presents information that will assist
the test user to answer these and other questions.

When one considers the number of standardized and teacher-made tests,
the number of achievement tests annually administered easily surpasses all
others. Literally hundreds of standardized achievement tests are available to
the classroom teacher, counselor, school psychologist, and administrator.
Some are norm-referenced (NRT), while others are criterion-referenced
(CRT). Some purportedly yield both norm- and criterion-referenced information. Some measure only a single subject, whereas others consist of a
battery of tests measuring performance in a variety of content areas. Some
are designed for only the upper grades; others are made up of an articulated
series ranging from K to 12. Some provide survey-type information, while
others yield diagnostic data. Most standardized achievement tests are group-

administered, but some, especially those designed for the handicapped, are individually administered.

To try to cover a substantial portion of them here would be an exercise in futility. We have selected only a few of the more representative ones in order that we might comment on their properties—properties that every user should examine when selecting a standardized test. The tests discussed here are generally of high quality. However, there are many other standardized achievement tests of equally high quality, and it should *not* be assumed that the tests discussed in this chapter are the best ones available. In the long run, the best test is the one that best measures the user's instructional or curricular objectives most validly, reliably, efficiently, and economically.

After studying this chapter, the student should be able to do the following:

1. Understand the similarities and differences between standardized and teacher-made achievement tests.
2. Compare the three major types of standardized achievement tests—diagnostic, single-subject-matter, and survey battery—in terms of purposes, coverage, and construction.
3. Have a better conception of the newer type of standardized criterion-referenced tests and of how they can be useful in the diagnosis of student learning problems as well as helpful in planning for optimal instruction.
4. Recognize that most standardized achievement tests are more similar than dissimilar.
5. Critically evaluate a standardized achievement test.
6. Understand the factors to be considered in selecting a standardized achievement test.
7. Understand and discuss the various instructional, guidance, and administrative uses of standardized achievement test data.
8. Recognize the supplemental value of standardized achievement test data to assist educators in their decision making.

DIFFERENCES BETWEEN STANDARDIZED AND TEACHER-MADE ACHIEVEMENT TESTS

Teacher-made and commercially published standardized achievement tests are more alike than different. Where there are differences, they are more a matter of degree than intent, since the purpose of each is to measure pupil knowledge, skills, and ability.

Any test that has a representative sampling of the relevant content (that is, possesses content validity) and that is designed to measure the extent of present knowledge and skills (from recall of factual material to the higher mental processes) is an achievement test, regardless of whether this test was constructed by the classroom teacher or by professional test makers. The

TABLE 8.1

COMPARISONS BETWEEN STANDARDIZED
AND TEACHER-MADE ACHIEVEMENT TESTS

Characteristic	Teacher-Made Achievement Tests	Standardized Achievement Tests
Directions for administration and scoring	Usually no uniform directions specified	Specific instructions standardize administration and scoring procedures
Sampling of content	Both content and sampling are determined by classroom teacher	Content determined by curriculum and subject-matter experts; involves extensive investigations of existing syllabi, textbooks, and programs (i.e., contains material covered in many, if not most, classrooms); sampling of content done systematically
Construction	May be hurried and haphazard; often no test blueprints, item tryouts, item analysis or revision; quality of test may be quite poor	Items written or at least edited by specialists. Developers use meticulous construction procedures that include constructing objectives and test blueprints, employing item tryouts, item analysis, and item revisions; only best items used
Reliability	Generally not known; can be high if test carefully made	Generally high, with reliability often over .90; small standard errors of measurement
Interpretive aids	None	Can be quite elaborate, ranging from a few suggestions to detailed remedial strategies
Norms	Only local classroom norms are available	Typically make available national, school district, and school building norms, in addition to local norms
Purposes and use	Best suited for measuring particular objectives set by teacher and for intra-class comparisons	Best suited for measuring broader curriculum objectives and for interclass, school, and national comparisons

major (but not the only) distinction between the standardized achievement test and the teacher-made test is that in a standardized achievement test the systematic sampling of performance (that is, the pupil's score) has been obtained under prescribed directions of administration. They also differ markedly in terms of their sampling of content, construction, norms, and purpose and use. The comparisons between teacher-made and standardized achievement tests are summarized in Table 8.1.

Sampling of Content

Standardized achievement tests normally cover much more material (although they need not have more items) than teacher-made tests because they are traditionally designed to assess more than one year's learning. Teacher-made achievement tests usually cover a single unit of work or that of a term. Standardized tests, in contrast to teacher-made tests, may not so readily reflect curricular changes, although test publishers attempt to "keep up with the times." (This is less of a problem with single-subject-matter tests than with survey batteries. It is easier, and often less expensive, to revise and renorm a single test than a survey battery.)

Whether a person should use a commercially published standardized test or a teacher-made test depends to a large degree on the particular objectives to be measured. Norm-referenced standardized tests are constructed to measure generally accepted goals rather than unique or particular classroom objectives. Criterion-referenced standardized tests and teacher-made tests usually measure more adequately the degree to which the objectives of a particular course for a particular teacher have been met. For example, let us assume that a teacher of eleventh-grade history wants to know the degree to which the pupils have an awareness of social conditions before the French Revolution. If this area is atypical of the conventional course curriculum, it should be readily evident that the teacher-made test would be more valid than the best standardized test that did not concern itself with this objective. In other words, test users must ask themselves, "How valid is this test for my objectives?" Generally, the teacher-made content test is more up-to-date vis-à-vis the curriculum, especially in the sciences.

Construction

Standardized achievement tests differ from teacher-made achievement tests in the relative amount of time, money, effort, and resources that are available to commercial test publishers. It is estimated that it costs from $50,000 to $100,000 for commercial test development (APA Monitor, 1984). The following example of how a standardized achievement test is constructed by test publishers may indicate why the teacher-made test is seldom as well-prepared as the standardized test.

First, the test publisher arranges a meeting of curriculum and subject-matter specialists. After a thorough study and analysis of syllabi, textbooks, and programs throughout the country, a list of objectives is prepared—what information students should have, what principles they should understand, and what skills they should possess. (Messick, 1984 has proposed a new approach to the development of achievement tests where, in place of instructional objectives, we use a developmental model.) These decisions concerning objectives to be sampled by the test are then reduced to a test outline or table of specifications (based on the judgments of the various experts involved in the test planning) that guides the test maker in constructing the test. Then, with the assistance of classroom teachers and subject-matter experts, a team of professional test writers prepares the items according to the specifications outlined in the grid.[1] After careful review and editing, the tryout or experimental items are arranged in a test booklet. Then, the general instructions (and specific instructions, if there are subparts) to both administrators and pupils are written and the tryout tests are given to a sample of pupils for whom the test is designed. After the answer sheets have been scored, an item analysis[2] is made in order to identify the poor items. In addition, comments from test administrators are noted insofar as they pertain to timing and clarity of instructions for both administrator and pupils. Further editing is then done on the basis of the item analysis (or more items are written if too many need to be discarded and the content validity is rechecked) and the test is then ready to be standardized.[3] After a representative sample of pupils has been selected, the refined test is administered and scored. Reliability and criterion-related validity evidence is obtained, and norms are prepared for the standardization sample.

This brief description should demonstrate how much time, effort, and expense go into the preparation of a standardized achievement test. Without minimizing the enthusiasm, interest, and dedication of classroom teachers in constructing their own tests, teacher-made tests seldom compare in technical aspects with commercially made standardized tests. The teacher alone constructs a test; the standardized test is constructed by test specialists in cooperation with subject-matter experts, curriculum specialists, and statisti-

[1] Inclusion of such a grid in the publisher's test manual would be very valuable to the user in ascertaining whether the test has content validity for him. Unfortunately, few publishers include the grid.

[2] Item analysis is the procedure used to compute the difficulty and discriminating power of each of the items on a test. See *Short-Cut Statistics for Teacher-Made Tests*. Princeton, N.J.: Educational Testing Service, Advisory Bulletin No. 5, 1964, for a simple treatment (this and other bulletins are available gratis from the publisher).

[3] It has commonly been assumed that reworking or rewriting test items on the basis of item analysis will improve the test. However, differential discarding of items could result in a biased test (such that the content validity is actually lowered). See Richard Cox, An Empirical Investigation of the Effect of Item Selection Techniques on Achievement Test Construction. Unpublished doctoral dissertation, Michigan State University, East Lansing, 1964.

cians. The teacher has a limited amount of time to devote to test construction; standardized test makers can spend as much as two or three years on the preparation of their tests. Teachers have little if any opportunity to examine their items in terms of difficulty and discrimination[4]; commercial test publishers have recourse to statistical tools in order to eliminate or to suggest ways to rewrite the poor items. Because teachers are often unable to try out their tests beforehand, they do not have the opportunity (1) to clarify ambiguous directions and/or (2) to alter the speededness of the test by either increasing or decreasing the number of items. The commercial test publisher tries out the items in experimental or preliminary editions and is able to ascertain how well the test and the items function. Generally, standardized achievement tests are more reliable than teacher-made achievement tests. On the whole, then, it should be readily evident that commercial standardized achievement tests are superior in terms of technical features to teacher-made achievement tests. This does not imply that teacher-made achievement tests cannot be technically as sound as commercial tests. They can be, but because of the time, money, effort, and technical skill involved in preparing a good test, they normally are not.

Classroom teachers should not develop an inferiority complex because of the preceding remarks. They should recognize that they have been trained to be teachers and not test makers.

Interpretive Aids

Another distinguishing feature between the traditional teacher-made and standardized test concerns the ancillary material accompanying the test to assist the classroom teacher in undertaking remediation of material that has not been learned by the pupils. Although some of the standardized single-subject-matter tests have little, if any, material to aid the teacher in interpreting the pupils' performance and then undertaking corrective action, some of the standardized survey achievement batteries, such as the Metropolitan, Stanford, and California Test of Basic Skills, have separate manuals devoted solely to providing suggestions to the classroom teacher for teaching/reteaching the concept(s) the pupils do not understand. Teacher-made tests have no such provisions, of course.

Norms

Another feature distinguishing most standardized tests from teacher-made achievement tests is that, generally, standardized tests contain norms of one type or another: sex, rural–urban, grade, age, type of school (public, pri-

---

[4] An item that is either too easy or too difficult is generally a poor item. Moreover, if the better pupils fail to answer an item correctly while the poorer or less able pupils give the correct answer, this item is also a weak or poor item.

vate, parochial). Their value is dependent upon the manner in which they have been constructed. With national norms, the classroom teacher, school psychologist, counselor, or others concerned with the pupil's education will be in a position to make numerous comparisons of the performance of individual pupils, classes, grades, schools, and school districts with the academic progress of pupils throughout the country. Naturally, the kinds of comparisons that can be made depend upon the types of norms furnished by the test publisher. Although teacher-made tests may have norms, they usually do not.

Purposes and Use

Standardized achievement tests, especially survey batteries, have a broad sampling of content, and may be too general in scope to meet most of the specific educational objectives of a particular school or teacher. Teacher-made achievement tests, on the other hand, will usually have narrow content sampling (although what is sampled may be covered thoroughly)—especially those tests prepared for just a single unit of material or for material covered in a single semester. This does not imply that the standardized achievement test is superior to the teacher-made achievement test. Because of the emphasis placed upon the various course objectives, the standardized achievement test may be superior to the teacher-made test in one instance and not in another. Both standardized and teacher-made achievement tests serve a common function: the assessment of the pupil's knowledge and skills at a particular time. However, because standardized and teacher-made achievement tests often differ in scope and content (as well as in the normative data provided), they also differ in their uses. It is usually agreed that the teacher-made achievement test will assess specific classroom objectives more satisfactorily than does the standardized achievement test. It should be noted, however, that all educational decisions—assignment of course grades, vocational and educational guidance, promotion, placement, teacher evaluation, instruction, and research, to mention just a few—should be based on as much empirical data as possible. Because the standardized and teacher-made achievement tests serve different purposes, school personnel should consider the supplemental value of standardized achievement test scores to teacher-made test scores and teacher observations and judgments, rather than argue that one measurement device is better than the other or that one should replace the other.

To compare the pupils in one school with those in another school, a standardized achievement test would be appropriate. To determine whether Betty has learned her addition skills in Mr. Jones' third grade may be better accomplished by using a teacher-made test. To measure pupils' basic skills, a standardized achievement test is the better choice. To measure pupil's knowledge in some content areas such as science, geography, and civics, a teacher-made test may be more appropriate, since the content in these areas may become outdated quickly and the locally constructed test can keep up with the times more easily. Thus, the functions or uses of the two kinds of achievement tests vary.

In addition, standardized achievement tests (in contrast to teacher-made tests), often have equivalent forms which allows one to measure growth without administering the same items to the examinees, or to obtain a "score" on one form if an error was made on another form. Many of the newer standardized survey batteries have an articulated series of levels so that one can obtain comparable measures from K through 12. Finally, more and more survey batteries are standardized concurrently with an aptitude measure, thereby permitting one to interpret an examinee's achievement in relation to his or her ability. We consider the uses of standardized achievement tests further in the concluding section of this chapter.

CLASSIFICATION OF STANDARDIZED ACHIEVEMENT TESTS

There are different kinds of standardized achievement tests: *diagnostic* tests, which are designed to isolate a pupil's specific strengths and weaknesses in some particular field of knowledge; *single-subject-matter* achievement tests, which are concerned with measuring the pupil's educational accomplishments in a single content area; and *survey batteries,* which consist of a group of tests in different content areas standardized on the same population so that the results of the various components may be meaningfully compared. (Some measurement texts include *prognostic* tests as a subset of achievement tests, but we prefer to discuss them under aptitude tests.)

These three types—diagnostic, single-subject-matter, and survey battery—of standardized achievement tests differ in their purposes, coverage, and construction. They differ primarily because they are designed to measure different aspects or segments of the pupil's knowledge.

Since we also discuss criterion-referenced tests (CRTs), it might be construed that there are four types of standardized achievement tests. We have purposely avoided this classification scheme, since any of the three types could be norm-referenced, criterion-referenced, or both.

Purpose and Use

All standardized achievement tests are designed to assess pupils' knowledge and skills at a particular point in time. This is true for diagnostic tests, single-subject-matter tests, and survey batteries, whether they be norm-referenced or criterion-referenced. If we are interested in learning whether Bill has the prerequisite entry skills that will enable him to profit maximally from reading

Theodore Lownik Library
Illinois Benedictine College

instruction, we will give him a reading readiness test. If we are interested in learning what Mary's specific strengths or weaknesses are in, say, reading or spelling, we will use a diagnostic test.[5] If we are interested in making a thorough evaluation of Mary's achievement in spelling, we should use a standardized spelling test rather than the spelling subtest of a survey battery, because the survey battery subtest will ordinarily be shorter, thereby being less reliable and of more limited coverage. If we are interested in learning whether Mary is a better speller than she is a reader, we should use a standardized survey battery, where the total test has been standardized on the same sample. If different subject-matter tests have norms based on different samples, direct comparisons cannot be made because the samples might not be equivalent.

For guidance purposes, it may be advisable to use the results of both a survey battery (which will indicate the relative strengths and weaknesses in many different subject-matter fields) and a single-subject-matter test that gives more thorough information in a particular area. For example, pupils can initially be given a survey battery as a preliminary screening device. Then, certain pupils can be identified for more thorough investigation and be given a single-subject-matter and/or diagnostic test in the area of suspected weaknesses. The use of such a sequential testing (that is, using the survey battery for an initial screening and a single survey test and/or a diagnostic test for only a few individuals) is an economical approach. If the results are used properly, sequential testing is of great help to classroom teachers or counselors in obtaining relevant data to assist them in providing optimal learning conditions. In the end, everyone benefits—pupils, teachers, and counselors.

Coverage and Construction

Standardized achievement test batteries attempt to measure pupils' knowledge in many diverse areas; single-subject-matter tests are restricted to only a single area of knowledge such as grade 11 physics, grade 4 spelling, or grade 6 language arts. Both types of tests measure the important skills, knowledge, and course objectives. Normally, single-subject-matter tests are a little more thorough in their coverage. For example, if a spelling test requires 1 hour and the spelling subtest of a battery requires 40 minutes, there is more opportunity for the single test to have more items and thereby to increase the content sampling.

Although the survey battery is more convenient to administer than an equal number of single tests and although, for the most part, the survey

---

[5] The teacher must interpret the results of a diagnostic test cautiously. The test does not provide an absolute and irrevocable explanation for the problem (deficiency or weakness) but offers only some suggestions. The psychometric quality of the data provided by these tests is typically inadequate.

battery is fairly valid for the average classroom teacher, some of the subtests may lack the degree of validity desired because of their more limited sampling of tasks. The general consensus, however, is that, despite the more limited sampling of tasks, survey batteries are preferred over a combination of many single-subject-matter tests. This is so because the survey battery (1) gives a fairly reliable index of a pupil's relative strengths and weaknesses, since it has been standardized on the same population, whereas this is seldom the case for single-subject-matter tests (even those prepared by the same publisher); (2) is more efficient timewise; (3) is usually more economical; and (4) young children generally find it easier to take the tests in a battery rather than as separate single-subject-matter tests because of the common format in the battery.

Diagnostic tests may differ markedly from the survey battery or single-subject-matter test, depending upon their use. Recall that diagnostic tests are designed primarily to assist the teacher in locating or attempting to isolate the genesis of some deficiency. Thus, we expect the diagnostic test to have a thorough coverage of a limited area. For example, both a standardized achievement test of arithmetic skills and/or the arithmetic subtest of a survey battery are concerned with measuring general goals and objectives of the arithmetic curriculum. Hence, both types of arithmetic tests contain a variety of items on many different arithmetic topics. A diagnostic test, however, may be restrictive in the sense that it is concerned only with one or two aspects of arithmetic, such as addition and subtraction. Moreover, the diagnostic test is more concerned with measuring the components that are important in developing knowledge of a complex skill.

There is no appreciable difference among the various types of achievement tests in the technical and mechanical factors involved in their preparation. In many instances, it is not possible to identify the type of test solely on the basis of the item format. That is, a test item such as "What percent of 36 is 9?" could conceivably be found in a survey, a single-subject-matter, or a diagnostic test. About the only way in which the various types of achievement tests may be distinguished is to make a study of the breadth or intensity of their coverage.

Summary

The major distinctions between the various types of standardized achievement tests are in their purpose and ultimate use (and for that reason, they differ slightly in the range of material covered). If an overall assessment in many different areas is desired and if comparisons are to be made for an individual's relative strengths and weaknesses in various subject-matter areas, a survey battery is desired. If only an assessment in a single area is desired, either a single-subject-matter test or a subtest of the battery will suffice. A teacher who is interested in obtaining a clearer picture of particular strengths and/or weaknesses should use a diagnostic test. To describe levels of performance, a criterion-referenced test (CRT) should be used. To make interindividual comparisons, a norm-referenced test (NRT) should be used. At this time it should be emphasized that the final decision regarding the selection of one test over another should be made by the person(s) using the test. It is essential that the test be valid for the users' purposes—they are in the best position to know what use will be made of the test results.

EXAMPLES OF STANDARDIZED ACHIEVEMENT TESTS

In the preceding section we were concerned with comparing and contrasting the different kinds of standardized achievement tests. In this section we present some examples of diagnostic tests, criterion-referenced achievement tests, single-subject-matter achievement tests, and standardized achievement-test survey batteries that are commonly used in the public schools. We also consider some of the factors that are relevant in determining the choice of one achievement test or battery over another.

Diagnostic Tests

We must, at the outset, differentiate between medical and educational diagnosis lest misunderstanding occur. Educational diagnosis generally refers to the identification of a student's weakness or learning difficulty—for instance, Allan is unable to do long division. This differs markedly from medical diagnosis, which is concerned with the identification of the underlying cause(s) of a problem or weakness—for example, Allan has a pain in his chest. Some probable causes are a heart attack, muscle contraction, or gall bladder attack. These hypotheses are further examined, in an effort to identify the probable cause(s) of the problem.

Diagnostic tests are primarily concerned with measuring the skills or abilities (for example, reading, arithmetic) that the subject-matter experts believe are essential in learning a particular subject. For example, an arithmetic diagnostic test will be concerned with factors that experts in teaching arithmetic believe enter into the arithmetic process. A legitimate question that could be raised is as follows: Since we know that survey batteries, especially the newer ones, provide diagnostic-type information (we can see that Billy is having difficulty in adding with carrying, but is doing all right in word problems), why is it necessary to have a separate diagnostic test? Basically, because of the limited sampling of content in the survey battery. Diagnostic achievement tests provide a variety of exercises and problems in a somewhat restricted range of instructional objectives, thereby giving the student considerable opportunity to commit errors that indicate a potential deficiency. In other words, rather than ask one or two items on, say, addition with carrying, a variety of such problems are presented in a diagnostic test. Moreover, the items in diagnostic tests are often graded in difficulty.

Diagnostic tests have much in common with criterion-referenced tests, because (1) both attempt to obtain information about a person's performance in highly specific skills and relate this information to instructional prescriptions, and (2) both have to be sharply focused. In fact, some diagnostic tests are essentially mastery tests, that is, perfect or near-perfect performance is expected. For example, by the end of the first grade the average pupil is expected to demonstrate a left-right orientation in decoding, and failure to do so indicates a deficiency in that skill.

The development of a valid diagnostic[6] test is predicated on satisfying two major assumptions: (1) the ability to analyze skills or knowledge into component subskills and (2) the ability to develop test items that will validly measure these subskills. In fact, a major weakness of diagnostic reading tests is the low reliabilities and high intercorrelations among the separate subtests. The low reliability is particularly significant in some of the shorter diagnostic tests, since this deficiency reduces the test's diagnostic value. The high intercorrelations suggest that the subtests are measuring *similar* skills.

Because reading is an integral component of the learning process and because reading skills have been identified, the majority of diagnostic tests are for reading. Diagnostic reading tests range from the conventional paper-and-pencil test, where the student reads a sentence and records the error in the sentence, to the oral procedure, where the examiner carefully notes, for example, mispronunciations, omissions, repetitions, substitutions, and reversals of letters. In the oral, or "thinking aloud," approach, the examiner is in a better position to observe and record errors as they occur and thus to see whether there is any pattern to the errors. Not only understanding the kinds of errors made but also obtaining some insight into how the pupil responds and reacts can prove invaluable for future remedial work. For example, in the oral approach, the examiner may note that the pupil is nervous, wary, concerned, and so forth. Diagnostic tests range from those which have just two or three subtests and function more like a survey battery, to those which have many subtests that provide for detailed clinical analysis. Some are completely verbal; others employ equipment such as a tachistoscope for controlling the rate of exposure of printed matter; others employ elaborate photographic apparatus to record eye movements while the subject is reading.

---

[6] Bejar (1984) conceptualizes the development of diagnostic tests as being either (1) an example of deficit measurement—that is, diagnosis is seen as the measurement of discrepancies from some "expected" value; (2) an example of error analysis—that it, diagnosis involves more than collecting symptoms; examinees are categorized on the basis of the types of errors they make; or (3) an instance of the cognitive approach, which goes beyond error analysis and attempts to ascribe causal relations so that appropriate remediation can be undertaken. As of now, the major work in developing standardized diagnostic tests exemplifies the error analysis approach and/or the cognitive approach. Accordingly, our discussion to follow is predicated by those methods.

Although most diagnostic tests are individually administered, a recent development has been the inclusion of a *group*-administered diagnostic test such as the Stanford Diagnostic Mathematics Test and the Stanford Diagnostic Reading Test as part of the Stanford Achievement Tests or the three batteries of Instructional Tests—reading, mathematics, and language—as part of the Metropolitan Achievement Tests. We should caution the reader regarding the use of group-administered diagnostic tests, however. Although these tests serve as excellent screening devices to identify pupils needing further attention, the diagnosis of learning disabilities and subsequent remedial prescriptions should be relegated to skilled clinicians, who invariably will employ individual tests to determine how the examinee behaves in the testing situation. Also, with individually administered tests it is easier to establish rapport, and one can probe if necessary.

The purpose of diagnosis, and hence of a diagnostic test, is to help in selecting proper treatment. Saying that Paul, a fifth-grader, has a grade equivalent of 4.8 on the Metropolitan Mathematics Test tells us very little about Paul's specific strengths and weaknesses. We do know, however, that he is performing below grade level in mathematics. But Paul's classroom teacher needs to know more. What kind of items did Paul fail/pass? Is there any pattern? Does Paul consistently demonstrate errors in addition or subtraction? With carrying? With multidigit items?

A good diagnostic test not only will inform the teacher that a pupil is weak or deficient in reading or arithmetic; it will also point out what areas are weak, such as word comprehension or addition with carrying. However, it will *not* establish causal relationships. The teacher might learn *what* the difficulty is but *not why* the problem is there. For example, let us say that Salvador is weak in algebra. This weakness may be due to his intellectual ability, poor reading skills, poor vision, psychomotor difficulties, poor study skills, emotional problems, inability to deal with polynomials, and other factors. The teacher must consider such factors to arrive at a reasonable solution to the problem. If not, the immediate difficulty with algebra may be remedied, but the etiological factors (having not been considered) may manifest themselves in other learning situations.[7]

We would be remiss if we did not caution prospective users of diagnostic tests (regardless of how well they have been constructed) to be somewhat pessimistic about the value of the test's results. Diagnostic tests may point out a student's strengths and weaknesses in, say, reading or arithmetic. They may indicate, for example, that Lois has difficulty adding with carrying but has mastered converting decimals to percentages, or that Chuck is weak in reading comprehension but performs above average in his rate of reading.

---

[7] The diagnosis of learning problems requires trained specialists—school psychologists and often social workers, physicians, and psychiatrists. The remedial program to be initiated will require special-education teachers. Because of this requirement, classroom teachers should leave this area to the specialists, especially for moderate or severe cases.

This does *not* mean that remedial work for Lois in addition with carrying or special attention to Chuck will result in an improvement in their arithmetic and reading test scores. In fact, research has demonstrated that we do not know what constitutes effective diagnosis and remediation (Gill, Vinsonhaler, & Sherman, 1979). Of what value then are diagnostic tests? We believe that they serve as hypothesis generators in that they suggest possible courses of action to the teacher.

The manuals of some achievement-test batteries suggest that some of their subtests may be used for diagnostic purposes. We caution the user not to consider these subtests as diagnostic. Before a diagnostic test can be considered valid, (1) the component skills subtests should emphasize only a single type of error (such as word reversal in a reading diagnotic test) and (2) the subtest difference scores should be reliable. This second point can be achieved only by having subtests that have high reliabilities in themselves and low intertest correlations. Achievement-test batteries or single-subject-matter tests seldom display these characteristics. Finally, before accepting a test as being diagnostic even though it may be labeled as such or claimed to be such by the publisher, ask yourself whether the subtests identify skill deficiencies that are amenable to remediation. For example, if a child does poorly on Quantitative Language (a subtest of the Metropolitan Readiness Tests), what guidance, if any, is given the teacher for remedial action? Should the pupil do more work with numbers? Should the pupil read more sentences dealing with quantitative concepts? Unless answers to such questions are forthcoming, the diagnostic test may not be of much educational value.

Although both teacher-made and standardized tests are (and should be) used for diagnostic purposes, the latter have proven especially valuable. It is not possible to consider in very much detail here the variety of diagnostic tests available to the classroom teacher. We have described some of the different methods used to construct diagnostic tests; we have attempted to caution the user to be wary in the interpretation of diagnostic test results (because they are not elegant psychometric instruments with high validity and complete normative data); and we have taken the view that the teacher must be certain every avenue has been explored in attempting to remedy an evident defect. This section concludes with a very brief description of three of the more popular diagnostic tests available in the elementary grades. Possibly because of the technical difficulties involved, there is a paucity of *valid* diagnostic tests.

Reading Diagnostic Tests   Reading is a complex behavior consisting of many skills. Accordingly, reading diagnostic tests generally measure such factors as rate, comprehension (literal, inferential, listening), visual and auditory discrimination, word attack skills, and motor skills. As will be evident when reading readiness tests are discussed, the skills measured by reading,

reading readiness, and reading diagnostic tests are very similar, as one would expect. The major difference among them is in the range of material covered, the intensity of coverage, and the method of administration. For example, the Stanford Diagnostic Reading Test (SDRT) is group-administered, while the Durrell Analysis of Reading Difficulty is individually administered. It should be noted that the majority of diagnostic reading tests are individually administered, thereby giving the examiner ample opportunity to observe the student as he or she approaches the tasks. A major limitation is that they are time-consuming.

There appears to be some disagreement among reading experts and psychometricians regarding the value of reading diagnostic tests. Some maintain that diagnostic tests are valid and aid the classroom teacher immeasurably in screening out pupils who are in need of remediation. Others, like Spache (1976), are very critical of many reading diagnostic tests, claiming that, in large part, they fail to demonstrate validity. We feel that some of the newer reading diagnostic tests are beginning to overcome this deficit.

Q. Do all reading diagnostic tests measure the same thing?

A. No! Although there are more similarities than differences among most standardized reading diagnostic tests, there are nevertheless some basic differences. For example, the Durrell Analysis of Reading Difficulty and the Gates-McKillop Reading Diagnostic Tests are both individually administered. Both measure various factors involved in the reading process, but do so in markedly different ways. In the Gates-McKillop, the subtests are analogous to power tests in that the exercises vary in their degree of difficulty. In the Durrell, this is not so. On the other hand, the Gates-McKillop includes tests of the child's word-attack skills, but the Durrell does not. The strength of the Durrell is in two sets of paragraphs; the Gates-McKillop has eight separate subtests.

Q. How valid are the interpretations that can be made with a reading diagnostic test?

A. This depends on the test—how the items were selected (or prepared), the test's psychometric qualities, and the adequacy of the norming group. For some tests such as the Gates-McKillop, the training and experience of the examiner plays a vital role. The older Gates Reading Diagnostic Tests can be interpreted easily by classroom teachers. The types of interpretations that can be made are governed to a large extent by the range of material the test covers. The practical clinical value of the interpretation depends to a large extent on the checklist of errors (and their validity) the publisher provides.

Stanford Diagnostic Reading Test (SDRT).[8]   This test, published by the Psychological Corporation (1978), has two forms. Four overlapping levels

---

[8] A third edition was scheduled for publication in 1984 but was not available when this text went to press.

span grades 1.6–13. It is group-administered; there are six, seven, or eight scores depending on the level. Working time varies according to level but approximately two hours are required for each level. Both timed and untimed tests are contained in each level, the number of strictly timed tests increasing as one moves from the lower to higher levels.

Factors measured in *all* four batteries are phonetic analysis, vocabulary, and reading comprehension, although different techniques are used to measure these factors depending upon the grade level. As might be expected, at only the upper grade levels are reading rate, scanning and skimming, and reading vocabulary measured. Some examples of the types of items used in the SDRT are presented in Figure 8.1.

Content and criterion-related (concurrent) validity were emphasized in the test's construction. K-R 20 reliability is reported using raw scores, and standard errors of measurement are reported for both raw and scaled scores. Alternate-form reliability estimates are also reported.

Each of the subtest and total scores can be expressed and interpreted in terms of *both* a within-grade criterion- (content-) referenced mode (raw scores and Progress Indicators) or norm-referenced mode (percentile ranks, stanines, grade equivalents, and scaled scores).

A variety of reports are available, and with the test manual provide helpful information to aid in the interpretation of the pupils' or classes' performance. The authors provide a variety of instructional strategies which they feel will help ameliorate the pupils' deficiencies. Evidence as to the efficacy of these instructional strategies is missing. The manual is concisely written and is teacher-oriented, although attention is also paid to how the test scores can be used for making administrative decisions.

Users of the publisher's scoring service are given an Instructional Placement Report (IPR) that reports *level-based* rather than grade-based stanines. This type of reporting provides a profile analysis in terms of the pupils' basic instructional needs regardless of their grade placement. In addition, pupils are identified either as being in need of specific remedial instruction or as progressing satisfactorily. On each computer-generated IPR brief instructional strategies are given.

The revised SDRT at each level reports or classifies the test items by objective and item cluster, provides the difficulty level of each item, and designates a Progress Indicator Cut-Off Score. Progress Indicators (PI), although not a test score per se, are cutoff scores that have been established for each SDRT Skill Domain and Item cluster to identify those pupils who have mastered or have not mastered minimum competencies in those areas deemed to be vital in the reading process development sequence. We caution users *not* to consider the PI as an absolute standard but to interpret the score in terms of their instructional objectives.

The revised SDRT is a well-constructed and standardized test. It is attractively packaged, has clear directions, provides a rationale underlying each of the subtests, and has an excellent manual to help the teacher. The type and

TEST 1:   Auditory Vocabulary

Look at the first shaded box, box A, at the top of the page. (Demonstrate.) Look at the pictures in the box. The pictures are of a rock, a dog, and a plant. (Pause.) Now I'm going to read a question to you about these pictures. Find the picture that answers the question. Ready? Here is the question: "Which one is an *animal?*" Which picture shows an *animal?*

Pause. Encourage replies. Then say:

Yes, it is the second picture, the picture of the dog, because a dog is an animal. The answer space under the picture of the dog has been filled in to show that it is the right answer.

TEST 1:   Auditory Vocabulary (continued)

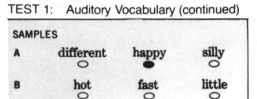

Look at the three words in line A, inside the shaded box. I am going to read a sentence to you. You are to choose one word from these three words that best completes the sentence. Here is the sentence: "To be glad is to be ... different ... happy ... silly." Which word best completes the sentence?

Pause for replies. Then say:

Yes, the best choice is "happy." That is why the space under "happy" has been filled in in your booklet.

TEST 2:   Auditory Discrimination

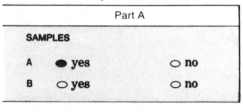

I am going to read two words to you. Listen to the words, and tell me if they begin with the same sound. The two words are: name ... night. Do "name" and "night" begin with the same sound?

Pause for replies. Then say:

Yes, they both begin with the same sound. That is why the space in front of "yes" has been filled in in your booklet.

TEST 3:   Phonetic Analysis   Part A

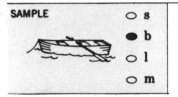

Look at the shaded box at the top of the page, where you see a picture of a boat. Think of the beginning sound of the word "boat" ... "boat." What is the first sound in "boat"?

Pause for replies.

Yes, it is /b/ ("buh"). "Boat" begins with the /b/ sound. Which letter in the shaded box stands for the /b/ sound?

Pause for replies.

Yes, it is "b" ("bee"); that is why the space next to the "b" has been filled in in your booklet. You will do the same with the other questions on this page. I will tell you what the picture is. Then you will fill in the answer space in front of the letter or group of letters that stands for the beginning sound or sounds of the word I say. Mark only one letter or group of letters for each picture. Does everyone understand what to do?

Figure 8.1   Sample items from Stanford Diagnostic Reading Test. (Copyright © 1976 by Harcourt Brace Jovanovich, Inc. Reproduced by special permission of the publisher.)

TEST 3:   Phonetic Analysis Part B

TEST 4:   Word Reading

TEST 5:   Reading Comprehension   Part A

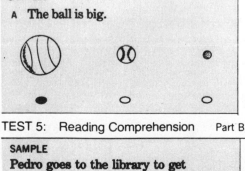

TEST 5:   Reading Comprehension   Part B

SAMPLE

Pedro goes to the library to get

Figure 8.1   (*continued*)

Look at the picture in the shaded box at the top of the page. (Demonstrate.) You see a picture of a cat. What letter tells the *ending* sound of the word "cat"?

Pause for replies. Then say:

Yes, "cat" ends with the /t/ sound of the letter "t." That is why the space next to the letter "t" has been filled in in your booklet. You'll do the same with the other questions on this page. I will tell you what each picture is. This time you will fill in the space next to the letter or group of letters that tells the *ending* sound or sounds of the word I say. You are to mark only one letter or group of letters for each picture. Does everyone understand what we're going to do?

We are going to look at some pictures and then find the words that tell about each picture. Look at the shaded box at the top of the page. (Demonstrate.) You see a picture of some children at a birthday party. (Pause.) Now look at the three lines of words below the picture. In each line, there is one word that goes with the picture. You are to pick out the word in each line that goes with the picture. Look at the first line. Read the words to yourself as I read them aloud: "yes ... cake ... cow." Which word goes with the picture?

Pause. Encourage replies.

Yes, the word "cake" goes with the picture. That's why the space under "cake" has been filled in in your booklet. (Pause.) Now look at line B. Read the three words to yourself. (Pause.) Which word goes with the picture?

Pause for replies.

Yes, the word "party" does. The three words are "dark," "away," and "party." The answer space under "party" has been filled in in your booklet. (Pause.) Now read the words in line C to yourself. (Pause.) Which word goes with the picture?

Pause for replies.

Yes, the right word is "fun." The children are having fun at the party. The space under "fun" has been filled in.

Look at the first shaded box at the top of the page. (Demonstrate.) Inside the box you see a sentence and three pictures. Read the sentence to yourself while I read it aloud: "The ball is big." One of the pictures goes with the sentence. Which picture is it?

Pause for replies.

Yes, the first picture is the one that goes with the sentence because the first ball is big. That's why the space under the first ball has been filled in in your booklet.

On this page, there are some stories for you to read. Look at the story in the shaded box. Read the first sentence to yourself as I read it aloud: "Pedro goes to the library to get ... food ... books ... flowers." Which word best completes the sentence?

Pause for replies. Then say:

Yes, "books" is the best answer. That is why the space under "books" has been filled in in your booklet.

variety of instructional strategies provided do indeed make this a diagnostic-prescriptive test. As mentioned earlier, however, the value of the instructional strategies has not been demonstrated. Although the classroom teacher can administer, score, and interpret the test, we strongly recommend that, where feasible, an experienced reading specialist do the actual interpretation and, in conjunction with the classroom teacher, develop the appropriate corrective action.

Woodcock Reading Mastery Tests (WRMT).   Published by the American Guidance Service (1973), the tests cover grades K through 12. The two forms, A and B, are individually administered. The five subtests include Letter Identification (45 items); Word Identification (150 items—*not* a vocabulary test but a pronunciation test); Word Attack (50 items—assesses the examinees' ability to pronounce phonetically a series of nonsense words); Word Comprehension (70 items—tests both verbal reasoning skills and reading comprehension); and Passage Comprehension (85 items—not a test of reading comprehension per se, because examinees fill in orally a missing word in a passage rather than explain the meaning of the passage). There are separate scores for each subtest as well as a total reading score (which, incidentally, the author believes gives the most reliable index of reading skill). The Word Attack and Passage Comprehension titles may be misnomers because, as noted, they do not measure what the names imply. Rather, they measure punctuation skills and only a smattering of reading comprehension, respectively. In fact, the two comprehension tests do not measure comprehension as we would define the term.

Raw scores can be converted to grade scores, age scores, standard scores, and three mastery scores (which are really derived scores)—again a misnomer, since they do not indicate the degree of mastery of learning. These mastery scores are then expressed as (1) reading grade scores, (2) easy reading level, and (3) failure reading level. An "achievement index" score and percentile ranks within grades are also available. Separate sex and SES-adjusted norms are provided.

Split-half and alternate form reliabilities are reported for second- and seventh-grade samples, with the second-grade reliability higher than that for the seventh grade. The test–retest reliabilities are not bad for group decision making but are not exceptional for an individual measure in general, and a diagnostic test in particular.

Validity data are conspicuous by their weaknesses. For example, over 25 percent of the test items use pictures, but aren't we interested in the pupils' *reading* skills? The author himself seems to question the value of the multi-method-multitrait matrix data. And where's the *predictive* validity? We also question the content validity of the Word Comprehension and Paragraph Comprehension in terms of both the analogy format used and the use of the "modified cloze procedure." Additionally, evidence is given to support predictive validity, but the technique used is for ascertaining parallel-form reliability.

The manual is clear and concise. The directions are easy to follow. The "open-ended" format may be better than the traditional multiple-choice format for a diagnostic test. The easel format is also good.

Presently, we would be remiss if we did not caution prospective users of the WRMT. The claims for predictive validity and criterion-referenced interpretation are not supported; the value of the Letter Identification and the comprehension is questionable. The WRMT *may* be useful in the hands of a skilled clinician or reading diagnostician. It is *not* recommended for the regular classroom teacher.

Some Other Examples.   Some other examples of diagnostic reading tests are the Durrell Analysis of Reading Difficulty, the Durrell Listening-Reading Series, the Diagnostic Reading Scales, the Gates-McKillop Reading Diagnostic Tests, the Gilmore Oral Reading Test, the Reading Recognition and Reading Comprehension subtests of the Peabody Individual Achievement Test, the Slingerland Test of Specific Language Disability, and the Word Recognition subtest of the Wide Range Achievement Test. These are all popular tests, and more information can be obtained about them and other tests by consulting the *Buros' Mental Measurements Yearbooks* and the publishers' catalogs.

Diagnostic Arithmetic Tests   With the exception of the teaching of reading, probably no subject has been more intensively studied than the teaching of arithmetic. Yet very few new arithmetic tests have been published and even fewer new diagnostic tests in the preceding decade. Certain fundamental skills in arithmetic are taught at the primary level, and regardless of the method of instruction employed, most diagnostic arithmetic tests employ similar kinds of items.

Diagnostic Tests and Self-Helps in Arithmetic.   Published by CTB/Mc-Graw-Hill (1955), the test covers grades 3–12. There is one form, four screening tests, and 23 diagnostic tests. It is untimed and has no norms.

Each of the 23 diagnostic tests is accompanied by a self-help unit that is on the back of the diagnostic test. Six major areas are surveyed by the series: basic facts (five tests); fundamental operations with whole numbers (five tests); operations with percentages (one test); fundamental operations with decimal fractions (four tests); operations with measures (one test); and fundamental operations with common fractions (seven tests). The four screening tests are designed to measure pupil achievements in whole numbers, fractions, decimals, and general arithmetic skills and knowledge. On the basis of the pupil's performance on one (or more) of the first three screening tests, the appropriate diagnostic test(s) is administered. For example, pupils who do poorly on Screening Test II, Screening Test in Fractions (the test author suggests that one or more errors is indicative of further testing) would be given one or more of the Diagnostic Tests in Common Fractions. The screening test, because it contains only a few examples of the skills needed, would have to be supplemented by a separate test that contains many examples.

The diagnostic tests are essentially power tests that begin with very simple items and then progress in difficulty. Because there are many items dealing with the same concept or skill, the probability of committing an error is maximized, something that is desired in a diagnostic test. The separate diagnostic tests are cross-referenced to assist the teacher in locating the nature of the difficulty. For example, a pupil who multiples 640 by 23 may arrive at an incorrect answer for a variety of reasons: (1) by placing the products incorrectly; (2) by not adding the columns correctly; or (3) by not knowing how to add with carrying. Therefore, if performance on the screening test suggested that a pupil had difficulty with multiplication, the teacher would have to administer one or more diagnostic tests to try and learn why. Pupils who multiplied 640 by 23 and arrived at an incorrect answer because they did not add properly could be given Test 1, Addition Facts, and/or Test 6, Addition of Whole Numbers.

The diagnostic self-helps are keyed to the diagnostic test items. The self-helps are in a sense remedial exercises that have been worked out in detail. They indicate to the pupil the correct procedure to be used in answering that kind of item. For example, in Test 12, Addition of Like Fractions, the self-help exercises on the addition of fractions with no carrying would be as follows:

$$\begin{array}{l} \frac{1}{8} \\ \underline{\frac{1}{8}} \\ \frac{2}{8} = \frac{1}{4} \end{array}$$ Add the numerators, 1 and 1
Write the sum over the denominator, 8

Then, $\dfrac{1 + 1}{8} = \frac{2}{8}$

Reduce $\frac{2}{8}$; $\dfrac{2 \div 2}{8 \div 2} = \frac{1}{4}$

After working through the self-help exercises, pupils are encouraged to rework the items that they answered incorrectly.

No reliability and validity data are reported. The test author states that reliability was increased by having numerous items of the same kind. Content validity was stressed in constructing the test. The test author attempted to analyze the skills needed to perform a particular task. It would have been desirable to present more information about how these skills were analyzed, and on what basis the analysis was done. Do the self-help exercises contribute to learning? Do the diagnostic tests really assist the teacher in locating the nature of the pupils' difficulties, or could essentially similar information be obtained from the arithmetic subtest of a standardized achievement test? Answers to these questions are absent from the manual.

The test manual contains numerous suggestions for the effective use of the test results. It also provides the user with a list of the more common errors in operations with whole numbers, common fractions, and decimals.

The Diagnostic Tests and Self-Helps in Arithmetic seems to do an adequate job in surveying specific weaknesses in fundamental arithmetic skills. The first four diagnostic tests contain 100 arithmetic operations involving digits 0 to 9. The basic facts, then, are covered thoroughly. However, there is inadequate provision for the measurement of arithmetic meaning or problem-solving ability. The value of these tests could possibly be increased by having some of the items responded to orally. In this way, the teacher, listening to the pupil "work the problem out loud," could obtain additional information regarding the pupil's work habits. Moreover, provision of a more complete error list could prove to be beneficial insofar as the teacher's instructional program is concerned.

Key Math Diagnostic Arithmetic Test (KMDAT).   Published by the American Guidance Service (1976), the test covers preschool to grade 6. It has one form. Developed originally for testing educable mentally retarded children, this individually administered test can be given, scored, and interpreted by classroom teachers who have studied the manual.

The test is divided into three major areas (content, operations, and applications) and 15 subtests, each having from 7 to 31 items. The subtests (with the number of items shown in parentheses) are as follows:

A. Content
   1. Numeration (24)
   2. Fractions (11)
   3. Geometry & Symbols (20)
B. Operations
   1. Addition (15)
   2. Subtraction (15)
   3. Multiplication (11)
   4. Division (10)
   5. Mental Computation (10), which also involves memory for digits
   6. Numerical Reasoning (12)
C. Applications
   1. Word Problems (14)
   2. Missing Elements (7)
   3. Money (15)
   4. Measurement (27)
   5. Time (19)
   6. Metric Supplement (31)

The items require almost no writing or reading ability.

With the exception of the Metric Supplement subtest, raw scores are converted to grade equivalents. These GEs can then be compared with the total score and strengths and weaknesses plotted. We caution the reader here because a change in only one or two answers can have a significant effect on the derived score and subsequent interpretation.

The validity and reliability data presented are acceptable.

The test is accompanied by an excellent manual which provides clear directions for administration and scoring as well as behavioral objectives for each item. The test format is good and the illustrations are exceptional in their use of color and attractiveness. A major criticism is the limited number of items in each of the subtests. This effect is the more serious in that a diagnostic test should have extensive sampling of the instructional objectives.

Some other examples of arithmetic diagnostic tests are the Buswell-John Diagnostic Test for Fundamental Processes in Arithmetic, the Individual Pupil Monitoring System: Mathematics, the Individualized Mathematics Program, and the Stanford Diagnostic Arithmetic Test.

CRITERION-REFERENCED STANDARDIZED ACHIEVEMENT TESTS

In recent years, accountability, performance contracting, formative evaluation, computer-assisted instruction, individually prescribed instruction, mastery learning, and the like have spawned an interest in and need for new kinds of tests—criterion-referenced tests (CRTs), or, as some prefer to say, content-domain- or objectives-based tests.[9] Test publishers are now paying more attention to the development of CRTs, since many educators believe that norm-referenced tests (because they are concerned with making *inter*-individual comparisons) are inadequate for individualized instruction decision-making purposes because they do not give specific descriptions of pupil performance.

The item-writing rules and principles are essentially the *same* for both CRT and NRT achievement tests. However, the tests do *differ* in purpose, use, and content sampling. In fact, traditional models for test construction and interpretation of NRTs appear to be less useful for CRTs. (See Durnan & Scandura, 1973.)

As mentioned in Chapter 1, a multitude of definitions have been advanced for a criterion-referenced test. But regardless of the definition one wishes to accept, users of a CRT must ask themselves three major questions when selecting a test: (1) Are the test items free from irrelevant sources of diffi-

[9] It should *not* be inferred that norm-referenced achievement tests (NRTs) are not based on objectives. In order for an achievement test to be valid, be it a CRT or an NRT, there must be objectives on which the test items are based.

culty? For example, an arithmetic computation test should not be overly verbal, since we are *not* measuring reading ability but whether the pupils have mastered computational skills. (2) Was a content domain specified and were the items generated from that domain representative of the domain being sampled? That is, in a test on fractions, there should be test items dealing with the division of, multiplication of, addition of, and subtraction of fractions, and *not* only items dealing with, say, the division of fractions. (3) Is the test short enough so that it is not too time-consuming (this is especially significant in formative evaluation where the pupils may be tested two or three times per week) and yet be long enough so that a valid score is obtained? Unless satisfactory answers are received to these three questions, CRT users should consider other tests.

Because instructional objectives in the basic skills of reading and arithmetic at the elementary level are more amenable to fine subdivisions, and because at this level the instructional objectives are of a hierarchial nature (that is, the acquisition of elementary skills are a necessary prerequisite for learning the higher order skills), CRTs are more common in the lower grades.

As of now, the majority of criterion-referenced achievement tests are teacher-made. But in the past few years commercial test publishers have begun preparing such tests. Today commercially prepared standardized criterion-referenced achievement tests are generally in reading and arithmetic, although agencies are available that will produce tailor-made criterion-referenced achievement tests in a variety of subject-matter fields at different grade levels (Westinghouse Learning Corporation, Instructional Objectives Exchange, CTB/McGraw-Hill, and Riverside Press).

Criterion-referenced tests vary from the single test to a battery of "mini-tests" that are designed to measure the pupils' knowledge of the various instructional objectives in detail. Moreover, test and textbook publishers are beginning to prepare complete instructional systems using a survey test, a diagnostic test(s), and a set of prescriptions (suggested instructional activities). One of the most comprehensive instructional systems has been developed by Science Research Associates in Reading and Mathematics.

The SRA package or "lab" in reading[10] consists of 34 Probes, or criterion-referenced diagnostic tests measuring instructional objectives normally covered in grades 1–4; six cassettes that make for self-administration of the Probes; a Survey Test that indicates the students' strengths and weaknesses and indicates what Probes, if any, should be taken; a Prescription Guide that keys the instructional objectives measured by a particular Probe (for instance, letter recognition, consonant blends, homographs) to major reading tests or supplementary activities; and a Class Progress Chart.

---

[10] SRA also has a program (which differs from its "lab") called "Mastery: Custom Program," where users can select reading and mathematics objectives from a list of over 1000 items. Criterion-referenced tests are then built, with three items/instructional objective.

School Curriculum Objective-Referenced Evaluation (SCORE). Published by Riverside Press, SCORE is an objective-based testing program where over 8000 instructional objectives in reading, language arts, and mathematics for grades 1 and upward have been catalogued and classified. To measure these objectives, over 5000 test items are available.

SCORE differs from the conventional standardized test in that the program will tailor a test to teachers' specifications. After teachers select their objectives, the type of item format desired, the item difficulty wanted, and the like, Riverside Press "customizes" a test to measure the objectives identified with item characteristics meeting prescribed criteria. The items are then assembled and printed in a test booklet with accompanying directions. Or, if the teachers wish, they can specify objectives that are unique to their course, and Riverside Press will produce and print appropriate items. A variety of report forms—for example, class list, building summary, district summary, percentile distribution by building and district—are available.

Objectives-Referenced Bank of Items and Tests (ORBIT). Published by California Test Bureau/McGraw-Hill, ORBIT is somewhat similar to SCORE. ORBIT offers 581 Mathematics objectives, 357 Reading and Communication Skills objectives, and 15 Social Studies objectives, from which users can select and have built for them customized CRTs. There are four items per objective. A valuable feature of ORBIT is the inclusion of an "I don't know" response. This should help minimize wild guessing and encourage remedial rather than punitive use of the scores. The specific objectives are grouped into category or general objectives.

Prescriptive Reading Inventory (PRI) and Diagnostic Mathematics Inventory (DMI).[11] Published by CTB/McGraw-Hill, the PRI and DMI exemplify a new approach in building criterion-referenced diagnostic tests. Both tests are designed to identify pupils with difficulties in reading and/or mathematics. Then, after appropriate remedial instruction has been given, the DMI or PRI is followed up with a criterion-referenced mastery test (Interim Evaluation Test) to ascertain the degree to which the pupil has mastered the minimal instructional objectives. Although untimed, each test takes about $2\frac{3}{4}$ hours working time. In both the DMI and PRI, each test item is referenced to commonly used textbooks. In this way, the teacher is assisted in developing appropriate remedial instruction.

A rather novel feature of the DMI is the manner in which pupils record their answers: pupils do their work in the test booklet and write their answer in "unique, item-specific" machine-scorable answer grids.

---

[11] The PMI and DMI are part of an instructional management system and are sometimes referred to as PMI/MS and DMI/MS. Also included in the system are the Writing Proficiency Program (WPP) and the Writing Proficiency Program/Intermediate System (WPP/IS). We realize that the DMI and PRI, because they are diagnostic tests, could have been discussed earlier. However, since they are objectives-based in development and because of their relationship to the Interim Tests, we decided to cover the series together.

Content validity was stressed in the construction of the DMI, PRI, and the respective Interim Evaluation Tests.

Both the DMI and PRI have a variety of reports available to pupils and teachers. The PRI has an Individual Diagnostic Map, a Class Diagnostic Map, an Individual Study Guide, a Program Reference Guide, a Class Grouping Report, and an Interpretive Handbook.

The Individual Diagnostic Map (see Figure 8.2) displays the student's score on each objective in the form of a "diagnostic map." The + indicates mastery of a particular instructional objective; the − indicates nonmastery; the R indicates that review is warranted. A blank indicates that the student omitted the items related to that objective.

The Class Diagnostic Map can be used for class or group instruction. It reports average class scores on each objective.

The Individual Study Guide uses the information from the Diagnostic Map to furnish individual prescriptions for the student. For those instructional objectives not mastered, pages in the text to be studied are noted.

The Program Reference Guides direct the teacher to appropriate resource and reference materials. Guides are available for each of the reading programs keyed to the PRI.

For levels A through D, there is a Class Grouping Report which identifies (and groups) students who fail to show mastery of 60 percent of the objectives in a particular category. The teacher can then provide appropriate remediation for various groupings of student deficiencies.

The DMI has an Objective Mastery Report, a Pre-Mastery Analysis, an Individual Diagnostic Report, a Group Diagnostic Report, a Mastery Reference Guide, a Guide to Ancillary Materials, and a Learning Activities Guide. The PRI's Interpretive Handbook and the DMI's Guides contain useful suggested activities and instructional strategies that teachers can use. All test questions are keyed to the appropriate objective being measured and most of the printouts reference the objective to a particular textbook page.

The Interim Evaluation Tests' (IET) objectives (and hence items) are organized as in the DMI or PRI except that there is no IET for DMI Level C (grades 7–8). Each objective, whether in reading or in mathematics, is measured with four to six items. Guidelines for determining whether the student has mastered the objective being tested or needs to review an objective are presented in the Examiner's Manual. This manual also suggests appropriate instructional activities that might be used to build mastery of the objective. A variety of output data is furnished. The test authors recommend that the IET (whether it be the total test, part of the test, or just a single objective section) "be administered not earlier than a full day and no later than a week" after appropriate remedial instruction has been given.

Use of the DMI or PRI and their respective Interim Tests permits a teacher to ascertain which students are in need of further instruction on a particular objective(s) and then to see whether, after remedial instruction,

PRI Reading Systems

Individual Diagnostic Map

Applications
System 2, Levels C, D, and E

DIRECTIONS

Name _____

Teacher _____

Grade _____ Date _____

The items that test a specific objective are listed by number in the ITEM NUMBERS column. To fill in the box under each item number, refer to the student's corrected test booklet or answer sheet for the *PRI Reading Systems Applications Test.* Record C for correct, X for incorrect, or 0 for item omitted. Add the number of correct items for each objective and enter that number on the line in the RAW SCORE column. Use the raw score to determine Mastery (+ = 3 or 4), Review (R = 2), or Nonmastery (- = 0 or 1). Enter a +, R, or - for each objective in the box in the last column.

Study Skills

SKILL AREA	OBJECTIVE NUMBER AND NAME	ITEM NUMBERS Enter C, X, or O	RAW SCORE	+ = 3, 4 R = 2 - = 0, 1
Level C	66 Front, Back Matter	1 2 3 4	____	☐
Level D	64 Paragraph Structure	17 18 19 20	____	☐
	65 Outlines	21 22 23 24	____	☐
	67 Bibliography	5 6 7 8	____	☐
	68 Dictionary	9 10 11 12	____	☐
	69 Library Resources	13 14 15 16	____	☐
Level E	64 Paragraph Structure	29 30 31 32	____	☐
	65 Outlines	33 34 35 36	____	☐
	69 Library Resources	25 26 27 28	____	☐

Content Area Reading

SKILL AREA	OBJECTIVE NUMBER AND NAME	ITEM NUMBERS Enter C, X, or O	RAW SCORE	+ = 3, 4 R = 2 - = 0, 1
Level C	70 Directions (Social Studies)	3 4 11 12	____	☐
	71 Vocabulary (Social Studies)	5 6 9 10	____	☐
	72 Graphic Displays (Social Studies)	1 2 7 8	____	☐
	73 Directions (Science)	25 26 35 36	____	☐
	74 Vocabulary (Science)	27 28 33 34	____	☐
	75 Graphic Displays (Science)	29 30 31 32	____	☐
	76 Directions (Mathematics)	13 14 23 24	____	☐
	77 Vocabulary (Mathematics)	17 18 21 22	____	☐
	78 Graphic Displays (Mathematics)	15 16 19 20	____	☐

Content Area Reading

SKILL AREA	OBJECTIVE NUMBER AND NAME	ITEM NUMBERS Enter C, X, or O	RAW SCORE	+ = 3, 4 R = 2 - = 0, 1
Level D	70 Directions (Social Studies)	63 68 69 70	____	☐
	71 Vocabulary (Social Studies)	62 66 67 71	____	☐
	72 Graphic Displays (Social Studies)	61 64 65 72	____	☐
	73 Directions (Science)	49 56 57 58	____	☐
	74 Vocabulary (Science)	51 54 55 60	____	☐
	75 Graphic Displays (Science)	50 52 53 59	____	☐
	76 Directions (Mathematics)	38 39 43 44	____	☐
	77 Vocabulary (Mathematics)	40 42 47 48	____	☐
	78 Graphic Displays (Mathematics)	37 41 45 46	____	☐
Level E	70 Directions (Social Studies)	85 86 95 96	____	☐
	71 Vocabulary (Social Studies)	89 90 91 92	____	☐
	72 Graphic Displays (Social Studies)	87 88 93 94	____	☐
	73 Directions (Science)	99 100 105 106	____	☐
	74 Vocabulary (Science)	101 102 107 108	____	☐
	75 Graphic Displays (Science)	97 98 103 104	____	☐
	76 Directions (Mathematics)	75 76 79 80	____	☐
	77 Vocabulary (Mathematics)	77 78 81 82	____	☐
	78 Graphic Displays (Mathematics)	73 74 83 84	____	☐

Figure 8.2 Individual Diagnostic Map. (Reproduced from the Prescriptive Reading Inventory. Copyright © 1976 by CTB/McGraw-Hill. Reproduced by special permission of the publisher.)

the student has mastered the objective(s). In a way, these tests can be considered part of an individualized instructional program. The rationale underlying their development is that sound and extensive work was done to identify objectives and select items. The various reports issued to the teacher and the numerous suggested instructional aids offered are excellent.

The Skills Monitoring System (SMS). Published by the Psychological Corporation, the SMS is another example of a broad-range diagnostic-prescriptive screening test that covers a multitude of instructional objectives with as few as one item per objective. Then, on the basis of the student's performance, more intensive testing can be done with a series of tests covering a single objective. Presently, there is only an SMS in Reading for grades 3–5. Each grade level has a Skill Locator and from 40 to 60 "Skill-Minis" containing eight to 12 items on a single objective; a Teacher Handbook providing suggested activities; Class and Learner Skill Records, which permit progress monitoring; and a Grouping Guide, which assists the teacher in forming groups for appropriate instruction. A novel feature of the SMS is how students respond. By means of chemically treated crayons and latent images, the student is able to obtain immediate feedback regarding the correctness of the answer. If the box marked is the correct answer, the word "Yes" appears; otherwise the student continues selecting responses until the correct answer is given.

Other Tests

Other standardized CRTs commercially available are Individual Pupil Monitoring System—Mathematics and Reading (IPMS) and Customized Objective Monitoring Service—Reading and Mathematics (COMS), published by Riverside Press; the Performance Assessment in Reading (PAIR), the Assessment of Skills in Computation (ASC), the Test of Performance in Computational Skills (TOPICS), the Writing Skills Test, and the Everyday Skills Test, published by CTB/McGraw-Hill; the Basic Skills Assessment Program (BSA), published by Addison-Wesley; and the tests accompanying the Harper & Row Reading Series. The IPMS, like the SRA and CTB/McGraw-Hill tests discussed earlier, key their instructional objectives to commonly used textbooks. The COMS, like ORBIT and SCORE, tailors a test to the teachers' specifications using validated test items.

A Word of Caution about CRTs

Although we are favorably disposed to the use of criterion-referenced testing, especially in formative evaluation and in computer-assisted or individually prescribed instruction where instruction is closely integrated with testing, we must admit that we have some reservations about many CRTs, especially their reliability and validity. How valid and reliable is a test that contains one to four items per objective? What can a teacher conclude if Irvin gets the right (or wrong) answer to "2 + 2"? Does this mean that Irvin would answer items of this type correctly (or incorrectly)? How far can we generalize? Has the total domain of this objective been delineated? Has there been sampling from this domain? What technical data pertaining to validity and reliability evidence are presented in the manual? (Hambleton & Eignor [1978] were somewhat perturbed about the paucity of such information in the test manuals they surveyed.) How was the "passing score" obtained? These are just some of the questions that have been raised about criterion-referenced tests. Those interested in greater coverage of the short-comings of CRTs should consult Hambleton & Eignor (1978) and Berk (1980b).

We are also concerned when the same test purportedly provides for both criterion- and norm-referenced interpretation, as claimed, for example, by the Boehm Test of Basic Concepts and the Tests of Basic Experiences. We caution test users to be very wary in accepting a test publisher's claim of providing criterion- or domain-referenced information. Relating individual test items to specific instructional objectives is not sufficient for establishing criterion-related validity, although it is a step in the right direction. Until the publisher can furnish evidence regarding the generalizability of the student's performance in the skill or knowledge domains being tested, we must interpret the scores cautiously.

We must warn the user of tests in general, and definitely diagnostic prescriptive tests in particular, to be on guard and to exercise extreme caution in interpreting the test results. Implementing sometimes radical prescriptive measures (remedial instruction, placement in special classes) on the basis of limited data is precarious.

We would be remiss if we did not mention that some test publishers are heeding the complaints of well-intentioned psychometricians regarding the weaknesses of CRTs. The 1978 Metropolitan Achievement Tests, for example, cover the same basic skills areas—reading, language, and mathematics—with both Survey and Instructional tests. The latter are longer—that is, have more items (whereas the survey reading test has 60 items, the Instructional reading test has between 120 and 237 items, depending upon the grade level). In fact, the items in the Survey Test Battery are a sample of those found in the Instructional Test. The larger number of items in the Instructional Tests (there are more test items for each cluster/objective measured) provides for more reliable criterion-referenced interpretation. Although both norm-referenced and criterion-referenced interpretation is possible for each of the tests, we strongly suggest that criterion-referenced interpretation is appropriate for the Instructional Tests, norm-referenced interpretation for the Survey Test Battery.

Summary

It is evident, then, that test publishers have jumped on the bandwagon in the past few years to produce criterion-referenced standardized achievement tests. These tests are primarily in reading and mathematics for the elementary grades, although we anticipate such tests in other content areas. And in many instances these tests are designed to provide diagnostic-prescriptive information, although SCORE, ORBIT, and COMS typify the conventional purpose of achievement tests—whether criterion- or norm-referenced—to describe the knowledge and skills possessed by a pupil in some content area(s).

STANDARDIZED ACHIEVEMENT TESTS IN SPECIFIC SUBJECTS

Standardized achievement tests are available for nearly every subject (agriculture to zoology) and for every grade level (kindergarten to professional and graduate school). There are, for example, reading readiness tests; reading tests; arithmetic, spelling, and science tests; product scales; and vocational achievement tests. For the most part, reading and arithmetic tests (as well as readiness tests in these respective subjects) are restricted to the primary grades because (1) these skills are primarily developed there and the major emphasis in the first few years of formal schooling is on reading and arithmetic, and (2) the relatively uniform curriculum of the elementary school makes it possible for the survey battery adequately to cover the measurement of the important objectives of instruction. In the secondary grades, because of the nonuniform nature of the curriculum, specialized tests covering a particular course such as Latin, Greek, or psychology are the predominant type.

As noted earlier, the major advantages of a single-subject-matter test such as algebra or science over a survey battery are that the single-subject-matter tests may provide a more valid measure of a student's achievement in a specific content area because they (1) are usually longer and thus permit more adequate content sampling; (2) are generally more reliable; (3) may better fit the classroom teacher's instructional objectives; and (4) generally are more up-to-date vis-à-vis the changing curriculum. The major limitation of the single-subject-matter test is that since different standardization samples are used, scores on different tests are *not* comparable. For example, unless the norms groups are comparable, we cannot say that Ilene does better in English than she does in social studies.

In the next section, we will focus on reading readiness tests. Although a variety of tests have been developed to assess the child's readiness for learning—the Cooperative Preschool Inventory, the Boehm Test of Basic Concepts, the Stanford Early School Achievement Test, and the Tests of Basic Experiences, to name a few—reading readiness tests are probably the most familiar and most frequently used in the elementary grades.

Reading Readiness Tests[12]

Usually the first type of standardized achievement test that a pupil receives is a reading readiness test. This test is administered either at or near the end of the kindergarten year or very early in the first grade. The test is often considered one of the most important achievement tests that the child takes during his or her school years. Since efficient and adequate reading skills play a vital role in subsequent learning, anything that can be done (section-

---

[12] Readiness, or prognostic, tests are sometimes considered aptitude tests because they are used to predict how well the individual will profit from instruction or training.

ing, placement, and remedial instruction) to provide optimal reading instruction should reap benefits insofar as future learning is concerned.

The major purposes of a reading readiness test are (1) to identify the children who possess the knowledge and skills reading specialists say are needed to learn to read, and (2) to identify, for grouping purposes, the children who are at essentially the same level of readiness. This grouping will then assist the teacher in providing appropriate reading or prereading instruction. Reading readiness tests are *not* designed to predict reading achievement in, say, the sixth or seventh grade. They do provide valuable information insofar as reading ability in the first and second grades is concerned. Reading readiness tests should not be confused with reading diagnostic tests. Although they may indicate weaknesses in certain general broad areas, such as word recognition or vocabulary, they are not designed to isolate specific reading defects. However, reading readiness and diagnostic tests contain many item *types* that are similar—visual discrimination, vocabulary, motor coordination, and the like.

There is a general consensus among reading specialists that a child's readiness to participate in reading and the extent to which he or she will learn how to read depend upon a variety of factors: (1) intellectual ability, (2) eye-hand coordination, (3) motivation to learn how to read, (4) perceptual and visual skills, and (5) knowledge of colors, names of common things, and concepts of time and space. Although there are variations among the many reading readiness tests commercially published, all have several of the following types of items:

1. *Motor skills.* Examinees are required to draw lines, complete a circle, underline words, go through a finger maze.
2. *Auditory discrimination.* The children are asked either to pronounce words after they have been read to them or to select which of several similar-sounding words identify a picture.
3. *Visual discrimination.* The children are required to choose similarities or differences in words, letters, numbers, or pictures.
4. *Vocabulary.* Children's knowledge of the meaning of words is assessed by asking them either to define a word, name various objects of the same or different class, or to select the correct word to describe a picture.
5. *Memory.* The children may be asked to reproduce a geometrical figure to which they have been exposed for a certain length of time; they may be asked to repeat a story that has been read to them; or they may be required to carry out in sequence a series of instructions that have been presented to them.
6. *Drawing/copying.* The children demonstrate their skill in copying or drawing a letter, a number, or a form.
7. *Recognition of numbers, words, and letters.* The children are required to identify numbers, words, or alphabetical letters.

Although all the reading readiness tests vary in the type and degree of coverage of these skills, all are designed to assess whether the child is ready to learn to read. It should be noted at the outset that a child requires *more* than those skills measured by even the most valid reading readiness test before we can say with any degree of confidence that the youngster is ready for reading instruction. Factors such as the child's interest, motivation, general aptitude, and the like must also be considered.

Although test validity and reliability are a *sine qua non* for any standardized test, the type(s) of validity evidence vary depending upon the type of test being considered. Since readiness tests in general and reading readiness tests in particular are intended to be used for predictive purposes, it is essential that they possess (and the test manual report evidence of) predictive validity.

The results from only a reading readiness test will not be sufficient to answer all questions about a child's readiness to learn to read, but they will provide valuable supplementary information to that gathered by observing the child. As we have constantly reiterated throughout this text, the results of any test are best considered as supplementary and complementary information for decision making. Some questions that may be raised regarding reading readiness tests are as follows:

Q. If there is a high correlation between reading test scores and intelligence test scores, why administer a reading readiness test?

A. Because intelligence tests do not survey all the skills and traits the child must have in order to learn to read. Intelligence tests, by their very nature, are not designed to provide specific information on the child's ability to handle words, whether or not the child can use and manipulate words, whether or not the child has adequate muscular coordination. Reading readiness tests are specifically designed to assess those skills deemed important in the reading process. For this reason, it is recommended that a reading readiness test be administered to kindergarten children, and the intelligence test be postponed to the first or second grade. (Research has shown that reading readiness tests given in kindergarten predict reading achievement in grade 1 *better* than aptitude tests but that aptitude tests given in kindergarten predict reading achievement in grades 4 and 5 better than do reading readiness tests.)

Q. Do all reading readiness tests measure the same thing?

A. No! Although many of them look as if they are doing so because they contain vocabulary items, or paragraph reading, or reproduction of objects, there is usually something unique or different about each of the reading readiness tests available. For example, the Harrison-Stroud Reading Readiness Profiles has a test of auditory discrimination, but the American School Reading Readiness Test does not. The Harrison-Stroud and Gates-MacGinitie have a test on word recognition; the Lee-Clark, Metropolitan, and Murphy-Durrell do not.

Q. How are items selected for reading readiness tests?

A. Once again, there are differences among the various tests. Harrison and Stroud attempted to make a task analysis—that is, they specified the skills they believed were important in the reading process and then prepared a test on the basis of this analysis. A somewhat different procedure was employed by the constructors of the Gates and American School tests. On the basis of previously used items and those suggested by experts in the field, they assembled a preliminary pool of items, administered the items, and then selected the items that were statistically sound. Both methods are valid, and no one can say that one is better than the other.

There is a growing trend among textbook publishers to develop tests for their reading series textbooks. In the past, the test materials were presented in workbooks and were not readiness tests per se. Harper & Row, for example, has developed a series of readiness and achievement tests for one of their reading-text series—the 1966 Harper & Row Basic Reading Program. The child (in grades K–6) is first given a readiness test at the beginning of the school year and, on the basis of his test score, is assigned to a particular reader. Then, after completing the reader, he or she is given an achievement test based on the reader's content. Although these tests are not so elegantly standardized as other achievement tests, such tests do serve a valuable purpose.

Q. How do I know whether an existing test is valid for my purposes?

A. You don't until you study it carefully. You must study the text manual thoroughly and determine whether the test's objectives are in agreement with your goals. All that test makers can do is to indicate what they think is important. It is up to the users to judge not only whether they agree with the test's purposes but also whether the manner in which the test was constructed was valid. For example, the authors of the American School Reading Readiness Test felt that auditory discrimination was not important. The Metropolitan Readiness Tests require the pupil to draw a man. The Harrison-Stroud and American School tests do not contain such an item. Users who believe that auditory discrimination is essential should consider a test other than the American. Similarly, if users feel that the ability to draw a man is vital to the reading process, they are advised to consider a test other than the Harrison-Stroud or the American. Users must also make a thorough analysis of the test items. The purpose of a test cannot be judged by merely looking at the items. As mentioned earlier, both the Harrison-Stroud and the American School tests include items designed to measure the child's ability to follow directions. In the former, this type of item is found as a peripheral task, whereas in the latter there is a specific subtest designed to measure this skill. Once again, we reiterate—do not judge a test by the names of the subtests.

Q. When should a readiness test be administered?

A. School personnel often ask whether a reading readiness test (or any readiness test for that matter) can be administered before a child enters the first grade and still have predictive validity. Rubin (1974) administered the Metropolitan Readiness Tests (MRT) to a group of pupils *prior* to kindergarten entrance and again prior to entering grade 1 and reported a one-year test–retest reliability of 0.65. She also found that the correlations between the Reading and Spelling scores on the Wide Range Achievement Test and Pre-Kindergarten MRT scores compared favorably with the correlations for the pre-first-grade and end-of-first-grade WRAT scores despite the 12-month interval between predictor and criterion measures.

The results strongly suggest that the MRT can be validly used in the first few months prior to kindergarten entrance to predict first-grade achievement in reading, spelling, and arithmetic (although not as well as for the latter two) instead of waiting to administer them at the end of kindergarten or early in the first grade as normally is the case. The implications of these findings, if they are substantiated by further research, are that (1) pupils with school readiness deficiencies can be identified early, and consequently appropriate remedial instruction can be initiated before grade 1 and (2) pupils who are not ready to enter grade 1 can be identified.

Reading readiness tests employ a variety of procedures. Generally, all are given orally, but on one section of the Harrison-Stroud, the pupils work independently. Numerous examples or practice exercises are provided so that the children will understand what they are to do and how they are to do it. All work is done in the test booklet. The examiner should constantly check the pupils to be sure that they understand the directions. This should not be difficult, because most of the tests are untimed and should under normal circumstances be administered in small groups or individually. Some examples of reading readiness tests and illustrative items are shown in Figure 8.3.

Some other examples of standardized reading readiness tests are the Analysis of Readiness Skills: Reading; the Initial Survey Tests; the Macmillan Reading Readiness Tests; the PMA Readiness Level; and the School Readiness Survey.

Uses of Reading Readiness Tests   The primary use of a reading readiness test is to furnish the teacher with basic information about the child's reading skills so that optimal learning conditions can be provided. On the basis of a reading readiness test, classroom teachers can tailor their teaching program to best fit the needs of each pupil. For example, Paul may be deficient in his ability to recognize similarities and differences, whereas Ilene may have

TEST 1: AUDITORY MEMORY

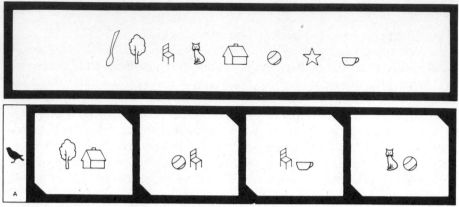

Look at the row of pictures at the top of the page (pointing to the top row). Let's name them together. SPOON, TREE, CHAIR, CAT, HOUSE, BALL, STAR, CUP. Now we all know what these pictures are.

This is what we're going to do. First, I'll tell you where to put your finger so you can find the right row. Then, you'll keep your finger there and close your eyes while I tell you what to mark.

A. Now put your finger on the little black BIRD. Close your eyes. Don't peek! Listen. CHAIR CUP. Open your eyes. Mark the right box.

You should have marked this box (pointing to the third box), because I said CHAIR CUP and this box has a CHAIR and then a CUP in it.

TEST 2: RHYMING

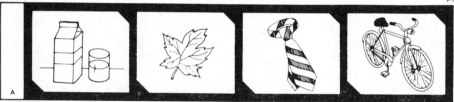

Listen to the words I say: LATE, DATE, GATE. Say each word with me. LATE, DATE, GATE.

Did you notice that all these words sound alike? Listen again: LATE, DATE, GATE. These words do not begin with the same sound, but they sound the same in the middle and at the end, so we say they RHYME.

I am going to say some more words. Tell me if they rhyme: BOOM, ROOM.

Pause for response.

Yes, BOOM and ROOM rhyme.

Tell me if these words rhyme: BIKE, BEAD.

Pause for response.

No, BIKE and BEAD do not rhyme.

A. Put your finger by the top row. The pictures are MILK, LEAF, TIE, BIKE. Listen to the word I say: LIKE. Mark the one that rhymes with LIKE, the one that rhymes with LIKE.

You should have marked the BIKE because BIKE rhymes with LIKE.

Figure 8.3 Types of items used on Reading Readiness Tests. Sample items, reprinted from the Metropolitan Readiness Tests. (Copyright © 1976 by the Psychological Corporation. Reproduced by special permission of the publisher.)

TEST 3: LETTER RECOGNITION

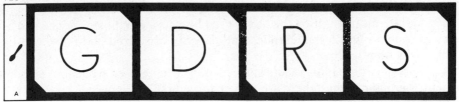

A. Put your finger on the little black SPOON at the beginning of the top row. Look at the letters in this row. Mark the S ... the S.

You should have marked this (pointing to the fourth box), the last letter in this row. That is the letter S.

TEST 4: VISUAL MATCHING

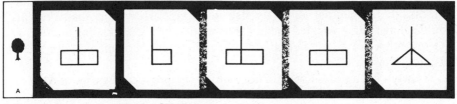

A. Put your finger on the little black TREE. Look at what is in the red box. Then look over at the other shapes in the row. Find the one that is just like the one in the red box, and mark that box. Remember, the shape must be just the same in every way as the one you see in the red box. It must MATCH it.

You should have marked this box (pointing to the next-to-last box). The shape in it is exactly like the one in the red box.

TEST 5: SCHOOL LANGUAGE AND LISTENING

A. Put your finger on the little black BALL. Mark the picture that shows this: The duck is beside the flower ... The duck is beside the flower.

You should have marked this picture (pointing to the last picture), because it is the only picture that shows a duck beside a flower.

TEST 6: QUANTITATIVE LANGUAGE

A. Put your finger on the little black HAND. Look at the rabbit in the red box. Now look over at the other rabbits. Mark the rabbit that is BIGGER THAN the rabbit in the red box ... Mark the rabbit that is BIGGER THAN the rabbit in the red box.

You should have marked this rabbit (pointing to the next-to-last one) because it is the only rabbit that is BIGGER THAN the rabbit in the red box.

Figure 8.3 (continued)

trouble reading numbers. After ascertaining that the deficiencies are not due to any physical factors, the teacher can institute remedial action where needed. In this illustration the test is used both as a prognostic device and as a criterion on which the learning materials are organized and presented by the classroom teacher.

The results of reading readiness tests may also be used by school personnel for grouping when there are two or three first-grade classes, so that the pupils who are at about the same level can be grouped together for instructional purposes. It is much easier to teach groups that have similar abilities. Naturally, for homogeneous grouping, the teacher should also consider other factors. But in the first grade, reading readiness may well be the most important. Intellectual ability is also important. However, many research studies have demonstrated the high correlation between reading and IQ. The IQ tests that are highly verbal are especially highly correlated with reading readiness tests.

We would be remiss if we did not caution the prospective user of readiness test results to be very wary of their potential *misuse*. As of now, the empirical evidence regarding the predictive validity of the readiness test scores is very weak (Henderson & Long, 1970).

Because readiness test score results appear to play such an important role in determining teacher expectancies, it is vital that *all* test users be thoroughly educated on the *limitations* of tests they are using or planning to use. And, as Long & Henderson (1974, p. 145) state: "If teachers are *overly* [italics added] influenced by relatively invalid tests [sic] scores, it might be better if children entering school were not tested at all."

Reading Tests

The ability to communicate by means of language is fundamental in today's society. Reading is one form of communication that must be developed in our pupils. If one examines the curriculum in the primary grades, it is readily obvious that the development of communicative skills—reading, writing, and speaking—makes up a major portion of the curriculum. In any survey battery there will be at least one or more subtests for the assessment of reading skills. The subtests may be classified in a variety of ways—reading comprehension, language arts, language skills—but regardless of the rubric used, they are essentially tests of the pupil's ability to read.

Because all survey batteries, regardless of grade level, have subtests for measuring the students' reading proficiency, we might well ask why it is necessary to have and use a separate reading test. Is it because the reading tests of the survey battery are invalid? Is it because they are unreliable? Not really. The major reasons for using separate tests for reading skills are: (1)

Using a survey battery to obtain an estimate of an examinee's reading ability is neither time- nor cost-efficient; (2) survey batteries are not as thorough in their coverage in any one area as are separate subject-matter (or skills) tests; therefore (3) reading tests should be used if the scores from a survey battery indicate that the pupil is weak in the area.

All reading tests use essentially similar procedures for measuring the pupils' reading ability. Pupils are typically required to read a series of paragraphs and answer questions about them. They are given items to determine whether they are facile with words and sentences. Some tests use short passages; others use long passages with many sentences. Some tests may employ prose selections only; others may use both prose and poetry to measure comprehension. Some focus on the lower levels of comprehension, while others stress interpretation. Some of the tests are oral; others are of the silent-reading type and can be administered in a group setting. Once again, regardless of the manner of assessment, reading tests all serve a common purpose—to see how well the individual can read. As we have mentioned earlier, the reading process is an extremely complex task and involves a variety of factors, some of which are continually interacting and cannot be isolated as distinct entities. No single test attempts to measure all these factors. Some of the factors, such as attitudes involved in reading or adult reading habits, are unlikely to be assessed by any test. Because opinions differ about the skills deemed important in the reading process, we see different kinds of reading tests. This is not to say that one standardized reading test is more valid than another. The evaluation of any standardized reading (actually, any achievement) test depends upon the similarity of the user's and test constructor's objectives. In selecting a test, users alone must decide whether the objectives they deem important are measured by the test and how well their objectives are measured.

Recognizing that reading tests differ in the skills they measure as well as in the emphasis they place on each of the skills in the reading process, we will now look at one of the more popular reading tests in greater detail.

Gates-MacGinitie Reading Tests, Second Edition   Published by Riverside Press in 1978, this replaced the familiar Gates Reading Tests. It consists of seven separate tests for grades 1–12: Basic R (grade 1.0–1.9), Level A (grade 1.5–1.9), Level B (grade 2), Level C (grade 3), Level D (grades 4–6), Level E (grades 7–9), and Level F (grades 10–12). Levels D and E have three forms each; all other levels have two forms each. With the exception of the Basic R level, which yields a total raw score (although subscores can be obtained in letter sound, vocabulary, letter recognition, and comprehension), all other levels provide scores in vocabulary and comprehension as well as a total score. The testing time for the vocabulary and comprehension subtests is 20 and 35 minutes respectively for Levels A–F. For Basic R, the test is untimed, although it is suggested that it requires about 65 minutes' testing time and that it be administered in two sittings.

The Vocabulary Test at all levels measures the child's ability to recognize or analyze isolated words. The vocabulary tests in Basic R and Levels A and B are primarily tests of decoding skills. In Basic R and Levels A and B, vocabulary is measured with pictures and words—each question consists of a picture followed by four words. The examinee has to select the word that corresponds to the picture by "sounding out" each word. Since most of the questions require that the examinee know the sound that corresponds to a specific letter or letter sequence in order to select the correct word, this can be of invaluable assistance to the teacher in helping identify specific decoding skills that the child has not yet mastered. Level C uses the same format as those of Levels A and B. However, this level is a test of the child's reading vocabulary and word knowledge rather than decoding skills. Whereas Level C asks the examinee to select the one of four words or phrases that comes closest in meaning to the "test" word, Levels D, E, and F use five words or phrases. The exercises are graduated in difficulty.

Comprehension at all levels measures the child's ability to read whole sentences and paragraphs with understanding. This is done by means of a series of reading passages that vary in length and complexity. For Basic R and Levels A and B, each passage is accompanied by four pictures from which the examinee selects the one that explains the passage, or answers questions about the passage. For Levels C to F, the Comprehension Test measures the child's ability to read complete prose passages (varying in number, length, and difficulty) with understanding. The examinee is asked from two to five questions on each passage. There are both literal and inferential questions, the percentage of the latter increasing from 10 percent in Level A to 45 percent in Levels D, E, and F.

The Vocabulary and Comprehension tests at all levels except Basic R (where the easy and difficult items are interspersed throughout the test) are power tests in the sense that the tasks become increasingly difficult. On the surface, it would appear that at the higher grade levels, the Comprehension Test may also be a speed test, considering the number of passages to be read, the number of questions asked, and the emphasis on inferential questions, which require the student to deduce rather than to recognize.

In addition to the Vocabulary and Comprehension tests, Basic R, because it is designed to measure general reading achievement as well as particular reading skills needed to read well, also has subtests in letter sound and letter recognition. However, only a total reading score is obtained.

As is true in any test that attempts to span two or three grades, it is extremely difficult to control the difficulty of the items so that they are not too easy for the upper-level students or too difficult for the lower-level students. The Gates-MacGinitie tests are no exception, but they do show marked improvement over the older Gates Reading Tests.

Validity evidence as such is not presented. We concur with the authors that users evaluate the test in relation to their instructional objectives and curriculum, that is, content validity. Although the authors describe in a very general fashion the rationale for the tests and the manner in which the tests were constructed (for instance, they indicate what texts were surveyed to select vocabulary words), no test blueprint is provided to enable the user to judge the content validity of a specific test. The authors state there was an initial tryout of the items, that minority group consultants were used, and that many more items were written than used. However, neither descriptive data concerning the tryout sample nor information concerning the item analyses performed is reported.

Three reliability estimates are reported—internal consistency (K-R 20), alternate-form, and test–retest. Standard errors of measurement are also provided. With the exception of three reliability coefficients, all K-R 20 reliabilities are in the .90s. Norms were developed on a stratified random sample of about 65,000 pupils for each of the two standardization programs—beginning and end of the school year. The first and second editions of the tests were equated so that scores on alternate forms and adjacent levels could be meaningfully compared. With the exception of Basic R, where raw scores are expressed as high, average, or low (because the subtests are very short), raw scores are expressed as percentile ranks, stanines, grade equivalents, extended scale scores, and normal curve equivalents. A variety of output data are available. The tests are accompanied by a Technical Manual and a Teacher's Manual. The latter contains brief, succinct descriptions of the meanings of the various derived scores, as well as an extremely brief section on the use of the test scores.

The Gates-MacGinitie Reading Tests, Second Edition, reflect many of the strengths of the earlier edition. The newer edition also pays more attention to testing in the first grade, which is as it should be, since this level is so important in the child's reading development. Another feature is a series of levels that provides for continuous measurement of reading achievement with a group of articulated tests from grades 1 to 12. The tests are attractively printed, use color appropriately, are printed in machine-scorable and hand-scorable versions, and are easy for teachers to administer and score. Unfortunately as in the first edition, the norms tables, the description of validity, and the standardization sample are inadequate. The content *appears* to reflect current trends in the teaching of reading, especially that there is a difference between vocabulary and comprehension. The Teacher's Manual is easy to follow.

Other Standardized Reading Tests   Other examples of standardized reading tests, in addition to the reading subtest of survey batteries that are appropriate for the elementary and secondary grades, are the Nelson Reading Skills Test, the Skills Monitoring System—Reading, the Durrell Listening-Reading Series, and the Gray Oral Reading Tests. For those who wish to assess the reading proficiency of persons who have completed high school, the Nelson-Denny Reading Test and the Iowa Silent Reading Tests can be used. As noted earlier, although there are differences among the various reading tests, they measure essentially the same core factors deemed important—for example, comprehension, vocabulary, and word usage.

Uses of Reading Tests   Reading tests, like other standardized achievement tests, are designed to measure an examinee's strengths and weaknesses. Specifically, however, reading test results can be used to help explain the reasons behind a pupil's underachievement in, say, science or mathematics. For example, Mary may be doing poorly in school not because she does not have an aptitude for learning, or the ability to learn, but because she is a poor reader. The results of reading tests can and should be used as *partial* evidence to evaluate the effectiveness of reading instruction. (Note: We did *not* say that they should be used to evaluate the teacher. In a later section we shall elaborate on the use of test scores for teacher evaluation.) And if Mr. Jones sees that his pupils are not doing well on his own or some standardized reading test, he can at least begin to advance some hypothesis(es) to explain why this is so. Finally, the results of a reading test can be used to identify, albeit tentatively, those students who are having difficulty and should be given a reading diagnostic test.

Summary   Thus the decision whether to use a single-subject-matter test, such as reading or mathematics or science, rather than the subtest of a survey battery depends upon the ultimate use of the test results. A survey test for a special-subject-matter area does not differ in principle from a battery subtest covering the same subject. Both are concerned with assessing the individual's present state of knowledge and contain much the same material. They do differ, however, in their degree or intensity of coverage. For example, an achievement test for arithmetic would contain more items and cover more aspects of arithmetic than would be possible in the battery's arithmetic subtest. Another advantage of the single-subject-matter test is that a particular school's objectives might be more in harmony with the objectives of a specific content test than with the subtest of a battery. There are other reasons for using single-subject-matter tests. One is to obtain more information about a pupil who has done poorly on the subtest of a battery. Another is to guide and counsel. Finally, because high schools have less of a uniform curriculum than do elementary schools, conventional test batteries will not have subtests for unique subjects such as Latin, Spanish, or psychology. Also, single-subject-matter tests normally reflect curricular changes sooner than batteries do.

STANDARDIZED ACHIEVEMENT TEST SURVEY BATTERIES

Survey batteries are the most comprehensive way to measure educational achievement. Their major purpose is to determine examinees' *normative* performance (some of the newer batteries also are concerned with criterion-referenced performance) rather than to isolate specific strengths and weaknesses, despite the fact that some survey battery authors claim their tests can be used for diagnostic purposes and purport to give prescriptive information.

Because survey batteries lend themselves best to a level where there is a common core of subjects and objectives, we find the largest number at the primary and elementary levels, although there are survey batteries at all other levels.

When we examine the numerous survey batteries that have been published for the primary and elementary grades, we find more similarities than differences among them. These survey batteries typically contain subtests in spelling, language usage, reading knowledge, vocabulary, arithmetic reasoning, arithmetic fundamentals, science, and social studies, no doubt, because the curriculum at the primary and elementary levels tends to be similar regardless of the state, region, or city in which schools are located. Because of the greater flexibility high school pupils have in selecting their courses, because of the diversity of courses offered, and because of differences in the content of courses that have the same name, test publishers find it extremely difficult to develop a common core survey achievement test battery for general high school use. Accordingly, various approaches have been used to try and develop a common core. One approach has been to build tests like the Stanford Achievement Test that measure the basic skills of reading, language, mathematics, and study. Another approach is to build tests like the Tests of Achievement and Proficiency (designed for grades 9 to 12 only) that emphasize the content—mathematics, science, English, and social studies—stressed in high schools. Still another approach is to build tests that are designed to measure skills and abilities which are not dependent on a particular curriculum or course of study such as the Sequential Tests of Educational Progress (STEP III). All these approaches have their advantages as well as limitations. For example, tests like the TAP are valid only for inferences regarding competence in a traditional curriculum. Achievement batteries like the STEP III, designed to measure general educational development and stressing critical thinking and interpretation rather than particular bits of information, are more valid for inferences regarding those skills. Survey batteries, regardless of their classification, often provide a total score as well as subscores. They often contain two or more parallel (equivalent) forms, take from 2 to 3 hours to administer (although some of the high school batteries take about five hours), and, for the younger pupils, have practice tests. Most of the batteries provide for both in-level and out-of-level testing (in out-of-level testing, a pupil in, say, the fifth grade may be given the test booklet that corresponds to, or includes, the fourth grade).

Although nearly all the survey batteries have interpretive information in either the general Manual or a Teacher's Manual, some of the batteries such as the California Achievement Tests and the Stanford Achievement Test have detailed procedures for the teacher to follow when interpreting a pupil's score and undertaking remediation. Batteries designed for the primary grades have the pupils respond directly in the test booklet; those for the upper elementary and above have answer sheets that are either hand- or machine-scorable. Standardized achievement test survey batteries often provide separate norms (sex, grade, age) to enable the user to make various comparisons. They provide for the conversion of raw scores to standard scores to assist in test interpretation. The most common method of expressing test scores is in terms of grade equivalents, although percentiles are frequently given. In the newer tests, stanines are reported. A still newer trend is to report scores in terms of normal curve equivalents (NCEs) (see Chapter 5). The latest editions of the major survey batteries provide both objective-referenced and norm-referenced data. An example of a printout of an objective-referenced report from a norm-referenced test is given in Figure 8.4. From such a printout one obtains both norm-referenced information in the form of the various derived scores and the pupil's performance on each of the objectives measured by the test. The latter is expressed in terms of the level of mastery (a ''+'' indicates mastery, a ''−'' nonmastery, and a ''P'' partial mastery).

As mentioned earlier, because of the large number of subtests in survey batteries, the content sampling is limited. As might be expected, not all the subtests are of equal reliability, and some of the subtests may not be valid for Miss Smith's inferences while others are. The major advantage of the battery is that since all the subtests have been normed on the same sample, a pupil's performance on different subtests can be compared directly. Also, many of the survey batteries are now being normed concurrently with an aptitude test (for example, STEP III and SCAT III; the Metropolitan with the Otis-Lennon), thereby enabling the user to compare pupils' achievement with their ability.

A major trend in survey achievement test batteries over the past decade has been their emphasis on the *application* and *interpretation* of knowledge rather than on simple recall of facts.

We will now consider some of the survey batteries most frequently used in the elementary and secondary grades, beginning with a detailed review of the Stanford Achievement Test and followed by brief reviews of other commonly used survey achievement batteries. Although standardized achieve-

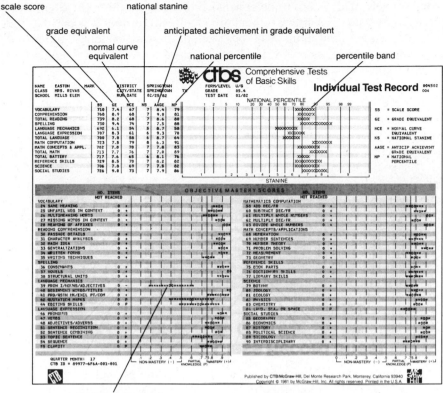

Figure 8.4   Individual Test Record from Comprehensive Test of Basic Skills, Form C. Reproduced by permission of the publisher. CTB/McGraw-Hill, Del Monte Research Park, Monterey, CA. 93940. Copyright © 1981 by McGraw-Hill, Inc. All rights reserved. Printed in the U.S.A.

ment survey batteries are available for college, graduate, and professional school, these will not be considered here.

Critical Evaluation of the 1982 Stanford Achievement Test[13]

We have selected the Stanford for our detailed review because it is one of the most popular and useful standardized survey achievement test batteries used

[13] The seventh edition (1982) is published by the Psychological Corporation. The authors of SESAT, Second Edition, are Eric F. Gardner, Richard Madden, and Cathy S. Collins. The authors of the Primary through Advanced batteries are Gardner, Herbert C. Rudman, Bjorn Karlsen, and Jack C. Merwin. The authors of the Test of Academic Skills, Second Edition (TASK) are Gardner, Rudman, Merwin, and Robert Callis. SESAT has two levels: Level 1

in our schools. This is not to be construed as signifying that the Stanford is the only good survey battery (others are available), or that it is perfect (that there are some limitations will be evident in the ensuing discussion). However, it represents one of the better test batteries for surveying school achievement from kindergarten to high school.

Grade Level and Content   Table 8.2 presents the subtests, number of items, and administration time by grade level. For each of the levels in Primary 1 through Advanced, there are both Complete and Basic Skills batteries. Complete batteries and Basic batteries differ in that the latter do not have subtests in social science and science. There are two forms (E, F) for the Complete battery for Primary 2 through TASK 2. SESAT (Stanford Early School Achievement Test) 1 and 2 have one form (E), while Primary 1 has three forms (E, F, G). Form G combines, in a single booklet, the reading tests of Primary 2 (F) with the remaining subtests of Primary 1 (F). Form G, therefore, is suitable for testing in high achievement classrooms at 1.8 and 2.1 or in low-achieving classes at 2.5 and 2.9 as an alternate to Primary 2.

The Stanford Achievement Test Series (hereafter referred to as the Stanford) is concerned at all grade levels with measuring the outcomes of a core curriculum—vocabulary, reading comprehension, spelling, listening comprehension, and arithmetic skills. The test items were prepared after consultation with subject-matter specialists and after a careful and thorough analysis of textbooks, word counts, and syllabi.

All subtests concerned with reading (e.g., Sounds and Letters, Word Reading, Vocabulary, and Reading Comprehension) are found at all levels. As expected, those tests concerned with assessing the skills needed before beginning reading instruction are available only at SESAT 1 and 2. The Language/English subtest (which has an optional Writing Assessment Program) is found at Primary 3 through TASK 2. Beginning with Primary 3, all complete batteries also measure science and social science. Spelling is measured at all levels beginning with Primary 1.

The Environment subtest in SESAT and Primary 1 is designed to measure pupils' understanding of basic concepts of (1) one's social environment, such as the ways in which people live together and the neighborhood, and (2) one's natural environment, such as the earth/sun relationship and the way plants and animals relate. In other words, this test attempts to measure science and social science concepts.

(K.0–K.9) and Level 2 (K.5–1.9) with five subtests common to both levels: Environment, Mathematics, Sounds and Letters, Word Reading, and Listening to Words & Stories. Level 2 has, in addition, sentence reading, which is measured by the Reading Comprehension subtest. Separate subtest and total score for each level. There is one form (E). Nine sittings are suggested for either level (130 and 145 minutes' testing time for Levels 1 and 2 respectively). With SESAT and TASK, the 1982 Stanford provides for an articulated measure of skills and knowledge in various content areas from grades K through 13.

The Sounds and Letters and Listening to Words & Stories subtests are found only at the SESAT 1 and 2 levels. The Sounds and Letters test consists of two parts: (1) auditory perception (the pupil's ability to match beginning or ending sounds in words) and (2) symbol perception (the pupil's ability to recognize upper- and lower-case letters and match them to the sounds they most frequently represent).

The Listening to Words & Stories subtest also consists of two parts. In one part, the pupil's knowledge of the meaning of words is measured (this resembles a vocabulary test). In the other part, the student's ability to answer questions based on short passages read to them is measured. The latter part requires the student not only to understand what has been read but also to remember the material, to follow directions, and to identify cause and effect.

Word Study Skills subtests are found in all the Primary and Intermediate batteries. At the Primary 1 level, the test is actually a measure of word recognition. In the Primary 2 battery and above, the test has two parts: one to measure the pupil's knowledge of phonics, the other to measure the pupil's abilities in structural analysis (the decoding of words through the analysis of their parts). The former is measured by having students select from a letter or letters underlined in a stimulus word, a letter or letter combination sound from a group of three or four words. A variety of letter–sound combinations are tested, such as single consonant sounds, digraphs, common affixes, short and complex vowel sounds, and the like. To measure the students' skill in structural analysis, a word is divided into syllables in four different ways and the student has to decide the correct way in which to divide the word. The test authors claim that pupils' performance is not markedly influenced by the size of their sight vocabulary, since the words used in the test are generally within the pupils' listening vocabulary.

Reading is measured at all levels from SESAT 1 through TASK 2, either in terms of a series of separate subtest scores, a reading score, or a total reading score. The combination of subtest scores comprising the Reading/ Total Reading scores varies depending upon the level (grade) tested. For example, the reading test score in SESAT 1 consists of the Word Reading and Sentence Reading subtest scores; for Primary 1 and 2 it consists of the Word Reading and Reading Comprehension scores; and for TASK 1 and 2 it is made up of the Reading Vocabulary and Reading Comprehension subtest scores. Similarly, the composition of the subtests making up the Total Reading score varies according to the level tested. In SESAT 2, Reading Comprehension is measured by the Sentence Reading Test. In the latter, children identify pictures illustrating sentences "that contain basic syntactic patterns" found in contemporary primers and first-grade readers.

The Word Reading subtest found in SESAT 1 and 2 and in Primary 1 and 2 is actually a test of the pupils' ability to *recognize* words. A novel technique was used to test for Word Reading. In one approach, the pupil matches a

TABLE 8.2

LIST OF TESTS BY BATTERY LEVEL AND NUMBER OF ITEMS AND
ADMINISTRATION TIME PER TEST FOR THE 1982 STANFORD ACHIEVEMENT TESTS

Test Levels and Recommended Grade Ranges

Complete Battery[a] Tests by Level and Scores	SESAT 1 K.0–K.9 Items	Time*	SESAT 2 K.5–1.9 Items	Time*	Primary 1 1.5–2.9 Items	Time*	Primary 2 2.5–3.9 Items	Time*	Primary 3 3.5–4.9 Items	Time*	Inter-mediate 1 4.5–5.9 Items	Time*	Inter-mediate 2 5.5–7.9 Items	Time*	Advanced 7.0–9.9 Items	Time*	TASK 1 8.0–12.9 Items	Time*	TASK 2 0.0–13 Items	Time*
Sounds and Letters	44	30	45	25																
Word Study Skills					36	20	48	25	54	30	60	35	60	35						
Word Reading			38	20	33	20	33	20												
Reading Comprehension			30	20**	40	25	40	25	60	30	60	30	60	30	60	30	50	30	50	30
Vocabulary					35	20	38	20	38	20	36	20	36	20	40	20	37	20	37	20
Listening to Words & Stories	45	30	45	30																
Listening Comprehension					28	20	30	20	40	30	40	30	40	30	40	30				
Spelling					30	20	30	20	36	15	40	15	50	15	50	15	40	15	40	15
Language/English†									46	30	53	30	53	30	59	30	54	30	54	30

Concepts of Number					34	25	34	20	34	20	34	20	34	20	34	20				
Mathematics Computation					45	45	38	30	42	35	44	40	44	40	44	40				
Mathematics Applications							36	25	38	35	40	35	40	35	40	35				
Mathematics[b]	40	30	50	30													48	40	48	40
Environment	38	25	40	20	27	20	27	20												
Science									44	25	60	30	60	30	60	30	50	25	50	25
Social Science									44	25	60	30	60	30	60	30	50	25	50	25
Total Basic Battery									388	4 hrs. 5 min.	407	4 hrs. 15 min.	417	4 hrs. 15 min.	367	3 hrs. 40 min.	229	2 hrs. 15 min.	229	2 hrs. 15 min.
Total Complete Battery	197	2 hrs. 10 min.	248	2 hrs. 25 min.	311	3 hrs. 35 min.	351	3 hrs. 45 min.	476	4 hrs. 55 min.	527	5 hrs. 15 min.	537	5 hrs. 15 min.	487	4 hrs. 40 min.	329	3 hrs. 5 min.	329	3 hrs. 5 min.

* Time for each subtest is in minutes.

** Sentence Reading at SESAT 2 level.

† An optional Writing Test is also available at levels Primary 3 through TASK 2.

[a] Basic Battery at all levels includes all subtests *except* social science and science.

[b] Mathematics at SESAT 1 and 2 and TASK 1 and 2 is measured by a single test. At all other levels, three separate subtests are used.

Reproduced from the Stanford Achievement Test Series, copyright © 1982 by the Psychological Corporation. Reproduced by special permission of the publisher.

spoken and a printed word. In another approach, the pupil identifies a word that names a particular illustration. In a third approach, the pupil identifies a printed word that tells something about the picture shown. The words used (both the correct answer and the distracters) were sampled from those generally taught in grades 1 and 2. Although some pupils could use phonics to arrive at the correct answer, Word Reading is *not* a phonics test. Since the words tested are in the average child's listening and speaking vocabulary, we essentially have a measure of the child's ability to go from the written to the spoken word.

The Reading Comprehension subtest in Primary 1 consists of a series of pictures (e.g., a dog on a table) with one or more questions based on the picture asked (e.g., It [the dog] was on the _____). The passages gradually increase in length. A modified cloze format is used, which is good since pupils respond in a way that simulates their reading process. In Primary 2, the first three test items use the same cloze format as Primary 1. Thereafter, the items used are based on the six passages the student reads. For each passage, the pupil selects one of four words to make the sentence correct (that is, answer the question). The vocabulary used for both levels is limited to those words taught in the primary grades.

Reading Comprehension for the Primary 3 through TASK 2 levels is measured in one of two ways: (1) comprehension as it relates to the types of questions asked—that is, some of the questions tap the students' inferential comprehension skills while others assess the students' literal comprehension skills, and (2) comprehension as it relates to the type—textual, functional, or recreational—of material read. Reading Comprehension is measured by having the pupil read a story or poem (the content is varied and the reading vocabulary is appropriate for the age level tested) and then answer questions based on the selection read. In the Intermediate and Advanced batteries, the selections range from 11 to 29 lines in length, and from 6 to 11 questions are asked per selection. Phonics and vocabulary skills are deemphasized, the major stress being on measuring the pupil's ability to gather information from connected discourse. The ability of the student to make inferences, to comprehend the content, and to ascertain what *should* be inferred from the content is also measured. As expected, emphasis on the higher-order mental skills (e.g., drawing inferences, using context for word and paragraph meaning) increases according to the grade level tested.

In TASK, a series of five passages and a poem measure whether the student is able to make inferences and to comprehend the content. From seven to 10 questions are asked per selection.

In summary, one's reading ability can be expressed in terms of separate subtest scores, a Reading score, or a Total Reading score. The combination of the subtest scores making up a particular score varies depending upon the level (grade) tested. For example, although vocabulary is measured at all levels beginning with Primary 1, it is considered as part of the Reading score only in TASK.

Vocabulary is measured with a separate subtest and yields a separate score at all levels from Primary 1 through TASK 2. (The Vocabulary score in the 1973 edition of TASK was part of the English Test score.) In SESAT 1 through Advanced, the teacher dictates three or four words and the pupil selects the one (of the three or four words given) that best completes a sentence read by the teacher. (The Vocabulary items, except for TASK, are read by the examiner to give a measure of the pupils' verbal development independent of their reading ability.) The authors state that the test words used "were selected to represent the various parts of speech, as well as the vocabulary encountered in school and in ordinary conversation" (p. 6, Intermediate 2 Directions for Administering). For TASK, the majority of words used will have been encountered by the eighth or ninth grade. We would have preferred to see the authors employ the technique used in the 1973 edition. There, the test words used were selected by sampling word counts in science, social studies, arts and crafts (for primary level batteries) plus words common to fiction, nonfiction, and reference books (intermediate levels and above). One-half of the items in the elementary batteries were content-dependent (those encountered in school subjects per se). The other half were general vocabulary found in the language arts.

The Vocabulary subtest is basically a measure of the verbal competency the child brings to school as well as those concepts taught in school. For this, the test can be diagnostically useful, especially in the lower grades.

Mathematics is measured by a single subtest in SESAT and TASK. At all other levels, three subtests—Concepts of Number, Mathematics Computation, and Mathematics Applications—are used. One obtains a separate score for each subtest as well as a Total Mathematics score.

The Mathematics subtest in SESAT measures the pupils' understanding of the basic number concepts such as counting and recognizing geometric shapes, rather than just their ability to carry out numerical operations; their understanding of mathematical language; and their knowledge of the basic addition and subtraction facts, with sums to 9 and 18 for SESAT 1 and 2 respectively.

The Concepts of Number subtest at the Primary, Intermediate, and Advanced levels measures the pupils' understanding of the basic number concepts such as counting, ordering, place value, part–whole relationships, and so on, rather than just skill in carrying out numerical operations. In addition, at the Intermediate and Advanced levels, concepts and operations of fractional and rational numbers also are measured. For the Primary levels, the teacher reads the questions aloud to the pupils to minimize the influence of reading ability. Even at the upper levels, the language used is kept simple so as to focus on measuring knowledge of mathematics rather than on reading ability. Both the "new" and "old" mathematics curricula are reflected in the test. The pupil's ability to read graphs and charts is tested as early as the first grade.

The Mathematics Computation subtest is found at all levels from Primary 1 through Advanced and contains items to measure the pupil's knowledge of fundamental arithmetic processes—addition, subtraction, multiplication, and division—both by verbal problems and in the conventional format (3 + 3 = ?). As one progresses to the higher levels, basic arithmetic operations involving decimals and fractions, estimation, and the solution of proportions and linear equations also are included.

The Mathematics Applications subtest is found at all levels from Primary 1 (where it is part of the Computation subtest) to Advanced. The tests rely heavily on verbal problems to assess the pupil's knowledge of fundamental arithmetic processes and concepts. Many of the problems stress computational ability to solve problems that occur in real-life situations. As one progresses from the Primary to Advanced level, there is more emphasis on the interpretation of graphed data, reading of charts and tables, use of maps and scales, and English and metric measures.

In TASK, mathematics computation, application, and concepts are evaluated by a single subtest designed "to measure general mathematical competence." About one-half of the test is devoted to the measurement of computational skills and the application of numerical concepts and skills to problem-solving situations. The other half assesses basic principles of algebra, geometry, and measurement. There is little emphasis on the "new" math. The authors claim that for Level 1, most pupils should have been exposed to the content tested by the time they have completed grades 7 or 8. After making a thorough content analysis, we feel that the authors are justified in making this claim.

Spelling is tested at all levels beginning in Primary 1. We commend the authors for making Spelling a separate subtest in TASK instead of part of the English test score as in the 1973 edition. In the Primary 1 battery, the teacher reads the word to be spelled both as a separate word, then again in a sentence context, and once again as a separate word. In the Primary 2 and 3 and Intermediate 1 levels, the pupil selects the incorrectly spelled word contained in a set of four words. At the Intermediate 2 and Advanced levels, a series of four phrases, each with a word underlined, is presented; pupils select the incorrectly spelled word from those underlined. In TASK, spelling is measured in two ways: by selecting the incorrectly spelled word contained (1) in a set of four words or (2) in a group of four phrases. According to the test authors, the mistakes to be detected represent errors that result from the improper use of phonetic or structural principles. We are concerned that at no time do pupils write out the correct spelling of a word; they need only *recognize* an incorrectly spelled word. We contend that spelling is more than just recognition; specifically, in written expression the individual must recall correct spelling rather than just identify it.

Language is measured in the Primary 3 through Advanced levels with a separate subtest and yields a separate score (another change from the 1973 edition, in which no separate score was obtained). The subtest is organized into three parts. In one, the pupils' knowledge of capitalization and punctuation is measured by presenting a group of statements that could be made into complete sentences by correct punctuation or capitalization. In another, the pupils' knowledge of grammar is assessed. In the final section, students are asked to identify complete or run-on sentences and sentence fragments. In addition, there are separate sections to measure the pupil's knowledge of dictionary usage, word meaning, different types of reference books, literary concepts, knowledge of morphemes, and grammatical concepts.

The Writing Assessment Program (an optional subtest) is available at the Primary 3 through TASK 2 levels. Whereas the mechanics of writing are measured by the Language and English subtests, the best way to assess students' writing style (organization, coherence, wording, etc.) is to examine a sample of their writing. Four different writing samples are obtained/measured: describing, narrating, explaining, and reasoning. Suggested topics for each type are given, as are the directions for administration and holistic scoring. Samples and ratings of each type of writing are given.

In TASK, language is part of the English subtest. The English subtest consists of four sections designed to measure the pupil's knowledge and effective use of the English language. The first section deals with the use of a dictionary and reference materials and is more like a vocabulary test than an English test per se. The second section requires the student to identify errors, if any, in punctuation, grammar, and capitalization. A novel approach is used here. Pupils are given a selection which may contain a variety of errors and must decide whether (1) there is an error in grammar, (2) in punctuation, (3) in capitalization, or (4) there is no error. This testing approach differs from the conventional one, such as that found in other achievement tests, where a set of items that are either correct or incorrect for a specific part of language such as punctuation or grammar is presented. The third section tests English expression by having four compound words or complex sentences from which the student selects the one that best conveys an idea. The final section consists of four jumbled sentences that the examinee must arrange to present an idea clearly.

Listening Comprehension (LC) is measured from the Primary 1 through Advanced levels. The LC subtest is designed to measure pupils' ability to "process information that has been heard, both in terms of the retention of specific details and the organization, or understanding of the material as a whole" (Primary 1 Manual of Directions, p. 7). The stimulus material represents both school-related and non-school-related information. The objectives measured by the LC test are similar to those assessed by the Reading subtest, but the skills used may differ. Collectively, the LC and Reading subtests provide a global measure of the "comprehension" of communication.

Listening Comprehension is measured by the teacher reading a short story or poem and then asking the pupils one or more questions based on the material read. In many instances the pupils are required to make an inference, but we question whether too much reliance is placed on the pupils' memory, especially for young children. Although there are some factual questions, other questions require the pupils to use interpretive skills, to perceive relationships and concepts, and to see implied meaning. The LC test is definitely *not* a vocabulary test, and because the selections vary in content, they should appeal to most pupils, regardless of their interests. For example, in the Intermediate 2 battery, the content comes from the sciences, the social sciences, poetry, and current events.

Beginning with Primary 3, two additional subtests common to all the complete batteries are the Science and Social Studies subtests. The Social Studies subtest measures critical thinking ability and map-reading skills as early as the Intermediate level. At all levels there are items on history, geography, sociology, anthropology, economics, and political science. Although the lower levels have some vocabulary-type items to measure the pupil's knowledge of social studies concepts, at the Intermediate level and above, emphasis is placed on measuring knowledge as well as the pupil's ability to predict, infer, conclude, and reason by means of maps, charts, and graphs. At the Intermediate and Advanced levels and in TASK, the items reflect the modern curriculum, which stresses critical thinking and the relationship between content and structure of the social sciences. In fact, in the Advanced level, newer social studies concepts are tested (the pupil's ability to relate knowledge of economics to the interpretation of maps, predicting future trends, and so forth).

The Science subtests are designed to measure the pupils' ability to apply their knowledge of scientific concepts and principles, to make inferences and estimates, and to measure. There are items on the life sciences, chemistry, physics, conservation, and the scientific method. The authors say they stress the use of inquiry skills. As one progresses from the lower to higher levels, it is apparent that more attention is paid to the measurement of the higher mental processes. We would like to see still greater emphasis on tests of the students' ability to draw conclusions based on experimental data.

Figure 8.5 illustrates some of the types of items used in the Intermediate 2 battery. Although the subtests of the other levels have not been illustrated, the reader should now have a general knowledge of the types of items used. Only after examining and taking the test will the user be able to determine how well adapted the test will be to his or her purpose.

Word Study Skills

DIRECTIONS
In each question the same word is divided into syllables in four different ways. Decide which is the correct way to divide the word. Then mark the space for the answer you have chosen.

SAMPLES

A a un – cert – ain
   b un – cer – tain
   c unc – er – tain
   d unc – ert – ain

B f mi – ner – al
   g min – e – ral
   h mi – ne – ral
   j min – er – al

Word Study Skills

DIRECTIONS
Look at the word with the underlined letter or letters. The underlined letter or letters stand for a sound. Decide which of the other three words has the same sound in it. Then mark the space for the answer you have chosen.

SAMPLE C

d<u>i</u>d

   a bud
   b him
   c by

Mathematics Computation

DIRECTIONS
Read each question and choose the best answer. Then mark the space for the answer you have chosen. If a correct answer is *not here*, mark the space for NH.

SAMPLE

$$\begin{array}{r} 25 \\ + 4 \\ \hline \end{array}$$

   a 27
   b 28
   c 29
   d 30
   e NH

Concepts of Number

DIRECTIONS
Read each question. Choose the best answer. Then mark the space for the answer you have chosen.

SAMPLE

Which numeral has the greatest value?

   a 7   c 8
   b 9   d 3

Science

DIRECTIONS
Read each question and choose the best answer. Then mark the space for the answer you have chosen.

SAMPLE

Mars and Venus are —

   a stars   c planets
   b moons   d comets

Language

DIRECTIONS
Read each sentence. Look carefully at the underlined word or group of words. If there is no error in capitalization or punctuation, mark the answer space for "Correct." If there is an error, choose the answer that is correctly capitalized and punctuated. Then mark the space for the answer you have chosen.

SAMPLE A

Where are the <u>children playing.</u>

   a Correct
   b children playing
   c children playing?
   d children playing,

DIRECTIONS
Read each sentence. Decide which word or group of words belongs in the blank. Then mark the space for the answer you have chosen.

SAMPLE B

George ____ the letter.

   a have wrote
   b has wrote
   c have written
   d has written

Language

DIRECTIONS
Read each group of words. Some groups are complete sentences; others are not. Punctuation and capitalization have been left out purposely.

If the group of words is a complete sentence, even though you might be able to add something else to it, mark the answer space for "Complete sentence."

If the group of words makes up more than one sentence, mark the answer space for "Run-on sentence."

If the group of words is not a complete sentence, decide which group of words can be added before or after the original group to make a complete sentence. Then mark the space for the answer you have chosen.

SAMPLE C

are playing at the beach

   a Complete sentence
   b Run-on sentence
   c the children
   d having fun

Figure 8.5 Sample items reprinted from the Intermediate 2 battery of the Stanford Achievement Test. (Copyright © 1982 by the Psychological Corporation. Reproduced by special permission of the publisher.)

Administration   The Stanford Achievement Test can be administered by the classroom teacher without any formal training. The manuals accompanying each battery are well written, complete, and concise for both examiner and examinees. For the pupils, there are examples that are worked out as well as practice items to be worked out before the test actually begins. New to the 1982 edition are Practice Tests for students taking the Primary and Intermediate levels. If necessary, the examiner should give the examinees assistance on the practice items.

We have a reservation regarding the directions given to the examiner for the "timed" tests. Examiners are told, "After exactly _____ minutes (or sooner if all have finished), say: Stop! . . ." We assume that in the norming study, all examinees were given the full time allotment. Accordingly, in order to use the test norms, the times specified in the Manual must be strictly adhered to. Pupils should not be penalized because the examiner "thinks" they have finished.

Scoring   NCS and MRC machine-scorable booklets are available for SE-SAT 1 through Primary 3. (The publisher recommends that answer sheets *not* be used below grade 4.) The Primary 3 through TASK 2 batteries, in addition, can be hand- or machine-scored. The decision on which scoring format to use often depends upon the output data desired from the publisher. The directions for scoring are clear and can be easily followed.

Types of Scores   Five types of scores are reported: percentile ranks, stanines, grade equivalents, scaled scores, and normal curve equivalents. Norms are reported for only percentile ranks, grade equivalents, and stanines. Scaled scores are a quasi-ratio scale of measurement and provide approximately equal units on a continuous scale. With them, it is possible to convert all the raw scores to a single common scale. Accordingly, with a single subtest area such as, say, Reading, scaled scores are comparable from grade to grade, battery to battery, and form to form. This permits the user to make meaningful comparisons of growth. Scaled scores are *not* comparable from one subtest area to another.

Norming   Much of the information on norming, especially the technical details, is to be reported in the Technical Data Report scheduled for publication in mid-1986. Some of the more salient points, however, are covered in the various norms booklets.

All norms were empirically determined for the beginning and end of the year at all grade levels and for the middle of the year for grades K and 1. Nonempirical midyear norms and interpolated week-of-testing norms are available at all grade levels. We commend the test authors for the cautions given regarding the interpretation of grade equivalents (Gardner et al., 1983, p. 14).

Two standardization programs were undertaken: one for public school students, the other for non-public school students. For the non-public schools approximately 20,000 students were used. Unfortunately, the number of schools used is not reported. For the public school standardization program a stratified sample of 300 school districts provided about 250,000 students for the fall and 200,000 students for the spring standardization programs for all levels except TASK. In addition, 15,000 kindergarten and grade 1 pupils were used for a midyear standardization for SESAT because it was felt that the rapid achievement growth during these years would not be accurately reflected in an October–May testing. Since two preliminary forms were developed for all levels except SESAT, it was decided to standardize the two forms simultaneously in both the spring and fall testings (to reflect end-of-year and beginning-of-year performance, respectively). It is unclear whether the same students were tested in both the fall and spring, and if they were, why there was a decrease in the sample size.

Pupils in K–3 answered questions in the machine-scorable test booklets. Separate answer sheets were used for all other levels. The standardization sample (except kindergartners) took the Stanford as well as the appropriate level of the Otis-Lennon School Ability Test (OLSAT). This provides the user with a means whereby the pupils' achievement-test score can be compared with their intelligence scores. It should also be noted that in the norming procedure, all students taking SESAT 1 through Intermediate 2 took a practice test before the actual test administration. Whether this procedure (which incidentally is to be commended because it puts the examinees at ease and familiarizes them with the task at hand) might affect the student who doesn't take the practice test is a matter of conjecture.

After collecting the data, weighting procedures were used to permit individual grade level norms that were comparable in mental ability to the OLSAT norms groups. By this procedure a Stanford norm group is provided for each grade level with a normal IQ distribution, and a mean OLSAT deviation IQ where the mean is 100 and the standard deviation is 16.

In the 1982 edition, as was the case for the 1963 and 1974 editions, no information is given on the cooperation rate of the schools invited to participate. Since this information can have a marked effect on the users' interpretation of the adequacy of the standardization sample as well as on their interpretation of the norms table itself, we hope that the publisher will provide these data in the forthcoming publication of the Technical Data Report. We also hope that the publisher will provide, as was true in 1963, special norms groups for the college preparatory, special semester, and different curriculum groups.

For TASK, there are separate norms for high school students by grade (8–12) and Junior/Community college freshmen. As was the case for the other levels, the TASK norms are based on a fall and spring testing. About 34,000 students in grades 8–13 comprised the standardization sample. Although caution and thoroughness were used to standardize the Stanford, it would be most desirable for the publisher to provide more descriptive and demographic information about the stratification variables used and about the characteristics of the standardization sample. In the norms booklets we are given only the total marginals for all levels combined. We hope that this type of information will be supplied in the to-be-published Technical Data Report.

It would also be useful to know why the publisher decided to have *both* a fall and a spring testing, since the 1973 edition had only a fall testing; the contention then was that previous research had indicated one testing would suffice. We commend the publisher for this shift. But what changed the publisher's mind? Was there any new research that could account for this? Explanations for the change would be of value.

Reliability   All reliability data are in the form of alternate-form reliability coefficients, K-R 20 estimates, and standard errors of measurement. Of the more than 200 estimates/coefficients reported, most are above 0.80, the range being from 0.45 to 0.97. All in all, the reliabilities of the various subtests, excepting the Environment test, are quite respectable. The lower reliabilities occur at the lower levels. Whether this is because the lower levels are based on more homogeneous samples or whether it is an artifact of the test is a matter of conjecture. Although no stability information is presented, we are not overly concerned, since growth in achievement takes place at varying rates, especially for young children.

For TASK, the alternate-form and K-R 20 coefficients and standard errors of measurement are reported for the beginning (fall only) of grades 8 through 12. Of the 100 coefficients reported, all but 20 are above .90 and none are below .85. The standard errors of measurement range from 1.8 to 4.6, with nearly 75 percent below 3.0.

On the whole, the test reliabilities are quite high. We regret that the publisher did not report grade-score standard errors of measurement, since grade scores are reported.

Validity   Content validity was stressed during the construction of the Stanford Achievement Test. The authors state that a major goal was to make sure that the test content would be in harmony with present-day school objectives and would measure what is actually being taught in today's schools. To achieve this, they made an extensive curricular study by (1) a thorough review of widely used textbooks, course syllabi, and state guidelines in the various content areas; (2) a review of research in developmental and educational psychology concerning children's concepts, experiences, and vocabulary at successive age levels; and (3) a consultation with subject-matter specialists. In addition, item analysis data from the experimental editions (about 100,000 pupils from 50 school systems were used in the tryout phase) guided the test constructors in their attempt to obtain high content validity.

A variety of editing procedures were employed in constructing the 1982 edition. All items were reviewed by subject-matter specialists, test construction experts, general editors, members of minority groups, and teachers, for clarity, style, and bias (gender, racial, and ethnic). Each form was reviewed to ensure that appropriate item-writing guidelines (e.g., one item not cluing the answer to another) were rigorously followed. (The authors state that they prepared twice as many complete forms at each level as were actually needed so as to ensure adequate content validity.)

Construct validity was also stressed in the development of the test. To be considered for final inclusion, the items had to be passed by a larger proportion of pupils at the higher grade levels (this is both good and bad since we would expect a seventh-grader to know more than a sixth-grader, but we fail to consider that forgetting can and does occur over time, especially information that is seldom used); had to correlate well with other editions of the Stanford as well as other achievement tests; and each subtest had to have high internal consistency. Care was taken to obtain average item difficulty across forms, to have items that varied in difficulty (no item in the middle range of difficulty was chosen unless the biserial correlation—that is, the correlation between the item and the subtest—was at least $+.35$), and to build skill clusters that were parallel in coverage.

The Manual states that the test authors wanted to construct a battery that would measure the knowledge, skills, and understanding commonly considered important in our public schools. The test authors felt that recent, extensive curriculum research and the results of item analyses demonstrated the test's reflection of current instructional goals, materials, and methods. They also indicated that appropriate weight is given both to traditional objectives and to recent curriculum trends. On the whole the tests reflect some of "the significant changes that had occurred in the elementary grades" in the previous 13 years. The major claim for validity is made on the basis of the description of content sampling. Perhaps the authors place too much emphasis upon the user's judgment, which, although commendable, is not entirely defensible. Also, if the test is to be used for more than assessment, it must demonstrate predictive validity.

The statistical analyses performed and the test construction procedures used in the 1982 edition were thorough and complete, as was the case for previous editions.

Format   The tests and administrator's manuals for each of the 10 levels are presented in $8\frac{1}{2}$-by-11-inch booklets. The quality of paper, reproduction, and illustrations is excellent.

On the back page of the Primary batteries, and on the hand-scored answer sheets, there are boxes to record the scores (number right, scaled score, grade equivalent, percentile rank, and stanine) separately for each subtest, as well as the four types of total scores (Reading, Mathematics, Language, and Listening). In addition, the content cluster scores for each of the nine tests and their respective subparts (e.g., Reading Comprehension is further subdivided into textual reading, functional reading, recreational reading, literal comprehension, and inferential comprehension) can be plotted in terms of below-average, average, and above-average performance.

Interpretation and Use   A variety of score reports are available, depending on (1) who will use the report—teacher, principal, curriculum director, and so on; (2) for what educational purpose(s) the report(s) will be used—grouping pupils for instruction, obtaining the reading needs for a pupil, class, or school; and (c) whether student, class, or summary (building or system) results are desired. For instructional decision making, the Pupil Skills Analysis and Group Skills Analysis Report for class, school, or system are appropriate. These reports (referred to by the publisher as Package 1) provide individual pupil reports and include detailed analyses of performances on the various subtest objectives. Another set of reports (called Package 2) consists of the Master List of Test Results and the Summaries for class, school, and system and "provides data on subtests and totals, but not on clusters within subtests" (Stanford Information Services Booklet, n.d.).

For administrative-type decisions, the 1982 Stanford provides other reports such as the (1) Master List of Teacher Results: Summary, (2) Administrator's Data Summary, (3) Ranked List of Three Scores, (4) Group Item Analysis, (5) Administrator's Graphic Summary: Percentile Graph, and (6) Socio-Economic Status Profile. Other "customized" reports are available from the publisher.

In this section, we will consider the various reports provided by the publisher (some at an additional cost) to assist users—teachers, pupils, parents, principals, curriculum specialists, and other educators—in interpreting and using the Stanford test scores to assist them in making valid and reliable instructional, counseling and guidance, and administrative decisions. In addition, we will comment on some of the 1982 Stanford's strengths and weaknesses and describe how these relate to the ultimate value and use of the test scores in the decision-making process.

Instructional Use.   A major advantage of the battery is that it provides for a continuous measurement of skills, knowledge, and understanding in the fundamental or core curriculum subjects from grades 1.5 to 9.9. (If we consider, and we should, SESAT and TASK as part of the battery, we have an articulated set of tests covering grades K through 13.) The continuous articulation of content permits the teacher, principal, or counselor (1) to readily locate the pupil's persistent strengths and weaknesses, and (2) to obtain a global concept of the pupil's growth in the various content areas. The user, then, after plotting the pupils' performance, will have a chart that will permit "identification of areas of strength and weakness, as well as the magnitude of the departure from average performance in the various subtests and domains'' (Gardner et al., 1983, p. 13).

The test authors contend that the Stanford Achievement Test measures what is being taught in our schools today, that appropriate attention is given to both the traditional and modern curricula, and that teachers may use this test to ascertain whether their goals of instruction are compatible with those measured by the Stanford. However, teachers must be cautious in their use of the Stanford as the sole criterion of what should be taught in their class.

Let us now consider a hypothetical pupil, Billy, who has taken the Primary 3 level of the 1982 Stanford. What information does the teacher, Mrs. Sanders, have, and what can be done with that information to help her provide optimal instruction? First, assuming a hand-scored edition was used (if machine scoring is used, the data to be entered by the teacher would be contained in the Pupil Skills Analysis report furnished to the teacher by the publisher), the teacher can plot the pupil's various scores in the Pupil Information Box located on the back page of the test booklet.[14] Then Mrs. Sanders can plot the stanines and prepare a profile depicting the pupil's strengths and weaknesses. Let us assume that Billy has an IQ of 135 on the Otis-Lennon; stanines in the normal range (4–6) for Reading, Concepts of Number, Mathematics Computation, Mathematics Applications, Spelling, Listening Comprehension, and the four total scores (Battery, Auditory, Reading, and Mathematics). Let us further assume that Billy evidences weakness in Vocabulary, Word Study Skills, Science, and Social Science. Here are some clues: Billy is above average in ability, so the problem is not because of a lack of ability. Low scores on the Reading and Listening Comprehension tests suggest a lack of language competency and that Billy should be given added instruction in these areas. But in what specific areas? Mrs. Sanders can refer to Billy's answer for each item and ascertain the objective(s) that is (are) causing Billy's problems—that is, the items answered incorrectly. Now, if this substantiates the teacher's impressions gained by observation, she can then initiate remedial instruction accordingly, using either her own method or those suggested in the Manual (each item is geared to a particular objective so it is possible to "zero in" on the problem).

Billy's weakness in Science and Social Science may be a reflection of a lack of understanding of verbal material as much as lack of knowledge in Science or Social Science. However, if Billy had low Science and Social Science scores but a very high Vocabulary score, this would suggest that the problem is subject-matter-related. This procedure in essence should be followed when interpreting the results of any test score. The Stanford is of

---

[14] In addition to presenting the separate subject and domain scores, the PSA expresses the pupils' performance on skills clusters within each subtest content area as below average, average, or above average. Finally, the Reading Skills Group designation provides the teacher with information for grouping pupils who are in need of similar instruction.

additional value in that it provides the teacher with specific classroom instructional activities to be used, depending upon the problem(s) at hand.

With the Class Group Skills Analysis Report, class rather than individual performance is plotted. Once again, subtest and domain performance is profiled in terms of national group stanine bands. This permits teachers to compare the performance of their class with other classroom groups. For each subtest and skill cluster, this report gives the percentage of pupils scoring in the below-average, average, and above-average range—information that should aid the teacher in identifying areas in which a significant proportion of the class is encountering difficulty. With the data indicating the number and percentage of pupils assigned to each Reading Skills Group, the classroom teacher has information that should help in grouping students for optimal reading instruction.

The Master List of Test Results provides norm-referenced scores for each pupil in a class on one set of sheets. (It is also available for a classroom, school, or system.) This report, in combination with the Pupil and/or Group Skills Analysis reports, provides the classroom teacher with a set of data that are most useful for analyzing and interpreting pupil performance. The teacher is provided with information that not only presents individual performance but also the class' performance in terms of the number of pupils (and who they are) who are in need of further instruction, the number performing at the average level, and the number of pupils doing well. The information provided also permits teachers to (1) compare their pupils' performance with that of others in the same grade level, (2) see subject area strengths and weaknesses in comparison to national achievement, (3) identify individual pupils who might benefit from extra instruction, and (4) see the interrelationships among the various subtests.

Some additional, optional reports are the Classroom Instructional Analysis, the Pupil Profile, the Narrative, and the Pupil Analysis Reports. The Classroom Instructional Analysis is really a series of reports, since there is one for each domain, such as Total Language or Total Reading. In each of the reports, every pupil is evaluated, in terms of skill performance on the subtest and content clusters, as either above average, average, or below average. In addition, the percentage of the class above average, average, or below average for each cluster is given. This report enables the classroom teacher to see which pupils need help in each objective, and to identify those objectives that are causing difficulty for the whole class. The Pupil Profile Report presents individual pupil test results as national percentile ranks, stanines, and national percentile bands. The reverse side of the report explains what each test measures and how the scores are to be interpreted. The pupil's performance can be reported in a Narrative Report if one wishes. The Group Item Analysis Report presents pupil performance (whether the item was answered correctly, or not answered, or, if answered incorrectly, the response selected) for items grouped by cluster objectives. Again, such information is useful for making grouping and instructional decisions.

Two booklets designed specifically for the classroom teacher to assist in providing for optimal instruction are the Guide for Classroom Planning and the Handbook of Instructional Strategies. The Guide considers the various kinds of decisions classroom teachers must make, such as grouping, planning and evaluation, and promotion. And attempts to illustrate, with examples, how the Stanford test results and the various reports can be used to make more valid decisions. In addition, brief but lucid explanations are given for the various types of scores reported. The authors are to be commended for the cautions they give regarding grade equivalents. The final section of the Guide discusses some of the more informal assessment approaches such as checklists, rating scales, and ancecdotal records and describes how they, in concert with teacher-made test scores and the Stanford test scores, can be of help in making more valid decisions. The Handbook contains brief descriptions of the subtests and explains how they were developed. Attempting to offer instructional strategies for all tests at all levels is, unfortunately, a herculean task at best. Apparently because of space limitations, only a cursory treatment is offered. Nevertheless, what is done is done well.

Guidance and Counseling Use.   The Stanford Achievement Test is valuable to the counselor in several ways. (1) It provides for a cumulative measurement. (2) It allows for a ready identification of strengths and weaknesses because of the profile feature. (3) It permits a comparison of pupils' achievement with their capacity. With test scores from the Stanford, the counselor can assist the students in making a more sound educational or vocational decision than if these data were not available. However, very cautious predictions should be made because the Stanford's predictive validity has not as yet been demonstrated.

Administrative Uses.   Although results from the Stanford Achievement Test can be used for a multitude of administrative decisions, the more common ones are (1) student selection, classification, and placement, and (2) curriculum planning and evaluation.

Selection, classification, and placement. Although the Stanford Achievement Test results may be used to select, classify, or place students for particular programs or instructional purposes, the reader should be cognizant of the fact that scores at either extreme (high or low) may be very misleading and could conceivably result in misclassification. In actual practice, we recommend that when either a very high or very low test score is obtained for a pupil, the student should be given either the next higher or lower level battery in a retest situation so that a more valid estimate of performance can be obtained. For example, assume that when Johnny was given the Primary II tests, he scored very high. If the teacher wishes to ascertain whether the first score is a relatively accurate picture of his performance, Johnny should be given the next higher level, the Intermediate I battery. Then, if he performs (scores) fairly well on the Intermediate I, the teacher can feel fairly confident that the high score obtained on the Primary II battery is valid.

Any decisions pertaining to the classification, selection, or placement of students must be made with caution and with as much supporting data as possible. The results of any standardized survey battery should be used as supplementary and not absolute information.

Curriculum planning and evaluation. Quite frequently public schools are criticized for not keeping up with changing social conditions. It is claimed that they are behind the times. Although we do not feel that the Stanford Achievement Test (or any other standardized achievement test) should be the sole criterion for evaluating the school curriculum, standardized test results may be invaluable in helping make such decisions. Remember: a good standardized achievement test reflects the important objectives stressed throughout the country. Therefore, if teachers and administrators subscribe to the test objectives, they should be willing to evaluate their curriculum in the light of test scores obtained from that test. There is little doubt that the Stanford Achievement Test was meticulously constructed and standardized, and reflects the opinions of curriculum experts and teachers and syllabi throughout the country. However, the Stanford may not stress the application of knowledge as much as some other standardized tests or to the degree the teacher desires. It is composed of items requiring factual recall, application, and interpretation; it has kept pace with the changing curriculum, especially in modern mathematics, science, and social science programs; but it has been constructed by humans, who are fallible. Recognizing the deficiencies, the administrator using Stanford test scores should be guided in making decisions about curriculum revision.

The Guide for Organizational Planning resembles somewhat the Handbook of Instructional Strategies previously discussed. (Although the Guide contains suggestions relevant to instruction, we have chosen to discuss it here because most of the scenarios and questions involve administrative and institutional decisions rather than pupil/individual decisions.) The Guide offers examples to show how the administrator can use test results for assistance in educational planning at the building and district level. It also explains how the administrator can interpret test results to various audiences such as the school board, parents, and the community at large. There is a brief discussion of how the Stanford test results can be used for evaluation and accountability. A new and most welcome section, albeit too brief, is devoted to showing administrators how they can develop in-service test interpretation programs for their staffs, and how to develop "cut-off" scores. In nearly every instance, a major point is based upon a particular profile, chart, or table. The authors are to be commended for presenting a logical argument of the cautions that must be observed before using test results to rate teachers and instructional programs.

Research Use.   As noted previously, decisions in a variety of educational contexts are based on standardized test results. Possibly one of the most flattering if unobtrusive measures of a test's popularity and sound psychometric properties is its use as a dependent variable or as a covariate in research studies. Previous editions of the Stanford have been employed frequently in educational research. And in many funded programs, the Stanford has been used to assess the effectiveness of the program on pupil achievement.

Weaknesses and Strengths of the Stanford   There is no denying the fact that the 1982 Stanford, like its predecessors, is one of the most carefully constructed tests with respect to reflecting the curriculum of our public schools. This fact, however, does not negate the possibility that there are deficiencies in the test. Some of the specific criticisms of the 1982 Stanford that the user *must* consider in interpreting the pupils' scores are as follows:

1. There is too much reliance on memory in the Listening Comprehension tests, especially at the lower age levels. At the Intermediate 1 level, the student is read 23 prose passages and five poems ranging in length from six to 14 lines and asked two to five questions on each selection. Since many of the items call for drawing inferences, recognizing and remembering details, and perceiving concepts and relationships, we feel that this might be expecting too much from the average fourth- or fifth-grader.
2. The Environment test's reliability is so low that we question its value. Although validity may be more important than reliability in an achievement test, even for group decision-making purposes, one should hope for a reliability of at least 0.65.
3. The instructions for examiners to follow when timing a test (examiners can end a test before the allotted time has elapsed if they "think" that all pupils have finished) raise serious concerns about the use of normative data.
4. Although the Mathematics test in TASK was specifically designed to measure *general* mathematical competence, the authors' use of such items as the solution of algebraic equations, the transformation of word problems into mathematical language, and mensuration raises serious questions regarding the validity of the test as a measure of "general mathematical competence." It may be that the test is valid but not for the purpose for which it was designed.
5. A spelling test, we feel, should be one in which the pupil must recall and write the word rather than just be able to recognize whether a word is correctly spelled. Recognition does not assure knowledge of how to spell;

moreover, in their own writing, pupils must recall rather than merely identify.

6. For the Science tests, especially at the Intermediate levels and above, we feel that there should be more emphasis on testing the pupils' ability to draw conclusions based on experimental results.

7. The Listening Comprehension test requires the examiner to read the various passages at a slow, deliberate speed. But what is slow for one teacher may be fast for another, and vice versa. It would have been much better had the authors specified the amount of time to be spent reading each passage. As it is now, variations in pupils' performance may well be a reflection of the differences in examiners' reading rates.

8. Although the norms provided are adequate and are based on sound sampling techniques, it would have been helpful to have included more descriptive information about the standardization sample, especially the rate of cooperation of schools initially invited.

Many of these deficiencies can be readily corrected, and if these revisions were made, the Stanford Achievement Test would be more useful. They have been discussed primarily to caution users in their application and interpretation of the Stanford scores. In order to validly appraise their curriculum, method of teaching, and pupils' strengths and weaknesses, teachers should be cognizant of these and other deficiencies.

The Stanford is quite valid for evaluating pupil status and progress. For teachers who frequently like to obtain a cumulative index of their pupils' progress, the Stanford, with SESAT and TASK, provides a cumulative assessment of pupil knowledge with an articulated series of tests from grades K to 13.

Many instances arise when a teacher is interested in knowing whether their pupils are working at their capacity. The Stanford, because it was standardized with the Otis-Lennon School Ability Test, provides for such information.

The Stanford, as well as other survey batteries, can be used to evaluate the relative strengths and weaknesses of pupils because of its extensive set of subscores. However, provision of many subtests invariably results in short tests (because of time factors), some of which may have relatively low reliabilities. Therefore, although we may get an individual profile, it is difficult to interpret, and it may result in gross remedial errors.

Summary of the Stanford Achievement Test   Despite some minor criticisms of the Stanford noted above, we recommend it highly. The Stanford series were meticulously constructed and standardized. With SESAT and TASK they provide for continuous measurement with a series of articulated tests from grades K to 13. The various manuals contain many useful suggestions for the teacher, counselor, and administrator. The final decision, however, regarding the tests' validity must rest on the user's instructional objectives. Individuals wishing another perspective of the Stanford are advised to read Airaisian's (1985) critique.

Metropolitan Achievement Tests (MAT 6) 1984 Edition

Published by the Psychological Corporation for grades K–12.9, these tests consist of two forms for all levels except the Primer where there is only one form. The MAT 6 attempts to provide *both* diagnostic-prescriptive information for the instructional use of tests and general survey information in the major skill and content areas of the school curriculum. Actually then, the Metropolitan is *both* a norm-referenced and criterion-referenced battery with eight overlapping batteries spanning the Pre-Primer Grade (K.0–K.9) to Advanced 2 (Grade 10.0–12.9). Diagnostic tests in Reading, Mathematics, and Language that are statistically linked to the Survey Battery tests are scheduled for publication in 1986. At all levels, the MAT 6 measures Reading, Mathematics, and Language and provides a total score in each of these areas as well as a Total Basic Battery score. From Primary 1 through Advanced 2, tests and scores are available in social science and science. From Elementary through Advanced 2, a research skills score (this is not a test, per se, but is a score derived from items already embedded in other tests) is available. Content cluster scores for each test domain and the components making up that domain (e.g., reading comprehension consists of literal, inferential, and critical reading scores) are available. An optional writing test is also available. In summary, then, eight scores are provided—one in each content area, a research skills score, a total basic battery score, and a total composite battery score. Testing time varies from 98 to 190 minutes and from 190 to 254 minutes for the Total Basic and Total Complete Battery respectively. Responses for the Preprimer, Primer, and Primary 1 levels are marked directly in the test booklet; for the other levels, a separate answer sheet is used.

Content validity was stressed in the development of the tests. Specific instructional objectives were derived from extensive analyses of textbook series, state guidelines, and school system syllabi. Items were written by curriculum and measurement authorities and then were edited by persons with classroom experience. Items were reviewed by educators, including a panel of minority educators. *Both* language and illustrations were screened and edited to remove potential ethnic, cultural, regional, and class bias. Extensive preliminary testing and item analyses were undertaken to select the "best " items. The authors say that criterion-related and construct validity will also be studied.

K-R 20 reliability estimates and standard errors of measurement in terms of raw scores and scaled scores are provided for both the fall and spring standardizations. No reliability data were available but the test authors believe that the MAT 6's reliability will be consistent with other high-quality survey achievement test batteries.

Raw scores may be converted to scaled scores, percentile ranks, stanines, grade equivalents, and normal curve equivalents. Percentile rank and stanine norms tables are available for both fall and spring testing. Over 500,000 students were used in the standardization program for the different phases.

A good feature of the 1984 Metro is the provision of an Instructional Reading Level (IRL) and Instructional Mathematics Level (IML). The authors state that the IRL, which incidentally was provided in the 1978 edition (the IML, however, is new in the 1984 edition), is "the best single indicator of a particular student's reading achievement." The IRL and IML scores are criterion-referenced and are used to select appropriate reading instructional and mathematics instructional materials respectively for the student. As noted earlier, the IML is new in the MAT 6. The authors are careful to point out that the IML is another way (norm and objectives-referenced scores are also available) of interpreting a student's performance in mathematics. The IML, like the IRL, is useful in that it helps the teacher select the most appropriate level and learning materials. The students' performance in reading and mathematics is "matched" to graded basal readers and mathematics textbooks respectively. The MAT 6 was normed concurrently with the OLSAT (see Chapter 7). This permits one to transform the Metro scores into expectancies for the aptitude test scores (see Chapter 5).

Other commendable features of the 1984 Metro include (1) the cautions given and discussion of the fallability of grade equivalents, (2) an attractive format with two-color printing and attention to such details as spacing, type size, type face, and so on, to make the test more natural, (3) practice tests for all levels, (4) a variety of output data using the publisher's scoring service, (5) attention to minority concerns and sex bias, (6) school-based achievement "expectancy" based on SES data, (7) language tests at all levels from K–12, (8) the dictation of tests (excluding tests measuring reading) before Elementary to reduce the effects of reading ability, (9) emphasizing the instructional value of test results, (10) numerous cautions about interpreting test scores, (11) provision of a Reading Frustration and Independent Reading Level Score in addition to the IRL, (12) ease of administration, (13) emphasis on the "process" rather than factual recall in the science and social studies tests, (14) provision of a Research Skills score and a Higher Order Thinking Skills score, (15) the availability of an optional writing test, (16) the involvement of parents in the testing/learning process, (17) more than one test per domain—for example, at the lower levels, MAT 6 will have 3 reading, 3 mathematics, 2 language, 1 science, and 1 social studies test(s), (18) overlapping grades in the standardization program, (19) a "Purpose Question" preceding each Reading passage to try to motivate the students,

(20) more diagnostic information from the spelling, mathematics, and problem-solving tests, and (21) no transformational grammar.

In summary, the MAT 6 reflects the core curriculum. It was carefully constructed and standardized. Careful attention was paid to selecting items that were as free from bias as possible. Many of the criticisms of the previous editions appear to have been rectified (see Mehrens & Lehmann, 1969; Buros, 1965).

Iowa Tests of Basic Skills (ITBS)

Published by the Riverside Press (1978), the Multilevel Edition (Forms 7 and 8) is designed for grades K–9.[15] There are two forms. The test consists of 11 separate subtests—measuring skills in the five areas of vocabulary, reading comprehension, language skills, work-study skills, and mathematics skills—and yields 15 scores, the majority of which are in reading and language arts.[16] The complete and basic batteries require a working time of 244 and 119 minutes respectively.

The Iowa consists of a very thorough battery of tests designed to "provide for comprehensive and continuous measurement of growth in fundamental skills which are crucial to current day-to-day learning activities as well as to future educational development." Specific content areas such as science and social studies are covered in a separate test booklet. An asset of multilevel tests is that for most students they circumvent base or ceiling effects. A liability is that stopping and beginning at different places in the test can be very troublesome and confusing for young children. Split-half reliabilities and standard errors of measurement are reported by grade level for each of the five content areas, as well as the composite score and range from .86 to .98 and 1.3 to 6.5 respectively. Content and construct validity are stressed.

Three types of converted scores, each with its own percentile rank and stanine, are available separately for each level and each subtest: grade equivalent (GE), age equivalent, and standard scores. The Teacher's Manual contains average grade equivalents for the total language, total work-study skills, total mathematics, and composite score. It also gives national percentile norms for grade equivalents for the beginning, middle, and end of school year. The provision of percentile norms for different times permits flexibility in the school testing program. Schools using the ITBS need not restrict themselves to a single testing period, nor do they have to depend on

---

[15] The primary battery is to be used for grades 1 and 2. The Tests of Achievement and Proficiency (TAP) are an extension of the ITBS and are designed for grades 9–12. TAP measures reading comprehension, written expression, mathematics, use of information sources, social studies, and science.

[16] The Basic Battery consists of Vocabulary, Reading, Spelling, Mathematics Concepts, Mathematics Problem Solving, and Mathematics Computation tests.

extrapolation. Special GE percentile norm tables are also provided for regional areas, Catholic schools, high and low socioeconomic schools, and large city schools. Also available are national percentile norms for age equivalents for age groups and national percentile norms for standard scores. Teachers using the publisher's scoring service may select a variety of output data.

An added feature of the ITBS is that it has been standardized jointly with the Cognitive Abilities Test and the Tests of Achievement and Proficiency (an achievement test designed for use in grades 9–12). This permits the teacher to compare a pupil's achievement with that of pupils of similar academic aptitude for grades K–12.

As were previous editions, the current ITBS has been carefully constructed. The 1978 ITBS was carefully normed on a representative sample. The Multilevel Edition is attractively packaged in a reusable, spiral-bound booklet. The illustrations are clear and the type is easy to read. To accomodate more "tailor-made" individualized testing, new reporting services were developed. To assist those teachers whose pupils are mostly "out-of-level," the tests were prepared and packaged by age rather than by grade levels.

Notwithstanding the many admirable features of the 1978 ITBS, it has some limitations that the test user should consider in evaluating this battery. Specifically, these deficiencies are as follows:

1. The vocabulary test stresses only the knowledge of words, although it is purported to test basic skills.
2. The spelling test indicates only that students may recognize an incorrectly spelled word given out of context, but does not necessarily indicate that they know the correct spelling.
3. The language-skills test places more emphasis on spelling, capitalization, and punctuation than on language usage.
4. The work-study skills test may not be valid for those teachers who do not stress map reading as an instructional objective.
5. The work-study skills tests are so highly verbal that they may be measuring reading rather than work-study skills.
6. The mathematics concepts test has many faulty items, e.g., asking "What is the name for the number of books?" but presenting numerical foils, and having questions with two correct answers.
7. The mathematics problem-solving test is overly verbal.
8. The map-reading test may prove to be a little frustrating for the younger pupils.
9. The arithmetic-skills test leans quite heavily on content which is highly verbal.
10. The reliability data are reported only as internal-consistency estimates.
11. Criterion-related validity is based on earlier editions of the test.

Some Other Survey Batteries

Some other examples of standardized survey achievement test batteries are the Sequential Tests of Educational Progress (STEP III) and CIRCUS C and D, which provide the user with an articulated set of tests from nursery school to high school (these tests introduced a new testing and score interpretation system called the Grade Level Indicator), the Cooperative Primary Tests, the Tests of Basic Experiences 2 (TOBE 2), the SRA Achievement Series, the California Achievement Tests, and the Comprehensive Test of Basic Skills. Another test that has become available nationwide recently is the College Board's new Assessment and Placement Services Program, a survey battery containing subtests in Reading, Writing, Mathematics, and an Essay portion. This program is specifically designed to serve the community college population. The program also contains a Student Placement Inventory and can be used by the counselor to assist in recommending appropriate course selection and placement to the student.

Up to this point we have focused primarily on those achievement tests used in schools or community colleges. However, a significant portion of the adult population is illiterate or disadvantaged in such a way that conventional achievement tests are not valid for them. Tests are available to measure the basic skills of adults with inadequate educational backgrounds. One of these is the United States Employment Service's Basic Occupational Literacy Test (BOLT), which assesses a person's vocabulary, reading comprehension, arithmetic computation, and arithmetic reasoning skills. (Some psychologists, like Anastasi, 1982, classify BOLT as an aptitude test.) Other tests available for testing adults with poor educational backgrounds are SRA's Reading-Arithmetic Index and the Psychological Corporation's Adult Basic Learning Examination (ABLE).

Individually Administered Achievement Tests

Although group-administered survey achievement tests and test batteries are the most frequently used, recent federal legislation on the *mainstreaming* of handicapped children into the regular classroom (the assessment of the exceptional child will be covered in detail in Chapter 10) has spawned an interest in and need for the assessment of the handicapped/exceptional child's academic performance. Generally, the pupils respond by pointing or by answering orally, although, depending on the child's condition, some writing may be required. The various individually administered survey achievement batteries provide norm-referenced, criterion-referenced, or *both* types of scores (interpretation). Some of the more popular individually administered survey achievement test batteries are (1) the Peabody Individual Achievement Test (PIAT), which is designed for grade K to adult; (2) the Basic Achievement Skills Individual Screener (BASIS), which is designed for use in grades 1–12 and for post-high school adults; and (3) the Wide Range Achievement Test (WRAT), which is designed for grade 5 to adult. The PIAT and WRAT are generally used only for those persons who cannot take a group test—for instance, handicapped children, very nervous children. Users of any individually administered achievement test must be very careful when interpreting the pupils' score. Since these tests tend to cover a wide age range with a limited number of items, the depth of coverage is minimal, even less so than with a group-administered survey battery. We will now consider the PIAT and BASIS in more detail.

Peabody Individual Achievement Test (PIAT)   Published by the American Guidance Service (1970), it is intended for grades K–12 and adults. There is one form. Individually administered achievement subtests cover five basic areas: Mathematics (84 items), Reading Recognition (84 items), Reading Comprehension (66 items), Spelling (84 items), and General Information (84 items). The General Information subtest is the only one which does not use multiple-choice items. Although it is untimed, the test takes about 30–50 minutes.

In addition to a separate subtest score, there is a total score. Raw scores can be expressed in terms of developmental (grade and age equivalents) or derived deviation scores such as percentiles and normalized standard scores (the latter two, like the WRAT, have been adjusted so that the mean and standard deviation are consistent with the Wechsler scales). A score profile can be plotted that permits the user to compare an examinee's performance on each of the subtests with what would be "expected" in terms of his or her IQ.

Items were selected on the basis of conventional item statistics procedures—item difficulty and discrimination.

We believe that one of the major weaknesses of the PIAT relates to its consideration of validity. Concurrent and content validity was considered. Although we agree with the test authors that the *sine qua non* of an achievement test is content validity, this is *not* sufficient for a test that is specifically designed to be used to determine placement in special education. We need predictive validity evidence as well.

Only test–retest reliability data on small samples in grades K, 1, 3, 5, 8, and 12 are given, and they are "quasi" respectable. We would also have liked to see Kuder-Richardson reliability data.

There are some fine aspects of the PIAT: (1) It has an excellent Manual; (2) the Reading Comprehension test is pictorial and spatial, well suited for testing learning-disabled children who are deficient in verbal expression; (3) the format and illustrations are excellent and especially appropriate for persons with learning problems or handicaps; (4) the examinees indicate their responses either orally or by pointing; and (5) practice/training items for each subtest help ensure that the examinee understands what is to be done.

As with most good things, though, there are some weaknesses in the PIAT: (1) the test may be primarily one of *speed* (rather than power, as the test authors claim), considering the population that is being tested; (2) the "basal-ceiling" approach and rules establishing a basal point may cause problems; and (3) the low subtest reliabilities suggest that the PIAT be used only for screening purposes and not for any "hard" decision-making purposes such as referral to a remedial class.

Basic Achievement Skills Individual Screener (BASIS)   Published by the Psychological Corporation (1982), BASIS is one of the newer individually administered achievement tests and is designed for use with pupils in grades 1–12 and for post-high school adults. It is particularly useful with young children, nervous examinees, and special populations where individual educational plans (IEPs) are to be formulated and then evaluated.

BASIS provides both criterion-referenced and norm-referenced information. There are three required tests—Reading, Mathematics, and Spelling—and an optional Writing exercise that requires the examinee to produce a writing sample. (The Writing exercise is used in grades 3–8; the required tests in grades 1–8.) All the items for the Reading, Mathematics, and Spelling tests are grouped in grade-referenced clusters; each cluster is designed to reflect the curriculum at a particular grade level. The test, although untimed, takes about one hour to administer (this includes the writing exercise, which takes 10 minutes).

For each of the three skills tests, beginning-of-grade and interpolated end-of-grade norms are provided for grades 1–8; beginning-of-grade norms are provided for grades 9–12. Age and adult norms are also furnished. The norming sample appears to be representative of the school population enrolled in mainstreamed classes. The publishers made certain that disabled students were included in the norming sample, and they are to be commended for reporting both the incidence and the types of disabilities the students had.

K-R 20 and test–retest reliability estimates are reported, the former for each grade and age level found in the standardization sample, the latter for samples of second-, fifth-, and eighth-grade students. The K-R 20s were quite high and the Manual cautions the user regarding the spuriousness of the correlations. (It is a result of the type of scoring used. BASIS scoring is similar to the basal and ceiling age approach of the Stanford-Binet, where the examinee is given credit for passing all the items below and failing all the items above a particular point.) We wonder why the publisher reported this reliability, inasmuch as most users will tend to ignore the caveat or not understand its significance.

"Logical" validity was substantiated for the validity of each of the three skills tests. Of the three tests, the Mathematics test appears to be more valid than either the Reading or the Spelling tests, especially in terms of predicting grade-placement accurately. Very little empirical validity data, however, are reported. Although reference was made to the manner in which the validity of the Writing exercise was established, too many questions remain unanswered (the number of papers rated, the number and characteristics of the raters, the number of times each paper was rated, and so forth) to permit us to comment on the findings of the studies reported.

Raw scores for each of the three skills tests (these scores are indicators of text and grade placement) can be converted to within-grade-level percentile ranks and stanines for grades 1–12 and post-high school; for ages 6–18 and post-high school, grade and age equivalents are provided. Standard scores, NCEs, and Rasch scale scores are also available.

BASIS has many good things going for it. A comprehensive Manual contains a thorough discussion on establishing and maintaining rapport; the test booklet is reusable; the information describing the development of the test and the items is complete; and the skills tests have adequate validity to be used as part of a student's diagnostic assessment and for decisions relating to the student's individual educational plan (IEP).

Tests of Minimal Competency

Nearly every state in the nation has mandated the testing of pupils in the basic skills of reading, writing, language, and arithmetic. Many states have developed their own tests, but one commercial publisher at least—California Test Bureau/McGraw-Hill—has developed a series of tests that can be used to certify high school students as eligible for graduation. There also are some tests designed for the junior high grades to ascertain whether the pupils are making satisfactory progress in their basic and life skills. Some CTB tests are as follows:

For use in the junior high school grades
    Assessment Skills in Computation
    Performance Assessment in Reading
For use in the high school
    Senior High Assessment of Reading Performance
    Test of Performance in Computational Skills
    Test of Everyday Writing Skill

While the majority of the minimal competency tests are designed for an in-school population, some, like the USES Basic Occupational Literacy Test and ABLE, are appropriate for adults who have a poor educational background. As is true for any of the areas/tests discussed in this text, the reader is encouraged to consult the test catalogs of the various test publishers (listed in the Appendix) because some areas are so rapidly changing that a test reviewed or mentioned may be revised by the time you read about it.

Summary of Standardized Achievement Tests

Achievement tests run the gamut from readiness and diagnostic tests to prognostic content-oriented tests, from norm-referenced to criterion-referenced, and from pre-school to graduate and professional school. Regardless of their format, or types of knowledge and skills surveyed, or types of items used, however, all are designed to give an index of what the student knows at a particular point in time. There are differences (possibly more so for the diagnostic tests than for the others) among the various standardized achievement tests, reflecting the test authors' purposes and procedures.

Readiness tests are normally restricted to reading, whereas diagnostic tests are confined primarily to reading and arithmetic. These tests are used most frequently in the primary grades. Readiness and diagnostic tests differ from the conventional standardized achievement (subject-matter content) tests in that they are confined to very limited areas.

There are some differences, however, in standardized reading readiness tests—the differences reflecting the importance attributed to those facets deemed by the test authors to be important in beginning to learn to read. For example, one test author might feel that the beginning reader must be able to recognize similarities and differences in geometric shape. Another test author might feel that this skill is unimportant. Hence, there would be a difference in the kinds of items used in the tests.

Diagnostic tests seem to be more similar than readiness tests. Their major purpose is to help the teacher recognize the pupil's difficulties; therefore, diagnostic tests are constructed so that they permit pupils to maximize the number of errors they can make. There may be a difference of opinion whether a pupil is ready to learn to read, but there is very little disagreement as to whether he or she exhibits tendencies of reversals or omissions when reading. It is also important to remember that no single readiness or diagnostic test can assess all the skills and knowledge needed by the pupil to learn effectively.

We have considered a few of the more popular survey batteries used at the elementary and secondary levels as well as specific "tailor-made" criterion-referenced achievement tests such as the SCORE, COMS, and ORBIT programs. Teachers desiring a better picture of the pupil's knowledge in a specific content area should select a standardized achievement test in that particular subject. Single or specific achievement tests are also valuable to the counselor. For example, if Rona plans to become a doctor, it would be helpful to know how well she performs on specific biology and chemistry tests, because these two areas are of vital importance in medicine (or at least in medical education).

Some of the survey batteries, such as the Stanford and the California Achievement Tests, provide for continuous measurement from kindergarten through high school—and even adult. Others, such as CIRCUS and the Cooperative Preschool Inventory, span the preschool/nursery to primary grades. Still others, such as the STEP III, are intended for grades 3–12. The ITBS and others span the upper elementary and junior high grades. And still others are for only high school students (Tests of Achievement and Proficiency). A survey battery cannot adequately measure all or even most of the outcomes of every (or any) instructional program. However, all batteries attempt to provide measures of achievement in the core subjects by containing tests of vocabulary, arithmetic, spelling, reading, and language. The various batteries provide separate subtest scores as well as a total score. The raw scores are transformed to some form of standard score to permit meaningful comparisons among the various subtests.

There are other differences among the various survey batteries. At the primary level (grades 1–3) the content is similar, although the format may differ from one battery to another. After the fourth or fifth grade, the contents of the various batteries differ markedly. Some batteries measure work-study skills; others do not. Some batteries may devote 15 percent of the test to measuring reading comprehension; others will devote about 30 percent. Only the Stanford has a separate test of Listening Comprehension. The various batteries also differ in the number of subtests. For example, at the elementary level, the Stanford yields six to 11 scores, whereas the ITBS gives 15 separate scores. The ITBS and Stanford both measure the fundamental skills of reading, mathematics, and language.

Because of the nature of their construction, survey batteries should not be used to obtain a thorough estimate of a pupil's knowledge or skills in a specific area. Although a science or language art subscore can be obtained, this score will normally be influenced by the sample of tasks measured by that particular subtest.

Although the various batteries may differ slightly with respect to the fundamental educational goals emphasized, they all share a common purpose: to help students and teachers recognize strengths and weaknesses—the students in their learning, the teachers in their teaching.

In conclusion, there are strengths and weaknesses in *all* standardized achievement tests (for example, the content validity is good but predictive validity is poor; or the normative data are excellent but the test is too time-consuming; or the test is valid but the scoring is too complex and requires an experienced examiner to administer and interpret). Accordingly, their limitations must be carefully considered and weighed against their virtues in test selection. In the final analysis, the good is taken with the bad, but we want to be certain that we choose a test with minimum limitations and maximum advantages. We concur with Katz (1961), who states that "there is no single achievement test or test battery that will be 'best' for all pupil populations, all curriculum objectives, all purposes, and all uses. Even tests universally recognized as 'good' are not equally 'good' for different school settings, situations, or circumstances.''

USING ACHIEVEMENT TEST RESULTS

The authors of many of the better standardized achievement tests and batteries suggest specific uses, and supplement their tests with valuable interpretive examples. At the same time, the ingenious classroom teacher may discover a use that is applicable only in his or her classroom. The remarks that follow should be thought of as only some suggested uses of standardized achievement tests.

The purpose of any standardized achievement test is to provide the user with information concerning an individual's knowledge or skills so that the user can make decisions—of selection and classification, for academic and vocational counseling, about the relative effectiveness of two or more methods of instruction—that are more valid than they would be if such data had not been employed. Achievement-test results can be used to measure the outcomes of learning; to identify those pupils who are in need of remedial instruction; to identify those pupils who may lack certain fundamental skills (whether they be cognitive or psychomotor) needed before they can begin reading; to aid in the assignment of course grades; to facilitate learning by the pupils; to provide an external criterion in the evaluation of sponsored-research programs that require evidence of or information about academic performance; to provide a basis for certification and promotion decisions; and to provide a criterion in research designed to evaluate various instructional strategies. As Airasian & Madaus (1983) and Haertel & Calfee (1983) point out, achievement tests in general, but standardized tests in particular, lately have assumed greater importance in policy and curriculum decisions that have an impact on students, teachers, and other educators.

Achievement tests—be they teacher-made or standardized—are *not* designed to measure, even remotely, the affective components of our educational enterprise. They do not tell us anything about whether Allan or Ilene is interested in school, enjoys reading, or can interact effectively with peers. What achievement tests do, however—measuring the cognitive aims of instruction in an objective manner—they accomplish more validly and reliably than is possible with teachers' subjective judgments (Levine, 1976).

Although we consider the use of standardized achievement tests under such headings as instructional uses, guidance uses, administrative uses, and research uses, the reader should be aware that this classification imposes rigidity in treatment and may result in the fallacious assumption that there is little, if any, overlap. Seldom is there a situation in which standardized achievement-test results serve only a single purpose. There will be strengths and weaknesses in *all* standardized achievement tests.

Instructional Uses

Achievement-test results can be invaluable to the classroom teacher. For example, reading readiness test scores can assist the teacher in determining which pupils possess the skills and knowledge needed to begin the reading program. These test scores help the teacher group the pupils (tentatively, at least) for maximum instructional benefits. Students, who on the basis of other evidence demonstrate that they should be successful in reading or arithmetic but who are experiencing difficulty or score poorly on a subject-matter test, may benefit from a diagnostic test. The diagnostic test can aid the teacher in locating the nature of the difficulty. Diagnostic tests may also be used to identify those students who might benefit from additional remedial work. Diagnostic and readiness tests may be used as an initial screening device to be followed by a more thorough investigation if needed.

Standardized diagnostic tests not only provide a more systematic approach than that of the informal method used by the classroom teacher (although we strongly favor gathering such informal data), but some of the newer diagnostic tests offer suggestions to the teacher for remediation.

Single-subject-matter tests and survey batteries help teachers ascertain the strengths and weaknesses of their class and thereby suggest modification of instructional method or the reteaching of certain materials. Or teachers can reevaluate their goals if the data suggest this. They can evaluate the effectiveness of a specific teaching method by using achievement-test results.

Standardized achievement-test results, in combination with data gathered from aptitude tests, may aid in identifying the under- and over-achieving students. Be careful, though! The discrepancy between the students' performance on the different tests must be large and these data should only be part of the information used in making a decision. We agree with Messick (1984, p. 215) that "the interpretation and implications of educational achievement measures must be relative to interpersonal and situational contexts."

As will be discussed more fully in Chapter 10, Public Law 94-142, which deals with the equality of education for exceptional children, mandates that the academic progress of these children be monitored regularly. Standardized tests provide for such a systematic monitoring. In addition, exceptional children—the gifted, the mentally retarded, the physically handicapped, and the like—have unique needs and problems. Standardized achievement and aptitude tests can assist in the identification of these needs and problems.

Standardized achievement tests (excluding readiness and diagnostic tests) can also play an important role with respect to standardizing grading. Quite frequently we hear that Mr. Smith is an "easy grader" and that Miss Jones is a "hard grader." Although standardized achievement tests should not be used to assign course grades, they can be used by teachers to evaluate their grading practices. For example, when Mr. Smith, the easy grader, compares the achievement of his pupils on standardized tests to that of other teachers' pupils and learns that his class achieves less well, he can see that the high grades he assigned may be misleading. This does not imply, however, that standardized achievement-test results should be used as the only reference point in assigning course grades. They should be used to give the individual teacher some perspective. Many other factors must be considered before Mr. Smith concludes that he is too easy in his grading. The standardized achievement test should be used as supplementary data on which to build a valid estimate of the pupils' achievement and hence their final grade.

Achievement-test results can be used to help the teacher provide optimal learning conditions for every pupil. In order to do this, the teacher should know as much as possible about every student. Standardized achievement tests will provide some of this needed information. Tests results will assist in the grouping of pupils for instructional purposes. They will also be extremely valuable in assisting the teacher to fit the curriculum to each child in a class. Some children should get enriching experiences; others may require remedial work. Cox & Sterrett (1970) present a simple model of how standardized achievement-test results can be scored so that the classroom teacher may make both criterion- and norm-referenced interpretations of the test scores. For example, Mr. Pedagogy may classify the test items in a particular standardized achievement test according to his instructional objectives. He could end up with three groups: one consisting of items that his pupils have studied and are expected to know; one of items that have not been studied, but which the pupils will be expected to know at a later time; and one of items that are not relevant. The test can then be administered and scored to yield three scores: Ilene correctly answered 90 percent of the items she was expected to know, 45 percent of those not yet studied, and 5 percent of the remaining items. With this information for each pupil, Mr. Pedagogy can plan his instruction accordingly. (Note: If tests are to be used for grouping purposes, and if only one testing period is available, we recommend that there be an early fall testing so that the results will be most beneficial to both pupils and teachers.)

Evidence has lately emerged on the role of test scores in the academic expectancies of teachers toward pupils (Brophy & Good, 1970; Chaikin & Sigler, 1973; Long & Henderson, 1974; Rosenthal & Jacobson, 1968; Willis, 1973). The majority of these studies have shown that prior knowledge of pupils' test scores can have a marked influence on the teachers' expectancies (they may be realistic or biased) regarding their pupils' academic performance.

As mentioned earlier, commercial test publishers now provide reporting services (for a slight additional fee) that group pupils of similar abilities and offer the classroom teacher suggestions on the instructional strategy to be used with these groups; furnish item analysis data; report the number of items answered correctly by each pupil; and the like. (See Figures 8.6 and 8.7.) Increasingly, standardized achievement tests such as the Stanford, aptitude tests like the SAT, interest inventories like the Strong-Campbell, and personality inventories like the MMPI are providing computer-generated narrative test reports in addition to the various types of test scores. These reports are generally designed to report an *individual's* performance, but some standardized achievement tests produce a "class" report. Although narrative reports may lack the precision of test norms, they do afford an excellent medium for reporting test results to unsophisticated audiences.

With education moving more and more toward individualized instruction and with the gearing of standardized achievement tests to textbooks becoming more common, the results of achievement tests can aid appreciably in fitting the curriculum to the child rather than the child to the curriculum. Criterion-referenced (or -scored) standardized tests, if successfully developed, should permit the teacher to prescribe individual learning experiences appropriately. These tests provide the teacher with valuable supplementary information that may be difficult or impossible to obtain with norm-referenced achievement tests, which are usually given only at the end of the year.

Conventional standardized achievement test results should *not* be used for individual diagnosis, but they can (and should) be used effectively as a springboard for the teacher to explore areas of pupils' strengths and/or weaknesses. (With the newer types of programs and standardized criterion-referenced tests such as SCORE, DMI/PRI/IET, Diagnosis: An Aid to Instruction, and others, individual diagnosis is possible. But not too many such tests are available now.) Once students in need of remediation have been identified, their progress can be monitored using both teacher-made and standardized achievement tests.

Teachers will occasionally use the results of a standardized achievement test as the major criterion in determining the status of their pupils and will then plan their instructional program accordingly. They should *never* do this! Other factors need to be strongly considered. For example, how well do the test objectives meet those of the particular teacher? How reliable is a part score in a battery or, for that matter, how reliable are, say, the four or five items used to test the pupil's knowledge of simultaneous equations or atomic structure? Is the course structure centered on skills, on content, or on both? Because of these and other considerations, standardized achievement tests should not be (1) a major criterion in course planning or (2) the focus of the course content to be taught by the teacher. With few exceptions, the common single-subject-matter test, readiness test, survey test, or survey battery should not be used for *individual* diagnostic purposes.

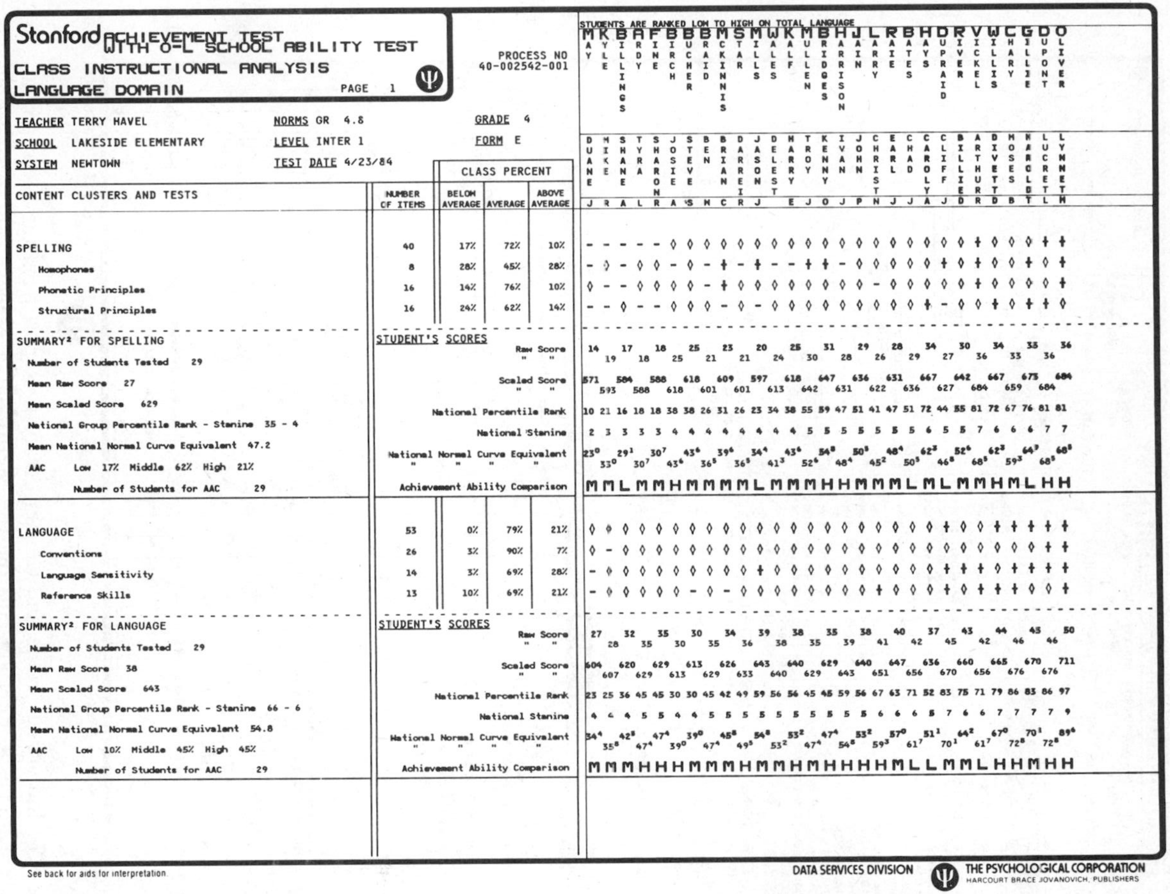

Figure 8.6 Class Instructional Analysis Report from the Stanford Achievement Test. Reproduced from the Stanford Achievement Test. Copyright © 1982 by the Psychological Corporation, Cleveland, Ohio. All rights reserved.

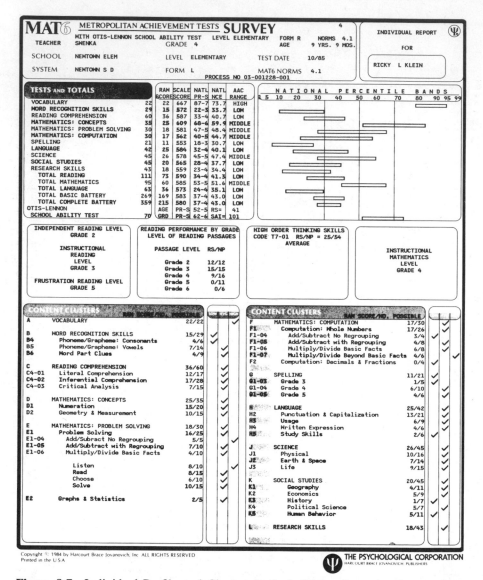

Figure 8.7 Individual Profile and Cluster Analysis Report from the Metropolitan Achievement Tests. Reproduced from the Metropolitan Achievement Test. Copyright © 1979 by the Psychological Corporation. All rights reserved.

Guidance and Counseling Uses

Achievement tests can be important in assisting the classroom teacher, principal, school counselor, or clinical psychologist in vocational and educational guidance. In combination with other data, achievement-test results can be used to help students plan their future educational or vocational program. It should be remembered that achievement-test data by themselves have limited meaning. They need to be augmented by other information—data about interests, aptitudes, and attitudes—to arrive at the best decision possible. An illustration may help clarify the situation.

Girder, a senior in high school, is interested in studying engineering. The school counselor has a variety of information about Girder. On the basis of the results from both survey batteries and single-subject-matter tests given Girder at the elementary, middle, and high school levels, a pattern is readily evident that Girder's strengths are in verbal skills and that he is deficient in science and mathematics. His interest test scores suggest that he possesses interests shared by journalists. His scholastic aptitude score indicates that he is of average ability. The counselor should use all these data in helping Girder arrive at a decision concerning the appropriateness of an engineering major in college. The counselor should point out that Girder must show marked improvement in science and mathematics in order to succeed in the engineering curriculum. Actually, what the counselor is doing here is making a tentative prediction of probable success on the basis of test data.

In conclusion, it must be remembered that achievement test results are not absolute measures and that success in vocational training, graduate, or professional school depends upon many factors, only one of which is prior achievement. Failure to consider these other vitally important factors will result in poor guidance and counseling.

Administrative Uses

Selection, Classification, and Placement   In many instances achievement test results are used to select individuals for a particular training program or for a specific vocation. In such cases the achievement test must demonstrate high predictive validity.

Selection is more common in industry and in higher education than it is in elementary and secondary schools. For example, a life insurance company may select agents on the basis of an achievement test if the company has found that the test is a good predictor of sales volume. Likewise, a college may select its entering freshmen on the basis of a standardized achievement test if it has been found that the test is a valid predictor.

Today more often than previously (because of people's greater mobility), administrators are confronted with determining where the transfer student should be placed. A fourth-grader from Los Angeles should not necessarily be placed in the fourth grade in Syracuse, because the schools in each area may require different levels of achievement. The results of a standardized achievement test can be used effectively to help the administrator evaluate the transfer student's past performance. This is especially true if the same test is used in both schools. If different tests are used and no comparisons are possible, the principal should administer the test used in his or her school.

The data presented in Table 8.3 are for a hypothetical 10-year-old transferring from an ungraded school in Los Angeles to a Syracuse city school in January. The pupil's test scores were obtained in the fall, when he entered the "fourth" grade. The norms in both schools are based on national norms.

What do we know about this pupil? We know that (1) he is below the average fourth-grader except in spelling, (2) he is more like Syracuse third-graders than fourth-graders, (3) he is more proficient in verbal skills than in arithmetic skills, and (4) if he is placed in the fourth grade, he may experience a great deal of competition, even to the extent that he might become frustrated and develop a negative attitude toward school.

Of what help can the data in Table 8.3 be to the principal? Would she be likely to make a more valid educational decision with these data than without them? With data such as these, the principal would exercise extreme caution before automatically placing the pupil in the fourth grade because of his age. The principal could either place the pupil in the fourth grade and recognize that the teacher will have to spend extra time with the pupil; or the principal could place the pupil in the third grade, aware that he may be out of place physiologically and psychologically. If the pupil is placed in the fourth grade, his teacher needs to understand that he may have difficulty at first,

TABLE 8.3
HYPOTHETICAL GRADE SCORE EQUIVALENTS ON THE STANFORD ACHIEVEMENT TEST, PRIMARY 3 BATTERY

Subtest	Transfer Student's Grade Score Equivalent	Mean Grade Score Equivalent for Syracuse Third-Graders	Mean Grade Score* Equivalent for Syracuse Fourth-Graders
Reading Comprehension	3.2	3.5	4.2
Paragraph Meaning	3.4	3.4	4.4
Vocabulary	3.4	3.7	4.8
Spelling	4.8	3.8	4.6
Word-Study Skills	3.6	3.6	4.9
Language/English	2.5	3.5	4.4

* Norms in both schools based on fall testing.

that remedial teaching will be in order, and that additional work will be needed before the pupil will absorb the material as readily as the average fourth-grader. Regardless of the decision made, it should be obvious that the principal must consult with the student's parents, since there may be problems associated with either decision.

As was discussed earlier, test results can be of help in decision making. In this example, two kinds of decisions must be made: (1) where to place the pupil and (2) how best to assist the pupil after the first decision has been made.

Another example of how standardized achievement tests can aid the user is in the classification or placement of students in special courses or programs. The kind of classification possible will depend upon the type of test used and the physical facilities available in the school. For example, if a survey battery is used, much information is provided. The results may suggest that a student take algebra in an average class, reading in a superior class, and social studies in a remedial class.

Comparing Test Scores   Although a variety of administrative decisions concerning selection, classification, and placement can be made on the basis of standardized achievement-test results, the examples discussed above pertain to the use of the *same* test. What kinds of decisions, if any, can be made with different survey battery or single-subject-matter test results? Can a pupil's performance be compared when two different tests are used? Can comparisons be made between scores obtained on the *same* subtest (content area) of *different* tests?

Comparing Scores on Different Tests.   Let us assume that Allan, who moved from an ungraded school in Los Angeles to an ungraded school in Syracuse, took the Gates-MacGinitie Reading Test in Los Angeles in September. Let us assume further that the Stanford Reading Test is used in Syracuse. Can Allan's new teacher in Syracuse translate the scores from the Gates-MacGinitie to equivalent scores on the Stanford? No! While scores from two different tests may be highly correlated, one cannot equate tests that measure, in part, different content. It is true, of course, that if Allan does very well (or very poorly) on the Gates-MacGinitie, it is reasonable to assume he might do very well (or very poorly) on the Stanford.

Comparing Scores on Similarly Named Subtests of Different Achievement Batteries.   Although it might be assumed that the Mathematics Computation subtest in the Stanford measures the *same* knowledge and skills as the Mathematics Computation test in the Metropolitan (especially since they were developed and published by the same publisher), such an assumption may be wholly unwarranted. On the surface, it might appear that the same instructional objectives (knowledge and skills) are being measured. But only a careful examination of the test manual and test blueprint will provide the information necessary to judge the comparability of the two subtests. Even this is *not* sufficient to judge the similarity of the Mathematics Computation subtests from the two survey batteries, however. The test items might differ in difficulty and discrimination power. The norming population may be (and often is) different. The validity and reliability of the subtests may be dissimilar. Even though it has been shown that there is a high correlation between the *total* scores obtained on the Stanford and the Metropolitan, it has also been demonstrated that there is a low correlation between similarly named subtests in these two batteries (Goolsby, 1971). Only by carefully studying the subtests themselves as well as the respective test manuals can the user ascertain whether the subtests are similar.

Evaluation of Instruction and Teachers[17]   One of the *mis*uses of standardized achievement tests is in making educational decisions (regarding the effectiveness of a teacher, of an instructional technique such as a film, of the school curriculum, or of a class or school) *solely* on the basis of standardized achievement-test results. We are especially concerned about this inappropriate test use because we feel that the recent flurry of federal reports and commissions on the state of American education may result in some drastic measures being taken to evaluate the educational enterprise—one such drastic response being the use of standardized achievement test results for the evaluation of teachers and instruction. Teacher effectiveness should not be determined solely on the basis of test results and definitely *not* on the results of one test.

It would be extremely difficult to compare Miss Garcia and Mr. Jackson, both third-grade teachers in the same school, when we know that one classroom contains an overabundance of bright pupils and the other contains many slower pupils. Even assuming that the average ability of the two classes is comparable, how can we rate the teachers when Miss Garcia, for example, feels certain skills are more easily learned at the end of the term, whereas Mr. Jackson prefers to teach these skills at the beginning of the term, although we administer our tests in the middle of the term? Also, is it not conceivable that the instructional objectives stressed by Mr. Jackson are only minimally reflected in the test but those emphasized by Miss Garcia are highlighted in the test (that is, the test is more valid for Miss Garcia than for Mr. Jackson)? Remember that even in the most valid test, we only have a sampling of a teacher's instructional objectives.

Not only can a multitude of factors affect learning and, hence, the evaluation of instruction and teachers, but we have statistical problems in inter-

[17] Gronlund (1974) and Wrightstone, Hogan, & Abbott (1972) present a thorough discussion of how achievement-test results can be used as one of the criteria in accountability. See Conklin, Burstein, & Keesling (1979) for a discussion of the pitfalls of using gain scores to evaluate educational programs.

preting "gain scores," since the reliability of the "gain score" is often substantially lower than the reliability of either the pre- or posttest scores.

Achievement-test results, regardless of their nature, are measures that depend on past learning. In other words, if Miss Milanski's sixth-graders are weak in certain arithmetic skills, the weakness may be due to the fact that the essential components of this skill were not developed in an earlier grade. Hence, blaming Miss Milanski because her pupils score below national norms would be utterly ridiculous. There is no doubt that teachers are instrumental in determining how well their pupils score on achievement tests. However, this is *not* analogous to the claim that *only* achievement test results (be they norm or criterion referenced) be used to rate teachers.

When achievement test results are used to rate teachers, they frequently instill fear into the teachers. This fear conceivably may result in a reduction of teacher effectiveness and in a tendency for "test teaching." Teaching for a test may encourage undue emphasis on cognitive development, the end result being absence of concern for the social and emotional development of pupils.

We believe that standardized achievement test results can and should (where deemed appropriate) be used to improve the instructional program. Further, we feel that test results should be used to *help* teachers rather than to evaluate them. Such self-help can be of marked benefit to teachers. They can see the strengths and weaknesses of their class (either as a whole or for the individual pupils) if they use survey batteries. They can, by means of an item analysis, see what skills or facts have and have not been learned. They can, using national norms, make comparisons between their students and students in the same grade nationally. They can, with local norms, compare the status of their students with that of other students in the same school or in the same school system. They can compare the content of their courses with the content deemed appropriate by experts.

In summary, the results from standardized achievement tests should *not* be used as the *sole* criterion to evaluate teachers, since too many factors other than teacher competency can and do influence the test score a pupil receives. But we *do recommend* that standardized achievement-test scores be used judiciously as *one* of *many* variables in teacher evaluation.

Curriculum Evaluation   Achievement test results may also be used as one of the criteria on which to evaluate the curriculum. For example, 25 years ago it was common practice to delay the teaching of a foreign language until the student reached the seventh or eighth grade. However, it has been found that elementary school children are able to master a foreign language. It has also been demonstrated that with the same amount of training, elementary school pupils do as well on the foreign language achievement test as junior high school pupils. Findings such as these suggest that our curriculum must be flexible. Frequently, achievement test results provide evidence needed to instigate curriculum revision.

The preceding example of the use of achievement test results for studying the efficacy of introducing a foreign language in the primary grades is a somewhat simple one. In some instances, however, the data on which to base curriculum revision are not so clear-cut.

The profile depicted in Figure 8.8 is for the performance of sixth-graders in a particular school in contrast to the performance of sixth-graders in other schools in the same city. The score scale is essentially a grade equivalent with the decimals omitted (e.g., a GE of 6.3 is represented as 63). The profile is based on data collected on the Iowa Tests of Basic Skills, which was administered during the first week of class. The following conclusions appear to be warranted:

1. Students in the sixth grade in the Walnut Street school have an average scaled-score performance of about 35, in contrast with the mean scaled-score performance of all other sixth-graders of about 60. Also, the Walnut Street pupils appear to be more proficient in arithmetic skills than they are in either language or work-study skills.
2. The Walnut Street pupils received the highest and lowest scores on the arithmetic concepts and reading graphs and tables subtests, respectively. This does not mean, however, that they are necessarily better in one than in the other. Much depends upon the variability of the pupils and the subtest intercorrelations. (If you don't know why, go back to Chapter 3 and restudy the discussion of reliability of difference scores.)
3. Whether the principal should change the instructional program at the Walnut Street School is unclear. If the Walnut Street pupils come mainly from an impoverished environment, the decision made could be markedly different from that made if these pupils came from an average or above-average socioeconomic area. In the former, we would have an instance of a poor environment that may not permit pupils to experience verbal and language-type activities, at least the kind that are measured by this or any other standardized achievement test. If the pupils were above average in intelligence, the principal would have to consider the adequacy of the teachers, the motivation of the pupils, the validity of the test, and other factors before making a decision.

Some modification of the curriculum might be in order for the Walnut Street school. The kind of modification (namely, having more free reading, introducing pupils to the public library, or motivating the pupils to achieve at their maximum), however, would depend on the many factors that influence learning. It is conceivable that the curriculum may not have to be modified. Rather, the manner in which the curriculum is introduced may have to be altered. For example, if the test results at the end of the sixth grade showed that this discrepancy no longer exists, this would suggest that (1) the prepa-

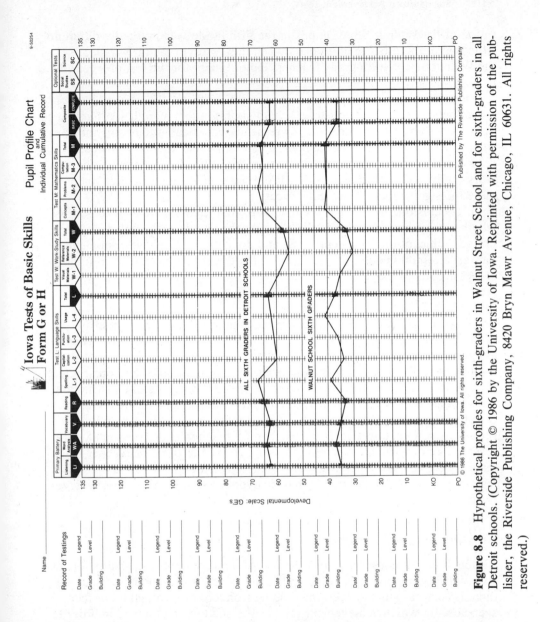

Figure 8.8 Hypothetical profiles for sixth-graders in Walnut Street School and for sixth-graders in all Detroit schools. (Copyright © 1986 by the University of Iowa. Reprinted with permission of the publisher, the Riverside Publishing Company, 8420 Bryn Mawr Avenue, Chicago, IL 60631. All rights reserved.)

309

ration of the Walnut Street pupils in the fifth grade was markedly different from that of the other sixth-graders when they were in the fifth grade, or (2) the Walnut Street sixth-grade teachers either taught for the test or were able to make up any deficiencies that existed.

An interesting feature of this hypothetical profile is the strange isomorphism between the Walnut Street school sixth-graders and all sixth-graders in the city. The peaks and valleys are nearly identical. Might this indicate something about the curriculum in all the schools? In other words, is it reasonable to expect that more attention might have to be paid to certain work-study skills? Not necessarily. From the profile, one is unable to determine the significance of the differences.

In conclusion, we must reemphasize that achievement test scores, whether they be from standardized or teacher-made tests, must be interpreted with caution. Test scores can and do serve as a valuable supplementary criterion on which to make more valid educational decisions. But these scores are supplementary and not absolute, and they are influenced by many factors.

Grading   In general, standardized achievement-test results should not be used to assign course grades. They may be used to assist the teacher in assigning the final course grade, provided the test reflects local objectives. As was pointed out earlier, standardized achievement tests are constructed so that they measure broad rather than specific outcomes of instruction. Hence, they may reflect and measure only a *small* part of a teacher's instructional goals. Also, the objectives of instruction may vary, not only from school to school but also from teacher to teacher. For these and other reasons, grades should typically be assigned on the basis of teacher-made tests. These tests, properly constructed, reflect the goals of the individual teacher to a much greater extent than do even the best standardized achievement tests.

Satisfying Federal Regulations

Although not directly related to the use of achievement-test results for instructional, guidance, or administrative purposes, as previously discussed, there is an area—that of securing funding from either local, state, or federal agencies—in which achievement-test results need to be obtained in order to evaluate particular programs. One such program is the Education Consolidation and Improvement Act of 1981 (it replaced the familiar "Titles" of the Elementary and Secondary Education Act), which requires the assessment and evaluation of compensatory education programs in order to receive funding. Further, this assessment and evaluation is to be realized through "comprehensive . . . testing programs in elementary and secondary schools . . . the administration of examinations to measure the proficiency of students . . . such evaluations shall include objective measurements of educational achievement in basic skills. . . ." It is true that these evaluations and assessments need not be addressed solely by means of standardized achievement tests, nor should they be. But, if for no other reason, standardized tests do lend an air of face validity to the assessment and evaluation of the program.

Research Uses

Standardized achievement-test results provide valuable information for researchers. For example, suppose that the Okemos High School mathematics faculty want to know whether providing ninth-graders with calculators will result in their obtaining higher arithmetic computation scores. At the beginning of the year two groups of ninth-grade algebra students could be tested with a standardized algebra achievement test. One group would be taught with the use of calculators; the other group would be taught without calculators. At the end of the term, a parallel form of the same algebra test would be administered to both groups. The pre- and posttest scores would be compared, and if the calculator group did the same as or better than the noncalculator group, we could say that further study is warranted. On the other hand, if the noncalculator group performed better than the calculator group, we would have some reservations about suggesting the purchase of calculators.[18] This is just one example of how standardized test results can be used for educational decision making.

Summary of Uses

In the preceding pages we have attempted to discuss some of the more common uses of standardized achievement-test results. Results of such tests can be, are, and should be used (1) for making predictions of future academic success, (2) for placing pupils in appropriate learning environments, (3) for diagnosing pupil strengths and weaknesses, (4) for assessing the effectiveness of instructional and curricular programs, (5) for evaluating new programs, and (6) for providing data for various reports to the administration, school board, parents, the media, and the like.

As we have stated, we have not treated all the possible uses. We have neglected to consider using standardized achievement test results for such purposes as (1) motivating pupils, and (2) demonstrating to students what is expected of them. We have tried to emphasize that test results provide only a limited amount of information. Good teachers derive much valuable information about pupils in their daily contact with, and observation of, them. We

---

[18] We are aware that we lack elegance in our experimental design. A myriad of factors could confound the study. We are presenting this study only as an example of the use of test results for research purposes.

hope that it is evident that the use of standardized achievement tests is limited only by the resourcefulness and ingenuity of the classroom teacher and that achievement-test results should be used as a supplement to other evidence, to make sound educational decisions.

SUMMARY

The principal ideas, suggestions, and recommendations made in this chapter are summarized in the following statements:

1. Standardized and teacher-made achievement tests differ markedly in terms of their purpose, method of construction, sampling of content, and availability of norms (although both have the goal of appraisal of present knowledge).
2. The trend today in standardized achievement tests is away from measuring factual knowledge and toward emphasizing application and interpretation.
3. Teacher-made and standardized achievement tests complement each other. It is futile to argue that one is more useful than the other.
4. Standardized achievement tests may be classified as diagnostic, single-subject-matter, and survey batteries and as criterion- or norm-referenced. Single-subject-matter tests may be further subdivided into readiness and prognostic tests.
5. Standardized achievement tests differ little in terms of their construction and technical features. They do differ markedly in their purpose. To determine whether a kindergarten child is ready for the first grade, a reading readiness test should be used. To obtain an indication of a pupil's strengths and weaknesses, a diagnostic test is recommended. To learn whether a pupil is proficient in a subject-matter area such as history or physics, a single-subject-matter test should be used. To ascertain the strengths and weaknesses (actually plot a profile) of pupils in the various core subjects, a survey battery should be used.
6. Within the past few years, commercial test publishers and other firms have begun to pay more attention to producing criterion-referenced standardized achievement tests; very specific, prescriptive diagnostic tests; mastery tests; and "tailor-made" tests.
7. Standardized-test publishers are paying more attention to providing teachers with prescriptive suggestions on the basis of their pupils' achievement-test performance.
8. Standardized-test publishers are providing a variety of output data (for a slight additional fee) to users. Various item analyses, grouping students of similar abilities with suggestions of instructional strategies to be used with these groups, and keying items to objectives and commonly used textbooks are some of the reporting services available.

9. Various examples were given to suggest the different uses of standardized achievement-test results for instructional, guidance, administrative, and research uses.

POINTS TO PONDER

1. Compare and contrast standardized and teacher-made achievement tests. List three specific situations where each would be preferable.
2. Of what value would it be to know the intercorrelations of the subtests in an achievement battery?
3. Which type of validity is most important in an achievement test? Why?
4. You are an elementary school guidance counselor. Your principal assigns you the task of choosing an achievement battery. How do you proceed in your task?
5. First-grade pupils are frequently grouped for instructional purposes on the basis of reading readiness tests. This grouping is not always effective. Does this suggest the elimination of reading readiness tests? Support your answer.
6. There seems to be general consensus, but not universal agreement, on the elementary curriculum. What role should standardized achievement tests play in reducing or increasing the diversity of this curriculum?
7. Mary Poppins scored at the 89th percentile (national norms) on the language subtest of the Stanford Achievement Test. However, she received only a grade of C in language arts. How can this be accounted for?
8. Discuss this statement: The California Achievement Tests subscores can be used for diagnostic purposes.
9. What problems are associated with using standardized achievement-test results to evaluate teacher effectiveness?
10. Given both aptitude- and achievement-tests results for a sixth-grade class, how would you select individuals for an enriched program? What other information would be desirable? What potential dangers exist in using test results for this selection procedure?
11. In what situations would you be more likely to use a criterion-referenced standardized achievement test over a norm-referenced test? Support your answer.
12. A survey battery manual states that the test can be used for diagnostic purposes. What kinds of evidence should you look for to ascertain whether it is a valid diagnostic test?
13. Your school board has jumped on the minimal competency bandwagon. What advantages and disadvantages are there in using (a) a test constructed by the school's research bureau, (b) a test constructed by the

teaching staff, and (c) a commercially published standardized achievement test to determine competency?

14. In Roy Wilkin's Middle School, eighth-graders are randomly assigned to algebra sections. The superintendent of schools, studying the grade distributions, notices that there is a marked discrepancy in grades given by the different teachers. Would you use the results of a standardized algebra test to study this problem? Defend your answer.

15. Do you concur with the argument advanced by some critics of standardized achievement tests that "their continued use will result in a national or uniform curriculum"? Why do you feel this way?

CHAPTER 9

Interest, Personality, and Attitude Inventories

INTRODUCTION
PROBLEMS OF MEASURING NONCOGNITIVE CHARACTERISTICS
MEASUREMENT OF INTERESTS
CAREER AWARENESS AND DEVELOPMENT
PERSONALITY ASSESSMENT
ATTITUDE AND VALUE ASSESSMENT

Should Girder be encouraged to study engineering in college? What are Allan's interests? How can we explain why Beth, who scored at the 95th percentile on the WISC, scored only at the 25th percentile on the Stanford Achievement Test? Is Ilene really an aggressive and hostile child? Are Ruth's concerns about peer acceptance atypical for an average 13-year-old? What are problem check lists? Should teachers interpret noncognitive inventories? Are there some noncognitive inventories that should be barred from the classroom? Does the information derived from interest, personality, and attitude inventories help educators make more valid decisions than could be made if such data were not used? These are some of the questions that are discussed in this chapter.

Typically, schools have tread softly in this area of assessment for three reasons: (1) the instruments available lack the psychometric elegance of many of our cognitive measures, (2) many educators, parents, and students (especially older ones) are concerned about invasion of privacy and "big brother" spying, and (3) many people attach little importance to the attainment of wholesome affective behavior as an objective of the schools.

How familiar are comments such as "Irvin has the ability but is still failing in school," "Ruth isn't too bright, but she gets through on perseverance"? One cannot dismiss the interaction between affective behavior—be it defined as interests, attitudes, values, or personality—and academic success. Educators cannot ignore the affective domain and still be effective.

Noncognitive characteristics can be ascertained in a variety of ways: directly from the person—that is, self-report (using either standardized or locally constructed instruments)—or from someone else (using rating scales, anecdotal records, other observational techniques). Although we might expect that the self-report method is the best source of information about people, this method has two major disadvantages: (1) we assume that the individuals know themselves and can therefore report their feelings, and (2) we assume that individuals will be truthful in their responses, considering people's concerns about invasion of their privacy, computer storage of data, and the like. Even though we have a test such as the Social Desirability Scale to measure bias, we cannot eliminate it (Crowne & Marlowe, 1964). On the other hand, data obtained from someone else may not be too objective. For example, would you expect the mother of an autistic child to be completely objective in her description of the child's behavior? In both approaches we must recognize that there may be problems of validity and reliability. In the "self-report," the data may be distorted by accident, by misunderstanding, or by design. In the "other report," the data may be distorted depending upon the scale used.

In this chapter we concern ourselves only with standardized noncognitive inventories, recognizing that there are many locally constructed affective tests and inventories. Observational techniques such as rating scales and anecdotal records are useful methods, especially for adults. Although they provide much valuable data, they may not provide data as valid as those obtained from standardized inventories. Standardized noncognitive inventories are uniformly administered and, in general, objectively scored. Many of them also have valuable normative data that permit valid comparisons between a pupil in one community and pupils throughout the country. With standardized noncognitive inventories, it may be ascertained whether Ilene is abnormally aggressive or whether Ruth's concerns about peer acceptance are natural.

At this point, it may be argued that these questions could be answered by natural observation that would have an additional feature over a testing situation: People are more likely to display their true behavior in natural settings that are informal, unstructured, and nonthreatening. Teachers are able to observe their students in real-life situations. But are their observations valid? Are teachers objective? Do they know what behavior is significant and what can be overlooked? Can teachers draw correct inferences from observed behavior? As imprecise as noncognitive inventories may appear to be, they do provide valuable information about the pupil, information that the teacher cannot acquire through observation but which may be necessary to understand the pupil's behavior. Some educators argue that test scores should be used only to supplement teachers' observations. Others argue the converse. The important thing to remember is that both teachers' observations and test data provide information about the pupils' behavior, and both should be used.

After studying this chapter, the student should be able to do the following:

1. Recognize the value to teachers of information about pupil interests, attitudes, and personality.
2. Understand that noncognitive measures are not so psychometrically elegant as cognitive measures.
3. Recognize the problems involved in measuring noncognitive characteristics—problems of definition, response set, faking, validity, reliability, and interpretation.
4. Recognize the three most commonly used procedures for constructing and keying noncognitive inventories—empirical, homogeneous, and logical.
5. Differentiate between attitudes and interests.
6. Discuss the major approaches used to measure interests.
7. Evaluate the more popular interest inventories in terms of their construction, grade level, content, administration, scoring, validity, reliability, and interpretability.
8. Recognize how interest test results can be used for instructional and guidance purposes.
9. Appreciate the use of career-awareness inventories.
10. Understand the various ways in which personality can be assessed.
11. Recognize the limitations of personality inventories.
12. Evaluate attitude scales.
13. Appreciate the value of study-habits inventories.

INTRODUCTION

It is generally agreed that everyone concerned with the education of children must understand them in their totality in order that optimal learning conditions may be provided. This totality goes beyond academic skills and knowledge. Although affective measures do not contribute as much to the prediction of academic and vocational success as do our cognitive measures (tests of *maximum* performance are clearly the best predictors), they do provide useful information to the classroom teacher.

The development of a healthy personality is essential to success in school. A student's mental health has direct relevance to ability to learn, interest in learning, and attitudes toward the value of an education. Quite frequently, learning difficulties are related to a student's personality (Rutkowski & Domino, 1975; Calsyn & Kenny, 1977; Edwards, 1977), and any attempt to correct the difficulty is doomed to failure if the student's total strengths and weaknesses are not considered in both the cognitive and the noncognitive areas. Whether teachers realize it or not, they *are* influenced by their students' attitudes, values, interests, and general makeup. If teachers know that their students dislike history, they could (and, it is hoped, would) employ a variety of techniques to motivate them—films, playacting, and humorous skits—to try to instill a positive attitude toward the value of studying history. If they know that some students who are poor readers are interested in mechanics, they might use stories with a mechanical flavor in the reading program. Teachers can and do capitalize on the interests and attitudes of their pupils. (Messick, 1979, presents a discussion of the uses and misuses of affective variables in educational decision making.) However, before teachers are able to apply knowledge, they must obtain it. Before teachers can use data about their pupils' interests, attitudes, values, and general personality makeup, they must obtain these data.

The classroom teacher and counselor should be able to administer problem checklists, interest inventories, and general personality tests, with minimal training. The counselor should be able to interpret the results of interest inventories without too much difficulty. No one, however, who has not had considerable training and experience should attempt to interpret measures designed to depict abnormality or maladjustment.

Classroom teachers, as members of a professional team vitally concerned with both cognitive and noncognitive behavior, must, in order to be effective team members, speak the language. Otherwise, they will not be able to communicate effectively with other team members—school psychologist, clinician, and counselor. In order to do so, they must know something about noncognitive inventories—what they are, what they can and cannot do, the different kinds of noncognitive inventories, and so forth—and about the behaviors they measure.

By helping establish optimal, positive test-taking attitudes, teachers through their knowledge of noncognitive assessment can indirectly help the counselor to work with the students. Rapport is essential in any testing situation. But it may be more vital in noncognitive assessment, especially when the test is envisaged by the testee as threatening. Also, in noncognitive inventories the pupil can fake either good or bad, and the teacher can aid greatly in diminishing faking by establishing rapport. The pupils may be more likely to trust their teacher, with whom they are in daily contact, than they are to trust the counselor or clinician, whom they see infrequently. Classroom teachers, especially the ones who are trusted and accepted by their pupils, can aid the clinician by breaking the ice and helping the children accept the clinician as someone who is trying to help them.

In summary, knowledge about pupils' interests, personalities, and attitudes is important to educators to help them understand pupils better and to help them communicate effectively with other professionals. Knowledge of affective characteristics is also important because they are a means to an end (for example, if we know that Billy likes sports, we might have him read sports magazines in order to help him improve his reading speed) as well as an end in themselves (that is, as a desired goal of instruction such as the development of tolerance). Knowledge about noncognitive instruments (especially interest inventories) is important because such inventories are being used in our schools, especially in the secondary grades, with increasing frequency. Interest inventories are valid insofar as they provide some information about a pupil's vocational or avocational interests; are more objective than the informal observational approach; and are frequently used in research on learning. We must reiterate that despite their limitations, standardized noncognitive inventories can play an important role in education (see Cronbach & Snow, 1977; Bloom, 1978; and Messick, 1979). Interest inventories are also popular in nonclassroom settings. A study by Zytowski & Warman (1982) indicated that of the 25 most frequently used tests in counseling centers, the Strong-Campbell Interest Inventory (SCII) and the Self-Directed Search (SDS), which is also an interest inventory, were in the top 10 in usage. In fact, they found that tests of *typical* performance (affective measures) were replacing tests of *maximum* performance (cognitive measures).

Before discussing the various procedures and tests available to measure noncognitive traits, their advantages and limitations, and their uses and misuses, we must consider some of the methodological problems associated with noncognitive inventories.

PROBLEMS OF MEASURING NONCOGNITIVE CHARACTERISTICS[1]

There are many unresolved problems in the assessment of noncognitive traits: problems of definition, response set, faking, low validity and reliability, interpretation, and sex bias. To observe that the measurement of affect poses methodological problems not encountered in cognitive assessment is deceptively simple. Because noncognitive assessment (or for that matter any assessment) involves the differences among individuals as well as changes in behavior over time, validity and reliability are of vital importance. It should be evident that until these problems are resolved, noncognitive assessment will be subject to much suspicion and criticism.

---

[1] For a thorough and thought-provoking discussion of the principles to be considered in the development and use of interest inventories (many of the principles, however, are pertinent to any noncognitive inventory), see Kuder (1970). Fiske (1963), Holtzman (1964), and Anastasi (1982) discuss the measurement problems involved in assessing noncognitive characteristics. Anderson (1981) has written an excellent book for assessing affective characteristics.

Problems of Definition

Noncognitive tests, even more than aptitude or achievement tests, present the problem of definition. Allport (1963) considered at least 50 definitions of personality before he advanced his own. This fact contributes no doubt to the inconclusive and often contradictory findings in noncognitive research. Frequently, different researchers arrived at different conclusions because they were studying different variables, even though the variables studied were all labeled the same—for example, *honesty* or *aestheticism*. To some, the terms *attitudes, beliefs, values,* and *interests* are used synonymously. To others, there are definite demarcations among the terms. To still others, attitudes and values are considered one category, beliefs and opinions another, and interests still another. The concept of personality has multiple and complex meanings, the various definitions are at best crude, and the techniques for evaluation are sometimes lacking in scientific rigor. Yet we cannot give up our research or interest in the area of affective development. Grandiose and ethereal constructs such as honesty, beauty, truth, and virtue can be translated to behavioral terms. Once this is done, an attempt can be made to measure these behavioral traits.

Just as we must talk about a specific kind of validity (such as content or predictive) or reliability (stability or equivalence), so, when we discuss a personality trait such as authoritarianism, we must be specific and refer to it as, for example, the "*F* Scale's authoritarianism" or "Rokeach's authoritarianism." Until we are able to develop definitions for noncognitive constructs, we will be looking for a needle in a haystack without knowing what a needle looks like.

Problems of Response Set

All noncognitive tests are susceptible to response set—that is, the tendency of an individual to reply in a particular direction, almost independent of content.[2] Individuals exhibiting response set will answer identical questions (but presented in different formats) differently. For example, some people may be predisposed to select the neutral category if a disagree-agree continuum is used, or the "true" statement in true-false items; or they may guess on all items they are unsure of. There are many types of response set: acquiescence, social desirability, guessing, and sacrificing accuracy for speed (or vice versa).

The response set that has been of most concern in noncognitive measurement is *social desirability* (Edwards, 1957). This is the tendency for individuals to respond favorably to the items that they feel are socially accepted,

---

[2] Response sets may also be present in cognitive measures. However, in cognitive tests the response sets can be controlled more easily. For example, guessing can be controlled in an achievement test through clear directions and correction formulas.

such as, "People should be concerned with how their behavior affects others," or "Open-housing legislation should be enacted by Congress." Here, subjects may answer not on the basis of how they truly feel but on the basis of what they think is a socially acceptable or desirable answer.

The original goal in the study of response sets such as social desirability was to devise a means whereby their effects could be eliminated (as much as possible) as scaling artifacts. It appears that a controversy exists as to whether we can automatically assume the existence of response sets and, if they do exist, whether response sets should be measured or eliminated from noncognitive tests (Cronbach, 1946, 1950; Crowne & Marlowe, 1960; Jackson & Messick, 1962; Rorer, 1965). For example, the California F Scale consists of strongly worded opinions, most of which express a critical attitude toward human nature. Hence, any tendency to accept these statements may in itself be an indication of authoritarianism, and any attempt to eliminate acquiescence may eliminate or prevent measurement of this important behavioral trait (Gage et al., 1957). There is also some disagreement on whether response set is a general or specific factor (Morf & Jackson, 1972).

If, however, one decides it is valuable, steps can be taken to try to control for response set. Cronbach (1950) found that response set is particularly prevalent on tests that (1) contain ambiguous items, (2) require the individual to respond on a disagree-agree continuum, and (3) lend themselves to responses in either a favorable or an unfavorable direction. Various techniques (such as using the forced-choice format, randomly ordering the items, keeping the instrument relatively short, insuring anonymity of the respondents, having an equal number of positively and negatively worded statements [Larkins & Shaver, 1968, recommend having more negative statements]) have been used in an attempt to control response set. These techniques have not eliminated the problem completely. In fact, some research indicates that the forced-choice approach is not as good as we initially thought as a control for faking and social desirability and may actually be detrimental when it yields ipsative scores (Anastasi, 1982).

Those using personality, attitude, value, and interest tests must pay particular attention to the presence of response sets and must govern their conclusions and recommendations accordingly. More research is needed on response sets: What kinds of people are susceptible? What kinds of items lend themselves to this? Why are some tests affected and others are not? Can (or should) their influence be neutralized?

Faking

Faking can and does occur on cognitive as well as noncognitive tests, but it is more common on the latter. One psychologist aptly said, "As long as a subject has sufficient education to enable him to answer a personality inventory, however, he probably has the ability to alter his score appreciably in the desired direction" (Anastasi, 1968, p. 456). Although individuals can fake either good or bad on a noncognitive test, they can fake only bad on a cognitive test (ignorance can be faked, but knowledge cannot). The tendency to fake is a characteristic inherent in the individual rather than a test artifact.

Although examiners expect a subject to give valid information, they do not always receive it. Subjects come to the test and will either be truthful or will lie, depending upon the purpose of the test and their perception of how the test results will be used.[3] Often responses may be rationalizations or unconscious modifications rather than deliberate lies. A candidate for college admission might try to fake good if inventory results might affect the chances for admission. Quite frequently, people are motivated to lie when they know that their selection or consideration for a particular job depends upon the types of answers they give on an interest or personality test. Hence, in their attempt to obtain the position, subjects will do everything possible to create the desired impression (Green, 1951, Wesman, 1952). Ben, a high school senior, because of his stereotypic impression of a surgeon's life (glamor and prestige), may try to convince his guidance counselor that he likes medicine, or may fake some interest tests to indicate that he has a liking for medicine.

Although subjects will most often try to present themselves in a favorable light, there are instances when subjects fake their scores so that they will appear maladjusted or abnormal. Criminals may go out of their way to exhibit tendencies of maladjustment so that they will be judged insane and unfit to stand trial.

Various procedures have been studied and are used to combat faking. One such procedure (perhaps the best) is to establish rapport with the subjects and to convince them that in the long run they will be better off if they give truthful responses. Another method is to attempt to disguise the purpose of the test. This does not always work, especially with intelligent subjects who may see through the disguise by the nature of the test items. However, in some instances it is possible to disguise the purpose of the test. For example, a researcher interested in studying honesty may prepare a list of book titles, some of which are fictitious. Students are asked to check those book titles they have read. On the surface, the test looks as though it is measuring reading interests, but it really is not. It is actually measuring honesty. If a student indicates that he has read one of the books that does not actually exist, then the student is obviously lying. Disguising the purpose of a test, though, can result in some ethical and practical problems, affect the image of psychologists and counselors, and destroy future attempts at establishing rapport.

Another approach to combat faking is to use the forced-choice technique.

---

[3] Because of faking, it is very difficult in clinical psychotherapy to evaluate the effect of the treatment from test-taking behavioral changes.

Here, two or more equally desirable or undesirable statements are presented together, such as

A. I like to read good novels.
B. I like to watch good movies.

The subject is required to choose one answer from the set. One of the answers, however, is a better indicator of the criterion being studied than is the other(s). The forced-choice method, unfortunately, also has its defects. It requires more time to obtain an equal number of responses; it is sometimes resisted by examinees (and may result in negative attitudes toward future testing and/or the counseling interview); and it may lower the reliability, because the choice is more difficult to make.

Still another approach is the construction of scales to *detect* rather than *prevent* faking. Tests such as the Minnesota Multiphasic Personality Inventory (MMPI), the Edwards Personal Preference Schedule (EPPS), and the Kuder Occupational Interest Surveys contain special subtests to detect the faker. Of the three, only the verification score of the MMPI is used to adjust the obtained score.

In conclusion, whatever elaborate procedures are employed by the test maker to minimize distortion—whether it be by response set, faking, or cheating—we must realize that the subject will provide only the information he is able and willing to report. People interpreting both cognitive and affective tests (more so the latter) must consider this.

Reliability and Validity

The reliability of noncognitive tests tends to be much lower than that of cognitive tests of the same length. For example, in studying stability reliability, how individuals behave—that is, how they respond to an affective-type item—is governed, in part at least, by the momentary situation. For example, a person with liberal attitudes toward blacks, if interviewed a few hours after being attacked by a black, might respond in a bigoted fashion. Because of the susceptibility of affective items to the momentary situation, the reliabilities of some items might be very low. Moreover, some of the more common procedures for studying reliability may be inappropriate. Because human behavior is vacillating rather than constant, reliability coefficients derived from test–retest methods (coefficient of stability) tend to be spuriously low and misleading in judging the test's precision. Inconsistency in test responses may be either an important aspect of an individual's personality or a test artifact. The split-half, coefficient alpha, and Kuder-Richardson methods (measures of internal consistency) are most frequently used to study the reliability of noncognitive tests. When low reliabilities are found, careful attention must be paid to the interpretation of difference scores in a test profile, because only marked differences may suggest true intraindividual differences.

For noncognitive measures, we generally are more concerned with *construct* validity than with predictive validity. Although we are interested in predictive validity, it is difficult to ascertain the predictive validity of a noncognitive measure because adequate external-criterion data are often lacking.

The research conducted with noncognitive inventories has led to many attempts to improve their validity. Some of the approaches applied are (1) using correction scores rather than discarding inventories that appear to be suspect; (2) disguising the purpose of the test; (3) randomly assigning items throughout the test rather than presenting them in blocks, so that the traits being measured do not appear obvious to the examinee; (4) using verification scores to reveal test-taking attitudes; and (5) selecting test items on the basis of empirical rather than a priori grounds. Although these and other approaches are used to improve the validity of personality tests and interest inventories, the evidence today indicates that noncognitive tests still do not approach the criterion-related validity of cognitive measures, mainly, perhaps, because of the problem of valid external-criterion data.

Rather than conclude that noncognitive tests do not have the desired degree of validity and reliability needed for making valid educational decisions, we should ask how much information we can get from the inventory and how it will help us. Another way to look at it is in terms of a cost analysis. In the long run, does the use of noncognitive inventories reduce the incidence of costly error?

Problems of Interpretation

Noncognitive tests are really not tests in the sense that aptitude and achievement tests are, because there are not necessarily any right answers. Noncognitive tests are generally interpreted in relation to the traits held by "normal" ("average") people. Hence, a Canadian exhibiting modal, normal behavior in Canada could, if behaving the same way in Peru, appear abnormal, even though, according to his own Canadian subcultural modes, he is behaving normally.

Another problem in the interpretation of noncognitive tests, especially attitude scales, reflects the kinds of responses permitted. Most attitude-scale responses provide for a neutral response. But what do neutral responses mean? Do they mean that the individual is really neutral, or do they mean that the subjects are unwilling to commit themselves? How is a neutral response interpreted? One way to circumvent the problem of neutral responses is to eliminate this type of response. But if we do so, might we be eliminating the measurement of a true neutral behavioral trait, or might we end up with untrue measurement?

An additional problem in interpreting the results from affective inventories is that there may be intervening factors that affect how an individual responds to a particular personality inventory item (Kuncel, 1973).

Of the various noncognitive tests, the problem of interpretation is most acute for projective tests, especially those that are unstructured. For example, in the Rorschach, is a subject's response "The picture shows two people fighting with knives" indicative of aggressive or hostile behavior?

Perhaps one of the more serious problems in interpreting noncognitive tests is that associated with ipsative forced-choice tests.

Assume subjects are given forced-choice items such as

A. I like to build model airplanes.
B. I like to play bridge.
C. I like to collect stamps.

and are required to select the one statement in the triad that they like the most. Each of the three possible choices is keyed under a different subscale. Thus, if they pick A, they may receive a point on the scientific scale. If they select B, they may receive a point on the sociability scale. If they choose C, they may receive a point on the clerical scale. The essential characteristic of such items is that when subjects make a choice in favor of one subscale (by choosing a particular item), they are at the same time rejecting the other subscales. A test composed of such items (where one is forced to make a choice) produces an ipsative scale, and the scores are ipsative scores. Although multiple-choice cognitive tests also require the individual to make a choice, there is only one correct answer for everyone. Hence, problems associated with ipsative forced-choice tests are unique only to some noncognitive tests.

The essential characteristic of an ipsative scale is that the total score summing across all the subscales is the same for all persons. Ipsative scores do not reflect the intensity of the subject's feeling, and yet this is something that would be of extreme value in interpreting an individual's responses. For example, three boys purchase vanilla ice cream cones. Does this imply that they all like vanilla ice cream to the same degree? Not necessarily so. Or if each of the three boys purchased a different flavor, does this signify that the boy who wanted and chose vanilla likes vanilla more than the boy who chose chocolate? Not necessarily!

Ipsative scales permit only intraindividual comparisons. In an ipsative scale, an individual will probably have some high scores and some low scores (he could have all scores at the mean). All his scores cannot be either high or low. Some psychometrists contend that the ipsative forced-choice technique parallels real life in that a person is always forced to choose between activity A and activity B. For example, a child, when offered some ice cream, must choose, normally, among a variety of flavors. Others argue that this forced choice can sometimes induce frustration in the subject, especially when all the statements (choices) are equally desirable or unde-sirable.

Interpreting a forced-choice profile is very difficult. How does a person interpret to a student the profile of an ipsative interest test with ten sub-scales? The tester cannot say that the student's interest in outdoor activities is higher than his or her interest in musical activities (even though the stu-dent may have had a higher score on the outdoor scale), because the scores are not absolute. We cannot say that two persons who rank at the 90th percentile in terms of the national norm group have equal outdoor interests because the scores are ipsative.

Problems of Sex Bias

Although sex bias has been discussed in other sections, we briefly reintro-duce it because much of the ferver on sex bias has been directed primarily toward interest measurement.[4] In fact, Campbell—possibly because of pres-sure—revised the Strong Vocational Interest Blank (SVIB) (Campbell, 1974) so that it avoided all sexual stereotypes, eliminated sexist language, and had scores reported for males and females for all but 8 of the 162 Occupational Scales. The issue at hand is not whether a test differentiates among individ-uals—be it blacks versus whites, males versus females, high socioeconomic versus low socioeconomic—as long as it does so validly. In fact, the major purpose of a test, be it criterion or norm-referenced, but particularly the latter, has as its major purpose one of differentiation. Just because research has shown that males tend to be more quantitative whereas females tend to be more verbal (Macoby & Jacklin, 1974; Strassberg-Rosenberg & Donlon, 1975), this is not prima facie evidence that the tests used are biased in favor of one sex over the other. Some psychologists maintain that differences in interests between males and females are the result of *basic differences* in the interests between the sexes rather than sex bias per se (Prediger, Roth, & Noeth, 1975; Shaffer, 1976) or differences in aptitude (Cegelka, Omvig, & Larimore, 1974).

If the test is valid, it is supposed to point up any differences between and/or among groups or individuals. But a test is biased if the item content is in terms of sexual stereotypes that affect the performance of males and females differentially or if a test is *deliberately* constructed so that male scores are separated from female scores invalidly.

---

[4] Good discussions on sex bias in interest measurement are found in AMEG (1973); Diamond (1975a,b); Harmon (1973, 1974); Tanney (1974); Tittle (1973); Godfredson (1976); Hanson, Prediger, & Schussel (1977); and Tittle & Zytowski (1978). Donlon & Eckhart (1979) discuss sex bias in standardized achievement tests. Flaugher (1978) and Gardner (1978) present general discussions of bias. Graham & Lilly (1984) discuss sex bias research in ability, interest, and personality tests and conclude that sex bias research is inconclusive for personality tests but that sex bias exists for cognitive and interest tests.

Construction and Keying

Constructing and keying (scoring) noncognitive tests also present problems. Because it is sometimes extremely difficult to distinguish between a particular technique used to construct and to key a test, both operations are considered together. Cognitive tests have only a single, accepted correct (or best) answer. Noncognitive tests, on the other hand, need not always be amenable to a "correct" answer. In a noncognitive test, especially one that has been empirically keyed, an item may be keyed one way as the "correct" answer for plumbers, but it may be incorrect for some other group. Three procedures are commonly used to construct and key noncognitive tests: empirical, homogeneous, and logical. It should be noted that few interest inventories are "pure" examples of only one approach.

Empirical Construction   In the empirical or criterion method, the scoring key is developed in reference to some external criterion. One makes no assumption about the traits or characteristics of people in different groups but attempts to develop items that will discriminate people in one group from those in another group. (Prediger, 1977, discusses the alternatives to using group membership as a criterion for validating interest inventories.) Each item is evaluated in terms of its relationship to some criterion. The criterion, say, for a test of paranoia might be those patients in a mental institution who have been diagnosed as paranoiacs. The control group (or normals) could be those people who come to visit the paranoiacs. In a criterion-keyed interest inventory, a person's interests are compared with the interests held by people successful in various occupations (only those items that empirically differentiate among different groups are selected—the items are not selected on sheer faith, as in logical keying).

Items used in the Strong-Campbell Interest Inventory, the Kuder Occupational Interest Survey, and the Minnesota Multiphasic Personality Inventory were empirically selected and keyed. Although the scoring is usually in terms of unitary weights, differential weights can be assigned in proportion to the difference in responses between the criterion groups.

One virtue of empirical construction (and keying) is that it is very difficult for the examinee to fake a response. This is true because the examinee does not know how the criterion group responded to the various items.

Homogeneous Construction   The test constructor employing the homogeneous method first begins with a large number of items. Then, through a technique called factor analysis, clusters are identified, and the items are organized to fit the identified clusters. A psychometric characteristic of a homogeneous-keyed test is that the items of any one scale have high intra-correlations—that is, a common factor runs throughout that scale; the scale intercorrelations are relatively low (or they should be if more than one trait or cluster has been identified).

Logical Construction   In the logical method the items are selected and keyed on a logical or rational basis rather than on empirical grounds. The test constructor specifies the traits or skills or knowledge needed for the task and then prepares appropriate items. The items are then scored in accordance with the test maker's perception of the underlying psychological theory. For example, let us assume that a tester prepares an interest scale and includes the following question: "I like to read blueprints." Logically, it would be expected that engineers like to read blueprints, and if logical keying was used, a + 1 would be given on the engineering scale to those who responded affirmatively. It is conceivable, however, that engineers do not like to read blueprints. If empirical keying had been used to key the test and if it was found that engineers do not like this activity, then a + 1 would not be assigned on the engineering scale to those who responded affirmatively to this item.

MEASUREMENT OF INTERESTS

As was previously mentioned, teachers must be concerned not only with *what* students learn but also with *how* and *why* they learn. People have a tendency to excel in, or at least to devote more effort and energy to, the activities they like. In order for classroom teachers to best capitalize on the likes and dislikes of their students, it is necessary that they know something of their interests. Interest inventories assist them in gaining this knowledge. A counselor who is familiar with interest measurement may be better able to help students in making vocational and educational plans.

Teachers should certainly strive to make their objectives (whether they be cognitive skills, factual knowledge, or wholesome attitudes and values) palatable and interesting to their students. The teacher of ninth-grade social studies might explore students' interests (or at least have the students think about their interests) as they are related to various occupations when discussing the world of work. The high school teacher who knows that Bill is a poor reader may attempt to provide meaningful learning experiences by capitalizing on Bill's interests and may assign books that are related to Bill's interests. The fifth-grade teacher working on addition or subtraction skills may exploit students' interests insofar as the types of story problems used. The important thing to remember is that because the interests of students can influence how well they learn, teachers must be concerned with interest measurement.

Counselors too must be concerned with how and why students learn; it may be even more important to know why they do *not* learn. In addition, the various interest inventories can provide answers to some of the vocational and career-choice questions that students ask counselors. Questions such as "What kind of work am I suited for?" or "Should I major in chemical engineering?'' can or should be answered in terms both of the person's ability and of his or her likes and dislikes.

Knowledge of an individual's interests provides a sound basis for educational and vocational guidance. Interest inventory results may help the classroom teacher and counselor understand why a bright pupil is performing poorly academically. These results can be of assistance to the students if only to make them think more about their future.

The study of interests has received its greatest impetus from educational and vocational counseling. School and industrial psychologists share the common concern that the application of test results may permit better decisions to be made (1) by the individual selecting an occupation and (2) by the firm selecting job applicants.

Interest inventories have progressed a great deal from the initial attempts of G. Stanley Hall in 1907 to develop a questionnaire to measure children's recreational interests. In the 1920s, 1930s, and 1940s, the emphasis of researchers such as Strong and Kuder were on developing interest inventories that measured only vocational interests. But now we have inventories that measure both vocational and avocational interests; we have inventories that measure the interests of students who are not college-bound; and we have inventories such as the Hall Occupational Orientation Inventory and Holland's Vocational Preference Inventory that conceptualize interests and vocational choice as an expression of an individual's personality.

Although not directly related to the measurement of interests per se, the field of vocational maturity measurement and career interest and planning programs has generated much interest in the preceding two decades. In 1965 Crites constructed the Vocational Development Inventory, which was designed to measure "the dispositional factor in the construct of vocational maturity." In 1971 Super et al. developed the Career Development Inventory, which "represents an overall measure of vocational maturity as defined by the individual scales." In 1971 Westbrook constructed the Cognitive Vocational Maturity Test, designed to measure career knowledge and abilities in six areas of the cognitive domain of vocational maturity. All three scales differ markedly in item content and method of construction. (For an excellent comparison of these three scales, see Westbrook & Mastie, 1973.) In 1978, Crites developed his Career Maturity Inventory. (The latter two are examples of diagnostic scales.) In 1979, Super & Thompson developed a new inventory to assess adolescent vocational maturity and the U.S. Employment Service published its Interest Check List and Interest Inventory and accompanying Guide for Occupational Exploration.

Although interest inventories and the study of interest and career development have progressed in the preceding decade and a half, much still remains to be done. We still need better theoretical foundations regarding the development of interests; more knowledge about the relationship of interests to other aspects of human behavior, such as ability, intelligence, and personality; and more evidence regarding the construct of interests. Fortunately, much research is being conducted in the area of interests, and some answers should be forthcoming in the near future (see Holland et al., 1981; Kapes & Mastie, 1982).

Attitudes versus Interests

Attitudes and interests are both concerned with likes and dislikes. Both can be related to preferences for activities, social institutions, or groups. Both involve personal feelings about something. It is this "something" that distinguishes attitudes from interests. An attitude is typically conceptualized as being a feeling toward an *object, a social institution,* or *a group*. An interest, on the other hand, is conceptualized as being a feeling toward an *activity*.

Attitude and interest inventories share many things in common. They are both highly susceptible to faking, require frank responses from the subject, and are therefore able to assess only the characteristics that the individual is able to, or wishes to, reveal.

Types of Standardized Interest Inventories

An individual's interests (likes and dislikes, preferences and aversions) can be ascertained in a variety of ways. Super & Crites (1962, pp. 377–379) suggest four approaches that can be used to ascertain an individual's interests: (1) direct questioning, (2) direct observation, (3) tested interests, and (4) interest inventories. (Becker, 1977, discusses how expressed and inventoried interests may be discrepant because of the person's personality.) Measuring a person's interests by means of interest inventories has proved to be the most fruitful, encouraging, and valid approach and is the only approach discussed here. Although recent research has shown that asking people about their vocational aspirations is as predictive as interest inventories, their joint use leads to more valid predictions (Bartling, 1979; Gottfredson, 1979). The interest inventory contains statements about various occupations and activities. These statements may be presented singly, in pairs, or in triads. Subjects respond to each statement in terms of their preference for, or aversion to, the activity or occupation.

At least two dozen standardized interest inventories are commercially published, some of which are designed for vocational guidance only, others for educational guidance only, and others for both educational and vocational guidance. Some are designed for use with high school seniors, college students, and adults; others, with junior high school children. Some are applicable only to students who intend to go to college; others are appropriate for adolescents not bound for college. Some are verbal; others, pictorial. Although research has shown the validity of biographical scales and keys for predicting vocational preferences, psychologists have shown very little interest in incorporating them in their interest inventories.

Some authors, such as Strong (1966), have developed interest inventories on the assumption that interests are not a unitary trait but a complex interaction of many traits. Other authors, such as Kuder (1969), have conceptualized interests as an assortment of unitary traits, and this is reflected in the homogeneity of each of Kuder's interest scales. Still other authors have constructed their interest inventories on the basis of logical validity. In spite of the different construction approaches (criterion keying, homogeneous keying, and logical keying), all interest inventories share the common purpose of assessing an individual's preferences for various activities. Most interest inventories are based on some common assumptions regarding interests: (1) interests, rather than being innate, are learned as a result of the individual's being engaged in an activity; (2) interests tend to be relatively unstable for young children, but after about age 20 they tend to become stabilized, with little change occurring after age 25; (3) people in different occupations share similar likes and dislikes regarding activities; (4) interests vary in intensity from one person to another; and (5) interests motivate the individual to action.

Despite their limitations, in the late 1970s nearly 4 million interest inventories were administered annually (Tittle & Zytowski, 1978), a point which suggests that they are among the most commonly used tests in the country. Considering the fact that these data were gathered about a decade ago, we can estimate that with today's popularity of career development and exploration programs, the number of interest inventories given annually may be approaching the 5 million mark.

Because of space limitations we must restrict our discussion of interest inventories to those most frequently used in our schools. The examples of interest inventories discussed illustrate the different methods of construction and keying (that is, the different constructs of interests).

Empirically Keyed Interest Inventories

Strong-Campbell Interest Inventory (SCII). A revision of the 1974 Strong Vocational Interest Blank, it is published by Stanford University Press (1981). Intended for 14-year-olds and over, it has six General Occupational Themes (GOT), 23 Basic Interest Scales (BIS), and 162 Occupational Scales (OS), of which 99 are entirely new. In addition, it provides three types of Administrative Indexes and two Special Scales. It is untimed but takes from 20 to 60 minutes to complete. There is one form (a Spanish edition is available).

According to a brochure discussing the 1981 revision, the major goals "were to match all extant male-normed Occupational Scales with corresponding new female-normed scales, and vice versa; to obtain new criterion samples for all scales; and to add new occupations. . . . A corollary of these efforts was a comprehensive revision of the Manual'' (Stanford University Press, n.d., p. 1).

The three greatest changes from its predecessor, the Strong Vocational Interest Blank (SVIB), are (1) adopting Holland's Occupational Classification Scheme as a theoretical framework for interpreting the test scores, (2) merging the men's and women's forms, and (3) developing homogeneous scales (the Basic Interest Scales and the General Occupational Themes—to be discussed later on). Because of the severe criticism leveled at interest tests in general, and at the Strong Vocational Interest Blank in particular, regarding the SVIB's sex bias (see Campbell, Chrichton, & Webber, 1974; Cole, 1973; Johansson & Harmon, 1972), the 1966 Form for Men and the 1969 Form for Women have been replaced by a single form, the SCII. The SCII is essentially a neuterized version of the SVIB. The SCII uses *both* empirical and homogeneous scales, and "Holland's codes" in interpreting the profile.

The SCII is suitable for older adolescents and adults considering higher-level professional or skilled occupations. The SCII contains 325 items (the *best* items from the original SVIB male and female forms), which are grouped into the following sections:

1. Occupations. Subjects respond in one of three ways—Like (L), Indifferent (I), or Dislike (D)—to each of 131 occupational titles.
2. School Subjects. Test takers indicate their L/I/D to each of 36 school subjects.
3. Activities. Subjects respond L/I/D to each of 51 general occupational activities.
4. Amusements. Subjects indicate their L/I/D to each of 39 hobbies or amusements.
5. Types of People. To each of 24 kinds of people, subjects indicate their L/I/D.
6. Preference Between Activities. For each of 30 pairs of activities, subjects indicate their preference between the activity on the (R)ight, (L)eft, or (?) No Preference.
7. Your Characteristics—a quasi-personality inventory. Subjects respond Yes, No, or ? to each of 14 characteristics/traits as being *self*-descriptive.

The items are both vocational and avocational, the subject responding to most of the items (281) by means of a three-element key: like, dislike, or indifferent. Care was taken to select items that (1) were free from sexual stereotypes (e.g., stewardess); (2) were balanced in terms of favoring one sex over the other (actually, there are a few more items favoring females); (3) were culture free; (4) were neither highly popular nor unpopular; (5) were not influenced or dependent upon previous work experience but on activities that the average adolescent could be expected to know about or at least imagine; (6) covered a wide range of occupational content; (7) were easy to read and comprehend (the SCII has a reading level of about grade 7); and (8) were interesting.

Strong conceived an interest inventory as a group of items that discriminate people in specific occupations from a general group of similar-age subjects (but not in that occupation). To be included in Strong's criterion group (as a member of a specific occupation), the individual had to be between the ages of 25 and 55, employed in that occupation for at least three years, and have indicated a liking for his or her work. For each of the items, the percentage of men (or women) responding "like, dislike, indifferent" was compared with the percentage of "men (or women)-in-general" responding in a similar manner. (The *new* "in-general" sample, now called the General Reference Sample, or GRS, was not selected in as meticulous a fashion as the former reference groups.) The responses were then assigned weights ranging from $+1$ to -1. A person who receives a high score on the engineer scale, say, displays interests similar to engineers in the norming sample. This is not analogous to saying that the individual would like to be an engineer, or would be successful as a professional engineer, or should study engineering in college. Rather, the test score indicates only the similarity of interests shared by the subject and the engineers selected in the norming sample.

The General Occupational Themes based on Holland's typology provide an organizing structure that aids the counselor in interpreting the Basic Interest Scales and Occupational Scales (see Figures 9.1 and 9.2). Holland (1973) has developed an occupational-classification system that postulates that people can be categorized in terms of six types—realistic, investigative, artistic, social, enterprising, or conventional—such that each person is characterized by one, or some combination, of these types. Now, instead of talking to counselors in terms of over 100 different occupations and/or clusters, the counselor can provide the counselees with a global picture of their occupational orientation. High scores on the GOT scales *suggest* the general kind of activities the counselees will enjoy, the type of occupational environment where they will be most comfortable, the kinds of activities they will be most willing to deal with, and the kinds of persons who will be found most appealing as co-workers. Research indicates that the themes possess adequate validity and short-term (30-day) stability.

The Basic Interest Scales, like the GOTs, aid the user in obtaining a better understanding of the Occupational Scales. Because of the heterogeneity of the occupational scales, the authors collected items into somewhat homogeneous subsets and refer to these subsets as BIS (there are 23 of them grouped under Holland's six themes, with one to five items in each theme; see Figure 9.1). Some of the BIS categories are Public Speaking, Office Practices, and Religious Activities. It was felt that the BIS would be more easily understood than the occupational scales (because one interprets a homogeneous

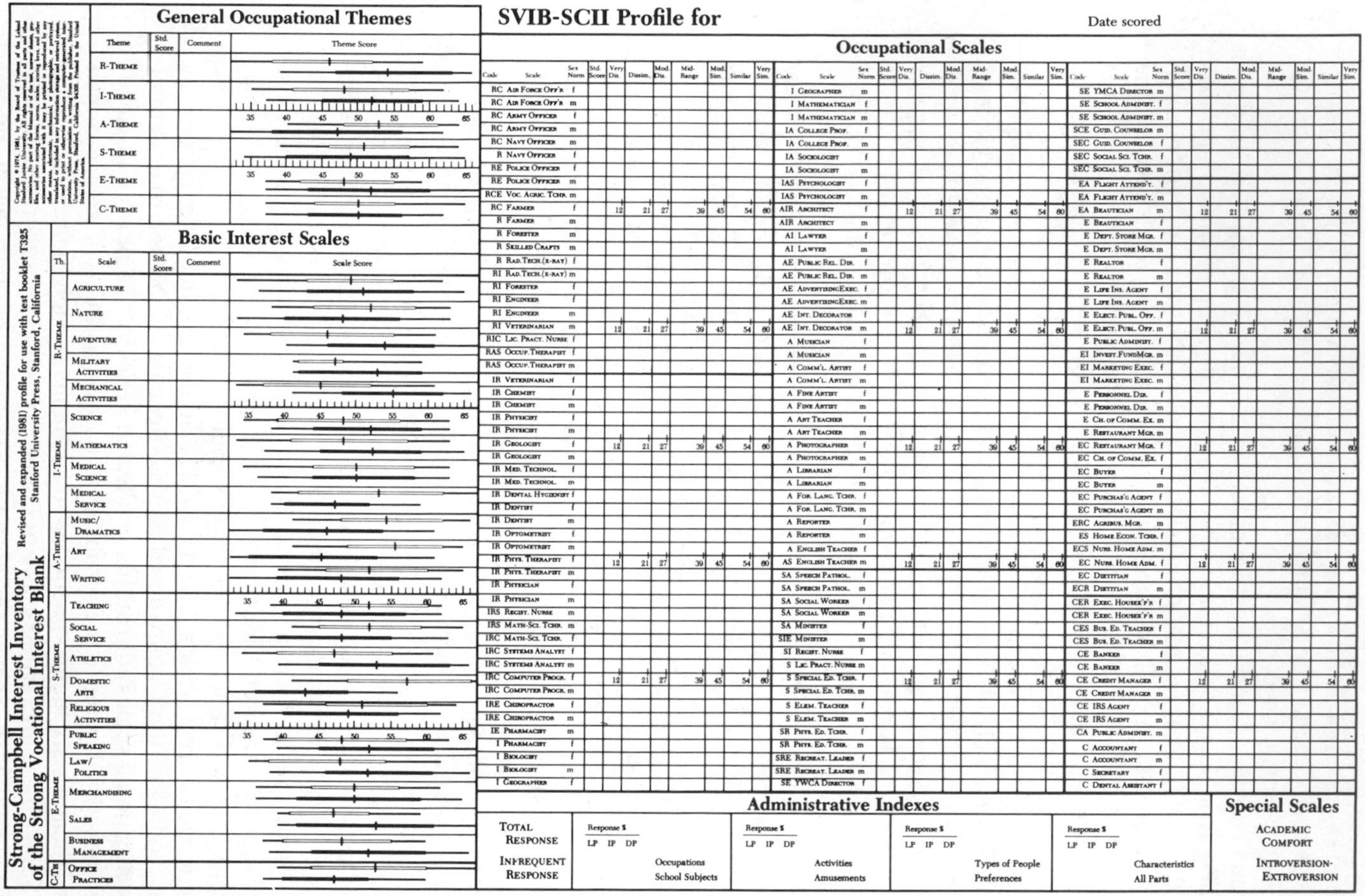

Figure 9.1 *Profile of scores on the Strong-Campbell Interest Inventory.* (Adapted by Consulting Psychologists Press from the profile in the *Manual for the Strong-Campbell Interest Inventory*, Third Edition, by David P. Campbell and Jo-Ida C. Hansen, with the permission of the publishers, Stanford University Press, Copyright © 1974, 1981 by the Board of Trustees of the Leland Stanford Junior University.)

set of items) and would reduce the need for endless revisions of the existing occupational scales. Since the BIS constitute a major focus in interpreting the SCII—they are to be inspected first because this is the "most important interpretive step" (Campbell, 1969, p. 22)—it is essential that more empirical evidence be presented to demonstrate the relationship between the BIS and the earlier SVIB occupational scales, as well as between BIS and the GOT. Despite their brevity BIS are highly reliable over short time periods.

The *Occupational Scales* (there are 162) are the most valid and reliable scales of the SCII and have been the bulwark of the Strong since it was first published in 1927. Because of societal changes, many modifications were made for the 1981 revision. For example, 12 new occupations (24 scales) have been added to the profile. Of the new scales, 17 are female scales developed to match existing male scales (for instance, chiropractor, forester), and 11 new male scales have been developed to match existing female scales (for example, flight attendant, physical education teacher). Other changes made in the 1981 revision are as follows: The profile scores are organized into Holland's system, new In-General samples have been drawn, criteria for selecting and weighting the items for a specific occupation have been modified from the earlier rules, and new norms have been prepared. Although the ultimate goal is to have male and female samples for each criterion group, this still has not been achieved (four scales are normed only for males; and four only for females) because it is difficult to obtain a sufficiently large number of women in some occupations (for example, pilot), or of men in others (for instance, secretary). Nevertheless, there are 77 matched-pair scales (based on *both* male- and female-normed groups), more than double the number in the 1974 SCII. Of the 325 items in the 1981 SCII, only two are competely new; 180 items are common to both of the earlier booklets; 74 appeared only on the Men's form; and 69 appeared only on the Women's form. In the earlier editions, each sex had its own booklet and scoring keys. In the SCII, the counselor has the option of scoring the inventory on either the male scales, the female scales, or both, and interpreting the scores accordingly. Campbell & Hansen (1981) contend that separately normed scales should be used if one wishes to maximize validity. The profile is organized so that scores on both same-sex and opposite-sex scales can be represented. In this way, all scores are available, but at the same time normative information appropriate for each sex is presented.

In addition to the GOT, BIS, and OS previously discussed, there are two empirically derived Special (nonoccupational) scales to detect response-set problems, careless test taking, and scoring errors. These are Academic Comfort (AC) and Introversion-Extroversion (IE). Further, there are three types of Administrative Indexes (AI): Total Responses (TR), Infrequent Responses (IR), and like percentage, dislike percentage, and indifferent percentage (LP, DP, and IP).

The AC replaces the former Academic Achievement scale and is a "mea-

STRONG VOCATIONAL INTEREST BLANK
STRONG–CAMPBELL INTEREST INVENTORY RESULTS FOR

** CHARLOTTE HANSEN **

 THE FOLLOWING STATISTICAL RESULTS HAVE BEEN COMPILED FROM YOUR
ANSWERS TO THIS INVENTORY.

THREE TYPES OF INFORMATION ARE PRESENTED—

    1) YOUR SCORES ON 6 GENERAL OCCUPATIONAL THEMES. THESE GIVE
       SOME IDEA OF YOUR OVERALL OCCUPATIONAL OUTLOOK.

    2) YOUR SCORES IN 23 BASIC INTEREST AREAS. THESE SHOW THE CON-
       SISTENCY, OR LACK OF IT, OF YOUR INTERESTS IN EACH OF THESE
       SPECIFIC AREAS.

    3) YOUR SCORES ON 162 OCCUPATIONAL SCALES. THESE TELL YOU HOW
       SIMILAR YOUR INTERESTS ARE TO THOSE OF EXPERIENCED WORKERS
       IN THE DESIGNATED OCCUPATIONS.

 FIRST, A CAUTION. THERE IS NO MAGIC HERE. THIS REPORT WILL GIVE
YOU SOME SYSTEMATIC INFORMATION ABOUT YOURSELF BUT YOU SHOULD
NOT EXPECT MIRACLES. YOUR SCORES ARE BASED SIMPLY ON WHAT YOU
SAID YOU LIKED OR DISLIKED.

 MOST IMPORTANTLY—THIS TEST DOES NOT MEASURE YOUR ABILITIES—
IT IS CONCERNED ONLY WITH YOUR INTERESTS.

THE GENERAL OCCUPATIONAL THEMES

 PSYCHOLOGICAL RESEARCH HAS SHOWN THAT OCCUPATIONS CAN BE
GROUPED INTO SIX GENERAL THEMES. ALTHOUGH THESE ARE CRUDE, THEY
DO PROVIDE USEFUL GUIDELINES. HERE IS AN ANALYSIS OF HOW YOUR
INTERESTS COMPARE WITH EACH OF THESE THEMES—

R–THEME–THIS TYPE IS RUGGED, ROBUST, PRACTICAL, STRONG, AND
          FREQUENTLY AGGRESSIVE IN OUTLOOK. THEY HAVE GOOD
          PHYSICAL SKILLS BUT SOMETIMES HAVE TROUBLE COMMUNI-
          CATING THEIR FEELINGS TO OTHERS. THEY LIKE TO WORK OUT-
          DOORS AND WITH TOOLS, ESPECIALLY WITH LARGE POWERFUL
          MACHINES. THEY PREFER TO DEAL WITH THINGS RATHER THAN

Figure 9.2 SVIB-SCII interpretive profile, sample generated and printed by computer (first sheet only)

sure of probable persistence in an academic setting'' rather than a predictor
of grades. The IE replaces the former Occupational Introversion-Extroversion scale. The IE scale provides useful clinical information and has been
shown to discriminate successfully between people-oriented and non-peo-
ple-oriented occupations. The TR index indicates the total number of responses marked and suggests action only if it is less than 310. The IR index is

WITH IDEAS OR PEOPLE. THEY USUALLY HAVE CONVENTIONAL
POLITICAL AND ECONOMIC OPINIONS, LIKE TO CREATE THINGS
WITH THEIR HANDS, AND PREFER OCCUPATIONS SUCH AS ME-
CHANIC, LABORATORY TECHNICIAN, SOME ENGINEERING SPE-
CIALTIES, FARMER, OR POLICE OFFICER. THE TERM "REAL-
ISTIC" IS USED TO SUMMARIZE THIS PATTERN, THUS,
R-THEME.

YOUR ANSWERS SHOW THAT FOR YOUR SEX YOU ARE HIGH IN
THESE CHARACTERISTICS AS YOUR STANDARD SCORE WAS 57.

COPYRIGHT © 1974, 1981 BY THE BOARD OF TRUSTEES OF THE LELAND
STANFORD JUNIOR UNIVERSITY. ALL RIGHTS RESERVED IN ALL PARTS AND
ACCESSORIES. NO PART OF THE MANUAL OR OF THE TEST, ANSWER SHEETS,
PROFILES, AND OTHER SCORING FORMS, NORMS, SCALES, SCOPING KEYS,
AND OTHER ACCESSORIES ASSOCIATED WITH IT MAY BE PRINTED OR REPRO-
DUCED BY ANY OTHER MEANS, ELECTRONIC, MECHANICAL, OR PHOTO-
GRAPHIC, OR PORTRAYED, TRANSLATED, OR INCLUDED IN ANY INFORMA-
TION STORAGE AND RETRIEVAL SYSTEM, OR USED TO PRINT OR OTHERWISE
REPRODUCE A COMPUTER-GENERATED INTERPRETATION, WITHOUT PER-
MISSION IN WRITING FROM THE PUBLISHER, STANFORD UNIVERSITY
PRESS, STANFORD, CALIFORNIA 94305. PRINTED IN THE UNITED STATES
OF AMERICA.

Figure 9.2   (*continued*)

based on responses infrequently selected by the GRS. The purpose of the IR
index is to identify the responses that may be incorrectly marked. Although
a high score suggests that a problem exists, it does *not* indicate *why*. The LP,
DP, and IP indices are used to detect errors that *might* be the result of
incorrect scoring, a mismarked answer sheet, or misunderstood directions.
On the other hand, they might indicate the subject's response style. In any
event, the three AIs should be checked *before* attempting to interpret an
examinee's scores on any of the other scales, since the AIs provide a preliminary check on the validity of the responses.

Reference is made in the manual to the validity and reliability of the
various scales of the SCII. Since the bulk of the data are based on the SVIB,
they are found in the *Handbook* (Campbell, 1971), which contains a cornucopia of information that should be *required* reading for every SCII user.
Additional technical information is found in the SVIB/SCII Manual (Campbell & Hansen, 1981). On inspection, the items appear to have good face
validity, and the reliability and criterion-related evidences presented are
acceptable. The BIS have lower concurrent and predictive validity than the
Occupational Scales, which have higher internal consistency but slightly
lower consistency over time. The predictive validity of the SCII (which can
be inferred from research with the SVIB) is equally good for very able black

and white students. The SVIB did *not* demonstrate any racial bias (Borgen, 1972; Borgen & Harper, 1973).

The 1981 manual contains case studies illustrating both common and unusual profiles as well as a user's guide for determining the Holland codes across the scales. The manual clearly states that separate sex norms should be used "as a means of expanding options, not limiting them (Campbell & Hansen, 1981, p. 81). Another change from the previous procedure is to report cross-gender occupational scale scores both numerically and graphically rather than just numerically. If there is one area in which the manual can be faulted it is in its inattentiveness to how interest inventories can be effectively used in counseling.

The SCII can be scored only by computer agencies licensed by the publisher. Since some of these commercial firms may process certain types of answer sheets (namely their own) more efficiently than others or score only their own, users of the SCII should check with the scoring agency before administering the test. To assist the teacher, counselor, or student in interpreting the test scores, raw scores on the BIS and OS are converted to T scores. A computer-generated, printed interpretive profile is also provided. In addition, the SCII profile has, for the BIS, bars printed to represent the middle-half or the GRS distribution; for each occupation, there is a shaded area to represent the "average" range (see Figures 9.1 and 9.2). These "bands" should assist in making decisions about the significance of an interest score.

In summary, the SCII contains the "best" from the most recent revisions of the SVIB. The SCII is about 20 percent shorter than the SVIB; items have been reworded so that the grammar and vocabulary are neutral; only one form is used for both men and women; sexual stereotypes have been removed; the distribution of items favoring one sex over the other has been roughly balanced; the scoring has been altered so that both sexes can be scored on the same booklet; scores on the profile have been reorganized into Holland's occupational classification system; the number of occupations has been increased; there are new administrative indexes; greater emphasis is placed on the Basic Interest Scales; the profile sheet has been redesigned; and hand scoring is no longer possible. The SCII is characterized by careful construction with up-to-date, unambiguous, low reading-ability-needed items. Some questions or potential problems are as follows. (1) Will the fact that the printed standard score is based on the combined male-female sample, whereas the printed interpretive statement is based on the distribution of scores for the examiner's sex, result in confusion? (2) What effect, if any, does the sampling design used to develop the new general-reference groups have on the validity of the Occupational Scales? It is evident from the material presented in the manual that further research is underway. (3) Does the fact that the items making up the individual scales are not reported (for security reasons) constitute a prohibition on research dealing with the test's psychometric properties? (4) Where is the evidence to support the claim made in the manual that those persons with high AC scores will be comfortable in an academic environment? (5) There is very little validity evidence for the IE scale. Despite the weaknesses noted, we believe the SCII to be the best vocational interest inventory available for those seeking managerial and professional occupations. Readers interested in a thorough critique of the 1981 edition should see Borgen & Bernard (1982) and Lilly (1984).

Minnesota Vocational Interest Inventory (MVII). Published by the Psychological Corporation (1965), it contains one form. There are two editions. One is intended for high school males and one for adult males. Although it is untimed, it takes about 45 minutes to administer. It has 21 occupational scales and nine "homogeneous" scales (of highly intercorrelated items) similar to the BIS of the SCII. Designed for those people who do not aspire to professional vocations, it has a reading level at about ninth grade.

The MVII suffers from an inadequate standardization and although published in 1965, it still has too few empirical studies to support any real claim for validity and reliability. It is easy to administer and score; the quality and format are good; many counselors' suggestions are contained in the manual; and it can be used with ninth-graders, although it must be recognized that the interest of young teenagers may still not be crystallized.

We have some serious reservations about the wisdom of providing the examinee with a profile sheet for self-interpretation of the MVII, even though the intent and scales are described with clarity and appropriate caution. Why should we sanction the opportunity for distortion? All in all, teachers and counselors in systems where the majority of students enter into skilled or semiskilled nonprofessional occupations might wish to consider the MVII.

Kuder Occupational Interest Survey (OIS), Form DD. Published by Science Research Associates (1964), it replaces the Kuder Preference Record Occupational (Form D). Manual and interpretive leaflet were revised in 1982 and 1979 respectively. It is intended for high school students and adults. There is one form. It is untimed, but takes about 30 minutes to complete. The vocabulary level is at about the sixth grade. There are 30 core scales, 126 occupational scales—e.g., bookkeeper, chemist, farmer—52 with male norms only, 20 with female norms only, and 54 (27 occupations) with *both* male and female norm groups. It covers 48 college majors—e.g., nursing, architecture—divided into 29 male and 19 female groups. In 1979, the first five of a number of additional scales with emphasis on nontraditional occupations were added.

In each of 100 triads of activities, the examinee selects the one most liked and least liked. The OIS has a verification key that can assist the counselor in ascertaining how honest and careful the examinee was in responding to the inventory. Although Kuder contends that the OIS scores are related to vocational maturity, no evidence is presented to support this (Stahmann & Matheson, 1973). Reliability evidence is satisfactory.

It should be noted that the OIS differs from the SCII in that it does not use a general reference group, as was done in all the Strong inventories. Rather, in the OIS, responses were correlated with membership in occupational groups.

The OIS has been carefully constructed and includes some features not found in other tests. It contains a well-written interpretive leaflet for the examinee. The 1979 manual is well written and contains some useful suggestions for the counselor. There are separate norms for men and women. The discussion on the development of the test and the description of the criterion groups are clear and should be valuable to the counselor considering the use of the OIS. A major advantage of the OIS is that new scales are being added continuously and the manual is periodically revised. A major disadvantage of the test is that it can be scored only by the publisher.

In comparison to the SCII, the Kuder DD has the following advantages: (1) scoring of college-major interests, (2) a broader range of occupations (more technical and trade level), and (3) scores for females on selected men's occupational and college-major scales. The major advantages of the SCII are that it shows more evidence of predictive validity (Zytowski, 1976), has more reliability data, and is easier to interpret (although the data presented in the 1979 manual indicate that the differences are lessening considerably). Studies have shown congruent validity between the same and similarly named scales of the OIS and SCII (Johnson, 1971; Zytowski, 1972). However, although the SCII and OIS have some similarly named scales, under *no* circumstances should they be interpreted in the same way (Kuder, 1969; Lefkowitz, 1970), because they were designed for different purposes and measure a different domain of interests. O'Shea & Harrington (1971) go even further and say that both instruments should *not* be used with the same client, since the results may serve only to confuse the undecided even further. And, like the SCII but unlike other interest inventories, the same form is used for both men and women. The OIS also resembles the SCII somewhat, in that those occupations which present opportunities for either sex (for example, medicine) report scores on the basis of data for the male groups. In fact, the new report form should make cross-sex interpretation much simpler.

Homogeneous Keyed Inventories

Kuder General Interest Survey (GIS), Form E.   Published by Science Research Associates, it was revised in 1976. It covers grades 6 through 12. There is one form. Although it is untimed, it takes about 1 hour to administer. It provides 11 scores, one of which is a verification score.

The GIS is suitable for students in grades 6–12, and research is under way to ascertain its validity for adults. It is intended to stimulate career exploration and suggest career possibilities. The GIS compares the examinees' interests in activities in 10 broad occupational/vocational areas with the interests of a national sample of persons in grades 6–12. Its reading level is sufficiently low to permit its use with high school students who have a limited vocabulary. The GIS consists of 552 statements grouped into 184 triads. The subject selects the statement or activity liked "most" and the one liked "least" in each of the triads. Kuder (1966) contends that the scoring is such that the GIS is not a purely ipsative scale, even though it is of a forced-choice format. Kuder (1966) offers some rational arguments concerning the nonipsative nature of the GIS, but we feel he has stretched the point in his argument. The GIS has been constructed with younger people in mind: (1) It has a vocabulary that is at the sixth-grade level; (2) it attempts to avoid using occupational titles (the meanings associated with them are relatively unstable, especially for younger people). The GIS differs from the Kuder Occupational Interest Survey and the SCII in that it expresses vocational preferences only as cluster areas rather than specific occupational choices (and this makes it better suited for younger people who either have limited experiential background or are not yet ready to focus on specific occupational exploration. There are 10 occupational scales: outdoor, mechanical, computational, scientific, persuasive, artistic, literary, musical, social service, and clerical. There is also a verification scale. The number of items assigned to a particular scale varies from 16 in the musical scale to 70 in the persuasive scale. Because the scales do not contain an equal number of items, the raw scores not only *can* vary from individual to individual but also *do* vary from one scale to another. Although this may not confuse the trained counselor, it will probably confuse the student because the GIS can supposedly be self-administered, self-scored, and self-interpreted.

The activities referred to in the inventory are biased in favor of middle-class American values. Only a few items relate to activities which the underprivileged could be expected to experience. This strongly suggests that the GIS not be used in poverty areas or in schools in which a major proportion of their pupils come from a racial or economic ghetto. Although homogeneous keying attempts to produce scales that have highly intracorrelated items but low intercorrelations (among the scales), we are unable to explain some of the intercorrelations among the scales. For example, should there be a substantial correlation between the musical and the artistic interest scales? Even with an ipsative scale where one obtains low intertest correlations, we would expect to find correlations higher than .02 or .03 between the musical and artistic scales. Inasmuch as the profile leaflet encourages self-interpretation, this dependence upon the relatedness (or unrelatedness) of the constructs measured can result in misuse and should be clarified.

The validity data for the GIS resembles that presented for its predecessor (Kuder Form C)—that is, it is woefully inadequate with respect to specific occupational criterion data.

The reliability estimates provided are in terms of stability data and Kuder-Richardson measures of internal consistency. The average test–retest (six-week-interval) correlations for boys and girls are .50 and .43, respectively. This would therefore severely limit the use of the GIS for making individual predictions. It would be of value to have data demonstrating whether over a longer period of time the highest scores tend to remain high and the lowest scores tend to remain low. Such data are especially significant in vocational and educational counseling.

There are separate sex norms (and profile sheets) for grades 6–8 and 9–12. This makes it possible for members of each sex to compare their interests with others who have similar role-sex experiences. The normative data are adequately presented in the manual. The descriptions of the sampling procedures used and the nature of the standardization sample are clear. The publishers exercised care in attempting to obtain a fairly representative sample, although some of the geographical regions are slightly under- or over-represented.

Percentile scores can be plotted on *both* the male and the female profile forms. Raw scores are converted to percentiles, and these percentile scores are then used to prepare the test profile. This procedure does not eliminate the possibility that the reported score may be an inaccurate representation of the subject's interest. For example, an individual can obtain a high percentile score and still have little interest in the area, and vice versa, because of the ipsative nature of the scales. This makes us somewhat uncomfortable, since the author suggests that a PR (Percentile Rank) of 75 or greater or 25 or less on the GIS scale be interpreted as a high and low interest respectively, in those areas.

A somewhat disturbing feature of the profile leaflet is the description of the various interest areas. Specific references are made to occupations or vocations, and these occupations are then grouped within a larger interest cluster. For example, in defining a persuasive interest the publishers say that most salespeople, personnel managers, and buyers have high persuasive interest. Yet no empirical evidence is presented in the manual to support such a claim. For this reason we feel that the user should exercise extreme caution in interpreting the test profile. We further suggest that because of possible misinterpretation of the profile leaflet (especially by younger pupils), the counselor or teacher does the actual interpretation.

In conclusion, we are pleased that an attempt has been made to measure the interests of younger people in the Kuder General Interest Survey. Our knowledge of the development and stability of interests is not complete, but this should not dissuade us from trying to measure them. Our interest, however, in the development of such an inventory should not cause us to sacrifice quality. For the early high school years, the GIS may be appropriate, but for older high school students who aspire to college, the new SCII appears to be superior.

Vocational Preference Inventory (VPI).   Published by Consulting Psychologists Press (1970), the inventory is in its sixth revision. There is one form. The VPI can be used for persons 14 years of age and older. It is self-administering and untimed, but takes from 15 to 30 minutes to complete. The inventory yields 11 scores—6 of which (Realistic, Intellectual, Social, Conventional, Enterprising, and Artistic) measure specific interests and relate them to learning environments; and 5 of which (Self-Control, Masculinity, Status, Infrequency, and Acquiescence) yield information about the subject's personality. Holland states that "its most desirable use" is as a "brief screening inventory" for high school and college students and for employed adults.

The rationale underlying Holland's VPI is that our environment can be classified into six types of combinations and that humans can also be classified into one or a combination of these six types. Holland claims that people of a particular type seek out a compatible environment of that same type, thereby giving us a person-environment match. The goodness of the match between the person and his environment depends upon a variety of factors.

The subject responds to each of the 160 occupational titles presented in terms of a "Yes" (interest in that occupation) or "No" (lack of interest in that occupation) format. The highest score represents a dominant personality type; the four highest scores yield a personality interest pattern.

The test–retest reliabilities are moderate to high (.62 to .98) but have been computed on very small samples. Internal-consistency coefficients for eight of the scales range from .64 to .89, suggesting that their content is relatively homogeneous. The other three scales—Masculinity, Status, and Infrequency—have low internal consistency estimates, which Holland claims is to be expected.

Most of the validity studies cited by Holland (1973) are of the construct, concurrent, and predictive type and indicate that (1) the VPI scales measure essentially similar constructs to some of those assessed by the California Psychological Inventory, the MMPI, and the SCII; (2) the VPI scores differentiate between men and women, persons in different occupations, and normal and abnormal people; (3) students' self-descriptions are consistent with their scale scores; and (4) VPI scores are correlated with such things as supervisor's ratings, choice of vocation, choice of major field, and psychiatric versus nonpsychiatric patients. Although the validity studies are highly favorable (Lucy, 1976; McLaughlin & Tiedeman, 1974; Toenjes & Borgen, 1974), more research is needed (and no doubt will be conducted) on noncollege persons. (Much of Holland's original research was conducted with National Merit Scholars, a very bright group. It is conceivable that a more heterogeneous group might yield different results.)

Generally, the numerous validity studies lend support to Holland's hypothesis of the relationship between occupational preferences and personality, as well as to the meaning of the scales (Cole & Hanson, 1971; Folsom, 1973). Three major limitations of the VPI are that (1) there appears to be a sex bias, with many of the occupational titles not being appropriate for women; (2) the VPI, unlike the SCII or OIS, does *not* give subjects information on how their likes or dislikes compare with those of people in other occupations; and (3) some of the younger students might not be familiar with occupational titles such as Speculator or Financial Analyst. Two additional limitations are that (1) there is some question whether the Acquiescence scale is valid (Jacobs, 1972) and (2) as already mentioned, the subjects Holland used in the development of his instrument were very homogeneous.

The manual is very good and outlines a clinical interpretation for each scale, presents a conceptual definition for each variable, and discusses some actual case studies.

The VPI is a very promising scale. It is quick, nonthreatening, and somewhat enjoyable to take. It is based on the hypothesis that individuals' choice of an occupation is an expression of their personality (that is, the subjects "project" themselves into an occupational title, thereby making the VPI a structured personality inventory as well as an occupational-interest inventory); that personal stability, career satisfaction, or stable career pattern depends greatly on the "goodness of fit" between individuals' personalities and the environment in which they work; that each occupation has an environment characteristic of the people in it; and that people in a particular vocation have similar personalities. These assumptions have been tested, and the data generally support Holland's thesis.

Holland's theory (and hence the VPI) differs markedly from the conception of interests held by others such as Strong and Kuder. And, as Campbell (1974) states, "Holland's ideas have already had a substantial impact on research in the areas of vocational counseling, the measurement of interests, and occupational typology." It is our belief, however, that Holland's Self-Directed Search and VIESA (Vocational, Interest, Experience, and Skill Assessment) are much better than the SCII and OIS for vocational planning with younger people. (VIESA is discussed in a later section.)

Logically Keyed Interest Inventories

Ohio Vocational Interest Survey, Second Edition, (OVIS II).   Published by the Psychological Corporation, it was revised in 1981. It covers grades 7-12, college, and adult. There is one form and one level. Untimed, it usually takes about 35 to 60 minutes to administer. It has 23 scales.

The OVIS II is a popular, well-constructed, and well-standardized vocational interest inventory for use with high school and college students, and adults. The rationale underlying the development of the OVIS was based on the *Dictionary of Occupational Titles' (DOT)*[5] cubistic model of involvement of data, people, and things. The OVIS II consists of three parts: (1) a student information questionnaire of six items—one requiring the student to indicate first and second choices from 23 job descriptions, one asking for first and second choices of school subjects liked, one on the type of high school program enrolled in (or contemplated), two questions on future plans, and one item of the student's first and second choices of 32 high school business and vocational programs (for example, bookkeeping, appliance repair, drafting); (2) a local survey information section, in which the user is given an opportunity to ask one to 18 questions of local concern or interest; and (3) an interest inventory. The interest inventory consists of 253 items (based on the fourth edition of the *DOT*), which are grouped into clusters of five or six items. All items are scored jointly for males and females (a departure from the first edition). The 253 items used were based on refinement of the 114 homogeneous areas of the *DOT* into 23 broad-interest categories (scales), with each scale being represented by 11 homogeneous items.[6] Of the 23 scales, 18 are common to both men and women, and five contain items differentiated by sex. To each item, the subject responds by means of a five-element key: would like the activity very much, would like, neutral, would dislike, and would dislike very much. The responses are weighted +5 to +1 respectively. Hence a subject's score on any one scale may vary from 11 to 55.

Although the *DOT* model has three levels for each of data, people, and things for a total of 27 cells, the OVIS II has only 23 scales. The missing four scales have been purposefully omitted, since the OVIS scales are based only on the real world of work, and in the *real* world some jobs would never exist in a practical sense, although they could be portrayed theoretically.

Five of the cells are represented by two or more scales, because it was found that to describe accurately the job groups represented—a combination of data-people-things—one would have to use two (or more) scales rather than one.

Extensive and detailed planning went into the development and standardization of the original and revised OVIS. The authors are to be commended for their painstaking efforts in developing and standardizing the OVIS and OVIS II.

Although predictive and concurrent validity are of value in interest inventories, no such data are presented. Construct validity was illustrated, and a

[5] Published by the United States Employment Service (USES); contains descriptions of virtually all occupations.

[6] The elaborate procedure used to select items and to develop the scales is thoroughly described in the manual.

mimeographed supplement from the publisher describes the scales in detail. However, if, as the manual states, validity is to be assessed by determining the extent to which realistic plans for the student's future are developed, then evidence *must* be presented to demonstrate this. We realize that longitudinal data are needed for some types of validity (especially to determine the long-range utility of the OVIS), but criterion-related validity could and should have been presented before the test was published, even if only on the experimental editions. The OVIS is not the only culprit. Many test publishers place their product on the market before satisfying the minimal standards adopted by the APA-AERA-NCME Committee on Test Standards (see American Psychological Association, 1985).

Reliability was ascertained by means of stability estimates. Lacking in the manual are internal-consistency estimates.

Normative data—including means, standard deviations, and scores at five different percentile points—are reported for each scale by sex, grade, and geographical region. Each student's raw scores, percentiles, stanines, and clarity indices (a clarity index on a given scale indicates the degree of consistency in responses to the 11 job activities on that scale) are available to the student in a personalized report folder. (As we commented for the MVII, we question the advisability of such an approach, especially for interest inventories.)

All in all, the OVIS may well be one of the best interest tests of the future, inasmuch as so much attention is placed on entering occupations as depicted by the *DOT*. Most of the problems discussed—including absence of validity data—can be remedied. We are confident that they will be. The major question to which the test authors must address themselves surrounds the rationale and implementation of the data-people-things model of interests.

Work Values Inventory (WVI).   Published by Riverside Press (1970), the inventory contains one form and covers grades 7 through college and adult. It measures 15 values (for instance, independence, creativity, altruism) deemed significant for vocational satisfaction and success. Although it is untimed, it takes 10 to 15 minutes to complete. Super (the WVI author) believes that interests are related to values and that we must be concerned with the factors that motivate people to work. The values measured are *extrinsic to* and *intrinsic in* work. The WVI contains 45 items (developed from job satisfaction research) to which the subject responds by means of a five-point scale. Content, construct, concurrent, and predictive validity were studied. Test–retest reliability reported for grade 10 only. Although the reliability coefficients are not high (in the low .80s), we must remember that there are only three items per value. Scores are expressed as percentiles. There are separate sex norms for grades 7–12 only. We would prefer more psychometric data before recommending the WVI for individual counseling.

Comparisons Among Selected Interest Inventories   There is very little difference, if any, among the various interest inventories with respect to their general purpose. All are concerned with an assessment of likes and dislikes for various occupations so that the examinee, with the help of a trained counselor, will be encouraged to engage in career exploration activities and, based on all the data acquired, can make more valid decisions regarding future educational or vocational plans than if interest inventory data were not available. There are, however, some marked differences between the various standardized interest inventories with respect to their method of construction, scoring, ease of administration, and ease of interpretation. Also, they differ in the grade level at which they can be used. We will now consider briefly the inventories previously discussed. (Those interested in a very comprehensive treatment of the purpose, method of construction, technical features, and interpretations possible of the inventories discussed here, except the SCII, should see Zytowski, 1973.)

Method of Construction.   The Strong-Campbell Interest Inventory (SCII), Minnesota Vocational Interest Inventory (MVII), and Kuder Occupational Interest Survey (OIS) employed criterion keying (contrasted groups). The SCII and MVII used as their criterion groups men-and-women-in-general, whereas the OIS compared the examinees' responses with the modal responses of those persons in each occupation and in each college major. The Work Values Inventory (WVI), and the Ohio Vocational Interest Survey, second edition (OVIS II) employed logical keying. The Kuder General Interest Survey (GIS) and the Vocational Preference Inventory (VPI) used homogeneous keying.

Grade Level and Content.   The SCII should not be used below junior high school. The OIS should not be used for students who are not at least juniors in high school. The MVII and VPI can be used for pupils in the ninth grade (about 15 or 16 years old). The OVIS can be used with eighth-graders. The WVI can be used for seventh-graders, but the results should be interpreted cautiously. The Kuder GIS can be used for bright sixth-graders.

With respect to content, there is very little difference, if any, between the Kuder OIS and the SCII. They stress activities and interests related to professional occupations and vocations. These inventories, however, differ from the OVIS II and the MVII, which are concerned more with nonprofessional occupations, especially the MVII. Because the OVIS II is based on the *Dictionary of Occupational Titles (DOT)*, it may sample many activities with which the student has little knowledge or experience. The Kuder scales are the only ones that contain a verification key per se, although the SCII has six administrative indices scores to detect examinee errors in responding.

The most marked difference is between the WVI and the other scales in that the WVI is concerned with measuring values, while the other inventories can be thought of as measuring interests per se. On the other hand, the VPI relates one's personality and the job environment to measured interests.

Administration and Scoring.   All interest inventories are untimed, but they take from about 10 to 90 minutes to administer. None requires any formal training for either administration or scoring. All are group-administered. Interest inventories are, in a sense, self-administering.

The inventories discussed here differ markedly in their ease of scoring. The WVI and GIS are relatively easy to score and can be either hand- or machine-scored. The SCII, OVIS II, and OIS are complex to score, and can be scored only by the publisher (SCII can be scored only by companies licensed by the publisher). The MVII and VPI are between the two extremes.

Validity and Reliability.   The degree of confidence that users can place in their interpretation is directly related to both the validity and stability of the instrument(s) employed. The amount of evidence supporting claims for validity and reliability differs among the interest inventories. If one were to conceptualize a continuum running from most to least empirical evidence in support of reliability and validity data, the results would be as depicted in Figure 9.3. Although the Kuder GIS does not have much data to lend support to its predictive validity, it does have a little more than the WVI or OVIS II. It is understandable why OVIS II does not have too much predictive data—it is a relatively new instrument. But at least the authors are cognizant of this and promise that predictive validity data will be forthcoming. Recency cannot be used as an explanation for lack of predictive validity by the authors of the VPI or the WVI.

Interpretation.   One may think that the less complex an inventory, the easier is its interpretation. This does not hold true, at least for interest inventories. All interest inventories are difficult to interpret properly. If they are to be used for more than exploratory purposes, they should be interpreted only by a trained counselor or psychologist. Of the seven inventories discussed earlier, the GIS conveys more general (rather than specific) information and hence may be frustrating to some students. It is one thing to tell Britt that she exhibits the interests shared by chemists or lawyers, but is is something else when you tell her that she has scientific interests. What are scientific inter-

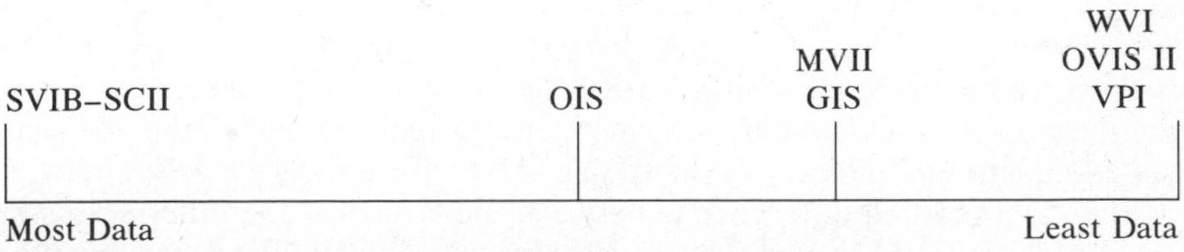

		MVII	WVI OVIS II
SVIB–SCII	OIS	GIS	VPI

Most Data   Least Data

Figure 9.3   Empirical evidence for validity and reliability.

ests? In using the SCII, the OIS, or the MVII, the counselor can be both specific (using the separate occupational scores) and general (using the cluster or area interest scores), but with the GIS, the counselor can be only general in evaluating the examinee's interests. Interpretations of WVI scores are a little different, since the WVI, rather than measuring interests per se, describes the individual's value orientation, and the scores are interpreted in a clinical fashion. The VPI, although it gives an indication of the individual's likes and dislikes for various occupations, may be conceived as being rooted in personality theory to explain one's vocational preferences.

The SCII, OIS, and MVII are better for job orientation because the scores tell one what people in a specific vocation or profession (as well as people in broad areas such as scientific, mechanical, and business) like and dislike. Unlike the GIS, we do not have to infer an individual's interests from a general scale such as personal-social or computational. The OVIS II, because it was constructed according to the *DOT,* is more applicable to specific occupations than is the GIS.

With regard to interpretation, one must keep in mind that the Kuder tests and the MVII, because they are forced-choice inventories, are ipsative scales. This means that the choice of one response automatically results in the rejection of the other(s). In other words, an ipsative scale results in a high score in one scale to be accompanied by a low score in another scale.

The VPI may be more susceptible than the other scales to responses being made in terms of stereotypes that the examinee holds rather than in terms of interests per se. In addition, the OVIS II and MVII are not so applicable to higher-level professional occupations as is either the Kuder OIS or the SCII. In comparison to the MVII, the OVIS II has broader application to the entering occupations described in the *DOT.*

Although similar labels, such as *scientific,* may be attached to scales in the various interest inventories, the counselor must be cautious in inferring that scales having the same designation are measuring exactly the same trait or characteristic. Just as one should not judge a book by its cover, the counselor should not interpret a scale by its name. The counselor must be thoroughly familiar with the test, the operational definitions of the terms used to describe the scale, and the theoretical orientation of the test constructor. All these cautions reinforce our position that, for other than exploratory information, the user be trained in terms of both formal course work and practical experience.

Users of the WVI have been cautioned by Super to avoid ascribing their own meanings to the scores. In interpreting the WVI, the user should look for patterns of scores. For example, a high independence score accompanied by high creativity and intellectual stimulation scores would suggest that the respondent's independence and intellectualism might lead to the pursuit of a research career. But, on the other hand, a high independence score coupled with high variety and economic return scores would suggest that the respondent's independence is of a financial nature, which might lead to satisfaction in selling bonds or life insurance.

The OIS and SCII are relatively unsatisfactory for people entering occupations that are below the professional-managerial level, even though there are many scales that are occupational in nature. Of the two tests, the OIS is more suitable for persons contemplating lower-level occupations. This is not to imply that Kuder and Strong believed the measurement of interests for skilled workers to be futile. Indeed, this was not the case. Strong (1966) went so far as to recommend some inventories to be used with individuals contemplating skilled, nonprofessional occupations. The nature of the research conducted in the development of the Strong and the OIS was such that the inventories are biased in favor of professional and managerial people. Use of either the SCII or the OIS for high school seniors who intend to enter the apprenticeship program of skilled craftsmen is strongly discouraged. In fact, using these inventories for these persons is a misuse (the MVII or OVIS II would be appropriate here).

Other Interest Inventories   Some of the newer interest inventories are the Interest Determination Exploration and Assessment System (IDEAS), the World of Work Inventory (WWI), and the Career Assessment Inventory (CAI), all published by NCS/Interpretive Scoring System. In fact, the IDEAS items were drawn from the CAI item pool. All are designed for use with younger pupils and all are designed to assist students in exploring their vocational interests. They yield from 14 to 60 scores. As is the case with many interest inventories, predictive validity evidence is lacking. Of the three, the CAI is expensive to score and can only be machine-scored. Of the three, the CAI (which is patterned after the SCII) is suited for students seeking careers that do not require a college degree (such as, electronics technician or dental technician). We might go so far as to say that the CAI is for blue-collar workers what the SCII is for professional and business people.

Another example of an interest inventory which is a combination self-assessment/interest inventory is the Harrington-O'Shea Career Decision-Making System, published by the American Guidance Services. In keeping with technological changes, we have been informed that a microcomputer edition is forthcoming.

Two additional interest inventories are the Jackson Vocational Interest Survey (JVIS) and the California Occupational Preference System (COPS). The JVIS resembles the SCII in that they both use empirical and homogeneous keying/construction approaches. However, the JVIS differs markedly from the SCII in that it (1) used construct validity approaches in its development, (2) utilizes *broad* rather than narrow interest areas, (3) reflects a theory-based approach to test construction, and (4) employed sophisticated statistical analysis procedures. The COPS is designed to assist persons (ranging from middle school students to adults) in career decision making. The COPS Professional Interest Inventory is specifically designed for adult and college populations; the COPS II and COPS-R for those with a fourth-grade and a sixth-grade reading level respectively.

Although not considered here in any great detail there are interest inventories for the exceptional child, such as the AAMD-Becker Reading-Free Vocational Interest Inventory for the educable mentally retarded; the Vocational Information and Evaluation Work Samples (VIEWS) for the severely mentally retarded; inventories such as the Wide-Range Interest Opinion Test for those persons who do not read English fluently; and the Jewish Employment Vocational Service Work Sample System (JEVS) for physically and mentally handicapped populations. The psychometric properties of these special inventories do not approach those of other interest inventories. They do show some promise, however, and although they should be interpreted with extreme caution, they fill a void in a vital area of assessment. Those wishing thorough but succinct reviews of these and other inventories for special populations should consult Kapes & Mastie (1982).

In addition to these interest inventories, there are some children's interest scales such as the Career Awareness Inventory and the Interest Inventory for Elementary Grades. There are also a limited number of interest inventories such as the Geist Picture Interest Inventory for use with the culturally and educationally disadvantaged.

Summary of Types of Interest Inventories   In summary, there are both similarities and differences among the various interest inventories. Although Kuder and Strong originally approached the measurement of interests differently, their inventories are now very similar—Strong adopting the interest clusters advocated by Kuder and Kuder adopting the specific interest areas used by Strong. There is, however, very little difference, if any, among the various interest inventories with respect to their general purpose. All are concerned with an assessment of a person's likes and dislikes for various occupations so that the examinee, with the help of a trained counselor, can make more valid decisions regarding future educational or vocational plans than if interest inventory data were not available. There are, however, some marked differences between the various standardized interest inventories with respect to their method of construction, scoring, ease of administration, and ease of interpretation. They differ in the types of reports produced and the ancillary materials accompanying them. They differ in the grade level at which they can be used. And they differ with respect to their validity, especially predictive validity, and the data used to support their claim to validity. Those interested in a very comprehensive treatment of the possible purpose, method of construction, technical features, and interpretations of the various vocational guidance instruments, assessment programs, and interest inventories for special populations in addition to those discussed here should consult Zytowski (1973) and Kapes & Mastie (1982).

Using Interest Inventory Results

As might be expected, the greatest utility of interest inventory results is for guidance and counseling—occupational, educational, and personal. (For a discussion on the use of tests for career guidance and counseling, see the July 1982 issue of *Measurement and Evaluation in Guidance*.) Used appropriately, the scores of these tests may help individuals crystallize their interests by encouraging them to think about their future plans, or may clarify some misconceptions that individuals have about future occupational or vocational goals. It should be stressed here that it is not the test scores per se that help achieve this self-discovery. It is the professional interpretation made of the test scores. Those who interpret interest test scores must be thoroughly trained and familiar with interest inventories: their uses and misuses, their fallibility, and their general value in helping make sound educational and vocational decisions.

Before considering the various instructional and guidance uses of inventory test results by educators, we feel that it is appropriate to summarize what research has shown regarding the nature of interests and interest inventories.

1. Interests tend to become progressively more stable with age (particularly after adolescence), but they are never permanently fixed. Although a broad area of interest, such as medicine, may not change, there can be a shift in a person's interests regarding general practice versus specialization or regarding different specialties. Using interest inventory results to counsel students who are not yet high school juniors into making specific vocational decisions is to be discouraged, because interests are changeable at this age. This does not mean that interest inventory results for adolescents are not reliable. On the contrary. Although the interests of adults tend to be more stable than those of adolescents, the test–retest correlations for adolescents are substantial (Kleinberg, 1976; Dolliver & Will, 1977). Interest test scores can and should be used in discussions about various occupations and professions. Only the Strong has demonstrated empirically that its results are quite reliable (in terms of long-term stability) for individuals around age 25.

2. Interest inventories are susceptible to response set and faking, some more so than others. The user should therefore interpret the results of interest inventories accordingly.

3. Interest inventory scores can be affected by the ambiguity of the questions asked. For example, two people may respond to the item "Like to play

bridge" in the same way but for different reasons. One person may answer "Like" because it affords him an opportunity to meet people and establish future contacts, even though he may dislike bridge. Another person might answer "Like" for different reasons. She may like bridge because of the challenge it offers; yet this person might not like people and may generally avoid them. Responses to interest inventory items are relative rather than absolute indicators of likes and dislikes. It is of vital importance that interest inventories be carefully constructed so as to remove the influence of ambiguity as much as possible.

4. Interest inventories are verbal. The examinees must be able to comprehend what is being asked of them. Although the reading levels of the interest inventories vary, nearly all assume that the examinee can read at least at the sixth-grade level. This therefore precludes the use of such inventories as the SCII, OIS, and GIS for illiterates and students who have a reading deficiency.

5. There is disagreement among interest inventory authors with respect to the kinds of items that are most valid. Kuder (1970) says that "activities" are more valid; Holland (1973) contends that "occupational titles" are more valid. Since interest inventory authors agree that vocational interests in occupations are sex-related (Holland, 1973; Campbell, 1974), and since we are concerned with sex stereotyping and bias, the kinds of items used can be significant.

6. Interest inventories are not very satisfactory in predicting job success, academic success, job satisfaction, or personality adjustment. No interest test on the market will permit one to say that Johnny should become a doctor, lawyer, or carpenter. No interest inventory will indicate whether or not Johnny will be happy or successful in vocations or occupations in which he has obtained high scores. This does not mean that interest inventories have no predictive validity. They do, but they are not as valid as cognitive measures. There is a slight relationship between interest inventory scores and academic success (correlations normally are about .40). And there is a slight relationship between interest scores and such things as job success and personality. This, however, should not necessarily be interpreted as evidence of a relationship that is of practical significance (even though it may be of statistical significance), nor should it be construed as a cause-and-effect relationship. In predicting job satisfaction, it should be remembered that many factors must be considered, of which interests are but one factor. The relationship between interest scores and job success is vague, partly because of the problem of obtaining a valid measure of job success. Interest inventory scores may be related to various measures of job and/or academic success and satisfaction. However, the nature of the relationship is such that interest scores alone should never be used to predict future success or satisfaction. It is because the untrained user may make exaggerated statements

about the probability or degree of success (or satisfaction) in a profession or vocation that we find interest inventories being severely and unduly criticized. Once again, we reiterate that in many instances the instrument is made the scapegoat.

7. Some empirically constructed interest inventories may be more susceptible to sex bias than those constructed by the homogeneous method (Johansson & Harmon, 1972; Cole, 1973).

8. We must be very cautious in making interpretations of interest inventory results. Research has shown that markedly different interpretations (and hence the suggestions that might be given students regarding potential careers) are possible depending upon the type of score used. When raw scores (which, incidentally, are widely used) or combined sex norms are used, highly divergent career suggestions are given men and women. But when same-sex standard scores are used the career suggestions given men and women are very similar.

Although people may have a natural tendency to accent the negative and eliminate or forget the positive, we hope that this tendency is not exercised where interest inventories are concerned. Properly used, interest inventory results can provide valuable information for the teacher and the counselor—information that is more valid than that obtained by nonstandardized approaches—so that they will better understand the pupils' cognitive and noncognitive behavior.

Guidance Purposes   After cognitive measures, interest inventory results play the most important role in occupational and educational counseling. Interest inventory results are beneficial to both the counselor and the counselee. The counselor can use the results as an introduction to the interview. The interest inventory may be used as a gambit in situations where it is difficult to establish rapport. The counselor can use the results to help open the way to discussion of other problems such as academic difficulty, personal-social relationships, and the like. The counselees, on the other hand, have an opportunity to view themselves as they described themselves. They can look at their present plans and with the assistance of the counselor see whether their aspirations are realistic and confirm their feelings, and then do some "reality testing." (An elaborate study by Flanagan, Tiedeman, & Willis, 1973, involving thousands of high school seniors reported that, by and large, young people have unrealistic career plans and that they desire more career awareness and occupational information. Additionally, they desired more counseling opportunities in high school.) The counselee can use the test results as leads for further consideration. The counselees and the counselor can both use the inventory results to see whether the expressed interests are related or unrelated (whether they all fit into a pattern such as humanitarian or technical, or whether they are distinct), whether the programs that the counselees are intending to follow is compatible with their profile of interests and abilities, and whether their vocational or avocational goal will be realized by the program they are now following.

Interest inventory results can also be valuable in working with students who have unrealistic *academic* expectations. For example, Gregory, a pre-med student who is receiving grades of C and D in his science courses and who has an MCAT (Medical College Aptitude Test) score at the 10th percentile and still aspires to be admitted to a prestigious medical school, may be very unrealistic. Gregory may be in pre-med for a variety of reasons: (1) his parents, who are both physicians and who come from a family of physicians, want their only child to follow in their footsteps; (2) Gregory has an unrealistic picture of the glamor of a doctor's life (it isn't always peaches and cream when you are awakened at 3:00 A.M., again at 4:15 A.M. and 5:30 A.M., and then have to be in surgery for 12 hours); or (3) a combination of these and other factors. Interest inventory results (the SCII, for instance, has a scale which reflects how compatible and comfortable one would be in various work settings) can help students like Gregory if only to make them think more realistically about their future (see Althen & Stott, 1983).

Interest inventory results, if used cautiously, can help individuals find themselves in terms of the activities they feel are important and interesting. Interest inventory results should not be used for classroom selection purposes (though they may be useful for classification). They should not be used to tell Fred that he should enter the field of engineering. They should not be used as a major criterion in occupational and educational counseling. High scores on an interest inventory are not analogous to saying that the individual has either the aptitude or the potential for success in a particular vocation. The test scores provide only a relative index of the individual's likes and dislikes, and for some inventories it is possible to compare the student's interests with those of individuals who are successful in a vocation or profession. In actual practice, interest inventory results should be used only for their valuable ancillary information. Other factors such as ability, aptitude, motivation, and the like must be considered. The total profile rather than just part of it must be considered so that as complete a picture as possible of the individual's interests can be obtained. Finally, we should not argue whether *expressed* vocational interests are more valid than inventoried interests. Rather, we should consider *both* when counseling students.

Instructional Purposes   Although interest inventory results can be used for grouping students, they normally are not intended for this purpose. In a somewhat indirect fashion, interest inventory results can be used by the classroom teacher to provide optimal learning conditions. Take, for example, the junior high school student who is a poor reader. Recognizing the limitations of interest inventory scores for junior high school students, the teacher who knows that Betsy likes mechanics may attempt to motivate her to read more by suggesting books, magazines, or articles of mechanical content. Hence, although the test score is not used as an instructional device per se, it is used to provide a learning experience that may be quite beneficial insofar as Betsy's reading is concerned.

Interest inventories can be used as a learning device. For example, in the unit on "Work" in Social Studies, the teacher may have the students take an interest test. This technique can help get the students to think systematically about the relationships between personal interests and occupational choice. Any interest inventory used in a group fashion should be used for discussion purposes only. Hopefully, divergent thinking rather than convergent thinking will ensue.

Summary of Interest Measurement

The three techniques most frequently used to construct interest inventories are logical keying, homogeneous keying, and criterion-keying. Although the men most renowned for their work in the area of interest measurement, Strong and Kuder, employed different approaches in the initial development of their inventories, the revised editions of the Strong and Kuder are more similar than different. The interest patterns or clusters identified or at least designated by Kuder and Strong have, in the main, been confirmed by empirical research.

Despite the fact that interest inventories have certain limitations (are fakable, are susceptible to response set, may be answered on the basis of stereotypes, and may be difficult to interpret especially if they are ipsative forced-choice tests), they do have much value in occupational and educational counseling *if* and *when* used properly.

Some inventories, such as the Kuder OIS and SCII, are designed for individuals who plan to attend college and aspire to managerial or professional roles. Other inventories, such as the MVII, are designed for students who plan to enter into apprenticeship programs after leaving high school. Still other inventories, such as the CAI, are best suited for persons who seek careers that do not require a college degree. Inventories such as OVIS II can be used in the eighth grade; the IDEAS is designed to be used in the sixth grade.

More research is needed about the relationship among the scores of the various inventories. In many instances discrepancies have been reported in the literature. Research directed toward resolving such discrepancies will permit the counselor to make a more valid interpretation of the test profile.

Interest inventories have come a long way from Strong's initial attempts in the 1920s. Not only are they becoming more refined, but interest inventory authors are beginning to emphasize or at least recognize the need for a theoretical position on the development of interests. Interest inventories can assist the counselor in establishing rapport. They can help students by giving them something to consider or reflect upon and by providing them with some ideas that they can develop more fully by reading and discussion. They can help the teacher organize meaningful learning experiences. All in all, they can help school personnel obtain a more complete picture of individuals by providing valuable data about their likes and dislikes. Such data are best obtained from standardized interest inventories.

CAREER AWARENESS AND DEVELOPMENT

It is becoming increasingly evident that a person requires *more* than merely an interest in, and possibly an aptitude or ability for, a particular vocation in order to be counseled for that vocation. Career planning is the most sought-after service by college students (Carney, Savitz, & Weiskott, 1979) and is given high priority by high school students (Prediger, Roth, & Noeth, 1974). Between 1958, when ETS published its Guidance Inquiry, and 1968 there was a void in the development and publication of standardized instruments to measure the various aspects of career development—cognitive, affective, and psychomotor—all of which are involved in the decision-making process engaged in by the counselor and the counselee in examining career choices. Since 1968, however, at least six major career-planning programs have been initiated; two national and several state assessment programs in the career and occupational development area have been conducted (see National Assessment of Educational Progress, 1977); numerous articles have been written (McClure & Buan [1973] present a collection of essays on career education); a comprehensive monograph on vocational guidance instruments and career assessment programs was published (Kapes & Mastie, 1982); and at least eleven career-development/vocational maturity standardized tests have been published or revised: Readiness for Vocational Planning Test (1968); Cognitive Maturity Test (1970); Assessment of Career Development (1973); Career Development Inventory (1979 for the school form, 1981 for the college form); Self-Directed Search (1970, 1973, 1979); Planning Career Goals (1976); Vocational Interest, Experience and Skills Assessment (1977); Programs for Assessing Youth Employment Skills (1978); Career Awareness Inventory (1974 for elementary, 1979 for advanced); Career Skills Assessment Program (1978); and Career Maturity Inventory (1973, 1978). (For more information on career maturity, see Super et al., 1972; Super & Crites, 1962; Westbrook & Parry-Hill, 1973; Westbrook, 1976a, b, c; and Peters & Hansen, 1977. For a discussion of the methodological problems in measuring career maturity, see Crites, 1974.)

Although all these instruments are designed to measure those factors deemed important for career development, it is not surprising to find that they differ markedly in terms of the constructs measured. An analysis by Westbrook (1974) showed that the inventories differed (widely at times) in their coverage (1) of cognitive, affective, and psychomotor behaviors, and

(2) of specific behaviors within a given component. These findings are different from, say, an analysis of reading readiness tests, no doubt because our state of knowledge of the reading process is at a more advanced level than that for career development or vocational maturity. On the other hand, analyses by Jepsen & Prediger (1981) and Kapes & Mastie (1982) suggest that the various career maturity inventories are more similar than dissimilar. In fact, Jepsen & Prediger found four factors that were common among the various inventories: decision-making style, systematic involvement in career decision making, decision-making certainty, and cognitive resources needed for or involved in decision making. Research has also been initiated to study the effects of computer assistance and group counseling as aids to career maturity. Any conclusions, however, still await more definitive testing.

Career-Planning Programs

Within the past two decades there has been increased interest by commercial test publishers in developing assessment batteries and programs that would aid both the student and the counselor in vocational and educational planning. This is especially commendable since it has been shown that a person's vocational aspirations can be affected by the kind and amount of information given (Haase et al., 1978; Malett et al., 1978). Three such programs are the Career Planning Program (CPP), sponsored by the American College Testing Program; the Career Development Program (CDP), conducted by Science Research Associates; and the Career Skills Assessment Program (CSAP), conducted by the College Board. There are many similarities among the three programs, the most striking one being that they are more than aptitude and achievement tests. They consider, in addition, such factors as interests, aspirations, career-related experiences, and work preferences. All three programs provide useful information for the student who knows his or her future plans, as well as for the student who is undecided. The CPP also sends information to the institution(s) selected by the student. We will now consider these three programs briefly. Those interested in a more comprehensive treatment of career education and development programs should see Krumboltz & Hamel (1982).

Career Planning Program (CPP)   Published by the American College Testing Program (1983), the CPP is really two programs in one: an *assessment* component (grades 8–11) and a *career-guidance* component (CPP Level 1 for grades 8–10; CPP Level 2 for grades 11–adult).[7] The CPP Level 2 (Postsecondary) Program is designed "to help students and adults 'check-up' on

---

[7] Although our discussion centers primarily on the CPP, the material is also relevant, with minor modifications, to the CPP Level 2.

their development and plans, and motivate themselves to complete their career objectives with a renewed sense of purpose and goals.'' Both levels of the CPP are comprehensive packages of aptitude (it was renormed in 1983) and interest tests as well as career-related experiences designed to ''stimulate and facilitate self and career exploration, including the exploration of self in relation to career'' in one articulated program. Besides the Vocational Interest Profile, Form A, which reports the subject's interest in six areas, and six ability scales, there is a Student Information Report (self-report measures of a variety of things such as job values, occupational preferences, certainty of occupational preferences, working-condition preferences, educational plans, and self-rated abilities). In 1978, a Building and System Summary Report was made available. It provides counselors with a ''comprehensive overview of students' abilities, interests, career-related experiences, and congruence of student traits.'' Test–retest and internal consistency reliability estimates are reported, and they appear to be respectable. Construct and criterion-related validity were studied and reported. The format is good. The directions for both administrator and student are very clear.

In 1983, a personal computer-generated report was introduced. The report not only contains the results of the ability measures but provides the counselor and counselee with a narrative report, a synthesis of the assessment results, and suggested resource materials, to name a few interpretive aids provided.

The CPP has an excellent Handbook, which discusses in clear fashion the development and use of the program, contains an annotated bibliography of career-guidance materials, and provides a complete lesson plan outline for a nine-unit Mini Course in Career Planning. The Handbook also contains a variety of norm tables.

The Student Report is well written and should be understood by nearly all students. It gives the student step-by-step suggestions on how to interpret the information and how to go about exploring suggested career options.

An adjunct of the CPP is the Assessment of Career Development for grades 8–12. On the basis of students' responses to 42 critical questions (the user can add up to 12 locally developed questions), a school can evaluate its career-development program and modify it, if necessary, to meet students' needs.

In summary, the CPP is a well-designed instrument program that provides measures of peoples' interests, abilities, and career-related experiences *all* normed on the *same* group. The test's technical qualities are acceptable, although we regret that the publisher did *not* provide empirical data to permit evaluation of the guidance component of the program. It serves both the student and the school: The former receives information that should be of assistance in career exploration and educational planning; the latter receives information on its student body that may be of value in the development or modification (as well as evaluation) of its career-guidance program. (For a review of the CPP, see Mehrens, 1982.)

Career Development Program (CDP)   Published by Science Research Associates (1975), the program is applicable for grades 9–12 and adults. The CDP is a system consisting of a planning notebook and a career development inventory. The planning notebook is the "heart" of the program and is designed to stimulate examinees to explore and consider careers either by themselves or with the aid of a teacher or a counselor. An optional feature to the notebook is the Career Development Inventory (CDI), which consists of a personal, biographical inventory of 46 items, and the Kuder Career Interest Inventory (CII) (although it has the same items as the Kuder OIS, Form DD, it has five new scales and is scored and interpreted differently).

The CDI results are plotted in the Career Development Profile in a 3 (the educational level associated with an occupational entry) -by-6 (the occupational clusters that resemble the six Holland RIASEC categories) grid. Within each of the 17 cells (one is empty), the examinee's profile indicates a score of either low, moderate, or high to indicate relative congruence of interests to people in occupations in each cell. This scoring system suggests the degree of consideration an examinee should give to occupations falling in that cell. The new scoring system also yields occupational cluster scores that are applied to occupational fields rather than to single occupations, as is the case with the KOIS.

The Technical Manual presents data on the reliability, concurrent validity, and factor structure of the occupational cluster scores. No reliability or validity data are reported on either the career development profile scores or the biographical items. Lacking and definitely needed for such a program are data relevant to establishing the test's predictive validity. Although the new scoring system was designed to reduce sex differences in scores, it seems that the authors were not as successful as the advertising copy writers would have us believe.

The CDP appears to be a valuable program for assisting individuals in career exploration. It combines the best of the KOIS with newest advances in, and knowledge about, interests, psychometrics, and career counseling; moreover, it is attractively packaged. Considering that the CDP is a self-directed career-assessment and career-exploration program, it should be evaluated with reference to Holland's Self-Directed Search (SDS), which is less expensive and more convenient, and to VIESA; both are also self-scoring. (VIESA is described briefly in a later section.)

It should be recognized at the outset that neither the CPP nor the CDP is intended to replace the counselor. However, if the results are used judiciously, they should assist the counselor in dealing more effectively with students by encouraging career exploration and by helping them make realistic, viable, and valid decisions regarding their future educational and vocational plans.

Career Skills Assessment Program (CSAP)   Published by the College Board (1978), the CSAP measures the students' skills in six areas—self-evaluation and career-development skills, career-awareness skills, career decision-making skills, employment-seeking skills, work effectiveness skills, and personal-economics skills. The CSAP is based on the assumption that career-development skills can be taught and learned. Each area or module is measured by a 60-item multiple-choice test, which is untimed. A variety of stimuli are used—graphs, pictures, cartoons—to create interest. It is supposedly free of sex bias. A unique three-ply answer sheet is included: the top is used for machine scoring, the middle for hand scoring, and the bottom permits students to compare their responses to "preferred" responses.

The CSAP emphasizes follow-up guidance activities by means of a Guide in each of the six content areas. The guide is really a minicurriculum which contains activities to help students develop and strengthen their skills, and is designed for *both* individuals and institutions.

The CSAP includes a Handbook, which describes the program, presents statistical information, and contains directions for administration, scoring, and interpretation. The program also includes a filmstrip kit to give teachers and students an understanding of the program and how it can be used.

Other Programs   Other career-exploration/development programs are SRA's Career Development Program, IPAT's Self-Motivated Career Planning, and the Psychological Corporation's Guided Career Exploration Program. More detailed information on these and the other instruments we have discussed can be found in Buros and the various publishers' catalogs.

Newer Approaches

Within the past few years, there have also been published what might be referred to as a total career-planning program or system. Although not standardized tests, per se, career-exploration and career-development programs (and hence materials) often incorporate an interest inventory and one or more cognitive measures (such as an aptitude and/or achievement test) into a package or module that can be used effectively in a unit or course on career exploration. These prepackaged units vary from programs that use no test materials, such as SRA's Introducing Career Concepts, to those that use a combination of workbooks, filmstrips, and standardized interest inventories, as exemplified in CTB/McGraw-Hill's Careers in Focus. Although the majority of career-exploration/development programs are designed for upper middle school and high school students, a few are intended for use in the elementary grades. On this latter point, we have some reservations. We are *not* against the use of materials or discussions about careers or employment opportunities and the like in the elementary and junior high school. In fact, we strongly endorse the inclusion of such materials as early as possible in the child's schooling. If anything, we regret that many of our syllabi and curricula, even at the high school level, pay only lip-service to career-development/exploration courses. We firmly believe, however, that any career-planning program used in the elementary grades which contains an interest inventory should be interpreted with extreme caution because of the instability of interests at that age. We will now briefly discuss three systems.

California Test Bureau/McGraw-Hill publishes a career planning system which consists of Careers in Focus (1976), Planning Career Goals (1975), and the Career Maturity Inventory (1978). These materials are integrated so as to provide an assessment and a teaching/learning component.

Careers in Focus is a learning system consisting of student manuals, worksheets, sound filmstrips, and interview cassettes. It is intended for students' career-exploration activities in grades 6–10. With this system, students can explore over 350 occupations. The program is integrated with Planning Career Goals and the Career Maturity Inventory.

Planning Career Goals is a single system that obtains measures of ability, interests, life and career plans, and general information. It is recommended for use in grades 8–12. The PCG permits students to compare their abilities, preferences, and information with those of people who are employed in a variety of careers. In this way, it somewhat resembles the SCII.

The Career Maturity Inventory is designed to provide "information for individuals and groups on the attitudes and competencies that are important for mature career decision making." It is recommended for grades 6–12. The CMI has an Attitude Scale (a Screening and Counseling Form) and a Competence Test.

Another approach is Riverside Press' Vocational, Interest, Experience, and Skill Assessment (VIESA) program, which was published in 1977. VIESA is designed for students in grades 8–12. It is untimed, but takes about 45 minutes. There is one form. The battery consists of a standardized interest inventory with sex-balanced scales, a standardized experience inventory which assesses experiences related to interests, and a structured guide for student self-appraisal of career-related skills. Students can make interpretations related to 6 job clusters, 25 job families, and 650 occupations. Scores are represented in a graphical Job Clusters on a World-of-Work Map. Students are given suggestions of what occupations to explore, as well as references to consult. VIESA is compatible with the Career Planning Program described earlier.

Commercial test publishers, in addition to publishing the various career-development/maturity programs and inventories previously discussed, are now beginning to pay more attention to the development of courses in career exploration. One such course is Guided Career Exploration, published by the Psychological Corporation in 1979. The GCE contains teaching materials that can be used in a one-semester course (minimum of 30 hours excluding testing time) in career exploration in grades 8–12. The course has been constructed so that students can (1) explore their own career potential, (2) learn about the various occupations available to them and how to obtain information about them, and (3) develop optimal strategies for decision making.

The GCE curriculum package consists of a Professional Manual, Posters, Cassette Recordings, and a Student Workbook. The Student Workbook contains an Occupational Selector Chart, which summarizes over 250 occupations in terms of work characteristics, educational requirements, and relevant aptitudes, values, and interests. The chart is intended to help students identify occupations that meet their requirements. The curriculum also consists of six teaching units—Learning About Career Development, Learning About Myself, Learning About Occupations, Learning About Decision Making, Making a List of Occupational Activities, and Drafting a Personal Career Plan—to guide students through the stages of career exploration. All but one of the units—Learning About Myself—are taught by self-contained materials. Learning About Myself consists of students' exploring their aptitudes, interests, and values. These are measured by the DAT Career Planning Program (which is an integral part of the program and is required by all students) and the OVIS (which is optional).

The GCE system is too new to be evaluated for its effectiveness, but on the surface it appears to be a well-designed program.

PERSONALITY ASSESSMENT

Personality characteristics are or should be of concern to educators. It is generally agreed that education must be concerned with attitudes, values, and interests just as it is concerned with the development of cognitive skills and knowledge. What values will accrue to society from individuals who can solve a quadratic equation or are able to detect the components of LSD, but who are hostile or aggressive? Education should be concerned with developing a well-rounded individual. Although there are major disagreements in defining, understanding, and measuring what we call personality, these disagreements should not prevent us from considering this important area and its relevance to the learning process.

Personality Defined

Analogous somewhat to the saying that "Intelligence is what intelligence tests measure," the definition of *personality* depends upon the psychologist one questions. In fact, the saying goes that if you ask 100 psychologists to give their definition of personality, you will receive at least 101 because one of the psychologists will have at least two definitions. The definition of personality is somewhat amorphous. To the politician, personality may be defined in terms of one's charisma; to the theologian, it may be courage or honesty; and to the college student taking an introductory social psychology course, it may be "one's predisposition to act in a certain way." To the behavioral psychologist, personality is an external pattern of behavior characteristics of an individual.

Although a variety of definitions of personality have been posited, they all share the common theme that it subsumes the *total* individual—both cognitive and noncognitive traits. We restrict our discussion of personality assessment, however, to problem check lists, general adjustment inventories, and projective tests. We recognize that the interests, attitudes, and opinions of individuals are an integral component of their general makeup (as are their cognitive traits).

We must emphasize that personality inventories should not be interpreted by the classroom teacher. The assessment of an individual's behavior depends upon the synthesis of many particles of information. Valid synthesis should and can be undertaken only by persons trained in this area.

During the preceding decade or so, personality assessment research has tended to focus less on techniques and more on the development of a theory of personality. Today, emphasis in personality testing is directed toward the assessment of normal behavior. Emerging trends are (1) a diminution of ideological posturing, (2) more rigorous definition of terms, (3) greater use of mathematical modeling and computer simulation, (4) integration of measurement and experimental approaches to personality, (5) the tightening of standards for the construction of personality measures, (6) a focus on process over product, and (7) a growing awareness of the functional role of "biases" (Jackson & Paunonen, 1980).

Types of Standardized Personality-Assessment Devices

Personality can be measured in a variety of ways. Three commonly used approaches to the study of personality are to see (1) what the individual says about himself or herself (self-report inventories), (2) what others say about the individual (sociometric inventories), and (3) what the individual does in a particular kind of situation (observational techniques).

Another way in which personality tests can be classified is in terms of the method by which one's behavior is studied or of the manner in which the stimuli are presented. Stimuli can be presented as either *structured* or *unstructured*. The structured test consists of items or questions that can be interpreted in relatively the same way by all examinees (for example, "Do you daydream?"). The unstructured test (sometimes referred to as the projective test, although projective devices can be either completely unstructured or semistructured) consists of ambiguous pictures or ink blots to which the examinee responds according to his or her interpretation of the stimulus. In the unstructured test, the subject projects his or her feelings when describing the ambiguous stimulus or completing the incomplete statement or word. Unstructured tests differ from structured tests in that they are usually not quantitatively scored, although they could be. Structured personality tests are objectively scored with predetermined keys.

Personality tests can further be classified in terms of their method of construction. As discussed later in the chapter, three common approaches used to construct personality tests are (1) criterion keying (used in the MMPI and the California Psychological Inventory), (2) factor analysis (used in the many Cattell personality tests), and (3) the logical approach (used in the Bernreuter Personality Inventory). In essence, then, personality tests can be differentiated in terms of *how* they do what they do. However, it is essential that the reader be aware of *what* they do. That is, does the test attempt to isolate problems, or does it attempt to give an indication of possible adjustment?

There are basic problems associated with the use of personality inventories that make their results somewhat questionable. Some of these problems are as follows: (1) generally, they are highly verbal and are therefore not suited for children who cannot read or have difficulty reading, (2) they are susceptible to faking, and (3) because the items tend to reflect a white, middle-class, Protestant ethic, they may be culturally biased.

In this chapter, we consider only the self-report inventories, recognizing that although other techniques provide valuable information, they are typically locally constructed, rather than commercially standardized, tests.

Structured Self-Report Inventories

Structured self-report inventories are the most common type of personality tests used in schools (and industry) today. They are a basic tool in the diagnosis of "illness," whether it be physical or mental. Just as the physician will ask what hurts you and where and when the pain started, the psychiatrist and clinician will ask you whether you have nightmares, a tendency to daydream, or similar questions. Over the years, the answers to these kinds of questions have been found to be more indicative of maladjustment than those to other questions that could be asked. When such questions are selected and put together in a list to be checked off by the examinee, it is a test or an inventory. Self-report inventories can be classified into either problem checklists or general adjustments inventories. They can also be classified in terms of their method of construction; criterion groups, factor analysis, or logical approach. All, however, are structured.

Problem Checklists

Problem checklists are the most applicable personality measure in our public schools because of their limited demand on formal training and experience for the examiner. In fact, we can go so far as to say that no formal training is required to administer and score a problem checklist. Interpretation, on the other hand, demands training, sophistication, and experience. It is one thing to administer a checklist and still another to interpret it. For example, let us assume that Elaine indicates she has difficulty with her brothers and sisters. What can, should, or does the teacher do? Naturally, the untrained teacher should obtain professional assistance in whatever action is undertaken. In fact, we strongly recommend that assistance in the interpretation of, and subsequent action to, a problem check list be obtained from a qualified counselor or clinician. Sibling rivalry in Elaine's case may appear, on the surface, easy to deal with. However, sibling rivalry is usually more complex and may require professional assistance.

Problem checklists can be used by classroom teachers to confirm some of their subjective impressions that were obtained by observation. For example, in Elaine's case the teacher may have noticed that Elaine is depressed or moody, whereas a few months earlier she was a happy child. Problem check lists can be used by the teacher (or counselor) to obtain a better understanding of the pupil—her problems, her behavior. It is quite conceivable that a pupil such as Elaine will suddenly begin doing poor, sloppy work. Possibly, from the results of a problem checklist the teacher working with the counselor will be able to learn that Elaine's performance is the result of something that is bothering her, rather than because of laziness. Problem check lists, especially when administered to the whole class, will make pupils less self-conscious and willing to reveal their problems. This is especially true if the teacher discusses the *general* findings. At no time should individual responses or pupils be identified and discussed. With discussion centering on general findings, a pupil like Elaine is able to see that she is not atypical, that other pupils are also bothered or concerned about a variety of things. Problem check lists also serve as excellent screening devices for the counselor. On the basis of their results and an interview, the counselor may suggest more thorough treatment if needed.

It should be remembered that problem checklists are just that—they do not make any claims to measuring personality traits. In fact, problem checklist authors caution users to avoid adopting this view. In problem checklists, individuals check only the statements that are applicable to them, and of which they are aware and willing to check. The greatest value of problem checklists is as communication vehicles between the pupil and the counselor. The test results can help save the counselor much valuable time by indicating what the problem seems to be, and can help establish rapport between the pupil and the counselor.

Problem checklists are often accepted at face value. They are composed of items that tend to be representative of problems that people face in different areas, such as family, peer relationships, finances, study skills, health, and relations with adults. Even so, they differ slightly in their format. In some problem checklists, the pupils check only the statements that they perceive as problems. In others, the pupils indicate the degree of severity: minor, moderate, severe. In still others, the pupils write a statement about their problems. The responses to problem checklists should not be considered as a test or subtest score. The teacher and the counselor should use the responses as a guide for further exploration. If used in this way, problem checklists are quite helpful.

Problem checklists are primarily used to identify individuals who are concerned with social and personal relationships. Another type of structured self-report inventory is the adjustment inventory. This type is concerned primarily with the identification of neuroticism and pathological deviation. In addition, structured self-report inventories have been developed that are most concerned with the assessment of narrowly defined behavior characteristics such as sociability, masculinity-femininity, and introversion-extroversion. These latter inventories place major emphasis on the measurement of individual differences within the normal range of deviation. They are not discussed here because of their limited educational value.

General Adjustment Inventories

It is not our intent to delve too deeply into the measurement of personality by means of general adjustment inventories. However, we do feel that educators should have at least a rudimentary knowledge of the different types, as well as some awareness of their strengths and weaknesses.

General adjustment inventories are of value because they (1) help establish rapport between counselor and counselee by having some basis on which to begin an interview, (2) permit examinees to express problems that are of relevance (or those which he thinks are of relevance or importance) to them, and (3) provide the counselor or clinician with more information about the individual so that he or she may have a global picture of the individual. Three methods often used to construct general adjustment inventories are (1) using criterion groups, (2) using factorial scales, and (3) using the logical approach.

General Adjustment Inventories: Criterion Groups

The Adjustment Inventory. Published by Consulting Psychologists Press (1963), it has one form and two levels: student form for grades 9–16 (research edition published in 1962) and adult form (published in 1938). The revised student form has six scores: Home, Health, Submissiveness, Emotionality, Hostility, and Masculinity. The adult form also provides six scores: Home, Occupational, Health, Social, Emotional, and a total score. It is untimed but requires about 30 minutes to administer.

The Adjustment Inventory consists of 200 items that are answered Yes, No, or ?. In the revised form, three criteria were used to select items: (1) correlating the scale against external criteria such as similar scales and ratings of experts, (2) eliminating items that have little intrascale correlations, and (3) writing items on rational or a priori grounds. Hence, we may say that the revised scale contains some items that have predictive validity evidence and other items that have logical validity evidence. Concurrent validity was studied by correlating the subscores with those of similar tests, and the resulting correlations are quite high, being about .72 (with the exception of the Bell masculinity-femininity scale and those of the MF scales of the Minnesota Multiphasic Personality Inventory (MMPI) where the r's were .38 for women and .13 for men). The split-half reliabilities are all in the .80s.

The test is accompanied by an excellent manual with many interpretative guidelines. The normative data are still scanty. Percentile norms are given for 295 boys and 372 girls in grades 10 to 12; college norms are based on 316 men and 347 women in their freshman to junior year. Unfortunately, both standardization samples are biased because of geographical limitations. The adult form contains the same number of questions, is answered in the same way, and was constructed with the same general principles as the revised student form. Odd-even reliability coefficients range from .80 to .89.

It should be emphasized that the validity of the Adjustment Inventory is as good as, and better than, most pencil-and-paper adjustment inventories. The student form is used more extensively than the adult form. The items were carefully selected and were randomly placed throughout the test to prevent or minimize acquiescence. Its principal functions are as an indicator of subjects requiring counseling, as a guide to help the trained clinician conduct the interview, and as an aid to a better understanding of the individual.

Minnesota Multiphasic Personality Inventory (MMPI).   Published by the Psychological Corporation (1943–1967), the MMPI is one of the most widely used instruments and possibly the most researched and referenced (over 5,000 references are found in Buros) self-report personality inventories.[8] There are three forms (a Group Form and two Individual Forms). It is untimed but takes from 45–90 minutes to complete. It is appropriate for ages 16 and over. The inventory provides 14 scores—4 validity scores, which assess the examinee's truthfulness and test-taking attitude, and 10 scale

[8] Since the original publication there have been over 300 new scales developed by users/ researchers.

scores, as follows (the numbers in parentheses refer to the number of items in the scale):

Hypochondriasis (33)   Depression (60)
Hysteria (60)   Psychopathic Deviate (50)
Masculinity-Femininity (60)   Schizophrenia (78)
Paranoia (40)   Hypomania (46)
Psychasthenia (48)   Social Introversion (70)

The authors attempt to assess psychopathology with 550 affirmative statements, to which the examinee responds, "True," "False," or "Cannot say." (Only 400 of the items contribute to the 14 scores.) In the Individual Form, each statement is printed on a separate card which the examinee sorts into the appropriate category. In the Group Form, the statements are printed in a booklet and the examinees' responses are recorded on separate answer sheets. Some examples of the type of items used are as follows:

"I have chest pains several times a week."
"I do not tire quickly."
"I am worried about sex matters."

Criterion keying was employed in the test's construction/scoring. With the exception of the Masculinity-Femininity and Social Introversion scales, items were selected on the basis of their ability to differentiate between a group of "normals" and a specified clinical group.

Reliability estimates were obtained using test–retest and split-half procedures. Although some of the scales possess adequate reliabilities, some do not, and this reduces the effectiveness of the profile analysis.

Interpretation of the MMPI is difficult and complex, to say the least, and requires an experienced clinician. To aid in the diagnostic interpretation, the authors prepared an *Atlas for the Clinical Use of the MMPI* (Hathaway & Meehl, 1951). The *Atlas* provides short case histories and coded profiles of nearly 1000 patients grouped according to the similarity of their profiles. Other *Atlases* have been developed for high school populations (Hathaway & Monachesi, 1961, 1963) and for college populations (Drake & Oetting, 1959).

To circumvent the complexity of profile interpretation, some agencies have developed computer-generated interpretations and actuarial analyses which may provide clinicians with valuable information that they may overlook. Is this good or bad? It depends. If the trend toward automation results in the interpretation of MMPI profiles by poorly trained and unqualified users, that's bad. However, if computer-generated interpretations will give clinicians more time to study the report intensively and provide them with additional diagnostic information, that is good.

Despite the many valuable aspects of, and the cornucopia of research on, the MMPI, there are some serious limitations:

1. The low reliability of some of the scales.
2. The inadequate size, recency, and representativeness of the standardization samples (only about 700 Minneapolis adults were tested in the original standardization) makes the norms suspect.
3. Lack of norms for various age and ethnic groups.
4. High enough interscale correlations for some scales to suggest overlap.

In summary, the MMPI has its shortcomings. Nevertheless, it is a valuable clinical instrument for assessing psychopathology. Notwithstanding the availability of computer-generated interpretations, we are adamant in our belief that its use should be restricted to skilled clinicians.

California Psychological Inventory (CPI).   Published by Consulting Psychologists Press (1975), the test has one form. It is untimed but requires about 1 hour to complete. The inventory is appropriate for ages 13 and over. It provides 18 scores: Dominance, Capacity for Status, Sociability, Social Presence, Self-Acceptance, Sense of Well-Being, Responsibility, Socialization, Self-Control, Tolerance, Good Impression, Communality, Achievement via Conformance, Achievement via Independence, Intellectual Efficiency, Psychological-Mindedness, Flexibility, and Femininity. The 18 scales are grouped into four categories. Three of the scales—Sense of Well-Being, Communality, and Good Impression—are validity scales.

The author attempted to construct an instrument that would provide for a comprehensive, multidimensional assessment of normal persons in various settings—in contrast to the MMPI, which emphasizes maladjustment and psychiatric disorders. The CPI consists of 480 statements (about half of which come from the MMPI) that are responded to on a true-false dichotomy. The number of items in each scale varies from 22 to 56, the median being 37. Eleven of the scales were constructed on the basis of criterion-group performance. Pupils were initially labeled as dominant or sociable by their high school principals, and the test scores were studied to see if they differentiated between these two groups. Cross-validation samples were then used to see whether the scales were valid. The other 10 scales were constructed by the same procedure, and it would appear that they are quite valid when judged against actual behavior criteria of contrasted groups. Three scales were empirically derived to provide the verification scales. Four of the scales were based on rational grounds. The author claims that personality traits can be classified into four categories: (1) measures of poise, ascendancy, and self-assurance; (2) measures of socialization, maturity, and responsibility; (3) measures of achievement potential and intellectual efficiency; and (4) measures of intellectual and interest modes. Later factor analytic studies, however, demonstrated that five scores would be needed to glean the information from the 18 scales. Possibly more important was that these studies suggest that some of the scales are improperly classified.

The test–retest and internal consistency reliabilities compare favorably with those of other well-constructed personality inventories. The norms are based on 6000 males and 7000 females from a wide geographical area, differing in age and socioeconomic status. In addition, separate mean profiles for high school and college students of each sex are presented. Total scores are also presented for 30 special groups for each of the 18 scores.

Although the author might have indicated more confidence in his inventory's reliability than is justified by the evidence, one cannot deny that it is one of the best personality inventories available. It was carefully constructed, is supported by much empirical evidence (see Megargee, 1972), has an excellent manual, and reports intercorrelations between the CPI and other widely used personality tests such as the MMPI and the Bernreuter. A computerized interpretive profile is available from the publisher.

Personality Inventory for Children (PIC).   Published by Western Psychological Services (1977), it has one form. Although designed primarily for children and adolescents from ages 6 through 16, it can be used with children as young as 3 years old. The PIC, like the CPI, is another MMPI clone. The PIC is unique in its administration in that the parents of the examinee respond to 600 items about their child. In this way, the PIC is not a self-report inventory and is subject to observer/reporter bias. Scores are obtained on 13 clinical and screening scales and three validating scales. Of the 13 clinical scales, one (Adjustment) serves as a "screen" to identify children needing psychological validation. Some of the scales were empirically constructed; other scales employed content validation methods. An extensive interpretive guide is available, as is a computer-generated report.

General Adjustment Inventories: Factorial Scales   If one subscribes to the definition of personality as a multitude of traits continually acting and interacting, it is necessary that some method be devised to isolate and measure these traits. And in order to measure these traits, it is necessary to select appropriate items. One procedure used to identify the existence of traits is termed *factor analysis*. Factor analysis attempts to account for the interrelationships among a number of items in terms of some underlying factors. Test makers normally begin with a construct, prepare a number of items, and administer these items to a group of subjects. Then they use factor analysis to ascertain whether the items selected do in fact measure the underlying traits that they specified. This approach has been used by Eysenck, Guilford, Thurstone, and Cattell to construct their personality tests. Factor analysis has done much to increase our understanding of the components of aptitude, achievement, and personality and has resulted in purer measures of these components.

Thurstone Temperament Schedule.   Published by Science Research Associates (1953), it is suitable for students in grades 9 to 16 and adults. There is one form and is untimed, but takes about 15 minutes to complete.

Prior to developing this test, Thurstone factor-analyzed some of Guilford's scales and found that only 7 of his 13 factors accounted for most of the test variance. He then proceeded to construct his schedule to measure these 7 factors, which he labeled Active, Vigorous, Impulsive, Dominant, Stable, Sociable, and Reflective. The test contains 140 items—20 for each trait. Responses are made in terms of Yes, No, ?. The schedule is self-administering. Because it is based upon the responses of normal individuals, it does not lay any claim to abnormal personality classification. The reliabilities of the seven scales vary from .45 to .86, with a median reliability of .64. This low reliability is to be expected when only 20 items are used in each scale. The manual contains norms for various occupational groups and would no doubt be of value to personnel directors. If some validity data could be gathered for educational decision making, the schedule may prove to be a valuable instrument in a high school counseling situation.

General Adjustment Inventories: Logical Approach   Some authors employ criterion groups to select their items. Others employ factor analysis to assist them in selecting their items. Still others use no empirical evidence per se, but construct their test on the basis of a logical or armchair philosophy. In other words, they conceive of a construct as manifesting itself in a particular type of behavior and then prepare items to measure that behavior.

The Personality Inventory.   Published by the Consulting Psychologists Press (1938), it has one level, suitable for grades 9 to 16 and adults. Although untimed, it requires less than 30 minutes to complete. Six scores are provided: Self-Sufficiency, Neurotic Tendency, Introversion-Extroversion, Dominance-Submission, Confidence, and Sociability.

The test consists of 125 items to which the examinee responds by means of a three-element key: Yes, No, ?. The items were selected from four existing inventories. The correlations between the Personality Inventory and these four scales varied from .67 to .94. Validity for such a test must necessarily be based on its predictive power. The manual contains very little validity evidence (actually, only a correlation table between the original four tests and the marker scales that were used to derive the weighting scheme). The voluminous research gathered with this inventory has produced negative findings. Reliability coefficients reported in the manual (split-halves) range from .85 to .92 for college samples and from .78 to .86 for high school samples. Test–retest coefficients reported in the literature are somewhat lower. The 1938 norms are percentile equivalents and are provided for high school boys and girls, college men and women, and adult men and women. Excellent features of this test are that it takes relatively little time to administer and that there has been a great deal of data collected with it.[9] There are, however, many defects that warrant serious consideration before using it. Specifically, some of the more pronounced deficiencies are as follows: (1) It is not recommended for selection programs because it is too susceptible to faking; (2) it really measures only two traits, even though six scores are provided; (3) the scoring is cumbersome; and (4) the normative data are dated (the manual still reports data gathered in 1935). About the only commendable feature of this test is that it has information based on nearly 50 years of experience with it, and all information points out the same thing: Look for another personality test.

Evaluation of General Adjustment Inventories   Throughout the preceding discussion we have stressed that the user be very cautious in the interpretation of noncognitive test results. Problems of validity, reliability, language (ambiguity and/or interpretation made of such words as *usually* or *good*), faking, response set, scoring, and interpretation exist. Nevertheless, as discussed earlier in this chapter, educators must know something about the area of personality and personality assessment in order to provide for optimal learning conditions. We feel that it is just as (if not more so) valuable for the teacher and counselor to know what is bad about tests as it is for them to know what is good about tests. In addition, as we mentioned earlier, teachers and counselors must realize that they are still able to obtain more reliable and valid information about the noncognitive characteristics of their pupils with tests than they can by other means. It is for this reason that we have spent some time discussing general adjustment inventories.

Unstructured Inventories

Structured self-report inventories are not the only manner in which an individual's behavior can be measured. Another standardized approach to the assessment of personality is the one frequently used by the clinican: the unstructured or projective test. Whereas self-report structured inventories require subjects to describe themselves, projective tests require individuals to interpret objects other than themselves. These objects may be pictures, incomplete sentences, drawings, and the like. Anastasi (1982) classifies projective techniques into five types: the various unstructured inkblot techniques (Rorschach Inkblot Test, Holtzman Inkblot Technique), which one might call *associative* techniques; the more highly structured *picture* techniques (Thematic Apperception Test and Children's Apperception Test); *verbal* techniques (various word association and sentence completion tasks

---

[9] An early factor analysis by Flanagan and subsequent research has demonstrated only two independent factors (self-confidence and solitariness). Therefore, instead of these six scores, there should be but two, those based on the factor analytic studies.

such as the Rotter Incomplete Sentence Test); *pictorial* techniques (the Picture Frustration Study); and *expressive* techniques (Machover Draw-A-Person Test). Projective tests may be differentiated from self-report inventories in many other ways: (1) Projective tests normally present unstructured stimuli, whereas self-report inventories are predominantly structured. The unstructured task permits individuals to project their feelings, which reflect their needs, motives, and concerns. (2) Projective tests are more resistant to faking and the influence of response set than are self-report inventories.[10] (3) Projective tests are interesting and novel and hence can easily be used with young children or with persons who are afraid of a formal pencil-and-paper test. (4) Projective tests can be either verbal or nonverbal, but self-report inventories are verbal and hence are not applicable to illiterates and very young children. (5) Self-report inventories, at least most of them, can be objectively scored, but projective tests are very susceptible to the subjective feelings of the scorer, even when certain guidelines are used in the scoring. (6) Projective tests are usually based on or reflect psychoanalytic theory such as that of Jung or Freud. (7) Projective tests normally utilize a global approach in the assessment of personality,[11] and often go beyond personality syndromes per se and concern themselves with creativity and critical-thinking ability.

Projective tests and self-report inventories share many things in common: (1) They have relatively low validity and reliability; (2) they provide some of the information needed to obtain a better understanding of the individual; (3) scoring systems vary from elaborate multifactor systems with profiles to nonquantifiable interpretive information; (4) most have inadequate norms; and (5) they can be administered either individually or in groups. Both structured and unstructured personality tests should be interpreted only by qualified persons. Because the administration, scoring, and interpretation of projective tests is complex and because of the formal training and experience needed to work with them, we will dispense with their further evaluation.

Summary of Personality Inventories

In summary, personality inventories (adjustment inventories) are intrinsically crude instruments, are not yet ready for general use in our schools, and should not be part of the test battery that is normally and routinely administered in school testing programs. Even the best of them must be used with caution and only by trained and experienced counselors or clinicians. With the exception of the problem checklists, we may go as far as to say that personality assessment should be withheld from the classroom teacher. This

---

[10] Even though a maladjusted person may attempt to fake a response, it is quite conceivable that the faked response will indicate that the individual is maladjusted.

[11] Color, movement, size, and so forth are frequently considered when interpreting a test protocol.

does not imply, however, that personality assessment should be barred from the public school. In order to gather empirical data, it is necessary to administer tests in general to pupils. The test results, however, should be used primarily for counseling and research rather than for making instructional decisions. Until personality tests achieve the stature of our cognitive measures and of some of the interest scales, they should be handled with great caution.

ATTITUDE AND VALUE ASSESSMENT

Although affective measurement encompasses the totality of the individual's personality, of which attitudes are just a segment, we focus our attention on the measurement of attitudes, since many aspects of personality assessment are beyond the scope of the classroom teacher.

Attitudes are learned. Because they are learned, they can be changed if deemed necessary. However, before people can alter, modify, or reinforce something, they must know the status of that "something." In fact, as early in the school year as possible, teachers should try to identify students who have positive and negative attitudes and implement appropriate strategies so as to accentuate the positive and eliminate the negative. Despite the methodological problems associated with attitude measurement, teachers should know something about attitudes and how they can be measured. The remainder of this chapter considers (1) the general characteristics of attitudes, (2) the evaluation of attitude scales, and (3) the assessment of pupil study habits inventories.

General Characteristics of Attitudes

Relevant to, and to be considered in, attitude measurement are certain traits or characteristics. These are listed below:[12]

1. Attitudes are predispositions to respond overtly to social objects.
2. A variety of definitions have been posited for attitudes, but all share a common theme that attitudes guide and direct an individual's behavior. For this reason, it is imperative for teachers to know something about attitudes, how they are formed, how they are changed, and how they relate to the teaching-learning process.
3. Attitudes, per se, are *not* directly observable but are inferred from a person's overt behavior, both verbal and nonverbal. You cannot see prejudice but you can observe the behavior of one who is prejudiced. Thus, on the basis of observations of someone's consistent behavior pattern to a stimulus, we would conclude that the individual displays

[12] See Shaw & Wright (1967) for a fuller treatment of the characteristics of attitudes.

this or that attitude (Shaw, 1973). It should be noted that these observations can be either *unstructured*—the teacher makes no particular effort to observe some behavioral trait, but when the teacher does see it, the situation, event, and behavior are noted—or *structured*—the teacher is interested in learning, for example, what Mary's attitude toward reading is. The teacher then purposely contrives a situation (places some books on a table, maneuvers Mary in front of the table) and observes/records Mary's behavior. Still another approach is to measure a person's attitude(s) by means of an attitude scale.

4. Attitude scales can be constructed in a variety of ways, the most common ones being the Thurstone, Likert, Guttman, and Semantic Differential methods.

5. Attitude scales are highly susceptible to faking, and therefore any interpretation of this type of self-report behavior should be made accordingly.

6. Attitude scales, like any affective instrument, are beset with a multitude of methodological problems that make their interpretation dubious.

7. Attitudes are evaluative and can be represented on some continuum of "favorableness."

8. Attitudes vary in intensity (strength of feeling) and direction. Two persons may have the same attitude toward abortion, but they may differ in how strongly they feel about the issue. Or they may be at completely opposite ends of the "favorableness" continuum but with the *same* degree of intensity. (For example, on the abortion issue, Alan may strongly agree and Ilene may strongly disagree. Both Alan and Ilene feel strongly about their position, but they are diametrically opposed.)

9. Attitudes vary in affective saliency—that is, some attitudes (such as toward abortion) are accompanied by or connected with a person's emotions.

10. Attitudes represent varying degrees of embeddedness or interrelatedness to other attitudes. As would be expected, attitudes related to similar objects, such as integration and equality of education, are more likely to be interconnected than attitudes toward dissimilar objects, such as capital punishment and women's liberation.

11. Attitudes are relatively stable, especially in adults. This does not mean that they cannot be changed or modified. Rather, it is more difficult to change the attitudes of an adult than of an adolescent or young child. The fact that attitudes are relatively stable supports the belief of many social psychologists that attitude scales can provide reliable measures, although possibly less so than for tests of cognitive skills or knowledge.

12. Despite the variety of problems associated with affective measurement, despite the fact that the validity and reliability of attitude scales are lower than for cognitive measures, and despite the reluctance of many teachers to pay appropriate attention to affective instructional/learning objectives, attitude scales can often be used effectively by the classroom

teacher to obtain a better understanding of pupils. The results obtained from attitude scales can be useful in educational planning and evaluation. Acquisition of desirable attitudes is one of the major goals in our schools. Without knowledge of the prevailing attitudes of the pupil, class, or school, it would be difficult to plan accordingly.

Evaluation of Attitude Scales

The usefulness of any test or scale depends upon its reliability, validity, norms, and ease of administration, scoring, and interpretation. We now briefly summarize how these factors relate to attitude scales.

Reliability. Attitude scales, by and large, have reliabilities around .75. This is much less than those obtained for cognitive measures, and hence the results obtained from attitude scales should be used primarily for group guidance and discussion.

Validity. In general, attitude measures have less validity data available than do other noncognitive measures. This is partly because of the problems inherent in measuring attitudes and partly because many of the measures were constructed primarily for research purposes.

The correlations obtained between the scale scores and observed behavior are typically low. Nevertheless, knowledge of the disparities between expressed attitudes and actual behavior is useful in understanding and working with the individual.

Norms. In the majority of instances no norms accompany standardized attitude scales. The user must be careful in the interpretation of the test scores. Naturally local norms can be prepared. Even if appropriate sampling techniques have been employed to select the standardization sample and even if the normative data are adequate, the fact that conditions affecting attitudes are so variable suggests that very recent norms be used. For example, American attitudes toward Japan were markedly different on December 6 and December 8, 1941.

Administration, scoring, and interpretation. In contrast to the projective tests considered in the previous section, attitude scales are easy to administer and score. They require no formal training and can be handled easily by the classroom teacher. The interpretation of attitude-test scores, on the other hand, is an entirely different matter. Because of psychometric problems, the user should be cautious in interpreting the data.

Assessment of Pupil Study Habits and Attitudes Toward School

As has been mentioned at various points in this text, the matter of how well a student does on an aptitude or achievement test depends upon factors other than basic ability or intelligence. Some of the factors that must be considered in assessing or appraising an individual's academic performance are (1) mental maturity; (2) motivation; (3) study habits; (4) study skills; and (5) attitudes toward the value of an education, teachers, school, and courses. Gene, a very bright student (speaking in terms of scholastic aptitude), may be performing at a somewhat mediocre level. He may be getting Cs and Ds, whereas we would predict from a valid measure of his scholastic aptitude that he should be receiving As and Bs. On the other hand, Pam, who is less intellectually gifted, might be getting Bs, although we would predict that she would obtain Cs. Why the discrepancy between predicted achievement and realized achievement? No doubt, how pupils study and what their attitudes toward education are play a significant role in an explanation of such discrepancies.

We now briefly consider one standardized study-habits and skills inventory.

Survey of Study Habits and Attitudes (SSHA)   Published by the Psychological Corporation (1965), the work has two forms: H (for grades 7–12) and C (for college students and high school seniors). It is untimed, but majority of students complete the SSHA within 20 to 35 minutes. Seven scores (based on four basic scales) include the following: Delay Avoidance (DA), Work Methods (WM), Study Habits (SH = DA + WM), Teacher Approval (TA), Educational Acceptance (EA), Study Attitudes (SA = TA + EA), and Study Orientation (SO = SH + SA or the total of the four basic scales).

The SSHA was designed (1) to identify the differences in study habits and attitudes between students who do well in their academic work and those who do poorly, (2) to assist students who might benefit from improved study habits (this improvement may result from counseling and/or instruction on how to study), and (3) to predict academic success for high school and college students. The authors recommend using it for screening, diagnosis, research, and as a teaching aid. The SSHA consists of 100 items such as the following, which attempt to assess the "motivation for study and attitudes toward academic work" syndromes rather than merely the mechanics of study:

Daydreaming distracts my attention from my lessons while I am studying (DA).
My teachers criticize my written work for being poorly planned or hurriedly written (WM).
My teachers make their subjects interesting and meaningful to me (TA).
I feel that I would study harder if I were given more freedom to choose subjects that I like (EA).[13]

The authors' intent to go *beyond* measuring mechanics of study is perhaps the most differentiating factor of the SSHA from other study-habit invento-

[13] Reproduced by permission. Copyright © 1953, 1965, the Psychological Corporation, Cleveland, Ohio. All rights reserved.

ries. Subjects respond to each item by means of a five-element key ranging from Rarely (0–15 percent of the time) to Almost Always (86–100 percent of the time). In an attempt to control for response set, the "acceptable" (keyed) responses are randomly distributed at both ends of the continuum. The extreme positions are weighted twice that of the near-extreme positions. That is, if a negative item is keyed Rarely, it is given a weight of 2; a Sometimes response is given a weight of 1.

Both logical and empirical validities were stressed in the test's development. Items were chosen on the basis of interviews with students, and each item was empirically validated (correlations of the SSHA with grades, teachers' ratings, and aptitude scores) as to its applicability to the problem. For Form H (grades 7–12), student advice was obtained so that the language would be clear and meaningful to junior and senior high school students. The validity data presented in the test manual show that the SSHA is independent of scholastic achievement and that there is an increase in the predictive efficiency of grades when the SSHA is used in combination with aptitude test scores. Internal consistency (.87–.89) and test–retest (.83–.88) reliability estimates are reported for Form C. Test–retest reliabilities for Form H vary from .93 to .95. It is unfortunate that these data are based on only Texas students, especially because the correlation data reported for Form C show differences between college students in Texas and those in other parts of the country. Percentile norms are reported separately for each of the seven scores. For Form H, norms are provided for grades 7–9 combined and grades 10–12 combined. The Form H norming sample appears to be heavily weighted in favor of students from Texas and the southwestern region of the country.

To aid in test interpretation, the percentile scores can be plotted on the diagnostic profile sheet (on the reverse side of the answer sheet—see Figure 9.4). The pupil's scores can then be compared with the performance of the norm group and his strengths and weaknesses identified. A separate counseling key is provided. This key enables the teacher or counselor to identify critical responses—the items that differentiate between high and low scholastic achievers. Still, the test authors recommend that the counselor and student make a detailed, item-by-item analysis of the responses. It would have been desirable if the test authors had presented more descriptive information on the development of this key.

The SSHA was well conceived. It is easy for the pupil to understand and complete the inventory. It is easy to administer and score. It stresses the motivational and attitudinal aspects of study more than any other study-habits inventory.

Some other study habits and attitudes toward school are the Quality of School Life Scale, the Study Skills Test of the McGraw-Hill Basic Skills System, and some of the subtests of survey achievement batteries.

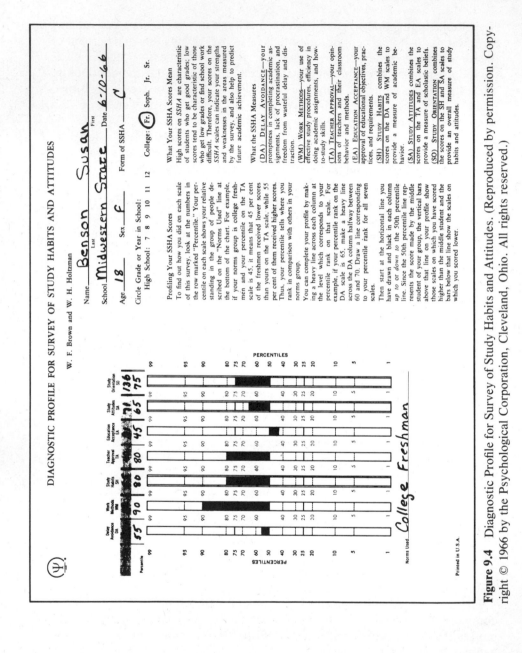

Figure 9.4 Diagnostic Profile for Survey of Study Habits and Attitudes. (Reproduced by permission. Copyright © 1966 by the Psychological Corporation, Cleveland, Ohio. All rights reserved.)

In conclusion, study-habit inventories have a place in the classroom and can be administered, scored, and interpreted by the classroom teacher. Although the majority of them stress the process of locating information, the Survey of Study Habits and Attitudes stresses attitudes and motivational aspects. Study-habit inventories, as with all self-report techniques, are dependent upon the respondent's honesty—they are only surveys of self-report. The essential question, "Do the results of a study-habit inventory in combination with previous GPA yield a higher cross-validated multiple R than do only previous GPA?" remains unanswered for most study-habit inventories.

SUMMARY

The principal ideas, suggestions, and recommendations of this chapter are summarized in the following statements:

1. Classroom teachers need to know about their pupils' attitudes, values, interests, and personality. This will not only give them a better understanding about the pupils' behavior (both cognitive and noncognitive) but will permit them to communicate with other professionals, such as the school diagnostician, psychologist, psychometrist, and psychiatrist.
2. With no formal training, the classroom teacher should be able to administer problem checklists, rating scales, observational schedules, and interest inventories. The classroom teacher can also interpret rating scales. Interest inventories, problem checklists, and personality tests should be interpreted only by specially trained personnel.
3. The major obstacles in measuring noncognitive characteristics are problems of (a) definition, (b) response set, (c) faking, (d) reliability and validity, and (e) interpretation.
4. Noncognitive assessment devices are not so psychometrically elegant as cognitive tests. Despite the limitation of noncognitive tools, they do provide useful information that cannot often be obtained by other means.
5. Three commonly used procedures for keying and constructing noncognitive tests are empirical, homogeneous, and logical.
6. Attitudes and interests are both concerned with likes and dislikes. Whereas attitudes have groups and social situations as their referent objects, interests are related to activities.
7. Interest inventories were originally concerned with a person's vocation and were designed primarily for college-bound high school youth. Today's inventories measure avocational interests, can be used with junior high school students, and not all are geared to college-bound students.

8. Earlier interest inventories have focused on the subject's likes and dislikes. Today more attention is being paid to other traits—motivation and personality—as they relate to interests.
9. More attention is now being paid to the study of vocational maturity and the development of inventories that will be useful in career development.
10. Although interest inventories differ in their content, their predictive validity, reliability, ease of scoring, and interpretation, they all share a common purpose of helping the user make better vocational and educational decisions. Despite the many similarities among interest inventories, there are nevertheless marked differences among them. The user must study the inventories carefully before adapting one.
11. Interests become more stable with age, but they are never permanently fixed. Thus, interest inventory results obtained in junior high school or for elementary school children should be interpreted with extreme caution.
12. Interest inventories are *not* designed to predict job success, academic success, job satisfaction, or personality adjustment. They are designed to encourage career exploration and to guide the teacher or counselor in helping students make vocational and educational decisions based on the similarity of their interests with persons successful in a particular vocation or avocation.
13. Interest inventory results can be helpful to classroom teachers in terms of helping them develop teaching strategies that will be most relevant to their pupils' interests.
14. Within the past two decades, much interest has been demonstrated in the study of career development and vocational maturity. Since 1970, at least eight standardized tests related to these areas have been published (or revised) and three large-scale career development programs initiated. Some of the tests are concerned with the subject's value orientation, some with personality, and some with motivation.
15. Personality inventories can be classified as either structured or unstructured, as well as in terms of their method of construction.
16. Problem checklists are essentially structured self-report inventories which provide the user with information the subject feels is of concern or a cause of worry. Problem checklists have no right or wrong answers and are not intended to measure personality per se.
17. Personality inventories can assist in identifying those persons who are in need of assistance and may help in ascertaining where or what their problems are. Despite their shortcomings, if used judiciously and if proper rapport is established and maintained, these inventories do permit the user to obtain a more complete understanding of the subject. They also provide subjects an opportunity to express and discuss their feelings.

18. Attitude scales are much less reliable and valid than are cognitive measures. They usually do not have norms. Although they can be administered by the classroom teacher, their interpretation is complex and questionable. Like many other affective measures, they provide the user with a better understanding of the individual, *provided* the subject has been truthful. Tests of study habits and attitudes were briefly discussed.

POINTS TO PONDER

1. Approximately 50 percent of the variance in grades among individuals can be accounted for by aptitude and achievement tests. Using noncognitive tests in addition does not increase this percentage very much. How do you account for this?
2. Write definitions for the following terms: *truthfulness, aggressiveness, rigidity, assistance,* and *deference.* Compare your definitions with those of your classmates. Do your definitions differ? If so, does this mean you would interpret personality inventories measuring these traits differently?
3. Should response set be controlled in personality inventories? (You may wish to do a thorough review of the literature before discussing the question.)
4. How would you employ empirical keying for the Strong Vocational Interest Blank so that it might be used to differentiate the interests of "good credit risks" from those of "poor credit risks"?
5. What would be the problems in developing a predictive interest inventory for fifth-graders?
6. Consider the following interest inventories: Strong-Campbell, Kuder OIS, Kuder GIS, Minnesota Vocational Interest Inventory, Vocational Preference Inventory, and Career Assessment Inventory. Which one(s) would you recommend for each of the following uses? Give reasons for your choices.
   a. An inventory is needed for an eleventh-grade course exploring careers and occupational choices.
   b. An inventory is required for use with eighth-grade students who desire careers that do not require a college degree.
   c. An inventory to be used in a technical-vocational high school where none of the students go on to college.
   d. An inventory that considers occupational choices as broad rather than specific areas.
   e. As the personnel manager for a large automobile manufacturer, you wish to use an interest inventory that will help you select assembly-line workers who will enjoy their work.

7. Interest and general adjustment inventories have not been found to be very useful in personnel selection uses. Why do you feel that they are of little value for this purpose?

8. If interests of adolescents are not very stable, can you in any way justify their use in junior or senior high school? Please explain.

9. The Kuder OIS is said to be ipsative. What significance does this have regarding its validity?

10. Is there a place for projective tests in (a) elementary school, (b) junior high school, and (c) senior high school? Defend your answer.

11. Rank the following types of standardized tests in terms of the necessity for frequent revision: achievement, aptitude, attitude, interest, problem checklists, projective, and self-adjustment inventories. Give reasons for your ranking.

12. What instructional use would you make of the results of a problem checklist?

13. As a new counselor, you find that your predecessor had been routinely administering a self-adjustment inventory as part of the school testing program. You are called to a school board meeting to explain the various tests used. Would you defend the use of the self-adjustment inventory? Why?

14. Recognizing the limitations of noncognitive tests, what arguments can you present to support their use in the public schools?

15. Develop a 20-item scale to measure teachers' attitudes toward culturally deprived children. What type of reliability estimate should you gather? How would you validate such a scale?

CHAPTER 10

Assessing Exceptionality[1]

INTRODUCTION
EQUALITY OF EDUCATION AND THE HANDICAPPED
ASSESSING THE EXCEPTIONAL CHILD
TYPES OF SPECIAL EDUCATION
MOTOR DEVELOPMENT MEASURES
SOME OTHER MEASURES
THE GIFTED
PUTTING IT ALL TOGETHER
A CASE STUDY: ALLAN

Frank, a fifth-grader, has a WISC-R IQ of 140 but has a percentile rank of 7 on the Gates-MacGinitie Reading Test. Frank has had reading problems since he began school. He is also overly aggressive, constantly getting into arguments (and sometimes fisticuffs) both on and off the playground, is surly, not interested in language arts and reading but very interested in science and mathematics. Is Frank learning-disabled (LD)? The discrepancy between his IQ and reading test scores is so marked that one must consider the possibility that Frank is LD. But how does one validly determine whether Frank is LD? Although the authors cannot provide any cookbook diagnostic recipes, one suggestion they can make is that a variety of information must be gathered in order to obtain a comprehensive picture of Frank. Some of this information will be culled from IQ tests, some from adaptive behavior inventories, some from achievement tests, some from checklists, rating scales, and other observational tools, and so forth. And depending on the condition studied, perceptual and motor skills tests may also be used. Then, and only then, should the teacher hypothesize possible causal relations and take appropriate action.

A legitimate question that you might have raised a decade ago is "I'm not a special-education teacher, so why do I have to know anything about tests

[1] Exceptionality is used in an all-inclusive sense. Although major emphasis is placed on ways to deal with children having deficiencies of one kind or another, we are aware that the gifted and talented also have special needs. Hence, the latter will also be considered in this chapter.

in this area?'' Such a question would not be asked today, because federal and state legislation has mandated that special-education students, where possible, be taught in the least restrictive environment, which is often the *regular* classroom (that is, these students are *mainstreamed*). In the 1977–1978 school year, about 67 percent of handicapped children and about 37 percent of the mentally retarded received their primary educational services in regular classrooms. As we will see in later sections, early initial identification and assessment of exceptional children is often done by regular classroom teachers. Therefore, it is imperative that they be knowledgeable about and actively involved in educating and testing handicapped children. The preceding discussion should *not* be interpreted as implying that only classroom teachers need be cognizant of special-education students and issues. The counselor, school psychologist, and other educators also play a vital role, as will be seen later.

The purpose of this chapter is twofold: (1) to acquaint you with some of the legislation (Public Law 94-142 in particular) dealing with the assessment and education of handicapped children, and (2) to introduce you to some of the standardized assessment tools that are used in the screening and diagnosis of exceptional children.

Although you need not become a legal scholar in order to understand recent federal regulations like PL 94-142 concerning the education of exceptional (handicapped) children, you should have minimal acquaintance with such legislation. Nor is it the intent of this chapter to make you a skilled clinician who is qualified to interpret some of the tests used. Rather, you should know something about the more commonly used tests so that you will be able to communicate effectively with other professionals and be able to use the test results to guide you in the development, delivery, and evaluation of an individual educational plan (IEP), which is mandated in PL 94-142.

Only within the last few decades has there been a concerted effort made to accommodate in our schools children who are handicapped because of physical, mental, or emotional deficiencies. In fact, until the early part of the twentieth century, handicapped children were either hidden at home or were institutionalized. In any event, they were relegated to isolation, especially insofar as their educational needs were concerned.

Of the nearly 9 million handicapped children in the United States today, less than one-half are receiving adequate educational services. This is indeed to be regretted in a country that has always prided itself in its educational system. Fortunately, however, with special programs and training given special-education teachers in teacher-training institutions today, and because of new legislation specifically aimed at improving the lot of the handicapped, the education received by these children is improving.

In this chapter, we are going to go beyond testing and will be concerned with assessment. Testing and assessment are *not* synonymous. Testing, as we have been using the term, may or may not be part of a larger process called assessment. Assessment is always an evaluative, interpretive appraisal of an individual's performance. Assessment, at least in the educational arena, is a multifaceted process that considers a variety of factors, such as extrapersonal, current life circumstances, and developmental history, when interpreting an individual's performance or behavior. Assessment considers the past as well as the present; utilizes systematic and nonsystematic observations; qualitative and quantitative data; and judgments.

After studying this chapter, the student should be able to do the following:

1. Recall the provisions of Public Law 94-142.
2. Understand the various categories of special education, as well as the various classifications within each category.
3. Discuss the various tests, scales, inventories, and other assessment tools used for special-education purposes.
4. Know what the ordinary classroom teacher should know about measurement in order to be able to deal effectively with "mainstreaming."

INTRODUCTION

It is assumed that you have had, or will have, a basic course in educational psychology. Accordingly, we have minimized our focus on the etiology and classification of the various handicaps as well as the definition of terms and will emphasize the techniques teachers can use in working with children with special needs. Also, we are not concerned with the educational/instructional strategies that can be used with exceptional children (there are a variety of excellent texts dealing with this). What we are concerned with in this chapter is the screening/diagnosis and subsequent assessment of exceptional children.

Writers in the learning problems area generally agree that there are three assessment levels: (1) the *screening* or *survey* level, in which group tests play a significant role; (2) the *intermediate* level, where diagnostic tests focus on a specific skill or ability; and (3) the *case study* method, in which a detailed workup of the child is made. Some of the tests that are appropriate for the screening and intermediate levels have been considered in previous chapters and will only be referred to here. Others will be discussed in more detail in the following sections.

Since the major national effort in dealing with the handicapped is an outgrowth of our concern with the equality of education for the handicapped and the resultant legislation and litigation, we will spend a few minutes discussing these areas.

EQUALITY OF EDUCATION AND THE HANDICAPPED

A movement toward equality of education for the handicapped came about through a series of landmark legal decisions which affirmed that all handicapped children, even the most severely debilitated, have the right to (1) an appropriate education, (2) due process of law, (3) nondiscriminatory testing and evaluation procedures, (4) a *free* public education, and (5) placement in the least restrictive environment. For the purpose of our discussion here, we are mainly concerned with the issue of nondiscriminatory testing and evaluation procedures, since that impinges on the role of the teacher, whether a regular or a special-education teacher. We are also concerned in this chapter with placement insofar as it relates to using assessment results in making valid placement decisions. The other three issues, although of importance, are more relevant to the school administrator than to the classroom teacher.

Nondiscriminatory Testing and Evaluation

As previously discussed, standardized tests in general, and scholastic aptitude tests in particular, have been severely criticized, and litigation has taken place in relation to the testing, identification, and placement of mentally retarded students. Two landmark California decisions were *Diana* v. *State Board of Education* (Civil Action No. C-70 37 R.F.P. N. D. Cal., Jan. 7, 1970, and June 18, 1973), and the oft-quoted *Larry P. v. Riles* (Civil Action No. 6-71-2270 343 F. Supp. 1036, N.D. Cal., 1972). The former case resulted in an agreement being reached whereby children were henceforth to be tested in their native language, and interpreters were to be used if bilingual examiners were not available. California was also directed to develop a standardized test that was valid for minority, nonwhite students. Finally, Chinese and Mexican-American children presently in classes for the educable mentally retarded were to be retested and reevaluated. In the *Larry P.* case, the judge ruled that traditional IQ tests discriminated against black students in diagnosing their mental handicaps. The judge further ruled that the San Francisco School District was not permitted to place black children in classes for the mentally retarded solely on the basis of IQ tests, if such placement resulted in a racial imbalance in these classes. A case similar to that of *Larry P.* was the one in Chicago (*PASE* v. *Hannon,* 1980) in which Judge Grady contradicted the decision made in the *Larry P.* case.

Although the consequences of these legal decisions are not clear-cut at the time of writing because the cases are at the appellate level and no doubt will go to the Supreme Court, it would appear that, for the time being, in California at least, factors other than a scholastic aptitude score have to be used for placing a student in a class for the mentally retarded or in some other special-education program. In addition, individually administered intelligence tests have to be used; if the tests are verbal, they must be in the examinee's native language; any assessment has to include estimates of the child's adaptive behavior; the examiner has to be fluent in the examinee's native language; the tests used must be free from any racial or cultural bias; and no test that has some manipulative tasks can be used when testing the physically handicapped. The cases previously cited no doubt played a large part in the enactment of Public Law 94-142, with the attendant regulations that were printed in the *Federal Register* of August 23, 1977. (See Lidz, 1981, for a discussion of the educational implications of PL 94-142. For a fuller discussion of court rulings related to the discussion of whether testing discriminates against minorities and the handicapped, see Bersoff, 1984.)

Public Law 94-142

Perhaps the most sweeping legislation since the Elementary and Secondary Education Act is Public Law 94-142, which became law in 1975. This law, also referred to as the Education for All Children Act, and the concept of *mainstreaming* have drawn all teachers—not only the special-education teachers—into the arena of evaluating and providing for the handicapped. Ordinary classroom teachers must now be, or quickly become, familiar with the various techniques available to identify the handicapped, the procedures available to monitor the progress of the handicapped, and the services available to help meet their educational needs.

The major provisions of PL 94-142 are as follows:

1. All handicapped children between the ages of 3 and 21 are entitled to free public education.
2. The early identification and intervention of handicapped children between the ages of 3 and 5 is encouraged by providing financial incentive grants to those that provide such children with special education.
3. A contract is drawn up so that an individually prescribed educational program is developed by a school official, the child's teacher and parents, and, where possible, the child. This contract must identify the child's strengths and weaknesses, short- and long-term goals, and the services that will be used to reach those goals. Also, the contract is to indicate the amount of time the child is to spend in the regular classroom and the manner in which the child's progress is to be assessed and monitored.
4. All tests, scales, inventories, and assessment tools used to diagnose, classify, and place handicapped children must be free from racial and cultural bias. All testing is to be done in the child's native tongue.
5. Handicapped and nonhandicapped children will be taught together as long as possible. This is referred to as "mainstreaming." Handicapped children will be placed in special classes only when the type or severity of the handicap is such as to preclude them from obtaining maximally effective instruction in the regular classroom.

6. All handicapped children must be identified through preliminary screening instruments.
7. Each child is to be reevaluated regularly in the program.
8. The diagnostic assessment is to be done by a team composed of school psychologists, resource specialists, administrators, and *teachers*—with parent participation—utilizing a variety of techniques.

One can readily see that in order to comply with these mandates, achievement and aptitude tests must be administered to exceptional children. It should be obvious that most of the conventional, group-administered (and, sometimes, individually administered) aptitude and achievement tests previously discussed are invalid when dealing with exceptional children. For example, can a blind child deal with the performance subtests of the WISC-R? Can a deaf child be given the verbal portion of the WISC-R or the Stanford-Binet? Would a child who is orthopedically handicapped be able to write his or her answers to any of our pencil-and-paper tests? The answer to these and similar questions is in the negative. Accordingly, special tests, or modifications of existing tests, are available for assessing the cognitive skills and abilities of exceptional children. In the next sections, we will review some of the tests used to assess exceptional children.

PL 94-142 and the Regular Classroom Teacher   Where do regular classroom teachers fit into the implementation of PL 94-142? What do they have to know about testing? According to the law, the regular classroom teacher has responsibilities in the following areas:

1. *Identification.* Is Gregory a slow learner, or is he learning-disabled? This differentiation is vital, since PL 94-142 covers the latter (and provides commensurate financial support for education) but not the former. In order to make this distinction, *both* aptitude and achievement data are needed.
2. *Individual Assessment.* The regular classroom teacher has the responsibility of gathering data about the child's competencies. This assessment will normally consider the mental, physical, language, psychomotor, adaptive, and sociological functioning of the child. Some of these data are obtained from informal classroom assessments, while other information is obtained from standardized tests. But which standardized tests? Should one use data obtained from a group or an individual test? Why? Which test(s) is (are) most valid? We will answer these questions in later sections.
3. *Developing and Implementing an Individual Educational Plan.* The data gathered above determine, in large part, the child's educational objectives and the instructional strategies to be used. Generally, assessment of the degree of accomplishment of these goals is made with informal, teacher-made tests.

In any of the activities noted above, standardized tests often play a significant role, especially in the identification, diagnosis, and learning assessment of exceptional children. Because regular classroom teachers play such an important role today in the education of the exceptional child, they must be cognizant of the measurement tools available and possess the measurement skills needed.

Before discussing the types of special education and some of the methods in which special-education students can be diagnosed, we should spend a few minutes considering some of the problems involved when assessing children with special needs.

ASSESSING THE EXCEPTIONAL CHILD

Although there are difficulties inherent in the assessment of ordinary or "normal" children, there are even more problems when dealing with the exceptional child.[2] First, most of the standardized aptitude and achievement tests have been normed using normal children—that is, the norms have been developed on the basis of performance of children who are not at one extreme or the other, such as hyperactive, emotionally disturbed, or hard-of-hearing. Hence, the norms of standardized tests when used with special-education students might not be appropriate and could raise unrealistic expectations. Second, observation is one of the most important tools that can be used to diagnose children with special needs. However, the observational approach under ordinary circumstances (but possibly more so when used with special-education students) is fraught with many problems, particularly that of bias. Third, children with learning difficulties or behavior problems, especially the latter, may vary greatly in their behavior. Johnny may be hyperactive today and tomorrow but next week may be normal. Or Mary may be grossly uncoordinated on the playground today but behave differently tomorrow when a new game is played. Remember, too, that when dealing with the exceptional child, you are dealing with the extremes, be it of learning ability, personality behavior, or physical coordination. This often results in measurement that is not as reliable as would be obtained if one were dealing with the average child. In dealing with the exceptional child, particularly with the learning-disabled, where we invariably have many scores, we must be cognizant of the unreliability of difference scores.

Another problem associated with the testing of the handicapped is the question of whether modifying the directions or the stimuli (such as using large type or Braille for the visually handicapped; oral procedures for the blind; nonverbal directions and tests for the deaf) affects the test's validity.

---

[2] For a refreshing and unique way of looking at exceptional children from birth through old age, see Cleland & Swartz, (1982).

As of now, little empirical evidence is available to answer this question with any degree of certainty. The 1985 *Standards for Educational and Psychological Testing,* addressing the problems associated with using modified standardized tests for the handicapped, carefully points out that test publishers have a responsibility for issuing appropriate caveats in their manuals vis-à-vis test interpretation; that they should explain what modifications have been made and how they might affect the test's validity when used with a handicapped population; that the modified test's validity and reliability are to be reported; and that special norms be available when interhandicapper comparisons are to be made. (See Laing & Farmer, 1984, for a discussion of the modifications made by the ACT Program for testing the handicapped.) Finally, the examiner effect, which may be operative when dealing with normal as well as handicapped persons, appears to be exacerbated when testing the handicapped. Fuchs, Featherstone, Garwicj, & Fuchs, 1984, reported that for speech and language-handicapped children, their performance was significantly higher when they knew the examiner. These researchers found a significant task complexity by response mode (gestural v. verbal) interaction, suggesting that those tests requiring verbal responses may spuriously underestimate examinees' abilities, especially those of handicapped children. We should be aware of this, since many of our screening, diagnostic, and IQ tests, even for exceptional children, employ a verbal response mode.

Strain, Sainto, & Mahan (1984) report research which suggests that current standardized tests (for reasons such as those mentioned above) may have limited value in assessing the ability and achievement of seriously handicapped persons. In fact, Gerber & Semmel (1984) contend that teachers' observations may yield more valid data than do our standardized tests. Does this mean that the seriously handicapped are untestable or that the situation is hopeless? Definitely not! It does suggest, however, that we will have to use different approaches.[3]

Ysseldyke & Thurlow (1984) contrast the norm-referenced approach (which relies almost exclusively on standardized assessment tools) and the continuous-monitoring approach (which relies heavily on more subjective data gathered from observations and parental input) for making decisions about the mildly handicapped and propose a modified norm-referenced approach that combines the two methods for making diagnoses and referral decisions.

Thus it is obvious that there are inherent problems in the assessment of exceptional children and adults. This, however, should not dissuade us in

[3] Although we firmly believe that the classroom teacher, by virtue of daily contacts with students, is in the *best* position to make a preliminary screening and identification of the exceptional child, we agree with the courts that teacher observation, per se, is insufficient to identify learning-disabled children and should be supplemented with standardized test data (Frederick, 1977).

our attempts to study such individuals. Rather, it should spur professional test makers to improve existing instrumentation and should force psychologists and educators to temper their conclusions based on the results of their tests.

TYPES OF SPECIAL EDUCATION

There are different categories of students needing special education—such as the physically and visually handicapped, the speech impaired, the mentally retarded, the hard-of-hearing, the deaf, the gifted, the learning-disabled, the emotionally disturbed, and any others needing special attention and assistance—which reflect different social, emotional, physical, and mental conditions among children. For that reason, we cannot refer to special-education students in an all-inclusive sense. Rather, we must carefully specify the type of special-education student with which we are dealing.

In a few instances, the initial diagnosis and referral is made by a specialist rather than by the regular classroom teacher.[4] But in many, if not most, instances, the initial diagnosis and referral is made by an observant teacher who notices that a pupil is not behaving normally. For example, Mary's eyes are always tearing, or Peter frequently cocks his head to the left, or Allan always appears to be tired. The tests used to diagnose children in need of special assistance can range from the highly sophisticated CAT scanner to the simple and familiar Snellen Eye Chart. Regardless of who makes the initial referral or diagnosis, the ordinary classroom teacher becomes an integral part of the treatment, since he or she is responsible for the development and monitoring of the educational program prescribed for the special education student. This places an added incentive for the regular classroom teacher to be aware of the different methods, tests, and instruments for assessing the special-education student.

The categories of special education to be considered in this chapter are as follows: *mentally retarded, emotionally disturbed, sensory handicapped* (visual, speech, hearing), *physically handicapped, learning-disabled,* and *gifted*. It should be noted that although we are discussing the various types of special-education students separately, it should *not* be implied that they are mutually exclusive. In fact, in many instances there is an interrelationship between one or more of the handicaps.

Mentally Retarded

Four categories of mental retardation are commonly used: slow learners, educable mentally retarded, trainable mentally retarded, and severely men-

---

[4] A complete educational assessment program for the handicapped requires a team effort of classroom teacher, diagnostician, school psychologist, and medical personnel.

tally retarded. Pupils in the first three categories are generally placed in special-education or regular (mainstreamed) classes, while the severely mentally retarded (IQ levels below 25) are generally institutionalized early in life and require constant attention.

Critics have charged that people are classified as mentally retarded solely on the basis of an IQ score. In fact, it has been asserted that up until the 1970s, a standardized IQ test such as the Stanford-Binet or the Wechsler Scales was the *sine qua non* for determining mental retardation. We deplore such an approach! Today, there is less rigid reliance on IQ than in the past, and greater consideration of adaptive behavior, social and developmental history, and contemporary functioning in a variety of settings (see Haywood et al., 1982; Grossman, 1973, 1977, 1981). This is evident from the current American Association of Mental Deficiency (AAMD) definition that ''mental retardation refers to significantly subaverage intellectual functioning existing concurrently with deficits in adaptive behavior and manifested during the developmental period'' (Grossman, 1977, p. 5). The IQ score ranges used for the classifications are somewhat arbitrary and may vary from one school system to another. Some of the more commonly used individual intelligence tests for diagnosis and classification are the Wechsler Intelligence Test for Children—Revised, the Bayley Scales of Infant Development, and the McCarthy Scales of Children's Abilities. In some instances, an initial diagnosis is made by screening pupils with a group intelligence test such as the Otis-Lennon or Differential Aptitude Tests. (See Buros, 1978, for a discussion of these and other tests described in this chapter.)

Generally speaking, the slow learner and educable mentally retarded are not diagnosed until the child enters school. At that time, parents and teachers may begin noticing symptoms that will be confirmed by the child's performance on regular school tests. (Note: Mental retardation is more easily seen than measured.) In contrast, the trainable mentally retarded usually and the severely mentally retarded definitely are identified early in life. For example, hydrocephalics can be identified at birth and occasionally in the fetal stage. Children who are slow walkers or slow talkers, or generally late in their physical and mental development, can be readily identified before they enter school. Hence, the identification is made early in the child's life while at home or at birth or sometimes even before birth, with the final diagnosis being made by a specialist such as a neurologist or psychologist.

Although comprehensive assessment is an important ingredient for normal children, it is even more significant for the mentally retarded, in order to provide them with appropriate educational and therapeutic programs. Assessment programs for the mentally retarded generally include some measure of adaptive behavior in daily living situations, such as the Vineland Social Maturity Scale or the Adaptive Behavior Scale; some measure of motor development, such as the Bruininks-Oseretsky Test of Motor Proficiency; and some pluralistic assessment measure, such as System of Multicultural Pluralistic Assessment (SOMPA) (see pp. 199–201), which includes the WISC-R (or WPPSI for younger children), in addition to standardized measures of the examinee's social competence in his or her environment and the examinee's physical condition (neurological and physiological).

Of the more than 100 adaptive behavior scales, three of the more commonly used are the Vineland Social Maturity Scale (VSMS), the Adaptive Behavior Inventory for Children (ABIC), and the American Association for Mental Deficiency Adaptive Behavior Scale (AAMD/ABS). We will now discuss the three in greater detail, paying particular attention to the Vineland.

Vineland Adaptive Behavior Scale (VABS)   Published by the American Guidance Service (1984), VABS is a revision of the perennial Vineland Social Maturity Scale. It has three forms. The Survey Form (297 items), which is most similar to the original Vineland Scale, and the Expanded Form (577 items, of which 297 are from the Survey) are designed to assess the adaptive behavior of persons from birth to 18 years, 11 months of age. The Classroom Form (244 items, some of which are found in the other forms) is for those students who range from 3 years to 12 years, 11 months of age. Responses are obtained by interviewing either the child's parent, primary guardian, or teacher about the child's *usual* abilities. In fact, one can collect data from each of these sources and interpret the child's behavior from each perspective.

The VABS is especially designed for the mentally retarded but can be used with other handicapped and nonhandicapped persons.

Adaptive behavior is assessed in the following four domains and subdomains:

Communication
- Receptive (what child understands)
- Expressive (what child says)
- Written (what child reads and writes)

Daily Living Skills
- Personal (personal hygiene, eating habits)
- Domestic (household tasks performed)
- Community (how child uses money, telephone, time)

Socialization
- Interpersonal Relations (interaction with others)
- Play and Leisure Time
- Coping Skills (sensitivity)

Motor Skills
- Gross (use of arms and legs for movement)
- Fine (use of hands and fingers for manipulation)

A total Adaptive Behavior Composite score is the combination of the four domains. A Maladaptive Behavior domain is included in *both* the Survey and Expanded forms and consists of items that represent undesirable behavior.

The Survey Form is a semistructured interview of a parent or care-giver and must be administered by a trained interviewer. Whereas the Survey Form gives a general assessment of adaptive behavior, the Expanded Form provides for a more comprehensive assessment.

The Classroom edition is independently completed by teachers and contains items related to basic academic functioning. However, interpretation should be done only by trained clinicians.

The Technical and Interpretive manuals give good directions for administering, scoring, and interpreting the results and contain informative technical data. In addition, the manual and program planning report provide valuable suggestions for prescriptive educational treatment, or habilitative programs.

The VABS is standardized on *stratified representative* national samples using 1980 census data. Supplementary norms developed with residential and nonresidential samples of emotionally disturbed, hearing-impaired, and hearing-handicapped children are available for the Survey and Expanded forms. For each of the four major domain scores and total composite score, standard scores, national percentile ranks, stanines, and age equivalents are available, as is an *adaptive level* (high, adequate, or low performance categorization). For the subdomains, adaptive levels and age equivalents are provided. A variety of other norms are provided in the Interpretive Manual.

Reliability estimates were computed using internal-consistency, test–retest, and interrater procedures. Validity studies are also reported.

Reports to parents are available for each form. They explain the child's derived scores in relation to his or her strengths and weaknesses. Space is also available for parental recommendations.

Six commendable features of the VABS are (1) an audiocassette that presents sample interviews; (2) substantial overlap between the standardization samples of the Survey and Expanded versions and the Classroom edition, which allows for direct comparisons of scores; (3) substantial overlap between the standardization samples of the VABS and K-ABC; (4) a computer software program (ASSIST) that permits rapid score conversion and profiling as well as effective record keeping; (5) a Maladaptive Scale; and (6) the use of noninstitutionalized as well as institutionalized subjects for the standardization.

It is still too early to poll the jury regarding the scale's predictive validity. On the surface, the VABS is a most prominent addition to the measurement and diagnosis of adaptive behavior.

Adaptive Behavior Inventory for Children (ABIC)   Published by the Psychological Corporation (1978), there is one form and 242 items. It is intended for ages 5–11. The ABIC is one of the three assessment models of SOMPA (see pp. 199–201). Six areas of adaptive behavior are measured: Family, Peers,

Community, School, Earner/Consumer, and Self-Maintenance. That is, the ABIC measures role behavior in the home, neighborhood, and community. Some of the items are as follows:

"How does the child get along with the children in the neighborhood?"
"Does the child use a can or bottle opener?"

The examiner interviews the principal guardian of the child (generally the mother). All respondents are asked the first 35 items.

The 207 items in Part II are grouped by age and only those items appropriate for the child are asked. A five-point scale is used. Provision is made for indicating inability to answer because of lack of knowledge. Raw and scaled scores are obtained for each of the six area scores, as is a total score.

Because the ABIC was standardized on a random sample of California children, the norms are of questionable worth, vis-à-vis generalizability to the nation's children. Split-half reliabilities for the scaled scores were computed for each age level and for each of three ethnic groups and are satisfactory.

Validity, according to Mercer (1979, p. 109), is "judged by its ability to reflect accurately the extent to which the child is meeting the expectations of the members of the social systems covered in the scales. . . ." Unfortunately, the examiner may find it difficult if not impossible to ascertain the community's expectations and therefore will be unable to ascertain validly whether the child has adapted effectively. In studying validity, various correlations were computed between the ABIC and various aptitude, achievement, and sociocultural scales. It is hoped that more empirical validity data will be forthcoming.

Adaptive Behavior Scale (ABS)   The program is published by the American Association for Mental Deficiency (revised 1974). Although designed primarily for the mentally retarded, it can be used effectively with emotionally maladjusted and handicapped persons. There is one form, applicable from ages 3 to 69. It takes from 15 to 30 minutes to administer. Two types of competencies are assessed: affective and behavioral. Like the Vineland Scale, the information needed is based on the observations of the examinees' everyday behavior and can be completed by anyone who has close contact with and knowledge about the examinee.

The ABS has 110 items grouped into two parts. Part I (66 items) is a developmental scale covering 10 behavioral domains concerning basic survival skills and habits deemed important to the maintenance of personal independence. For some of the 10 domains, there are further subdivisions. For example, Independent Functioning is further categorized into eating, toilet use, care of clothing, etc. Provision is made in scoring of questions dealing with activities the examinee has not had an opportunity to experience (e.g., eating in a restaurant). Part II (44 items) covers 14 behavior domains that focus primarily on maladaptive behavior related to personality and behavioral disorders, such as hyperactivity and withdrawal. In each of the 14 domains, a 1 is assigned to those behaviors (e.g., bites others) that occur occasionally, a 2 if occurrence is frequent.

The fact that the test was standardized on an institutionally based mentally retarded population limits the generalizability of the normative data and raises other psychometric questions. Percentile norms for 11 age groups, from 3 to 69 years, are presented. The Manual does not provide any reliability data other than interrater reliabilities, which range from .71 to .98 for Part I and from .37 to .77 for Part II. Evidence suggests that most of the domains do not overlap. A paucity of data are furnished to demonstrate the scale's validity.

Clear administration and scoring instructions are given in the Manual. In addition, the scale's authors caution the user in interpreting the scores. According to the authors, it is of paramount importance to interpret an examinee's scores relative to his or her ability to function in the environment.

The Public School Version (grades 2–6) is identical to the 1974 ABS except for the 15 items deleted to conform to public school settings. The only other marked departure from the ABS is that the rater uses a different scoring system.

Whereas Salvia & Ysseldyke (1978) are not too positive in their evaluation of either the ABS or the Public School, Speat (1980) is not overly critical, contending that the ABS provides "valid estimates of group membership."

Other examples of adaptive behavior scales are Watson's Behavior Modification Technology, Balthazar's Scale of Adaptive Behavior, the TMR Social Competency Tests, and the Cain-Levine Social Competency Scales. The latter two are especially designed to assess the social competency of *trainable* mentally retarded persons.

Problems in Assessing Adaptive Behavior   It would appear that regardless of the scale used to measure adaptive behavior, there are two inherent problems: (1) the traditional adaptive behavior scales lean heavily on information gathered from "third-parties," and this information may be either incorrect, biased, or both, and (2) because many retarded persons have difficulty in communication, securing valid measures and information from them is very difficult, sometimes even impossible.

Assessing the learning potential of the mentally retarded has been a challenging endeavor. For a variety of reasons, the contemporary scholastic aptitude measures are being replaced by *dynamic assessment* tools that are concerned with the measurement of learning and cognitive *processes* (see Feuerstein, Rand, & Hoffman, 1979; Anastasi, 1980; and Switzky, 1981).

In summary, we can say that presently there are no standardized and well-normed tests of adaptive behavior covering infancy through adulthood. Unfortunately, many of the scales have been normed on an institutionalized and/or retarded population. It should also be noted that there is no single, all-inclusive adaptive behavior scale that covers all areas of behavior—social, motor, and the like. Accordingly, users wishing to assess adaptive behavior must select the most valid scale. Care must also be exercised in ascertaining the relevancy of the standardization sample for a particular examinee. For example, one shouldn't use the ABS for a noninstitutional examinee. Nor should the ABS even be considered if the examinee is not emotionally maladjusted or developmentally disabled.

Emotionally Disturbed

Another handicapped group worthy of special attention and consideration are those children who are classified as emotionally disturbed. There is disagreement as to both the definition of and the causes of emotional disturbance. Most children exhibit symptoms of emotional disturbance sometime in their life. Have we all not fantasized or hit our head on the wall at one time? No doubt we have. But should children who exhibit such behavior be classified as emotionally disturbed? We believe not. We do believe, however, that it is necessary for the ordinary classroom teacher to be observant of what might be termed abnormal behavior. We feel that teachers should be cognizant of the various stages of development and recognize that fighting, arguing, withdrawing, and bullying are not necessarily abnormal. Only when such behaviors are the general pattern rather than the exception to the rule should we become concerned. In other words, the teacher's judgment is very important in the identification stage.

There are no special tests, inventories, or scales that classroom teachers can use to help in their identification of emotionally disturbed children. All we are able to say is that teachers must be observant and then, if they have any suspicions, should call in professionals.

Sensory Handicapped

Classified as sensory handicapped are children with vision, hearing, and speech defects.

One of the first things teachers should do if they suspect that a pupil is experiencing either social or academic difficulty is to check the child's visual and hearing acuity. A child who has difficulty seeing or hearing, or both, will undoubtedly have difficulty in learning. Students who cannot see the board will not be able to read what is written on it and may incorrectly answer questions written on the board, because they have *misread* the questions, not necessarily because they do not know the correct response. And if there are many instances where the student gives an incorrect answer because of a hearing or sight problem, the student may be labeled as stupid or a smart aleck.

Visually Handicapped   There are two categories of visually handicapped— *partially sighted* and *blind*—depending upon their degree of vision expressed in terms of how well the person is able to read letters from 20 feet that a normal person can read from 20 feet. For example, a person with 20/40 vision is able to read letters at 20 feet that a normal person is able to read at 40 feet. A very simple screening test is the familiar Snellen Wall Chart.

There are three ways in which vision may be limited: (1) color vision problems, (2) field of vision (tunnel vision) limitations, and (3) visual acuity weakness. Although there are a variety of tests and instruments available for diagnostic screening for visual problems—such as the Snellen Wall Chart, the Massachusetts Vision Test, the Fitneus Vision Tester, the Dvorine Pseudo-Isochromatic Plates, and the Ishahara Color Blind Test—the observant teacher once again is the initial screener. Children complaining of frequent dizzy spells, with red or watery eyes, sloppy, unaligned written work, tilted heads or the habit of squinting when reading, and letter reversals in reading may be suffering from vision problems.[5] An alert teacher generally is able to see the problem(s) and request additional testing by a specialist.

It should be evident that performance tests and tests that require extensive reading, such as paragraph comprehension, are not appropriate for assessing the aptitude or achievement level of blind examinees (although the material could be read to the examinees, they would need a phenomenal memory, especially for multiple-choice items). The most suitable procedures for testing the blind are oral examinations, although adaptations of existing tests can be used (the Binet and Wechsler have Braille editions; the SAT, the SCAT, and portions of the GRE have large-type editions). An aptitude test specifically designed for the blind is the Blind Learning Aptitude Test (BLAT). The BLAT, a tactile test, uses a bas-relief format and is designed for children between 6 and 12 years of age. Only the test directions are verbal; the child can respond by pointing. Two scores are obtained: a learning–aptitude test age, and a learning–aptitude test quotient. BLAT was standardized on blind children in residential and day schools. The internal consistency and test–retest reliability reported compares favorably with other special population tests. Regrettably, the validity data are woefully inadequate.

Another type of visual handicap is related to visual perception, such as eye-hand coordination, visual attention to detail, and discrimination of shapes and colors. The WISC-R in its Picture Completion, Block Design, Coding, and Object-Assembly subtests, and the Illinois Test of Perceptual Abilities' Visual Memory, Visual Association, Visual Reception, and Visual

---

[5] See *Helping the Partially Sighted Child in the Classroom* (Publication T-300, National Society for the Prevention of Blindness, New York, 1965) for a list of 10 behavioral signs that may be indicative of a visual problem.

Closure subtests measure certain facets of visual perception. However, there are two commercially published tests that were specifically developed to assess visual-perceptual skills—the Bender-Visual Motor Gestalt Test and the Frostig Developmental Test of Visual Perception. Although Bender and Frostig approached their tasks from different theoretical orientations, both were concerned with measuring skills deemed to be important in reading so that remediation of the defects would result in improved reading ability. Unfortunately, the empirical evidence shows very little improvement in reading skill as a result of remediation in the weakness(es) shown by the tests.

Some other visual perception tests are the Primary Visual Motor Test, the Revised Visual Retention Test, and the Illinois Test of Psycholinguistic Abilities.

Hearing Handicapped   There are two categories of hearing handicapped children—*hard of hearing* (those children whose loss of hearing does not interfere with or affect language development) and *deaf* (children with a hearing loss so severe that language development does *not* occur. There are some who advocate the classification of deafness into two categories depending upon when the hearing loss occurred. Furthermore, degree of deafness is dependent upon frequency and intensity of sound.

Because many learning problems have as their genesis some form of auditory weaknesses, the early detection of hearing problems is imperative so that appropriate remediation can be initiated. Just think for a moment of what transpires in the classroom. Ms. Krone asks a question and Charles is expected to answer the question. But regardless of how bright Charles may be, he may either not answer the question or answer it incorrectly because he did not hear the question. Take Mary, who appears to be very aloof, is not accepted by her peers, is a loner, and eventually becomes a behavior problem. It is quite conceivable that Mary's behavior is not the result of some personality quirk but rather the manifestation of a hearing problem. Similarly, children experiencing difficulty with speech, language, and reading, and those often performing below their academic potential and possibly in time becoming retarded, may well be suffering from some form of hearing problem.

A teacher who suspects that a child has a hearing problem might use some of the subtests of the WISC-R or the Illinois Test of Psycholinguistic Abilities. It would be better to use the Goldman-Fristoe-Woodcock Auditory Test Battery or the Wepman Auditory Discrimination Test, which were specifically designed to measure auditory perception. The former consists of four major tests. The latter is very simple—the examiner says two words and the examinee indicates whether the sounds are the same or different. Preliminary research is encouraging with respect to the Auditory Test Battery. Some other auditory perception measures are the Auditory Memory Span

Test, the Auditory Sequential Memory Test, the Flowers Test of Selective Attention (Experimental Edition), and the Kansas State University Speech Discrimination Test. Some of the tests can be administered by the ordinary classroom teacher. Others require a trained clinician. We believe that the teacher who suspects the child has a hearing problem should refer the child to a specialist for actual diagnosis and treatment.

Again, what is important is not the definition of, or the causal factors associated with, a hearing handicap. Rather, of vital importance is what, if anything, teachers can do, or use to initially identify children with hearing problems. (The final determination and treatment is left to the specialist.) Most mild hearing defects go undetected in classrooms because the children are able to talk. But many children who are inattentive, are low achievers, or have poor listening skills may have a hearing problem rather than an emotional problem or low intelligence.

A problem in testing the deaf is that they are generally handicapped when taking verbal exams because their language development has been negatively affected. The early performance tests such as the Pintner-Paterson and the Arthur Performance Scale were especially developed to test the deaf. Although the Wechsler Scales have been adapted for testing the deaf, the use of the norms and the tests' psychometric properties may be suspect because they have been standardized on examinees with normal hearing. To circumvent this problem, some instruments, like the Hiskey-Nebraska Test of Learning Aptitude (HNTLA), were developed for and standardized on the hard-of-hearing.

The HNTLA is an individually administered intelligence test designed for deaf and hard-of-hearing children ranging in age from 3 to 16 years. The test is administered in pantomime. Practice exercises are available. The HNTLA has 12 performance subtests. There are separate norms for the deaf and for the hard-of-hearing. The split-half reliabilities are in the .90s. Again, as with most of the tests designed for special populations, the validity evidence is sparse. Because of limited technical data, the test scores must be judiciously interpreted.

Speech Handicapped   Speech is fundamental to the communication process. Frequently, a speech defect may be the result of some other form of handicap (for instance, deafness). And in some instances a speech impairment might cause some other type of behavior (for example, severe shyness/withdrawal). Some speech disorders, such as cleft palate or stuttering, are readily detectable. Others, such as a slight huskiness, may be ignored because they are so mild. Regardless of the severity of the disorder, it is the teacher's observational skills that play a vital role. Only after an initial screening—for which no test, per se, exists—is the child referred to a specialist for further testing and diagnosis. Some of the more commonly used instruments are the Templin-Darley Test of Articulation and the Goldman-

Fristoe Test of Articulation, both of which should be administered only by a specialist.

Physically Handicapped

Although speech, vision, and hearing defects could conceivably be classified as types of physical handicap and have a neurological or orthopedic basis, we have purposely treated them as sensory handicaps. Accordingly, we restrict our consideration of the physically handicapped to those whose impairments are not sensory. Also, we have selected for discussion (from the myriad of physical handicaps) the two that teachers generally will encounter: *epilepsy* and the orthopedically handicapped.

Epilepsy   Epilepsy is characterized by the victim having a seizure. The seizures can be severe (grand mal) or of a less serious nature (petit mal). Although the seizures themselves are due to electrochemical disturbances in the brain, there is the belief that the causes of epilepsy may be rooted in a variety of neurological disorders. Once again, classroom teachers are dependent upon their skill of observation and their knowledge of some of the symptoms associated with an epileptic seizure. The final diagnosis and treatment is best left to professionals.

Some other types of physical disability are cystic fibrosis, muscular dystrophy, diabetes, and congenital heart problems. Unless the disability is fairly severe, most children manifesting these illnesses are able to function well in the ordinary classroom. Granted, there may be some types of activities, such as strenuous sports or running, where such children should not be required or expected to participate as do the other class members, but these are generally exceptions to the rule.

Orthopedically Handicapped   The orthopedically handicapped, especially the severely cerebral palsied,[6] pose the greatest assessment problems.

These students generally have problems working with performance tests, since their motor coordination is severely affected; the tension that they may be working under makes the validity of their test scores suspect; and if they suffer from severe speech defects, both verbal and oral testing is nearly impossible. In addition to these problems, the examinees' susceptibility to rapid fatigue makes it imperative to have many brief testing sessions.

Most of the assessment devices developed for the orthopedically handicapped are adaptations of tests such as the Stanford-Binet, the Porteous Mazes, and the Leiter International Performance Scale, all of which were

[6] We recognize that cerebral palsy is a neurological disorder. However, since it is restricted to disturbances of the voluntary motor system and manifests itself in uncoordinated muscular behavior, we refer to it as a type of orthopedic handicap.

originally designed for testing normal people. Unfortunately, validity data for special populations is lacking.

The future holds some promise, however, because tests are being developed that require the examinees only to point, to nod their head when the correct response is read, and so on. For this reason, pictorial scales like the Peabody Picture Vocabulary Test and the Columbia Mental Maturity Scale have been found to be useful and valid tests for the orthopedically handicapped (see Dunn & Dunn, 1981).

Learning-Disabled

There are many children who have no sensory or physical handicap, and who are of average or above-average intelligence but have difficulty in learning. Such children are categorized as *learning-disabled,* and they are recognized by the fact that there is a severe discrepancy between their academic achievement and their aptitude potential, as measured by some type of achievement and aptitude test respectively. A major problem here centers on the method of computing this discrepancy (see Berk, 1984). As with the categories of special education, the definition of learning disability is fraught with controversy. Some definitions specifically exclude children whose learning problem(s) may be due to mental retardation or a visual handicap. Some definitions consider sociological factors. We subscribe to the definition given by Kirk & Bateman (1962, p. 263), because it offers suggestions for remediation. Their definition is as follows:

> *A learning disability refers to a retardation, disorder, or delayed development in one or more of the processes of speech, language, reading, writing, arithmetic, or other school subjects resulting from a psychological handicap caused by possible cerebral disfunctions and/or emotional or behavioral disturbances. It is not the result of mental retardation, sensory deprivation, or cultural or instructional factors.*

If one accepts the definition that excludes mental retardation; severe emotional disturbances; cultural, environmental, economic, or educational deprivation; and sensory loss or weakness, it should be evident that the common diagnostic instruments available will not readily identify the child with a learning disability.

We would be remiss if we did not at least mention that some critical measurement issues are involved in the assessment of learning disability. In addition to the definition of a "severe discrepancy between aptitude and achievement" mentioned above, there is the problem of the validity of the tests used to screen and diagnose LD persons. As of now, many of the instruments used for exceptional children are woefully inadequate with respect to their validity and reliability.

Once again, we are dependent on the observant classroom teacher. Although parents should notice whether or not their child has poor motor coordination, is restless, and has a poor memory, this is seldom the case. The observant teacher, especially the kindergarten or first-grade teacher, is usually the first person to recognize the symptoms of learning disability. And if these teachers do not, surely the second- and third-grade teachers should notice children who, although of average or above-average intelligence, are having difficulty with their schoolwork and do not seem to be working up to their potential.

Generally, the assessment of children with learning disabilities is a team effort and involves a variety of tests, inventories, and other instruments. The classroom teacher will normally administer a group test, such as the Jastak Wide Range Achievement Test, for screening purposes. (Although a group test is appropriate for screening, we concur with Reynolds & Clark, 1983, that for young children especially, an individual test would provide a qualified examiner with much valuable clinical data.) The teacher will also provide the team with data gathered from the child's cumulative folder, which, if properly kept, will contain anecdotal-type information, previous reports by other psychologists and teachers, health records, academic records, and the like. At this point, various specialists will come into play. A psychologist may then be called upon to administer and interpret an individual scholastic aptitude test to assess the child's academic potential. It may be a verbal test such as the Stanford-Binet, the WISC-R, the WPPSI, or a nonverbal test such as the United States Employment Services Nonreading Aptitude Test or the Goodenough-Harris Drawing Test. Not only do tests such as the WISC-R, the WPPSI, and the McCarthy Scales provide a global index of aptitude to help one differentiate between learning disabilities and mental retardation, but the subtests furnish valuable information about specific deficiencies such as memory span and visual perception.

To obtain measures of a child's academic performance, we may use teacher-made tests or standardized achievement batteries such as the SE-SAT, CIRCUS, the Kaufman ABC test, or the primary levels of some of the achievement batteries discussed earlier. To assist the teacher in diagnosing pupils' strengths and weaknesses, there are a variety of readiness and diagnostic tests available that, on close examination, show that their items closely resemble specially designed tests of learning disability such as the Frostig Developmental Test of Visual Perception, the Benton Visual Retention Test (Revised), and the Auditory Discrimination Test.

Up to this point, our discussion of the various tests available for assessing a child's intellectual capacity has been of those that are used routinely. These, however, may be inappropriate for testing people who, for one reason or another, have difficulty responding to traditional tests. To accommodate these persons, three approaches have been used: (1) Adapting existing test procedures (for example, using the large-type or Braille edition of the SCAT and aptitude test of the Graduate Record Examination, or not timing a timed test. Unfortunately, such procedures invalidate the use of existing norms.). (2) Using tests to which a handicapped person can respond. (For example, a deaf examinee can answer items on the Peabody because it uses pictures. But once again we have a problem analogous to the one before in that the test has been standardized on nonhandicapped subjects.) (3) Using specially designated tests.

We have purposely focused, at least in the tests of learning ability (aptitude/IQ), on individually administered tests for the following reason: Individually administered tests provide an experienced and insightful examiner with a wealth of clinical information beyond the examinee's performance or score—data on such factors as motivation, anxiety, verbal facility, and problem solving—that not only have an impact on the examinee's performance but that should be considered in the test interpretation. Some of the more commonly used individual aptitude tests are the Wechsler Scales (WISC-R, WAIS, WPPSI), the Stanford-Binet (SB), the McCarthy Scales of Children's Abilities, the Illinois Test of Psycholinguistic Abilities (ITPA), the Slosson Intelligence Test, and the Peabody Picture Vocabulary Test, Revised Edition (PPVT-R). There are two other instruments that differ markedly from these. One, the Cognitive Skills Assessment Battery (CSAB), is a CRT, whereas the others are norm-referenced. The other is the System of Multicultural Pluralistic Assessment (SOMPA), which bases the interpretation of the examinees' performance in the light of their cultural background.

In addition to the aptitude and achievement test data gathered, the battery of tests which frequently are used to identify the LD include assessments of short-term memory and perception as measured by the Benton Visual Retention Test and the Bender-Gestalt Test respectively; measures of aphasia; and measures of language facility. All the data would be collated to assist in diagnosing the nature of the learning disability. An attempt is then made to establish the causal nature of the learning disability. For example, if it is suspected that the disability is the result of a cerebral dysfunction, the child would undoubtedly be referred to a neurologist, who might conceivably administer an electroencephalograph test (EEG). Or we would have to ascertain whether the problem is the result of an emotional disturbance, a behavioral disturbance, or a combination of these and other factors. Although some valuable data can be provided by the regular classroom teacher by means of careful, systematic observation, it should be obvious that the diagnosis and remediation of learning disability is best left to the professional clinician.

In closing, we are happy to report that tests have been developed especially for children with learning disabilities. Those interested are referred to Buros (1985) as well as test publisher catalogues. (If you use Buros, you should consult the "Speech and Hearing Tests" and the "Sensory and Motor Tests" sections.) We concur with Anastasi (1982, p. 480), who says

"These tests should be regarded not as psychometric instruments but as observational aids for the clinical psychologist and learning disabilities specialist."

Cutting across the various types of handicaps are those that result from some form of motor disability. We will now spend a few minutes on this topic.

MOTOR DEVELOPMENT MEASURES

Increasingly greater attention is being paid to motor development. Whether the impetus came from Piaget's work, which emphasizes the role of sensorimotor skills in human development, or from research findings, which have shown that there is an interaction between motor development and both cognitive and affective development, is unclear at this time. In fact, if one thinks about the Stanford-Binet, the Wechsler scales, or the McCarthy Scales, it is evident that these authors believed motor development played an important role in school readiness and intellectual development.

Once again, we are plagued with the recurring dilemma of definition or skill analysis. What do we mean by *motor development*? Are we talking about large or small muscle control? Are we talking about coordination and, if so, what kind of coordination? One of the few measures specifically designed to assess motor development is the Bruininks-Oseretsky Test of Motor Proficiency.

Bruininks-Oseretsky Test of Motor Proficiency

Published by the American Guidance Services (1978), it was originally issued by Oseretsky in 1923 in Russia and adapted and translated by Doll in 1946. It contains eight separate motor proficiency tests—Running Speed and Agility (1 item), Balance (8), Bilateral Coordination (8), Strength (3), Upper Limb Coordination (9), Response Speed (to a moving visual stimulus), Visual Motor Control (8), and Upper Limb Speed and Dexterity (8)—are measured with 46 items. It is designed to measure gross and fine motor functioning of children from $4\frac{1}{2}$ to $14\frac{1}{2}$ years of age, and has one form. It is individually administered and takes from 45 to 60 minutes. There is a 14-item Short Form which takes from 15 to 20 minutes and yields a single index of general motor proficiency. Three scores—a Gross Motor Skills Composite (dealing with large muscles), a Fine Motor Skills Composite, and a Total Battery Score—are produced.

A stratified sample of 765 children was used as the standardization sample. For each of the three composite scores, scores can be expressed as standard scores, percentile ranks, or stanines. Age equivalents are available for each of the eight subtests. Test–retest reliabilities range from .86 to .89

for the Battery Composite and from .68 to .88 for the Fine and Gross Motor composites. The Gross Motor composite has somewhat higher reliabilities than the Fine Motor composite. Average standard errors of measurement range from 4.0 to 4.7. The individual subtest reliabilities are so low that the practitioner is cautioned in using them for clinical interpretation. Factor analysis and a comparison of normal with learning-disabled children were used to support the claim to validity.

Some other sensorimotor tests are the Bender-Purdue Reflex Test, the Southern California Sensory Integration Tests, and the Motor Problems Inventory. Some examples of psychomotor tests, although not motor-development measures per se, are the Stromberg Dexterity Test and the Crawford Small Parts Dexterity Test. Those wishing more information about these and other tests should consult Buros (1985).

SOME OTHER MEASURES

In addition to the individual aptitude and achievement tests discussed in Chapters 7 and 8, and the adaptive, visual, perceptual acuity, and psychomotor tests discussed earlier in this chapter, there are instances, especially when one is dealing with the screening/diagnosis of handicapped children, where it is desirable to obtain a measure of the child's language ability, listening ability, and oral language performance. Although these latter measures are especially useful when dealing with the learning-disabled, they are not restricted to this special population. Hence, we discuss them here rather than in the LD section.

Language Tests

In addition to the language subtests of the major survey achievement batteries, we have specific language tests such as the Goldman-Fristoe Test of Articulation, the Peabody Picture Vocabulary Test, Revised Edition, and the Illinois Test of Psycholinguistic Abilities which are individually administered and use either a picture stimulus completely or one as part of a total stimulus mode. Of the three, the validity and norms of the ITPA are questionable (Salvia & Ysseldyke, 1981) and should not be used to select the learning-disabled for remedial programs.

Listening Tests

Compared with the number of reading readiness, reading, and reading diagnostic tests available to evaluate the child's reading potential, performance, or weaknesses, there are relatively few listening skills tests. Whether this is the result of the absence of a clear definition, the problem of delineating those skills involved in listening, the difficulty in measurement, or a combination of these and other factors, is a matter of conjecture. Some examples of listening tests (in addition to the general listening comprehension subtests of the Durrell Analysis of Reading Difficulties and the Sequential Tests of Educational Progress II) are the Brown-Carlsen Listening Comprehension Test and the Assessment of Children's Language Comprehension.

Assessment of Oral Language Performance

Many tests are available to measure and subsequently diagnose oral language performance. Most of the tests require the subject to respond to a stimulus (either verbal or pictorial) with a word or sentence. Some of the tests, like the Oral Vocabulary subtest of the Gates-McKillop Reading Diagnostic Test, use a multiple-choice and sentence-completion format. Others, like the Auditory Association subtest of the ITPA, use verbal analogies such as, "I cut with a saw, I pound with a _____." Some of the more commonly used oral language tests are the Goldman-Fristoe Test of Articulation, the Auditory Discrimination Test, and the Denver Developmental Schedule. Many of them are individually administered. Regrettably, the psychometric properties of most of these tests, with the possible exception of survey subtests, leave much to be desired (Sattler, 1982; Salvia & Ysseldyke, 1981).

Some other measures designed especially to assess the aptitude of exceptional children are as follows:

1. The Arthur Adaptation of the Leitner International Performance Scale. Useful for deaf and speech-impaired subjects or any others who have difficulty responding verbally. Psychometric data are woefully lacking.
2. The Pictorial Test of Intelligence. Can be used for both normal and handicapped children. Especially suited for orthopedically handicapped children. Requires no verbal stimuli or response. Also good for children who have speech or language problems.
3. The Columbia Mental Maturity Scale. Originally designed for cerebral-palsied children. May be used with children who have difficulty responding verbally. The examinee makes visual-perceptual discriminations. Technically adequate. Must be interpreted cautiously since it measures only two kinds of intellectual behavior—classification and discrimination.

THE GIFTED

The continuum of exceptionality or of children with special needs can range from those who are mentally retarded and handicapped to those who are gifted. Both extremes have special needs that must be considered by the regular classroom teacher, although treatments for the two groups differ markedly. One definition of gifted focuses on creativity and intellectual superiority, while another focuses on outstanding prowess in any field. For the former, the individually administered scholastic aptitude test is generally used to identify the gifted. Whereas teacher observations play a vital, if not the most significant, role in identifying the mentally retarded or handicapped child, teachers do not do too well in identifying the gifted. In fact, there are some instances where very creative children are branded as nuisances or troublemakers because they may be bored in class.

Noppe (1980) classifies instruments for assessing creativity as follows: (1) projective tests such as the Rorschach, (2) personality scales such as the California Psychological Inventory, (3) self-report methods, (4) reports of others, (5) cognitive tests such as Torrance's Tests of Creativity, and (6) miscellaneous instruments.

As of now, there are no standardized tests of creativity that possess adequate reliability and validity to bear recommendation. There are, however, a number of experimental or research creativity tests on the market. Some of the more popular ones are Torrance's Tests of Creative Thinking, the Mednick's Remote Associates Test, Thinking Creatively with Sounds and Words (Research Edition), Watson-Glaser Critical Thinking Appraisal, and the Kit of Factor-Referenced Appraisal.

PUTTING IT ALL TOGETHER

The most exotic spices, the finest milled wheat, the purest of ingredients, and the most advanced electronic oven will by themselves or even collectively *not* result in a cake that would win first prize or even place in a bakeoff. What is important is the skill of the baker in blending everything. In the same way, the ultimate value that will accrue to those dealing with children with special needs, and hence to the children themselves, will be the manner in which all the data are collected, collated, and interpreted. At best, we should only expect our data, regardless of the manner in which it was collected—standardized aptitude and achievement tests, observational schedules, standardized personality measures, and teacher-made tools—to provide teachers with the information with which to generate hypotheses. These hypotheses can then be the framework of an individual educational plan.[7]

---

[7] Two excellent sources of case histories are Mahan & Mahan (1981) and Salvia & Ysseldyke (1981).

A CASE STUDY: ALLAN

Allan is a third-grader. He is the only child from a working, lower-middle-class family. His mother and father both work and Allan stays by himself for about two hours after returning from school. Allan's mother had a normal pregnancy and delivery. Allan's medical history indicates no unusual illnesses other than such childhood diseases as mumps and chickenpox. Other than a single case of an overdose of medication as an infant, there is nothing in Allan's medical record to be a cause for alarm. Allan is very passive in the classroom and makes little effort to enter into class discussions. This is markedly different from his behavior on the playground, where Allan has a tendency to throw temper tantrums when he becomes frustrated. Allan does not seem to be interested in school, especially when reading instruction is given. Allan performs quite well in the quantitative areas such as science and mathematics. When asked a question, Allan invariably asks that it be repeated. Allan complains of frequent headaches and dizzy spells. He always appears to favor his right side.

It should be evident that a series of questions, and, it is hoped, hypotheses will be generated by the teacher. Some of these are as follows:

1. Is Allan's behavior in class and on the playground so diametrically opposed that it is indicative of abnormal behavior?
2. Is Allan basically a shy, reserved child who is introverted by nature but is seeking approval?
3. Is Allan's learning problem the result of some learning disability(ies) or physical handicap such as being hard-of-hearing?
4. Is Allan's lack of interest in reading a manifestation of some problem(s) or weakness in reading or is it just a lack of interest in the subject?
5. Is the fact that Allan is an only child and alone much of the time a plausible explanation for some of his problems?
6. Does Allan need remedial work in reading and, if so, what are his verbal strengths and weaknesses? Will any remediation result in Allan becoming a better reader, for example, as shown by a higher reading test score?
7. Is Allan's performance in the quantitative areas sufficiently better than his performance in the verbal areas?

In order to obtain answers to these and other questions, a cooperative effort would have to be made by the classroom teacher, the school psychologist, and other professionals. As a starter, the teacher, Ms. Greene, could administer (or have administered) a battery of tests to Allan. In addition, she could observe Allan's behavior more closely in an attempt to obtain certain kinds of information. Ms. Greene might even request a meeting with Allan's parents to learn more about Allan's home environment and his behavior out of school. Some of the tests that might be given Allan are as follows:

1. The WISC-R, so that both a verbal and a performance IQ score could be obtained. This will permit the teacher to obtain a measure of performance on a variety of tasks as well as obtain some global picture by means of the Kaufman (1979) factor scores (verbal comprehension, perceptual organization, and freedom from distractability).
2. The Children's Personality Questionnaire could be used to provide information on 14 factors, such as Allan's anxiety, assertiveness, and shyness. This information could then be used to supplement that already gathered by interviews and observations.
3. The Peabody Picture Vocabulary Test, Revised Edition, could be used to check the teacher's hypothesis that Allan is weak in verbal skills. This could also be confirmed by the WISC-R and Kaufman factor scores. If any weakness is found, diagnostic tests such as the Stanford Diagnostic Reading Test or the Diagnostic Reading Scales could be used to identify particular strengths and weaknesses.
4. An audiometry test could be given Allan to see whether he suffers from any hearing loss.
5. The Stanford Achievement Test, which provides scores in spelling, reading, and arithmetic, and the Woodcock Reading Mastery Tests could be used to confirm the teacher's suspicion that Allan has difficulty with verbal-type materials and hence may be uninterested in language activities because he is a poor reader.

These are only some of the tests and inventories and tools that can be used when making a diagnosis. As stated earlier, it was not our intent to make you an expert in either testing or teaching children with special needs. Rather, it was to provide you with the information needed to be a more effective teacher because you understand your pupils better and to enable you to interact with other professionals such as the school psychologist and the teacher of learning-disability children. The latter is even more important today because of our emphasis on mainstreaming.

Finally, we reiterate that the major function of assessment tools and techniques as related to children with special needs is *not* to give hard-and-fast answers or to dispense prescriptions and treatments to cure the malady of pupils such as Allan. Rather, it is to provide you with sufficient information about tests so that you will be able to generate plausible, testable hypotheses when dealing with children with special needs.

In conclusion, we would like to reiterate that meeting the needs of special-education students—ranging from the handicapped to the gifted—is a matter of concern for every teacher and *not* just the specialist. This is even more true today with the legislation mandating mainstreaming. We are well aware that the ordinary classroom teacher is not trained to administer many of the tests used to diagnose special needs. Nevertheless, the ordinary classroom teacher must know how to assess exceptionality as well as how to deal with such students in his or her classroom.

SUMMARY

The principal ideas, conclusions, and implications of this chapter are summarized in the following statements:

1. *Assessment* is a more inclusive term than *testing* or *measurement* and involves observations, data, and judgments.
2. Although ordinary classroom teachers are not trained to administer and interpret many of the tools used to diagnose special needs, they still must be knowledgeable in this area so that they can communicate intelligently with specialists and provide for optimal learning.
3. A complete educational assessment program for the handicapped requires a team effort of classroom teacher, diagnostician, school psychologist, and medical personnel.
4. The movement toward equality of education for the handicapped came about through litigation and culminated in the passage of Public Law 94-142.
5. Three landmark cases concerned with nondiscriminatory testing were the *Diana* v. *State Board of Education,* the *Larry P.* case, and the *PASE* v. *Hannon* case.
6. Public Law 94-142 has placed responsibilities on the regular classroom teacher in dealing with the handicapped student.
7. The concept of *mainstreaming* mandates that children with special needs be taught in the regular classroom as long as possible.
8. A variety of tests, scales, and inventories are used to assess children with special needs. They may range from a relatively simple checklist to a complex electroencephalograph. Generally speaking, educational and psychological tests are less reliable than many of our physical tests.
9. There are many problems associated with assessing the exceptional child, such as using tests that have been normed on normal children; dealing with behavior that is variable, thereby making any interpretation of difference scores difficult; and dealing with extremes, which makes measurement less reliable.
10. The major classifications of special education are as follows: mentally retarded, emotionally disturbed, sensory handicapped, physically handicapped, learning-disabled, and gifted.
11. There are four classifications of mentally retarded: slow learners, educable mentally retarded, trainable mentally retarded, and severely mentally retarded. Classification is made on the basis of a scholastic aptitude score.

12. Assessment programs for the mentally retarded generally include a measure of adaptive behavior as well as a measure of motor development.
13. Of the more than 100 adaptive behavior scales, none tests persons over 20 years of age. Also, the majority have been standardized on institutionalized samples, which makes their norms suspect when we are dealing with noninstitutionalized individuals.
14. Emotional disturbance cannot be identified by a test, per se. It requires a trained medical or psychological specialist.
15. The sensory handicapped child has some type of vision, hearing, or speech defect. There are further classifications within the visually handicapped (partially sighted and blind) and the hearing handicapped (hard-of-hearing and deaf).
16. The two most common types of physical handicap that the teacher encounters are cerebral palsy and epilepsy.
17. The learning-disabled child has no sensory or physical handicap and is of average or better than average intelligence, but still has difficulty in learning.
18. Increased attention is being paid to motor development, which, research has shown, plays an important role in cognitive development.
19. Some special tests such as the Hiskey-Nebraska Test of Learning Aptitude, the Blind Learning Aptitude Test, and the Arthur Adaptation of the Leitner International Performance Scale have been specifically developed to assess the scholastic aptitude of handicapped subjects.
20. The gifted child is generally classified on the basis of a scholastic aptitude score. As of now, there are no standardized creativity tests, although there are some experimental forms, such as the Mednick Remote Associates Test, available.
21. Possibly the most important stage in assessing the exceptional child is collating the different kinds of data and putting it together into a meaningful whole.

POINTS TO PONDER

1. What effect, if any, has Public Law 94-142 had on the preparation of teachers with respect to their measurement competencies?
2. Do you think that Public Law 94-142 has been a boon or a bane for exceptional children? Why?
3. The assessment of the exceptional child includes a variety of tests, inventories, and scales. One of the measures prescribed by the law is an estimate of the child's adaptive behavior. What is meant by adaptive behavior? How is it measured? How valid are the tests presently being used?

4. One of the provisions of Public Law 94-142 is that the tests used must be free from racial and cultural bias. Can we meet this requirement considering our present state of the art in measurement? How would you proceed to prevent legal action being taken against you?

5. Discuss some of the major problems in assessing the exceptional child? Can any of these problems be circumvented? How?

6. Should the child with a learning disability such as dyslexia be classified as an exceptional child? Defend your position.

7. If the diagnosis of exceptionality is so technical that it should be left to specialists, what need is there for the ordinary classroom teacher to be cognizant of the various assessment tools and techniques?

8. If you were to develop a course in Tests and Measurement for Special-Education Teachers, what would your course objectives be? What would be the course content? What type of evaluation would you use for the students?

9. In what way does educational diagnosis differ from medical diagnosis? Illustrate.

10. Tim is a third-grader. He is morose, aggressive, and has a predilection to using foul language. He appears to be of average ability but does not do well in his classroom achievement tests. When you confront Tim's parents with your observations, they become very hostile and accuse you of being a racist. What would you do to support your position that Tim is in need of special help?

CHAPTER 11

Accountability: Testing and Evaluation Programs

ACCOUNTABILITY
PROGRAM EVALUATION
INTERNAL TESTING AND EVALUATION PROGRAMS
EXTERNAL TESTING PROGRAMS

In this chapter we discuss some philosophical and measurement concerns related to accountability and some possible consequences of accountability. Next we discuss the related field of program evaluation and two types of internal evaluation programs: standardized testing programs and evaluation for individualized instruction. Both types of programs can provide limited accountability data, although neither one was implemented as a response to the demand for accountability. Then we discuss two kinds of external testing programs: college selection and placement programs and state assessment programs; the latter is an outgrowth of the demand for accountability.

After studying this chapter, the student should be able to do the following:

1. Define *accountability*.
2. Recognize the reasons for the popularity of the accountability concept.
3. Recognize the philosophical concerns related to accountability.
4. Understand the measurement problems of accountability programs.
5. Judge various accountability programs with respect to their philosophical and measurement limitations.
6. Understand the distinctions between and similarities of program evaluation and student evaluation.
7. Recognize some differences and similarities between program evaluation and experimental research.
8. Understand the dangers of evaluation bias.
9. Understand the importance of watching for unintended outcomes in program evaluation.
10. Differentiate between formative and summative evaluation.

11. Appreciate the necessity for cooperative planning in setting up a testing program.
12. Understand the various steps necessary in planning and administering a testing program.
13. Propose and defend a standardized testing program.
14. Recognize the various evaluation needs in individualized instruction.
15. Differentiate between internal and external evaluation (testing) programs.
16. Understand the functions of college selection and placement programs.
17. Recognize some priorities and trends in, and reasons for, state assessment programs.

ACCOUNTABILITY

Accountability means different things to different people; the term has been defined in many ways (Barro, 1970; Bell, 1971; Cunningham, 1971; Gooler, 1971; Lessinger, 1970a, b; Lindman, 1971; Locke, 1971; Porter, 1971; Saretsky, 1973). A typical definition of accountability would include *setting* correct goals; *evaluating* their degree of achievement (we discuss program evaluation in the next section) and at what price; *presenting and interpreting* this information to the public; and *accepting responsibility* for any results that are perceived inadequate. A few users of the term would evidently allow educators to attempt to explain why all failures may not be their fault. In the abstract, accountability is basically the process of justifying costs by presenting the positive effects derived from expenditures. Perhaps in the concrete it boils down to (1) who gets hanged when things go wrong and (2) who does the hanging (Browder, 1971, p. 19).

Reactions to accountability among educators have been mixed. It has been said that any new idea passes through the following stages: (1) indignant rejection, (2) reasoned objection, (3) qualified opposition, (4) tentative acceptance, (5) qualified endorsement, (6) judicious modification, (7) cautious adoption, (8) impassioned espousal, (9) proud parenthood, and (10) dogmatic propagation. As Browder, Atkins, & Kaya (1973, p. vi) suggest with respect to accountability, some legislators, school boards, and commercial hucksters short-circuited the evolutionary sequence and reached a point of impassioned espousal rapidly. Many others are still at the point of indignant rejection.

What does all this have to do with the contents of a textbook on standardized tests? Simply this: Accountability depends upon good measurement and the correct uses of that measurement data. As accountability procedures are implemented, educators and prospective educators should be alerted to the various philosophical and measurement aspects inherent in such programs in order to maximize their values and minimize their dangers. We, and probably most educators, are in favor of the abstract principle of accountability. But it is impossible to say in the abstract whether accountability is a blessing or a burden, a miracle or a mirage, a milestone or a millstone, and potential problems arise when we try to move from the abstract to the specific. What are some of the philosophical and measurement concerns educators should be alert to, and what are some of the potential approaches to and consequences of accountability?

Philosophical Concerns

Basically the philosophical concerns center on who are accountable and for what they are accountable. We are not suggesting that we have the answers, but we can present some different dimensions that pertain to the questions.

Who Is Accountable?   There is certainly no current agreement about who is presently being held accountable in education or who should be. Deterline (1971, p. 16) said that educators operate so that "all failures and ineffective aspects of our instruction are slyly laid on the students, in the form of a grade or rating, [and] we never really have to face the facts of our own incompetence in the field of instruction." He suggested that students are held accountable if they do not learn—in spite of any failures, deficiencies, and incompetence in our teaching—and he welcomed educational accountability as a countervailing force.

Campbell argued that Deterline was guilty of fighting yesterday's wars instead of today's:

> There was a time when teachers were scarcely held accountable for their shortcomings as instructors, but this has not been the state of affairs I have noted in my 20 years in education. Rather, there has been a drumfire of extramural criticism and intramural breast-beating rising to the present crescendo. Through every possible medium, including his professional journals, the teacher receives the same message: "You are a failure. You are incompetent at best and probably insensitive, unimaginative, lazy, and cruel as well." His grade is a straight F/U.
>
> By constrast, "failure" for students is like the death penalty—still legal, but seldom applied. (Campbell, 1971, p. 176)

It seems to us that the pendulum has swung too far toward holding educators accountable for lack of pupil learning in spite of any failure, deficiencies, and incompetence in the pupils and/or parents. The definition of teaching for many educational critics has changed from an activity *intended* to induce learning to an activity that *does* induce learning. Although it seems condescending to assume that students have no responsibility for their own learning, most writers on educational accountability do not mention students' (or parents') accountability. Yet, "substituting the teacher . . . for the pupil as the *only* accountable party is an example of reactionary thinking" (Campbell, 1971, p. 177). Educators *alone* cannot be held accountable for a product when they have virtually no control over their resources or raw material.

> *When students are regarded as "products" of the school, it is implied that the school is a factory and should be fully accountable for the behavior of its products. Yet, without the power to select its raw material and reject defective products, the school cannot guarantee its product. (Lindman, 1971, p. B-4)*

The foregoing paragraph is not meant to let educators off the hook. Just because educators are not accountable for everything does not mean they are not accountable for anything. But we need to be somewhat moderate in any approach to accountability. We have to recognize that: "Each participant [including students and teachers] in the educational process should be held responsible only for those educational outcomes that he can affect by his actions or decisions and only to the extent that he can affect them" (Barro, 1970, p. 199).

Educators, then, should be held accountable for some aspects of children's learning, but there is no easy way to discern which portions are under their control. Accountability programs must keep this in mind. The "who is accountable" question cannot at present be answered, and until (and if) it is answered, we must remember that the purpose of accountability programs should not be punitive, but rather should be accepted as a means of quality control.

Accountable for What?   Perhaps even more difficult than the question of who should be held accountable is the question of "accountable for what?" The simpleminded answer is that we should be held accountable for the pupils' attainments of our educational objectives. But although there is a consensus about many desired outcomes, there still remain diverse goals or objectives held by our educational systems. Some people maintain "good citizenship" or "healthy self-concepts" are more important than reading skills. Others assert just the opposite. This difference of opinion causes considerable difficulty in instituting accountability. And since we can measure some objectives more readily than others, accountability programs may tend to focus narrowly on these easily measured objectives. We discuss this further in the section on measurement problems related to accountability.

Opinions differ not only about what the outcome objectives should be but also about what the *distribution* of these results should be. Downs (1968) discussed four diverse goals regarding distribution.

1. The *minimum-citizenship (level) goal.* All students should be brought up to some basic *minimum* level of proficiency.

2. The *maximum-system-output goal*. The total capabilities of all students considered as a group (perhaps best measured by their total resulting productivity) should be made as large as possible.
3. The *equal-opportunity (really equal-outcome) goal*. *All* students emerging from the system (say, on high school graduation) should have approximately the same capabilities for entering into the postschooling portion of their lives.[1]
4. The *maximum-individual-advancement goal*. Each student should be given as much development of his or her individual potential as possible.

As Downs has pointed out:

> . . . *pursuing each of the above goals exclusively, without regard to the others, would result in very different allocations of publicly-supplied educational inputs. At one extreme, the equal-opportunity goal would require a heavy concentration of resources among the poorest and most culturally-deprived students. They would receive much higher inputs than children from higher-income and more advantaged homes. . . . In contrast . . . the maximum system output goal would concentrate publicly-supplied inputs on the best qualified students. This would result in the greatest total gain in technical proficiency per dollar invested.* (Downs, 1968, pp. 16, 17)

It seems to us that people advocating accountability are, in general, operating as if their goal were the *minimum citizenship* mentioned (see Lessinger, 1971; Porter, 1971). However, sometimes the stated minimum goal is to bring everyone up to average. This is, in effect, the equal-opportunity (read "outcome") goal. Many educators seem to be unaware that, by definition, half the pupils will always fall below the median unless all obtain the same score. We are continually amazed that so many people operate as if they are not aware of this basic fact. For example, Lessinger (1970a, p. 220) spoke of the right of all children to read at their grade level. (See the definition of grade equivalents in Chapter 5 if you cannot see what is wrong with his statement.)

We should not leave this topic before stating that the fourth goal regarding distribution of outcomes is idealistic and can never be achieved as long as resources—goods, services, time, energy, and money—are limited. We simply cannot do as much as possible for each child, and educators should stop acting as if it were feasible (for example, when discussing how we will account for individual differences).

Other writers (Dyer, 1970; Harmes, 1971; Lindman, 1971; Shanker, 1971; and Tye, 1971) approach "accountability for what" in a different way. Dyer (1970, p. 206), for example, emphasized a *process* accountability rather than

[1] This would coincide with the definition Coleman et al. (1966) have given to equal opportunity as the equality of outcome.

a *product* accountability. This seems more in agreement with the definition of teaching, which states that the *intent* of teaching is to induce learning.

We are strong advocates of the position that the role of educators is to facilitate certain types of pupil learning. We believe that educators need to measure student outcomes in order to make wise educational decisions. But this position is not analogous to blaming teachers for any specified lack of pupil performance. Whether one wishes to say they are *accountable* for pupil outcomes depends in part on how one wishes to define accountability and in part upon philosophical/political considerations.

Thus there are considerable differences of opinion on the *what* issues. Whether we should assess basic cognitive skills or affective objectives, what the ideal distribution of educational results is, and whether we should have process or product assessment are the three issues we have briefly discussed.

Measurement Concerns

The measurement problems in accountability are very difficult to surmount. We do not intend to discuss all these problems in detail. Rather, we wish to introduce the reader to a few key concerns. As a professional, you almost invariably will be subject to some accountability programs, and therefore you should be alert to some of the more pressing measurement problems involved. You may wish to refer to the problems of obtaining reliable gain measures as discussed in Chapter 3. As mentioned there, many accountability programs try to use such gain measures in their assessment. (See Wrightstone, Hogan, & Abbott, 1972, for a further treatment of the measurement problems.)

Establishing Causal Relations   The attempt to determine causal relationships is directly related to the philosophical issue of *who* is to be held accountable. The abstract answer is that people should be held responsible only for those outcomes they can affect. Concrete details of how to determine that are at best incomplete. But even if we determine that a teacher can and should affect reading skills, how can we determine that a student who reads well does so because of the teacher's efforts?

Specialists in educational measurement and evaluation have historically concentrated their efforts on determining *what is,* rather than *who is, responsible* or *accountable* for what is. Many problems still exist in the first determination, such as measurement in the affective domain. However, by comparison, we can do a fairly accurate job of measuring what is. What we cannot do very well is to establish causal relationships between these outcomes and various input and process variables. To do this requires something more than measurement; it requires a research design.

Dyer (1970, p. 207) referred to four groups of variables that must be taken into account in any thorough accountability research design:

1. *Input variables,* or the characteristics of the *pupils* as they *enter* a particular phase of schooling—their health, level of achievement, self-concept, aspirations, and other considerations.
2. *Surrounding conditions* within which the school operates, including the home, community, and school conditions.
3. The *educational process.*
4. *Output variables,* or the characteristics of the pupils as they emerge from a particular phase of schooling.

However, it is difficult to take the first three variables into account, and many accountability programs are not likely to do so. Thus there is a danger that schools (and teachers) in those districts where surrounding conditions are poor will be unduly chastised for low outputs. This problem was magnified during a recent period in our society when some vociferous critics of education hold the naive belief that the school can and should be held accountable for overcoming poor input and negative surrounding variables. Yet research shows quite clearly that a large proportion of the variance in performance levels is accounted for by out-of-school variables, such as pupils' socioeconomic status and home environments.

Validity   Just as the measurement problem of establishing causal relations is related to the philosophical issue of who is to be held accountable, the measurement problem of validity is related to the "what is to be assessed" issue. Because basic-skill areas are very important as well as the easiest areas to assess, many accountability programs focus only on these areas. Since the school's objectives are ordinarily much broader than attainment of basic skills alone, the assessment tools may have inadequate content validity. Although poor content validity is always deplorable, it is particularly troublesome when the results of an assessment device are used to hold the schools (or teachers) accountable.

Consequences of Accountability

Accountability has forced schools to do a better job of specifying and evaluating objectives. There has been an increased focus on the relationship between outcomes, input, and process variables. School have worked toward adopting better management techniques and fiscal controls. There have been more concerted efforts to keep the public informed of educational objectives, expenses, processes, and results. All this seems commendable.

Accountability may also lead to increased teaching "toward the test," which could be counterproductive. The question under what circumstances is teaching for the test a harmful educational practice deserves careful consideration. Whenever the performance tested is only a sample (or indicant) of our objectives, teaching directly for the test (that is, teaching for those specific questions on the test) is inappropriate. If a test indeed covers accepted objectives, it is appropriate to teach for the general topics covered by the test. But when the objectives covered by the test are much more narrow in focus than the objectives of the school, it would be inappropriate to stress only the general objectives covered by the test, and to do so could seriously alter the overall substance of the educational product.

Various evaluation programs are discussed in the next three sections. Some of these programs were in existence long before the recent use of the term *accountability*. Others have been undertaken largely in response to the accountability issue.

PROGRAM EVALUATION

Whether or not educators wish to use the term *accountability,* they are typically involved in curriculum and instructional decision making. And to make these decisions, *program evaluations* are necessary. The basic distinction between program evaluation and student evaluation is related to the kinds of decisions that are to be made. If we wish to make a decision about an individual—for example, when we ask whether Susan should take advanced algebra or how she did in first-year French—we are concerned with student evaluation. When we wonder whether nongraded classrooms such as those operating in elementary school A should be introduced in school B, we are concerned with program evaluation. Whether French should be taught in fourth grade or whether a programmed text should be used in ninth-grade algebra are program decisions. The decision whether to continue any experimental program (such as using the Initial Teaching Alphabet) requires program evaluation.

Thus program evaluation is considerably broader than student evaluation. Student evaluation involves the determination of whether a student is making appropriate progress toward stated goals. Students' progress toward goals is but one dimension of program evaluation—though probably the most important.

In program evaluation we are concerned with such things as why the student goals were, or were not, achieved, the evaluation of the goals (objectives) themselves, the need to be particularly alert to unintended outcomes, the impact of the curriculum on persons other than the students, obtaining measures of cost effectiveness, and formative as well as summative evaluation.

Although school personnel have always made implicit evaluations of their curriculum (that is, they have made decisions about their curriculum), historically they have been ill-equipped to handle the more formal, explicit aspects of program evaluation. They have been unsure of what the term encompasses, how program evaluation differs from student evaluation, and what procedures are appropriate.

We do not attempt in this introductory book to cover all aspects of program evaluation. It is a fairly complex topic, and to become an expert in it would require knowledge in statistics, research design, and educational philosophy, as well as extensive reading in the area of program evaluation per se. Every school district should have a program evaluation expert, and most large districts do. However, this book intends simply to introduce our readers to this growing and important field of program evaluation in the hope that some will continue their education in the area. (See Payne, 1974, pp. 9–10, and Worthen, 1975, pp. 14–16, for lists of the required skills or competencies of evaluation experts.) Moreover, all educators—from teachers to administrators—should be cognizant of the dimensions and importance of this field. Good program evaluation requires the cooperation of many people. Educators will be better able and more willing to assist if they have at least some exposure to the topic.

Evaluation versus Research

Much has been written about the distinctions and similarities between evaluation and research. Not all authors take the same position about this. In our opinion Worthen & Sanders (1973) present one of the clearest discussions of this issue. As they suggest, evaluation and research serve somewhat different purposes. The purpose of research is to produce new knowledge, whereas the purpose of evaluation is to judge the worth or social utility of the program. While the techniques of investigation are often quite similar for evaluation and research, better control may be possible in pure research than in program evaluation. This may limit the causal inferences that can be made from program evaluation. Such a drawback is not as serious in evaluation as in research, however, because the major goal of evaluation is not to produce new knowledge that is generalizable but, as we said, to weigh the social usefulness of a program. Nevertheless, in evaluating the causal effects of curriculum (or instructional procedures), one needs to be concerned with the activities that preceded (and, inferentially, produced) the outcomes. There is some disagreement about how rigorous one's "research design" need be—or whether, indeed, program evaluation should be classified as research—but the inference (correct or incorrect) is usually made that certain student outcomes are the result of the teaching-learning activities, that preceded them (see Guba, 1969, and Stanley, 1969). If one wished to view program evaluation as research, it probably comes closest to what Corey (1953) calls action research or what Cronbach & Suppes (1969) call decision-oriented research.

Politics, Evaluation, and Evaluation Bias

One major early impetus for increased evaluation came from the various governmental funding agencies. It follows that much evaluation occurs in a political context. Further, many evaluation results indicate that programs dealing with social and educational problems fail to accomplish their goals. Since program founders and administrators, as well as many evaluators, are uncomfortable when negative or inconclusive evaluation findings are used to justify an end to spending on social or educational programs, we must recognize the ever-present danger of evaluation bias. Scriven (1975) has written about the problem of evaluation bias and its control. One major step in attempting to reduce bias is to use an external, independent evaluator. These are two separate points. An external evaluator is not necessarily independent.

> *Suppose you do hire an outside firm for evaluating a project, a firm whose headquarters are in a distant state. This* looks *like real independence. But ask yourself what the reward system is for that firm. It isn't any more rewarding for them if your project is successful or not,* per se—*and that's why you value their opinion, why they appear independent. But look a little deeper, or* longer. *What is rewarding to them* over the years? *Success in their business, which of course requires a continued flow of contracts. Since such firms are very well aware of the power of the grapevine in getting further clients, they are often well aware that an evaluation which shows the client in a good light is much more conducive to later contracts than a critical evaluation. The reverse side of this coin was brought home to me when communicating with a network of evaluators on a USOE grant. I heard more than one sad tale of "blackballing" an evaluator who gave a deservedly critical evaluation. In short, the "independence" of an external evaluator can be seriously compromised by the constraints of business success. (Scriven, 1975, p. 17)*

One way to help combat the problem of bias for internal and external (but not independent) evaluations is through employing what Scriven terms Meta-Evaluation—the evaluation of evaluations or evaluators. If evaluators know that they and their reports are subject to evaluation, this should do much to minimize the bias of their reports! (See Stufflebeam, 1974, for more on Meta-Evaluation.)

Evaluating Program Goals

As we have mentioned, program evaluation is broader than evaluating the degree to which—and reasons why—we have achieved certain outcomes. It also involved determining whether the stated goals are appropriate. As

Scriven (1967, p. 52) points out, "It is obvious that if the goals aren't worth achieving then it is uninteresting how well they are achieved." Because new curricula (or instructional procedures) have somewhat different goals from those of the old curricula, comparing the efficacy of different curricula is difficult. Existing standardized achievement tests, for example, which are generally considered to be quite adequate measures of particular kinds of student achievement, may not be sufficient for comparing two different curricula. The evaluation of the goals must take into account their realism and relevance. The needs of the learner as well as the community and society as a whole must be considered.

Unintended Outcomes

In evaluating a program we must be particularly alert to the side effects or the unintended outcomes for students. As Dyer (1967, p. 20) emphasizes, "Evaluating the side effects of an educational program may be even more important than evaluating its intended effects." A student may learn more arithmetic under a new program, but may also develop a hatred toward it. A student may become a better convergent thinker, but a poorer divergent thinker. Teachers should be alert to measuring these unintended outcomes. For example, in Project PLAN (Flanagan, 1971) the teachers were requested to report critical incidents that they believed resulted from use of the PLAN system. This is one way to assist the teachers in evaluating unintended outcomes.

Other program side effects are the effects on teachers, effects on students not in that particular program or curriculum, and effects on parents and taxpayers. Are teachers' knowledges updated with a new curriculum? Do teachers suffer from more fatigue? Have they become more enthusiastic about teaching? Scriven (1967, p. 77), for example, points out that some programmed texts have left teachers feeling less important. Are other teachers in the system forced to teach less attractive courses or to increase their work load as a result of the new curriculum program? Is there jealousy, or are these other teachers stimulated through association with the teachers in the new program? Do students who are not in the new program feel discriminated against? Are there positive side effects such as improved library facilities or an improved teacher/student ratio? How does the community at large react to the new program? The controversy on sex education in the schools is a good example of the importance of considering public attitudes.

Cost

In evaluating a program, one must certainly also consider cost factors. As Alkin (1970, p. 221) stated: "To be in a situation in which costs can be disregarded is certainly not the reality of today." Two types of cost-benefit factors must be considered. Before engaging in an evaluation, one must weigh the likely benefits of the evaluation against its costs. If it appears that the information produced by the evaluation will be sufficient to justify the costs, then the evaluator can proceed. When the evaluation is being done, cost-benefit factors must again be considered—that is, the costs of the program itself must be taken into account.

There are a variety of cost-benefit and cost-effectiveness models. Basically in cost-benefit models all costs and all benefits are stated in dollar amounts. In cost-effectiveness analyses, on the other hand, the values do not need to be stated in monetary units. Of course comparable units need to be used. Cost-effectivness analyses are the more useful in most social programs because it is not always possible to calculate the price of the benefits. Thus, for example, one might express benefits in terms of "gains in reading comprehension" rather than attempting to place a monetary value on those gains. While it is logically just as important to consider costs when choosing an educational program as when deciding which car to buy, it is much more difficult in the former situation. Evaluators should have some special training in cost-benefit and/or cost-effectiveness procedures.

Formative and Summative Program Evaluation

One final topic that should be discussed is the distinction between formative and summative evaluations (Scriven, 1967). The gathering of data during the time the program is being developed for the purpose of guiding the developmental process is called *formative evaluation*. Making an overall assessment or decision with regard to the program is termed *summative evaluation*. New curricular innovations are not born fully developed, nor are they ever perfected. A person who is continually evaluating a program will find many things that can be changed for the better during the operation of the program. Most educators feel it unprofessional not to make these improvements, even though they may upset the "research design." However, these formative evaluations—accompanied by shifts in the program's operations—can hinder the process of making causal inferences about outcomes from processes.

Summary of Program Evaluation

As can be seen, there are a multitude of factors to be considered in program evaluation. Various models have been developed that emphasize different evaluation tasks. Although evaluation and research differ in purpose, there are many similarities in the methods used. However, at times the methodology one must use in evaluation does not, strictly speaking, allow one to make causal inferences. Politics plays a role in evaluation, and this may lead to evaluation bias. Evaluation goes beyond the measurement of student outcome data and includes evaluating goals, unintended outcomes, and cost effectiveness.

Often we cannot easily obtain measurements of all the factors that have the important properties of reliability, validity, and objectivity. However, if enough different types of data are obtained, the quality of any single set of data becomes somewhat less important. Also, in program evaluation we are not using data to make decisions about a single individual, and therefore the data need not have such high reliability and validity. Of course, in program evaluation, the highest quality of data possible should be obtained, but since the quality will not always be uniformly high, we are suggesting that it is important to obtain a wide variety of data.

INTERNAL TESTING AND EVALUATION PROGRAMS

Internal testing/evaluation programs are those over which the local school district has full control. The school selects the instruments, determines the scheduling, administers the tests, and determines what to do with the results. We discuss two topics in this section: standardized testing programs and testing programs used in individualized instruction programs.

Standardized Testing Programs

In this section we discuss who should plan, direct, and administer the program; present steps in planning the total program; give an example of a typical school testing program; and discuss the dissemination and interpretation of the results. An excellent resource book for those wishing further coverage is the *Guide for School Testing Programs,* edited by Ward, Backman, Hall, & Mazur (n.d.).

Who Should Be Involved?   A good school testing program should be a cooperative venture from the planning stage through the recording, interpretation, and dissemination of the results. Teachers, administrators, counselors, and, to some extent, parents and students all need to understand the program and to realize that it is designed for the benefit of all groups. Without cooperative involvement the program cannot achieve its full potential. If the original program planning is conducted by only a single individual or a special-interest group, the rest of the professional staff, the parents, and the students cannot necessarily be expected to endorse and adopt the program with enthusiasm.

Cooperative planning should lead not only to more enthusiastic test use but also to a better and more complete program. Teachers, counselors, administrators, parents, and students have overlapping yet somewhat unique needs to be met from testing programs. The special needs of each group may not be well known to others. For example, the instructional decisions of teachers require somewhat different data from those needed for curricular decisions made by administrators. If a member of each group does not have an opportunity to assist in the planning of a program, that program will more than likely be incomplete. Thus a committee representing all interest groups should actively participate in the planning of a testing program.

Though it is extremely important that many subgroups be represented in the planning so that a variety of viewpoints is obtained, competent planning is of more importance than the cooperative planning, and the final specific decisions (for example, which achievement battery should be used) should be the responsibility of the professional staff. The actual administration of the program should be made the responsibility of only a single professional person. This individual should be one who (1) is well trained in tests and measurements and is dedicated to the philosophy of measurements (that is, that test results *do* aid in decision-making processes); (2) can communicate and cooperate with the various interest groups in the school; and (3) has at least a little tolerance for, and expertise in, administrative duties, since the total program from planning to ordering tests, administering tests, seeing to the scoring, analysis, recording, and appropriate distribution and interpretation of results does require administrative know-how. This role is typically filled by a counselor who has a special interest and training in testing. Since directing a testing program is a time-consuming task, the director should be given released time from other duties to handle the program.

Steps in Planning the Program   Several steps are necessary in planning a good testing program. The first and probably the most important step is that the planning committee specify as clearly as possible the purposes of the testing program for their school. As has been repeatedly emphasized, different tests serve different purposes. Without some purposes in mind the committee would be hard put even to designate areas to be covered by the program, let alone select the best instruments. Although schools will surely have some different purposes, there are many commonalities. Most schools will expect their testing programs to serve some instruction, guidance, and administrative purposes. It is hoped that all schools will also use their testing programs for research purposes, although it may be that no test would be selected solely for its research uses (except, of course, when the research has been funded by an external agency).

Second, after thorough consideration has been given to what a testing program should accomplish, the committee must consider the practical aspects of the testing program. There are always unfortunate limitations such as not enough money and too few or inadequately trained personnel. Once priorities have been set, the committee is ready to make some decisions about what specific tests should be given; the when, how, and who of administration, scoring, and analysis; the system of record keeping; and the methods of distributing and interpreting results. Table 11.1 provides a sample

TABLE 11.1

**A CHECKLIST OF FACTORS AFFECTING THE SUCCESS
OF A TESTING PROGRAM**

	Check
1. Purposes of the program:	
Clearly defined	_____
Understood by parties involved	_____
2. Choice of tests:	
Valid	_____
Reliable	_____
Appropriate difficulty level	_____
Adequate norms	_____
Easy to administer and score	_____
Economical	_____
Best available for purpose	_____
3. Administration and scoring:	
Administrators well trained	_____
All necessary information provided	_____
Scorers adequately instructed	_____
Scoring carefully checked	_____
4. Physical conditions:	
Sufficient space	_____
Sufficient time	_____
Conveniently scheduled	_____
5. Utilization of test results:	
Definite plans for use of results	_____
Provision for giving teachers all necessary help in using scorers	_____
Provision for systematic follow-up on use of results	_____
6. System of records:	
Necessary for purpose	_____
Sufficient for purpose	_____
Convenient form for use	_____
7. Personnel:	
Adequately trained for the purpose	_____
8. Affiliated research:	
Full advantage taken of results	_____
Provision for special studies, analyses, or other work	_____

SOURCE: Reproduced from Roger T. Lennon, "Planning a Testing Program," *Test Service Bulletin No. 55*, issued by Harcourt Brace Jovanovich, Inc. Reproduced by special permission of the publisher.

checklist for the committee and/or administrator to follow in a testing program. (See also Chapter 1 under "Practical Aspects of Testing.")

A Typical School Testing Program   As mentioned, testing programs can and should vary, depending upon such characteristics as the size of the school, the characteristics of the student body, and the number and quality of the pupil personnel workers. Nevertheless, surveys of school testing programs show a great many similarities.

One might conceptualize a typical testing program (to be routinely administered to all students) as illustrated in Table 11.2. This typical program is not necessarily the best pattern for all schools. Other tests such as individual intelligence tests, special aptitude and achievement tests, diagnostic tests, and various types of interest, value, attitude, and personality inventories should be available for use with individual students.

The specific tests chosen depend upon the characteristics and needs of each school district, but we strongly recommend that the *same* achievement battery be used at the designated grade levels to provide some continuity. Naturally, if the content validity of a specific test used at the lower grades is inappropriate in a higher grade, use of an alternate achievement battery is warranted. Also, it is helpful if schools use scholastic aptitude tests that have been normed on the same population as the achievement battery. This will permit the user to meaningfully compare scores on the two types of tests.

Because various states have different testing requirements, programs may differ from the one given. We have mixed feelings regarding these external

TABLE 11.2
A TYPICAL SCHOOL TESTING PROGRAM

Grade	Kind of Test
K	Reading readiness test
1 or 2	Reading test
2 or 3	Scholastic aptitude test
4	Achievement battery
5	Achievement battery
5	Scholastic aptitude test
6	Achievement battery
7	Achievement battery
8	Achievement battery
8, 9, 10, or 11	Multifactor aptitude test
10	Achievement battery
9, 10, 11, or 12	Interest inventory

state regulations. They do serve a useful purpose by forcing schools to maintain minimum testing programs. On the other hand, external regulations always mean a certain amoung of rigidity, and there is the danger of being forced to administer tests that the schools will not use, either because they have no objectives relevant to those tests or because they are inadequately staffed to use the results correctly. It may also lead to duplication of testing. Moreover, a few schools overtest.

A more recent phenomenon related to state-imposed requirements for certain standardized tests is for states actually to administer their own testing programs. We discuss this further under "External Testing Programs." One potential consequence of state testing programs is that some schools may feel they no longer need internal testing programs. This is not true. Many state programs are quite limited. Even if they expand considerably in future years, they are not likely to replace the need for local schools to administer the unique tests that are necessary for local decision making. Just as there can be too much overlap between local and state programs, there also can be such a concern with overlap that valuable local testing programs are overcurtailed.

If all schools would adopt the position that a test not be given unless the results are to be used, there would be less testing. *However, what is needed in most schools is probably not less testing but better use of the tests now being given.* Nevertheless, many existing testing programs overlap. For example, schools will occasionally administer both the DAT and a general intelligence test in the same grade, even though research shows fairly conclusively that the VR + NA score of the DAT correlates very well with scores from most group intelligence tests. Any unnecessary duplication of testing or administration of tests whose results remain unused should be eliminated. This is a waste of valuable time and materials, and results in a negative attitude toward testing by all involved—pupils, teachers, parents, and taxpayers.

Dissemination, Recording, and Interpreting Standardized Test Results   If standardized test results are to be used effectively, they must (1) be made available to (and interpreted to or by) the users as quickly as possible and (2) be recorded and filed in a way that facilitates their use. How test results are disseminated and recorded will vary from school to school, because school facilities differ. However, for each test, the school personnel must decide (1) to whom the test results should be distributed and (2) a method of disseminating information that will be efficient and yet ensure correct and adequate communication.

Dissemination.   We take as a given that properly interpreted results should be disseminated to the pupils who have taken standardized tests and who are old enough to understand the interpretation. In this section we discuss who else should be told of the test results.

The public correctly has two somewhat conflicting concerns about the dissemination of test information. It is concerned with how the schools are doing and feels that the schools should release data so that it can judge the school's performance. Parents also want to know how their own particular children are doing in school and some reasons for whatever performance level is reached. Thus, there is a general feeling that data should be released. On the other hand, the public correctly is concerned about schools releasing information to the wrong people. Thus, schools have to tread carefully between releasing information to those who should have it and withholding it from those who should not. Various guidelines have been written on the topic of releasing information. One of the best guidelines is by the Russell Sage Foundation (1970).

Those guidelines advocate five major principles for the collection and dissemination of pupil records. First, there should be informed consent for the collection of data. Second, pupil data should be classified into categories according to potential sensitivity, and these categories should be treated differently in terms of access. Third, all data kept should be verified for accuracy. Fourth, parents and pupils should have access to the data. Fifth, no agency or persons other than the parent or school personnel who deal directly with the child concerned should have access to pupil data without parental or pupil permission.

The Family Educational Rights and Privacy Act of 1974 (Section 513 of Public Law 93-380), which was passed by Congress and became effective in November 1974, prohibits giving federal funds to any educational institution

. . . which has a policy of denying, or which effectively prevents, the parents of students attending any school of such agency, or attending such institution of higher education, community college, school, preschool, or other educational institution, the right to inspect and review any and all official records, files, and data directly related to their children, including all material that is incorporated into each student's cumulative record folder, and intended for school use or to be available to parties outside the school or school system, and specifically including, but not necessarily limited to, identifying data, academic work completed, level of achievement (grades, standardized achievement test scores), attendance data, scores on standardized intelligence, aptitude, and psychological tests, interest inventory results, health data, family background information, teacher or counselor rating and observations, and verified reports of serious or recurrent behavior patterns. Where such records or data include information on more than one student the parents of any student shall be entitled to receive, or be informed of, that part of such record or data as pertains to their child. Each recipient shall establish appropriate procedures for the granting of a request by parents for access to their child's school records within a reasonable period of time, but in no case more than forty-five days after the request has been made.

Parents shall have an opportunity for a hearing to challenge the content of their child's school records, to insure that the records are not inaccurate, misleading, or otherwise in violation of the privacy or other rights of students, and to provide an opportunity for the correction or deletion of any such inaccurate, misleading, or otherwise inappropriate data contained therein. (p. 89)

The law not only states that parents (or students over 18) will have access to records and a right to challenge their accuracy; it also specifies a policy on the releasing of personal records. In general, the policy states that no personal records should be released without written parental (or student if over 18) consent except to certain authorities such as school officials or state educational authorities.

Although most educators support the intent behind the act, there is less unanimity in the value of its consequences. For example, what effect, if any, has this law had on letters of recommendations? Or suppose a high school senior has received below-average scores on several standardized aptitude and achievement tests throughout his school career. He (or his parents) may challenge the accuracy of those scores and request they be deleted. Even though the school believes the records are accurate, they may delete them rather than go through litigation. Now, what inferences would prospective employers and college admissions officers make regarding the quality of the missing data? Would it not be reasonable to infer that the removed data were negative? Would such removal benefit the student? Although many questions remain unanswered, school personnel who help develop policy regarding the release of school data should study both the Russell Sage Foundation guidelines and Public Law 93-380.

Aptitude and Achievement Test Data. We do not regard results of aptitude or achievement tests as private information between the test taker and some other single individual such as the school psychologist. We take the position that the results of all achievement and aptitude tests should be disseminated to all professional staff members in the school, the individuals who were tested, and the parents of those individuals. In fact, there is precedent (*Van Allen* v. *McCleary,* 1961, Public Law 93-380, Sec. 513) for the opinion that parents have a legal right to the test information contained in the official school record. (This right may not apply for students over 18, unless the student gives his or her permission to release the data to the parents.)

Goslin (1967, pp. 19, 77, 92) found that over 60 percent of the public secondary school students and parents of elementary school children sampled believed that intelligence-test information should be routinely reported to them. In contrast, he found that approximately half the teachers in his sample had never given pupils even a general idea of their intelligence, although nearly all teachers felt they, as teachers, should have free access to such information about their students. Goslin used this type of evidence to conclude that there is a "need for a clear statement of policy regarding the dissemination of test scores and information resulting from test scores, both by teachers and other school personnel" (p. 26). We certainly concur with that statement. Such a clear statement of policy should come from the local school district, and not from textbook writers. The policy should depend upon such school characteristics as student-counselor ratio, measurement competencies of the teachers, and whether or not in-service training is available for measurement-naive teachers. The important point is that some *professional* interpretation of aptitude and achievement test scores should be made available to every parent and child.

Aptitude and achievement test scores should also be made available to other school systems (primary, secondary, or college) in which the student intends to enroll. It is probably advisable to receive consent from parents (or students, if over 18) before such a release, but we would not deem it absolutely essential. In general, schools should *not* release the aptitude or achievement test scores of a pupil to any other person or agency (such as a prospective employer, a physician, or psychiatrist) without written permission.

A common practice is for schools to release group achievement-test results to the press. The demands for accountability data and the increased number of state-supported testing programs have served as incentives to this procedure. We have no objection to this general release of data as long as some explanatory and cautionary interpretive exposition accompanies the data. The release should *not* identify particular students' scores or the average score of any single class. (See Frechtling, in press, for a thorough discussion of how to report test scores to different audiences.)

Interest Inventory Data.   Interest inventory results should, in general, be made available (that is, recorded where all would have access to it) to professional staff, students, and parents, but the information should be disseminated to and discussed only with the students. Naturally, any concerned parents should be able to receive professional interpretation of their child's interest test scores. Teachers should know what kind of interest inventory information is available and where it can be obtained. They should be strongly urged to avail themselves of this information and to use it, much as they would other data in the cumulative record, to help in the full understanding of each individual child. No interest inventory data should be released to other agencies without the written consent of the child or parent.

Personality Inventory Data.   As a matter of normal routine, personality and attitude inventory results should not be made available to anyone except the student without his or her explicit permission. One way to minimize faking is to alleviate anxiety about who will have access to the test results and about how they will be used. If a counselor or a school psychologist wishes to obtain an accurate measure from a student, the confidential nature of the information should be emphasized. If confidentiality is promised or even implied, it should not be broken. Often, however, the professional who gathered the information will deem it beneficial for the student to share the information with others, such as parents or teachers. If so, the student's permission to release the data should be obtained. Recall that Public Law 93-380 specifies that parents have the right to "inspect and review any and all official records, files, and data directly related to their children" (p. 89). These records could also be subpoenaed. Counselors might argue, however, that their records (including personality test scores) are not part of the official school records.

Recording.   The recording of the test results not considered private information can be done by trained clerks. Even these results, however, are *not* in the public domain, and the clerks should be cautioned to treat the results as confidential. Test results are generally stored in pupils' cumulative folders. In the future they will no doubt be placed in computer storage. In either case, one must somehow ensure that the information is readily available to those who should have access to it and is not available to those who should not have access to it. These two goals are hard to reach simultaneously. Test results must be kept under lock and key, but teachers should have easy access to them and be encouraged to use them. Of course some teachers are not knowledgeable enough to use test results correctly. This places us somewhat in an ethical dilemma when we suggest that aptitude, achievement, and interest test results be made available to all the professional staff. It is really the teachers' ethical responsibility, however, to know how to use most, if not all, of the scores in the areas mentioned. If teachers do not know how, they should surely recognize their limitations in the area and not use the information without obtaining guidance.

All data on file should be reviewed periodically to determine their present usefulness and accuracy. For most pupils aptitude and achievement-test data should probably be retained throughout secondary school. However, there are occasions where test scores are of doubtful validity or almost assuredly far from correct. These scores should be deleted from the record. (For example, if a student is obviously very ill while taking an exam, the test results should certainly not be made a part of the record.) Interest inventory scores are not likely to be useful for more than three or four years. There is no reason to retain (except perhaps in a very secure file for research purposes) such scores on a pupil's record once he has graduated. As we have mentioned, personality inventory data should not be a regular part of the pupil's records. Anecdotal data should be reviewed annually and discarded when no longer useful.

Interpreting Test Information to Others.   Just as the parent and pupil have a right to certain kinds of test information, the school has the responsibility to communicate this information so that it will be understood correctly and used appropriately. The major aspects to be communicated are (1) the type of information provided by the test score, (2) the precision of this information, and (3) the way the information can be used appropriately.

Confusion often exists as to what information the test score provides. This may be due to one of two reasons: (1) the type of score (that is, percentile rank, stanine, and so on) may not be understood and (2) the construct being measured may not be understood. These problems can be overcome, but the educator needs to be sufficiently aware of the confusion that may occur in a parent's or a pupil's mind. Confusion concerning the type of score may result from mistaking percentile ranks for percentages; misunderstanding of a construct may be the result of confusing aptitude with interest. Even administrators, counselors, and teachers are guilty of these misinterpretations. If a professional can make such a mistake, it reinforces our belief that we must be very careful in interpreting to others what the test is measuring.

The precision of the test information is another important aspect of test interpretation. What needs to be interpreted is an accurate impression of test score accuracy. This, of course, varies from test to test. There has been much concern in the past about the public not being aware of the imprecision of tests. The attempt by some to differentiate between IQs only one point apart illustrates insensitivity to the concept of errors of measurement. One should guard against this danger of overinterpretation. Although teachers or counselors cannot teach a parent or a student about the theoretical concepts of reliability or the standard error of measurement, they certainly can and should communicate the general idea. A good way to do this is through band interpretation. Presenting a range of values encompassing $\pm 1 S_e$ from the observed score as indicating where the individual would probably score if he or she retook the test, usually gets across the point of imprecision. The idea of band interpretation is most often conveyed by using percentile bands, although raw-score or z or T score bands could be used. Percentile bands are reported for the better constructed tests. If they are not reported, they can be easily computed for any test that reports percentile ranks and a standard error of measurement. A person simply looks up the percentile ranks that correspond to $X \pm 1 S_e$. One can be about 68 percent confident that a student's true percentile will be within this range. A possible misinterpretation of percentile bands is that a person unsophisticated in this type of score may think that the percentile corresponding to an observed score is halfway between the two percentile end points of the confidence band. (Or, as mentioned earlier, it is possible to confuse percentiles and percentages.) Because percentile ranks are rectangularly distributed and observed scores are typically distributed in a fairly normal fashion, this interpretation will not be the case except when an observed score is equal to the mean of the distribution. Thus, if percentile bands are used, the percentile for the observed score should be given along with the two end percentiles.

Although many people overinterpret small differences in scores, it is also true that other people place too little faith in test results and *underinterpret* score differences. This has probably become even more true because of the criticisms of testing that have received so much space in the press. In particular, students who score poorly on tests have a tendency to discount the results. Although a teacher or a counselor should not argue with a parent or student over the accuracy of a test score, the precision of a test should not be underplayed. There has been much talk about the importance of a good self-concept. This is fine, but there is no evidence to suggest that persons who have an inaccurately high self-concept will make better decisions than persons who perceive themselves accurately. A good decision, by definition, is dependent upon an accurate self-concept, not a good self-concept.

People may understand what characteristic has been measured and how accurately it has been measured without understanding how this information is useful to them. For example, the knowledge that a person is at about the 80th percentile on a test that measures creativity may not be particularly useful to that person. It is up to the test interpreter to help the individual understand how that information is related to the decisions he or she must make.

It is probably acceptable to present interpretations of achievement and aptitude test results to groups of teachers, but such group interpretation is not ideal. Parents and students who are somewhat less sophisticated with regard to test interpretation should receive more individualized interpretations.

Some schools routinely send home the results of standardized achievement tests accompanied by short brochures (prepared by the test publishers or the local school) that describe the test and explain the meaning of the scores in terms parents can understand. We have mixed feelings about such a practice. The advantage is that it ensures broad dissemination of information. A possible disadvantage is that the information will be either incompletely understood or misunderstood. Another approach is to announce in the school paper or through direct mailings to parents that the results are available and a counselor or homeroom teacher will explain the information if the parents wish to visit the school. Another possibility is to explain the scores at one of the regularly held parent–teacher conferences.[2]

Interest inventories are best interpreted individually, although group interpretations of some interest inventories are appropriate. If the purpose of the interest inventory is primarily to start students thinking about how their interests relate to their educational plans and the world of work, then group interpretation is appropriate. If the interest inventory data are to be used to assist the individual in an immediate educational or vocational decision, then individual interpretation of the data in a counseling situation is necessary.

---

[2] This forcefully illustrates why classroom teachers should be knowledgeable about the interpretation of standardized test scores.

Personality inventory results should be interpreted in an individual interview by qualified personnel. Problems inherent in personality measurement lead us to strongly recommend that the results of such inventories be discussed only in general terms.

Any sharing of information between parents (or students) and teachers (or counselors) regarding test score results is subject to misinterpretation. The following guidelines should be useful in minimizing the problems (Lien, 1976, pp. 297–300):

1. *Make sure that both you and the person to whom you are interpreting the test results have a clear, immediate goal in mind which will serve as a reason for the interpretation.*
2. *Never discuss the implication of the scores in terms of absolute answers (for example, "This score shows you won't get through college").*
3. *Try to concentrate on increasing understanding rather than posing as an expert. Use simple nontechnical terms whenever possible.*
4. *Remember that understanding and acceptance are two different concepts.*
5. *Never compare one student with another particular student.*

Much more could be said concerning specific techniques of test interpretation (see Ricks, 1959). Separate courses should be taken by counselors in test interpretation beyond an introductory course. The main point to be made here is that, in any interpretation of test data, the focus should always be on the student, *not* on the test score. For a further discussion of test interpretation in counseling see Goldman (1971).

Evaluation for Individualized Instruction

Psychologists and educators have long recognized individual differences and the implications of these differences for instruction, and many schools have set up formal individualized instruction programs.

Regardless of the particular type of individualized instruction program, a teacher's job ideally involves undertaking (or assisting the pupil in undertaking) several basic tasks (Heathers, 1971).

1. Specifying in behavioral terminology the desired objectives.
2. Assessing the extent to which the student already has mastered the objectives.
3. Assessing the student's learning characteristics (or learning styles) to determine the best media for achieving the objectives.
4. Using the assessment data mentioned in 2 and 3 above to develop a specific plan with the student.
5. Monitoring the pupil's progress, assessing his or her mastery of the tasks, and determining whether the student is ready to select further tasks.

As can be seen, an individualized program demands considerable evaluative skills on the part of a teacher. Determining and specifying objectives, measuring present student inputs (including both levels of achievement on the objectives and data on learning styles), and continually monitoring the progress of each of 25 to 40 pupils in order to guide the subsequent learning tasks are demanding jobs. The fact that evaluation is so necessary and yet so demanding for a truly individualized instruction program accounts for the attention given to it in many recently developed programs.

All programs should require extensive pretesting to determine the entry behavior of an individual, both with respect to subject-matter achievement and styles of learning. The pupils' progress should be frequently tested or monitored while the pupils are in a program, and they should be given a posttest to determine their final achievement. In most cases the achievement tests are criterion-referenced, since in individualized instruction the intent is to compare a pupil's level of achievement to a specified set of objectives, *not* to a norm group. Data gathered on styles of learning may well be norm-referenced. Most programs emphasize detailed objectives and frequent feedback to students regarding their progress. Computer facilities are often used to assist in collecting, analyzing, storing, and disseminating test information. Usually, decision rules are established to assist in using the test data.

Many of the evaluative techniques *needed* for individualized instruction are also *useful* in group instruction. Objectives should be specified, there should be frequent monitoring and feedback regarding pupils' progress, a posttest should be given, and computers could be used to assist in instruction, testing, and record keeping. Pretesting would also be useful in group instruction for grouping purposes. Usually, however, in group instruction we would wish to norm-reference the results of the posttests, although (as we pointed out in Chapter 1) every norm-referenced test score is also related to objectives.

EXTERNAL TESTING PROGRAMS

By *external testing programs* we mean those administered under the control of agencies other than the school. These programs are often administered in the school by school personnel, but the school is not officially in charge. We discuss three such types of programs: college selection and placement programs, state assessment programs, and national assessment.

College Selection and Placement Programs

Some colleges have limited resources and cannot admit everyone who applies. In general, college admission officers have felt that their job was to admit those who have the greatest probability of success in college. The criterion for judging success has typically been grades in college. Time and time again it has been shown that high school grades are the best single predictor of college grades, that scholastic aptitude tests are the second best predictors, and that the two predictors combined in a multiple regression equation give a significantly better prediction than either one alone. The average correlation between high school performance and first-year college grades is around .50 and .55. When scholastic aptitude tests are added as a predictor, the multiple correlation is raised from .05 to .10 points (Astin, 1971; Hills, 1964). Research suggests that biographical data, interviews, references, personality variables, and work samples have seldom added any practical precision to the prediction process (Hills, 1971, p. 694). Thus, research clearly shows that if the admissions staff wishes to admit students on the basis of predicted success in college, scholastic aptitude tests are useful.

There have been some severe critics of college admission procedures, however. Some critics feel that it is the right of all high school graduates to attend regardless of their chances of success. They argue for an open-admissions policy. The desirability of this policy is debated, but much of the debate is purely academic, since some colleges simply do not have the money to admit all who wish to attend college and others have routinely admitted all high school graduates. An average of four out of five applicants at four-year public and private colleges are being accepted and at nine out of 10 two-year colleges *every* applicant is accepted (*Newsfront,* 1980).

Other critics argue that admissions decisions should be based on a quota system. In either case, testing for college entrance would still be useful. Under an open-admissions policy, tests are needed to assist in placement decisions (and, of course, the facilities to adapt treatments to student needs). (In the absence of open-admissions policies, placement decisions need to be made in addition to selection decisions.) Under a quota system, one would still probably wish to select, within each subgroup, those who are most likely to succeed. Thus, selection tests are useful. Existing aptitude tests predict about as well within one subgroup as another (for a fuller discussion of this point, see the section on "Fairness of Tests to Minority Groups" in Chapter 12).

The two major organizations in this country that provide college selection and placement programs are the College Entrance Examination Board (CEEB) and the American College Testing Program (ACT) (see Chapter 7). About one-third of each year's crop of high school seniors takes the CEEB Scholastic Aptitude Test (SAT), and about one-third takes the ACT test. These two tests are not taken by exactly the same third, but many students do take both batteries. The reason students may take both tests is that different colleges have different requirements, so unless students know for sure what college they will be attending, they end up being forced to take more than one test. There has been some concern from school personnel

(Joint Committee on Testing, 1962) about the overlap and the amount of student time and money these tests consume. The SAT and ACT tests do overlap somewhat, and many persons have wondered whether the tests could not be equated statistically so that only one of these tests need be taken and the score on it converted into equivalent scores on the other test. The problems of equating tests have been discussed considerably in the literature (Angoff, 1964; Lindquist, 1964), and the consensus of the psychometric experts is that such tests cannot be equated completely, because they measure, in part, different constructs. Nevertheless, transformation tables have been built allowing conversions of scores on one test to the other (for example, Astin, 1971). Since the two tests are highly correlated and since tests are seldom used as the sole criterion, it seems that some flexibility by colleges regarding which test was taken is justifiable.

State Assessment Programs

"Clearly the action in testing and assessment in 1984 is in state departments of education" (Womer, 1984, p. 3). Anderson & Pipho report that "by the summer of 1984, 40 states were actively pursuing some form of minimum competency testing. Nineteen states are now implementing tests for high school graduation, and five states are using tests for some form of grade promotion" (1984, pp. 210–211).

Why the push for such mandated programs? Womer (1981) identified five categories of social and educational forces for these state tests: locus of control, the strengthening of state educational agencies, educational equity, accountability, and the decline in educational attainment.

Certainly the demand for accountability and the concern the public has shown for the quality of public school education have served as impetuses. Many recent reports on the condition of education in the country have called for, and resulted in, state legislative and board of education actions for mandated testing programs. For example, one of the recommendations from the report *A Nation at Risk* was that

> *standardized tests of achievement (not to be confused with aptitude tests) should be administered at major transition points from one level of schooling to another and particularly from high school to college or work. (National Commission on Excellence in Education, 1983, p. 28)*

Womer stated: "Lay persons and legislators who control education see testing/assessment as a panacea for solving our concerns about excellence in education" (1984, p. 3). While we suspect that such people know indeed that it is not a cure-all, it is clear that many are hoping that testing/assessment will serve as a positive force in educational quality.

Basically the initiative for mandated assessment programs has come about because many persons believe that the evidence suggests (1) the quality of our children's education is deteriorating and (2) minimum competency testing will improve the educational quality (or reverse the deteriorating process if the first point is true). Both points are debatable.

There are two main variations of what is typically meant by minimum competency measurement. Both involve a systematic test over some basic competencies. In one case the outcome is used to control grade-to-grade promotions; in the other it is used to determine high school graduation (or type of diploma).

There is currently debate around the nation about whether such state-mandated programs will have positive or negative effects. There is even some debate as to the legality of withholding diplomas from students who do not pass minimum competency exams. This topic is addressed at more length in Chapter 12.

National Assessment of Educational Progress (NAEP)

The National Assessment of Educational Progress (NAEP) is the most extensive assessment project ever initiated in the United States. Although NAEP testing began in 1969, the concept of a national assessment program probably began as far back as 1867 with the establishment of the United States Office of Education (USOE). One of the charges then given the commissioners was to determine the progress of education.

The original purpose of NAEP was to "gather data which will help answer the question, how much good is the expenditure of so much money doing, in terms of what Americans know and can do?" (NAEP, 1969).

Knowledge, skills, and attitudes originally were assessed in 10 subject-matter areas—art, career and occupational development, citizenship, literature, mathematics, music, reading, science, social studies, and writing. Tests were given in these areas periodically, with reassessment in later years to determine any changes over time. The tests were administered to four age groups: 9, 13, 17, and young adults.

The reports to the public have been by separate exercises as well as by small subsets that measure the same objectives and/or produce similar results. National p-values (the proportion getting the correct answer) and group differences from the national p-value are reported for all exercises. Some of the actual exercises are released to the public; others remain unreleased so they can be reused in subsequent assessments for growth comparisons. Relevant comparisons have been made across the categories of age, geographic region, type of community, sex, socioeducational status, and race. The original sampling plan was intentionally set up to preclude any state-by-state comparisons.

Recently, NAEP's headquarters has been moved from the Commission of the States to the Educational Testing Service. Concomitant with this change, there have been some shifts in the assessment program itself. Because of the political climate at the time NAEP began, the original program was intentionally designed to limit its scope. As mentioned, sampling did not permit state-by-state comparisons. Also, the students who were assessed were sampled by age rather than by grade, thus reducing any perceived pressure on the teachers of specific grades. Reports were purposely descriptive rather than evaluative by nature, and cause-and-effect inferences were avoided. Under the current political climate there is a demand for information that will be more useful in an accountability sense. The redesigned NAEP, for instance, samples by grade (fourth, eighth, and eleventh) as well as by age. More background questions are asked of the students; and teachers and administrators are asked to answer questions regarding curricula, teaching materials, and instructional practices.

There have also been some recent changes in the subjects to be assessed and the frequency of the testing. Assessments are to be conducted every two years, and reading will be measured each time because of its importance to education. Three or four subject-matter areas will be included in each assessment. Reading and writing were assessed during 1983–1984. The 1985–1986 assessment will cover reading, mathematics, science, and computer understanding.

The political climate now is such that many people are advocating that the NAEP program be conducted to allow for state-by-state comparisons. For example, the Southern Regional Educational Board (1984) suggested that "a missing link in assessing student achievement in the schools is the existence of publicly accepted, nationwide measures by which states can gauge their relative progress" (p. iii). At the 1984 Education Commission of the States' Large-Scale Assessment Conference, William Pierce, director of the Council of Chief State School Officers, indicated that "the 'chiefs' have endorsed the idea of state-by-state rankings based on results from the proposed administration of National Assessment test items to samples of students in each of the 50 states" (Womer, 1984, p. 3). Whether or not this is a good idea is clearly debatable. In an audience of about 150 (mostly professionals in educational measurement) at the opening session of the conference, only three or four indicated that they favored a state-by-state ranking (Womer, 1984). However, because of current demand, the federal government is already ranking states based on poorer data. One can argue that states should not be ranked. However, several governors and commissioners of education in Southeastern states have vowed to raise the educational quality of their states in comparison to other states. For example, Florida has made a commitment to rank in the top 10 states. How can they determine whether or not they have achieved that goal unless there is some way to compare states?

Currently schools (both secondary schools and colleges) are ranked either within states (secondary) or across states (college) on quality of specific athletic teams. At times, the rankings are questioned. They are not always based on sound comparative data. For example, as this is being written,

Brigham Young University (BYU) has been declared number 1 in football among major college teams for 1984. This ranking has been debated on the basis that BYU had "an easier schedule" and therefore its undefeated season did not mean that it was superior to some other teams who were defeated during the year but had played tougher competition. What has been the impact of the debate regarding the accuracy of the rating? Washington, who some claim should have been ranked number 1, happens to play BYU for its first game next season. The competition during that game no doubt will be more intense than if no rankings had been made.

Some people have argued that, whether the rankings in athletics be correct or not, they have been counterproductive because they have resulted in too much emphasis on athletics in college. Perhaps some will argue that state-by-state rankings in educational quality, whether the rankings are accurate or not, will be counterproductive because they will result in too much emphasis being placed on educational quality in the states! In our view, the ranking of states on educational quality is, in an abstract sense, a good thing. Whether good or ill comes from any particular ranking depends on whether the data are *actually* reflective of educational quality. If they are, and states compete to do better on the variables from which the data are gathered, that seems fine. On the other hand, if the data do *not* actually reflect educational quality, then striving to do better may indeed be counterproductive. A good example of that is the use of average SAT scores within the states. If states wished to achieve a higher ranking on that variable, the easiest way would be to discourage all but the very brightest from taking the test. While that would raise the mean for the state, it would not result in increased quality of education. Clearly the mean performance on NAEP data would represent better quality data than mean SAT scores, which are currently being used as an indicator of quality.

SUMMARY

The major ideas, conclusions, and implications of this chapter are summarized in the following statements:

1. Accountability in education means different things to different people. However, the term usually encompasses setting correct goals, evaluating whether they have been achieved and at what price, releasing this information to the public, and accepting responsibility for any results that are perceived inadequate.
2. Each participant in the educational process should be held responsible only for those educational outcomes that he or she can affect.
3. There is a tendency for accountability programs to focus on the objectives that are more easily measured.

4. Opinions differ on what the distribution of educational outcomes should be.
5. In general, it seems that most people advocating accountability operate as if their goal is to bring all students up to some minimum level.
6. A good accountability program should assess input variables, surrounding conditions, and the educational process as well as the output variables, and should attempt to establish causal relations between the first three and the last. This is an extremely difficult task.
7. In program evaluation one would hope to be able to make inferences about what conditions lead to certain outcomes.
8. The politics of program evaluation is a potential cause of evaluation bias.
9. Program evaluation involves evaluating goal appropriateness as well as outcome achievement.
10. In program evaluation we must be alert to the side effects or unintended outcomes.
11. Formative evaluation is the gathering of data during the time a program is being developed, for the purpose of guiding that developmental process.
12. Summative evaluation is the process of making an overall assessment or decision about the program.
13. A good school testing program should be a cooperative venture among teachers, administrators, counselors, students, and parents.
14. Both faculty and students need to be prepared for the administration of standardized tests.
15. More evaluation is necessary in a program of individualized instruction than in traditional instruction procedures.
16. All individualized instruction programs require extensive pretesting to determine the entry behavior of an individual, with respect both to subject-matter achievement and styles of learning. There should be frequent testing or monitoring of a pupil's progress and a posttest to determine final achievement.
17. There is considerable empirical evidence that college selection and placement programs assist in individual and institutional decision making.
18. The demands for accountability have resulted in an increased number of state minimum-competency assessment programs.

POINTS TO PONDER

1. In this chapter we have suggested that pupils, parents, and teachers all be involved in setting up the school testing program. What part should each play? What are the dangers of such a heterogeneous committee?

2. Assume you are in a financially troubled school district and are allowed to give only one aptitude test and two achievement batteries in grades K to 12. At which grade levels would you administer the tests?
3. Some states have a uniform statewide testing program. Are you in favor of such programs? Explain your position.
4. What does the decline of admission test scores say, if anything, about the overall quality of public schools?

CHAPTER 12

Public Concerns About and Future Trends in Evaluation

PUBLIC CONCERNS ABOUT MEASUREMENT AND EVALUATION
FUTURE TRENDS IN EVALUATION

Many topics that could be classified as issues or trends have already been discussed in this text. *Issues* would include such topics as

1. Should norm- or criterion-referenced tests predominate?
2. What is the definition and structure of intelligence?
3. What is the etiology of intellectual differences?
4. How stable are intelligence test scores?
5. Do we have, or should we develop, culture-fair tests?
6. Should standardized tests be used in schools?
7. Is accountability a good concept, and if so, how should we set up accountability programs?
8. What does the regular classroom teacher have to know about measurement because of mainstreaming?

Current *trends* discussed have included (1) criterion-referenced tests; (2) expanded report forms; (3) program evaluation; (4) testing for individualized instruction programs; and (5) testing children with special needs.

In this final chapter we wish to discuss several public concerns about measurement and evaluation. (By public we mean all nonmeasurement specialists. This would include teachers, counselors, and administrators as well as the lay public.) We do not mean to suggest that the public has been unconcerned about some of the previously discussed topics. They have been concerned about some issues but have been largely unaware of other issues. We will also briefly mention some of the more recent and predicted future

448

trends and give some appropriate references for those who wish to read more about these topics.

After studying this chapter the student should be able to do the following:

1. Recognize several public concerns about testing.
2. Understand some of the motivating factors behind these concerns.
3. Discuss the rationale behind and likely consequences of truth-in-testing legislation.
4. Define minimum competency testing and discuss reasons for its prevalence and controversial nature.
5. Recognize the relevant and irrelevant concerns of the invasion-of-privacy issue.
6. Discuss the concept of "cultural fairness."
7. Recognize some recent and predicted future trends in measurement and evaluation.

PUBLIC CONCERNS ABOUT MEASUREMENT AND EVALUATION

With an increase in testing in schools, industry, and government, it is natural and appropriate for the public to show interest in, and concern for, this enterprise. In the early 1960s many writers criticized tests in what became a typical journalistic exposé fashion (Gross, 1962; Hoffmann, 1962; Black, 1963). The phrase *antitest revolt* was often used to express public concern. By the late 1970s much of the general public became more in favor of testing than against it, and current concern is more likely to be from special-interest groups rather than the general public.

One example of a special-interest group's attack on testing is in the articles found in the *National Elementary Principal* and *Today's Education*. Most of the criticism about testing in those publications was directed at scholastic aptitude tests. Another example of a special-interest group's attack on testing is *The Reign of ETS: The Corporation That Makes Up Minds* (Nairn et al., 1980). Published and promoted by Nader it is commonly referred to as the Nairn/Nader report. Although it received considerable public press coverage, it is considered by professional measurement experts to be quite unscholarly and biased. (See Hargadon, 1980, and Mehrens, 1981, for sample professional reviews of the publication. Mehrens concluded that in writing the truth about testing the Nairn/Nader report had reached a nadir.)

Haney (1980) discussed some of the recent concerns about testing. He suggested that minimum competency tests, truth in testing legislation, use of tests as gatekeepers, and bias in testing are issues that are intensely political. Lerner (1980) charged that the war on testing comes from three main groups: the National Education Association, the National Association for the Advancement of Colored People, and the Nader conglomerate. Ebel (1976, pp.

2–3) essentially agreed. He suggested that the criticism of tests and testing comes primarily from three special-interest groups:

1. Professional educators who are uneasy about the accountability associated with standardized tests and external testing in general.
2. Reformers who regard testing as part of an unsuccessful and outmoded instructional process.
3. Free-lance writers whose best sellers purport to expose scandals in important human institutions.

We believe there is considerable truth to both Lerner's and Ebel's positions.

As we pointed out in Chapter 1, the leaders of the two major teachers' unions take quite different positions on standardized tests. The American Federation of Teachers (AFT) strongly supports testing, while the National Education Association's (NEA) leadership favored a moratorium on standardized testing. Teachers, as a group, are much closer to the AFT position. Stetz & Beck (1981) report that only 10 percent of a national sample of teachers supported a moratorium. A survey by Ward (1980) also found that teachers support standardized tests. There is thus considerable evidence to suggest that the opposition comes mainly from a vocal minority of professional educators.

Although the critics raise a few valid concerns, in general they also do not understand much about the field of measurement, and the result is that their criticisms are frequently invalid. As Page (1976) points out, measurement is a technical field, and it cannot be understood, let alone criticized intelligently, without some mastery of the content. In terms of technical competence many of the critics are analogous to the "flat earthers" who attacked the heliocentric theory.

Even though the validity of the criticisms expressed in the numerous books and articles is probably inversely proportional to the public acclaim they have received, all these criticisms have been of value—if for no other reason than that of forcing psychometricians to examine the criticisms, then change practices where advisable, and to defend themselves against the sometimes unjust criticisms. Glaser & Bond suggest that "in the heat of the current controversy, it is especially necessary to be our own sternest critics" (1981, p. 997). We would also remind you of the Anderson quote in Chapter 1, which suggests that we also must recognize and label some of the attacks for what they are: "*vicious, destructive, deliberately misleading,* but also *sustained, well organized,* and *well-financed*" (Anderson, 1980, p. 5, italics in original). As professionals we have a responsibility to improve our procedures. We also have a responsibility to educate the public to the educational and social benefits of measurement and evaluation.

Since public concern encompasses so many specific yet interrelated aspects of testing, it is difficult to present the topic completely in any tightly organized fashion. Therefore we have chosen to discuss five issues that seem of most concern to the public: (1) the use (or misuse) of test scores for making decisions about individuals, (2) truth in testing, (3) minimum competency testing for students and teachers, (4) the invasion-of-privacy issue, and (5) the fairness of tests to minority groups. These issues are neither mutually exclusive nor exhaustive.

Use (or Misuse) of Test Scores

As mentioned in Chapter 1, concern with the correct use of test scores has focused mainly on using standardized tests. We are not suggesting by this statement that data gathered from classroom evaluation procedures cannot be misused also. They can, but in general the critics are unaware or unconcerned about misuse of data from nonstandardized tests. This seems unfortunate. As Hargadon points out, the courses students take and the grades received in high school have a greater effect on educational and life chances than College Boards, there is great variation in the standards and quality of those courses and grades, and students take more teacher-made tests in a single year in high school than standardized tests in a lifetime (Hargadon, 1980). Students express more anxiety about teacher-made tests and find them to be more difficult than standardized tests (Stetz & Beck, 1981).

At any rate, all types of data can be misused. The consequences of misusing tests can be quite severe and examples abound, although probably not with the frequency critics suggest. Using test scores to label or categorize a child as a nonlearner instead of helping one understand a person is an accusation mentioned very frequently. Research, however, suggests that teachers do not do this to any great extent. Research has shown that a child's classroom behavior counts more than standardized tests in teacher judgments about students. Teachers tend to discount standardized test scores *below* what they would predict from classroom performance and use *higher* scores as an indication that classroom performance was perhaps an inaccurate indicator. Thus, teachers who receive standardized test information are more apt to raise their ratings of students than teachers who do not receive such information (Kellaghan, Madaus, and Airasian, 1980; Salmon-Cox, 1981).

The important point is that misuse of tests can occur. This does not lead us to the conclusion that testing is bad; rather it makes us aware that we must concentrate our energies toward the goal of *educating* people on the *correct* use of tests results. Most of the problems regarding test misuse relate to the overgeneralizations made by users, not to the fact that the tests per se are invalid. Most standardized test constructors display integrity and professional honesty in stipulating how these tests can be used. However, educators are not being professionally honest when they use tests they are not qualified to use.

Educators' incompetence in testing is due to several factors. First, a basic measurement course is not required in all undergraduate teacher training institutions, or even in some graduate training programs. Second, preservice teachers do not flock to the measurement courses as electives because they are often seen as harder than other courses that may be selected. There have been some attempts to have inservice (professional development) programs on measurement and evaluation, but again, teachers do not typically select these programs if they have a choice. Furthermore, measurement and evaluation has a bit too much substance to be covered in a one- or two-hour (or even one- or two-day) inservice program.

Specialists in measurement and evaluation are aware of the educators' lack of appropriate training and have made a variety of attempts to minimize the misuse of tests by educators. For example, the *Standards for Educational and Psychological Testing* (AERA-APA-NCME, 1985) contains many guidelines on appropriate test use. By and large, this book was written so that educators can understand at least major portions of it even though they are not highly trained in measurement. Publishers of standardized tests put out a variety of materials designed to promote correct use of test data and discourage the incorrect use of test data. The National Institute of Education and the Department of Defense Dependents Schools funded a two-year research and development project to examine the relationship between assessment and instruction. "The ultimate goal of this project was to increase teachers' use of assessment data in the classroom by focusing on various methods for integrating assessment data into classroom instructional decisions" (Wanous & Mehrens, 1981, p. 3). One of the outcomes of this project was *The Data Box* (Rudman, Mehrens, & Wanous, 1983), an integrated set of materials that enable teachers to investigate the use of assessment data in a variety of instructional decision-making situations. Most large school districts have a measurement and evaluation unit that offers workshops to teachers on the correct uses of measurement data. Some of the states that have implemented a minimum competency test for teachers have a portion of the test devoted to measurement competencies. This should serve as an impetus for colleges of education in those states to teach some measurement courses, and for education students to take such courses.

Despite the various efforts we have discussed, not all educators know enough about testing to avoid all misuses. In the final analysis, educators must be sufficiently professional to seek out training in areas where they need instruction and not to take on projects that are beyond their professional competence.

Many people criticize the faulty decisions made through the misuse of test information. Fewer people realize that a far more costly misuse of tests is not to use them at all. Too many critics evaluate tests against nonexistent ideal predictors. Even if only a few better decisions were made with the help of test information than would have been made without that information, the long-term benefits would likely outweigh the initial costs of testing. As mentioned earlier, Hunter (1983) estimated that the potential increase in workforce productivity by the optimal use of tests in employment decisions would be $80 billion per year. While tests do not predict perfectly, they certainly can result in considerable benefits! We have indicated in Chapter 7 that tests are more useful in prediction decisions than most other alternatives. Lennon (1981) had this to say about the alternatives:

> *Those who find fault with standardized testing have continually urged the search for alternatives to it. In their conferences and in their publications, they call for reduced dependence on standardized tests in favor of use of alternative ways of gathering information about subjects. . . . And each time these alternatives are advanced as if our literature were not replete with demonstrations that they compare very poorly indeed with standardized tests by any conventional measures of reliability or validity. To encourage the innocent to root around in the rubble of discredited modes of study of human behavior, in search of some overlooked assessment "jewels," is to dispatch a new band of Argonauts in quest of a nonexistent Golden Fleece." (pp. 3–4)*

Probably the concern with imperfect test validity would be less if tests were not seen as gatekeepers to better education and a better way of life. Tests are frequently designed to measure differences among individuals, and this information may help in making decisions about the allocation of limited resources or opportunities. But the limited resources are not always allocated to those who score high on tests. Compensatory education programs are obvious exceptions. Who deserves limited resources and what should be done about individual differences are *policy* questions. Tests simply provide information about what differences exist. It is not appropriate to call a test *unfair* (or invalid) because data from it are used to allocate resources in a manner that runs opposite to our personal philosophies. If it is believed that admission to a college having limited enrollment should be based on predicted academic success, if test scores increased the predictive accuracy (they do), and if the admissions offices use the test scores *correctly* in a regression equation (or set of regression equations—differentiated on ethnicity, sex, or whatever other demographic variable would increase predictive efficiency) to help predict success, then we would argue that the test was not unfair nor were the test data misused in any *measurement sense*. The correctness of the philosophy to limit enrollment based on predicted success can be debated, but *that* argument is independent of, and of a different order from, whether the test data are useful, given the philosophical stance. But the above comments are surely not to suggest that tests cannot be misused.

Correct test use involves all aspects of testing, from selection to interpretation. But we wish to stress again that if test information is used correctly, it is impossible to make (in the long run) poorer decisions by using this additional information. Thus, if the public desires accurate decision making, their concern should not be whether tests should be used but whether tests are used properly. As previously stated, users of tests have an ethical responsibility to be qualified to administer, score, and interpret tests properly. Unfortunately, many test users do not assume this responsibility. A pertinent question is *who* should stipulate users' qualifications? Is it the responsibility of the test publishers to be sure unqualified users do not obtain copies of tests? Should a professional organization such as the American Psychological Association set up standards? Should states have certification requirements? (Although many states have certification requirements for psychologists, this does not really control access to, and potential misuse of, test data.) Should a federal agency exert control? Any suggested answer to this last question would probably raise as much controversy as one that decided who should assume responsibility for our safety while we ride in automobiles.

"Truth-in-Testing" Legislation

At the time of this writing, New York and California are the only states to have "truth-in-testing" laws. The New York law requires, among other things, that for tests used for post-secondary or professional school admission, the actual questions and answers be available for public scrutiny within 30 days of the test's administration. The California law, which took effect on July 1, 1982, requires test disclosure for only *some* of the undergraduate entrance exams. Federal test-disclosure legislation has been under consideration for the past several years, but no bill has yet made it out of committee. These bills, by and large, have been similar to the bill passed in New York. In addition, several other states have considered similar bills and some may have been passed by the time you read this.

Generally the bills require (1) that a test taker on request be able to see a copy of the corrected test; (2) that the test publisher file information of test-development procedures and evidence of reliability and validity with some governmental agent; and (3) that test takers be told, in advance, the intended use of the tests. If the bills were written by someone knowledgeable in measurement, provisions 2 and 3 would not be troublesome. Unfortunately, the bills are written by nonmeasurement people and can call for ill-defined or unavailable information.

The provision of these bills that has caused the most concern among measurement experts is the requirement that items must be disclosed after the test is given. The reason for the concern should be obvious. Once items are in the public domain there is a real reluctance to reuse them. Any new test should have at most only a very few items that were used previously. Thus, the requirement calls for the writing of many more items—an expensive and time-consuming process. Krumboltz (1981) has suggested that if the legislation had been labeled the "Expensive Test Item Giveaway" legislation, the outcomes would have been different.

Why have such bills been introduced? It certainly has not been due to general public dissatisfaction with previous testing practices. A summary of 10 opinion surveys of the public's attitudes toward testing points to just the opposite conclusion (Lerner, 1981a). The bills have been pushed by special-interest groups "who confuse arrogance with idealism by insisting that they are . . . representatives of a public whose views they scorn" (p. 275). The *stated* purposes of the bills are acceptable. These generally relate to such positive goals as making tests better and fairer.

However, laws are not needed to fulfill these purposes. Further, they are not likely to facilitate the accomplishment of those purposes, but will probably seriously hamper efforts to achieve some of them (such as greater accuracy, validity, and reliability in testing).

The legislation passed and being proposed is consistent with the efforts by some to do away with, or at least seriously weaken, standardized testing. There is abundant research evidence showing that should these efforts succeed, the result would be poorer educational decision making. In fact, it should be obvious to anyone that better decisions are made with data than without data.

The effect of the New York law on the College Boards' Scholastic Aptitude Test is that the costs in New York are up slightly and the services have been reduced somewhat (fewer test dates are scheduled in New York). Fewer than 5 percent of those tested in New York requested the SAT questions and answers, suggesting considerably less public interest than the sponsors of the bill had claimed (*The College Board News,* 1981). Further, the evidence suggests that these 5 percent disproportionally represent "students who are already better off—scholastically, financially, and in terms of their test scores and their plans to attend college. Release of items and answers may serve only to widen the gap between disadvantaged students and those who are already 'test-wise' and advantaged in other respects" (Committee on Psychological Tests and Assessment, 1984, p. 5).

Since disclosure is required in New York, the College Board has made some copies of the SAT (and PSAT) available for everyone. Beginning in 1981–1982, the College Board offered nationally five SAT test dates on which students could obtain questions and answers for the test they took as well as their own answers. *Before* taking the SAT every registrant receives a sample copy of the SAT, its answers, test-taking advice, and so on (this was available *prior* to any legislation). Will disclosure of test items benefit anyone? We are inclined to doubt it. Advocates of the various bills have made much of the discovery of three flawed test questions, suggesting that disclosure provisions made such discovery possible and that such discovery will result in subsequently less flawed exams. Actually one should be amazed that only three out of more than 1500 questions placed under public scrutiny were found to be flawed! This suggests good previous quality control. As ETS must now develop more test questions with less time to pilot them extensively, it is more likely that quality control subsequent to item disclosure will go down rather than up. Item disclosure is simply not likely to result in better exams. The argument that prior to item disclosure students did not know the general content of the exams or types of questions asked is simply false. There was abundant free information available to students regarding the SATs, including sample tests, prior to any legislation. Research (Stricker, 1984) suggests that access to disclosed material has no appreciable effects on retest performance.

In general, measurement specialists have been opposed to the so-called Truth in Testing ("Expensive Test Item Giveaway") legislation. Evidence for this can be seen by some brief quotes from the statements of professional measurement associations. For example, the National Council on Measurement in Education (NCME) statement on Educational Admissions Testing states the following: "Making all test questions and answers public poses problems for the test developer that may result in increased costs and diminished services for the test taker" (NCME, 1980). The Association for Measurement and Evaluation in Guidance (AMEG) statement says: "we do not believe legislative action regarding testing is necessary or desirable" (AMEG, 1980). The statement specifically recommends *against* the enactment of legislation that requires disclosure of items following testing. The statement of the American Psychological Association's Division of Evaluation and Measurement on the 1979 Truth in Testing Act says: "Disclosure of items used on standardized tests has many disadvantages." Later the statement says: "We believe that students, themselves, would be the principal losers if the provisions of Section 5 of H.R. 4949 were to become law." (That was a reference to the disclosure-of-items section of H.R. 4949—see Glaser & Eyde, 1979.) The Committee on Psychological Tests and Assessment of the American Psychological Association stated: "We oppose total disclosure of items from low volume tests or tests where item domains are finite. . . . We oppose disclosure of tests where interpretation is dependent upon a long history of research" (1984, p. 5).

We agree with the statements quoted. We admit that the assertions made regarding the likely harmful effects of such legislation cannot be proven beyond a shadow of a doubt, but these assertions are made by three major professional associations. They are seriously thought out, informed opinions by the leading experts in the field. You should not take their views lightly. Certainly, since the passage of the New York law and the current policies of the College Board to release test items of some tests, further legislation of this sort seems totally unnecessary.

Minimum Competency Testing

Minimum competency testing (MCT) is certainly one of the most controversial topics in measurement, indeed in all of education, today. In the summer of 1981 the National Institute of Education (NIE) sponsored a three-day adversary evaluation hearing on the topic (Thurstone & House, 1981). To educate the public, all testimony from both the pro and con sides was videotaped and edited for four 60-minute programs aired by the Public Broadcasting System.

What is minimum competency testing and why has it caused so much turmoil? Many definitions of the phrase exist. We quote here the one used in the NIE hearings:

> *Minimum competency testing refers to programs mandated by a state or local body which have the following characteristics: (1) All or almost all students of designated grades are required to take paper-and-pencil tests designed to measure basic academic skills, life or survival skills, or functional literacy; (2) a passing score or standard for acceptable levels of student performance has been established; and (3) test results may be used to certify students for grade promotion, graduation, or diploma award; to classify students for or to place students in remedial or other special services; to allocate compensatory funds to districts; to evaluate or to certify schools or school districts; or to evaluate teachers. (Thurstone & House, 1981, p. 87)*

Minimum competency testing has been around for a long time. A very early minimum competency exam was when the Gilead Guards challenged the fugitives from Ephraim who tried to cross the Jordan river.

"Are you a member of the tribe of Ephraim?" they asked. If the man replied that he was not, then they demanded, "Say Shibboleth." But if he could not pronounce the "sh" and said Sibboleth instead of Shibboleth, he was dragged away and killed. As a result, 42,000 people of Ephraim died there at that time (Judges 12:5–6, *The Living Bible*).

Nothing is reported concerning the debates that may have gone on among the guards regarding what competencies to measure, how to measure them, when to measure, how to set the minimum standard, or indeed what should be done with the incompetent. We do not know the ratio of false acceptances to false rejections or the relative costs of the two types of errors. We do know that a very minimum competency exam was given that 42,000 people failed—with no chance of a retake. And some people think our public school students have it bad! But there have been other, less drastic competency exams—for example, those for certifying or licensing professionals and those for obtaining a driver's license.

If not a new concept, why so much fuss? Never before have state and local agencies been so active in setting the minimum competency standards for elementary and secondary students. For example, by 1984, 40 states were actively pursuing some form of minimum competency testing. Nineteen states were using tests for high school graduation decisions, and five states were using tests for grade-to-grade promotion (Anderson & Pipho, 1984). In May 1983, about 1300 high school seniors in Florida did not receive diplomas because they failed the state's minimum competency test (Citron, 1983). Several large-city school districts—including, for example, Detroit, Philadelphia, and New York—have also implemented some type of minimum competency testing program.

General Questions About Minimum Competency Tests   Over the past several years a multitude of questions have been raised about minimum competency testing: (1) Why have them at all? (2) What competencies should be measured? (3) When should we measure the competencies? (4) Who should set the minimum standard? (5) How should the minimum standard be determined? and (6) What should be done with the incompetent? These questions are all related. The answer given for one has implications for the answers to the others. We will discuss briefly some aspects of these questions. Further details regarding one of the authors' views of these and other questions can be found in Mehrens (1979).

(1) Why Have Standards at All?   As mentioned in Chapter 1, 71 percent of the American people believe that children should be promoted from grade to grade only if they pass examinations, and 65 percent think that all high school students in the United States should be required to pass a standardized *nationwide* examination in order to get a high school diploma (Gallup, 1984). It is reasonable to assume the percentage would have been even higher had the word *nationwide* been left out of the question, because many people may prefer a state or local examination.

Why the big push for minimum competency tests with specified standards? Many individuals believe the evidence suggests that the general quality of our children's education is deteriorating and that far too many children are not learning adequately the basic skills. Many feel that minimum competency testing will improve educational quality (or reverse any deterioration). Both points are debatable. We believe the first—some of you may not. The evidence is on our side. Lerner (1981b) summarizes some of the relevant data and concludes that 20 percent of American 17-year-olds are illiterate and 60 percent semiliterate. On the second point, that minimum competency testing will improve our educational system, we would prefer to reserve judgment, but there is some supportive evidence reported in the literature. For example, Klein (1984) stated that in a doctoral dissertation Wagner (1983) concluded that minimum competency has improved instruction through clearer goals, better-focused teaching, and better inservice training.

Of course there are many perceived costs as well as perceived benefits of minimum competency testing. Perkins (in Gorth & Perkins, 1979) has compiled two very complete lists. We will present five examples from each side of the debate.

PERCEIVED COSTS OF MINIMUM COMPETENCY TESTING

1. Causes less attention to be paid to difficult-to-measure learning outcomes.
2. Promotes teaching to the test.
3. Will cause "minimums" to become "maximums" thus failing to provide enough instructional challenge in school.
4. May unfairly label students and cause more of the "less able" to be retained.
5. Can be costly, especially where implementation and remediation are concerned.

PERCEIVED BENEFITS OF MINIMUM COMPETENCY TESTING

1. Restores meaning to a high school diploma.
2. Certifies that students have specific minimum competencies.
3. Defines more precisely what skills must be taught and learned for students, parents, and teachers.
4. Motivates students to master basic reading, mathematics, and writing skills.
5. Provides an opportunity to remedy the effects of discrimination by identifying learning problems early in the educational process.

(2) What Competencies Should Be Measured?   The answer to the question of what competencies should be measured in a minimum competency program is related directly to the purposes of the test—that is, what inferences we wish to make about a person who "passes"—and much less directly about the "purposes of the school." Many people apparently do not make enough of this distinction.

Although there exists a reasonable consensus about desirable adult characteristics, there is considerable diversity of opinion about their relative importance and about the role of the school in promoting those characteristics. Some people maintain that good citizenship or healthy self-concepts are more important in life than reading skills. Others assert just the opposite. And some who believe the former do not believe it is the primary purpose of the school to promote those characteristics. We will never reach agreement on what characteristics we "need" in our society and on the role of the school in teaching, establishing, or nurturing those characteristics. But that should not deter us from determining general content for a minimum competency test. No test can be designed to assess the degree to which all the purposes of education have been achieved or even to assess whether students have achieved a level of minimal competency in all areas.

Surely no one would infer that all purposes of education have been achieved if students pass a minimum competency test. Would any reasonable citizen infer—or would we want it to be inferred—that a passing score means the person has "survival skills" for life? Life is very varied, and so are the skills needed to survive. We cannot believe the populace is so unrealistic or naive as to think in such grandiose terms. Schools do not and cannot teach all survival skills. Such skills cannot even be adequately enumerated (or defined), and thus they cannot be adequately measured. Since we do not want any "survival skills" inference to be drawn from a test, we should not build a test to measure such defined competencies.

The focus of most minimum competency programs is on the basic skill areas of writing, mathematics, and language arts. But if we measure only basic skills (applied to life settings), would not other areas of school suffer? Not necessarily. Remember, there is a distinction between the purpose of school and the purposes of a minimum competency test. The purpose of the latter can never be to assess all the objectives of school. We all know that. Of course not all skills are basic and we do not want minimums to become maximums. Few would be happy to see high school graduates who lacked maturity, self-discipline, and some understanding of their own value systems. But if we keep in mind the limitations of the inferences to be drawn from passing (or failing) a minimum competency test, such limited testing should not have deleterious effects.

We should not assume that minimum competency standards can do much to define the goals and objectives of education. They only set a lower limit of acceptable standards in certain basic skill areas. This certainly suggests that passing the minimum competency test should not be the only requirement for high school graduation. Other graduation requirements could assure breadth in other areas. In specifying the domain of basic skills, we need to keep in mind the relationship between the tested domain and what is taught in school. We should *not* be testing content that is not taught. Both logic and court rulings make this very clear. On the other hand, we should not attempt to randomly sample *all* that is taught. The tested domain must be a *subset* of materials taught in the curriculum.

(3) When Should the Competencies Be Measured?   The answer to the question when to measure (like the answer to every other question) depends on the purpose(s) of testing. Of course, the primary reason for minimum competency testing is to identify students who have not achieved the minimum. But identify for what purpose? To help the students identified through remediation programs? To motivate students through "fear of failure"? To make a high school diploma more meaningful?

We believe there should be periodic but *not* every-grade testing. Minimum competency programs will be more cost-effective if tests are given approximately three times during the K–12 portion of a student's schooling—for example in grades 4, 7, and 10. Teachers, of course, gather almost continuous data. They often have already identified those students achieving inadequately. The formal tests supplement the teachers' measures and confirm or disconfirm previous judgments. This formal identification is useful. Tests are credible instruments, help motivate students (and teachers), and help assign a minimum competency meaning to a diploma or certificate.

We are opposed to every-grade testing for *minimum competencies* because it is not cost-effective. (We are not opposed to every-grade testing with a more general achievement measure.) Only a very few students, we hope, will be identified as not achieving at a minimum level, and at any rate those identified in fourth grade would very likely overlap considerably with those in third or fifth grade.

Finally, let us stress that if minimum competency tests are used for high school certification or graduation, there must be opportunities for students who have not passed to retake the exams. Further, no test should be used for such a purpose the first year it is given. To be fair to students there should be a phase-in period.

(4) Who Sets the Minimum?   Obviously, the minimums must be determined by those who have the authority to do so. This will be an agency such as a state board of education or a local school board. It is more difficult to decide who should represent this agency. Of course all constituents should be involved, but measurement experts need to be involved as well. Although setting the minimum is arbitrary, measurement experts can have some useful suggestions.

(5) How Should the Minimum Standard Be Determined?   The actual choice of a minimum is arbitrary. Different methods of setting the minimum lead to different cutoff scores, and one cannot say in the abstract that one method (or one cutoff score) is superior to another. Glass makes the point as follows:

> *I have read the writings of those who claim the ability to make the determination of mastery or competency in statistical or psychological ways. They can't. At least, they cannot determine "criterion levels" or standards other than arbitarily. . . . the language of performance standards is pseudoquantification, a meaningless application of numbers to a question not prepared for quantitative analysis. (Glass, 1978a, p. 602)*

So, admittedly, setting the standard is arbitrary. (But that does not necessarily mean it is capricious.) Further, it is politically and economically influenced. If the standards are too high and too many students fail, then there will surely be a public outcry about the quality of the schools and the unreasonableness of the standards. Moreover, if one is committed to remediation, the costs of remediation could be very high. If the standards are set too low then the program becomes meaningless, and if people become aware of the ridiculously low standards, they will again present an outcry about the quality of the schools. The standard setters will be damned either way.

Glass raises the question of whether a criterion-referenced testing procedure entailing mastery levels is appropriate. He answers in the negative, stating that "nothing may be safer than an arbitrary something" (Glass, 1978b, p. 258). Now, we certainly admire Glass and indeed, we might be "safer" with nothing rather than an arbitrary something. But let us take the other side.

There is no question but that we make categorical decisions in life. If some students graduate from high school and others do not, a categorical decision has been made whether or not one uses a minimum competency exam. Even if everyone graduates, it is still a categorical decision if the philosophical or practical *possibility* of failure exists. If one can *conceptualize* performance so poor the performer should not graduate, then theoretically a cutoff score exists. The proponents of minimum competency exams seem to believe, at least philosophically, that there is a level of incompetence too low to tolerate, and that they ought to define that level so it is less abstract, less subjective, and perhaps a little less arbitrary than the way decisions are currently made.

The above is not an argument for using a minimum competency test alone as a graduation requirement. Nor is it an argument for using a dichotomous (as opposed to continous) test score as one of the factors in that decision. What we are trying to make very clear is that ultimately—after combining data in some fashion—a dichotomous categorization exists: those who receive a diploma and those who do not. No matter what type of equation is used, linear or nonlinear, no matter what variables go into the equation, no matter what coefficients precede their values, the final decision is dichotomous and arbitrary. The argument against minimum competency exams cannot be that they lead to an arbitrary decision unless one truly believes that all individuals—no matter what their level of performance—belong in the same category.

If it has been decided to set a minimum test score, how should it be done? Practically, there are many different ways that have been suggested, and we have mentioned a few of these in Chapter 5. We have not discussed them in sufficient detail for those who must actually choose and implement a method. However, they are thoroughly discussed in readily available literature, and readers wishing a more thorough presentation should check Millman (1974), Glass (1978b), Nassif (Chapter 4 in Gorth & Perkins, 1979), Hambleton (Chapter 4 in Berk, 1980b), and Shepard (1980).

(6) What to Do with the Incompetent?   If we are going to spend money to identify the incompetent through testing, we surely ought to have a follow-up plan. The testing alone will not educate the children.

There are a variety of options—the desirability of most somewhat debatable.

Schools might do one or more of the following:

1. Give students another chance to take the exam.
2. Encourage incompetents to drop out of school.
3. Not allow them to graduate.
4. Not allow them to receive a *regular* high school diploma.
5. Give everyone a regular diploma but give those who pass the exam a special certificate of attainment.
6. Not allow such students to be promoted from one grade level to the other.
7. Assign such students to a less-demanding curriculum or track.
8. Provide special instructional assistance in areas of specific weaknesses.
9. Make such students attend summer school.
10. Work with parents to teach them how to help their children learn basic skills.

Now these 10 are surely neither mutually exclusive nor exhaustive options. They do reasonably represent those advocated by other writers in the field. We happen to favor 1; 3, 4, or 5; 8; 9; and 10. (We are opposed to 2 and 6, although they do have some merit.)

You will recall that we favor testing in about three different grades—with opportunities for retakes in between. It does not seem wise to have students who fail *repeat a whole grade*. They should receive special attention. What kind of special attention? That is a question to be answered by instructional experts—not measurement experts. But let us make several points:

1. A test designed to be effective in certifying competence is not an effective *diagnostic* test. Separate measures would be needed to pinpoint specific weaknesses.
2. Remediation takes time, money, trained staff, and a planned curriculum.
3. Schools should not allocate so disproportionate an amount of time, money, and staff to the less competent that the education of the vast majority of competent students is neglected.
4. Some students may never pass a minimum competency exam. For others, the costs may simply be higher than the benefits. Schools need to consider how to minimize the adverse effects of such failures.
5. If remediation is started early, there would, it is hoped, be very few students who never make it.
6. The number who do not make it is partially dependent upon the effectiveness of remediation.
7. In the final analysis, the effectiveness of remediation is dependent upon the student. As Ebel has stated: "Learning cannot be imposed. It must be

pursued. . . . the best a school or teacher can do is provide opportunities for learning and create conditions that make learning attractive"
(1978, p. 548).
8. To have no minimum standards in the basic skills for high school certification may well be a greater disservice to the youth of our nation than to
insist on such minimum competence. As Jordan (1979) stated: "If we try
to defend our right to be incompetent, we lose" (p. 27).

Minimum Competency Testing for Teachers   While the notion of minimum
competency testing was first revitalized for students, it has spread to teachers. Currently 27 states require (or are going to require next year) the passing
of a test as one of the requirements for an initial teaching certificate. Twelve
additional states are contemplating a teacher competency examination
(Lehmann & Phillips, 1985). Several of the states require the National
Teacher Examination (NTE); others are constructing their own tests or are
contracting with test publishers. The motivating factor behind such teacher
competency tests is that the public believes our teacher-training institutions
have granted diplomas to, and states have certified, teachers who are not
minimally competent. They believe our colleges have failed as gatekeepers,
that social promotion in colleges is as prevalent as social promotion in the
public schools. Considerable evidence exists for both beliefs. For example,
Feistritzer reported that "never before in the nation's history has the caliber
of those entering the teaching profession been as low as it is today" (1983, p.
112). In speaking of the results of research done for the National Center for
Educational Information, Feistritzer was quoted as saying: "The certification of classroom teachers in the U.S. is a mess. There are far too many
colleges where a student can show up with a high-school diploma and a
checkbook and get out with a bachelor's degree in education" (*U.S. News,*
1984, p. 14). She goes on to say that one-third to one-half of the colleges
operating teacher-training programs "ought to be shut down."

    An earlier *Time* article (1980) reported that 20 percent of all teachers had
not mastered the basic skills they were supposed to teach. In 1978 the Dallas
Independent School District gave the Wesman Personnel Classification Test
(WPCT) to 535 first-year teachers and a volunteer group of high school
juniors and seniors. The students outperformed the teachers, and more than
half the teachers fell below the score considered acceptable by the district.
Of course, one could argue that the WPCT is not a teacher competency test
at all. It is a test of verbal and quantitative ability. As Webster pointed out,
the WPCT "makes no pretense of testing the substantive knowledge presumed necessary for good teaching. . . . It was assumed, however, that
persons who scored very low on the WPCT would be expected to encounter
more-than-average difficulty in a profession that depends so much on one's
ability to communicate" (1984, p. 4). On a teacher competency test in Hous-
ton, job applicants scored lower than high school juniors in mathematics

achievement (Benderson, 1982). We know of at least one state, which we will leave unidentified, in which some college graduates score *at the chance level* on the state's teacher competency test! We suspect this finding may be fairly common across the states.

There is evidence that colleges tend to fail as gatekeepers; there is also evidence that the most competent graduates of colleges of education are not the ones most likely to be hired (Perry, 1981). Webster (1984) shows that the WPCT does correlate with a variety of criterion measures of classroom instruction (including student achievement), whereas the structured interview does not. However, the interview traditionally contributed most to the hiring decisions.

The public is dismayed at the semiliterate letters teachers send home. (Copies have made big news in various papers across the nation. One example, reprinted in *Time* (1980), was as follows: "Scott wont pass in his assignment at all, he had a poem to learn and he fell tu do it.") People find it distressing that elementary school teachers have not all mastered elementary school arithmetic. The public believes that teachers should be able to read, write, and do simple arithmetic. If colleges do not weed out those teacher candidates who cannot perform the basic functions they will be charged with teaching others, state exams are the only recourse to which the public can turn.

Gallup (1984) polls indicate that 89 percent of the public (and 63 percent of the teachers) believe that teachers "should be required to pass a state board examination to prove their knowledge in the subjects they will teach." An Educational Research Service (ERS) poll of teachers and principals indicated that 82 percent of the teachers and 86 percent of the principals agree that new teachers should be required to pass exams in their subject areas. After 75 percent of both teachers and principals also feel that new teachers should be tested on knowledge of teaching methods (*Newsnotes,* 1984).

It is easy to understand why most teachers favor such exams. Most teachers *are* qualified to teach. Most teachers *do* know the basics. Most teachers *would* pass the examinations with ease. They recognize that the examinations will provide some quality control by weeding out the incompetent. The exams should increase the public's confidence in the profession and the status of the teaching profession.

Shanker, president of the American Federation of Teachers, and Ward, its director of research, make the following points:

> We think it is perfectly appropriate and desirable to test new entrants in the teaching field to insure that they meet minimum standards. . . . If you do not know something, you cannot teach something. . . . Specifically AFT advocates a series of written examinations to test fundamental knowledge in language and computational skills, knowledge in general education and the subject area to be taught, and knowledge of pedagogy. (Shanker & Ward, 1982)

Despite the popularity, among both teachers and the public, of teacher competency examinations, some educators deplore this movement (Hodgkins & McKenna, 1982). While opponents, of course, are not in favor of incompetence, they do argue against the use of *measures* of competence. Their main argument is that there is no guarantee that someone who passes such a test will be a good teacher. That is true but totally irrelevant. (One wonders if such an argument is not evidence for a need for a minimum competency test in logic!) The tests are not designed to be predictive among the competent or to ensure that all certified teachers will be good teachers (although some predictive validity evidence does exist, as mentioned earlier). The tests are predicated on the notion that individuals cannot effectively teach what they have not learned. If they cannot read, write, or compute at a basic level, there is a strong likelihood that they will not be able to teach those basics. Even if people could teach knowledge and skill they had not personally acquired, their role model as educators would leave much to be desired. Thus, the reasoning goes, why grant such poor risks a teaching certificate?

Another point typically raised by the opponents of teacher competency testing is that it will reduce the pool of certified black teachers. There is indeed some evidence that this is true. The competency test in Louisiana has reduced the number of certified black teachers by more than 50 percent (Kauchak, 1984). Other states also find that a disproportionate number of blacks fail to pass. There are certainly societal reasons to explain this, including the quality of colleges attended. Nevertheless, Raspberry, a black columnist who frequently speaks and writes about educational issues, wrote the following in support of such testing:

> There's a lot we don't know about educating our children, particularly disadvantaged children. That's a failure of information, which is bad enough.
>
> But we know a lot more than we are willing to act on. That is a failure of guts, which is worse. . . .
>
> We know that a lot of our teachers aren't as good as they ought to be. But we—and here I mean specifically the civil rights leadership—balk at insisting that incompetent teachers be weeded out, particularly if they are minorities. We'd rather feel sorry for them, as victims of society, than hold them to standards that would improve the quality of the schools for our children. . . .
>
> We can have well-educated children or ignorant teachers. We cannot have both. (Raspberry, 1983)

All of this is surely *not* meant to argue for all tests of teacher competency. Each one must be judged against the standards discussed in this book (such as reliability and validity). However, to argue against them in an abstract sense, and to use illogical arguments to attack them will surely add to the public's belief that we as educators are afraid of the results. This will be likely to strengthen their belief that such tests are needed and strengthen their determination to require them.

Future of Minimum Competency Testing   The minimum competency movement has received considerable public and professional educator support. Of course, opinions can change. We cannot foresee the future. However, we believe that the future of MCT is likely to be decided in the courts. Lawsuits over MTC abound. An important and often-quoted case is the *Debra P*. v. *Turlington* case in Florida. In 1981 the Fifth Court of Appeals ruled that the state can impose graduation standards based on a test and that the Florida MCT was not biased. However, the court did require the state to show that the MCT accurately reflected what was taught in the classroom (this is the issue of curricular validity discussed in Chapter 4). Further, it required the state to show that there were no lingering effects of previous school desegregation. Two years later, the federal district court upheld the Florida testing program on both issues (*Debra P*. v. *Turlington*, 1983). In preparing for the defense, Florida conducted a massive four-part study and collected voluminous evidence that convinced the court that the test material was taught in the Florida schools. Not all states or local districts would necessarily be able to gather such extensive data. We do not know what types of evidence of curricular validity will be deemed sufficient in other cases. We suspect the future of MCT of students hinges more on this issue than on any other single factor.

Invasion-of-Privacy Issue

Assume you are a counselor in a school system and are working with a disturbed youngster. You believe that additional information about the youngster will enable you to deal with him more effectively. Do you have the right to ask him to answer "true" or "false" such questions[1] as the following?

1. I have never been in trouble because of my sexual behavior.
2. I have never indulged in any unusual sexual practices.
3. I believe there is a devil and a hell in afterlife.
4. I have had some very unusual religious experiences.
5. There is something wrong with my sex organs.

These are examples of some of the more personal questions taken from the Minnesota Multiphasic Personality Inventory (MMPI). Criticism comes from many people who are concerned that questions such as these are an

[1] From the Minnesota Multiphasic Personality Inventory. Reproduced by permission. Copyright 1943, renewed 1970 by the University of Minnesota. Published by the Psychological Corporation, New York, N.Y. All rights reserved.

invasion of privacy. Why should we tell anyone whether or not we have ever indulged in any unusual sexual practices? Some people have even suggested that the very asking of such questions is harmful to the person taking the test.

Suppose you wish to gather some data regarding the pupil's home background. Can you ask questions such as the following?

1. How much education does your mother have?
2. What does your father do for a living?
3. Do you have a set of encyclopedias at home?

Questions such as these have often been asked in an attempt to gain some information about an individual's socioeconomic status. Any accountability program that wishes to take into account such variables as home conditions needs to gather such data. But, again, many people object to such questions as being an invasion of privacy.

What really is the invasion-of-privacy issue? What is the fuss all about? It varies, of course, from person to person. Some people actually find it distasteful and degrading to read (or be asked) personal questions. The knowledge that some people feel this way suggests something to us about their psychological makeup. Their feelings of uneasiness, however, probably do not represent a valid objection to the asking of such questions. There is no known evidence to suggest that the reading of such questions makes a person more disturbed or less moral.

Other people object on different grounds. Some are concerned not about having to read or answer such questions but rather about how the answers will be used. This gets us into such problems as scorers' qualifications, their ethics, and storage of test information. What if the answer sheets to such tests as the MMPI are kept and filed? Who, then, will have access to these files? Ethical and knowledgeable users would never reveal to a third party an answer to a specific question. Seldom would they even interpret such an answer to the client. They would, instead, look at the patterns of responses as recorded on the profile sheet. But what about others who may have (or at some later date obtain) access to the files? Could not, for example, a lot of political hay be made by reporting a candidate's answers to the questions cited above? The merits of permanently storing data are that (1) we will have more information available to help make decisions about individual people and (2) we will be able to improve our tests and learn more about people in general by doing follow-up research. The dangers center on who does (or may in the future) have access to the stored information. Will clerks have access to the data? Can it be subpoenaed? The public concern about what information is kept on file and who has access to it are very real and important concerns, but these should be recognized as issues separate from the question of whether we have a right originally to ask personal questions.

Besides the matter of confidentiality, there is the issue of freedom versus coercion in responding to items. Some students may object to answering some questions, but feel they must comply because school authorities ask them to do so. Further, school authorities may never even tell students why the data are being gathered or how they will be used. Data are often collected from individuals in early elementary school, who may not be aware of the importance of the data. The American Psychological Association (1970, p. 266) position statement on psychological assessment and public policy asserts: "The right of an individual to decline to be assessed or to refuse to answer questions he considers improper or impertinent has never been and should not be questioned. This right should be pointed out to the examinee in the context of information about the confidentiality of the results."

An amendment to the Family Educational Rights and Privacy Act states:

> *No student shall be required, as part of any applicable program, to submit to psychiatric examination, testing, or treatment, in which the primary purpose is to reveal information concerning:*
>
> *(1) political affiliation; (2) mental and psychological problems potentially embarrassing to the student or his family; (3) sex behavior and attitudes; (4) illegal, anti-social, self-incriminating, and demeaning behavior; (5) critical appraisals of other individuals with whom respondents have close family relationships; (6) legally recognized privileged and analogous relationships, such as those of lawyers, physicians, and ministers; or (7) income. (Public Law 95-561, 1978, November 1)*

Educators, in general, have not been very alert to the kinds of questions or of wording that the public will find offensive. Investigations such as those conducted by the National Assessment of Educational Progress (NAEP) should alert educators to potential problem areas (Berdie, 1971). Questions on such topics as family finances, relationships between children and parents, religion, minority groups, and sexual practices are likely to be considered either offensive or an invasion of privacy. One state even prohibited NAEP from asking a cognitive question regarding the menstrual cycle.

Let us move briefly from the educational setting to the government and private employment setting. In making a personnel decision about a person, does an employer have a right to pry into the applicant's personality? If employers are going to invest time and money in training persons, will they not prefer stable persons with good work habits who can get along with other workers?

Most psychologists would argue yes. As Hathaway (1964) has pointed out, once you decide, for example, that maladjusted individuals should not be accepted as Peace Corps volunteers, how do you go about screening the applicants? If, for reasons of privacy, investigation of personal items is prevented, is not this analogous to the prudery that would not permit medical doctors to examine the body? It is our contention that this analogy holds, and our conclusion is that qualified psychologists should have the right to ask personal questions if the questions are pertinent. (We should not have to strip before the receptionist, only before the medical doctor, and we would object to having a medical doctor examine our body if the examination were irrelevant.) The problem is that the public has a hard time judging the relevancy of what a professional does. How do we know whether it is relevant for a medical doctor to check our blood pressure and perform a urinalysis? How do we know whether it is relevant for a psychologist to ask us if we love our mother? If tests are not relevant, they are invasions of privacy. If they are relevant, they are not invasions of privacy.

Commentators on the invasion-of-privacy topic should adhere to the important issues—that is, the relevancy of the information gathered, qualifications of the gatherer, immediate use to which information is put, and what is done about the storage of such information. They would thus find that they share the same concerns as professional psychologists. Some people carry their worries about invasion of privacy to the extreme. If we really were never allowed to find out anything about another person, then we would not even be allowed to give classroom achievement tests to find out how much the student has learned.

Fairness of Tests to Minority Groups

In Chapter 7 we discussed two topics—"Etiology of Intelligence Differences" and "Culture-Fair Tests"—that are related to this section, but here the discussion is directed more to the concerns of the fair use of tests with minorities (women are considered a minority for purposes of this discussion). It would be nice to believe that every logically thinking person in the United States is against unfairness of any sort. The question to be discussed is certainly not whether we should be fair but rather what is meant by fairness. What practices are and are not fair? Do tests discriminate against the disadvantaged? What is and is not discrimination? According to *Webster's* (1965), *to discriminate* is (1) "to make a distinction; to use good judgment," or (2) "to make a difference in treatment or favor on a basis other than individual merit."

Tests can and do help us make distinctions. Tests are often used to identify differences within and among individuals and within and among groups or classes of people. That is a major purpose of testing. If there were no differences in test scores (that is, if tests did not discriminate), they would be worthless.

Can tests discriminate in an unfair sense (that is, on the basis of the second definition of discrimination)? Suppose a company uses a selection test on which it can be shown that blacks typically do less well than whites. Is the test unfair for revealing this difference? Many would say so. The test is certainly discriminating under the first definition, but is it unfair discrimination? To be sure, we could use test results to help us unfairly discriminate.

For example, we could require that blacks receive higher scores in order to be hired (or vice versa, as some advocate). This would be discrimination of the second type. This, however, would be an example of unfair use of test results rather than the use of an unfair test.

Even if we do not set up this kind of differential standard, is the test still unfair just because blacks, on the average, do less well? This depends on the degree to which the test is relevant (or valid) for selecting prospective employees. If, indeed, there is a reasonable correlation between job success and test scores, it would seem to many that selection on the basis of test scores is a wise decision and is not unfair, even though members of some subcultures do better than members of other subcultures.

If, however, a test does tend to discriminate (differentiate) between races, sexes, or other subcultures, and if the differential scores are not related to what is being predicted (such as on-the-job success), then the test is unfair. This could occur. For example, the test may demand knowledge that depends upon having been raised in a certain cultural environment, whereas the criterion may not depend upon this knowledge. Thus, it can be seen that the question of test fairness is really one of test validity. A test may differentiate blacks from whites and be fair (valid) for some purposes and not for others. *Differentiation alone is not what makes a test unfair.*

Even a distinction based on validity is an oversimplification in determining if a test is fair or unfair. Cleary has offered the following, more precise, definition:

> *A test is biased for members of a subgroup of the population, if, in the prediction of a criterion for which the test was designed, consistent non-zero errors of prediction are made for members of the subgroup. In other words, the test is biased if the criterion score predicted from the common regression line is consistently too high or too low for members of the subgroup. With this definition of bias, there may be a connotation of "unfair," particularly if the use of the test produces a prediction that is too low. (1968, p. 115)*

This precise definition is an incomplete guideline, however. Hunter & Schmidt (1976) define three mutually incompatible ethical positions in regard to the fair and unbiased use of tests, present five *statistical* definitions of test bias, and show how they are related to the three ethical positions. These positions are (1) unqualified individualism, (2) qualified individualism, and (3) quotas. The *unqualified individualism* position in employment would be to give the job to the *person* best qualified to serve. Under this position it would be *unethical* not to use whatever information increases the predictive validity of performance even if such information is sex or ethnic group membership. The *unqualified individualist* interprets "discriminate" to mean *treat unfairly,* and to refuse to recognize that a difference between groups would result in *unfair* treatment. The *qualified individualist* believes it is *unethical* to use information about race, sex, and so on, even if it were scientifically valid to do so. "The qualified individualist interprets the word discriminate to mean *treat differently*" (p. 1054). The *quota* position is that the ethical position is to give every well-defined group (black, white; male, female; Protestant, Catholic, Jew) its "fair share" of desirable positions. "The person who endorses quotas interprets *discriminate* to mean *select a higher proportion of persons from one group than from the other group*" (Hunter & Schmidt, 1976, p. 1054).

The Cleary definition given above is an example of unqualified individualism, and it turns out that under her definition unreliable tests are biased against whites and in favor of blacks. Thorndike (1971) and Darlington (1971) have argued for different approaches, which Hunter & Schmidt show to be forms of quota setting. Darlington suggests that the term *cultural fairness* be replaced with the term *cultural optimality,* which would include a subjective policy-level decision on the relative importance of two goals; maximizing test validity and minimizing test discrimination.

The entire Spring 1976 issue of the *Journal of Educational Measurement* was devoted to the topic of bias in selection. Peterson & Novick (1976), in a detailed evaluation of the existing models for culture-fair selection, concluded that "the concepts of culture fairness and group parity are neither useful nor tenable. . . . The problem, we think, should be reconceptualized as a problem in maximizing expected utility" (see also Hunter, Schmidt, & Rauschenberger, 1977). Novick & Ellis (1977, p. 307) argue that "an acceptable solution must (a) be based on statistical decision theory, which emphasizes the concept of utility rather than fairness to groups; (b) address individuals as individuals without regard to race, sex, or ethnic origin, except under narrowly delineated conditions carefully defined; (c) take direct account of individual disadvantage in providing compensation; and (d) employ more effective methods than those of group parity when race, sex, or ethnic origin are required as classifiers." Since this is a continuing debate (see Flaugher, 1978), let us leave the models and discuss the uses in a more general fashion in employment and educational decisions.

In Employment   The whole issue of the cultural fairness of tests has been raised with respect to both educational decisions and employment decisions. We will discuss first the employment aspect of cultural fairness. The Supreme Court (*Griggs* v. *Duke Power Co.,* 1971) ruled that an employer is prohibited "from requiring a high school education or passing a standardized intelligence test as a condition of employment in or transfer to jobs when (a) neither standard is shown to be significantly related to successful job performance, (b) both requirements operate to disqualify Negroes at a substantially higher rate than white applicants, and (c) the jobs in question formerly have been filled only by white employees as part of a longstanding practice of giving preference to whites."

The ruling went on to state that

if an employment practice which operates to exclude Negroes cannot be shown to be related to job performance, the practice is prohibited.

. . . Nothing in the Act precludes the use of testing or measuring procedures; obviously they are useful. . . . Congress has not commanded that the less qualified be preferred over the better qualified simply because of minority origins. Far from disparaging job qualifications as such, Congress has made such qualifications the controlling factor, so that race, religion, nationality, and sex become irrelevant. What Congress has commanded is that any tests used must measure the person for the job and not the person in the abstract.

Although the quotes given above are no doubt reasonable, the Court ruling does present some problems. If "significantly related" is interpreted as statistical significance, then what should be the level of significance? If it means practical significance, how is this to be determined? The *Federal Register* (1970) contains a chapter on Equal Employment, with a part prescribing guidelines on employee-selection procedures. These guidelines were useful, but were just what the heading implies—guidelines. They did not spell out exact requirements. In 1973, in an attempt to improve the guidelines and the coordination across federal agencies, the Equal Employment Opportunity Coordinating Council (EEOCC), consisting of representatives of the Equal Employment Opportunity Commission, the Department of Justice, the Civil Service Commission, and the Department of Labor, began work on a uniform set of guidelines. The newest guidelines were published in the *Federal Register* on August 25, 1978 (Federal Executive Agency, 1978).

The new guidelines better represent professionally accepted standards for determining validity than the original EEOC guidelines. But, as with its predecessor, the new guidelines are just guidelines. It is only through repeated, time-consuming, and costly court tests that employers will fully understand what is expected of them in terms of validity evidence. Some courts will probably be reasonable with respect to validity evidence; others, unreasonable. And how readers of this book define reasonable evidence will vary, depending upon their perceptions of the whole issue.

The problem of fair employment is made even more complicated by the fact that a test may predict success in job *training* but *not* in *job performance*. And the lack of relationship between test scores and job performance may be due to inadequate criterion measures. Nevertheless, the Supreme Court ruling should reduce the misuse of tests. As the ruling makes clear, those best qualified to do a job should be selected, regardless of race, religion, nationality, or sex.

In Education   With respect to fairness of tests in educational uses, the major concerns seem to be in using tests either as predictors of future success (and therefore as screening devices), for certification or for placement into special-education programs. When achievement tests are used only as measures of *outcomes* of education, few people question their applicability to minority groups. In fact, results on achievement tests have been used as evidence that schools are doing a poor job of educating minority children.

As mentioned in Chapter 7, a few well-meaning psychologists have sought to devise culture-fair intelligence tests. Such tests have attempted to use only those items that do not differentiate among groups coming from different cultures. The advocates of such procedures argue that this gives them a test that is independent of environmental influences and as close as possible is a measure of innate ability. In general, these tests have not been well accepted by most psychologists. It is very doubtful whether we could ever devise a paper-and-pencil test to measure innate ability (whatever that is). Certainly, scores on present tests are influenced by environmental factors. There is no debate about that. But, does that make them unfair? Clifford, a black educator, has stated:

> *To disparage testing programs for revealing the inequities which still exist in the social, the economic, the educational, and cultural domains of American life is as erroneous as it would be for residents of Bismarck, North Dakota, to condemn the use of thermometers as biased, when, as this is being written, the temperature of Bismarck is −11°F and in Miami, Florida it is 83° (Clifford & Fishman, 1963, p. 27).*

It should be pointed out that Clifford's statement is based on the assumption that whoever interprets the intelligence test scores will realize that they are *not* direct measures of genetic capacity and that they are influenced by environmental conditions. Although the test is not unfair, it would be an unfair use of a test score to interpret it as irrefutable evidence of only genetic capacity.

Most psychologists take the position that "culture-fair" tests would be less useful (valid) predictors of educational achievement than present aptitude and achievement tests. If a person's previous environment is related to school success, then using a test that masks out environmental differences will likely result in a loss of some predictive power.

Actually, considerable research has been done on the predictability (or fairness) of scholastic aptitude tests for minority students. The studies show that tests are *not* biased (using Cleary's definition given earlier) against students with culturally disadvantaged backgrounds (Hills, Klock, & Lewis, 1963; Hills, 1964; Munday, 1965; Hills & Gladney, 1966; Stanley & Porter, 1967; Cleary, 1968; Kallingal, 1971; Pfeifer & Sedlacek, 1971; Temp, 1971; Wilson, 1978). In fact, several studies suggest that the test scores *overpredict* the performance of blacks in college (Breland, 1978; Cleary, 1968; Kallingal, 1971; Pfeifer & Sedlacek, 1971; Silverman, Barton, & Lyon, 1976; Temp, 1971). Findley & Bryan (1971) found much the same thing in reviewing the research on different tests used in the elementary grades. This over-prediction would be a test bias in one sense of the word, but certainly not unfair to the minority groups. Thomas & Stanley (1969) have clearly shown that scholastic aptitude tests are better than high school grades for predicting college grades of black students. This is the reverse of findings for white students. Stanley (1971a), in a thorough review of predicting college success of the educationally disadvantaged, has urged a reversal of the then current trend of waiving test scores in admitting disadvantaged applicants. He felt that the more disadvantaged an applicant, the more objective information one needs about the person.

The use of "intelligence" tests for placing students into programs for the mildly retarded has been the subject of much controversy in recent years. Two court cases, both in the appeal process, highlight this controversy (*Larry P.* v. *Riles,* 1979; and *PASE* v. *Hannon,* 1980). Both cases involved the overrepresentation of black students in programs for the mildly retarded and the role of intelligence testing. The rulings were on opposite sides. In *Larry P.,* Judge Peckham concluded that intelligence tests were biased against black students and that overrepresentation of blacks in such programs was illegal. In *PASE,* Judge Grady ruled that the tests were not biased and that overrepresentation was not illegal. While the issues are multifaceted, several things seem clear to us. (1) Overrepresentation, per se, in educational programs is not unacceptable to blacks. They are certainly over-represented in such programs as Head Start, Follow Through, and Title I programs. (2) Special-education placement leads to the expenditure of substantially more, not less, money on the student's education. (3) Overrepresentation is due to academic failure and behavioral problems, not intelligence tests. Prior to being referred for testing there must be some achievement or behavioral reason. Tests have either a neutral effect on disproportionality or tend to reduce it somewhat (Reschly, 1981). A moratorium on testing will not, in itself, reduce the disproportionate representation of blacks in such programs. (4) The concern of Judge Peckham in the *Larry P.* case was the quality of special-education classes. They were referred to as "dead-end," "inferior," and so on, 27 times in the written court opinion. (5) If indeed the programs were that poor, no student, regardless of race, should have been placed in them. (See Lambert, 1981, and Reschly, 1981, for elaboration and evidence on the points noted.)

Although various test critics may have reviewed the court cases as if the tests were on trial, a more accurate appraisal—at least in the *Larry P.* case—was that special programs were on trial. We are not in this book taking a position on the quality of special-education programs, although evidence suggests most are beneficial. Our expertise does not lie primarily in that area. (Yes, we realize that many educators and judges take what they pass off as expert positions on things they know little about. We think that is unfortunate.) Obviously no educator or measurement specialist would advocate using intelligence tests to place children into inferior but more expensive programs. Again, we have a prime example of the critics of testing confusing the issue of what decision should be made with the issue of what data we should use to assist in making the decision.

Summary of the Fairness Issue   Tests should not be considered unfair just because they discriminate. That is what tests are supposed to do. Tests, however, can be invalid and therefore unfair, or people can give unfair interpretations of the results (whether the tests were valid or invalid).

Although there would be important exceptions that should be investigated, the effect of using objective measures such as test data is to make social class barriers more permeable.

Tests cannot see if a youngster is black or white, rich or poor. Making decisions on the basis of objective measures is really more fair than making them on the affective reactions (positive or negative) we have toward different subcultures.

Conclusion on Public Concern About Evaluation

It is good that people feel free to voice their concerns about evaluations. Although many of these concerns are legitimate, many others are often neither logical nor relevant. If there are problems associated with test accuracy (there are), and if the misuse of tests has sometimes led to unfortunate consequences (it has), the appropriate procedure is to *correct the problems, not to stop testing.* We maintain that in many instances the issues of concern to the public such as invasion of privacy and unfair tests are problems associated with test use rather than with the psychometric properties of the tests. Psychologists and educators are partly to blame for this misuse. They have an obligation to inform the public as to how tests should be used and as to how they are being used. However, much of the negative feelings toward tests stem precisely from the fact that tests are used as they should be, to help make decisions. These decisions are not always pleasant to the people involved. Since tests help make decisions, they have been attacked. Unfortunately, some people assume that by doing away with tests we could *avoid making decisions.* That is not the case. Decisions must be made. Information helps us make decisions. Tests provide information. As professionals, we must ensure that valid tests are used for making appropriate decisions.

FUTURE TRENDS IN EVALUATION

We have already discussed such trends as program evaluation, state assessment programs, criterion-referenced tests, and testing for individualized instruction programs. Future trends are harder to discuss. It is always hard to predict. Even with tests carefully designed to help predict specific future behavior, we often cannot make accurate predictions. Yet the authors of this text—without the aid of specific test results—are audacious enough to make some tentative predictions about testing.

Increased Judicial and Legal Involvement in Testing

Legal scrutiny of educational and psychological measurement is both a present and a future reality. Several issues discussed in the last section are the primary areas in measurement that are being subjected to legal involvement. The so-called truth-in-testing legislation, minimum competency testing, and the use of tests for selection or placement purposes in either employment or education that results in disproportionate minority representation will, no doubt, continue to be legal issues. PL 94-142 may well be a source of future litigation.

Whether all the legal scrutiny is a good or bad thing in the long run is clearly debatable. Bersoff believes the intense legal scrutiny "should be viewed as both salutary and welcome" (1981, p. 1055). Lerner, in a discussion of minimum competency testing, argues that such issues are about educational policy choices and "should not be made by any branch of the federal government, least of all by the federal judiciary" (Lerner, 1981b, 1063). Turlington, the Florida commissioner of education, believes that the Florida state department of education "should not have to face continued harassment from professional litigators . . . who would seek . . . to impose their disproven philosophy upon Florida's schools and Florida's students" (Turlington, 1981, p. 204). Pullin, an attorney for the plaintiffs in the *Debra P.* case, would disagree (Pullin, 1981).

We as authors and you as readers can view all this legal scrutiny as either good or bad. But it will continue and all users of test information should be aware of the trend. However, we should point out that to do away with testing would not in the long run cut down on legal actions. They come about primarily because the plaintiffs do not agree with the decisions being made. If other sources of data, or no sources of data, were the bases for the decisions they too would be challenged in this era of litigation.

Computer-Aided Testing

Anyone who has read the technical manuals accompanying the better standardized tests realizes that computers already play a large role in the testing enterprise. Computers are employed in the development of tests by aiding in the processes of norming, deriving types of scores, computing item analyses, estimating reliability and validity, and in a host of other tasks. Computers are also used in the process of scoring and the reporting of results.

Recently test publishers have greatly expanded their services in these areas and will no doubt continue improving the services in the areas.

Predictions in this rapidly growing field are certainly difficult to make. Brzezinski (1984) reports: "In 1950, the RAND Corporation predicted that because computers were so large and expensive, no more than 12 corporations in the United States would ever need or be able to afford one" (p. 7). In 1983, the Educational Testing Service predicted that by 1985 there would be anywhere from 300,000 to 650,000 microcomputers in the schools (Educational Testing Service, 1983). The December 1984 issue of *Phi Delta Kappan* reported that in the fall of 1984, the country's 50 largest school districts alone had 73,570 microcomputers, up from 36,835 the year earlier (*Newsnotes*, 1984, p. 302). Given the history of conservative predictions on computer use, we trust that our statements will be interpreted in the light of the year we wrote them (early 1985). There is clearly a flurry of interest in the use of computers in testing and in education in general. For example, the November 1984 issue of the *Journal of Counseling and Development* was devoted to the topic of computers in counseling and development; the summer 1984 issue of *Educational Measurement: Issues and Practice* had a number of articles on microcomputers and testing; and the winter 1984 issue of the *Journal of Educational Measurement* examined in detail the application of computers to educational measurement. The revised *Standards for Educational and Psychological Testing* (1985) contains several guidelines specifically on the use of computers in testing. These and other recent references attest to the attention computers are receiving in education and testing.

An exciting area of research that may well have a significant and lasting impact is the use of computers to administer tests. An automated approach to testing has many advantages but also some potential problems. There is the clear advantage of cost effectiveness. Having a computer administer a test requires only a trained clerk for supervision and frees the professional staff to perform other tasks. Furthermore, computerized test administration will typically reduce the turn-around time for obtaining the results; it may well reduce scoring errors; and it will certainly allow flexibility in scheduling test administrations—something that would be particularly helpful in testing individual students (clients). The use of a computer in test administration should be of some benefit to individuals with various types of visual, auditory, and physical limitations (Sampson, 1983), although for some other handicapping conditions the computer might not be suitable. Finally, computer administration should allow for innovations in testing. The graphics and color capabilities, as well as the various input and output media (light pens, joysticks, touch sensitive screens, etc.), provide much more flexibility in item format. Johnson (1983) lists examples of tests in ballet that can be administered through videodiscs on which sequences of a step may be shown. Green (1983) suggests that situations could be presented on videodiscs for firefighters' or police officers' exams where the respondents could be asked questions regarding the situation. Obviously, memory could be tested by the use of successive frames.

As we said, though, there are also potential problems connected with computer administration of tests. One of these is the counterpart of efficiency of staff time. To the extent that a professional is not supervising students while they take the tests, the practitioner cannot learn from observing them. Personal observation has typically been considered a big advantage in using individual intelligence tests. Another disadvantage is that the test takers' scores may be based in part on their ability to use the computer. Some critics have suggested that females, minorities, and those from low socioeconomic backgrounds may be somewhat less familiar with computers than white males and thus may perform less well than they would on conventional modes of presentation. There are problems connected with the confidentiality of the information. Once they are stored in a computer's memory, data may be compromised. Other drawbacks involve the norms, the equivalence of forms, and the validity of the scores from computer-administered tests. Finally, there may be some staff resistance to the use of computers.

Some attempts have been made to develop standards for computerized testing. As mentioned earlier, the revised *Standards for Educational and Psychological Testing* addresses some of the issues. Another good reference is Bersoff (1983). However, at the time of this writing, it is generally felt that his document should be viewed as a working proposal that should be expanded and refined.

A particular type of computer-administered testing has become known as computer-adaptive testing. Computers can be programmed to present items of appropriate difficulty for an individual, as judged by that person's responses to previous items, thus providing "adaptive," "tailor-made," "flexilevel," or "response-contingent" tests. In an adaptive test, an examinee who answers an item correctly is administered a harder unanswered item (as judged by a difficulty index for group data). An examinee who misses an item would then be given an easier item, usually the most difficult of all the unanswered items that are easier than the one just missed. Research generally supports the notion that tailored tests are somewhat more efficient than conventional tests, because one does not need to ask an individual a whole set of items that the person is almost sure to get all right (or wrong). Typically only about one-half the number of items from a conventional test are needed on an adaptive test to produce equivalent reliability estimates. Thus testing time, boredom, and fatigue are all reduced. However, there are some potential problems with the use of adaptive testing. Because not all students take the same items, the students' scores must be accurately compared. Obviously the items have to be scaled in some fashion. Item response theory provides a way to do this but requires empirical information from a fairly large sample of students. Further, there is some concern, particularly among people not well versed in item response theory, that it is not "fair" to give different individuals different questions.

Commercial test publishers as well as the military are entering into computerized adaptive testing in greater numbers. The College Board is currently field-testing an adaptive college placement test in reading comprehension, sentence skills, arithmetic, and elementary algebra to ascertain whether prospective college students need remedial work in the basic skills. The College Board program can administer both conventional and adaptive tests and is amenable to various item formats ranging from free response to multiple choice. In addition to the computer-administration and scoring features, the usual reporting services are provided as separate packages. Those desiring further information should consult ETS (see *ETS Developments*, 1984). The military, on the other hand, is exploring the feasibility of employing an adaptive testing model for administration of its Armed Services Vocational Aptitude Battery.

Much more could be said about the exciting field of adaptive testing. For the interested reader, Green (1983), Green, Bock, Humphreys, Linn, & Reckase (1984), McBride (1980), Weiss (1980), and Wood (1976) present thorough reviews of this topic.

Yet there is no question that computers have gained a permanent place in the assessment arena. The use of computers in the school should facilitate teaching–learning–testing cooperation. The immediate storage, analysis, and printout of a student's examination results would help the teacher plan instructional processes. Using computer facilities in conjunction with expanded item banks will allow teachers to do more instructional testing without taking an inordinate amount of their time in preparing, administering, and scoring tests. Using an interactive mode, students, taking a test via computer, can be told immediately whether or not an answer is correct. In some cases it may be possible to determine why an answer is wrong and to offer, through the computer, an immediate learning sequence dealing with the precise problem (Bork, 1979, McArthur & Choppin, 1984).

An interesting commercial application of the computer in instruction is the software programs on the market designed to prepare students for taking college admissions tests. Silverman & Dunn (1983) reviewed 10 programs that prepare students for the Scholastic Aptitude Test. Others exist for the American College Testing Program. Prices range from $20 to $300 and the programs vary widely from drill and practice to the teaching of test-taking skills. We take no position on the efficacy of these programs. (See Ward (1984) for details.)

A variety of other computer programs for testing are also on the market. Tescar, Incorporated, for example, has a microcomputer scoring system that allows for local scoring of standardized achievement or ability tests as well as local teacher-made tests. CTB/McGraw-Hill has a software package called the Microcomputer Instructional Management System (MIMS), which should assist in the monitoring, diagnosis, and prescription process for individual pupils. Sampson (1984) presents a guide to microcomputer software programs in testing and assessment.

The use of computers to report and interpret test scores to examinees is also receiving attention. A study by Mathews (1973), comparing a traditional test report (national and local percentiles, and grade equivalents for the various subtests, summary scores, and a composite score) with a locally prepared computer-generated narrative report, indicated that classroom teachers rated the narrative format superior on 15 of 18 comparisons. Some writers suggest that computer interpretations are both more reliable and more valid (Burke & Normand, n.d.). Humans are not generally as consistent as computers, which do not have hangovers, family arguments before coming to work, and other such weaknesses. Burke & Normand summarize some research that shows that computer-generated reports are of equal or superior validity to clinical judgments. However, serious concerns have been raised about computer-based test interpretation.

The most pressing worry of practitioners is the accuracy of computerized test interpretation. . . . Used by those with little training or awareness of test interpretation validity, computerized testing can do more harm than good. . . . Because test scores and interpretations come from a computer, they give a false impression of infallibility. And because the tests are so easy to use . . . many who are untrained will use them incorrectly for decisions involving employment, educational placement, occupational counseling, mental health diagnosis, or brain deficiency assessments. (Turkington, 1984, pp. 7, 26)

Eyde & Kowal (1984) discuss both advantages and potential misuses of computer-based test interpretations. They point out that an American Psychological Association policy statement requires "professional-to-professional consultation." Thus, the interpretation from the computer would be for the professional, not to be given directly to the student (client). Further, they give an example of a Minnesota Multiphasic Personality Inventory (MMPI) profile as produced by four different computer software interpretation programs and by a clinican. There were some important differences. Clearly, caution must be observed in the use of computer-based test interpretations.

Quality versus Quantity

It is the authors' hope, if not their prediction, that the years ahead will bring a reduction in the number of tests designed to measure the same constructs. Far too many tests of poor quality are on the market. The fact that Buros (1978) lists 1189 tests, many of them scathingly criticized, indicates the extent of this problem. Buros (1972) suggested that at least half the tests on the market should never have been published. We would much prefer to see fewer tests, all of higher quality. Unfortunately, with the movement toward locally developed criterion-referenced tests, this is not occurring.

Probably the only way for our hope to materialize is for professionals to stop building and purchasing inadequate tests. This, of course, cannot occur unless consumers are capable of making good judgments, which leads to our last prediction.

Consumer Competence

Tests can be important and helpful tools. Used correctly by competent personnel, tests will continue to play an increasingly significant role in educational institutions. Tests used incorrectly by incompetent, unprofessional staffs may do more harm than good. There have been far too many instances of incorrect use of tests by school and industrial personnel. *It is our hopeful prediction that professionals' competencies in test use will increase to an acceptably high level.* If not, tests will continue to be misused.

It would be helpful if all preservice teacher-training programs included a required course in testing, measurement, and evaluation. Much use or potential misuse of test results is by classroom teachers, and regrettably, many of them are woefully and inadequately prepared. It behooves college administrators and possibly legislators to mandate such a course as a requirement for teacher certification. It would be helpful if teachers' unions would join us in our goal to increase the competence of educators in test use. This approach would be far more beneficial to education than the negative stances toward measurement frequently taken by the leaders of one teachers' union during the preceding decade.

SUMMARY

The major ideas, conclusions, and implications of this chapter are summarized in the following statements:

1. The public is concerned about measurement and evaluation in education. Some of these concerns are rational and relevant; others are irrational and irrelevant.
2. Tests have certainly been misused. Most of the problems related to test misuse bear on overgeneralizations made by users.
3. Many people criticize tests because their use has sometimes led to faulty decisions. What they fail to realize is that even more decisions would be faulty in the absence of test data.
4. Truth-in-testing legislation has led to increased costs. It will be likely to result in exams of somewhat poorer quality.

5. Minimum competency testing is currently both very popular and very controversial. The controversy involves legal questions as well as educational questions such as what competencies should be measured, who should set the minimum standards, how the standard should be determined, and what should be done with those not meeting the standard.
6. Whether tests invade one's privacy depends upon the relevancy of the information gathered, the qualifications of the gatherers, the use to which the information is put, and the confidentiality of the data.
7. The major purpose of tests is to differentiate (discriminate) among people. Differentiation alone does not make a test unfair.
8. There are a variety of definitions of *test bias*. Some are complementary, others are contradictory.
9. The major educational concern related to cultural fairness is the use of tests as screening or prediction devices. Few people suggest that achievement tests measuring the outcomes of education are unfair.
10. Culture-fair tests would probably be less valid predictors of educational achievement than present aptitude and achievement tests.
11. Research seems to show quite conclusively that, under the most common definitions of test bias, scholastic aptitude tests are *not* biased against students with culturally disadvantaged backgrounds.
12. The use of intelligence tests for placing students into special-education programs has been very controversial. There have been recent court decisions on both sides.
13. Several future trends in evaluation were discussed. These include (a) increased legal involvement in testing, (b) an increased use of computers in giving tests and storing and reporting test data, (c) higher quality in testing, and (d) greater user competence.

POINTS TO PONDER

1. Some states or local districts require the passing of a minimum competency examination for high school graduation. Are you in favor of such programs? Explain your position.
2. Should prospective teachers have to pass a basic skills test prior to being certified? Why or why not?
3. It is typical school policy to have students' cumulative records accompany them as they move from one grade to the next or from one school to another. What are the advantages and limitations of this policy? Under what conditions could it constitute an invasion of privacy?
4. Under what circumstances would it be appropriate to ask very personal questions in a standardized test?
5. Assume a test has been developed that can differentiate between pro-union and antiunion teachers. Does the school superintendent have a

right to use this instrument in helping decide whom (a) to hire and (b) to promote?

6. What would be the benefits to society of developing a test on which all subcultures perform equally well? How have you defined subculture?

7. A college uses test ABC for admission purposes. Research has demonstrated that the test is a reasonably valid predictor ($r = .58$) of college GPA. Research has also shown that some subcultures do less well on this test than others. What further evidence needs to be gathered to answer the question of whether the test discriminates unfairly?

8. If it is possible for a test to be administered by either a teacher or a computer, are two sets of norms necessary? Why?

APPENDIX

Selective List of Test Publishers

Addison-Wesley Publishing Company, 2725 Sand Hill Road, Menlo Park, California, 94025
American College Testing Program, P.O. Box 168, Iowa City, Iowa, 52240
American Guidance Service, Publishers' Building, Circle Pines, Minnesota, 55014
Australian Council for Educational Research, Frederick Street, Hawthorn, Victoria, 3122 Australia
Bobbs-Merrill Company, P.O. Box 7080, 4300 West 62nd Street, Indianapolis, Indiana, 46268
California Test Bureau/McGraw-Hill, Del Monte Research Park, Monterey, California, 93940
Committee on Diagnostic Reading Tests, Mountain Home, North Carolina, 28758
Consulting Psychologists Press, 577 College Avenue, Palo Alto, California, 94306
Cooperative Tests and Services, Educational Testing Service, Princeton, New Jersey, 08540
Educational and Industrial Testing Service, P.O. Box 7234, San Diego, California, 92107
Educational Testing Service, Princeton, New Jersey, 08540
Guidance Centre, Ontario College of Education, University of Toronto, 1000 Yonge Street, Toronto 289, Ontario, Canada
Houghton Mifflin Company, One Beacon Street, Boston, Massachusetts, 02107
Institute for Personality and Ability Testing, 1602 Coronado Drive, Champaign, Illinois, 61820
Personnel Press, 20 Nassau Street, Princeton, New Jersey, 08540
Psychological Corporation, 555 Academic Court, San Antonio, Texas, 78204-0952
Riverside Publishing Company, 8420 Bryn Mawr Avenue, Chicago, Illinois, 60631
Scholastic Testing Service, 480 Meyer Road, Bensenville, Illinois, 60106
Science Research Associates, 155 North Wacker Drive, Chicago, Illinois, 60606
Stanford University Press, Stanford, California, 94305
Teachers College Press, 1234 Amsterdam Avenue, New York, New York, 10027
University of London Press, St. Paul's House, Warwick Square, London E.C.4, England
Western Psychological Services, 12031 Wilshire Boulevard, Los Angeles, California, 90025

References

ACT. (1979). *Using the ACT Assessment on Campus*. Iowa City, Iowa: American College Testing Program.

ACT. (1983). *Using the ACT Assessment on Campus*, Iowa City: The American College Testing Program.

ACT. (1984). *Counselor's Handbook*. Iowa City: The American College Testing Program.

Adams, G. S. (1964). *Measurement and Evaluation in Education, Psychology, and Guidance*. New York: Holt, Rinehart and Winston.

AERA-APA-NCME. (1985). *Standards for Educational and Psychological Testing*. Final review draft. Washington D.C.: American Psychological Association.

Airasian, P. W. (1979). A Perspective on the Uses and Misuses of Standardized Achievement Tests. *Measurement in Education, 10*(3), 1–12.

Airasian, P. W., T. Kellaghan, G. F. Madaus, and J. J. Pedulla. (1977). Proportion and Direction of Teacher Rating Changes of Pupils' Progress Attributable to Standardized Text Information. *Journal of Educational Psychology, 69*(6), 702–709.

Airasian, P. W., and G. F. Madaus. (Summer 1983). "Linking Testing and Instruction," *Journal of Educational Measurement, 20*(2), 103–118.

Alderman, D. L., and D. E. Powers. (1980). The Effects of Special Preparation on SAT-Verbal Scores. *American Educational Research Journal, 17*, 239–253.

Alkin, M. (1970). Evaluating Net Cost-Effectiveness of Instructional Programs. In M. C. Wittrock and D. E. Wiley, *The Evaluation of Instruction: Issues and Problems*. New York: Holt, Rinehart and Winston.

Allport, G. W. (1963). *Pattern and Growth in Personality*. New York: Holt, Rinehart and Winston.

Alpert, R., and R. N. Haber. (1960). Anxiety in Academic Achievement Situations. *Journal of Abnormal and Social Psychology, 61*, 207–215.

Althen, G., and F. W. Stott. (June 1983). Advising and Counseling Students Who Have Unrealistic Academic Objectives. *The Personnel and Guidance Journal, 61*(10), 608–611.

AMEG. (1973). AMEG Commission Report on Sex Bias in Measurement. *Measurement and Evaluation in Guidance, 6*, 171–177.

American Psychological Association. (1970). Psychological Assessment and Public Policy. *American Psychologist, 25*, 264-266.

Anastasi, A. (1968). *Psychological Testing* (3rd ed.). New York: Macmillan.

Anastasi, A. (1973, May). *Common Fallacies About Heredity, Environment, and Human Behavior* (ACT Research Report No. 51). Iowa City, Iowa: American College Testing Program.

Anastasi, A. (1980). Review of R. Feuerstein, Y. Rand, and M. B. Hoffman, "The Dynamic Assessment of Retarded Performers: The Learning Potential Assessment Device, Theory, Instruments, and Techniques." *Rehabilitation Literature, 41*, 28–30.

Anastasi, A. (1981). Coaching, Test Sophistication, and Developed Abilities. *American Psychologist, 36*, 1086–1093.

Anastasi, A. (1982). *Psychological Testing* (5th ed.). New York: Macmillan.

Anderson, B., and C. Pipho. (1984). State-Mandated Testing and the Fate of Local Control. *Phi Delta Kappan, 66*(3), 209–212.

Anderson, L. W. (1981). *Assessing Affective Characteristics in the Schools.* Boston: Allyn-Bacon.

Anderson, S. B. (1980). Going Public. *Newsnotes, 15*(4), 1–5.

Angoff, W. H. (1964). Technical Problems of Obtaining Equivalent Scores on Tests. *Journal of Educational Measurement, 1,* 11–13.

Angoff, W. H. (1971). Scales, Norms, and Equivalent Scores. In R. L. Thorndike (Ed.). *Educational Measurement* (2nd ed.). Washington, D.C.: American Council on Education.

Arlin, M. (1984). Time, Equality, and Mastery Learning. *Review of Educational Research, 54*(1), 65–86.

Association for Measurement and Evaluation in Guidance. (1980, October). AMEG Statement on Legislation Affecting Testing for Selection in Educational and Occupational Programs. Author.

Astin, A. W. (1971). *Predicting Academic Performance in College.* New York: Free Press.

Ausubel, D. P. (1968). *Educational Psychology: A Cognitive View.* New York: Holt, Rinehart and Winston.

Baglin, R. F. (1981). Does "Nationally" Normed Really Mean Nationally? *Journal of Educational Measurement, 18*(2), 97–107.

Bajtelsmit, J. (1977). Test Wiseness and Systematic Desensitization Programs for Increasing Test-Taking Skills. *Journal of Educational Measurement, 14,* 335–342.

Baltes, P. B., and K. W. Schaie. (1976). On the Plasticity of Intelligence in Adulthood and Old Age: Where Horn and Donaldson Fail. *American Psychologist, 31*(10), 720–725.

Barber, T. X., and M. J. Silver. (1968). Fact, Fiction, and the Experimenter Bias Effect. *Psychological Bulletin Monograph Supplement, 70,* 1–29.

Barclay, J. R. (1968). *Controversial Issues in Testing,* Guidance Monograph Series III. Boston: Houghton Mifflin.

Barro, S. M. (1970). An Approach to Developing Accountability Measures for the Public Schools. *Phi Delta Kappan, 52,* 196–205.

Bartling, H. C. (1979). An Eleven-Year Follow-up Study of Measured Interest and Inventoried Choice. Unpublished doctoral dissertation. University of Iowa, Iowa City.

Bayley, N. (1949). Consistency and Variability in the Growth of Intelligence from Birth to Eighteen Years. *Journal of Genetic Psychology, 75,* 165–196.

Bayley, N. (1955). On the Growth of Intelligence. *American Psychologist, 10,* 805–818.

Becker, S. (1977). Personality Correlates of the Discrepancy Between Expressed and Inventoried Interest Scores. *Measurement and Evaluation in Guidance, 10*(1), 24–30.

Bejar, I. I. (1984). Educational Diagnostic Assessment. *Journal of Educational Measurement, 21*(2), 175–190.

Bell, T. (1971). The Means and Ends of Accountability. In *Proceedings of the Conference on Educational Accountability.* Princeton, N.J.: Educational Testing Service.

Benderson, A. (1982). The Teachers in America. *Focus, 10,* 1–5.

Bennett, G. K., H. G. Seashore, and A. G. Wesman. (1951). *Counseling from Profile—A Casebook for the Differential Aptitude Tests.* New York: Psychological Corporation.

Berdie, F. S. (1971). What Test Questions Are Likely to Offend the General Public. *Journal of Educational Measurement, 8*(2), 87–94.

Bereiter, C. E. (1963). Some Persistent Dilemmas in the Measurement of Change. In C. W. Harris (Ed.). *Problems in Measuring Change* (pp. 3–20). Madison: University of Wisconsin Press.

Berk, R. A. (1980a). A Consumers' Guide to Criterion-Referenced Test Reliability. *Journal of Educational Measurement, 17*(4), 323–349.

Berk, R. A. (Ed.). (1980b). *Criterion-Referenced Measurement: The State of the Art.* Baltimore: Johns Hopkins University Press.

Berk, R. A. (1984). *Screening and Diagnosis of Children with Learning Disabilities* (Chapter 4). Springfield, Ill.: Charles C. Thomas.

Bersoff, D. N. (1981). Testing and the Law. *American Psychologist, 36*(10), 1047–1056.

Bersoff, D. N. (1984). Legal Constraints on Test Use in the Schools. In C. W. Daves (Ed.). *The Uses and Misuses of Tests*. San Francisco: Jossey-Bass.

Biehler, R. F. (1971). *Psychology Applied to Teaching*. Boston: Houghton Mifflin.

Binet, A., and V. Henri. (1896). Le Psychologie Individuell. *Année Psychologique, 2,* 411–465.

Binet, A., and T. Simon. (1905). Methodes Nouvelles pour le Diagnostic du Niveau Intellectual des Anormaux. *Année Psychologique, 11,* 191–244.

Binet, A., and T. Simon. (1916). *The Development of Intelligence in Children* (Training School Publication No. 11, p. 192). Vineland, N.J.

Black, H. (1963). *They Shall Not Pass*. New York: Morrow.

Black, R., and R. H. Dana. (1977). Examiner Sex Bias and Wechsler Intelligence Scale for Children Scores. *Journal of Consulting and Clinical Psychology 45,* 500.

Bliss, L. B. (1980). A Test of Lord's Assumption Regarding Examinee Guessing Behavior on Multiple-Choice Tests Using Elementary School Children. *Journal of Educational Measurement, 17,* 2, 147–154.

Block, N. J., and G. Dworkin. (1974a). I.Q.: Heritability and Inequality—Part 1. *Philosophy and Public Affairs,* Summer, *3*(4), 331–409.

Block, N. J., and G. Dworkin. (1974b). I.Q.: Heritability and Inequality—Part 2. *Philosophy and Public Affairs, 4*(1), 40–99.

Bloom, B. S. (Ed.). (1956). *Taxonomy of Educational Objectives, Handbook I: The Cognitive Domain*. New York: McKay.

Bloom, B. S. (1964). *Stability and Change in Human Characteristics* (pp. 52–94). New York: Wiley.

Bloom, B. S. (1968). Learning for Mastery. *Evaluation Comment,* UCLA, CSEIP, May, *1,* 2.

Bloom, B. S. (1978). New Views of the Learner: Implications for Instruction and Curriculum. *Educational Leadership, 35,* 563–576.

Borgen, F. H. (1972). Predicting Career Choices of Able College Men from Occupational and Basic Interest Scales of the Strong Vocational Interest Blank. *Journal of Counseling Psychology, 19,* 202–211.

Borgen, F. H., and G. T. Harper. (1973). Predictive Validity for Measured Vocational Interests with Black and White College Men. *Measurement and Evaluation in Guidance, 6,* 19–27.

Borgen, F. H., and C. B. Bernard. (1982). Review of the Strong-Campbell Interest Inventory. *Journal of Educational Measurement 14,* 208–212.

Bork, A. (1979). Interactive Learning: Millikan Lecture, American Association of Physics Teachers. *American Journal of Physics, 47*(1), 5–10.

Bowles, S., and H. Gintis. (1974). IQ in the United States Class Structure. In A. Gartner, C. Greer, and F. Riessman (Eds.). *The New Assault on Equality* (pp. 7–84). New York: Harper & Row.

Breland, H. M. (1978). *Population Validity and College Entrance Measures*. Princeton, N.J.: Educational Testing Service.

Brophy, J. E., and T. L. Good. (1970). Teachers Communications of Differential Expectations for Children's Classroom Performance. *Journal of Educational Psychology, 61,* 365–374.

Browder, L. H., Jr. (1971). *Emerging Patterns of Administrative Accountability*. Berkeley, Calif.: McCutchan.

Browder, L. H., Jr., W. A. Atkins, and E. Kaya. (1973). *Developing an Educationally Accountable Program*. Berkeley, Calif.: McCutchan.

Brown, F. G. (1983). *Principles of Educational and Psychological Testing* (2d ed.). New York: Holt, Rinehart and Winston.

Brzezinski, E. J. (1984). Microcomputers and Testing: Where Are We and How Did We Get There? *Educational Measurement: Issues and Practice, 3*(2), 7–9.

Burke, M. J., and Normand, J. (n.d.). *Computerized Psychological Testing: State of the Art.* Xerox.

Burket, G. R. (1984). Response to Hoover. *Educational Measurement: Issues and Practice, 3*(4), 15–16.

Burns, R. W. (1972). *New Approaches to Behavioral Objectives.* Dubuque, Iowa: William C. Brown.

Buros, O. K. (Ed.). (1938). *The 1938 Mental Measurements Yearbook.* New Brunswick, N.J.: Rutgers University Press.

Buros, O. K. (Ed.). (1941). *The Nineteen-Forty Mental Measurements Yearbook.* New Brunswick, N.J.: Rutgers University Press.

Buros, O. K. (Ed.). (1949). *The Third Mental Measurements Yearbook.* New Brunswick, N.J.: Rutgers University Press.

Buros, O. K. (Ed.). (1953). *The Fourth Mental Measurements Yearbook.* Highland Park, N.J.: Gryphon Press.

Buros, O. K. (Ed.). (1959). *The Fifth Mental Measurements Yearbook.* Highland Park, N.J.: Gryphon Press.

Buros, O. K. (Ed.). (1965). *The Sixth Mental Measurements Yearbook.* Highland Park, N.J.: Gryphon Press.

Buros, O. K. (Ed.). (1972). *The Seventh Mental Measurements Yearbook.* Highland Park, N.J.: Gryphon Press.

Buros, O. K. (Ed.). (1978). *Eighth Mental Measurements Yearbook.* Highland Park, N.J.: Gryphon Press.

Butcher, H. J. (1968). *Human Intelligence: Its Nature and Assessment.* New York: Harper & Row.

Callenbach, C. (1973). The Effects of Instruction and Practice in Content-Independent Test-Taking Techniques upon the Standardized Reading Test Scores of Selected Second-Grade Students. *Journal of Educational Measurement, 10,* 25–30.

Calsyn, R. J., and D. A. Kenny. (1977). Self-Concept of Ability and Perceived Evaluation of Others: Cause or Effect of Academic Achievement? *Journal of Educational Psychology, 69*(2), 136–145.

Campbell D. P. (1969). *Strong Vocational Interest Blanks Manual—1969 Supplement.* Stanford, Calif.: Stanford University Press.

Campbell, D. P. (1974). *Manual for the SCII.* Stanford, Calif.: Stanford University Press.

Campbell, D. P., and J. I. C. Hansen. (1981). *Manual for the SVIB-SCII* (3rd ed.). Palo Alto, Calif.: Stanford University Press.

Campbell, D. P., J. I. Chrichton, and P. Webber. (1974). A New Edition of the SVIB: The Strong-Campbell Interest Inventory. *Measurement and Evaluation in Guidance, 7,* 92–94.

Campbell, R. E. (1971). Accountability and Stone Soup. *Phi Delta Kappan, 53,* 176–178.

Campione, J. C., and A. L. Brown. (1979). Toward a Theory of Intelligence: Contributions from Research with Retarded Children. In R. J. Sternberg and D. K. Detterman (Eds.). *Human Intelligence: Perspectives on Its Theory and Measurement* (Chapter 6). Norwood, N.J.: Ablex Publishing.

CAPTRENDS. (1984). Portland, Ore.: Center for Performance Assessment, Northwest Regional Educational Laboratory.

Carney, C. G., C. J. Savitz, and G. N. Weiskott. (1979). Students' Evaluations of a University Counseling Center and Their Intentions to Use Its Programs. *Journal of Counseling Psychology, 26,* 242–249.

Carroll, J. B. (1974). Fitting a Model of School Learning to Aptitude and Achievement Data over Grade Levels. In D. R. Green (Ed.). *The Aptitude–Achievement Distinction.* Monterey, Calif.: CTB/McGraw-Hill.

Carroll, J. B., and Horn, J. L. (1981). On a Scientific Basis of Ability Testing. *American Psychologist, 36*(10), 1012–1020.

Carver, R. P. (1974). Two Dimensions of Tests: Psychometric and Edumetric. *American Psychologist, 29,* 512–518.

Cashen, V. M., and G. C. Ramseyer. (1969). The Use of Separate Answer Sheets by Primary School Children. *Journal of Educational Measurement, 6,* 155–158.

Caswell, M. (1981). *A Guide to Test Taking.* Lansing: Michigan Educational Assessment Program, Michigan Department of Education.

Cattell, J. McK. (1890). Mental Tests and Measurements. *Mind, 15,* 373–381.

Cattell, R. B. (1963). Theory of Fluid and Crystallized Intelligence: A Critical Experiment. *Journal of Educational Psychology, 54,* 1–22.

Cattell, R. B. (1971). *Abilities: Their Structure, Growth, and Action.* Boston: Houghton Mifflin.

Cattell, R. B., and A. K. S. Cattell. (1973). *Handbook for the Individual or Group Culture-Fair Intelligence Test.* Champaign, Ill.: Institute for Personality and Ability Testing.

Cattell, R. B., and J. L. Horn. (1978). A Cross-Social Check on the Theory of Fluid and Crystallized Intelligence with Discovery of New Valid Subtest Designs. *Journal of Educational Measurement, 15*(3), 139–164.

Cegelka, P. T., C. Omvig, and D. L. Larimore. (1974). Effects of Attitude and Sex on Vocational Interests. *Measurement and Evaluation in Guidance, 7,* 106–111.

Chaikin, A. L., and E. Sigler. (1973). Non-verbal Mediators of Teacher Expectancy Effects. Paper presented at the annual meeting of the Eastern Psychological Association, Washington, D.C.

Chambers, A. C., K. D. Hopkins, and B. R. Hopkins. (1972). Anxiety, Physiologically and Psychologically Measured: Its Effects on Mental Test Performance. *Psychology in the Schools, 9,* 198–206.

Chi, M. T. H., R. Glaser, and R. Rees. (1982). Expertise in Problem Solving. Chapter 1 in R. J. Sternberg (Ed.). *Advances in the Psychology of Human Intelligence* (Vol. 1). Hillsdale, NJ: Lawrence Erlbaum.

Chun, K.-T., S. Cobb, and J. R. P. French, Jr. (1976). *Measures for Psychological Assessment.* Ann Arbor: Institute for Social Research, University of Michigan.

Cieutat, V. J., and G. L. Flick. (1967). Examiner Differences Among Stanford-Binet Items. *Psychological Reports 21,* 613–622.

Citron, C. H. (1983). Courts Provide Insight on Content Validity Requirements. *Educational Measurement: Issues and Practice, 2,* 4, 6–7.

Clarizio, H. F., and W. A. Mehrens. (1985). Psychometric Limitations of Guilford's Structure of Intellect Model for Identification and Programming the Gifted. *Gifted Child Quarterly, 29:* 3, 113–120.

Clark, C. A. (1968). The Use of Separate Answer Sheets in Testing Slow-Learning Pupils. *Journal of Educational Measurement, 5,* 61–64.

Cleary, T. A. (1968). Test Bias: Prediction of Grades of Negro and White Students in Integrated Colleges. *Journal of Educational Measurement, 5,* 115–124.

Cleary, T. A., L. G. Humphreys, A. S. Kendrick, and A. Wesman. (1975). Educational Uses of Tests with Disadvantaged Students. *American Psychologist, 30,* 15–41.

Cleland, C. C., and J. D. Swartz. (1982). *Exceptionalities Through the Lifespan.* New York: Macmillan.

Clemans, W. V. (1971). Test Administration. In R. L. Thorndike (Ed.). *Educational Measurement* (2nd ed.). Washington, D.C.: American Council on Education.

Clifford, P. I., and J. A. Fishman. (1963). The Impact of Testing Programs on College Preparation and Attendance. *The Impact and Improvement of School Testing Programs.* Yearbook LXII, Part II, NSSE, p. 87.

Coffman, W. E. (1969). Achievement Test. In R. L. Ebel (Ed.). *Encyclopedia of Educational Research* (4th ed.). New York: Macmillan.

Cohen, E. (1965). Examiner Differences with Individual Intelligence Tests. *Perceptual and Motor Skills, 20,* 1324.

Cole, N. S. (1973). On Measuring the Vocational Interests of Women. *Journal of Counseling Psychology, 20,* 105–112.

Cole, N. S. (1982, March). *Grade Equivalent Scores: To GE or Not to GE.* Vice Presidential Address to the meeting of the American Educational Research Association, New York City.

Cole, N. S., and G. R. Hanson. (1971). An Analysis of the Structure of Vocational Interests. *Journal of Counseling Psychology, 18,* 478–487.

Coleman, J. S., et al. (1966). *Equality of Educational Opportunity.* Washington, D.C.: Office of Education, Department of Health, Education and Welfare.

The College Board News. (1981, Spring). New York Experience: Fewer Than Five Percent Request SAT Questions and Answers, p. 1.

College Entrance Examination Board. (1978). *Taking the SAT: A Guide to the Scholastic Aptitude Test and the Test of Standard Written English.* New York: Author.

Committee on Psychological Tests and Assessment. (1984). Snares Lurk in Test Disclosure Laws, *APA Monitor, 15*(2), p. 5.

Comrey, A. L., T. E. Backer, and E. M. Glaser. (1973). *A Sourcebook for Mental Health Measures.* Los Angeles: Human Interaction Research Institute.

Conklin, J. E., L. Burstein, and J. W. Keesling. (1979). The Effects of Date of Testing and Method if Interpolation on the Use of Standardized Test Scores in the Valuation of Large-Scale Educational Programs. *Journal of Educational Measurement, 16*(4) 239–246.

Coolcy, W. W. (1971). Techniques for Considering Multiple Measurements. In Robert L. Thorndike (Ed.). *Educational Measurement* (2nd ed.). Washington, D.C.: American Council on Education.

Coombs, C. H. (1964). *A Theory of Data.* New York: Wiley.

Corey, S. M. (1953). *Action Research to Improve School Practices.* New York: Teachers College, Columbia University.

Cox, R. C. (1964). An Empirical Investigation of the Effect of Item Selection Techniques on Achievement Test Construction. Unpublished doctoral dissertation, Michigan State University, East Lansing.

Cox, R. C., and B. G. Sterrett. (1970). A Model for Increasing the Meaning of Test Scores. *Journal of Educational Measurement, 7,* 227–228.

Crites, J. O. (1974). Methodological Issues in the Measurement of Career Maturity. *Measurement and Evaluation in Guidance, 6,* 200–209.

Crockenberg, S. B. (1972). Creativity Tests: A Boon or Boondazzle for Education. *Review of Educational Research, 42,* 27–46.

Cronbach, L. J. (1946). Response Sets and Test Validity. *Educational and Psychological Measurement, 6,* 475–494.

Cronbach, L. J. (1950). Further Evidence on Response Sets and Test Design. *Educational and Psychological Measurement, 10,* 3–31.

Cronbach, L. J. (1951). Coefficient Alpha and the Internal Structure of Tests. *Psychometrika, 16,* 297–334.

Cronbach, L. J. (1963). Course Improvement Through Evaluation. *Teacher's College Record, 64,* 672–683.

Cronbach, L. J. (1969). Heredity, Environment, and Educational Policy. *Harvard Educational Review, 39,* 338–347.

Cronbach, L. J. (1970). *Essentials of Psychological Testing* (3rd ed.). New York: Harper & Row.

Cronbach, L. J. (1971). Test Validation. In R. L. Thorndike (Ed.). *Educational Measurement* (2d ed.). Washington, D.C.: American Council on Education.

Cronbach, L. J. (1975). Five Decades of Public Controversy over Public Testing. *American Psychologist, 30,* 1–14.

Cronbach, L. J. (1980). Validity on Parole: How Can We Go Straight? In W. B. Schrader (Ed.).

Measuring Achievement: Progress Over a Decade (No. 5 in *New Directions for Testing and Measurement*). San Francisco: Jossey-Bass.

Cronbach, L. J., and L. Furby. (1970). How We Should Measure "Change"—or Should We? *Psychological Bulletin, 74*(1), 68–80.

Cronbach, L. J., and G. C. Gleser. (1965). *Psychological Tests and Personnel Decisions* (2nd ed.). Urbana: University of Illinois Press.

Cronbach, L. J., G. C. Gleser, H. Nanda, and N. Rajaratnam. (1972). *The Dependability of Behavioral Measurements: Multifacet Studies of Generalizability.* New York: Wiley.

Cronbach, L. J., and P. E. Meehl. (1955). Construct Validity in Psychological Tests. *Psychological Bulletin, 52,* 281–302.

Cronbach, L. J., and R. E. Snow. (1969). *Final Report: Individual Differences in Learning Ability as a Function of Instructional Variables.* Stanford, Calif.: School of Education, Stanford University.

Cronbach, L. J., and R. E. Snow. (1977). *Aptitudes and Instructional Methods: A Handbook for Research on Interaction.* New York: Irvington.

Cronbach, L. J., and P. Suppes (Eds.). (1969). *Research for Tomorrow's Schools: Disciplined Inquiry for Education.* New York: Macmillan.

Cronin, J., et al. (1975). Race, Class, and Intelligence: A Critical Look at the I.Q. Controversy. *International Journal of Mental Health, 3*(4), 46–132.

Cross, L., and R. Frary. (1977). An Empirical Test of Lord's Theoretical Results Regarding Formula Scoring of Multiple-Choice Tests. *Journal of Educational Measurement, 14,* 313–322.

Crowne, D. P., and D. Marlowe. (1960). A New Scale of Social Desirability Independent of Psychopathology. *Journal of Consulting Psychology, 24,* 349–354.

Crowne, D. P., and D. Marlowe. (1964). *The Approval Motive: Studies in Evaluative Dependence.* New York: Wiley.

Cunningham, L. L. (1971). Our Accountability Problems. In L. H. Browder, Jr. (Ed.). *Emerging Patterns of Administrator Accountability.* Berkeley, Calif.: McCutchan.

Dahl, T. A. (1973). Test Review of the Boehm Test of Basic Concepts. *Measurement and Evaluation in Guidance, 6,* 63–65.

Daly, J. A., and F. Dickson-Markman. (1982). Contrast Effects in Evaluating Essays. *Journal of Educational Measurement, 19,* 309–316.

Darlington, R. B. (1971). Another Look at "Cultural Fairness." *Journal of Educational Measurement, 8,* 71–82.

DAT Manual (4th ed.). (1966). New York: Psychological Corporation.

Debra P. v. *Turlington.* (1981). 644 F. 2d 397, 5th Cir.

Debra P. v. *Turlington.* (1983, May 4). Case 78-892. Memorandum Opinion and order (M.D. Fla.).

Debra P. v. *Turlington.* (1983). 564 F. Supp. 177 (M.D. Fla.). (appeal pending).

Deterline, W. A. (1971). Applied Accountability. *Educational Technology, 11,* 15–20.

Diamond, E. E. (1975a). Guidelines for the Assessment of Sex Bias and Sex Fairness. *Measurement and Evaluation in Guidance, 8,* 7–11.

Diamond, E. E. (Ed.). (1975b). *Issues of Sex Bias and Sex Fairness in Career Interest Measurement.* Washington, D.C.: Government Printing Office.

Diamond, J. J., and W. J. Evans. (1972). An Investigation of the Cognitive Correlates of Test Wiseness. *Journal of Educational Measurement, 9,* 145–150.

Diana v. *State Board of Education.* (1970, January 7, and 1973, June 18). Civil No. C-70, 37 RFP (N.D. Cal.).

Dolliver, R. H., and J. A. Will. (1977). Ten-Year Follow-Up of the Tyler Vocational Card Sort and the Strong Vocational Interest Blank. *Journal of Counseling Psychology, 24,* 48–54.

Downs, A. (1968). Competition and Community Schools. Mimeograph.

Drake, L. E., and E. R. Oetting. (1959). *An MMPI Codebook for Counselors*. Minneapolis: University of Minnesota Press.

Dunn, L., and L. Dunn. (1981). *Peabody Picture Vocabulary Test Revised: Manual for Forms L and M*. Circle Pines, Minn.: American Guidance Services.

Durnan, J., and J. M. Scandura. (1973). An Algorithmic Approach to Assessing Behavior Potential: Comparison with Item Forms and Hierarchial Technologies. *Journal of Educational Psychology, 65,* 262–272.

Dyer, H. S. (1967). The Discovery and Development of Educational Goals. *Proceedings of the 1966 Invitational Conference on Testing Problems* (pp. 12–29). Princeton, N.J.: Educational Testing Service.

Dyer, H. S. (1970). Toward Objective Criteria of Professional Accountability in the Schools of New York City. *Phi Delta Kappan, 52,* 206–211.

Dyer, H. S. (1973). Recycling the Problems in Testing. *Proceedings of the 1972 Invitational Conference on Testing Problems* (pp. 85–95). Princeton, N.J.: Educational Testing Service.

Ebel, R. L. (1961). Must All Tests Be Valid? *American Psychologist, 15,* 640–647.

Ebel, R. L. (1962). Content Standard Test Scores. *Educational and Psychological Measurement, 22,* 15–25.

Ebel, R. L. (1965a). Confidence Weighting and Test Reliability. *Journal of Educational Measurements, 2,* 49–57.

Ebel, R. L. (1965b). *Measuring Educational Achievement*. Englewood Cliffs, N.J.: Prentice-Hall.

Ebel, R. L. (1969). The Relation Betweeh Curricula and Achievement Testing. Mimeograph, Michigan State University, East Lansing.

Ebel, R. L. (1972). *Essential of Educational Measurement*. Englewood Cliffs, N.J.: Prentice-Hall.

Ebel, R. L. (1974). And Still the Dryads Linger. *American Psychologist, 29,* 7, 485–492.

Ebel, R. L. (1975). Prediction? Validation? Construct Validity? Mimeograph.

Ebel, R. L. (1976). The Paradox of Educational Testing. *Measurement in Education, 7,* 4, 1–12.

Ebel, R. L. (1978). The Case for Minimum Competency Testing. *Phi Delta Kappan, 59*(8), 546–549.

Eckland, B. K. (1967). Genetics and Sociology: A Reconsideration. *American Sociological Review, 32,* 173–194.

Educational Testing Service. (1960). *Short-Cut Statistics for Teacher-Made Tests*. Princeton, N.J.: Author.

Educational Testing Service. (1983). *Focus: Computer Literacy*. Princeton, N.J.: Author.

Educational Testing Service. (1984, August). *ETS Developments*. Princeton, N.J.: Author.

Education Week. (1984). Author, 8-22, p. 7.

Edwards, A. L. (1957). *The Social Desirability Variable in Personality Assessment and Research*. New York: Holt, Rinehart and Winston.

Edwards, R. C. (1977). Personal Traits and "Success" in Schooling and Work. *Educational and Psychological Measurement, 37*(1), 125–138.

Elasoff, J., and R. E. Snow (Eds.). (1971). *Pygmalion Revisited*. Worthington, Ohio: C. A. Jones.

Engelmann, S., and T. Englemann. (1968). *Give Your Child a Superior Mind*. New York: Simon and Schuster.

Engen, H. B., R. R. Lamb, and D. J. Prediger. (1982). Are Secondary Schools Still Using Standardized Tests? *Personnel and Guidance Journal, 60*(5), 287–289.

Erlenmeyer-Kimling, L., and L. F. Jarvik. (1963, December). Genetics and Intelligence: A Review. *Science, 142,* 1477–1479.

Ethical Standards for Psychologists. (1973). Washington, D.C.: American Psychological Association.

Exner, J. E., Jr. (1966). Variations in WISC Performance as Influenced by Differences in Pretest Rapport. *Journal of General Psychology* 74, 299–306.

Eyde, L. D., and Kowal, D. M. (1984). *Ethical and Professional Concerns Regarding Computerized Test Interpretation Services and Users.* Paper presented at the meeting of the American Psychological Association, Toronto.

Eysenck, H. J. (1971). *The IQ Argument.* Freeport, N.Y.: Library Press.

Eysenck, H. J. (1979). *The Structure and Measurement of Intelligence.* New York: Springer-Verlag.

Federal Executive Agency. (1978, August 25). Uniform Guidelines on Employee Selection Procedures. *Federal Register, 43,* 166.

Federal Register. (1970), *35,* 149.

Feistritzer, C. M. (1983). *The condition of teaching.* Princeton, N.J.: The Carnegie Foundation for the advancement of teaching.

Feldt, L. A. (1967). Reliability of Differences Between Scores. *American Educational Research Journal, 4,* 139–145.

Feuerstein, R., Y. Rand, and M. B. Hoffman. (1979). *The Dynamic Assessment of Retarded Performers: The Learning Potential Device, Theory, Instruments, and Techniques.* Baltimore: University Park.

Findley, W. G. (1974). Ability Grouping. In G. R. Gredler (Ed.). *Ethical and Legal Factors in the Practice of School Psychology* (Chapter 3). Harrisburg: Pennsylvania State Department of Education.

Findley, W. G., and M. M. Bryan. (1971). *Ability Grouping: 1970 Status, Impact and Alternatives.* Athens, Ga.: Center for Educational Improvement, University of Georgia.

Fisher, Thomas H. (1983). Implementing an Instructional Validity Study of the Florida High School Graduation Test. *Educational Measurement: Issues and Practice, 2*(4), 8–9.

Fiske, E. B. (1976, February 18). New Test Developed to Replace I.Q. *The New York Times,* p. 28.

Flanagan, J. C. (1971, January 1–8). The Plan System for Individualizing Education. *Measurement in Education, 2*(2).

Flanagan, J. C., D. V. Tiedeman, and M. G. Willis. (1973). *The Career Data Book.* Palo Alto, Calif.: American Institutes for Research.

Flaugher, R. L. (1970). *Testing Practices, Minority Groups and Higher Education: A Review and Discussion of the Research* (Research Bulletin 70-41). Princeton, N.J.: Educational Testing Service.

Flaugher, R. L. (1974). Some Points of Confusion in Discussing the Testing of Black Students. In L. P. Miller. *The Testing of Black Students* (Chapter 2). Englewood Cliffs, N.J.: Prentice-Hall.

Flaugher, R. L. (1978). The Many Definitions of Test Bias. *American Psychologist, 33,* 671–679.

Folsom, C. H. (1973). Effects of Mental Abilities on Obtained Intercorrelations Among VPI Scales. *Measurement and Evaluation in Guidance, 6,* 74–81.

Frechtling, J. A. (in press). Administrative Uses of School Testing Programs. In R. L. Linn (Ed.). *Educational Measurement.* Washington, D.C.: American Council on Education.

Frederick, L. T. V. (1977). *Federal Reporter* (2nd Series, 557F. 2d. 373).

Fricke, B. G. (1975). *Grading, Testing, Standards, and All That.* Ann Arbor: Evaluation and Examinations Office, University of Michigan.

Fuchs, D., N. L. Featherstone, D. R. Garwicj, and L. S. Fuchs. (1984). Effects of Examiner Familiarity and Test Charateristics on Speech- and Language-Impaired Children's Test Performance. *Measurement and Evaluation in Guidance 16*(4), 198–204.

Gaffney, R. F., and T. O. Maguire. (1971). Use of Optically Scored Test Answer Sheets with Young Children. *Journal of Educational Measurement, 8,* 103–106.

Gage, N. L. (1972). I.Q. Heritability, Race Differences, and Educational Research. *Phi Delta Kappan, 53,* 308–312.

Gage, N. L., et al. (1957). The Psychological Meaning of Acquiescence Set for Authoritarianism. *Journal of Abnormal and Social Psychology, 55,* 98–103.

Gallup, A. (1984). The Gallup Poll of Teachers' Attitudes Toward the Public Schools. *Phi Delta Kappan, 66*(2), 97–107.

Gardner, E. F., R. Madden, H. C. Rudman, B. Karlsen, J. C. Merwin, R. Callis, and C. S. Collins. (1983). *Stanford Achievement Test Series: Multilevel Norms Booklet (National).* Cleveland, Oh.: Psychological Corporation.

Gerber, M. M., and M. I. Semmel. (1984). Teacher as Imperfect Test: Reconceptualizing the Referral Process. *Educational Psychologist, 3,* 137–148.

Getzels, J. W., and P. W. Jackson. (1962). *Creativity and Intelligence.* New York: Wiley.

Ghiselli, E. E. (1966). *The Validity of Occupational Aptitude Tests.* New York: Wiley.

Gibb, B. G. (1964). Test Wiseness as a Secondary Cue Response. Unpublished doctoral dissertation. Ann Arbor: University Microfilms, No. 64-7643.

Gill, D., J. Vinsonhaler, and G. Sherman. (1979). *Defining Reading Diagnosis: What, When, and How* (Research Series No. 46). East Lansing: Institute for Research on Teaching, Michigan State University.

Gladstone, R. (1975). Where Is Fashion Leading Us? *American Psychologist, 30,* 604–605.

Glaser, R. (1963). Instructional Technology and the Measurement of Learning Outcomes. *American Psychologist, 18,* 519–521.

Glaser, R. (1973). Individuals and Learning: The New Aptitudes. In M. C. Wittrock (Ed.). *Changing Education.* Englewood Cliffs, N.J.: Prentice-Hall.

Glaser, R., and L. Bond. (1981). Testing: Concepts, Policy, Practice, and Research. *American Psychologist, 36*(10), 997–1000.

Glaser, R., and L. Eyde. (1979). Statement of American Psychological Association's Division of Evaluation and Measurement on the Truth in Testing Act of 1979 (H.R. 3564) and the Educational Testing Act of 1979 (H.R. 4949) Before the Subcommittee on Elementary, Secondary and Vocational Education Committee on Education and Labor, U.S. House of Representatives.

Glaser, R., and A. K. Nitko. (1971). Measurement in Learning and Instruction. In R. L. Thorndike (Ed.). *Educational Measurement* (2nd ed.). Washington, D.C.: American Council on Education.

Glass, G. V. (1975). A Paradox About Excellence of Schools and the People in Them. *Educational Researcher, 4*(3), 9–12.

Glass, G. V. (1978a). Minimum Competence and Incompetence in Florida. *Phi Delta Kappan, 59,* 602–605.

Glass, G. V. (1978b). Standards and Criteria. *Journal of Educational Measurement, 15,* 237–261.

Goldman, L. (1971). *Using Tests in Counseling* (2nd ed.). New York: Appleton.

Goldman, B. A., and J. C. Busch. (Eds.). (1978). *Directory of Unpublished Experimental Mental Measures* (Vol. 2). New York: Human Sciences Press.

Goldman, B. A., and J. L. Saunders. (Eds.). (1974). *Directory of Unpublished Experimental Mental Measures* (Vol. 1). New York: Human Sciences Press.

Gooler, D. D. (1971). Some Uneasy Inquiries into Accountability. In L. M. Lessinger and R. W. Tyler (Eds.). *Accountability in Education.* Worthington, Ohio: C. A. Jones.

Goolsby, T. M. (1971). Appropriateness of Subtests in Achievement Test Selection. *Educational and Psychological Measurement, 31,* 967–972.

Gorth, W. P., and M. R. Perkins. (1979). *A Study of Minimum Competency Testing Programs: Final Program Development Resource Document.* Amherst, Mass.: National Evaluation Systems.

Goslin, D. A. (1967). *Teachers and Testing*. New York: Russell Sage.

Gottesman, I. I. (1968). Biogenetics of Race and Class. In M. Deutsch, I. Katz, and A. R. Jensen (Eds.). *Social Class, Race, and Psychological Development* (pp. 11–51). New York: Holt, Rinehart and Winston.

Gottfredson, L. S. (1979). Aspiration Job-Match: Age Trends in a Large Nationally Representative Sample of Young White Men. *Journal of Counseling Psychology, 26*, 319–328.

Graham, J. R., and R. S. Lilly. (1984). *Psychological Testing*. Englewood Cliffs, N.J.: Prentice-Hall.

Graziano, W. G., P. E. Varca, and J. C. Levy. (1982). Race of Examiner Effects and the Validity of Intelligence Tests. *Review of Educational Research, 52*(4), 469–497.

Green, B. F. (1983). Adaptive Testing by Computer. In R. B. Ekstrom (Ed.). *Measurement, Technology, and Individuality in Education* (No. 17 in *New Directions for Testing and Measurement*). San Francisco: Jossey-Bass.

Green, B. F., R. D. Bock, L. G. Humphreys, R. L. Linn, and M. D. Reckase. (1984). Technical Guidelines for Assessing Computerized Adaptive Tests. *Journal of Educational Measurement, 21*(4), 347–360.

Green, D. R. (1983, April). Content Validity of Standardized Achievement Tests and Test Curriculum Overlap. In D. Wanous (Chair), *National vs. Local Tests and Curriculum: Inferences to Which Domain and Why*. Symposium conducted at the annual meeting of the National Council on Measurement in Education, Montreal.

Green, R. F. (1951). Does a Selection Situation Induce Testees to Bias Their Answers on Interest and Temperament Test? *Educational and Psychological Measurement, 11*, 501–515.

Gronlund, N. E. (1971). *Measurement and Evaluation in Teaching* (2nd ed.). New York: Macmillan.

Gronlund, N. E. (1973). *Preparing Criterion-Referenced Tests for Classroom Instruction*. New York: Macmillan.

Gronlund, N. E. (1974). *Determining Accountability for Classroom Instruction*. New York: Macmillan.

Gronlund, N. E. (1978). *Stating Objectives for Classroom Instruction* (2nd ed.). New York: Macmillan.

Gronlund, N. E. (1981). *Measurement and Evaluation in Teaching* (4th ed.). New York: Macmillan.

Gross, M. L. (1962). *The Brain Watchers*. New York: Random House.

Grossman, H. J. (Ed.). (1977). *Manual on Terminology and Classification in Mental Retardation*. Washington, D.C.: American Association of Mental Deficiency.

Grossman, H. J. (Ed.). (1981). *Manual on Terminology and Classification in Mental Retardation* (1973, 1977, and 1981 editions). Washington, D.C.: American Association of Mental Deficiency.

Grosswald, J. (1973, April). The CRT vs. NRT Syndrome—A New Large City Plague. *Measurement News* (Official Newsletter of the National Council on Measurement in Education), *16*, 2, 4.

Guba, E. G. (1969). Significant Differences. *Educational Research, 20*(3), 4.

Guilford, J. P. (1959). Three Faces of Intellect. *American Psychologist, 14*, 469–479.

Guilford, J. P. (1967). *The Nature of Human Intelligence*. New York: McGraw-Hill.

Guilford, J. P. (1969). *Intelligence, Creativity and Their Educational Implications*. San Diego: Educational and Industrial Testing Service.

Guion, R. M. (1983, August). The Ambiguity of Validity: The Growth of My Discontent. Presidential Address to the Division of Evaluation and Measurement at the meeting of the American Psychological Association, Anaheim, California.

Haase, R. F., C. F. Reed, J. L. Winer, and J. L. Boden. (1979). Effects of Positive, Negative, and Mixed Occupational Information on Cognitive and Affective Complexity. *Journal of Vocational Behavior, 15,* 294–302.

Haertel, E., and R. Calfee. (Summer 1983). School Achievement: Thinking About What to Test. *Journal of Educational Measurement, 20*(2), 119–132.

Hakstian, A. R., and W. Kansup. (1975). A Comparison of Several Methods of Assessing Partial Knowledge in Multiple-Choice Tests: II. Testing Procedures. *Journal of Educational Measurement, 12,* 231–240.

Hambleton, R. K., and D. R. Eignor. (1978). Guidelines for Evaluating Criterion-Referenced Tests and Manuals. *Journal of Educational Measurement, 15,* 321–327.

Hambleton, R. K., and D. R. Eignor. (1979). Competency Test Development, Validation, and Standard Setting. In R. Jaeger and C. Tittle (Eds.). *Minimum Competency Testing.* Berkeley, Calif.: McCutchan.

Hambleton, R. K., and R. Novick. (1973). Towards an Integration of Theory and Method for Criterion-Referenced Tests. *Journal of Educational Measurement, 10,* 159–170.

Hambleton, R. K., H. Swaminathan, J. Algina, and D. Coulson. (1978). Criterion-Referenced Testing and Measurement: A Review of Technical Issues and Development. *Review of Educational Research, 48,* 1–48.

Haney, W. (1980, May). Trouble over Testing. *Educational Leadership,* 640–650.

Hansen, J. C. (1984). *Users' Guide for the SVIB-SCII.* Palo Alto, Calif.: Consulting Psychologists Press.

Hanson, G. R., D. S. Prediger, and R. H. Schussel. (1977). *Development and Validation of Sex-Balanced Interest Inventories* (ACT Research Report No. 78). Iowa City, Iowa: American College Testing Program.

Hardy, R. A. (1984). Measuring Instructional Validity: A Report of an Instructional Validity Study for the Alabama High School Graduation Examination. *Journal of Educational Measurement. 21*(3), 291–301.

Hargadon, F. A. (1980). Two Cheers. In *Commentaries on Testing.* Princeton: College Board.

Harmes, H. M. (1971). Specifying Objectives for Performance Contracts. *Educational Technology, 11,* 52–56.

Harris, C. W. (Ed.). (1963). *Problems in Measuring Change.* Madison: University of Wisconsin Press.

Harris, C. W., et al. (Eds.). (1974). *Problems in Criterion-Referenced Measurement* (CSE Monograph Series in Evaluation, No. 3). Los Angeles: Center for the Study of Evaluation, University of California.

Harris, M. L., and D. M. Stewart. (1971). Application of Classical Strategies to Criterion-Referenced Test Construction: An Example. Paper presented at the annual meeting of the American Educational Research Association, New York.

Harvard Educational Review. (1969). *Environment, Heredity, and Intelligence* (Reprint Series No. 2).

Hathaway, S. R. (1964). MMPI: Professional Use by Professional People. *American Psychologist, 19,* 204–210.

Hathaway, S. R., and P. E. Meehl. (1951). *An Atlas for the Clinical Interpretation of the MMPI.* Minneapolis: University of Minnesota Press.

Hathaway, S. R., and E. D. Monachesi. (1961). *An Atlas of Juvenile MMPI Profiles.* Minneapolis: University of Minnesota Press.

Hathaway, S. R., and E. D. Monachesi. (1963). *Adolescent Personality and Behavior.* Minneapolis: University of Minnesota Press.

Havighurst, R. J., and B. C. Neugarten. (1975). *Society and Education* (4th ed.). Boston: Allyn and Bacon.

Hays, W. A. (1973). *Statistics for Psychologists* (2nd ed.). New York: Holt, Rinehart and Winston.

Haywood, H. C., C. E. Meyers, and H. N. Switzky. (1982). Mental Retardation. In M. R. Rosenzweig and L. W. Porter (Eds.). *Annual Review of Psychology 33*, 327. Palo Alto, Calif.: Annual Reviews, Inc.

Heathers, G. (1971). A Definition of Individualized Education. Paper presented at the annual meeting of the American Educational Research Association, New York.

Henderson, E. H., and B. H. Long. (1970). Predictors of Success in Beginning Reading Among Negroes and Whites. In J. A. Figural (Ed.). *Reading Goals for the Disadvantaged* (pp. 30–42). Newark, Del.: International Reading Association.

Herrnstein, R. J. (1971, September). I.Q. *Atlantic Monthly*, pp. 43–64.

Herrnstein, R. J. (1973). *I.Q. in the Meritocracy*. Boston: Little, Brown.

Herrnstein, R. J. (August, 1982). IQ Testing and the Media. *Atlantic Monthly*, pp. 68–74.

Hills, J. (1981). *Flexing Your Test Muscles: A Guide to Developing Test-Taking Skills*. Tallahassee: Student Assessment Section, Florida Department of Education.

Hills, J. R. (1964). Prediction of College Grades for All Public Colleges of a State. *Journal of Educational Measurement, 1*, 155–159.

Hills, J. R. (1971). Use of Measurement in Selection and Placement. In Robert L. Thorndike (Ed.). *Educational Measurement* (2nd ed.). Washington, D.C.: American Council on Education.

Hills, J. R. (1981). *Measurement and Evaluation in the Classroom* (2nd ed.). Columbus, Ohio: Merrill.

Hills, J. R., and M. B. Gladney. (1966). Predicting Grades from Below Chance Test Scores (Research Bulletin 3-66, Office of Testing and Guidance). Atlanta: Board of Regents of the University System of Georgia.

Hills, J. R., J. C. Klock, and S. Lewis. (1963). *Freshman Norms for the University System of Georgia, 1961–1962*. Atlanta: Office of Testing and Guidance, Board of Regents of the University System of Georgia.

Hodgkins, R., and B. McKenna. (1982). Testing and Teacher Certification: An Explosive Combination. *Educational Measurement: Issues and Practice, 1*(2), 10–16.

Hodgson, M. L., and S. H. Cramer. (1977). The Relationship Between Selected Self-Estimated and Measured Abilities in Adolescents. *Measurement and Evaluation in Guidance, 10*(2), 98–103.

Hoffmann, B. (1962). *The Tyranny of Testing*. New York: Crowell-Collier-Macmillan.

Holland, J. L. (1973). *Making Vocational Choices: A Theory of Careers*. Englewood Cliffs, N.J.: Prentice-Hall.

Holland, J. L., T. M. Magoon, and A. R. Spokane. (1981). Counseling Psychology: Career Interventions, Research, and Theory. *Annual Review of Psychology, 32*, 279–305.

Honzik, M. P., J. W. Macfarlane, and L. Allen. (1948). The Stability of Mental Test Performance Between Two and Eighteen Years. *Journal of Experimental Education, 17*, 309–324.

Hoover, H. D. (1984). The Most Appropriate Scores for Measuring Educational Development in the Elementary Schools: GE's. *Educational Measurement: Issues and Practice, 3*(4), 8–14.

Hopkins, K. D., and G. H. Bracht. (1975). Ten-Year Stability of Verbal and Nonverbal IQ Scores. *American Educational Research Journal, 12*(4), 469–477.

Hopkins, K. D., and S. E. Hodge. (1984). Review of the Kaufman Assessment Battery (K-ABC) for Children. *Journal of Counseling and Development, 63*(2), 105–107.

Hopkins, K. D., and J. C. Stanley. (1981). *Educational and Psychological Measurement and Evaluation* (6th ed.). Englewood Cliffs, N.J.: Prentice-Hall.

Horn, J. L., and G. Donaldson. (1976). On the Myth of Intellectual Decline in Adulthood. *American Psychologist, 31*(10), 701–719.

Hoyt, C. J. (1941). Test Reliability Estimated by Analysis of Variance. *Psychometrika, 6*, 153–160.

Hughes, D. C., and B. Keeling. (1984). Model Essays and Context Effects. *Journal of Educational Measurement, 21,* 277–281.

Humphreys, L. G. (1967). Critique of Cattell, "Theory of Fluid and Crystallized Intelligence—A Critical Experiment." *Journal of Educational Psychology, 58,* 129–136.

Hunt, J. McV. (1961). *Intelligence and Experience.* New York: Ronald.

Hunter, J. E. (1980). Construct Validity and Validity Generalization. In *Construct Validity in Psychological Measurement. Proceedings of a Colloquium on Theory and Application in Education and Employment,* pp. 119–125. U.S. Office of Personnel Management and Educational Testing Service, Princeton, N.J.

Hunter, J. E. (1983). *The Dimensionality of the General Aptitude Test Battery (GATB) and the Dominance of General Factors over Specific Factors in the Prediction of Job Performance for the U.S. Employment Service* (USES Test Research Report No. 44). Division of Counseling and Test Development, Employment and Training Administration, Department of Labor, Washington, D.C.

Hunter, J. E., and R. F. Hunter. (1983). *The Validity and Utility of Alternative Predictors of Job Performance* (Office of Personnel Research and Development Report 83-4). Washington, D.C.

Hunter, J. E., and F. L. Schmidt. (1976). Critical Analysis of the Statistical and Ethical Implications of Various Definitions of Test Bias. *Psychological Bulletin, 83*(6), 1053–1071.

Hunter, J. E., and F. L. Schmidt. (1982). Fitting People to Jobs: The Impact of Personnel Selection on National Productivity. In M. D. Dunnette and E. A. Fleishman (Eds.). *Human Performance and Productivity: Human Capability Assessment.* Hillsdale, N.J.: Lawrence Erlbaum.

Hunter, J. E., F. L. Schmidt, and J. M. Rauschenberger. (1977). Fairness of Psychological Tests: Implications of Four Definitions for Selection Utility and Minority Hiring. *Journal of Applied Psychology, 62,* 3, 245–260.

Hutton, J. (1969). Practice Effects on Intelligence and School Readiness Tests for Preschool Children. *Training School Bulletin, 65,* 130–134.

Huynh, H. (1976). On Consistency of Decisions in Criterion-Referenced Testing. *Journal of Educational Measurement, 13,* 253–264.

Ivens, S. H. (1970). *An Investigation of Items Analysis, Reliability and Validity in Relation to Criterion-Referenced Tests.* Unpublished doctoral dissertation.

Jackson, D. N. (1977). *Jackson Vocational Interest Survey Manual.* Port Huron, Mich.: Research Psychologists Press.

Jackson, D. N., R. R. Holden, R. H. Locklin, and E. Marks. (1984). Taxonomy of Vocational Interests of Academic Major Areas. *Journal of Educational Measurement, 21*(3), 261–276.

Jackson, D. N., and S. Messick. (1962). Response Styles and the Assessment of Psychopathology." In S. Messick and J. Ross (Eds.). *Measurement in Personality and Cognition.* New York: Wiley.

Jackson, D. N., and S. V. Paunonen. (1980). Personality Structure and Assessment. *Annual Review of Psychology.* Palo Alto, Calif.: Annual Reviews, Inc.

Jackson, R. (1970, June). Developing Criterion-Referenced Tests. *ERIC Clearinghouse on Tests, Measurement, and Evaluation.*

Jackson, R. (1980). The Scholastic Aptitude Test: A Response To Slack and Porter's "Critical Appraisal." *Harvard Educational Review, 50,* 382–391.

Jacobs, S. S. (1972). A Validity Study of the Acquiescence Scale of the Holland Vocational Preference Inventory. *Educational and Psychological Measurement, 32,* 477–480.

Jaeger, R. M., and T. D. Freijo. (1975). Race and Sex as Concomitants of Composite Halo in Teachers' Evaluative Rating of Pupils. *Journal of Educational Psychology, 67,* 226–237.

Jarvik, L. F., C. Eisdorfer, and J. E. Blum (Eds.). (1973). *Intellectual Functioning in Adults: Psychological and Biological Influences.* New York: Springer.

Jenks, C. (1972). *Inequality: A Reassessment of the Effect of Family and Schooling in America.* New York: Harper & Row.

Jensen, A. R. (1968a). Patterns of Mental Ability and Socioeconomic Status. *Proceedings of the National Academy of Sciences of the United States of America, 60,* 1330–1337.

Jensen, A. R. (1968b). Social Class, Race, and Genetics: Implications for Education. *American Educational Research Journal, 5,* 1–42.

Jensen, A. R. (1969a). How Much Can We Boost IQ and Scholastic Achievement? *Harvard Educational Review, 39,* 1–123.

Jensen, A. R. (1969b). Reducing the Heredity-Environment Uncertainty. *Environment, Heredity, and Intelligence* (Reprint Series No. 2). *Harvard Educational Review.*

Jensen, A. R. (1970a). Hierarchical Theories of Mental Ability. In B. Dockrell (Ed.). *On Intelligence.* Toronto: Ontario Institute for Studies in Education.

Jensen, A. R. (1970b). IQ's of Identical Twins Reared Apart. *Behavioral Genetics, 2,* 133–146.

Jensen, A. R. (1973a). *Educability and Group Difference.* New York: Harper & Row.

Jensen, A. R. (1973b). *Genetics and Education.* New York: Harper & Row.

Jensen, A. R. (1973c). Let's Understand Skodal and Skeels, Finally. *Educational Psychologist, 10*(1), 30–35.

Jensen, A. R. (1975). The Meaning of Heritability in the Behavioral Sciences. *Educational Psychologist, 11*(3), 171–183.

Jensen, A. R. (1976). IQ Tests Are Not Culturally Biased for Blacks and Whites. *Phi Delta Kappan, 57,* 676.

Jensen, A. R. (1980). *Bias in Mental Testing.* New York: Free Press.

Jensen, A. R. (1982). The Chronometry of Intelligence. Chapter 6 in R. J. Sternberg. (Ed.). *Advances in the Psychology of Human Intelligence* (Vol. 1). Hillsdale, N.J.: Lawrence Erlbaum.

Jensen, A. R. (1984). Political Ideologies and Educational Research. *Phi Delta Kappan, 65*(7), 460–462.

Jensen, A. R., and E. Munro. (1978). Reaction Time, Movement Time, and Intelligence. Mimeograph.

Jepsen, D. A., and D. Prediger. (1981). *Dimensions of Adolescent Career Development: A Multi-Instrument Analysis.* Unpublished manuscript, University of Iowa, Iowa City.

Johansson, C. B., and L. W. Harmon. (1972). Strong Vocational Interest Blank: One Form or Two? *Journal of Counseling Psychology, 19,* 404–410.

Johnson, J. W. (1983). Things We Can Measure Through Technology That We Could Not Measure Before. In R. Ekstrom (Ed.). *Measurement, Technology, and Individuality in Education* (No. 17 in *New Directions for Testing and Measurement*). San Francisco: Jossey-Bass.

Johnson, O. G. (1976). *Tests and Measurement in Child Development: Handbook I and II.* San Francisco: Jossey-Bass.

Johnson, O. G., and J. W. Bommarito. (1971). *Tests and Measurements in Child Development: Handbook I.* San Francisco: Jossey-Bass.

Johnson, R. W. (1971). Congruence of Strong and Kuder Interest Profiles. *Journal of Consulting Psychology, 18,* 450–455.

Joint Committee on Standards for Educational Evaluation. (1981). *Standards for Evaluation of Educational Programs, Projects, and Materials.* New York: McGraw-Hill.

Joint Committee on Testing of the American Association of School Administrators. (1962). *Testing, Testing, Testing.* Washington, D.C.: National Education Association.

Jordon, M. C. (1979, October). How to Overcome. *Newsweek,* p. 27. *Journal of Educational Measurement.* (1976, Spring). *13.* Judges 12:5–6. *The Living Bible.*

Juni, S., and E. J. Koenig. (1982). Contingency Validity as a Requirement in Forced-Choice Item Construction: A Critique of the Jackson Vocational Interest Survey. *Measurement and Evaluation in Guidance, 14*(4), 202–207.

Juola, A. E. (1968). *Examination Skills and Techniques*. Lincoln, Neb.: Cliff's Notes.

Kaiser, J. F. (1974). The Chaldeans Speak: An Interpretive Summary. In D. R. Green (Ed.). *The Aptitude–Achievement Distinction*. Monterey, Calif.: CTB/McGraw-Hill.

Kalechstein, P., M. Kalechstein, and R. Docter. (1981). The Effects of Instruction on Test Taking Skills in Second-Grade Black Children. *Measurement and Evaluation in Guidance, 13*(4), 198–202.

Kallingal, A. (1971). The Prediction of Grades for Black and White Students at Michigan State University. *Journal of Educational Measurement, 8*, 263–266.

Kamin, L. J. (1974). *The Science and Politics of IQ*. Potomac, Md.: Erlbaum.

Kapes, J. T., and M. M. Mastie (Eds.). (1982). *A Counselor's Guide to Vocational Instruments*. Falls Church, Va.: National Vocational Guidance Association.

Karmos, A. H., and J. S. Karmos. (1984). Attitudes Toward Standardized Achievement Tests and Their Relation to Achievement Test Performance. *Measurement and Evaluation in Counseling and Development, 17*(2), 56–66.

Katoff, L., and J. Reuter. (1979). A Listing of Infant Tests. *Catalog of Selected Documents in Psychology, 9*, 56.

Katz, M. (1961). *Selecting an Achievement Test: Principles and Procedures*. Princeton, N.J.: Educational Testing Service.

Kauchak, D. (1984). Testing Teachers in Louisiana: A Closer Look. *Phi Delta Kappan, 65*(9), 626–628.

Kaufman, A. S. (1979). WISC-R Research: Implications for Interpretation. *School Psychology Digest, 8*, 5–27.

Kellaghan, T., G. F. Madaus, and P. W. Airasian. (1980). *Standardized Testing in Elementary Schools: Effects on Schools, Teachers, and Students*. Washington, D.C.: National Institute of Education, Department of Health, Education, and Welfare.

Kelley, T. L. (1927). *The Interpretation of Educational Measurement*. Yonkers-on-Hudson, N.Y.: World Book.

Kerlinger, F. N., and E. J. Pedhazur. (1973). *Multiple Regression in Behavioral Research*. New York: Holt, Rinehart and Winston.

Keyser, D. J., and R. C. Sweetland (Eds.). (1984). *Test Critiques* (Vol. 1). Kansas City, Mo.: Test Corporation of America.

Keysor, R. E., D. D. Williams, and A. P. VanMondfrans. (1979). The Effect of "Test Wiseness" on Professional School Screening Test Scores. Paper presented at the annual meeting of the National Council on Measurement in Education, San Francisco.

Kingsbury, G. G., and D. J. Weiss. (1979). An Adaptive Testing Strategy for Mastery Decisions (Research Report 79-5). Department of Psychology, Psychometric Methods Program, University of Minnesota.

Kirk, S. A., and B. Bateman. (1962). Diagnosis and Remediation of Learning Disabilities. *Exceptional Children, 29*, 73–78.

Klein, K. (1984). Minimum Competency Testing: Shaping and Reflecting Curricula. *Phi Delta Kappan, 65*(8), 565–567.

Kleinberg, J. L. (1976). Adolescent Correlates of Occupational Stability and Change. *Journal of Vocational Behavior, 9*, 219–232.

Klopfer, W. G., and E. S. Taulbee. (1976). Projective Tests. *Annual Review of Psychology, 27*, 543–568.

Kohn, S. D. (1975). The Numbers Game: How the Testing Industry Operates. *The National Elementary Principal, 54*(6), 11–23.

Kreit, L. H. (1968). The Effects of Test-Taking Practice on Pupil Test Performance. *American Educational Research Journal, 5*, 616–625.

Krumboltz, J. D. (1981). Tests and Guidance: What Students Need. Paper read at the Educational Testing Service Invitational Conference, New York.

Krumboltz, J. D., and D. A. Hamel (Eds.). (1982). *Assessing Career Development*. Palo Alto, Calif.: Mayfield.

Kuder, G. F. (1966). *Kuder Occupational Interest Survey General Manual*. Chicago: Science Research Associates.

Kuder, G. F. (1969). A Note on the Comparability of Occupational Scores from Different Interest Inventories. *Measurement and Evaluation in Guidance, 2*, 94–100.

Kuder, G. F. (1970). Some Principles of Interest Measurement. *Educational and Psychological Measurement, 30*, 205–226.

Kuncel, R. B. (1973). Response Processes and Relative Location of Subject and Item. *Educational and Psychological Measurement, 33*, 545–563.

Laing, J., and M. Farmer. (1984). *Use of the ACT Assessment by Examinees with Disabilities* (ACT Research Report No. 94). Iowa City, Iowa: American College Testing Program.

Lambert, N. M. (1981). Psychological Evidence in *Larry P.* v. *Wilson Riles:* An Evaluation by a Witness for the Defense. *American Psychologist, 36*(9), 937–952.

Lanyon, R. I., and L. D. Goodstein. (1982). *Personality Assessment* (rev. ed.). New York: Wiley.

Larkins, A. G., and J. P. Shaver. (1968). *Comparison of Yes-No, Matched Pairs, and All-No Scoring of a First-Grade Economics Achievement Test*. (ERIC Report No. ED 029701). Logan: Utah State University.

Larry P. v. *Riles*. (1972). 343 F. Supp. 130b (N.D. Cal.) (Preliminary Injunction), affirmed, 502 F. 2d 963 (9th Cer. 1974), Opinion Issued No. D-71-2270 RFP (N.D. Cal.).

Law School Admissions Test Council. (1970, October 27). *Statement on Pass–Fail Grading Systems* (Report No. HE–001–881).

Leacock, S. (1938, January 26). *The Daily Princetonian*. Princeton, N.J.: Princeton University.

Lefkowitz, D. (1970). Comparison of the Strong Vocational Interest Blank and the Kuder Occupational Interest Survey Scoring Procedures. *Journal of Counseling Psychology, 17*, 357–363.

Lehmann, I. J., and S. E. Phillips. (1985). *Teacher Competency Examination Programs: A National Survey*. Paper presented at the annual meeting of the National Council on Measurement in Education, Chicago, IL.

Lennon, R. T. (1956). Assumptions Underlying the Use of Content Validity. *Educational and Psychological Measurement, 16*, 294–304.

Lennon, R. T. (1980). The Anatomy of a Scholastic Aptitude Test. *Measurement in Education, 11*(2), 1–8.

Lennon, R. T. (1981). *A Time for Faith*. Presidential Address to the National Council on Measurement in Education, Los Angeles.

Lerner, B. (1980). The War on Testing: David, Goliath and Gallup. *The Public Interest, 60*, 119–147.

Lerner, B. (1981a). Representative Democracy, "Men of Zeal," and Testing Legislation. *American Psychologist, 36*(3), 270–275.

Lerner, B. (1981b). The Minimum Competence Testing Movement: Social, Scientific, and Legal Implications. *American Psychologist, 36*(10), 1057–1066.

Lessinger, L. M. (1970a). Engineering Accountability for Results in Public Education. *Phi Delta Kappan, 52*(4), 217–225.

Lessinger, L. M. (1970b). The Powerful Notions of Accountability in Education. *Journal of Secondary Education, 45*(8), 339–347.

Lessinger, L. M. (1971). Accountability for Results: A Basic Challenge for America's Schools. In L. M. Lessinger and R. W. Tyler (Eds.). *Accountability in Education*. Worthington, Ohio: Charles A. Jones.

Levine, M. (1976). The Academic Achievement Test: Its Historical Context and Social Functions. *American Psychologist, 31*, 228–238.

Lewis, J. (1975). The Relationship Between Academic Aptitude and Occupational Success for a Sample of University Graduates. *Educational and Psychological Measurement, 35,* 465–466.

Li, C. C. (1975). *Path Analysis: A Primer.* Pacific Grove, Calif.: Boxwood Press.

Lidz, C. S. (1981). *Improving Assessment of Schoolchildren.* San Francisco: Jossey-Bass.

Lien, A. J. (1976). *Measurement and Evaluation of Learning.* Dubuque, Iowa: William C. Brown.

Lindman, E. L. (1971). The Means and Ends of Accountability. *Proceedings of the Conference on Educational Accountability.* Princeton, N.J.: Educational Testing Service.

Lindquist, E. F. (1964). Equating Scores on Non-parallel Tests. *Journal of Educational Measurement, 1,* 5–9.

Lindvall, C. M., and J. O. Bolvin. (1967). Programmed Instruction in the Schools: An Application of Programmed Principles in Individually Prescribed Instruction. In P. Lange (Ed.), *Programmed Instruction.* 66th Yearbook, Part II. Chicago: National Society for the Study of Education.

Linn, R. L. (1980). Issues of Validity for Criterion-Referenced Measurement. *Applied Psychological Measurement, 4,* 4, 547, 561.

Livingston, S. A. (1972). Criterion-Referenced Applications of Classical Test Theory. *Journal of Educational Measurement, 9,* 13–26.

Livingston, S. A., and M. J. Zieky. (1982). *Passing Scores: A Manual for Setting Standards of Performance on Educational and Occupational Tests.* Princeton, N.J.: Educational Testing Service.

Locke, R. W. (1971). Accountability Yes, Performance Contracting Maybe. *Proceedings of the Conference on Educational Accountability.* Princeton, N.J.: Educational Testing Service.

Loehlin, J. C., et al. (1975). *Race Differences in Intelligence.* San Francisco: Freeman.

Long, B. H., and E. H. Henderson. (1974). Certain Determinants of Academic Expectancies Among Southern and Non-southern Teachers. *American Educational Research Journal, 11,* 137–147.

Lord, F. M. (1957). Do Tests of the Same Length Have the Same Standard Error of Measurement? *Educational and Psychological Measurement, 17,* 510–521.

Lord, F. M. (1963). Formula Scoring and Validity. *Educational and Psychological Measurement, 23,* 663–672.

Lucy, W. T. (1976). The Stability of Holland's Personality Types over Time. *Journal of College Student Personnel, 17,* 76–79.

Mackenzie, B. (1984). Explaining Race Differences in IQ: The Logic, the Methodology, and the Evidence. *American Psychologist, 39*(11), 1214–1233.

Madaus, G. (Ed.). (1983). *The Courts, Validity, and Minimum Competency Testing.* Hingham, Ma.: Kluwer-Nijhoff Publishing.

Magnusson, D., and G. Backteman. (1978). Longitudinal Stability of Person Characteristics: Intelligence and Creativity. *Applied Psychological Measurement, 2,* 481–490.

Mahan, T., and A. Mahan. (1981). *Assessing Children with Special Needs.* New York: Holt, Rinehart and Winston.

Malett, S. D., A. R. Spokane, and F. L. Vance. (1978). Effects of Vocationally Relevant Information on the Expressed and Measured Interests of Freshman Males. *Journal of Counseling Psychology, 25,* 292–298.

Masling, J. (1960). The Influence of Situational and Interpersonal Variables in Projective Testing. *Psychological Bulletin, 57,* 65–85.

Mathews, W. M. (1973). Narrative Format Testing Reports and Traditional Testing Reports: A Comparative Study. *Journal of Educational Measurement, 10,* 171–178.

McArthur, D. L., and B. H. Choppin. (1984). Computerized diagnostic testing. *Journal of Educational Measurement, 21*(4), 391–398.

McBride, J. R. (1980). Adaptive Verbal Ability Testing in a Military Setting. In D. Weiss (Ed.). *Proceedings of the 1979 Computerized Adaptive Testing Conference*. Minneapolis: Department of Psychology, University of Minnesota.

McCall, R. B. (1977). Childhood IQ's as Predictors of Adult Educational and Occupational Status. *Science, 197*, 482–483.

McCall, R. B. (1980). The Development of Intellectual Functioning in Infancy and the Prediction of Later IQ. In J. D. Osofsky (Ed.). *Handbook of Infant Development*. New York: Wiley.

McCall, R. B., M. I. Appelbaum, and P. S. Hogarty. (1973). Developmental Changes in Mental Performance. *Monographs of the Society of Research in Child Development, 38* (3, Serial No. 150).

McCall, R. B., P. S. Hogarty, and N. Hurlburt. (1972). Transitions in Infant Sensorimotor Development and the Prediction of Childhood IQ. *American Psychologist, 27*, 728–748.

McClure, L., and C. Buan (Eds.). (1973). *Essays on Career Education*. Portland, Ore.: Northwest Regional Educational Laboratory.

McKee, L. E. (1967). Third Grade Students Learn to Use Machine-Scored Answer Sheets. *The School Counselor, 15*, 52–53.

McLaughlin, D. H., and D. V. Tiedeman. (1974). Eleven-Year Stability and Change as Reflected in Project Talent Data Through the Flanagan, Holland, and Roe Occupational Classification Systems. *Journal of Vocational Behavior, 5*, 177–196.

McNemar, Q. (1964). Lost: Our Intelligence? Why? *American Psychologist, 19*, 871–882.

Meehl, P. E., and A. Rosen. (1955). Antecedent Probability and the Efficiency of Psychometric Signs, Patterns, or Cutting Scores. *Psychological Bulletin, 52*, 194–216.

Meeker, M. N. (1981). *Using SOI Test Results: A Teacher's Guide*. El Segundo, Calif.: Structure of Intelligence Institute.

Megargee, E. I. (1972). *The California Psychological Inventory*. San Francisco: Jossey-Bass.

Mehrens, W. A. (1979). The Technology of Competency Measurement. In R. B. Ingle, M. R. Carroll, and W. J. Gephart (Eds.). *Assessment of Student Competence*. Bloomington, Ind.: Phi Delta Kappa.

Mehrens, W. A. (1981a). ETS Versus Nairn/Nader: Who Reigns? *Measurement and Evaluation in Guidance, 14*(2), 61–70.

Mehrens, W. A. (1981b). *Setting Standards for Minimum Competency Tests*. Presentation given at the Michigan School Testing Conference, Ann Arbor.

Mehrens, W. A. (1984a). A Critical Analysis of the Psychometric Properties of the K-ABC. *Journal of Special Education, 18*(3), 297–310.

Mehrens, W. A. (1984b). National Tests and Local Curriculum: Match or Mismatch? *Educational Measurement: Issues and Practice, 3*(3), 9–15.

Mercer, J. (1977). *SOMPA, System of Multicultural Pluralistic Assessment*. New York: Psychological Corporation.

Messick, S. (1979). Potential Uses of Noncognitive Measurement in Education. *Journal of Educational Psychology, 71*, 281–289.

Messick, S. (1980a). Test Validity and the Ethics of Assessment. *American Psychologist, 35*(11), 1012–1027.

Messick, S. (1980b). *The Effectiveness of Coaching for the SAT: Review and Reanalysis of Research from the Fifties to the FTC*. Princeton, N.J.: Educational Testing Service.

Messick, S. (1981). The Controversy over Coaching: Issues of Effectiveness and Equity. In B. F. Green (Ed.). (No. 11 in *New Directions in Testing and Measurement: Issues in Testing, Coaching, Disclosure, and Ethnic Bias*). San Francisco: Jossey-Bass.

Messick, S. (1984). The Psychology of Educational Measurement. *Journal of Educational Measurement, 21*(3), 215–237.

Michigan State Board of Education. (n.d.). *A Guide to Test Taking as Easy as . . . 1 2 3*. Michigan State Board of Education.

Millman, J. (1966). *Test-Wiseness in Taking Objective Achievement and Aptitude Examinations: Final Report*. New York: College Entrance Examination Board.

Millman, J. (1974). Criterion-Referenced Measurement. In W. J. Popham (Ed.). *Evaluation in Education: Current Applications* (Chapter 6). Berkeley, Calif.: McCutchan.

Millman, J., C. H. Bishop, and R. L. Ebel. (1965). An Analysis of Test Wiseness. *Educational and Psychological Measurement, 25*, 707–726.

Millman, J., and W. Pauk. (1969). *How to Take Tests*. New York: McGraw-Hill.

Mitchell, J. V., Jr. (Ed.). (1983). *Tests in Print III*. Lincoln: Buros Institute of Mental Measurements, University of Nebraska.

Mitchell, J. V., Jr. (1984). What's New in Testing? Serving the Test User: New Developments from the Buros Institute. *Educational Measurement: Issues and Practice, 3*(2), 51–54.

Mitchell, J. V., Jr. (ed.). (1985). *The Ninth Mental Measurements Yearbook*. Lincoln, Nebraska: Buros Institute of Mental Measurements.

Moore, J. C. (1971). Test Wiseness and Analogy Test Performance. *Measurement and Evaluation in Guidance, 3*, 198–202.

Moore, R. (1960). Separate Answer Sheets for Primary Grades. In *17th Yearbook*, pp. 53–55. Ames, Iowa: National Council on Measurements Used in Education.

Morf, M. E., and D. N. Jackson. (1972). An Analysis of Two Response Styles: True Responding and Item Endorsement. *Educational and Psychological Measurement, 32*, 329–353.

Mosier, C. I. (1947). A Critical Examination of the Concepts of Face Validity. *Educational and Psychological Measurement, 7*, 191–205.

Munday, L. (1965). Predicting College Grades in Predominantly Negro Colleges, *Journal of Educational Measurement, 2*, 157–160.

Nairn, A., and Associates. (1980). *The Reign of ETS: The Corporation That Makes Up Minds*. Washington, D.C.: Author.

National Assessment of Educational Progress. (1969). Questions and Answers About National Assessment of Educational Progress, p. 1. Ann Arbor, Michigan.

National Assessment of Educational Progress. (1977). *Objectives for Career and Occupational Development: Second Assessment*. Denver: Education Commission of the States.

National Commission on Excellence in Education. (1983). *A Nation at Risk: The Imperative for Educational Reform*. Washington, D.C.: Government Printing Office.

National Council on Measurement in Education. (1980, April). NCME Statement on Educational Admissions Test. East Lansing, Michigan.

Nelson, C. H. (1958). *Let's Build Quality into Our Science Tests*. Washington, D.C.: National Science Teachers Association.

Nevo, B. (1976). The Effects of General Practice, Specific Practice, and Item Familiarization on Change in Aptitude Test Scores. *Measurement and Evaluation in Guidance, 91*, 16–20.

Newsfront. (1980). U.S. Colleges Are Becoming Less Choosy. *Phi Delta Kappan, 62*(1), 3.

Newsnotes. (1984). School Programs Are Changing in Response to Reform Reports: ERS. *Phi Delta Kappan, 66*(4), 301.

Nitko, A. J. (1980). "Criterion-Referencing Schemes." In S. T. Mayo (Ed.) *Interpreting Test Performance* (No. 6 in *New Directions for Testing and Measurement*). San Francisco: Jossey-Bass, pp. 35–71.

Nitko, A. J. (1983). *Educational Tests and Measurement: An Introduction*. New York: Harcourt Brace Jovanovich.

Noppe, L. D. (1980). Creative Thinking. In R. H. Woody (Ed.). *Encyclopedia of Clinical Assessment* (Vol. 2). San Francisco: Jossey-Bass.

Novick, M. R. (1980). Discussion of Hunter's Construct Validity and Validity Generalization Chapter in *Construct Validity in Psychological Measurement. Proceedings of a Colloquium on Theory and Application in Education and Employment*, pp. 125–129. U.S. Office of Personnel Management and Educational Testing Service, Princeton, N.J.

Novick, M. R., and D. D. Ellis, Jr. (1977). Equal Opportunity in Educational and Employment Selection. *American Psychologist, 32*(5), 306–320.

O'Bryan, K. G., and R. S. MacArthur. (1969). Reversibility, Intelligence, and Creativity in Nine-Year-Old Boys. *Child Development, 40,* 33–45.

O'Shea, J. F., and T. F. Harrington, (1971). Using the Strong Vocational Interest Blank and the Kuder Occupational Interest Survey, Form DD, with the Same Clients. *Journal of Counseling Psychology, 18,* 44–50.

Overall, J. A., and J. A. Woodward. (1975). Unreliability of Difference Scores: A Paradox for Measurement of Change. *Psychological Bulletin, 82,* 85–86.

Page, E. B. (1976). Nader v. E.T.S. [Letter to the editor]. *APA Monitor 7*(12), 2–3.

Parents in Action on Special Education (PASE) v. *Hannon.* (1980, July 16). No. 74-C-3586 (N.D. Ill.).

Payne, D. A. (Ed.). (1974). *Curriculum Evaluation.* Lexington, Mass.: Heath.

Perry, N. C. (1981). New Teachers: Do "The Best" Get Hired? *Phi Delta Kappan, 63*(2), 113–114.

Peters, H. J., and J. C. Hansen (Eds.). (1977). *Vocational Guidance and Career Development* (3rd. ed.). New York: Macmillan.

Peterson, N. S., and M. R. Novick. (1976). An Evaluation of Some Models for Culture-Fair Selection. *Journal of Educational Measurement, 13,* 3–30.

Pfeifer, C. M., Jr., and W. E. Sedlacek. (1971). The Validity of Academic Predictors for Black and White Students at a Predominantly White University. *Journal of Educational Measurement, 8,* 253–262.

Pinard, A., and E. Sharp. (1972, June). IQ and Point of View. *Psychology Today,* pp. 65–68, 90.

Pines, M. (1969, July 6). Why Some Three-Year-Olds Get A's—and Some C's. *New York Times Magazine,* pp. 4, 17.

Popham, W. J. (1976). Normative Data for Criterion-Referenced Tests? *Phi Delta Kappan, 57,* 593–594.

Popham, W. J. (1978). *Criterion-Referenced Measurement.* Englewood Cliffs, N.J.: Prentice-Hall, p. 94.

Popham, W. J. (1981). *Modern Educational Measurement.* Englewood Cliffs, N.J.: Prentice-Hall.

Porter, J. W. (1971). The Future of Accountability. In *Proceedings of the Conference on Educational Accountability.* Princeton, N.J.: Educational Testing Service.

Prediger, D. J. (1971). *Converting Test Data to Counseling Information* (ACT Research Report No. 44), Iowa City, Iowa: American College Testing Program.

Prediger, D. J. (1977). Alternatives for Validating Interest Inventories Against Group Membership Criteria. *Applied Psychological Measurement, 1,* 275–280.

Prediger, D. J., J. D. Roth, and R. J. Noeth. (1975). Career Development of Youth: A Nationwide Study. *Personnel and Guidance Journal, 53,* 97–104.

President's Commission on Higher Education. (1947). *Higher Education for American Democracy: vol. 1. Establishing the Goals.* Washington, D.C.: Government Printing Office.

Prescott, G. A., I. H. Balow, T. P. Hogan, and R. C. Farr. (1978). *Metropolitan Achievement Tests: Survey Battery Manual.* New York: Psychological Corporation.

Public Law 93-380. (1974, August 21).

Public Law 95-561. (1978, November 1).

Pullin, D. (1981). Minimum Competency Testing and the Demand for Accountability. *Phi Delta Kappan, 63*(1), 20–22.

Ramseyer, G. C., and V. M. Cashen. (1971). The Effect of Practice Sessions on the Use of Separate Answer Sheets by First and Second Graders. *Journal of Educational Measurement, 8,* 177–182.

Raspberry, W. (1983, April 29). Teachers Should Pass Tests, Too. *Washington Post.*

Report of the Commission on Tests: I. Righting the Balance. (1970). New York: College Entrance Examination Board.

Reschly, D. J. (1981). Psychological Testing in Educational Classification and Placement. *American Psychologist, 36*(10), 1094–1102.

Resnick, L. B. (Ed.). (1976). *The Nature of Intelligence.* Hillsdale, N.J.: Lawrence Erlbaum.

Reynolds, C. R. (1980). An Examination for Bias in a Preschool Test Battery Across Race and Sex. *Journal of Educational Measurement, 17*(2), 137–146.

Reynolds, C. R. (1982). The Problem of Bias in Psychological Assessment. In C. R. Reynolds and T. B. Gutkin (Eds.). *The Handbook of School Psychology.* New York: Wiley.

Reynolds, C. R., and J. H. Clark. (1983). Assessment of Cognitive Abilities. In K. D. Paget and B. Bracken (Eds.). *Psycho-Educational Assessment of Preschool Children.* New York: Grune and Stratton.

Ricks, J. H. (1959). *On Telling Parents About Test Results* (Test Service Bulletin No. 54). New York: Psychological Corporation.

Riverside Publishing Company. (1982). *Technical Manual: Cognitive Abilities Test.* Chicago: Riverside Publishing Company.

Rogosa, D., D. Brandt, and M. Zimowski. (1982). A Growth Curve Approach to the Measurement of Change. *Psychological Bulletin, 92*(3), 726–748.

Rorer, L. G. (1965). The Great Response-Style Myth. *Psychological Bulletin, 62,* 129–156.

Rosenholtz, S. J., and C. Simpson. (1984). The Formation of Ability Conceptions: Developmental Trend or Social Construction? *Review of Educational Research, 54*(1), 31–64.

Rosenthal, R., and L. Jacobson. (1968). *Pygmalion in the Classroom.* New York: Holt, Rinehart and Winston.

Rowley, G. L. (1974). Which Examinees Are Most Favored by the Use of Multiple-Choice Tests? *Journal of Educational Measurement, 11,* 15–23.

Rowley, G. L., and R. Traub. (1977). Formula Scoring, Number-Right Scoring, and Test Taking Strategy. *Journal of Educational Measurement, 14,* 15–22.

Rubin, R. A. (1974). Preschool Application of the Metropolitan Reading Tests: Validity, Reliability, and Preschool Norms. *Educational and Psychological Measurement, 34,* 417–422.

Rudman, H. C., W. A. Mehrens, and D. S. Wanous. (1983). *The Data Box.* Cleveland: Psychological Corporation.

Rudner, L. M. (1981). Conference Summary, Conclusions, and Recommendations. *Testing in Our Schools.* Washington D.C.: National Institute of Education, Department of Education.

Rulon, P. J., D. V. Tiedeman, M. M. Tatsuoka, and C. R. Langmuir. (1967). *Multivariate Statistics for Personnel Classification.* New York: Wiley.

Rumenik, D. K., D. R. Capasso, and C. Hendrick. (1977). Experimenter Sex Effects in Behavioral Research. *Psychological Bulletin, 84,* 852–877.

Russell Sage Foundation. (1970). *Guidelines for the Collection, Maintenance and Dissemination of Pupil Records.* New York: Author.

Rutkowski, K., and G. Domino. (1975). Interrelationship of Study Skills and Personality Variables in College Students. *Journal of Educational Psychology, 67,* 784–789.

Sabers, D. L., and L. S. Feldt. (1968). An Empirical Study of the Effect of the Correction for Chance Success on the Reliability and Validity of an Aptitude Test. *Journal of Educational Measurement, 5,* 251–258.

Salend, S., A. E. Blackhurst, and E. Kifer. (1982). Effects of Systematic Reinforcement Conditions on the Test Scores of Children Labeled Learning and Behaviorally Disordered. *Measurement and Evaluation in Guidance, 15*(2), 133–140.

Salmon-Cox, L. (1981). Teachers and Standardized Achievement Tests: What's Really Happening? *Phi Delta Kappan, 62*(9), 631–634.

Salvia, J., and J. E. Ysseldyke. (1981). *Assessment in Special and Remedial Education* (2nd ed.). Boston: Houghton Mifflin.

Sampson, J. P. (1983). Computer-Assisted Testing and Assessment: Current Status and Implications for the Future. *Measurement and Evaluation in Guidance, 15*(4), 293–299.

Sampson, J. P. (1984). Guide to Microcomputer Software in Testing and Assessment. *AMECD Newsnotes, 19*(3), 3–9.

Samuda, R. J. (1975). *Psychological Testing of American Minorities.* New York: Dodd, Mead.

Samuels, S. J., and G. E. Edwall. (1975). Measuring Reading Achievement: A Case for Criterion-Referenced Testing and Accountability. *Measurement in Education, 6,* 2.

Sarason, I. G. (Ed.). (1980). *Test Anxiety: Theory, Research and Application.* Hillsdale, N.J.: Lawrence Erlbaum.

Saretsky, G. (1973). The Strangely Significant Case of Peter Doe. *Phi Delta Kappan, 54,* 589–592.

Sarnacki, R. E. (1979). An Examination of Test Wiseness in the Cognitive Test Domain. *Review of Educational Research, 49,* 252–279.

Sattler, J. M. (1974). *Assessment of Children's Intelligence.* Philadelphia: Saunders.

Sattler, J. M. (1982). *Assessment of Children's Intelligence and Special Abilities.* Boston: Allyn and Bacon.

Sattler, J. M., and J. Gwynne. (1982). Ethnicity and Bender Visual Motor Performance. *Journal of School Psychology, 20,* 1, 18–24.

Sattler, J. M., and J. Gwynne. (1982). White Examiners Do Not Generally Impede Test Performance of Black Children: To Debunk a Myth. *Journal of Consulting and Clinical Psychology 50,* 196–208.

Sattler, J. M., W. A. Hillix, and L. Neher. (1970). Halo Effect of Examiner Scoring of Intelligence Test Responses. *Journal of Consulting and Clinical Psychology, 34,* 172–176.

Sattler, J. M., and B. M. Winget. (1970). Intelligence Test Procedures as Affected by Expectancy and I.Q. *Journal of Clinical Psychology, 26,* 446–448.

Schmidt, F. L., and J. E. Hunter. (1981). Employment Testing: Old Theories and New Research Findings. *American Psychologist, 36*(10), 1128–1137.

Schmidt, F. L., J. E. Hunter, R. C. McKenzie, and T. W. Muldrow. (1979). Impact of Valid Selection Procedures on Work Force Productivity. *Journal of Applied Psychology, 64,* 609–626.

Schoenfeldt, L. F. (1968). An Empirical Comparison of Various Procedures for Estimating Heritability. Paper presented at the annual meeting of the American Psychological Association.

Scriven, M. (1967). The Methodology of Evaluation. In Ralph Tyler et al. *Perspectives of Curriculum Evaluation.* (AERA Monograph Series on Curriculum Evaluation, No. 1, pp. 39–83). Skokie, Ill.: Rand McNally.

Scriven, M. (1975). *Evaluation Bias and Its Control* (Occasional Paper No. 4). Kalamazoo: Evaluation Center, College of Education, Western Michigan University.

Semmel, M. (1984). Introduction to Special Issue on Special Education. *Educational Psychologist, 19*(3), 121–122.

Shaffer, M. (1976). The Use of Item-Favorability Data as Evidence of Sex Bias in Interest Inventories. Paper presented at the annual meeting of the National Council On Measurement in Education, San Francisco.

Shanker, A. (1971). Possible Effects on Instructional Programs. In *Proceedings of the Conference on Educational Accountability.* Princeton, N.J.: Educational Testing Service.

Shanker, A. (1980, October 19). The Nonsense of Attacking Education Tests. *The Washington Post.*

Shanker, A., and J. G. Ward. (1982). Teacher Competency and Testing: A Natural Affinity. *Educational Measurement: Issues and Practice, 1*(2), 6–9, 26.

Shaw, M. E. (1973). *A Theory of Attitudes.* Unpublished manuscript, University of Florida, Gainesville.

Shaw, M. E., and J. M. Wright. (1967). *Scales for the Measurement of Attitudes*. New York: McGraw-Hill.

Shepard, L. (1980). Standard Setting Issues and Methods. *Applied Psychological Measurement, 4*(4), 447–467.

Sheriffs, A. C., and D. S. Boomer. (1954). Who Is Penalized by the Penalty for Guessing? *Journal of Educational Psychology, 45,* 81–90.

Shockley, W. (1971). Models, Mathematics, and the Moral Obligation to Diagnose the Origin of Negro I.Q. Deficits. *Review of Educational Research, 41,* 369–377.

Shockley, W. (1972). Dysgenics, Geneticity, Raciology: Challenges to the Intellectual Responsibility of Educators. *Phi Delta Kappan, 53,* 297–307.

Silverman, B. I., F. Barton, and M. Lyon. (1976). Minority Group Status and Bias in College Admissions Criteria. *Educational and Psychological Measurement, 36*(2), 401–407.

Silverman, S., and S. Dunn. (1983). Raising SAT Scores: How One School Did It. *Electronic Learning, 2,* 51–53.

Slack, W. V., and D. Porter. (1980a). The Scholastic Aptitude Test: A Critical Appraisal. *Harvard Educational Review, 50,* 154–175.

Slack, W. V., and D. Porter. (1980b). Training, Validity, and the Issue of Aptitude: A Reply to Jackson. *Harvard Educational Review, 50,* 392–401.

Slakter, M. J. (1968). The Penalty for Not Guessing. *Journal of Educational Measurement, 5,* 141–144.

Slakter, M. J., R. A. Koehler, and S. H. Hampton. (1970a). Grade Level, Sex, and Selected Aspects of Test Wiseness. *Journal of Educational Measurement, 7,* 119–122.

Slakter, M. J., R. A. Koehler, and S. H. Hampton. (1970b). Learning Test-Wiseness by Programmed Texts. *Journal of Educational Measurement, 7,* 247–254.

Snow, R. E. (1969). Review of Pygmalion in the Classroom. *Contemporary Psychology, 14,* 197–199.

Snow, R. E. (1984). Placing Children in Special Education: Some Comments. *Educational Researcher, 13*(3), 12–14.

Sommer, R., and B. A. Sommer. (1983). Mystery in Milwaukee: Early Intervention, IQ, and Psychology Textbooks. *American Psychologist, 38*(9), 982–985.

Southern Regional Education Board. (1984). *Measuring Educational Progress in the South: Student Achievement*. Atlanta: Author.

Spache, G. D. (1976). *Diagnosing and Correcting Reading Disabilities*. Boston: Allyn and Bacon.

Spearman, C. (1927). *The Abilities of Man*. New York: Macmillan.

Speat, W. I. (1980). The Adaptive Behavior Scale: A Study of Criterion Validity. *American Journal of Mental Deficiency, 85*(1), 61–68.

Spielberger, C. D., W. Anton, and J. R. Bedell. (1976). The Nature and Treatment of Test Anxiety. In M. Zuckerman and C. D. Spielberger (Eds.). *Emotions and Anxiety: New Concepts, Methods and Applications*. New York: Lawrence Erlbaum/Wiley.

Stanley, J. C. (1969). Reactions to the March Article on Significant Differences. *Educational Researcher, 20*(5), 8–9.

Stanley, J. C. (1971a, February). Predicting College Success of the Educationally Disadvantaged. *Science, 171,* 640–647.

Stanley, J. C. (1971b). Reliability. In R. L. Thorndike (Ed.). *Educational Measurement* (2nd ed.). Washington, D.C.: American Council on Education.

Stanley, J. C., and A. C. Porter. (1967). Correlation of Scholastic Aptitude Test Scores with College Grades for Negroes Versus Whites. *Journal of Educational Measurement, 4,* 199–218.

Sternberg, R. J. (1981). Intelligence and Nonentrenchment. *Journal of Educationl Psychology, 73*(1), 1–16.

Sternberg, R. J. (1984). What Should Intelligence Tests Test? Implications of a Triarchic Theory of Intelligence for Intelligence Testing. *Educational Researcher, 13*(1), 5–15.

Sternberg, R. J., B. E. Conway, J. L. Ketron, and M. Bernstein. (1980). *People's Conceptions of Intelligence* (Technical Report No. 28). Yale University, Department of Psychology, New Haven.

Stetz, F. P., and M. D. Beck. (1981). Attitudes Toward Standardized Tests: Students, Teachers and Measurement Specialists. *Measurement in Education, 12*(1), 1–11.

Stevens, S. S. (1946). On the Theory of Scales of Measurement. *Science, 103,* 677–680.

Stott, L. H., and R. S. Ball. (1965). Infant and Preschool Mental Tests: Review and Evaluation. *Monographs of Social Research in Child Development, 30*(3), 151.

Strain, P. S., D. M. Sainto, and L. Mahan. (1984). Toward a Functional Assessment of Severely Handicapped Learners. *Educational Psychologist, 19*(3), 180–187.

Strassberg-Rosenberg, B., and T. F. Donlon. (1975). Content Influences on Sex Differences in Performance on Aptitude Tests. Paper presented at the annual meeting of the National Council on Measurement in Education, Washington, D.C.

Stricker, L. J. (1984). Test Disclosure and Retest Performance on the SAT. *Applied Psychological Measurement, 8*(1), 81–88.

Strong, E. K. (1966). *Vocational Interest Blank for Men.* Stanford, Calif.: Stanford University Press.

Stufflebeam, D. L. (1974). *Meta-Evaluation* (Occasional Paper No. 3). Kalamazoo: Evaluation Center, College of Education, Western Michigan University.

Stufflebeam, D. L., et al. (1971). *Educational Evaluation and Decision Making.* Bloomington, Ind.: Phi Delta Kappa, 1971.

Subkoviak, M. J. (1976). Estimating Reliability from a Single Administration of a Mastery Test. *Journal of Educational Measurement, 13,* 265–276.

Super, D. E. (1972). The Future of Vocational Development Theory. In J. M. Whitely, (Ed.). *Perspectives in Vocational Development.* Washington, D.C.: American Personnel and Guidance Association.

Super, D. E., M. J. Bohn, D. J. Foster, J. P. Jordaan, R. H. Lindeman, and A. A. Thompson. (1972). *Career Development Inventory.* New York: Columbia University, Teachers College.

Super, D. E., and J. O. Crites. (1962). *Appraising Vocational Fitness by Means of Psychological Tests* (rev. ed.). New York: Harper & Row.

Supplement, *Journal of Educational Measurement.* (1967). *4*(1), 1–31.

Swaminathan, H., R. K. Hambleton, and J. Algina. (1975). A Bayesian Decision-Theoretic Procedure for Use with Criterion-Referenced Tests. *Journal of Educational Measurement, 12,* 87–98.

Switzky, H. N. (1981). Review of R. Feuerstein, Y. Rand, M. B. Hoffman, and R. Miller, "Instrumental Enrichment." *American Journal of Mental Deficiency.*

Tannenbaum, A. J. (1965). Review of the Culture-Fair Intelligence Tests. In O. K. Buros (Ed.). *The Sixth Mental Measurements Yearbook.* Highland Park, N.J.: Gryphon Press.

Taylor, C. and K. R. White. (1982). The Effect of Reinforcement and Training on Group Standardized Test Behavior. *Journal of Educational Measurement, 19*(3), 199–210.

Teachers Opinion Poll. (1974). *Today's Education, 63*(2), 4.

Temp, G. (1971). Validity of the SAT for Blacks and Whites in Thirteen Integrated Institutions. *Journal of Educational Measurement, 8,* 245–252.

Tenopyr, M. L. (1977). Content-Construct Confusion. *Personnel Psychology, 30,* 47–54.

Terman, L. M. (1916). *The Measurement of Intelligence.* Boston: Houghton Mifflin.

Terman, L. M., and M. A. Merrill. (1937). *Measuring Intelligence.* Boston: Houghton Mifflin.

Terman, L. M., and M. A. Merrill. (1960). *Stanford-Binet Intelligence Scale: Manual for the Third Revision* (Form L-M). Boston: Houghton Mifflin.

Thomas, C. L., and J. C. Stanley. (1969). Effectiveness of High School Grades for Predicting

College Grades of Black Students: A Review and Discussion. *Journal of Educational Measurement, 6,* 203–216.

Thorndike, R. L. (1971). Concepts of Cultural Fairness. *Journal of Educational Measurement, 8,* 63–70.

Thorndike, R. L. (1975). Mr. Binet's Test 70 Years Later. *Educational Researcher, 4*(5), 3–7.

Thorndike, R. L., and E. Hagen. (1977). *Measurement and Evaluation in Psychology and Education* (4th ed.). New York: Wiley.

Thorndike, R. L., and E. Hagen. (1982). *Preliminary Examiner's Manual for 1982 Edition: Cognitive Abilities Test.* Chicago: Riverside Publishing Company.

Thorndike, R. L., E. Hagen, and J. M. Sattler. (In Press). *Draft Manual of the Stanford-Binet Intelligence Test* (4th ed.). Chicago, Ill.: Riverside Publishing Company.

Thurstone, L. L. (1933). *The Theory of Multiple Factors.* Privately published.

Thurstone, P., and E. R. House. (1981). The NIE Adversary Hearing on Minimum Competency Testing. *Phi Delta Kappan, 63,* 87–89.

Time magazine. (1980, June 16). Help! Teachers Can't Teach.

Tinsley, H. E. A., and D. J. Weiss. (1975). Interrater Reliability and Agreement of Subjective Judgments. *Journal of Counseling Psychology, 22,* 358–376.

Tittle, C. K., and D. G. Zytowski (Eds.). (1978). *Sex-Fair Interest Measurement: Research and Implications.* Washington, D.C.: N.I.E.

Toenjes, C. M., and F. H. Borgen. (1974). Validity Generalization of Holland's Hexagonal Model. *Measurement and Evaluation in Guidance, 7,* 79–85.

Torrance, E. P. (1962). *Guiding Creative Talent.* Englewood Cliffs, N.J.: Prentice-Hall.

Torrance, E. P. (1965). *Reward Creative Behavior.* Englewood Cliffs, N.J.: Prentice-Hall.

Traub, R. E., R. K. Hambleton, and B. Singh. (1969). Effects of Promised Reward and Threatened Penalty on Performance on a Multiple-Choice Vocabulary Test. *Educational and Psychological Measurement, 29,* 847–861.

Traub, R. E., and G. L. Rowley. (1980). Reliability of Test Scores and Decisions. *Applied Psychological Measurement, 4*(4), 517–545.

Traub, R. E., and C. W. Fisher. (n.d.). *On the Equivalence of Constructed-Response and Multiple-Choice Tests.* Toronto, Canada: Ontario Institute for Studies in Education.

Tryon, G. S. (1980). The Measurement and Treatment of Test Anxiety. *Review of Educational Research, 50,* 343–372.

Turkington, C. (1984, January). The Growing Use and Abuse of Computer Testing. *APA Monitor,* pp. 7, 26.

Turlington, R. D. (1981). Florida's Testing Program: A Firm Foundation for Improvement. *Phi Delta Kappan, 63,* 3, 204.

Tye, K. A. (1971). Educational Accountability in an Era of Change. In L. H. Browder, Jr. (Ed.). *Emerging Patterns of Administrative Accountability.* Berkeley, Calif.: McCutchan.

Tyler, L. E. (1976). The Intelligence We Test. In L. B. Resnick (Ed.). *The Nature of Intelligence* (Chapter 2). Hillsdale, N.J.: Lawrence Erlbaum.

The Use of Multifactor Tests in Guidance. (1957). Reprint Series from *Personnel Guidance Journal.* Washington, D.C.: American Personnel and Guidance Association.

United States Employment Service. (1983). *Overview of Validity Generalization for the U.S. Employment Service* (USES Test Research Report No. 43). Division of Counseling and Test Development, Employment and Training Administration, Department of Labor, Washington, D.C.

U. S. News & World Report. (1984, September). Why Many Teachers Don't Measure Up. *10,* 14.

Uzgiris, I. C., and J. McV. Hunt. (1975). *Assessment in Infancy: Ordinal Scales of Psychological Development.* Urbana: University of Illinois Press.

Van Allen v. *McCleary.* (1961). 27, Misc. 2d 81, 211 NYS 2d 501 (Sup. Ct. Nassau CO.).

Vernon, P. E. (1961). *The Structure of Human Abilities* (2nd ed.). London: Methuen.

Vernon, P. E. (1964). Creativity and Intelligence. *Journal of Educational Research, 6,* 163–169.

Vernon, P. E. (1979). *Intelligence: Heredity and Environment.* San Francisco: Freeman.

Votaw, D. F. (1936). The Effect of "Do-Not-Guess" Directions on the Validity of True-False and Multiple-Choice Tests. *Journal of Educational Psychology, 27,* 699–704.

Wagner, L. (1983). *Organizational Heterogeneity and School Policy Response to Proficiency Assessment in California.* Unpublished doctoral dissertation, Stanford University, Stanford, Calif.

Wagner, R. K., and R. J. Sternberg. (1984). Alternative Conceptions of Intelligence and Their Implications for Education. *Review of Educational Research, 54*(2), 179–223.

Wahlstrom, M., and F. J. Boersma. (1968). The Influence of Test-Wiseness Upon Achievement. *Educational and Psychological Measurement, 28,* 413–420.

Wallach, M. A., and N. Kogan. (1965). *Modes of Thinking in Young Children.* New York: Holt, Rinehart and Winston.

Waller, J. H. (1971). Achievement and Social Mobility: Relationships Among IQ Score, Education and Occupation in Two Generations. *Social Biology, 18,* 252–259.

Wanous, D. S., and W. A. Mehrens. (1981). Helping Teachers Use Information: The Data Box Approach. *Measurement in Education, 12*(4), 1–10.

Ward, A. W., M. E. Backman, B. W. Hall, and J. L. Mazur. (n.d.). *Guide for School Testing Programs.* East Lansing, Mich.: National Council on Measurement in Education.

Ward, J. C. (1980). Teachers and Testing: A Survey of Knowledge and Attitudes. A report of the research department of the American Federation of Teachers, AFL-CIO.

Ward, W. C. (1984). Using Microcomputers to Administer Tests. *Educational Measurement: Issues and Practice, 3*(2), 16–19.

Webb, E. J., et al. (1981). *Nonreactive Measures in the Social Sciences* (2nd ed.). Boston: Houghton Mifflin.

Webster, W. J. (1984). *Five Years of Teacher Testing: A Retrospective Analysis.* Paper presented at the annual meeting of the American Educational Research Association, New Orleans.

Webster's Seventh New Collegiate Dictionary. (1965). Springfield, Mass.: Merriam.

Wechsler, D. (1955). *Wechsler Adult Intelligence Scale, Manual.* New York: Psychological Corporation.

Weiss, D. J. (1976). *Computerized Ability Testing 1972–1975* (Final Report of Project NR150-343, NOO 14-67-A-0113-0029). Minneapolis: University of Minnesota.

Weiss, D. J. (Ed.). (1980). *Proceedings of the 1979 Computerized Adaptive Testing Conference.* Minneapolis: Department of Psychology, University of Minnesota.

Wesman, A. G. (1952). Faking Personality Test Scores in a Simulated Employment Situation. *Journal of Applied Psychology, 36,* 112–113.

Westbrook, B. W. (1974). Content Analysis of Six Career Development Tests. *Educational and Psychological Measurement, 7,* 172–180.

Westbrook, B. W. (1976a). Interrelationships of Career Choice Competencies and Career Choice Attitude of Ninth-Grade Pupils: Testing Hypotheses Derived from Crites' Model of Career Maturity. *Journal of Vocational Behavior, 8,* 1–12.

Westbrook, B. W. (1976b). Criterion Related and Construct Validity of the Career Maturity Inventory Competence Test with Ninth-Grade Pupils. *Journal of Vocational Behavior, 9,* 377–383.

Westbrook, B. W., and M. M. Mastie. (1973). The Measurement of Vocational Maturity: A Beginning to Know About. *Measurement and Evaluation in Guidance, 6,* 8–16.

Westbrook, B. W., and J. W. J. Parry-Hill. (1973). The Measurement of Cognitive Vocational Maturity. *Journal of Vocational Behavior, 3*(3).

Willerman, L. (1979). *The Psychology of Individual and Group Differences.* San Francisco: Freeman.

Willis, S. L. (1973, May). Formations of Teachers' Expectations of Students' Academic Performance. *Dissertation Abstracts.*

Williams, R. L. (1974). Stimulus/Response: Scientific Racism and IQ—The Silent Mugging of the Black Community. *Psychology Today, 7*(12), 32, 34, 37–38, 41, 101.

Wilson, K. M. (1978). *Predicting the Long-Term Performance in College of Minority and Nonminority Students* (Research Bulletin RB-78-b). Princeton, N.J.: Educational Testing Service.

Wing, H. (1980). Practice Effects with Traditional Mental Test Items. *Applied Psychological Measurement, 4,* 144–155.

Womer, F. B. (1981). State-Level Testing: Where We Have Been May Not Tell Us Where We Are Going. In D. Carlson (Ed.). *Testing in the States Beyond Accountability* (No. 10 in *New Directions for Testing and Measurement*). San Francisco: Jossey-Bass.

Womer, F. B. (1984). Where's the Action? *Educational Measurement: Issues and Practice, 3*(3), 3.

Wood, R. (1976). Response-Contingent Testing. *Review of Educational Research, 43,* 4, 529–544.

Worthen, B. R. (1975). Competencies for Educational Research and Evaluation. *Educational Researcher, 4*(1), 13–16.

Worthen, B. R. and J. R. Sanders. (1973). *Educational Evaluation: Theory and Practice.* Worthington, Ohio: Charles A. Jones Publishing Company.

Wrightstone, J. W., T. P. Hogan, and M. M. Abbott. (1972). Accountability in Education and Associated Measurement Problems. *Test Service Notebook 33.* New York: Harcourt Brace Jovanovich.

Yalow, E. S., and W. J. Popham. (1983). Content Validity at the Crossroads. *Educational Researcher, 12*(8), 10–14, 21.

Yamamoto, K., and H. F. Dizney. (1965). Effects of Three Sets of Test Instructions on Scores on an Intelligence Scale. *Educational and Psychological Measurement, 25,* 87–94.

Yeh, J., J. Herman, and L. M. Rudner. (1980). A Survey of the Use of Various Achievement Tests. *Testing in Our Schools.* Washington D.C.: National Institute of Education, Department of Education.

Ysseldyke, J. E., and M. L. Thurlow. (1984). Assessment Practices in Special Education Adequacy and Appropriateness. *Educational Psychologist, 19*(3), 123–136.

Zigmond, N., and R. Silverman. (1984). Informal Assessment for Program Planning and Evaluation in Special Education. *Educational Psychologist, 19*(3), 163–171.

Zimmerman, D. W., and R. H. Williams. (1982). Gain Scores in Research Can Be Highly Reliable. *Journal of Educational Measurement, 19*(2), 149–154.

Zoref, L., and P. Williams. (1980). A Look at Content Bias in IQ Tests. *Journal of Educational Measurement, 17*(4), 313–322.

Zytowski, D. G. (1972). Equivalence of the Kuder Occupational Survey and the Strong Vocational Interest Blank Revisited. *Journal of Applied Psychology, 56,* 184–185.

Zytowski, D. G. (Ed.). (1973). *Contemporary Approaches to Interest Measurement.* Minneapolis: University of Minnesota Press.

Zytowski, D. G., and R. E. Warman. (1982). The Changing Use of Tests in Counseling. *Measurement and Evaluation in Guidance 15*(2), 147–152.

Name Index

Subject Index